Social Work Live

Social Work Live

Theory and Practice in Social Work Using Videos

By Carol Dorr, Ph.D.

OXFORD
UNIVERSITY PRESS

OXFORD

UNIVERSITY PRESS

Oxford University Press is a department of the University of
Oxford. It furthers the University's objective of excellence in research,
scholarship, and education by publishing worldwide.

Oxford   New York
Auckland   Cape Town   Dar es Salaam   Hong Kong   Karachi
Kuala Lumpur   Madrid   Melbourne   Mexico City   Nairobi
New Delhi   Shanghai   Taipei   Toronto

With offices in
Argentina   Austria   Brazil   Chile   Czech Republic   France   Greece
Guatemala   Hungary   Italy   Japan   Poland   Portugal   Singapore
South Korea   Switzerland   Thailand   Turkey   Ukraine   Vietnam

Oxford is a registered trademark of Oxford University Press
in the UK and certain other countries.

Published in the United States of America by
Oxford University Press
198 Madison Avenue, New York, NY 10016

Library of Congress Cataloging-in-Publication Data
Dorr, Carol.
Social work live : theory and practice in social work using videos / by Carol Dorr Ph.D.
     pages cm
ISBN 978–0–19–936893–8
1. Social service.   2. Social case work.   I. Title.
HV40.D677 2014
361.3—dc23
2014022086

9 8 7 6 5 4 3 2 1
Printed in the United States of America
on acid-free paper

Contents

Preface

This work is the result of many years of teaching social work practice and wanting to help students more easily integrate theory with practice. Although my students could often pass a test on theory, they had trouble identifying which theories they used in client interventions. I found that students often treated theory and practice as though they were separate areas of study. When I asked, "What knowledge base informed your work with a particular client?" or "What theory or theories guided your intervention strategies?" they looked puzzled. They were unable to articulate clearly their reasons for doing what they were doing, or to understand how their actions reflected a particular theory or practice skill.

Attempting to find another method to help students make this important link between theory and practice, I tried incorporating video recorded interviews into class. By watching a video, students could begin to reflect on what theories were being used and articulate better how they figured this out. I was frustrated with the available teaching videos, so I started recording my own mock-client interviews that could be used in the classroom. They soon became my focus for teaching students about clinical practice. The videos allowed students to study the conversation that occurred between clients and social workers, which opened up discussions about multiple aspects of practice in engaging and interactive ways. Watching the interviews and analyzing the transcripts absolutely helped students learn how to identify the theories and practice skills used with clients.

And so it is that after 20 years of teaching theory and practice in social work, I finally have found an approach that I feel really works with students. Although I have used videos in the classroom before, until recently I wasn't daring enough to think they could form the base for most of my practice coursework. In the past, I used traditional textbooks and added interviewing videos to class sections. Now, the interviewing videos, along with the curriculum I developed to support them, have become my primary method for teaching students about theory and practice.

My goals in writing this book are twofold: to provide you with classroom materials to make practice come alive and keep students awake; and to offer a method to facilitate students' identification of theory used in practice. This casebook is intended to teach social work students about the theory and practice of social work in an experiential, "hands-on" way using case studies. Rather than a traditional textbook that centers on the text, this approach uses an in-depth analysis of cases with video recorded interviews as the key teaching tool.

Using this method in my own classroom, I also made certain unintended yet serendipitous discoveries. In particular, I found that I could measure student outcomes by asking students to create their own video recorded interviews that could be viewed in class. The last two revisions in the Educational Policy and Accreditation Standards by the Council on Social Word Education (CSWE, 2008, 2015) emphasize the importance of assessing student competencies, and for the most part, social work educators have looked to the field for help with student assessment. That's in part because students are performing learned skills at their field placements, whereas supervisors are the ones to observe how they are meeting the standards. By having students produce their own video recorded interviews, faculty has a way to observe them performing skills in the classroom, providing educators with another valuable tool for assessment.

After students watch the skills demonstrated in the curriculum videos, teachers can have them practice what they've learned in their own mock-client interviews. In addition to producing the videos, students are assigned questions about their communication skills, client assessment, intervention strategy, and theories used, and they also reflect on what went well and what they could have done differently. Their written responses to these questions provide another means for assessment.

In the past, I had encountered one inevitable problem: The students didn't have access to the equipment they needed to complete their interviews successfully. However, advances in technology have bypassed this obstacle. In September 2012, Regis College, where I teach, decided to give all students an iPad, reflecting how mobile technology is transforming the classroom. Students can now use the camera feature on the iPad to video record their own role-plays and client interviews, and then project them on the larger screen in class for discussion and feedback. In my experience, students find these exercises fun, engaging, and extremely valuable for learning how to perform practice skills or demonstrate specific competencies. These class activities help students build their confidence to prepare them for work with future clients, and as I've mentioned already, are excellent tools for student assessment as it relates to CSWE standards.

With an iPad in the hands of every student, I saw the opportunity to make the equally bold decision of teaching practice completely using videos and the corresponding text—both the videos I have produced and those of the students. Although I wasn't completely sure how it would turn out, so far the results have exceeded my expectations, and I have been using this method seamlessly ever since to teach practice skills. After completing my first semester with this approach in fall 2012, I observed tremendous student progress with interviewing skills between the beginning of the semester and the end, and from fall to spring semesters. Students also noticed the difference. Their feedback was positive and enthusiastic. Students loved the practice class and looked forward to weekly seminars. I wondered why it took me so long to get to this point. After presenting my work at CSWE conferences, I was encouraged by participants to make this work available to others, and thus came the idea for this book. I hope you will try this method in your classrooms, and I look forward to your feedback and your stories about how this method is working for you.

Acknowledgments

As I reflect on my own process of constructing videos and writing this book, I realize it would not have been possible without the help of so many people. I appreciate everyone who volunteered to participate in the five video-recorded interviews, either playing the role of social worker or client. I believe they did a terrific job, despite comprising a hodgepodge of actors: former social work faculty, two BSW alumni, a welfare supervisor, and family members. I also want to thank Peter Schipelliti of the Media Technology Department at Regis College and his students in video production courses for taping three of the videos. When two of the five videos had to be re-taped at the last minute due to unforeseen problems, Basia Goszczynska came to the rescue. Although under tight deadlines, she stayed calm and eased my worries about making it happen. I am grateful for her help during a stressful time. Lastly, I want to thank my family for their never-ending support and belief in me and in my work on this book. They weathered many challenging moments with me, and times when I thought of giving up, but they always encouraged me to keep going. Last, I want to thank my daughter, Rebecca, for her creative editing of my manuscript and for making my ideas clearer.

Introduction

When I decided to write this book, I set out to create something that would be more engaging than the typical textbook yet still provide students with the knowledge, skills, and values needed for social work practice. I wanted students to experience direct practice in a visceral, hands-on, meaningful way that they could see, listen to, and feel in the classroom and that sparked lively discussion. As a result, the book is built around five hypothetical client cases. Of the eight chapters, five contain in-depth analysis of mock-client social work interviews that become the focus for teaching. They are video recorded and may be viewed with the DVD that accompanies the book. The text in the five case chapters includes excerpts from the interview transcripts, presented in the form of process recordings that look at the social worker's reflections and observations and also identify the theories and practice skills used in the interventions.

The first two chapters provide background information that will help the reader understand the basic practice skills, intervention strategies, and theories used in the later chapters. Think of these early chapters as an abbreviated review of social work's fundamental principles. Eventually, the practice concepts and theories receive further elaboration through the case examples, as students watch the videos, read and reflect on the transcripts and process recordings, and take part in class discussions and homework. The final chapter is the conclusion, where I discuss the key points I hope you will take away after reading the book.

Chapter 1, which surveys social work practice, includes sections on approaches to practice, assessment, and evidence-based research. It also discusses the important tenets of professional practice that guide social workers in their day-to-day work with clients, such as self-awareness, reflection, communication skills, and critical thinking. These skills are emphasized in the process recordings that appear later in the book, and look in depth at the worker–client interaction.

Chapter 2 provides a limited overview of social work theory, without going into much depth. It is expected that students have already been exposed to these theories in other human behavior or practice courses. I have summarized what I feel are the essential concepts behind each theory, realizing that other faculty might choose to emphasize different aspects. Students are encouraged to refer to their favorite theoretical texts for a more detailed understanding of theories and how they are used in social work practice. Also, faculty using the text may choose to include other theories not discussed in this book to open up further discussion of the case material.

The theories that I highlight in chapter 2 are psychodynamic, narrative, cognitive, behavioral, and systems theories. Under the section on psychodynamic, I include a description of ego psychology and object relations theories. I decided to discuss individual life cycle and developmental theories directly as they apply to the case vignettes in the later chapters. Because of the recent popularity of positive psychology and its compatibility with social work practice from a strengths perspective, I have incorporated this material into the section on cognitive theory. Information on mind–body approaches, stress management, and mindfulness are included in the section on behavioral theory. And under systems theories, you'll find details about structural family theory and multigenerational family theories. Although many clinicians think about cognitive-behavioral theory and intervention together, I discuss each theory separately to differentiate between them.

Chapter 3 covers practice with serious and life-threatening illness at an inpatient hospital. I discuss the first of five video recorded mock interviews, the case of Allen, who is a medical patient in an urban hospital waiting for open heart surgery. This case example provides an opportunity to learn about medical social work practice in the context of a hospital setting. It brings attention to some of the challenges social workers face when working with clients with serious and life-threatening illness. It also looks at specific ethical and practice issues that social workers confront in medical environments. The chapter discusses other areas of practice, as well: loss and meaning-making, meditative and mind–body techniques, individual and family life cycle assessment, DSM-V and panic disorder, and use of medical terminology.

Chapter 4 describes practice with at-risk populations and includes the case of Betty, an elderly woman applying for help at a public assistance office. It brings up issues of clients who feel discriminated against, marginalized, and alienated by society, and who possess less power and limited access to resources. In particular, it looks at diversity in two key areas: aging and poverty. The chapter includes material on the role of individualism in American society, poverty and social welfare policies, the history of public assistance programs, criminalization of poverty, healthcare policy, and age discrimination in the workplace.

Practice with children is discussed in chapter 5 using the case of Emily, who is meeting with a social worker in an outpatient medical setting. Emily, an 11-year-old girl, has been diagnosed with leukemia and is also dealing with parents who have recently separated and are planning to divorce. This chapter highlights the importance of using a multisystemic approach when working with children and demonstrates the effectiveness of engaging the child, siblings, parents, school, medical community, and other groups, such as friends, in working with Emily. The chapter also brings attention to special areas of social work knowledge and practice skills needed in Emily's case, such as developmental theory, resiliency, play and expressive therapy with children, the impact of divorce on children, and practice with leukemia and childhood cancer.

Chapter 6 is a continuation of chapter 5 and involves an interview with Lisa, the mother of Emily, who was featured in the previous chapter. It takes place in an outpatient hospital clinic and covers practice with families, particularly around parenting a child with leukemia. The interview demonstrates the impact a child's illness can have on the whole family system. During the session, Lisa addresses her reaction to Emily's diagnosis, her understanding of leukemia and the options for treatment, the effect of that treatment on the family, communication with hospital and clinic staff, parental stress and conflict, and how the illness affects a sibling. The chapter covers family life cycle and looks at how, in the case of Lisa's family, the life cycle is disrupted both by Emily's serious illness and Lisa's potential divorce from her spouse, Emily's father. The critical role of family beliefs about illness and optimism is discussed as having positive health outcomes and coping abilities for families.

Practice with domestic violence is the subject of chapter 7, which focuses on a mock-client interview with Nicole, a 25-year-old, single, African-American woman with two young children. Nicole seeks safety at a domestic violence shelter after leaving her fiancé, who has become more abusive and threatening to her. Nicole's case puts a spotlight on the problem of violence against women, viewing it through the lens of gender, race, ethnicity, culture, and poverty. The interview provides rich learning opportunities for practice in the areas of domestic violence, cultural competence and Intimate Partner Violence (IPV), and IPV screening.

After writing the final chapter on the case of Nicole, I was amazed at how the five cases touched on so many important and varied aspects of practice. They lend themselves to discussions on a wide range of subjects including, but not limited to, social work supervision, loss and life-threatening illness, poverty, advocacy, organizational culture, healthcare policy, discrimination, diversity, cultural competence, family belief systems, family communication, divorce, intimate partner violence (IPV), social welfare policies, criminalization of poverty, DSM-V, referral, and evidence-based practice. The cases provide examples of racism, sexism, ageism, and classism. They also demonstrate the professional role of the social worker in different settings and show how context shapes practice.

The five interviews cover wide territory in other ways, too. Each one demonstrates how to handle different individual life cycle and family life cycle issues and emphasizes the importance of considering these factors in practice, by including work with a child, an adolescent (brother of Emily), someone in early adulthood, at midlife, and later adulthood. I outline multiple forms of assessment for each case to help students become more comfortable writing their own case reports. The interviews focus on a variety of practice modalities, including individual, couples, family, play, and group therapy, and they illustrate, too, how social workers must collaborate with other disciplines. For example, in the case of Emily, the worker communicates with the schools, and refers Emily to community resources, both public and private; in the case of Betty, the worker assigns her an advocate so she can gain access to needed welfare programs. I highlight the social worker's role as part of the medical team and in multidisciplinary meetings in the cases of Allen, Emily, and her mother. I also explore new areas for social work practice that I hope will be embraced more in the future: mind–body approaches, holistic work, positive psychology, and spirituality.

The end-of-chapter resources include questions for students related to each of the five interviews that address student competencies emphasized by CSWE. Rather than refer to the competencies throughout the text, I have chosen to include them at the end of the chapter. I felt it was an appropriate way to demonstrate how students could apply and learn these important skills by answering questions about the cases. The questions can become homework, class discussion points, class exercises, or topics for individual, student, or group presentations.

I am often asked what student level I wrote this text for, BSW or MSW. This is a complicated question that I approach with certain broad guidelines. Many BSW students go on to graduate schools of social work with advanced standing, meaning that the foundation first year of graduate school is waived. I interpret this to mean that there is an overlap between undergraduate and graduate education and that the material that students get at the BSW level sometimes fulfills the requirements of first-year graduate work. Having said that, I also feel that some clinical material is appropriate at both levels. I believe my text is aimed at that intersection and can teach students in both undergraduate and graduate programs.

I find that using video recorded interviews works best in small classes that are practice seminars. This allows time for students to show their own video clips and get comments from other students and faculty. In this more intimate environment, students learn to tune in to each other, as well as the clients in their mock interviews, and create a caring environment that feels safe and genuine—embodying the vital qualities that must exist in any worker–client relationship that promotes growth.

Process recordings have always been the foundation of social work supervision, and for this reason, I have included them in the five interview chapters. They provide a window into how social workers think while doing practice and can be an important avenue for student learning. It encourages students to question on their own and with supervisors, whereas supervisors can use the material to give students valuable feedback. In the classroom, process recordings can be dissected by students and the instructor and become a valuable teaching tool. Some argue that process recordings are an older teaching method, and that it's too challenging for students to stay focused on long, detailed analyses of client–worker interactions. However, I have not found this to be the case. Students appreciate being able to observe the progression of a clinical interview because it gives them a better sense of what happens behind closed doors between social worker and client. Watching the videos and reading the transcripts and process recordings demystifies practice. It gives students something tangible to work with and demonstrates the skills of clinical practice and theories in action.

When I talk with field supervisors, many say they like using the long form of process recordings because it gives them a better sense of how a student is engaging with a client. It allows the supervisors to provide helpful feedback based on a closer representation of what actually happened in the clinical situation rather than a summary of what the student says happened. Process recordings are an effective way to measure how well students perform many of the skills expected of them in the field. They also help students develop their capacities for active listening, tuning in, and staying with the client during the interview, and later, they sharpen students' critical thinking skills as they reflect on their work with clients.

Students often wish for a technique or script they may follow when working with clients to deal with their initial anxiety about what to say. Unfortunately, there are no short cuts for learning effective clinical skills. The interviews you will find on the DVD were not scripted, so as to be more true to what social workers experience every day with clients. The people in the role-plays were only given a minimum of information and asked to let the interview evolve naturally in the moment. This resembles the real-life clinical situation in which the social worker has no idea ahead of time what the client will want to talk about.

As you watch the interviews and read the transcripts, it is important to understand that they do not represent perfect or model interviews. This gives students the message that they are not expected to be perfect either, and they will learn pivotal lessons by sharing their mistakes. By reflecting on the interviews in class, students can observe what went well and what didn't, and think about other interventions that could have been used. This exercise encourages students to use reflection and critical thinking skills, both of which are crucial components of good practice.

No one book can satisfy all the needs of an instructor or course. I encourage faculty to supplement this book with additional material and articles that can fill in any perceived gaps. This allows faculty to individualize courses to reflect their own teaching voices. I believe the book lends itself to side discussions on special topics that come up related to the five case studies. Seize these opportunities and touch on other areas of practice that interest you. The five interview chapters can become a jumping-off point for faculty to customize the book to meet their own needs and fulfill course requirements in new and creative ways.

Social Work Live

Overview of Practice in Social Work

This chapter highlights key ideas that will be helpful when thinking about practice and the case vignettes included in this book. It does not provide a complete overview of the concepts, values, and skills used in social work practice. In choosing what to include, I emphasize what I find most important; another clinical worker would write about different aspects of practice that reflect other views. Writing from a postmodernist and constructivist position, I assume that my personal values and biases influenced the text. I interchangeably use practitioner, worker, social worker, clinician, counselor, and therapist to reference the person doing the direct work with the client. I also alternate between the masculine and feminine gender for any hypothetical client in the text to avoid always saying "he or she."

What Is Direct Practice?

The field of social work has long struggled with how to reconcile two seemingly opposing tendencies, each with their accompanying goals and methods; that is, whether to focus on the needs of the individual or society. For most of the first half of the twentieth century, one faction preferred clinical work with individuals, families, and groups. Another concentrated its efforts on community organizing, advocacy, policy, and legislative action. Before the 1970s, social workers were also defined by the methods they used; they were caseworkers, group workers, community organizers, and psychiatric social workers. During the political unrest of the 1960s and 1970s, social work was criticized for its narrow clinical focus on individuals and families, a focus that ignored the larger social problems and needs of poor and oppressed groups.

Gradually the field changed and moved to a new, more comprehensive approach to practice. With these changes came a broader definition of practice that was more holistic and included client systems of all sizes, individual, family, group, community, and society (Hepworth et al., 2013). Accreditation standards mandated foundation courses in social work programs that would prepare students for generalist practice. Schools added curricula to provide social work students with the knowledge and skills to intervene at micro, mezzo, and macro levels.

And an acknowledgment was made: Although a social worker, at least on the surface, counsels an individual client, that same worker might also perform other roles, such as collaborating with other professionals, acting as advocate, and helping a client with a testimonial for legislative action.

Generalist or direct practice looks at the "person-in-situation," meaning that problems are understood in context and do not stand alone. It is holistic, because it looks at the whole person, including such factors as biology, psychology, socialization, interpersonal skills, emotions, culture, spiritual leanings, and the greater environment. Woods and Hollis (2000) describe the psychosocial approach, now common in social work practice, as a method to help clients with a variety of problems that could stem from inner or outer issues, psychological or interpersonal factors, or from pressures in the environment. The approach combines concepts from psychiatry, psychology, the social sciences, and social work. The basic values include concern for the well-being of the individual, the right to self-determination, maintaining an attitude of acceptance and empathy, and belief in the central role of the worker–client relationship.

Direct Practice, Generalist Practice, and Clinical Practice

There is a lot of confusion about these three terms. Direct social work practice includes work with individuals, couples, families, and groups in a variety of settings and includes many different tasks. The social worker is trained to perform diverse roles such as face-to-face counseling; collaboration with other professionals and organizations; advocacy; brokering; referral; group work; and so on. A strong foundation in generalist practice prepares students for direct practice.

The Council on Social Work Education (CSWE) requires that both undergraduate (BSW) and graduate social work programs (MSW) prepare students for generalist practice. As such, the curriculum for both BSW programs and the first year of MSW programs usually incorporate this broad approach to the field. This explains why students who graduate with a BSW may be accepted with advanced standing to a graduate school of social work; they are not expected to repeat first-year courses they've already covered. For the purpose of this book, I concentrate on direct practice at the generalist level, where BSW and MSW education overlap.

The second-year curriculum in social work graduate school includes specialization or a concentration in a particular field of practice, for example, child welfare, mental health, child and families, substance abuse, and aging. Clinical social work is frequently identified with engagement in the mental health field, and this also requires advanced practice training in the second year. Clinical social workers are found in multiple settings and often treat clients with mental, emotional, and behavioral disorders. Certain states recognize the distinction of the clinical social worker for licensing at an advanced level that makes practitioners eligible for third-party reimbursement. This requires an MSW, two years of supervised experience, and passage of a licensing exam.

Qualities of Worker–Client Relationship

You would be unlikely to pick up a book on direct practice that didn't emphasize the central role of the worker–client relationship in social work, or mention the specific worker characteristics that lead to successful outcomes. Research has found that personal qualities in the worker, such as being empathic, open, caring, accepting, trustworthy, and genuine are strongly correlated with both client satisfaction and client outcomes, and that these characteristics are what clients emphasize more than technical skills (Dong-Min et al., 2006; Lutz at al., 2007; Maluccio, 1979). Other studies enumerate similar findings. Positive outcomes are associated with clients who have hope and actively seek help, and therapists who are genuine and empathic (Lambert & Ogles, 2004), as well as workers who show caring and flexibility (Hopps et al., 1995).

What are the methods for teaching these skills? Some argue that you either have these personal characteristics or you don't, and that clinical instructors cannot impart them to students. I disagree and have found it is possible to help students engage more empathetically with clients by coaching them on the nuances of their interviewing skills. This can be done when observing students in role-plays, or in video-recorded interviews, where they practice listening and responding. These situations provide opportunities to observe and analyze student interactions with potential clients; the student, in turn, can receive constructive feedback from both instructors and peers on ways to improve. In my experience, students have appreciated these exercises that ask them to test their skills and then reflect on practical, hands-on suggestions about what they could do differently to build stronger relationships with clients. Using myself as a teaching tool, I also role-play with students and show them some of my video-recorded interviews with mock clients, giving them opportunities to offer me feedback as well. In this way, the classroom becomes a lab, where students can learn practice and communication skills, and demonstrate competencies that they are expected to possess upon graduation.

Recently I asked students to videotape themselves doing a mock client interview. After they completed the interview, they had to transcribe parts of it, do a process recording on it, and write a paper that reflected on their intervention and communication skills. While showing her video in class, one student shared that she didn't show much empathy with the client. She was right in her self-assessment, and as a class, we reviewed the process recording with her in detail and found moments when she could have responded differently. For example, rather than always rushing to respond, she needed to pause and reflect more on the meaning behind what was said, and tune in to the client's feelings. After a thoughtful pause, she could experiment with reflecting back feelings, exploring feelings, or helping to put the client's words into feelings. There were other times when she needed to fine-tune how she balanced listening with responding. At critical points in the interview, we stopped the video and brainstormed approaches that would help the student connect with the client in a more affective and effective way. These are the types of skills that strengthen the client–worker relationship, conveying warmth and genuine caring on the part of the social worker. And these skills can be demystified and learned in class.

Tuning in to the client and following one's intuition about where to go next dictates how interviews play out with clients. As the old adage goes, "social workers start where the client is." There is no way to know in advance what the client will want to discuss, so students need to wait to see how the client starts the session. The social worker's task is to stay present with the client in whatever way she needs in the here and now. The client–worker encounter happens spontaneously in the moment. The best tools are full concentration, and a genuine, honest, open approach. Mindfulness is crucial. As a social worker, you must let go of other distractions and worries when you enter a session, and truly stay in the present with the client. By doing this, the worker can use self (a concept discussed later in the chapter) in an effective manner by picking up on client cues about what is important and where the conversation will go next. Out of this intimate interaction will come a natural flow, the building of a caring and trusting relationship that will be the foundation for emotional healing.

Clinical Wisdom

Tacit knowledge refers to a worker's personal understanding and experiences that contribute to her ability to practice. Social work requires more than just theories. For the seasoned clinician, responses also come from a lifetime of work, and from the clinician comparing current clinical data with familiar schemas based on prior experience (Fleck-Henderson, 1989, p. 133). This type of "clinical wisdom," or collection of clinical experiences, does not derive from espoused theories directly, although theory shapes the clinician's perceptions and actions. These different ways of knowing, combining theoretical expertise with tacit knowledge and practice experience, lead to clinical wisdom and the art of practice. Effective practice requires that the social worker has knowledge from research, but also intuition and interpretive abilities that come from years of experience with clients (Graybeal, 2007).

With the current emphasis on evidence-based practice, there are some in the field who reject any concept of the art of practice; they say it doesn't fit with a stronger research orientation in social work because it can't be quantified and measured. Others disagree and believe that substantial evidence supports tacit knowledge and clinical wisdom; these clinicians feel strongly that social work competence can't be found by avoiding intuition, but instead by recognizing and developing it (England, 1986). From this viewpoint, art and science are two dimensions of an integrated and more meaningful whole; "acknowledging the artistic dimension of practice should not be seen as a refutation of science, but rather as an opportunity to enrich and expand the scope of inquiry, and thereby the potential contribution of science" (Graybeal, 2007, p. 521). Simple research on theories and techniques that work well with a particular diagnosis is not enough. We also need to understand how personal characteristics and other variables influence treatment outcomes, including: the unique traits of the client and social worker; unique elements of their collaboration; what makes some workers more effective than others; what makes certain clients recover in different ways; what characteristics enhance working relationships; and what clients define as success (Graybeal, 2007, p. 521).

These research questions require us to study the worker–client relationship in more depth and return to a discussion about the art of social work. We must look at "the capacity of the individual practitioner to form working alliances with clients, and to abstract from the generalities of accumulated knowledge to the particulars and the exigencies of a moment in time" (Graybeal, 2007, p. 521). This is at the heart of social work—belief in the relationship as a critical factor in a client's improvement. In the following passage, Graybeal compares social work to improvisational theater:

> The social worker enters, armed with theory and technique, experience and intuition, and a desire to be helpful. The client enters the stage as if from another play, having none of the assumptions or training, but with a lifetime of individual experience, and an expectation of being helped, or at the very least not to be harmed. There is no script. The two players must find a way to interact, to establish a meaningful and productive relationship. This collaboration, to be successful, will ultimately emerge from a synthesis of science and art…that builds on a broad base of knowledge and experience, and is highly improvisatory in nature. (Graybeal, 2007, p. 513)

Paying Attention to Content and Process in the Interview

Content and process are two concepts that explain different aspects of a client interview. Although content includes the substance of what is talked about between the client and worker, the process is what is happening in the moment with the client. Teaching students to pay attention to process in an interview involves attending to the relationship—the rapport the client and worker have with each other and how well the worker picks up on the client's feelings. Some questions the worker can ask herself relating to process are: What is the client's affect and has it changed from past meetings or during this session? Is there a natural flow, a give and take, to our conversation? Is the client showing signs of resistance, or reacting to something I have said? Am I off base with my understanding of what the client is telling me? How is our connection right now? Am I tuned in to what the client is feeling? Does the client seem far away, distracted, or fully engaged with me? How should I interpret the client being more silent in the meeting with me today? Sometimes the process is connected to the content, the discussion at hand. For example, a client may change the subject when he feels uncomfortable and finds the topic hard to broach. In such cases, it is important to recognize this and make the observation to the client.

When the worker perceives something different happening with the client during a session, especially if it represents a break in the working alliance, it is important to stop the conversation and process it. Workers must stay attuned to these important signals and not be afraid to talk about them openly with the client. The worker may process these moments by responding in any number of ways: "I notice that something feels different now in our discussion. Do you notice it too?" or "I seem to have lost you; are you thinking of something else?" or "I don't feel we're on the same wave length. What's going on with you now? What are you thinking right now?"

If the worker sees the client showing more feelings, then it would be important to recognize and comment on this observation. For example, if a client appears sad, the worker might pause, giving the client time to be in the feeling, and then gently comment, "You seem sad now. Could you share what is making you sad?" These direct statements show that the worker is tuned in to the client in the present moment and is sensitive to his feelings. Because the social worker shows authentic concern, commenting honestly on what he observes with the client, a stronger relationship is formed. What results is a more open and meaningful conversation between the worker and client that captures what is really going on in the session. The therapeutic alliance and the clinician's ongoing attention to the client's feelings about the intervention are the most significant attributes associated with successful treatment (Miller, Duncan, & Hubble, 2004).

Intersubjectivity

Worker sensitivity and awareness of the client's experience can also be referred to as intersubjectivity. Stern (1985) explains this as "capacities for sharing a focus of attention, for attributing intentions and motives to others and apprehending them correctly, and for attributing the states of feelings in others and sensing whether or not they are congruent with one's own state of feeling" (p. 27). A worker who has achieved this level of relatedness with a client will have an easier time reading the client, in essence is aligned and attuned with what the client feels. It is possible that intersubjective evidence can provide important information about the treatment process, an idea I'll return to later as a way to measure client progress.

Process Recordings

Process recordings are used to foster integration of theory and practice. Integrative practice refers to how students synthesize multiple concepts about practice, including theories, practice skills, and knowledge from other sources. When making this linkage, students often struggle with how to identify theories used in everyday interactions with clients. Few social workers practice from a single theoretical perspective. Instead, most draw from a base of many proven theories that are useful in working with different types of client problems. However, differentiating among these theories can be challenging. In this book, I use process recordings as a method to engage students in identifying theories and reflecting on practice interventions.

Often, social workers asked which theoretical base informs their practice dodge the question by saying they are eclectic. For some, this answer may result from a difficulty articulating their practice philosophy or preferred theories. From my experience teaching social work students, I have found that using process recordings helps them connect theories and practice and understand how their questions and responses to clients are related to particular theories. For this reason, I have included process recordings from each of the transcribed interviews included in this textbook as a teaching tool to facilitate integrating theory and practice in the classroom.

Process recordings are a time-honored tradition in clinical social work that result in the student learning about himself and the client (Cooper & Lesser, 2011). It involves having students "painstakingly" write down their conversations with clients, to the best of their abilities, aware that what they remember may be, in part, their construction of what was actually said. Regardless, I still believe process recordings are an essential tool for teaching students about self-reflection and critical thinking in practice, as well as how to identify theories used in intervention, and alternative ways of understanding and intervening with clients.

Up to now, process recordings mostly have been used in the field by supervisors with students. In this setting, they are positively correlated with students' satisfaction with their supervisors and feelings of preparedness to enter practice (Abramson & Fortune, 1990; Knight, 1996). Although highly valuable for teaching students the art of practice, the use of self, and the integration of theory and skills development, process recordings are underutilized in the classroom (Lovett, 2005; Neuman & Friedman, 1997).

One reason that process recordings are valuable is that they stay close to the written word, giving a clearer picture of what transpired during the interview. They also provide an opportunity to offer feedback on actual clinical work, gain insight into oneself through self-reflection, and, as I've said, connect interventions to particular theories. In this way, process recordings can help to educate students, while also addressing the standard for social workers to "use supervision and consultation" (CSWE, 2008).

Other social work standards come into play, as well. Students are engaged in a reflective analysis when they use process recordings and "apply critical thinking to inform and communicate professional judgments" (CSWE, 2008). Process recordings lead students to "distinguish, appraise, and integrate sources of knowledge, including research-based knowledge and practice wisdom" (CSWE, 2008). On their own and with clinical supervisors and instructors, students can evaluate if the intervention was successful, or question whether another approach would have been more effective. Students can review what they said and how the client responded. They can examine what theory or practice concept informed their intervention. They can ask, "What are some other responses or questions I could have used at that particular moment?"

Social workers today are being held more accountable, asked to explain the effectiveness of their interventions with clients and evaluate their practices. Much goes on behind closed doors, and there is a growing interest in demystifying the work that happens in the privacy of the clinician's office. Process recordings can provide some of this transparency. They are a way for workers to identify theories and practice approaches used with clients, and communicate what led to successful treatment. This gives more confidence to outside funders and third-party payers that we can articulate and evaluate our work. We can demonstrate how our interactions with clients are based on a body of knowledge that is well established, has undergone the rigors of scientific research, and is cited in professional journals. In this sense, social work is moving toward relying more heavily on evidence-based practice (CSWE, 2008).

Process recording templates for use with students vary. Many are organized around three sections: providing text of what was said between the social work intern and client; student analysis and questions; and the supervisor's comments and feedback. The format may range from less structured to more structured, and can be fine-tuned to include specific information related to assessment. For example, they can be arranged to focus on areas of student development (Neuman & Friedman, 1997), used for strengths assessment (Walsh, 2002), or used to record and understand play as communication in social work practice with children (Lovett, 2005). The format used in this book for the five interviews is a table made up of three columns. One column contains the actual words said by the social worker and the client; the next column includes the worker's observations and self-reflections; and the third column contains an analysis of the intervention looking at both theory and practice.

In the first column, the content is verbatim what the social worker and client say in the interview. As soon as the client leaves, the worker writes down as much as she can remember; the sooner this is done after the session ends, the more will be recovered of the conversation. It is crucial to recall exact words as well as possible and not summarize the main points. Staying as close to the narrative as possible will provide rich teaching opportunities in supervision. Avoid trying to look brilliant by changing what was said, because this prevents you learning from and understanding mistakes.

The second column, observations and reflections, emphasizes the importance of the social worker being in tune with herself and her client, and noticing what is happening in the moment. It includes the worker's self-dialogue, what she is thinking and feeling about how the session is going. Effective helping requires the ability to reflect and be self-aware. Social workers must acknowledge how they are influenced by their own thoughts, as well as biases that affect how they interact with clients. As part of professional practice, it is vital that social workers monitor their personal reactions to what clients say to ensure they are responding to clients' needs rather than their own.

The third column identifies the theories and practice knowledge the social worker uses when she intervenes with the client, either by making a statement or posing a question. As professionals, social workers must be prepared to explain their interventions with clients. In the moment, this requires that the social worker use critical thinking skills to evaluate multiple options and choose an intervention that will produce the best outcomes. Afterward, she must evaluate how it worked.

The following template explains how I use process recordings in most of the cases described in this book.

Content	Observation/Reflection	Analysis of Intervention: Theories and Practice Used
Includes the actual words of what the social worker and client say in each interaction in the interview. It is not a summary of what is said but is as close as possible to the spoken words.	Includes any observations the social worker makes of the client or nonverbal cues the client exhibits. Also includes social worker's own self-observations or self-reflection. Social worker notes how the intervention was received by the client.	Identifies theory or practice concepts used in intervention. How effective was the intervention? What are some other different responses or questions the social worker could have used at that particular moment? Social worker judges whether the intervention was successful or not.

Although the usefulness of process recordings is debated in social work education and thought outdated by some, I am a proponent of them. I believe there is no better way to know how a student is engaging with her client, reflecting on her work, critically reviewing practice skills and theories used in interventions, and evaluating practice. We can talk about what we do with clients, and espouse the theories we think we use in practice, but it is quite another experience to dissect what is really taking place. Rather than limiting the use of process recordings in social work education, I recommend using this valuable tool in an expanded way in the classroom, as well as in the field, for student self-evaluation and for measuring student competencies. In addition, I also highly recommend using video-recorded mock client interviews done by students as homework and then playing them back in class for discussion, reflection, and feedback.

Communication Skills

Communication skills are essential for building strong relationships with clients. How we communicate can either make or break the relationship. It can mean the difference between a client returning or stopping prematurely. As a result of its importance in all clinical work, this section is lengthy and discusses many facets of communication.

Students often worry about their first encounter with a client and knowing what to say. They wish they could follow scripts to help them navigate their way through the session and feel less anxious. What do they need to be prepared to sit and talk with a client? My answer is they need a combination of mindfulness communication skills—being present in the moment, knowing how to tune in to self and other, and using effective responding and listening skills. Although I include a lot of factual information about communication, there is another aspect of how we communicate that is difficult to articulate. It relates to the "art of practice" that occurs on an intuitive level and integrates knowledge from many sources. Graybeal (2007, p. 514) refers to this art of practice as an "informed art, born of a balance between the structured, general knowledge that prepares the practitioner for categories of concern, and the intuitive, improvisatory understanding that is expressed in the immeasurable details of being fully present to another human being."

A name I associate with communication training is Virginia Satir, a social worker and pioneer of the family therapy movement in the 1960s. One of her main interests was communication and how it related to self-worth, what she referred to as people's "pot level." Pot was an expression she used (before it referred to marijuana) to describe a person's self-esteem. She used this word with families, giving them an easy way to express feelings previously difficult to talk about. For example, a wife having a bad day and feeling inadequate could say to her husband, "Don't bother me. I am having a low pot day." Satir believed that feelings of worth are learned in the family and are strongly linked to communication. Until a child starts school at age 5 or 6, the child's pot is formed by the family; after, it's formed by school and other outside influences. A child with high-pot can handle many obstacles they experience at school and with peers, whereas a child with lot-pot carries around an overwhelming sense of low self-worth (Satir, 1972, pp. 20–24). Satir (1972) explains it as follows:

> I see communication as a huge umbrella that covers and affects all that goes on between human beings. Once a human being has arrived on this earth, communication is the largest single factor determining what kinds of relationships he makes with others and what happens to him in the world about him. How he manages his survival, how he develops intimacy, how productive he is, how he makes sense, how he connects with his own divinity—all are largely dependent on his communication skills.... Communication is the gauge by which two people measure one another's "pot level," and it is also the tool by which that level can be changed for them both. (p. 30)

When I was a young social worker, I once had trouble getting into a conference I had registered for with Virginia Satir. I was frustrated with the conference organizers, who were not going to admit me at first, and this colored how I experienced the first half of the program. During a break, I waited in line to speak with Virginia, and when it was my turn, I gave her some negative feedback about parts of her earlier presentation. She listened attentively to me, without interrupting or being defensive. When I finished, she simply said, "Thank you. That has been very helpful feedback."

Those few words left a lasting impression on me. I felt that she, in that moment, sensed what I needed from her. What I said was less important than just being heard. Having observed my difficulty getting in to the conference, she knew intuitively that I was looking for validation. She raised my "pot level" by closely listening to me without interruption and then responding in an incredibly supportive way. My frustration dissipated. I felt more alive, and wholeheartedly enjoyed the afternoon session with her. This story is a personal example of the link between self-worth, or pot level, and communication. I have never forgotten the experience and, although I listened to her for a whole day, I learned more from those simple words of affirmation than anything else, and have tried to model this wisdom with clients.

The field of communication skills addresses how we convey messages both verbally and nonverbally to others. It includes three areas: attending skills, listening skills, and responding skills. Attending skills are often (but not always) nonverbal signs that show you are listening and aware of what the client is saying; expressions and body movements are two examples. These skills emphasize the importance of maintaining regular eye contact, having good body posture, facing the other person, and showing an overall open presence. Facial expressions convey thoughts and feelings and should match the words being said by you and the client. Verbal attending skills are words such as—uh-huh, yeah, oh, yes, really, go on, can you say more—and are ways of encouraging the client to share more without interfering with the process.

Another component of attending skills is paying attention to the physical space between you and the client. The goal is to create an optimal balance of distance and closeness on a case-by-case basis. Leaning toward the other person can show you care, but too much leaning may cause the person to back away, feeling uncomfortable. On the flip side, if you're too distant, you may seem uncaring and "far away." Clients differ on how much closeness or distance they want. Schizophrenic clients, for example, are less trusting and may prefer more distance between them and the worker.

When sitting with a client, think about the effect of your body movements. For instance, crossing your legs frequently during a session may give a signal that you are uncomfortable or restless. Nodding during a session is a helpful way to show that you understand, but too much can be distracting and downright annoying. Pay attention to any tendency to fidget, perhaps playing with your hair, pen, or fingernails. I remember once sitting with my clinical supervisor who was fiddling with the elastic band on his watch during our entire conversation. It was bothersome and made it hard for me to concentrate.

Listening skills are another critical part of communication and are often undervalued. Students tend to place more emphasis on what they say and may need to learn how to balance talking with listening. I tell students they have only one mouth but two ears, so they need to listen more than speak. Some students feel pressure to be ready to advise clients, to solve their problems instantly; instead of listening, they are thinking of what they will say next, and this gets in the way of listening. In place of this anxiousness to speak, students must learn to appreciate the collaborative process, helping clients find their own answers through talking, reflecting, and gaining more understanding of their situations.

An example comes to mind from my work with a student. When showing his video-recorded interview of a mock client session in class, it became clear that he was struggling to define his role with the client. Although I felt he had a good rapport with the client, and he demonstrated good attending and engagement skills, I was concerned with his tendency to over-advise the client on what should be done. Another student role-played the client in the video. The mock client had changed her major in college from nursing to social work but had not told her mom. She was worried that her mother would be angry about her decision, and this was causing the client more anxiety. Toward the end of the mock session, the student role-playing the social worker gave a long monologue about what the client should do and the importance of being honest with her mother.

Although this assessment may be right, his response sounded "preachy" and involved a long passage of his talking on his own with no input from the client. Looking at the process recording reinforced this problem by bringing attention to the first column and the long section with only the worker speaking. When we discussed this interview in class, other students saw the problem and simultaneously identified with the tendency to take too much responsibility for the session. When I said to the student who conducted the interview that I thought he was working too hard, he understood what I was getting at. He realized that he fell into the trap of trying to be the expert and proscribe what the client needed rather than help her find the answer.

I tell students that sometimes the greatest gift they can give to a client is being fully present and listening. Although it may not feel like they are doing much, they are joining the client in a meaningful way that lets the client know someone cares enough to take the time to really listen and understand. If you have ever had the experience of being listened to in this way, you know what I mean. It can be very empowering and affirming.

As you learn to balance speaking with listening, stay aware of "how" you listen and what gets in the way. For example, you may not be listening carefully, because you are focusing on what to say next and trying to come up with a brilliant solution to the client's problem. By concentrating on the solution, you can't give full attention to what the client is saying and feeling. This was the case with the student I described in the preceding example, who felt he needed to advise his client about what to do. True listening is also hampered if the worker has stereotypes and preconceived ideas about the client and what he needs.

A practitioner's own personal issues can become obstacles to good listening as well. This explains why social work emphasizes the values of self-reflection and self-awareness, concepts that are discussed later in this chapter. Sometimes a client's problem may trigger thoughts of unresolved personal problems in the worker that cause him to be preoccupied with himself and not fully listening to the client. This can lead to further issues if the worker makes the false assumption that because their problems are similar, they require the same solution. Another potential problem area has to do with countertransference reactions. This is when a client reminds the social worker of someone else from her past and she reacts as if the client were this other person.

For example, I once supervised a young social worker who was working with a heterosexual couple who came to her for help with their relationship. Their presenting problem was that the woman wanted more closeness in the relationship, and the boyfriend felt smothered by her and wanted more space. The social worker described the woman in the relationship as being more dependent and rigid in her thinking, adhering to strict social norms and traditional expectations for marriage and family. In contrast, she described the boyfriend as more independent, enjoying being single, having few responsibilities and wanting to go out with his friends more.

Early in the treatment, the social worker noticed she was reacting negatively to the woman and had a tendency to side with the boyfriend. Realizing these feelings, she reflected on her reactions in supervision. It surfaced that this woman reminded her of her mother and sister who were dominating figures in her life growing up, and whom she also saw as rigid and dependent types. She felt pressured by them to conform to their way of thinking and behaving, and when she rebelled, they were very critical of her. Once the social worker became aware of this countertransference she was able to separate herself from the past and see her client differently.

Thus far I've discussed attending and listening skills, which leaves responding to clients. Practitioners can sometimes respond to clients in ways that are ineffective and alienating. These responses are often categorized as communication stoppers. Examples are: being judgmental or critical, advising, showing prejudicial or stereotypical thinking, interrupting, finishing a client's sentences, being sarcastic, sympathizing or pitying, jumping to conclusions or making assumptions before listening fully to what the client has to say, diverting or changing the subject in order to avoid talking about something that may make the worker uncomfortable. The latter is one of the most common struggles of students. When looking at video-recorded student interviews, or analyzing process recordings, these abrupt moments when the worker changes the subject stand out and become apparent to students. They occur when the student is not sure what to do with the feelings the client expresses. They can also happen if the student feels he needs to direct the conversation to make sure he gets the information needed for an assessment. Other times, the student simply is not listening closely to what the client is saying and goes off in another direction.

If I'm working with a class, and we notice a disruption in the process during a video-taped mock interview, we try to understand how it happened and ask the student to reflect on what he was thinking at the time. Then we come up with several options for responding differently to the client that would follow the client's lead and keep the conversation on track. Next, we might role-play these alternative interventions to see where they take us. Another recent example from a student illustrates the tendency new social workers have to change the subject prematurely and move into a new line of inquiry. During a mock interview with another student role-playing an undergraduate struggling with social anxiety, the student in the role of social worker changed the subject abruptly, which meant moving away from a potentially meaningful conversation.

The following example is part of the process recording where this happens:

Client: My mother was really overprotective with me and my brothers. I don't know she was always like super careful about everything, anxious about us going out or going to parties and stuff like that. I think socially she's kind of the same way too, being anxious in social situations.

Student social worker: Have you ever experienced any bullying or anything that would make you self-conscious?

Client: Not really. that's why I don't know where it comes from.

When I asked the student what made her ask that question, she responded that she had read recently that some people with social phobia have experienced bullying. This student came to understand that while the client was talking about something important, perhaps strongly related to the problem of social anxiety, she as the social worker was only thinking about what to ask next. By exploring the client's problem with questions based on what she had read, rather than listening to what the client was telling her, she missed a very important opportunity in the session. If she had followed up on the client's comment about her mother being overly protective and also possibly having social anxiety, the student might have learned more about the problem. This significant lesson for the student was made possible when she shared her video-recorded interview and process recording.

Another important communication assessment tool is the use of open- and closed-ended questions. In terms of how social workers pose questions to clients, it is important to distinguish between the two. Open-ended questions are conversation movers, because they allow clients to offer their own answers and feelings about a subject. Clients can choose among multiple possibilities to respond in a way that reflects their situation, as opposed to the social worker leading them in a certain direction. This frees clients to tell their story with the least interference.

Closed-ended questions can be answered with a yes, no, or one-word answer. There may be times when closed-ended questions are useful in gathering facts, but most of the time they restrict the conversation and limit how clients respond. Also, the practitioner can use closed-ended questions inadvertently in destructive ways to manipulate the client's story to reflect the worker's own opinions and choices. How the practitioner frames the question might provide him with the answer he wants, but it doesn't give a true picture of the situation from the client's perspective. It also doesn't allow the client to elaborate and give a fuller description of the situation.

Example of closed-ended question: You feel badly don't you?
Open-ended alternative: How do you feel about that?
Example of closed-ended question: Is your family upset about you going to the concert?
Open-ended alternative: How did your family feel about you going to the concert?
Example of closed-ended question: It's hard to think about that, isn't it?
Open-ended alternative: What do you think about it?

You can find a wealth of information on specific interviewing tactics in the counseling, communication, and social work literature, particularly when and how to use the various responding skills (Sevel et al., 1999; Shulman, 2009). Some of these common skills are tuning in, paraphrasing, reflecting back feelings, clarifying, exploring, containment, elaborating, information-giving, confronting, holding to focus, and summarizing. In each of the five mock client interviews discussed in this book, I define and discuss the communication skills used. It is helpful for students to practice these skills in role-plays and in their own video-recorded interviews.

Strengths Perspective

Acknowledging clients' strengths is central to social work practice. When clients come for help, they are feeling overwhelmed by their problems, and they may be unable to recognize their positive qualities, attributes, and abilities. As clients talk about their struggles and their stories unfold, social workers listen and inquire about aspects of their lives that demonstrate resilience, courage, talents, hobbies, personality characteristics, uniqueness, family supports, social networks, and other resources that can be enlisted to help them find creative solutions to their problems. By bringing attention to these competencies, social workers give back to clients a complete picture of themselves that restores their self-esteem and sense of hope about the future.

Saleebey looks at how we use the strengths perspective as a paradigm shift in social work knowledge and education, with profound implications for practice (2009, pp. 42–43). That's because our professional know-how, our role as expert, is challenged. It changes the orientation from a worker directing treatment to a collaborative effort. This means that the worker is available in a different way: It emphasizes his role in identifying clients' assets and asking questions about their strengths and resilience. The practitioner's approach shifts away from problems and deficits to a positive framework for understanding human development that looks for areas of competence, resiliency, and self-correction. The strengths perspective builds on the potential for change that exists in clients.

Until recently, the strengths perspective was used in assessment to identify strengths related to overcoming adversity and hadn't included explicit intervention strategies and treatment protocols. Rawana and Brownlee (2009) broaden how we think about strengths to include a more comprehensive strengths assessment followed by a plan for intervention that uses clients' assets. In this expansion stage, strengths can be turned into clients' capacity to make changes to address difficulties. Social workers use questions to enhance clients' understanding of how the strengths can be used in everyday interactions. As part of an intervention strategy, a worker may recommend that a client post a list of strengths in a prominent place as a constant reminder.

This strengths model has found success in work with youth. It includes specific guidelines that build upon the strengths of young people in different domains of functioning, not only those linked to overcoming adversity (MacArthur et al., 2011). Working with children and adolescents between the ages of 10 and 18, practitioners explore the young clients' lives across the board to find the positive characteristics and abilities that each client can enhance and then apply to daily life. Interventions involve frequent conversations with the children, and the significant people in their lives, about their strengths. This motivates youth to make positive changes and helps them to see the practitioner as an ally.

The Strengths Assessment Inventory is the tool mentioned in the preceding example to identify strengths of children and adolescents across multiple domains of daily functioning. Although strengths may reside within persons, the extent to which they are expressed often depends on the environmental context. In assessment, the worker evaluates "the strengths of the child as personal agency and the strengths in how the child interacts with their environment" (Brazeau et al., 2012, p. 385). The inventory includes questions related to personal development and within specific contexts, such as home, school, and the community. The advantage of this inventory is that it looks at strengths intrinsic to the individual, as well as strengths related to the individual's interaction with the environment. In clinical situations, the worker engages the family to visualize "in which domains the youth has many strengths, in which ones the youth is choosing not to develop or express strengths, and in which the youth may be facing substantial challenges or adversities" (MacArthur et al., 2011, p. 11). Workers involve families in innovative ways that take the discussion away from deficits. In this new conversation, the emphasis of family therapy shifts from how families have failed to how they can succeed (Walsh, 2012).

There are many similarities between the strengths perspective and narrative theory (narrative theory is discussed in chapter 2). They warn against a strict adherence to theories as facts that pathologize clients. By labeling, these theories blind us from seeing the whole client and how context shapes what we see. Both approaches encourage the social worker to assume a position of "not knowing" that takes the conversation away from the "saturated" problem into new areas. This allows other possibilities to emerge from the collaborative dialogue between worker and client that lead to "unique outcomes" and the construction of alternative narratives.

Assessment, if wielded unwisely, can be considered a political activity (Cowager, 1994). When assessment focuses on deficits, it creates obstacles for clients, exercising control and power over their personal and social lives. It renders clients helpless in finding their own solutions to problems. In contrast, assessment that emphasizes client strengths delivers another message with a different political agenda—one that gives the power back to clients. The role of the social worker is "to nourish, encourage, assist, enable, support, stimulate, and unleash the strengths within people" (Cowager, 1994, p. 264). This links assessment to empowerment and the belief that clients can take action on their own behalf to improve their lives.

Empowerment

I learned about the true meaning of empowerment working with Judy Lee at the University of Connecticut School of Social Work in the 1990s. After I completed my PhD in social work, she was instrumental in bringing me to the school, where I worked for two years as a part-time faculty member. Lee devoted her life to the principles of empowerment—writing, teaching, and practicing from this perspective. At the time, I was an ardent follower of narrative therapy, and Lee saw how my ideas about narrative connected to empowerment practice.

Lee (1994) saw empowerment as a new way of practicing social work and wrote extensively about its conceptual framework and knowledge base. She was concerned that the word "empowerment" was being applied inappropriately in direct practice, commonly used by social workers to describe most everything they did. Lee (1994) claims that: "the word empower is not intended to describe psychologically, interpersonally, or existentially oriented interventions with dominant group clients. Although the general population may also experience powerlessness at this time of constant societal change, our focus here is on members of stigmatized groups" (pp. 12–13). Instead, empowerment practice works with vulnerable populations to build community. It joins with them to challenge ways they have been oppressed and blocked from gaining access to necessary resources.

Lee (1994) describes three related and "interlocking" concepts of empowerment practice that are: "1) the development of a more positive and potent sense of self; 2) the construction of knowledge and capacity for more critical comprehension of the web of social and political realities of one's environment; and 3) the cultivation of resources and strategies, or more functional competence, for attainment of personal and collective goals" (p. 13). These goals lead to specific intervention strategies that include: work on an individual level to raise self-esteem, acknowledge personal assets, and build ego strengths and coping skills; work at multiple levels to teach directly about poverty, power and authority, oppression, social stratification, and so on; and work to remove power blocks and attain needed resources.

Lee (1994) provides a gripping example of empowerment practice in chapter 8 of her book that describes her work with a group of African-American homeless women, who called themselves "Successful Women" and resided in a Hartford area shelter. After meeting with Lee for almost two years, they celebrated many accomplishments for themselves and others who were homeless. They participated in national and state political action events, they attended coalition meetings on the problem of homelessness, they testified at the legislature to impact social policies, and they spoke to outside groups to educate the public on the problem of homelessness. Once the group ended and the women moved on with their separate lives, some members remained involved by reaching out to current residents in the shelter and advising shelter staff. The group experience empowered them and led to significant changes in their lives.

Diversity

Making the transition from a discussion of empowerment to diversity is an easy one. Empowerment practice often works with marginalized clients who appear different from the dominant culture. Diversity can relate to age, economic status, sexual orientation, disability, physical appearance, mental illness, gender, language, race, and ethnicity. These groups may experience prejudice, discrimination, and oppression on an ongoing basis by those more powerful and privileged, and have limited access to resources that would help them break free. One of the goals of social work is to overcome social and economic injustices by empowering vulnerable and oppressed populations to participate more fully in society.

We live in a multicultural society that demands that social workers be culturally competent. As the nation becomes more diverse, this becomes a more pressing need and an important part of social work education. The current European-American majority will soon be a minority. To prepare for multicultural practice, workers must be knowledgeable and open with clients "having many cultures, religions, family forms, strengths and challenges or migration stories. Multicultural practice recognizes, respects, and responds with informed thoughtfulness to the variety of differences within and between people" (Murphy & Dillon, 2011, p. 14). Practitioners should be attentive and sensitive to differences and willing to engage in direct discussion about them with clients, in a way that shows respect and a willingness to embrace diversity and not avoid it.

Current waves of immigration, and the ensuing political debate about immigration policy, reflect this growing transformation in our population. Delgado, Jones, and Rohani (2005) believe that "the United States is on the cusp of incredible changes in the next 50 years—changes that will alter the composition of the country as we know it and bring with it numerous languages that will be an integral part of the nation's social fabric" (p. xi). Social work's role in responding to the needs of refugee and immigrant populations will continue to grow. It calls out to new social workers to be creative and innovative to address the needs of this expanding community. For example, a recent alumna from the Regis College Social Work Program received a grant from a local foundation to train multilingual, diverse women who were poor and living in the Boston area to be translators. The goal is for the new trainees to get hired by local hospitals to provide services to patients who need translators. The benefits of this program are twofold: It provides an important communication bridge for patients who do not understand or speak English, and it also offers skills training and jobs for low-income, previously unemployed, diverse women.

The conversation about cultural diversity becomes even more complex when you consider multiracial and multiethnic peoples. This new aspect of diversity was recognized in the 2000 census, which allowed citizens to check off more than one box to identify their racial identity. I personally notice this changing landscape each year with my social work students when we discuss their racial and cultural identities in a class exercises to learn about diversity. Increasing numbers of them identify themselves as multiracial and multiethnic, and this allows them to become resources to each other in becoming more culturally competent.

Diversity issues impact assessment and how we see clients' stories. What may be normative in one culture may not be viewed the same way in another. Assessment must consider how issues of diversity impact understanding the person and the situation. It must also avoid worker bias. D. Mark Ragg (2011) warns against the risk of attributing meaning to clients' stories based on our own cultural bias. Ragg (2011) states: "Most of our knowledge and practice wisdom will be developed within our cultural cocoon. Cultural assumptions, priorities, and experiences silently influence our thinking, creating many unacknowledged biases in how we respond to client information" (p. 91).

Although it is important for social workers to have knowledge and acceptance of difference, they can also learn from clients by asking specific questions about the client's ethnic identity. Done in an empathic way, this demonstrates to clients that the worker is interested in them and appreciates ways in which they may be different. It can also give clients more confidence in the worker's ability to understand them. Another way of looking at cultural competence is that it "is a process by which social workers position themselves and become open to those with whom they work as key informants in their competence journey" (Hepworth et al., 2013, p. 462).

Values and Ethics

One way new social workers are socialized into the profession is through identification with the strongly held beliefs and values of the profession. Programs and schools have strict admission policies to ensure that potential candidates embody the values deemed crucial for practice. Professional values include: regard for individual worth and dignity; the right to self-determination; commitment to social and economic justice; helping clients obtain needed resources; making institutions more humane and responsive to human needs and; respect for diversity. From time to time, social work educators may identify students whose personal values conflict with those of the profession and who may need to find another area of study; for example, when a student blames welfare clients for their own problems or expresses prejudicial or disparaging comments about a minority group.

Self-reflection and self-awareness are critical practice skills to help social workers avoid unethical behavior or personal values interfering with client work. These pitfalls present themselves constantly. For example, a social worker might impose her own religious or political agenda on a client considering an abortion, on a wife struggling with whether to stay with a cheating husband, or with a daughter faced with terminating life support on an elderly mother. Many students struggle to maintain a nonjudgmental stance when sitting with abusive parents, substance abusers, pedophiles, or men in domestic violence disputes. They can express empathy for the victims of abuse, but they often have a harder time understanding the needs of those who have abused others. These feelings may be pronounced if students have had first-hand experience with abuse in their own families. If this comes up in supervision, students may be asked to reflect on their reactions and, in some cases, encouraged to seek outside counseling.

Closely related to social work values is ethics. Core social work values, referred to in the preceding example, are embedded in principles for ethical behavior. Students need to be competent in applying these principles to guide professional practice (CSWE, 2008). This requires managing personal values so they do not interfere with clinical work and making ethical decisions based on the National Association of Social Workers (NASW) Code of Ethics (please refer to the NASW website for a copy of the Code of Ethics). The Code includes a set of rules for ethical behavior that are standards for professional behavior. Some areas that the Code addresses are: issues of confidentiality; informed consent; duty to warn or report; specific expectations for responsible behavior with clients, such as keeping boundaries and dual relationships; incompetent behavior of colleagues; and conduct in the work setting. Although the NASW Code of Ethics can help social workers with certain ethical issues, it can also be unclear and difficult to apply to specific client situations. Rothman (2005) adds that "the Code appears purposively ambiguous, and the play of professional standards, laws, and personal ethical standards can be a fascinating, though often challenging, part of the professional social worker's decision-making process" (p. 14).

Ethical decision making is not a simple process of translating the guidelines into practice. Social workers are daily faced with complicated and unique client situations that pose ethical dilemmas for which the Code does not offer solutions. Dilemmas can result from competing values, such as self-determination, versus an obligation to serve the client's best interests; for example, imagine a practitioner working with an elderly client who adamantly wants to stay in his own home despite concern for his safety and well-being. Ethical dilemmas also could result from conflicting responsibilities or loyalties; for example, should social workers follow an agency's policy or do what they think is right for the client.

Social workers are expected to recognize and tolerate ambiguity in resolving ethical conflicts and apply strategies for ethical reasoning to make decisions (CSWE, 2008). Loewenberg and Dolgoff (1996) developed a decision-making model comprising 11 steps that can be applied to many clinical situations. It includes a number of ethical criteria that can be used when assessing decision alternatives; it orders principles by rank from the most important to the least important. To further clarify and integrate ethical aspects of decision making into social work practice, Loewenberg and Dolgoff (1996) offer additional screens: the ethical assessment screen, ethical rules screen, and ethical principles screen.

Even combining the Code of Ethics with other strategies for decision making, social workers are not given a crystal-clear ethics path. Practitioners also need to be engaged in open and ongoing dialogue with each other about ethical dilemmas. Rhodes (1986) states that, "what is needed is a much broader debate about the ethical and political basis of our work. Given the different points of view that exist in the profession, the Code could serve as a focal point for such dialogue" (pp. 182–183). Rhodes calls for the profession to have open discussion, disagreement, and questioning about ethical issues as they surface, without the expectation of consensus.

To help foster this important conversation about ethical dilemmas, social workers need resources, especially other professionals to talk to about these issues, so they aren't burdened by solving tricky questions on their own. The Massachusetts chapter of NASW has a committee that serves this purpose and consults with social workers struggling with ethical issues. Specific agencies and settings in which social workers practice should also recognize the need to support their staff in these areas.

Use of Self, Self-Reflection, and Self-Awareness

Use of self refers to a social worker's personal style of relating to clients. Social workers must find their own voice and style of doing clinical work that takes into account their personality, experiences, humor, and other unique features that make them who they are. When a worker practices from a style that resonates with her own person, this humanizes the therapeutic experience and makes the worker–client encounter more genuine. It allows for a natural, relaxed flow in communication that is flexible, dynamic, and adapts to each situation.

Students often begin in the field by modeling their supervisors, instructors, and other experienced social workers, who students see applying skills in distinct ways with clients. At first, the students may try to mimic exactly what they observe. Over time, and with more experience, they will become more comfortable with their skills and experiment with approaches that feel more natural. They also begin to judge when it is appropriate, or not, to use self-disclosure and personal experiences as metaphors to help clients cope with a similar experience.

The use of self also informs how we think about clients and how we make clinical decisions. It relates to practice wisdom and intuition, both different ways of knowing discussed earlier. From years of experience in direct practice, seasoned social workers can pick up on the nuances of what clients say and need by comparing their situations to other ones, and using those comparisons to help guide clinical action. Sometimes this can be articulated and is understood, and other times it is an automatic, unconscious response that is hard to explain.

Social work is a profession that uses the self in its practice, and this necessitates that clinicians fine-tune their skills of self-reflection. Practitioners need to understand themselves on a deeper level. We should be in touch with our values, our reactions to others, the influence of family-of-origin patterns, and our basic assumptions about culture and difference. It requires that we set aside time to think about the meaning of clinical work—how our personal experiences and biases may trigger reactions to clients that are unwarranted. We learn a lot about ourselves through practice; sometimes, we need outside help to address what issues arise for us as we work.

Although it's sometimes joked that people go into social work because they need help themselves, there is always some truth in sarcasm. I think all students should experience sitting in the client's chair for a period of time. They would gain valuable insight into themselves on an intrapsychic and interpersonal level that would contribute to greater self-awareness. This experience also allows workers to separate their personal issues from those of clients to avoid countertransference and projection. Countertransference, referenced earlier, is a distortion that occurs when the worker reacts to the client as if the client were someone from his own past. Sweitzer and King (2009) attribute self-understanding to helping social workers avoid projection: "The unconscious tendency to believe that you see in others feelings and beliefs that are actually your own, but you are unaware of them because of their unconscious nature. This tendency can affect your ability to understand, accept, and empathize with another person" (p. 65). For example if you are upset with a client, you may project this feeling onto the client and instead think the client is angry with you.

One of the core competencies in social work is to "identify as a professional social worker and conduct oneself accordingly" (CSWE, 2008). To do this, social workers must "practice personal reflection and self-correction to assure continual professional growth" (CSWE, 2008). Using process recordings and observing one's inner thoughts, feelings, and reactions to clients strengthens a student's skills of self-reflection. It leads to self-awareness and a more conscious use of self in clinical practice. Reviewing process recordings and interventions used also helps the practitioner ask questions and think about other more effective strategies, which leads to self-correction.

Evidence-Based Practice

There is a growing demand for clinicians to use evidence-based practice (EBP) in social work. In a short time, EBP has strongly influenced medical and mental health practice, research, and policy, and it has become a major part of clinical training in the mental health field (Drisko & Grady, 2012). However, because it is relatively new, challenges exist for understanding what it means and how it can be applied. In the past, social work practitioners have depended little on research findings to guide their practice (Proctor, 2007), and now find themselves ill prepared to respond to these new dictates. The push for EBP in mental health has come from third-party insurers asking for more accountability, the medical model that uses EBP with its patients, and the new Council on Social Work Education standards that emphasize engaging in research-informed practice and practice-informed research (CSWE, 2008).

One definition of evidence-based practice describes it as a "process of including the best available research evidence alongside practice wisdom to make clinical decisions, and evaluate the outcomes of your decisions" (Wharton & Bolland, 2012, p. 158). In the Social Worker's Desk Reference (Vandiver, 2002), evidence-based practice means that we use a variety of databases of systematic reviews on best practices to guide our interventions with clients to improve treatment outcomes.

Drisko and Grady's book on EBP seeks to address significant problems they found with current literature on the subject that made it difficult for social workers to apply the method to practice. Problems included: discordance with direct practice or a client-centered viewpoint; absence of lengthy case examples; technicalities well described, but not real people in real situations; lack of detailed, high-quality, systematic reviews; incomplete guidelines for what constituted good research; and an emphasis on "top down" outcome research, which showed limited collaboration between the client and clinician (2012, p. v).

Other studies done on practitioner use of EBP also cited obstacles to its implementation. Evidence-based practice research findings didn't fit every client, and diversity wasn't always acknowledged. There was a sense that certain theories got overemphasized in EBP, and many workers feared loss of flexibility (Wharton & Bolland, 2012). The studies found that clinicians were more likely to consult with peers or mentors than to seek relevant research before making practice decisions. These workers relied on their training and experience and clinical observations, and preferred to rely on common sense and an intuitive approach. "Practice-based evidence appeared to guide most of their practice decisions, because they believed that research is often produced outside of real-life settings" (Wharton & Bolland, 2012, p. 160). These same studies showed that clinicians were not opposed to empirical evidence but believed it should be considered along with practice wisdom, client preferences, client details, other research, and contextual issues (Wharton & Bolland, 2012).

Although EBP is associated with objective, quantitative data, there is growing recognition that there are other ways to measure evidence. One promising study suggests the use of qualitative, practice-based evidence to inform decisions about the goals and direction of client work. In this study, Arnd-Caddigan (2011) proposes intersubjective evidence as an alternative to quantitative proof of effective treatment. This evidence relies on the social worker's knowledge in the shared, intimate experience with the client and emphasizes the importance of the worker's reflections on the process to discover shifts that may be occurring.

Intersubjectivity, which I spoke about earlier in the chapter, refers to tuning in to the other's experience or knowing what the other's experience is, in terms of its meaning, goals, and emotions (Stern, 1985). By reflecting on the client's feelings, the practitioner can track important changes taking place in the client as evidence of progress. Arnd-Caddigan (2011) believes that intersubjective evidence should be recognized as a valid form of practice-based evidence. In the future, perhaps we'll come to a broadening definition of what constitutes evidence, making room for both quantitative and qualitative measures to determine positive treatment outcomes.

Although the debate continues about the merits of EBP, it appears that the movement is here to stay, because it is linked to accountability and third-party payers. However, Drisko and Grady (2012) caution social workers from reaching simple conclusions about what constitutes best practices and to stay aware of many points of view on the subject. Practitioners must use critical thinking skills to evaluate the research, how it was done, the methods used, the populations studied, how conclusions were made, and whether summaries of treatment leave out critical factors that may explain why treatments worked. Also, workers should involve clients in choosing treatment options. The list of questions that follows brings attention to the key issues you need to consider when applying EBP principles to work with clients and can help guide decisions regarding treatment.

"Does useful evidence exist on the topic I need to know about? Does the research address the specific kinds of outcomes I and my client seek? Is the research comprehensive and valid? Were the study participants like my client? Does the research point to a single best treatment? Are other treatments available which were not fully studied but which may be helpful to my client? How does my client view the best treatments reported in the literature? Are there cultural or practical factors that may make this treatment a poor fit for this client in the situation? Are these practices ethical? Can I deliver this treatment or are there other nearby services that can provide it?" (Drisko & Grady, 2012, p. 16).

Assessment

Assessment involves ascribing meaning to events. Dorothy Scott (1989) compares this process in social work to that of the ethnographer who seeks to understand the culture of another society (p. 38). She draws a parallel between practice and ethnographic research, "including validation of interpretations and the need for reflexivity." She argues that, "meaning-making is central to how social workers practice," and the worker attempts to "decipher what events mean to the client and significant others, both at the intrasubjective and intersubjective levels of analysis.... Through experience and application of theory, the practitioner develops cognitive schemata on categories of problems that facilitate the process of deciphering what events mean to clients and others" (Scott, 1989, p. 49).

Assessment requires understanding the client in a holistic way that elevates the importance of context in the construction of meaning. It is a collaborative activity done with the client. Some of the areas explored include the client's developmental history, present family, family-of-origin, school, work, medical and psychiatric history, culture, ethnicity, religion, friendship and support networks, strengths, community involvement, and significant events and people that have influenced the individual over time. Data collection refers to this compilation of information about (and with) the client from many sources that provide a comprehensive and in-depth understanding of the person and his situation.

The social worker learns more about the client with each meeting, which makes assessment continuous. It is a multidimensional concept that can be approached in many ways using different theoretical approaches. To make meaning out of the information, social workers look to theories as well as other sources of knowledge: generalist social work practice, the ecological and the bio/psycho/social/spiritual models, human behavior and developmental life span theories, family life cycle and family systems theories, knowledge of cultures, psychological theories, personality theories, and sociological theories. Assessment is an active and ongoing process between the client and social worker using these relevant theories and knowledge bases to make meaning out of the client's situation. Assessment leads to an understanding of the problem, what causes it and potential solutions, and has implications for intervention.

Ecological Method

The ecological model, although not referred to as a theory, is a lens through which social workers understand clients' problems. It views these problems contextually, as the result of difficult transactions between individuals and their social and/or physical surroundings. The relationship is reciprocal: The individual affects the environment and is affected by the environment. The social environment includes family, neighborhood, groups, organizations, and larger social systems. The physical environment might encompass issues such as poverty, inadequate space, poor living conditions, and lack of opportunity to experience nature. In this model, a person can influence the environment in many ways, that is, temperament, self-esteem, genetic predispositions, or mental or physical illness. Likewise, the environment can create hardships and stressors that impinge on the individual.

Problems are not seen as residing within the person or the environment. Instead, the problem is described as a poor fit between the two. For example, a child who learns best experientially may not perform well in a more traditional classroom setting. A child with a disability may not thrive or feel accepted in a family that has perfectionist tendencies. In both situations, the child may become disruptive in these settings, and by acting out, cause additional problems in each environment.

To study the transactions between a person and her environment, the social worker might choose to construct an eco-map with the client. The eco-map illustrates all systems involved in the client's life: extended family, schools, churches, public agencies, clinics, work, and friends. The eco-map also depicts the quality of the relationship between the individual and the various systems. It is an assessment tool through which the social worker and the client can identify problem areas, as well as sources of support and stress in the environment, and can lead to interventions aimed at increasing resources.

Diagnosis versus Assessment

Although the medical model emphasizes diagnosis, specifically linking a patient's symptoms to a diagnosis, social work uses the person-in-situation model that emphasizes a different type of assessment, one that looks at the whole person. Assessment goes beyond matching symptoms to a diagnosis and attempts to understand clients' problems in their context and from a life span developmental perspective. Assessment is done at the micro, mezzo, and macro levels and also understands issues of diversity.

When practitioners work in medical settings or in mental health, they may be forced to diagnose and use the terminology found in the Diagnostic and Statistical Manual (DSM). Barbara Probst (2012) believes that "new social workers need guidance on how to think diagnostically yet flexibly about clients who are mixtures rather than purebreds" (p. 255). To supplement the limited and depersonalized view of patients based on diagnosis, social workers can provide more background information, psychosocial histories that are added to medical records. This gives a more personal and humanistic picture of the patient, which can help foster empathy.

In the following pages I have included three outlines for assessment. They include the problem-solving method, psychosocial assessment and intervention strategy, and bio/psycho/social/spiritual assessment. I refer back to these outlines in later chapters as I apply them to each case study.

There are few differences between the three outlines, and there may be times when they are repetitive. Indeed, there are many ways in which they are similar: They all use an ecological approach that is collaborative, pay attention to client strengths, and stress the overall importance of assessment. Both the problem-solving and psychosocial assessments cover intervention strategies, evaluation, plans for termination, and follow-up. I appreciate that the problem-solving outline looks at how the client and social worker engage with each other, which highlights the value of the therapeutic relationship. Psychosocial assessment includes a statement about the presenting problem, a reminder that workers must stay aware of why the client wants help. There is also more emphasis on the client's functioning level and relevant past history.

The bio/psycho/social/spiritual assessment takes into account the constant interactions among systems that affect clients, and helps the social worker understand how each system affects the other. What I especially appreciate about this outline is its inclusion of the spiritual domain, an aspect of client's lives often neglected in social work practice. By addressing spirituality, workers can help clients tackle the larger questions they often seek help with, for example, meaning and purpose in life and understanding loss and death.

Problem-Solving Method

The basis of the problem-solving method is collaborative work with the client to define and resolve the problem for which the client seeks help. This approach looks at the different phases of the helping process, that is, engagement, assessment, planning, intervention, evaluation, termination, and follow-up. Although the method describes discrete phases, each stage is really ongoing and continuous. For example, the social worker is always engaging the client, assessing new information, and evaluating the process. Following are the steps in the problem-solving method.

1. Engagement is the initial step in the problem-solving method and involves building a relationship and an alliance with the client and defining the problem (or problems). This requires showing empathy and warmth toward the client and having genuine interest. It also involves using good communication skills that demonstrate you are listening and attuned to what the client is saying.

2. Assessment is the process of understanding and defining the problem in more depth based on the information gathered, the history, and any previous attempts to solve it. The social worker and the client prioritize the problems, which to address first, and set goals for their work together. Goals are described in specific, behavioral terms that can be measured. Assessment takes place on a micro, mezzo, and macro level and is sensitive to issues of diversity. Client strengths are identified.

3. Planning involves figuring out what to do next after assessing the problem with the client. The social worker and the client work together to plan the intervention. It asks the questions, "How will we achieve these goals?" and "What are the steps involved?"

4. Intervention is the process of carrying out the plan and is the action step. It is what the social worker and client do to achieve pre-set goals. Intervention is based on choosing the best strategies and approaches to deal with the problem(s).

5. During evaluation, the social worker and client review the goals and determine if they have been achieved. If they have not, the worker and client re-assess the definition of the problem, the goals, and the intervention. Were there other factors that were not considered? Were the goals achievable? Should the goals be changed? Was the intervention appropriate to meet these goals?

6. Termination involves a transition. It can mean the client ends the relationship with the social worker if the goals have been met. Or it can be unplanned, when either the social worker or client ends the relationship prematurely for different reasons, for example, moving, changing jobs, or leaving a field placement. A client may also choose to end treatment abruptly if he is not ready to address the problem.

7. Follow-up means contacting clients after termination to determine how they are progressing. This can be done with a phone call or a written survey in which clients evaluate the services they received and let you know how they are doing. Through follow-up, a worker may realize a client requires additional services. This step is often overlooked by social workers who are often busy concentrating on a heavy, active caseload.

Psychosocial Assessment and Intervention Strategy

The psychosocial assessment and intervention strategy is similar to the problem-solving method. It is a collaborative process done with the client and acknowledges client strengths, but it does not categorize assessment as a series of steps. Emphasis is on describing the client and the presenting problem, looking at current functioning and relevant past history, and coming up with a formulation based on the information collected, with implications for intervention. An evaluation of treatment outcomes follows termination. At the end of this outline, I have added a bullet point on theories. I include this to reinforce the importance of students reflecting on the theories used to make case formulations and to engage their critical thinking skills.

Identifying Data
- Basic demographic information: Age, gender, ethnicity, economic status, employment, and marital or family status. For macro students: describe the organization, agency, or community and key players involved.
- Brief physical description

Presenting Problem
- What is the reason for seeking services?
- What event or stressor led to the current request for help?
- Which risk factors or vulnerabilities are being addressed by the request for services?

Social Supports, Current Functioning, Strengths

- Access to family, friends, or other supportive persons
- Functioning level at work, school, or within the organization
- Strengths, risk factors, protective factors

Relevant Past History

- Include any information that relates to the current issues
- Relevant developmental events
- Prior coping or areas of mastery
- Past intervention

Formulation

- Start with restating key identifying information, presenting problem, and referral source
- Present your understanding of the problem, the causes, and what options for change are present

Intervention Strategy

- What is the plan for intervention? Who will be involved in treatment? What modality will be used (individual, couples, family or group treatment, or a combination of modalities)? How often and how long will treatment be?

Termination and Evaluation

- How will you evaluate the treatment? Will the client be referred to other services?

Theoretical Lens

- In making your assessment and formulation of the problem, what theories did you use and how did they help you?

Bio/Psycho/Social/Spiritual Assessment

The bio/psycho/social/spiritual approach is holistic and looks at the relationships among different systems that continually interact with each other. The social worker observes how an individual is influenced by biological, psychological, social, and spiritual systems. When examining a client's problem, it is important to consider how each system affects each other. For example, a teenager could be suffering from attention deficit hyperactivity disorder (biological) that causes him to have low self-esteem (psychological) and difficulty relating to his peers, his family, or being in school (social), which in turn causes him to feel alienated and disconnected (spiritual). It uses an ecological and systems approach to assessment.

The biological part of the assessment includes some of the following areas:

- History of attaining, or having difficulty with, developmental milestones
- Predispositions, temperament
- Present and past physical health issues

- General health status: level of physical activity, nutrition, weight, sleep patterns
- Any disability or physical handicap
- Any addiction, for example, alcohol, tobacco, drugs, sex, gambling
- Family genetic history
- Medication taken
- Any other health problem or physical symptoms not noted earlier

The psychological part of the assessment includes some of the following areas:

- Cognitive development: This involves the client's ability to learn. Areas to pay attention to would be the client's attention span, memory, capacity for abstract thought and insight, and problem solving.
- Communication: This is the client's ability to communicate effectively with others.
- Self-concept: This looks at the client's level of self-esteem, both how the client feels about himself and also how he perceives others feel about him.
- Emotions: This involves whether the client can express and manage feelings in an appropriate way.
- Taking the other's perspective: Is the client able to take the perspective of another and show a capacity for empathy?
- Reality testing: Here the worker assesses if the client is realistic and demonstrates a solid understanding of reality.
- Judgment and problem-solving skills: This asks if the client can make good decisions for himself and solve problems using reason and thoughtful processing of alternatives.
- Significant problem areas: Are there any signs of mental illness, early trauma, loss, child abuse, or other problem areas that need to be highlighted?

The social part of the assessment includes some of the following areas:

- Family: This looks at who is in the family and how they interact with each other. What roles do people play in the family? How close are family members? Is it an open or closed family system, enmeshed or disengaged? How differentiated are family members? How do family members communicate with each other? Are there any emotional cutoffs?
- Friends and supports: This involves assessing the quality of the client's friends and social support network.
- Groups: Does the client belong to any groups, and what is his relationship with each group? This could include school, work, activity groups, and so on.
- Organizations: The worker notes what institutional supports exist for the client, such as day care, welfare, support groups, and youth organizations.
- Multicultural: This requires learning whether the client identifies with a particular ethnicity and issues related to acculturation.
- Other considerations: This involves looking out for issues related to poverty, unemployment, discrimination, and any other concerns that may surface related to the social domain and larger system.

The spiritual part of the assessment includes some of the following areas:

- Meaning and purpose in life: The worker assesses whether the client wrestles with questions about his purpose and meaning in life.
- Transpersonal: Does the client struggle with his belief in a higher consciousness or being, a connection to something larger?
- Human energy system: This involves assessing the client's energy level and whether the client has an open, clear, well-balanced energy system supported by a well-aligned and flexible body.

Often, the spiritual aspect is missing in client assessments. Although the social work profession acknowledges the importance of addressing spiritual issues as they surface in the therapeutic conversation, social workers don't always pick up on clients' spiritual needs, or choose to avoid them. They may pass over this topic and move the discussion to more tangible and comfortable subjects they feel better equipped to handle. Practitioners, field instructors, and social work educators acknowledge the need for training on the significance of tackling religious and spiritual issues with clients (Cascio, 1999).

Talking to clients about spiritual issues sometimes triggers fear in social workers who find they cannot draw on specific behavioral techniques and intervention strategies with easy "how-to" formulas. It means sitting and reflecting with clients in a stripped-down human way, posing challenging questions, delving into issues of meaning and life purpose and connection to a larger being. It also means not knowing where the discussion will lead, accepting ambiguity and uncertainty in the clinical experience, and not having a stake in the outcome.

What Is Spirituality?

Simply stated, spirituality refers to an awareness of one's state of being and one's spirit. It is associated with the transpersonal, looking beyond the level of the individual toward how each human is an integral part of a larger whole. Religion and spirituality are not the same, but they share a belief in something greater than the self, a higher power that connects us. This desire to attain oneness of spirit with the larger universe provides some clients with a sense of peace, well-being, harmony, and fulfillment. This connection to something greater than oneself is the opposite of feeling disconnected, alienated, lonely, and without purpose or meaning in life.

Although some people consult religious leaders during times of personal and emotional turmoil, others seek help from a social worker. It may be a time when they are questioning their lives, their relationships, and the path they are on, and wanting a renewed sense of meaning and purpose. Clients might find it helpful to discuss these issues with a social worker in a way that touches upon the spiritual domain. These clients are perhaps striving to find their true self, and seeking to realign themselves somehow to find peace and fulfillment. When clients feel alienated and disconnected from others, re-connecting to something larger than themselves can bring great comfort.

Certain life crises and transitions may stimulate conversation about spirituality. With this in mind, it is useful to understand what spirituality has meant to clients at different points in the life cycle. For example, spirituality can play an important role in positive youth development and is sometimes tied to thriving amidst adversity; it can orient certain people to help others, understand social responsibility, and connect with what is most meaningful in life (Cheon & Canda, 2010). For African-American children in middle childhood, the church can serve as an important context for socialization and building competence and motivation; spirituality can also act as a protective factor for black children's exposure to racism (Haight & Taylor, 2007) and provide a strong message about God's love for all children.

Social workers would do clients a great disservice by not tuning into these needs or refusing to go down this road. Speaking openly and exploring clients' thoughts on the subject will help them find the answers they seek within themselves. A willingness to discuss spirituality with clients when they bring it up and to refrain from imposing one's own values is good practice.

How I Use Spirituality in My Practice

When I first began to practice social work more than thirty years ago, I was trained in the psychodynamic approach, which looked at ego development and the importance of helping the client become more differentiated from others. I wanted clients to find their sense of self and separate from others, with enhanced independence and self-reliance. As I age and get in touch with my own spirituality, I notice a shift taking place in what I pay attention to and what I choose to focus on. As I experience how spirituality impacts the quality of my life, I see the benefits of integrating it into my practice and have found that it resonates with clients.

I'll give an example from my recent work with a client, who I will disguise to maintain his anonymity and confidentiality. An older man came to see me about his daughter's death in a car accident. He was distraught and unable to find peace in this tragic loss. On his third visit, he recounted an odd experience about which he couldn't make sense. There was a particular song his daughter enjoyed listening to, and some of the words in this song, "we're gonna make it through alright," were added to the memorial card with her picture on it. On a day when he was feeling great sadness, he went to a local café for coffee, and as he sat down, he heard this song playing. Hearing it added to his sadness and he left the café. Later in the day, he went to another shop, and as he entered, he heard the song playing again. He had never heard this song played before in a store and didn't know what to make of it. As we talked about the meaning of this experience, it seemed clear that his daughter was trying to send him a message that she was all right and that her father didn't need to be sad anymore. I saw this father one more time and, as he realized his daughter was okay, he could move on and accept his daughter's death.

When sitting with this man, if I had dismissed the experience as coincidence and moved the discussion in another direction, he may have remained stuck in his grief. By discussing the meaning of this experience on a spiritual level, this man found comfort and resolution to the untimely loss of his daughter. Had we not spoken about it so openly, he may have remained in counseling indefinitely and been put on antidepressants and sleep medication. Instead, he found peace in knowing there was something greater in the universe that he and his daughter were connected to, and that at this level, all was well. Death was nothing to fear.

Another case example shows how clinical work can use a person's faith and religion to address treatment goals, and how religious counseling can operate in conjunction with traditional therapy to provide support for clients. I worked with a middle-aged, professional married woman with one daughter whose husband was alcoholic, verbally abusive, and very controlling. This client's daughter hated her father and pleaded with her mother to leave him. The mom was beginning to weigh the pros and cons of this decision in her mind and sought counseling for another opinion. As we discussed how difficult the situation was, I learned that she was very religious and that her family went to a Seventh-Day Adventist church every Saturday. Although her husband hadn't gone to church for more than a year, she and her daughter regularly attended and found it a source of great emotional, spiritual, and social support.

Because this woman felt close to the pastor and his wife, we discussed how it might help if she talked with them about what was happening at home. Up to that point, she had kept her family life private, and this created more internal stress. She agreed to speak with her pastor and continue meeting with me. For several weeks, we worked on some of her issues: how she could better care for herself, exert control over her life in little ways, tease out her finances from her husband's, separate physically from her husband when he was verbally abusive, find time outside of work to spend with a colleague who had befriended her, and open up about her problems to this friend, as well as to the pastor and his wife. Each week she came to our sessions feeling better and more self-confident. She felt the benefits of praying about her situation with the pastor and talking with me about ways she could improve her life and self-perceptions. Because her daughter would not see an outside counselor, she also began to meet with the pastor, with whom she was more comfortable.

One week, this client proudly shared a striking example of how she was changing. As she was driving away from home with her husband, he became verbally abusive and mean to her, upon which she stopped the car and let him out, much to her surprise and his. That week she had also made a date to meet her co-worker for dinner, the first time she had ever planned a meal out that excluded her husband. She had a more positive outlook on life with a renewed sense of hope for the future, and she believed she could make it on her own if necessary. The church continued to provide support to her and her daughter around the family issues. As they prayed for things to get better, the mother and I also kept up our sessions, looking for solutions in case there were no improvements with her husband's abusive and controlling behavior. I felt comfortable talking to her about the role of religion and prayer in her life and appreciated how her spirituality enhanced our work.

Social workers may find it easier to discuss spirituality with clients around issues of death and loss if it comes up naturally, for example, in discussion with a terminally ill patient. But such conversations can aid clients with everyday struggles as well. Helping clients to connect with their own spirit or spirituality might allow them to let go of conflicts that have directed their lives in unhealthy ways. Clients can begin to realize that certain attacks that put them on the offensive are merely illusions constructed in their minds. They are projections created within themselves by a belief in a separate ego and are not real. By letting go of the need for these ego defenses, clients can forgive the attacks and align themselves with their own true needs.

The ego is used very differently in this conversation than when talking about psychodynamic theory, which focuses on helping clients to differentiate and create a sense of self that is separate from others. From a spiritual perspective, the goal is quite the opposite: One should have "less ego" and let go of the notion of a separate self and, instead, acknowledge how we are all a part of something larger. We are each a piece of the puzzle that makes up the whole. Living with an awareness of a higher spirit has the power to bring peace to some clients.

In addition to bringing peace to clients, accessing this spiritual realm can also revitalize clients' life energy systems. A colleague of mine, Reema Safadi, believes that the human energy system and its effect on everything around us is one of life's best-kept secrets. In clinical practice, we characterize clients with depression as having low energy, no motivation, lethargy, and lack of interest or passion in life. One innovative way to view energy is as actual spirit. By integrating spirituality into clinical practice, part of the treatment for depressed clients could include improving their energy system.

Safadi states that to access the spirit, we need to recognize that our experiences in physical reality are meant to align us with the abundant source of energy. Each person's energy system is constantly interacting with that of a larger cosmic one, which is meant to clear, balance, and rejuvenate this energy. By growing in awareness and alignment with the principles of universal consciousness—the concept that there is only universal consciousness and that it expresses itself through each person—we can live to our highest potential. In this sense, attending to self-care means bolstering your life-energy system, and observing your attitudes and feelings to see if they affirm the goodness of life (Safadi, 2012).

One exercise that Safadi suggests to realign with the universal consciousness is grounded in the beauty and perfection of nature. She encourages us to reflect on what she calls a "wonder nature moment" (Safadi, 2012). Take a moment, she says, to reflect on a memory of when you were outdoors by yourself, enjoying the wondrous beauty of nature. What did you experience in this moment? Often people describe feeling peaceful, calm, expansive, uplifted, invigorated, free, and full of gratitude, as well as connected with a larger whole, oneness. This memory becomes like a reset button restoring well-being, allowing us to return to a state Safadi would call pure being. The more we can reinforce this state in our awareness, combined with meditation and deep breathing, the more we can transcend the limitations of our ego-self and connect to our infinite universal self.

Mindfulness practice is closely related to spirituality. Mindfulness meditation teaches us the importance of staying grounded in the present. Through awareness of each breath—breathing deeply, slowly, and evenly—we can become more alive in the present moment. This allows us to notice what is happening in the here and now. It means learning to let go and not attach to what surfaces in each moment but rather to enable the flow of experience with each breath. This practice can benefit clients who may be stuck in past conflicts by helping them to let go of the past and live more in the present. Mindfulness also helps us to transcend the self and be aware of a higher perspective beyond an individual state of being, connecting with spirituality.

There are many ways that integrating spirituality into practice can benefit clients. For example, social workers can teach clients about mindfulness meditation and try Safadi's "wonder nature moment" exercise as described. There are other affirmations and daily practices that can also help clients re-align with a universal source of being or higher consciousness. By tuning in to clients' spiritual needs, social workers can engage in therapeutic conversations about meaning and purpose in life that help clients to find their essence of being, sense of harmony, and fulfillment.

In the case vignettes in this book, there will be opportunities to identify ways to integrate spirituality into intervention strategies with clients. In addition, there may have been appropriate moments to address these issues in the interviews that the social workers actually missed in the role-plays. I've included student exercises that encourage you to find these moments and explore different ways of responding.

References

Abramson, J. & Fortune, A. (1990). Improving field instruction: An evaluation of a seminar for new field instructors, *Journal of Social Work Education, 26*(3), 273–286.

Arnd-Caddigan, M. (2011). Toward a broader definition of evidence-informed practice: Intersubjective evidence. *Families in Society, 92*(4), 372–376.

Brazeau, J., Teatero, M. L., Rawana, E. P., Brownlee, K., & Blanchette, L. R. (2012). The strengths assessment inventory: Reliability of a new measure of psychosocial strengths for youth. *Journal of Child and Family Studies, 21*, 384–390.

Cascio, T. (1999). Religion and spirituality: Diversity issues for the future. *Journal of Multicultural Social Work, 7*(3/4), 129–145.

Cheon, J. W. & Canda, E. R. (2010). The meaning and engagement of spirituality for positive youth development in social work. *Families in Society, 91*(2), 121–126.

Cooper, M. G. & Lesser, J. G. (2011). *Clinical social work practice: An integrative approach.* Boston: Pearson.

Council on Social Work Education. (2008). *Educational Policy and Accreditation Standards.* Alexandria, VA: Council on Social Work Education.

Cowager, C. (1994). Assessing client strengths: Clinical assessment for client empowerment. *Social Work, 39*(3), 262–268.

Delgado, M., Jones, K., & Rohani, M. (2005). *Social Work Practice with Refugee and Immigrant Youth in the United States.* Boston: Allyn & Bacon.

Dong-Min, K., Wampold, B. E., & Bolt, D. M. (2006). Therapist effects in psychotherapy: A random effects modeling of the National Institute of Mental Health treatment of depression, collaboration research program data. *Psychotherapy Research, 16*, 161–172.

Drisko, J. W. & O'Grady, M. D. (2012). *Evidence-Based Practice in Social Work.* New York: Springer.

England, H. (1986). *Social Work as Art.* London: Allen & Unwin.

Fleck-Henderson, A. (1989). Personality theory and clinical social work practice. *Clinical Social Work Journal, 17*(2), 128–137.

Graybeal, C. T. (2007). Evidence for the art of social work. *Families in Society: The Journal of Contemporary Social Sciences, 88*(4), 513–523.

Haight, W. L. & Taylor, E. H. (2007). *Human Behavior for Social Work Practice: A Developmental-Ecological Framework.* Chicago: Lyceum.

Hepworth, D. H., Rooney, R. H., Rooney, G. D., & Strom-Gottfried, K. (2013). *Direct Social Work Practice: Theory and Skills.* Belmont, CA: Cengage.

Hopps, J. G., Pinderhughes, E., & Shankar, R. (1995). *The Power to Care: Clinical Practice Effectiveness with Overwhelmed Clients.* New York: The Free Press.

Knight, C. (1996). A study of MSW and BSW students' perceptions of their field instructors. *Journal of Social Work Education, 32*(3), 399–414.

Lambert, M. J. & Ogles, B. M. (2004). The efficacy and effectiveness of psychotherapy. In Bergin A. E. & S. L. Garfield (Eds.), *Handbook of Psychotherapy and Behavior Change* (5th ed., pp. 139–193). New York: Wiley.

Lee, J. A. B. (1994). *The Empowerment Approach to Social Work Practice.* New York: Columbia University Press.

Lovett, B. B. (2005). Using process recordings to teach social work practice with children in BSW programs. *Arete, 29*(1), 86–92.

Loewenberg, F. M. & Dolgoff, R. (1996). *Ethical Decisions for Social Work Practice.* Chicago: Peacock.

Lutz, W., Leon, S. C., Martinovich, Z., Lyons, J. S., & Stiles, W. B. (2007). Therapist effects in outpatient psychotherapy: A three-level growth curve approach. *Journal of Counseling Psychology, 54,* 32–39.

MacArthur, J., Rawana, E., & Brownlee, K. (2011). Implementation of a strengths-based approach in the practice of child and youth care. *Relational Child and Youth Care Practice, 24*(3), 6–16.

Maluccio, A. N. (1979). *Learning from clients.* New York: Free Press.

Miller, S. D., Duncan, B. L., & Hubble, M. A. (2004). Beyond integration: Triumph of outcome over process in clinical practice. *Psychotherapy in Australia, 10,* 2–19.

Murphy, B. C. & Dillon, C. (2011). *Interviewing in action in a multicultural world.* Belmont, CA: Cengage.

Newman, K. & Friedman, B. (1997). Process recordings: Fine tuning an old instrument. *Journal of Social Work Education, 33*(2), 237–243.

Proctor, E. K. (2007). Implementing evidence-based practice in social work education: Principles, strategies, and partnerships. *Research on Social Work Practice, 17,* 583–591.

Ragg, D. M. (2011). *Developing Practice Competencies: A Foundation for Generalist Practice.* Hoboken, NJ: Wiley.

Rawana, E. P. & Brownlee, K. (2009). Making the possible probable: A strength-based assessment and intervention framework for clinical work with parents, children and adolescents. *Families in Society: The Journal of Contemporary Human Services, 90*(3), 255–260.

Rhodes, M. L. (1986). *Ethical Dilemmas in Social Work Practice.* Boston: Routledge & Kegal Paul.

Rothman, J. C. (2005). *From the Front Lines: Student Cases in Social Work Ethics.* Boston: Pearson.

Safadi, R. (2012). *Being Your Brilliance.* Unpublished manuscript.

Saleebey, D. (2009). *The Strengths Perspective in Social Work Practice.* Boston: Allyn & Bacon.

Satir, V. (1972). *Peoplemaking.* Palo Alto, CA: Science and Behavior Books.

Scott, D. (1989). Meaning construction and social work practice. *Social Service Review, 63*(1), 39–51.

Sevel, J., Cummins, L., & Madrigal, C. (1999). *Social Work Skills Demonstrated: Beginning Direct Practice.* Boston: Allyn & Bacon.

Sweitzer, H. F. & King, M. (2009). *The Successful Internship: Personal, Professional and Civic Development.* Belmont, CA: Cengage Learning.

Shulman, L. (2009). *The Skills of Helping Individuals, Families, Groups, and Communities.* Belmont, CA: Cengage Learning.

Stern, D. N. (1985). *The Interpersonal World of the Infant.* New York: Basic Books.

Vandiver, V. L. (2002). Step-by-step practice guidelines for using evidence-based practice and expert consensus in mental health settings. In A. R. Roberts & G. J. Greene (Eds.), *Social Workers' Desk Reference* (pp. 731–738). New York: Oxford University Press.

Walsh, T. C. (2002). Structured process recording: a comprehensive model that incorporates the strengths perspective. *Social Work Education, 21*(1), 23–34.

Walsh, F. (2012). *Normal Family Processes: Growing Diversity and Complexity.* New York: Guilford.

Wharton, T. & Bolland, K. (2012). Practitioner perspectives of evidenced-based practice. *Families in Society, 93*(3), 157–164.

Woods, M. & Hollis, F. (2000). *Casework: A Psychosocial Therapy.* Boston: McGraw-Hill.

2

Overview of Theories

The main purpose of this book is to concentrate on clinical interviews and how we can learn from them. As a result, this chapter serves as a limited overview of social work theory, without giving great depth or time to the subject. It is expected that students have already been exposed to these theories in other human behavior or practice courses. I have summarized what I feel are the important concepts behind each theory, cognizant that other authors might highlight different aspects. Students are encouraged to refer to their favorite theoretical texts for a more detailed understanding of theories and how they are used in social work practice.

The theories that I chose to highlight are: psychodynamic, narrative, cognitive, behavioral, and systems theories. Under the section on psychodynamic, I include a description of ego psychology and object relations theories. Under cognitive, I've highlighted the literature on positive psychology and cognitive restructuring. Under behavioral, there is information on mind–body approaches, stress management, and mindfulness. And under systems theories, you'll find material on structural family theory and multigenerational family theories. Although many clinicians think about cognitive-behavioral theory and intervention together, I discuss each theory separately to differentiate between them. Individual life cycle and developmental theories are also important in social work interventions, but I chose to discuss them directly as they apply to the case vignettes in the following chapters.

Use of Videotaped Recordings, Transcripts, and Process Recordings to Identify Theories

In the case study chapters that follow, I have included excerpts of transcripts from the video-recorded interviews. The transcripts are then analyzed using process recordings, which take a closer look at the theories used in each role-play session. I pulled the theories in this chapter from those that cropped up most often in the book's teaching examples. In the process recordings, I tend to assign broad theoretical perspectives to interactions, when specific theoretical terms also exist. For example, I might reference "psychodynamic theory" to explain an intervention, when it could also be called "object relations" or "ego psychology," both theories that fall under psychodynamic. I could use the term "behavioral theory," when the social worker is utilizing mindfulness and mind/body work, or family systems as shorthand for principles from structural family theory or multigenerational family theory. After the process recordings, I discuss in more detail the intricacies of the theories being applied.

A process recording is an important tool that helps identify theories used in interactions between clients and social workers. The third column in the process recording contains an analysis of the theories used by the social worker in the interviews. This analysis takes place after the interview with the client and is what Donald Shon (1983) refers to as reflection-on-action. This can be done by the social worker alone, or in supervision, and is an example of critical thinking. It is a way to reflect on the social worker's actions with the client to evaluate what went well and what could have been done better or differently. I use this analysis as a way to identify theories used by the social worker in each of the interventions you will find in the transcripts.

My interpretation of client stories, and identification of theories in this book's process recordings, may differ from how other social workers would understand what is happening. What I emphasize won't always match what others would. When you watch the videos or read the transcripts, you may find alternative ways to understand how the story is told and the theories that are used. The perspectives I present here are meant as a starting-off point, from which students and their instructors can then question and discuss interventions, and how they relate to theory, as part of the critical-thinking process. You are encouraged to critique my analysis. Find your own rationale, and think about other ways to make meaning out of these case studies. Let my analysis act as a guide, a beginning to the conversation.

This in-depth analysis of client interviews provides students with an experiential way of linking theory and practice. In my own teaching, I've found that students benefit from using case examples to understand how theories use language differently, rather than talking about theory in abstract ways. How social workers ask questions, and the words they use with clients, have different implications and purposes and are informed by theory in complicated ways. Often times, social workers, in the moment with the client, may be unaware of how their questions are linked to theory. When asked which theoretical frameworks they use in practice, they may espouse theories that in fact they do not use upon closer inspection. This points to the distinction between "espoused theories" and "theories in use;" the former refers to the theories we believe we use, whereas the later points to theories we actually do use in practice (Argyris & Shon, 1974).

Social workers are often surprised at what they learn by reviewing the transcript of a conversation with a client. Such review greatly raises awareness about how theories are used in action. Reflecting on process recordings enables social workers to clarify the theories they use in practice, theories tied to interventions rather than what they merely assume is happening. This results in a more "true" rationale for client outcomes and the effectiveness of interventions, based on what actually occurs between the social worker and client. This has important implications for evidence-based treatment that links effective treatment strategies to what clinicians merely say they are doing.

It isn't always easy to understand clinical action and what influences it. This requires paying closer attention to what we say and do on a regular basis. Fleck-Henderson (1989) states, "We need to attend to what we do with a client, our practical strategies based on tacit theory-in-use and more conscious reflection, and to how we reflect, outside the clinical session on the interaction and the client, our formulations" (p. 130). By thinking critically about the process recordings, students can reflect on other factors that affect interventions, "implicit assumptions about interpersonal behavior learned by lived experience in and out of the clinical situation, schemas about personality which are more particular and less abstract than personal theory, and clinical knowledge or wisdom constructed from prior experience" (Fleck-Henderson, 1989, p. 136). Additional influences on social workers could be their families, their culture, their education, and particular teachers and supervisors whose voices may be heard during clinical interventions.

Although there is no way to tell the story or make formulations without theoretical shaping (Fleck-Henderson, 1989, p. 134), we must also be careful not to let our theories shape what we see and observe with clients. Our personal biases and espoused theories can interfere with how we listen to clients' stories, and we may try to make what clients tell us fit into preconceived beliefs about them. Clinical formulations must be based on rich descriptions, on what we hear and observe, not on faulty assumptions far removed from the case material. Clinical data without such detail, distanced from case material and using jargon to interpret behavior, can present a false picture of the client. By giving you video-recorded interviews with transcripts and process recordings, I am providing you with a complete description of the clinical situation and encouraging you to look and listen to what is happening and find your own way of constructing meaning out of the case studies. I am also giving you a foundation of descriptive details and theoretical material, to open up the discussion and allow you to come up with alternative formulations. One theory is not better than another, and using multiple theories enriches our understanding of clients.

There are times when interventions identified with one theory could also be explained from other theoretical perspectives, or could be simply communication skills used to explore the problem as part of psychosocial assessment. For example, exploration could be seen as a communication skill. It could be seen as part of person-situation-reflection in psychodynamic theory, which uses exploration. And it could surely be used in other theoretical formulations. There are no right or wrong answers, but instead many ways to interpret what is happening. Students should reflect on their work with clients; transcribe interviews using process recordings; make sense of the interactions that took place with clients; and get meaningful feedback on both their strengths and what they could do better.

Use of Multiple Theories and Advantages of Combining Theories

It can be challenging for social workers to choose with confidence from the many different theories and techniques available to them. An important first step for students is to gain expertise on the major social work theories proved to be effective with clients. Rather than working from a single theoretical framework, most social workers use many theories in practice, often in combination with each other. It is more important to be flexible, choosing interventions that best fit the needs of clients and their unique situations. Consult the research literature on best practices. Evidence from practice effectiveness studies shows that successful social workers adjust their theories and practice interventions to fit with each client's presenting problem (Thomlinson, 1984).

There is no one theory that can claim to adequately describe all of human behavior. Similarly, there is no one theory that can fit all types of clients' problems or situations. Although one theory may work well for one client, it may not be effective with another. Research on best practices might indicate that a particular theoretical approach would be more effective for a specific diagnostic category than others. However, even this particular method, prescribed for specific circumstances, might not work well with every client. All clients are different. We benefit from having many theories to choose from and knowing how they can be combined to maximize the therapeutic benefits.

As you will notice in the process recordings, the social worker in each case uses multiple theories in her interventions with the clients. No interview is conducted from a single theoretical lens. This reflects what has been found in the literature: There is no one practice framework that is considered the domain of social work; rather, social workers combine concepts from a variety of theories (Miley et al., 2009; Norlin & Chess, 1997; Timberlake & Sabatino, 1997). What seems to be most important is "that a practitioner's ability to be effective with clients is largely due to having confidence in whatever theories and interventions he or she uses" (Walsh, 2010, p. 7).

There is reason to believe that combining psychodynamic and cognitive-behavioral approaches produces positive client outcomes (Heller & Northcut, 2011; Weinberger, 1995). Cognitive, behavioral, and psychodynamic can complement each other to provide a more holistic and integrative understanding of emotion, thoughts, and behavior. Psychodynamic theory concentrates on working with affect or feelings; cognitive theory focuses on thoughts; and behavioral theory looks at behavior.

Practicing from a psychodynamic foundation, Heller and Northcut (2011) found that insight alone didn't always change client outcomes. They found that integrating concepts from psychodynamic and cognitive-behavioral approaches was more successful. They provide case examples in their article of how they did so with good outcomes. Principles from psychodynamic theory contributed knowledge about resilience, the ego functions, and the capacity of the individual to adapt to the environment, along with client–worker relationship factors. Heller and Northcut also added three cognitive-behavioral concepts, strategies designed to work with cognitive distortions, impulse control problems, and clients' faulty schemas and attributions. When these cognitive and behavioral interventions were combined with the psychodynamic approach, this led to successful treatment that was integrative, flexible, and effective.

Warning About Techniques and Eclecticism

There are many interventions advertised to clinicians that do not fall under any particular theory but are specific techniques taught to social workers to use with clients. These are often attractive to new social workers who are not sure of how to sit and be in the moment with clients and are looking for specific "how to" manuals that can be applied to all clients. An over-emphasis on techniques can be to the detriment of sound clinical work, which embraces the central role of the relationship in the helping process. This, I would argue, is at the heart of social work, and is discussed more in chapter 1.

When asked what theories they use in practice, some social workers will respond that they are eclectic. What does eclectic mean? Sometimes, it means they don't know what theories they use, so they say eclectic to avoid answering the question. These social workers may not be able to articulate what theories they are using or how to differentiate between theories. Social workers taking this approach must be able to elaborate on what eclecticism means to them. They must be able to describe what theories they find helpful with clients and in which situations. When I refer to integration of theories, and combining different theories in practice, I am referring to a deliberate approach that uses theories from different orientations in an informed way.

Approach to Using Theories in Case Studies

The theories described in the following are all referenced in the five case studies that follow this chapter. They are theories that I identified in the process recordings, which led to their inclusion here. However, others may find the interventions in the process recordings originating from other sources. My choice of theories suggests my own biases and preferences based on what I tend to use in my own practice. Although theories are embedded in therapeutic conversations, it is not always easy to identify and differentiate between them. When you read my analysis of interventions in the process recordings, I challenge you to look at the interventions with fresh eyes and come to your own conclusions. You may even want to practice this exercise further, by reading other client transcripts and testing your ability to identify theories. Students can also practice with clients in their field placements by analyzing process recordings with supervisors. By using this exercise under supervision and with teachers, beginning students can become more confident in understanding theory and how to integrate it into their practice.

In addition to the theories I have included in this text, students and teachers alike may want to introduce other theories not described here, and role-play alternative interventions using them. I encourage you to explore different approaches that could be equally effective with the clients than the ones I identified. Using your critical thinking skills, ask yourselves, "What are some other ways to work with this client? How would I respond to this situation?" It is important to stay open to the idea that there are many potentially effective interventions, and not get caught up believing there is only one way to work with clients. Stay open to interacting in new ways with clients, especially when you feel stuck; it may help you find a new path forward that livens discussions and leads to progress.

Psychodynamic Theories

Psychodynamic theories attempt to understand what motivates behavior, why people behave the way they do. The Psychoanalytic Method originated with Sigmund Freud and continues today as a theory of human development that is concerned with personality, abnormal psychology, and treatment. There have been many changes since Freud's time. Rather than considering it a single theory, clinicians now refer to psychodynamic theories, plural, to distinguish between different schools of thought within the psychodynamic literature. Later, two psychodynamic theories, ego psychology and object relations, will be discussed in more detail.

Psychoanalytic personality theory sees people as a complex of drives, forming the id, which pushes us to act on our needs; the ego, which controls the id and keeps us from acting on impulses; and the superego, which guides the ego with moral principles. The original drives found in Freud's writings are those toward pleasure and aggression. These drives can cause conflict for people if they go against social norms, so the ego uses unconscious defense mechanisms to ward off unacceptable feelings, keeping them out of conscious thought, and keeping anxiety, guilt, and shame at bay. For example, a mother may feel it is unacceptable to express how there are times when she wants to throw the baby out with the bath water. Although she knows she won't act on this impulse, she may still feel guilty for having these feelings and go out of her way to show how much she actually loves her baby. In this case, she is using a defense called reaction-formation, which replaces an unacceptable impulse (wanting to throw her baby out with the bath water) with its opposite (an exaggerated expression of love) to cover up the unwanted thought.

There are certain concepts that all psychodynamic theories have in common. Those include a belief in the unconscious (some of our thoughts are hidden from our consciousness); psychic determinism (some of our actions and behaviors arise from our unconscious thought processes); and transference and countertransference (that past relationships affect how we see people in the present). The psychodynamic approach emphasizes this last tenet, that is the influence of the past on the present, and seeks to help patients gain insight into their behavior that will resolve internal conflicts and give them more conscious control over their lives. It looks at the relationship between the self and significant others, and between inner and outer reality, to reduce distortions in how people experience their worlds. The curative aspect of the therapeutic relationship is a central ingredient in all of psychodynamic therapy.

Interventions using ego psychology and object relations theories use many similar strategies, such as ego sustaining and ego modifying techniques. The former refers to techniques that help clients with healthy ego functioning to understand their motivations and behaviors more clearly and then become engaged to resolve current problems. Examples of ego sustaining interventions are: sustainment (promoting a positive client-worker relationship); exploration/description/ventilation (encouraging the client to express feelings about a problem for relief); and person-situation reflection (reflecting on the present problem to find solutions). One common ego modifying technique is developmental reflection, which connects present problems to experiences in childhood.

Woods and Hollis (2000) go into more depth about these interventions. Sustainment refers to the client-worker relationship and includes activities by the social worker to show interest, understanding, acceptance, and confidence in the client. Woods and Hollis (2000) state that, "sustaining procedures are those designed to reduce feelings of anxiety or lack of self-esteem or self-confidence by a direct expression of the worker's confidence or esteem for the client, or confidence that some external threat is not as dangerous as it seems, or—acceptance of the person and the desire to help" (p. 131). Relief comes less from self-understanding and more from the worker conveying a sense of reassurance to the client and giving the client confidence in the worker's knowledge and care. The therapist's qualities of acceptance, encouragement, and reaching out are the important variables that lead to positive outcomes. Interventions that use exploration, description, and ventilation encourage the client to express feelings that are causing stress.

Drawing clients into reflective consideration of their lives is the objective of two other interventions: person-situation reflection and developmental reflection (Woods & Hollis, 2000, p. 153). In person-situation reflection, the social worker uses comments, questions, explanations, and nonverbal communication to promote the client's reflection on the presenting problem. This approach does not spend time analyzing the client's early years with parents, but rather begins with adulthood and continues to the present. On the other hand, developmental-reflection looks at a client's history, from birth to about age 20. Ego modifying techniques such as this are used when clients have less mature levels of ego functioning and more problematic behavioral patterns that require a deeper exploration and understanding of childhood relationships and unconscious processes. In addition to using the ego-sustaining techniques, the social worker engages the client in discussions to reflect on the impact of past relationships and experiences on present problems. The goal is for the client to gain insight into this connection between past and present to change maladaptive behavior (Walsh, 2010, pp. 44–47). For example, a client comes for treatment because of repeated abusive relationships with men and gains insight into how observing her mother in similar situations caused her to follow that same pattern.

Berzoff (2012) believes that exploration of clients' inner worlds is invaluable no matter what the situation, that it helps social workers have more insight into and empathy for clients' problems. This refutes prevalent assumptions that psychodynamic approaches can only be applied to the "worried well" or educated clients from middle to upper socioeconomic groups and is not useful with poor, vulnerable clients with complex problems. Joan Berzoff gives examples in her book of social work students returning to school for post-masters work, looking for in-depth psychological knowledge missing in their previous training. Although they had strong backgrounds in solution-focused and systemic theories, and had been practicing for several years, they were still not satisfied. They wanted to understand how people's unconscious motivations were making it hard for them to "just" change, and how early experiences shaped their clients' lives. Berzoff and others see the social work field now revisiting teaching practices from a previous era, when psychodynamic theory held a key role in training students, and expect programs nationwide to add courses to make up for this somewhat neglected piece of theory.

Ego Psychology

Ego psychology pays more attention to ego functioning and ego defenses, whereas object relations theory emphasizes the quality of interpersonal relationships. Although the influence of the previously mentioned drives toward pleasure and aggression is not dismissed, ego psychology gives conscious thought greater attention (Walsh, 2010, p. 37). This approach holds that both past and present experiences are important to understand a person's social functioning. Also, not all drives are sources of conflict. White (1963) proposed that there are conflict-free drives that help us live in our environment. These include the drives toward mastery and competence. More recent writings in ego psychology place greater emphasis on adaptation, resilience, and coping mechanisms that are needed for survival. And because ego psychology also falls under the rubric of developmental theory, it is interested in studying a person's development throughout the life span, from birth to death, and does not concentrate on the early years alone.

The ego is described as having 12 functions, both conscious and unconscious, that include such areas as judgment, reality-testing, identity, impulse control, and interpersonal relationships. The ego functions are assessed in treatment to determine a patient's maturity level and to identify areas that require support for the patient to live with less conflict. Although the ego has these 12 functions, it is more than just the sum of its parts. Blanck and Blanck explain "that the ego is better defined, not simply by its functions, but by its functioning as an organizer" (1979, p. 18). The ego can only fulfill its organizing role when development is occurring normally. When there are disruptions in development, the ego cannot perform its organizing function, and the resulting deficits will cause the person to struggle more in life. People are said to have strong egos when they can manage relationships with other people in a consistent, rational pattern. If they can do this, they achieve "ego mastery."

Defense mechanisms, one of the 12 ego functions, are distortions of reality used by people to reduce anxiety at different times in their lives. By studying clients' use of defenses, ego psychologists understand what makes them act irrationally. Freud saw defenses as pathological, with the ego mediating between the id and superego to manage and protect against sexual and aggressive drives; he believed that to be fully analyzed, one had to give up defenses. George Vaillant (1997), drawing on his research on adult development, disagreed with Freud's conclusions. Vaillant refers to the "wisdom of the ego" to explain the ego's adaptive capacity, making sense out of inner and outer reality and providing clients with illusions to help them cope with the intolerable pain that accompanies life. Vaillant saw defenses functioning not to just protect against internal sexual and aggressive drives, but also against external threats that cause anxiety and depression, such as interpersonal relationships and everyday reality.

Vaillant (1997) states that the "ego possesses a remarkable capacity for life-preserving distortion" (1997, p. 9) and describes that defenses are "creative, healthy, comforting, coping, and yet often strike observers as downright peculiar" (p. 19). In one such example, Vaillant describes a conversation with an internist who took part in his longitudinal study of ego development. The doctor's mother had died three weeks earlier. Vaillant writes:

> I was interviewing an internist who had participated in the study for thirty years. He told me, with vividness and enthusiasm, about his hobby: growing tissue cultures in his basement. He then told me with still more enthusiasm that the cells for one of these tissue cultures had been taken from a lesion on his mother's leg. He described his interest in tissue culture as if it were the most ordinary pursuit in the world. But I have yet to describe his hobby to an audience without an uneasy ripple of laughter sweeping the room. Audiences have found that this doctor was growing his mother's cells in the basement, as a child might raise flowers, extraordinary, even pathological. (p. 17)

Knowing this man was fond of his mother, Vaillant asked how he had coped with her death. The man responded, using defenses of rationalization and altruism, by saying that he spent his time consoling his father. However, Vaillant identified the source of comfort as the knowledge that somehow his mother was still alive and living in his basement. Defenses are often erected to protect against overwhelming loss, to give us time to gradually internalize its meaning.

In another example from my own practice, a client was sharing concerns that she couldn't show more emotion about her son's recent suicidal gesture. Although intellectually she could talk about the experience, and knew she was upset about it, she couldn't understand what kept her from showing these feelings. As we discussed how her defenses were helping her cope with this event, I remembered how, in a similar way, I had used isolation as a defense for a period of time after my father died. "Such mental defenses creatively rearrange the sources of our conflicts so that they may become manageable and we may survive" (Vaillant, 1997, p. 1).

Ego psychologists are sensitive to a client's use of defense mechanisms and how they are used, because they provide insight into how the client can handle life's challenges. Defense mechanisms are considered adaptive when they are flexible, and used in healthy ways to reduce conflict and provide a sense of security. They are problematic when they are rigid, based too much on the past, and significantly distort reality (Walsh, 2010, p. 38). Vaillant (1997) proposes that if we use defenses well, we are considered mentally healthy, but if we use defenses badly, we are labeled mentally ill. Similarly, some defenses are considered more mature than others. Examples of less mature defense mechanisms are denial, displacement, and projection. More mature ones would be sublimation, intellectualization, and rationalization.

Ego psychologists also focus on how a person reacts to normal life transitions. This could be entering school, starting a new job, getting married, starting a family, or facing retirement. Social work interventions help the client build new ego strengths, or use existing ones better, to have greater self-understanding, resolve problems, and negotiate life's transitions. "The goals of intervention are to enhance the client's inner capacities through ego development....Clients are helped to acquire problem-solving and coping skills and to achieve insight (self-understanding) through reflection about their strengths, limitations and potential resources" (Walsh, 2010, p. 42).

Object Relations

The central concept in object relations theory is that human beings are motivated from the earliest moments of life by the need for significant relationships with others. "Object" refers to important people in our environment that are the targets of our attention and need for connection. As opposed to concentrating on drive theories (sex and aggression drives), object relations theory considers that making and maintaining personal relationships is the primary motivator for our behavior. Our experience in relationships is the basis for our internal lives and our perceptions of the world around us.

Object relations theory, like ego psychology, finds some of its basic principles in developmental theory, understanding the stages of a person's development. Object relations theory, in particular, was built on studying child behavior from birth onward. From these observations came theories of child development, described as a series of stages that children must go through to grow into mature and independent adults capable of healthy relationships. Problems at a specific early stage were thought to create issues later, and could make the difference between healthy or abnormal development. If a child were stuck at one stage, this would impede his ability to negotiate future stages.

Many of the terms used to understand child development were based on the research of Margaret Mahler, a psychiatrist who studied mothers and infants from birth to age 3. Mahler's theory describes the process of "separation-individuation" that all children go through to become independent. It is made up of a series of stages that, in healthy development, helps children to separate from their mothers or primary caregivers. At one end of the continuum is the child who is fused with the mother, or undifferentiated, described as a normal stage that occurs at birth. At the other end of the continuum is the child who has successfully gone through the developmental stages and learned to "individuate" or differentiate from the mother with a secure sense of self. As a result, the individual develops the capacity to maintain a sense of positive self-esteem and manage a wide range of emotions.

When a child makes it to the last stage and can separate successfully from the mother, somewhere between 24 to 36 months, the child has reached what Mahler refers to as "object constancy." At this stage, a child has a stable internal representation of the mother, whether the mother is physically present or not. When a child has this type of secure attachment with the mother, the child can express herself without fearing separation, abandonment, or loss of love. This differentiation allows the child to develop clear boundaries between self and other. The child can relate to others as separate, rather than as extensions of the self. Having a secure attachment with a significant figure in childhood, and then successfully passing through the stages of individuation and separation, has enormous implications for the relationships people can form in adulthood.

Indeed, where one ends up on this continuum of separation-individuation determines the quality of later relationships. It is believed that people form relationships with others that match the patterns established by their earlier experiences. For example, people who are overly dependent or attached to others may be repeating patterns they established with their mothers that reflected problems in separating when they were toddlers. A person who has not differentiated successfully from the primary caregiver may also tend to have poor boundaries with others. Instead of seeing people as whole complex persons, having both strengths and weaknesses, they may see others as only good or bad.

Attachment theory falls under object relations theory and explains the type of attachment that children develop with their parents. It looks at how early caregivers are able to gratify, or not, the needs of children in their formative years. How secure we are depends on how we experience these early connections. Parent-child relationships based on warmth, mutuality, consistency, and support help children form strong identities and develop a sense of trust in relationships. On the other hand, children from homes that lack these qualities and instead harbor instability, anger, frustration, abandonment, and loss, will form an insecure attachment and be distrustful of others.

Social workers using object relations theory are sensitive to important qualities in the worker-client relationship that foster change. They provide the client with a "facilitative environment" that helps the client to further her development. Winnicott (1975) refers to this as the "holding environment," a place created by the practitioner that feels secure, allowing the client to progress from being dependent to independent. Many of the optimal worker's characteristics described in object relations theory are consistent with the important role that social work gives overall to the client-worker relationship.

Daniel Stern studied the close relationship between mothers and their infants and young children to understand its important qualities, especially the characteristics that allowed mother and child to be attuned to each other's needs. He came up with the term intersubjectivity, which refers to "capacities for sharing a focus of attention, for attributing intentions and motives to others and apprehending them correctly, and for attributing the states of feelings in others and sensing whether or not they are congruent with one's own state of feeling" (1985, p. 27). This term is sometimes also applied to the worker's sensitivity and awareness of the client's experience. A worker who has achieved this level of relatedness with a client will have an easier time reading the client, in essence is aligned and attuned with what the client feels. It is possible that intersubjective evidence, data from the worker's observations of client changes during treatment, can be used in outcome studies contributing to research on best practices, an idea that was discussed in chapter 1.

Both ego psychology and objects relations theories have great relevance for social work practice and are widely used in clinical settings. For example, attachment theory is applied to children in the child welfare system who have experienced multiple disruptions in their early years. The theory provides insight about their behavior, and has implications for policy and practice. As mentioned earlier, psychodynamic theories are becoming more appreciated for what they have to offer practitioners, especially understanding clients' internal worlds and unconscious motivations of behavior.

Narrative Theory

Constructivism and meaning-making play an important role in narrative theory by bringing special attention to the nature of reality and what is true. Constructivism stems from the ideas of famous German philosopher Immanuel Kant in the eighteenth century. It sees all knowledge as subjective, created by the observer interacting with the environment. According to constructivism, we cannot know reality separate from our experience and interpretation of it. If we as social workers believe that there is no objective reality, only our personal constructions of it, this will have a profound effect on how we practice, especially how we approach assessment, treatment, and our ways of thinking about the therapeutic relationship (Dean, 1993). It also brings into question how we use theories as "truths," and take on the role of expert in people's lives. Taken to its extreme, this might lead to hasty assessments clinging too closely to theories, missing the subtleties and nuance of individual clients who do not fit a specific mold.

Constructivist ideas are embedded in narrative therapy; practitioners must be aware of how their ways of knowing influence their assessments. Social workers are encouraged to suspend their theories at times to listen to clients from a position of not-knowing, open to new interpretations. Narrative approaches also incorporate the important role of dominant culture in shaping theories and our assumptions about clients. This has implications for how social workers listen to clients' stories, with an appreciation for the intersection of culture, theory, and narrative (Bruner, 1990; Saleebey, 1994).

Human beings build themselves into the world by creating meaning, a way to understand their experience, and they get their ideas about how to construct this meaning out of culture (Bruner, 1990). As practitioners, we must understand the role culture plays in influencing how clients construct meanings in their lives. By doing so, we can turn clients into catalysts for their own revised stories, constructing new meanings, all of which has profound implications for practice (Saleebey, 1994). Practice informed by constructivism accepts the possibility that there are "multiple truths" or "multiple realities," and proposes that clients need not be subjugated to the dominant culture's version of "truth." How clients construct meaning relates to finding what is "true" for them and questioning what they have been told. As becomes evident, narrative theory has strong political implications and looks at issues of knowledge, power, and the dominant culture.

Michael White, a counselor from Australia, is a name often associated with narrative therapy. White (1995), in writing about narrative therapy, proposes that "human beings are interpreting beings—that we are active in the interpretations of our experiences as we live our lives…and that we live by the stories…that these stories actually shape our lives, constitutes our lives" (pp. 13–14). Narrative therapy looks at how "the lived" experience gets expressed through stories. Often people come to therapy when they are situated in stories that others have told about them and their relationships. They may be actively participating in these stories even though the narratives are unsatisfying and limiting, and contradict important aspects of their "lived" experiences. A successful outcome of therapy would be the generation of alternative stories that are enabling and create new meaning. The new stories include previously neglected aspects of their lives and opens up new possibilities for them.

In their groundbreaking book, *Narrative Means to Therapeutic Ends* (1990), White and David Epston apply Michel Foucault's ideas to therapy. Foucault was a French philosopher and social theorist who addressed the notion of power, and the manner in which it restricts knowledge and is a form of social control. These ideas, interpreted by White and Epston, show us how the stories of people who seek therapy are framed by a larger sociopolitical context that exerts power over how these people see themselves and their relationships. The authors' approach challenges the way the dominant culture controls the story, and instead works with clients to help construct new, more self-affirming stories. By externalizing the problem, locating it outside of themselves, clients are encouraged to go back and question their stories, and to come up with new interpretations that recognize their strengths and resilience. Clients also can explore with clinicians parts of their "lived experience" that have never been told to "resurrect subjugated knowledge" (White & Epston, 1990, p. 31). By finding new meanings for past events, and recovering previously neglected parts of their story, clients begin to tell a new narrative that gives a more complete picture of who they are.

Interventions using narrative theory employ questioning as a primary tool to help clients construct this new story. The therapist collaborates with the client and uses questions to open up new ways of seeing the problem and possible solutions. In particular, questions that invite the client to reflect on the situation can help to create new meanings going forward.

Practitioners pay attention to how clients use words and "story" their experiences. Clients are encouraged to challenge how their stories have been told, in order to separate themselves from the problem and from previous interpretations.

Using this approach, clients are first asked how the problem has influenced them. This line of questioning identifies the effects across different interfaces, that of other people and relationships. Next, clients are asked how they personally have influenced the problem. These questions encourage clients to see their own impact on the life of the problem. This process of questioning helps clients to map out the issue at hand, its influence on their lives, and the people involved; in essence, the social worker is helping them to externalize the problem. White and Epston (1990) believe that "externalizing the problem enables persons to separate from the dominant stories that have been shaping their lives and relationships" (pp. 40–41). In this way, clients open up and discover new possibilities about themselves, and begin to tell alternative stories that do not include the problem.

Beliefs are embedded in all stories and can be difficult to change. The promise of narrative therapy is that if you change the story, the "old beliefs are shattered," and the person may choose a new course based on emerging beliefs (Parry, 1991, p. 213). By adopting the postmodernist treatment of a story, it becomes endlessly inventive, a tool for enabling clients to shake off constraining beliefs so that they can move forward as they choose (Parry, 1991, p. 213). In narrative therapy, clients take an active role in deconstructing the old stories told about them and "re-storying" their lives. Rather than letting other voices dominate their narrative, essentially accepting other people's interpretations of their experiences, clients find their own voice and take charge of the story. In this reauthoring process, clients assume new beliefs about themselves.

When narrative therapy was first introduced, I saw great possibilities for its application to both social work teaching and practice. In one instance, I used narrative concepts to devise an icebreaker for the beginning of a new class. I would ask students to separate into pairs. Each partner had to tell the other a story about herself, one that was told to her growing up. I gave them an outline to follow with a list of questions to answer about the story: How do you interpret the story that was told about you? Who usually tells the story? When and under what circumstances is the story told? How do you react to hearing the story? How do others react? Has the story changed over time? Are there any other versions of the story? How are you portrayed in the story or series of stories (e.g., competent, incompetent, courageous, cowardly, dignified, silly, saintly?) What meaning does the story hold for you now? How does it affect your choices, relationships, and behaviors? How would you like to change the stories about you? How could you go about doing it? What stories would you like your grandchildren to tell about you? After students completed the exercise in pairs, we would process it together as a group, and I would invite them to share any reactions or revelations they had. This exercise generated a lot of discussion, and created a constructivist framework for future class assignments and discussions.

Since the introduction of narrative theory and therapy in the 1990s, it has become very popular and is used widely in many settings where social workers practice. It has great relevance for social work through its emphasis on understanding the impacts of oppression, and of social and economic injustice, on clients. By drawing on the theories of Michel Foucault, it sees truth, power, and knowledge as inseparable, and interprets the role of the dominant culture as one that advances certain "truths" or norms in order to subjugate others. These ideas from Foucault, embedded in narrative theory, can be used in clinical work to decipher ways clients have experienced oppression. Social workers can explore with clients how the clients' stories, unduly influenced by various sociopolitical contexts, do not fully capture their true narratives. Workers and clients can acknowledge this and begin to build another more fulfilling story based on new interpretations of the past. This approach also resonates with social work by emphasizing client strengths and empowerment. Clients are active participants, authoring both past and present stories, and choosing how the next chapter will be written.

Cognitive Theory

The basis of cognitive theory is that people's feelings and behavior are affected by the ways in which they think. To help people feel better, you need to tackle the problem where it starts—in their thoughts. Cognitive therapy focuses on understanding how peoples' belief systems affect their attitudes, experiences, and expectations in life. Interventions are aimed at helping clients question faulty ways of thinking about themselves and the world, and to encourage more realistic and self-affirming beliefs. Social workers help clients interpret events and construct reality in new ways, and engage in more effective problem-solving and decision-making behavior. Based on more rational information, clients can start to make better choices for themselves.

There are a number of distinct differences between cognitive theory and psychodynamic theories. Whereas the unconscious plays an important role in understanding behavior in the psychodynamic tradition, cognitive theory is more interested in conscious thought and improving rational thinking patterns. In contrast to psychodynamic approaches, the social worker using cognitive theory plays a more active, directive, and goal-oriented role in the client interview, asking detailed questions about the sequence of events that led up to the presenting problem. Clients are helped to identify and understand certain self-defeating behaviors and irrational thoughts, and replace them with more positive, realistic, and affirming ones. The thrust of the social worker's efforts is in changing misconceptions, unrealistic expectations, and faulty assumptions that have become habitual ways of thinking for clients.

Aaron Beck (1967, 1976) was one of the pioneers in the field of cognitive therapy. He looked at the relationship between depression and thinking, and found that depressed patients had difficulty recognizing their successes and were preoccupied with negative and distorted thoughts. Later, Burns (1980) outlined some of the common cognitive distortions that depressed patients often exhibit that lead to problems. At the start of therapy, depressed clients are sometimes given a handout to educate them about typical distortions. The goal is to help clients be more aware of when they are using them. Below is a list of these distortions as described by Burns (1990).

- "All or nothing thinking." People's tendency to perceive themselves and their experiences in extremes, all or nothing, all good or all bad.
- "Overgeneralization." People's tendency to take a single negative event and conclude that it will always happen.

- "Mental filtering." This is when a person isolates one negative part of a situation and focuses attention solely on this detail. For example, a person may focus on a mistake and ignore the overall successes.
- "Disqualifying the positive." People's tendency to see their positive experiences as trivial and not counting, even in the face of objective evidence to the contrary.
- "Jumping to conclusions." This happens when a person arbitrarily comes to a negative conclusion without any evidence to support this belief.
- "Magnification or minimization." This occurs when people exaggerate a situation, making it worse than it is, or minimize their ability to cope with the situation.
- "Emotional reasoning." This refers to how a person explains a situation based on her feelings rather than reason.
- "Labeling and mislabeling." This happens when an error in behavior is considered a permanent personal characteristic. For example, when people do something stupid and label themselves stupid instead of the behavior.
- "Personalization." This occurs when a person thinks that everything people do or say is somehow related to him. The person takes too much responsibility for negative events that happen.

Cognitive restructuring is used to describe interventions aimed at helping clients change their belief systems. Clients are encouraged to pay attention to what they say to themselves and how they use distortions in their daily life. "Self-talk" refers to repetitive things we say about ourselves and our lives, such as "I'm not good enough" and "I don't deserve this." It can become like an automatic tape running in our heads that plays constantly, without our realizing it, and gives us negative and self-defeating messages. One way to help clients become aware of this internal dialogue is to ask them to keep a notebook or daily log, marking down any time they notice themselves engaging in critical "self-talk." Next, they should try to compare and identify each incident to the Burns list of distortions. The social worker asks, "What feelings are associated with the distortion? How do these critical self-statements affect you?" Last, clients are challenged to come up with alternative thoughts or explanations based on more realistic and rational beliefs.

Albert Ellis is associated with a branch of cognitive therapy referred to as Rational Emotive Therapy. Ellis believes that people can deal with their emotional or mental problems by confronting their irrational thoughts. Ellis is most known for his ABC method, which helps clients rid themselves of cognitive distortions that interfere with optimal functioning and is now a technique used in cognitive restructuring. The method requires that clients pay attention to their thinking during stressful moments, especially their automatic thoughts, and submit to three steps: (A) During the intervention with the social worker, clients are asked about the assumptions or belief upon which the automatic thought was based. (B) Then the social worker asks what the consequences were for making these assumptions. (C) Last, the worker challenges them. For example, a client may think he will never get into a good school, (A) because he is not smart enough. (B) This makes him feel depressed and hopeless. (C) The social worker then works with the client to help him challenge the false belief and arrive at another self-appraisal that leads to more self-confidence and self-esteem.

Although both psychodynamic and cognitive therapies work with clients' distortions, they understand and treat them very differently. In psychodynamic theory, social workers help clients see how their distortions are based on past experiences; through insight gained in therapy, clients can make this connection, which helps them let go of the past and choose better ways of looking at the present. In cognitive therapies, there is less interest in talking about the client's childhood. The emphasis is on dealing with irrational thinking and replacing false beliefs with more accurate assessments of the situation.

Social workers use another technique called affirmations to help clients replace the negative "self-talk" with more positive statements. For example, clients may be asked to write down ten attributes they appreciate about themselves. They would be instructed to complete ten sentences that begin with, "I like that I. ..." Next, they would be asked to read aloud these ten sentences several times a day for several weeks. The goal is for clients to replace the automatic negative tapes running in their heads with more positive and self-affirming beliefs about themselves. In this way, clients become their own best coaches and learn to counteract negative internal messages whenever they surface.

Reframing and thought stopping are two other interventions used in cognitive therapy. Reframing is used to help a client view a situation differently. For example, a woman feeling badly about herself after a divorce is helped to see that she is not a failure, rather her husband was not able to appreciate her unique and wonderful qualities. Thought stopping refers to stopping obsessive self-criticisms and unwanted thoughts by yelling or saying to oneself, "Stop, stop!" or snapping a rubber band around one's wrist. This action is followed by an alternative, positive statement that counteracts the criticisms.

In addition to improving self-dialogue, cognitive therapy also helps clients develop their communication skills with others. Clients are encouraged to use language that is assertive, clear, and centers around "I" messages. They are also taught to be better listeners, by learning to reflect back and acknowledge what the other person is saying. This prevents clients from making false assumptions by jumping to the wrong conclusions, and lessens the chance for misunderstandings. Clients may rehearse or role-play situations with the social worker to practice these new skills, especially when there is a pressing issue with another person that needs to be resolved. This gives the client a chance to build her confidence before confronting the situation by trying out the new tactics and getting feedback. Teaching clients better communication skills that emphasize the importance of listening is very important. To know how to really listen from the other person's perspective is an essential life skill that promotes empathy and better understanding between people and leads to fewer conflicts.

Brainstorming is another technique used in cognitive therapy for improved problem solving. Clients are prompted to create as many possible solutions to a problem as possible. Once the client has created an exhaustive list of ideas, he evaluates each one with the social worker to determine which seems the best choice at the time. The client and social worker weigh out the pros and cons, costs and benefits, of each alternative before making a decision. This process helps to build problem-solving and critical-thinking skills that demonstrate good judgment.

Positive Psychology

A branch of cognitive theory, positive psychology looks at the importance of positive emotions and happiness as a means to alleviate suffering. It traces its beginnings to 1998 and Martin Seligman, a cognitive psychologist who was President of the American Psychological Association at the time. Although similar to social work's emphasis on the strengths perspective, positive psychology takes a broader approach and actually builds treatment around using positive emotions to help people feel better (Cooper & Lesser, 2011; Fredrickson, 2004). Research conducted on the effectiveness of treatment using principles from positive psychology has found it quite effective (Burton & King, 2004; Emmons & McCullough, 2003).

Instead of using the Diagnostic and Statistical Manual (DSM) to label patients based on deficits, Peterson and Seligman (2004) devised their own diagnostic guidelines, which they refer to as the "Character Strengths and Virtues Handbook and Classification." It comprises six virtues, each associated with a list of strengths, which I have included below:

1. Wisdom and knowledge (virtue) is associated with the strengths of creativity, curiosity, open-mindedness, love of learning, and perspective.
2. Courage (virtue) is associated with the strengths of authenticity, bravery, persistence, and zest.
3. Humanity (virtue) is associated with the strengths of kindness, love, and social intelligence.
4. Justice (virtue) is associated with the strengths of fairness, leadership, and teamwork.
5. Temperance (virtue) is associated with the strengths of forgiveness, modesty, prudence, and self-regulation.
6. Transcendence (virtue) is associated with the strengths of appreciation of beauty and excellence, gratitude, hope, humor, and religiousness.

One of positive psychology's significant contributions is its ease of use by the layperson. Many of the suggestions and techniques for improving mood and pursuing happiness can be practiced on one's own by applying the principles found in the literature. One book that I recommend, and that many of my clients have found helpful, is *The Pursuit of Happiness* (Ben-Shahar, 2007). I have also tried certain suggestions in the book with my students. For example, at the beginning of one class I asked students to reflect and write down five things they were grateful for in their lives. They enjoyed this task immensely; one student was so moved that even now, many years after her graduation, she tells me she continues to use this exercise.

Behavioral Theory

The premise behind behavioral theory is that all behavior is learned and can be studied in an empirical, scientific way. The primary goal is to change behavior, not to produce insight. Behaviorists are concerned with understanding actions that are observable, objective, and quantifiable. They are interested in looking for the simplest explanation of a client's problem.

It's possible that behaviorism grew out of a reaction to psychoanalysis, which was considered subjective and emphasized unconscious and hidden determinants of behavior.

John Watson is credited with the beginning of behavioral theory. A pioneer in the first half of the 20th century, he worked hard to make psychology a reputable, recognized science. He believed that "observation of behavior alone was able to provide the clear data needed for scientific activity," and that human behavior could "be reducible to the laws of physics" (Walsh, 2010, p. 124). The early experiments of Pavlov and Watson in the 1920s and 1930s studied the rudimentary stimulus and response reactions in behavior that are now described as classical conditioning. They looked at learned automatic responses, how a certain stimulus will evoke a particular consequence. Pavlov's famous experiments with dogs showed that when a bell was sounded in conjunction with showing the dog food, the dog would salivate. The bell became a conditioned stimulus that would produce the response by itself because it was linked to the main stimulus, food. Behaviors become conditioned when they are associated with a stimulus. If the association between the conditioned response and stimulus is not kept up, the conditioned response will fade or become extinct.

B. F. Skinner later introduced the concept of operant conditioning that looked at how reinforcement leads to a desired behavior. Operant conditioning took behaviorism to a new level by studying how to shape future behavior by setting up rewards and punishments that serve as positive and negative behavior reinforcements. Changing the contingencies that affect behaviors leads to new consequences. For example, if getting a bike is contingent on getting grades of B or better on a report card, a child will be motivated to study harder to get the bicycle; in this case, studying is the behavior being reinforced by the future reward of a bicycle, and the reward is contingent on good grades.

These principles have been widely used with children and adolescents who have behavioral problems to help modify behavior. They have also been taught to parents in parent-education programs. Residential programs for children with behavioral problems often use a token system to reinforce children's more appropriate behavior. Children in these settings will be given tokens for positive behavior, and once they have accumulated a certain number, they can redeem them for something they want. The goal is to help children learn more socially appropriate behavior by reinforcing the desired behavior with rewards.

Traditionally, this is how behavior modification has been used: to change behavior by manipulating stimulus and response, or through punishments and rewards. This straight behaviorism is effective in treating severe disorders like autism and schizophrenia. This approach alone is limited, though, and most social workers use cognitive-behavioral approaches that try to change behaviors and feelings while also changing thinking patterns. Cognitive-behavioral approaches with children help them think about whether their perceptions are justified (cognitive), then model ways to deal with stressful situations and rehearse competent responses (behavioral) (Fishman, 1991).

The concepts behind operant conditioning and classical or respondent conditioning provide a basis for behavioral analysis. Applied behavioral analysis (ABA) is a contemporary term used to describe what was formerly known as behavior modification. Behavioral analysts observe and study the relationship between behavior and the environment, with the goal of changing a problem behavior into more socially acceptable behavior. The techniques used in

ABA can be applied to a wide range of problems, but they are often associated with children with an autism spectrum disorder, developmental delays, or people with severe mental illness. Applied behavioral analysis has proved effective as a learning tool for helping this population acquire and maintain new skills. There are many graduate degree programs available in ABA, as well as advanced graduate certification programs. There is a high demand for special education professionals who have training in ABA.

Albert Bandura (1977) is a behaviorist known for promoting the concept of modeling in behavioral theory. Modeling is an important way that all people learn, especially children who observe their parents and siblings and can later be observed imitating them. Adolescents observe their peer group for social cues on how to behave and be accepted. Peer pressure is a negative example of modeling in which a dominant personality influences others to behave in a certain way to belong to the group. This can lead to problem behaviors associated with alcohol, drugs, and premature sex. Rehearsing is a concept related to modeling and can be used when a client is anxious about an approaching situation and the social worker wants to allay those fears by role-playing the event in advance. In the role-play, the social worker can first model ways to approach the situation by taking the role of the client. Next, they can reverse roles, and the client can rehearse the same scenario but play himself this time to gain confidence in mastering the interaction.

Often, young professionals starting out in a new career model supervisors or mentors by watching what they do and rehearsing or practicing these same behaviors. Nurse preceptors play an important role in educating new nurses and helping them make the transition from the classroom to a clinical setting. In a similar way, social work also emphasizes the importance of field supervisors in modeling professional practice for social work students, who often begin at a placement by shadowing social workers. After observing and rehearsing these skills, students are then expected to try them out with their own clients.

Closely related to modeling are skills-training programs. These are behavioral programs that teach specific skills to a variety of client groups to help them manage different and challenging situations. There are anger-management skill programs to teach clients ways to control and find acceptable outlets for overwhelming emotions. There are social skills programs to teach children how to behave in more socially acceptable ways with their peers to gain friends. There are stress-management programs to teach people skills to manage stress in their lives. There are time-management groups to teach the skills of managing time efficiently to get work completed on schedule. There are life skills groups for hospitalized psychiatric patients who are transitioning to independent living. Dialectical behavior therapy, a treatment for patients with borderline personality disorder, uses a combination of behavioral and cognitive techniques to teach affect management, coping mechanisms, interpersonal skills, and other important competencies.

Behavioral studies and therapy has also moved into the area of behavioral medicine. The connection between mind-body is widely recognized as an important factor in treating illness (Astin et al., 2003). There are a number of alternative therapies that have been proven effective in helping sick people that can be used as adjuncts to conventional medical practice. Meditation has been credited with lowering blood pressure. Herbert Benson (2000) argued for this relationship between hypertension and meditation in his groundbreaking book,

The Relaxation Response. Benson found a correlation between stress and hypertension and discovered that through meditation alone, a person can bring about striking physiological changes—drops in heart rate, metabolic rate, and breathing rate. Benson (2000) concluded that although stress triggers the fight or flight response, the mind does not have to race if it can become focused through meditation.

Benson's instructions for reaching the relaxation response are the following: (1) Repetition of a word, phrase, prayer, or muscular activity, and (2) Passively disregarding everyday thoughts that inevitably come to mind and returning to your repetition (Benson, 2000, p. 13). There are times when people can engage in a hobby or exercise that also elicits the relaxation response, making the given activity an effective stress management technique. Once the mind is preoccupied with a repetitive diversion, whether saying a word over and over in the mind, or engaging in a hobby such as gardening, it facilitates letting go of stressful thoughts and distractions that interfere with relaxation and affect blood pressure.

Another type of meditation practice that is similar to the relaxation response is mindfulness meditation. Like Benson's relaxation response, this meditation has been proven to promote well-being and decrease stress. Two key words that help describe qualities of mindfulness practice are awareness and attention. By focusing on the breath, the practitioner pays attention to what is happening in the present and maintains an awareness of this experience from moment to moment. One definition of mindfulness is as "enhanced attention to and awareness of current experience or reality" (Brown & Ryan, 2003, p. 822). "Mindfulness captures a quality of consciousness that is characterized by clarity and vividness of current experience and functioning and thus stands in contrast to the mindless, less awake states of habitual or automatic functioning that may be chronic for many individuals" (Brown & Ryan, 2003, p. 823). Brown and Ryan further state that by adding "clarity and vividness" to experience, mindfulness may contribute to well-being and happiness.

Teaching clients to meditate can be therapeutic for them in many situations. It has proved effective for dealing with stress and illness and helping the body heal itself. It has also been used to help clients manage anxiety by teaching them to stay focused on the present experience rather than jumping to future worries. For clients who suffer from post-traumatic stress and childhood trauma, meditation can help them deal with affect dysregulation, or difficulty controlling emotional responses. It may be challenging for these patients to tune out stimuli around them and find ways to calm themselves or self-soothe. They have dealt with trauma by becoming hypervigilant to their environments to ward off the possibility of future trauma. They focus on the external because that is where the danger is. A central problem for these clients may be the inability to go inward, to be attuned to their experience. These clients can be taught that in the here and now, they are not being traumatized. They can learn to let go of the difficult memory and be aware of their experience in the moment. People usually experience the present as pleasing, listening to sounds, being aware of their senses, noticing and not judging. For this reason, mindfulness meditation has important applications for social workers.

I have found mindfulness meditation very useful in my practice, both teaching it to clients and applying it to my own approach during a session. It helps me to stay centered in the moment, attentive to what is happening in the present. I can be nonjudgmental, accepting feelings and thoughts that surface naturally, which the client and I then come to understand together in the here and now. "Within the context of the therapeutic relationship, mindfulness is a way of paying attention with empathy, presence and deep listening that can be cultivated, sustained, and integrated in our work through the ongoing discipline of meditation practice" (Cooper & Lesser, 2011, pp. 14-15).

Another behavioral strategy that uses relaxation exercises is systematic desensitization. To help deal with a fear or phobia, clients are taught practical techniques of relaxation. Slowly, the unwanted stimulus is introduced using the relaxation exercise to ward off the anxiety (Payne, 2005, p. 124). The feared object or situation is desensitized so that the client no longer fears it. Biofeedback is another way to help clients track their physiological response to stress. Clients are attached to a monitoring apparatus that provides them with continuous feedback about their responses and heart rate. By practicing meditation and relaxation exercises, they can observe changes in their responses that reinforce the beneficial effects of these practices.

There are many practical applications of behavioral theories that can be used with clients in multiple settings. The principles of classical and operant conditioning and modeling have particular relevance in work with children and adolescents who have behavioral or emotional problems. The various skills programs are helpful to clients in school and psychiatric settings, and relaxation and meditation practices are important adjuncts to any therapy.

Systems Theory

Systems theory is an overarching theory that provides social workers with a conceptual framework or lens through which to view the world. A system is made up of many parts that are interrelated and function as a whole. Social workers must be conversant with systems of various sizes from the individual to the family to social groups to organizations and communities. The ecological perspective in social work evolved from systems theory, and although they are very similar, there are some differences. The ecological method emphasizes living, dynamic interactions, whereas systems theory is a much broader concept and can also refer to relationships between inanimate objects. Also, there are distinctions between the types of language used in the two theories. Systems theory uses such terms as "boundaries" and "subsystems," wherein the ecological perspective emphasizes transactions between the person and environment.

To understand problems from an ecological perspective, social workers look at the impact of the environment on the person and the reciprocal nature of this relationship. Systems theory also looks at how multiple systems interact with and affect each other, such as the individual, family, groups, community, and country. Families are considered systems because they are made up of many parts that are interrelated and function as a whole. Psychosocial assessment from a systems perspective looks at understanding problems in their context and includes information about a client's family.

Family Systems Theory

Social work has a long history of understanding clients' problems in terms of systems, and acknowledging the important influence of the family on the individual. Before family therapy was popular, social caseworkers were visiting clients in their homes and working with the family unit. Historians of social work will find that as far back as the early 1900s, the Charity Organization Societies had become increasingly oriented toward helping families. Many local chapters changed their names to Family Welfare Agency around the same time that the National Alliance for Organizing Charity was renamed the American Association for Organizing Family Social Work. By 1946, this organization was known as the Family Service Association of America, later renamed Family Service America FSA in 1983. This continues to be an important national social work agency with chapters throughout the country.

The family systems movement took off in the 1950s and 1960s as leaders in the fields of social work, psychology, and psychiatry resisted the idea that client problems resided within the person alone. Many movement leaders and family therapists came from the Child Guidance Clinics. These clinics were established on the premise that to prevent mental illness it was important to work with children early, when the problem started. In the beginning, children and parents were treated separately, but this proved unsuccessful. It became clear that the child's problems were related to what was going on in the family. Eventually, child guidance workers began to work with parents and children together, and family therapy took off.

Although there are many different family theories, only family emotional systems theory and structural family theory will be discussed in this chapter. When applying any theory to a family as part of assessment, it is important to pay attention to a family's culture and not force the key theoretical concepts onto every family. Social workers must use critical thinking and to be flexible in applying theories to clients. For example, when I discuss family emotional systems theory and the work of Murray Bowen, there is a strong emphasis on separation and differentiation. This concept may not have relevance in a culture in which there are very close family ties and multigenerational families live together as part of established tradition.

Family Emotional Systems Theory or Multigenerational Family Theory

Murray Bowen is the name most often associated with family emotional systems theory, because he played a central role in the family movement of the 1960s. Bowen (1978) saw the family as an emotional system composed not just of the nuclear family but the extended family as well, whether living or dead. He believed the emotional system of a family's previous generations continues in the present family, and that its influence should be recognized as part of the therapy. Although his writings date back 50 years, they are still relevant today, and many of his terms have become a part of mainstream thinking about families (Bregman & White, 2011). For example, key concepts such as triangulation, sibling position, differentiation of self, family projection system, and emotional cutoff are still used in modern-day assessment.

Having come out of the psychoanalytic tradition, Bowen used reflection with his patients to help them understand the importance of family history. He wanted clients to see how the past influenced them in the present, sometimes in unconscious ways. The goal of unlocking such history is to recognize how family patterns are passed down through generations. With this information, clients can see how they may be repeating destructive behaviors modeled in their families, and then make more conscious choices for themselves based on reason and not emotion. By acknowledging their history and making other choices, clients learn to differentiate from their families and become more autonomous. Bowen believed that a healthy family was one in which members were allowed to separate or differentiate from one another and be independent.

Differentiation is a key term in family emotional systems theory. It refers to the family's ability to accept change and difference on the part of its members, allowing autonomy. Differentiated people can separate themselves from emotional entanglements. They are flexible, adaptable, thoughtful, independent, and more self-sufficient. People who are differentiated have their own feelings and, although aware of the other's feelings, are able to maintain a degree of objectivity and emotional distance about what's outside of their own experience. The differentiated person is said to have a solid sense of self and operate on the basis of clearly defined beliefs, opinions, convictions, and principles. They do not change their positions to receive love or approval from others. They are free to hold opinions different from other family members and are not pressured to conform to the family's way of thinking or behaving.

The opposite of differentiation is fusion. A fused family resists new ideas from the outside and experiences change as a threat (Hartman & Laird, 1983, p. 234). The undifferentiated family, a state known as fusion, refers to a family's oneness. People who are undifferentiated from their families are more rigid and more emotionally dependent on others for their well-being. Family members are enmeshed. A fused person is trapped in a world of feelings and makes decisions on the basis of emotional pressure as opposed to reason. As a result, choices are inconsistent and change in order to please others. An undifferentiated person may be afraid of becoming too close to another person because it threatens what little sense of self exists. Unlike the differentiated person who has a solid sense of self, the undifferentiated person has a pseudo-self.

Another important concept in Bowen's family theory is triangulation. This refers to the process of a two-person system pulling in a third member of the family to create a triangle. Often, this happens when a couple is experiencing anxiety or conflict and they involve a third person, usually a child who is the most vulnerable member of the family, to take the attention away from their problem. By projecting the problem onto the child, the couple then focuses on the child, who becomes the family scapegoat. This is also called family projection, because the parents project their marital problems onto one or more of the children, thus triangulating them into the marital system. Family assessment looks for evidence of triangles in a family system. In a fused family, triangulation is more likely to occur.

Family assessment can take many forms. There are scales that measure levels of differentiation in families. There is also an assessment tool known as the genogram. Bowen used genograms to map family information. He would ask questions about the family that would go back at least three generations. In drawing the genogram, he would look for patterns and themes passed down unconsciously from one generation to the next. Bowen believed that our identities are strongly influenced by family members, whether they are grandparents, parents, siblings, aunts, uncles, etc. By bringing these influences to the surface, clients can separate from the past and are free to make better choices.

When social workers use genograms, they play the role of a Sherlock Holmes in collecting information about the family (Hartman & Laird, 1983, p. 218). The social worker would explore ethnic and religious backgrounds, losses, major family events, occupations, immigration, information about triangles and coalitions, emotional cutoffs, communication patterns, and family roles. However, when collecting information for a genogram, rather than just getting facts, it is important for the social worker to elicit whole stories to create a more living family narrative that gives meaning to the data. Following is a list of the kind of data gathered in a genogram. Much of the information included in this list is adapted from Ann Hartman and Joan Laird's book *Family Centered Social Work Practice* (1983, pp. 217–227).

- The Family Emotional System: What are relationships like in the family-of-origin? What role did the client play in her family? With whom did the parents identify? What were the parents' ambitions for her like? Were there family triangles? Are there people from whom the family has been cut off?
- Names: Names identify family members and suggest ethnic background, naming patterns, and important identifications. Was the client named after anyone? If so, what was this person like? What was the nature of the client's parents' relationship with this relative?
- Occupations: Occupations of family members show what their interests and talents are, the successes and failures of their work and careers, and the different levels of socioeconomic statuses found in families. Occupational patterns may point to identifications with past family members and may reflect family expectations.
- Dates: Dates of birth and death recorded on the genogram inform the social worker of the timing of important events. They indicate how early or late in a marriage kids were born, and the age of the parents at those births. It is important to discover all events that took place in the period surrounding the client's birth. What were the circumstances at the time of the client's birth? Major losses experienced in the family around the birth time can be important. The tendency to use newborn family members as replacements for lost members is common.
- Sibling Position: Dates of birth also identify sibling positions. It is important to list the siblings in order by age, with the oldest first. This makes it easy to identify visually those who occupy the same sibling position in different generations. An individual's place in the sibling group can have correlations to others in the family who occupied the same position. This can provide clues concerning possible hidden scripts for this individual. Some examples are: the competent daughter, the responsible eldest, the caretaker, the brilliant one, the patient one, the joker, the incompetent one, etc. Sibling position can also explain powerful affective relationships. How a mother felt about her oldest sister, the firstborn in her family of origin, can influence how she feels about her own firstborn daughter. For several generations, the middle child may have felt left out or, alternately, been the most successful.
- Place of Birth and Residence: Place of birth and residence provides insight on where families have lived and why. Were there major migrations and periods of loss or upheaval? Generations of a family may have stayed within a fairly small area or be spread out geographically. There may be a particular family member who stands out for moving away from the home base. Many families emigrate from their country of origin due to war, persecution, or a poor economy.

- Health and Sickness: Facts about family members' health and causes of death have an effect on the way clients see their own futures. Most people have an inner conviction concerning their own times and forms of death. Some families may organize around illness, which is used throughout generations to keep family members close. When exploring illness, it is important to look at both physical and mental illness and periods of hospitalization.

- Heroes and Villains: Information about people in the family who are idealized as well as devalued can provide clues concerning the family's values and aspirations, as well as the behavior it deplores.

- Alcohol and Drug Addiction, Sexual Assault, Rape, Incest, Suicide, Family Secrets: All families have someone hiding in the closet that they are reluctant or embarrassed to talk about. It is important to uncover these family secrets and understand the emotional toll they have played on the family. How have some of these events and family experiences affected the family unit?

- Losses: Loss can play a central role in family life and should be assessed for how it affects family behavior. A family member may identify with a person who died, a birth may signify a replacement of the lost person, and there may be new expectations placed on the family.

- Descriptions of Family Members: How would you describe family members? Is there a word or picture that comes to mind when you think about each person? Are there labels associated with one person or another, such as lazy, brilliant, stupid, weak, martyr, beautiful, caretaker. Are other people in the family assigned similar roles?

- Family Themes and Toxic Events: Certain themes or events may reemerge in successive generations. For example, there may be someone in each generation who sacrifices his own education or career for that of another. Or, one female in each generation may remain single and stay home to take care of aging parents. Fathers may leave their families, or alcoholism may appear throughout the system.

- Emotional Cutoffs: Cutoffs refer to breaks in family relationships whereby members no longer communicate with other members, usually due to conflict, unresolved problems, painful experiences, or family secrets. It may indicate that the family is undifferentiated or unable to tolerate different opinions. It could be a sign that a family cannot communicate openly with each other or accept different perspectives. Sometimes these cutoffs occur after a parent has died and there is anger about the will or distribution of family possessions. Sometimes there may be a family member who identifies with the person who is cut off. For example, the son of an alcoholic father who deserted the family many years ago may begin drinking heavily, or an adopted girl becomes pregnant out of wedlock, as did her own biological mother.

The genogram is an assessment tool but it is also an intervention. Social workers engage clients in the process and invite them to take part in the investigation. Clients discover important connections, repetitive family patterns, and influences that become the focus of further discussion and reflection. When the genogram is completed, the social worker spends time reviewing what the client learned from the exercise, what meaning it had for him. Sometimes the genogram work can span several sessions with the client. It's possible the client won't know parts of the family history, and the worker can encourage him to be in touch with other family members to fill in gaps. This can also lead to important insights. If used in this comprehensive way, the genogram becomes a valuable tool in treatment. It furthers the goal of differentiation by helping clients form a strong sense of self and identity.

Structural Family Theory

Structural family theory is another systemic approach to understanding clients' problems, and Salvador Minuchin is the clinician who helped develop the tenets behind the theory. He, like Murray Bowen, was at the forefront of the family therapy movement in the 1960s, and like Bowen, Minuchin's work is still relevant today. Minuchin was the director of the Philadelphia Child Guidance Clinic for 10 years, and his interest was working with children from multiproblem families and poor urban neighborhoods. Through his work, he started to develop a theory to deal with the type of family issues he confronted in the clinic: issues associated with poverty, family disruption, physical and mental illness, juvenile delinquency, drug addition, single parenthood, crime, and violence. What became structural theory evolved in response to the needs of these families experiencing multiple problems, and his interventions focused on family structure, with a high level of therapist activity that seemed particularly suited to the population (Walsh, 2010, p. 200).

Unlike family emotional systems theory, structural family theory is less interested in emotion and history, and more concerned with how the family is organized in the present. Minuchin believed that an individual's emotional problems are maintained, and sometimes created, by a family's dysfunctional organizational structure. Changing the structure of the family usually leads to the resolution of an individual's problem (Minuchin, 1974). When these structural barriers are removed, family members relate better to one another and are in a stronger position to solve their own issues (Minuchin & Fishman, 1981).

Minuchin (1974) thought of structural family therapy as a therapy of action. The family's problems are acted out with the therapist, and his job is to facilitate change in the present. To do this, the therapist joins with the family and uses himself to transform the system. At the start of a session, the therapist notices where family members sit when they enter the room, and he may decide to change the seating pattern. For example, if he sees that a child is sitting between the two parents, he may ask the child to sit with his siblings and have the parents sit next to each other. With some families, he may always work with the entire group, whereas with other families, he may select certain groupings or subgroups to meet with periodically to observe different family dynamics. When the therapist notices a coalition, he may break it up in the session. If he finds a certain family member always becoming the scapegoat, he may choose to align himself with this member in the session.

Structural therapy looks for the proper functioning of family subsystems. Attention is given to the system's boundaries, and the appropriateness of coalitions, triangles, and alliances (Ford, Durtschi, & Franklin, 2012). For example, dysfunction occurs in a couple when one or both partners are dissatisfied with the relationship, or when boundaries are violated. Problems can occur if detrimental coalitions, triangles, and alliances are formed, which also affect subsystem boundaries. This could happen when a child becomes a confidant to a parent and crosses the parent-child boundary, creating tension in the marital relationship. Outside coalitions may also create a systemic imbalance by creating a triangle with an inappropriate third member, for example when one person in the couple is having an affair. In both of these cases, the goal of structural family therapy is the realignment and restructuring of the couple. A therapist can accomplish this by creating opportunities for intimacy and closeness between spouses, actions that can become reinforcing and self-perpetuating (Ford, Durtschi, & Franklin, 2012).

In assessing the family structure, the practitioner first looks at the executive level of the family, the parents, who establish family rules. For a family unit to function well, the parents need to sit at the helm directing the ship. Are the parents working together as a subsystem, and do they assume power for decision-making in the family? Although the parents need to take charge, they should also show flexibility and listen to everyone's opinions. It is important that decisions are made in a fair way, with input from others. This is especially true when children reach adolescence and want to play an active role in the decision-making process, part of efforts to become more independent.

Here's an example of a problem that can occur at a family's executive level: The parents' position of authority is challenged by a child who begins to exert more power over mom and dad, who then feel helpless to do anything. Another structural problem occurs when a parent and child assume power in the family and weaken the second parent's role. This is a problematic alliance. It goes against proper subsystems interaction between adults and children, and also reflects poor boundaries between parents and their kids. In such cases, the practitioner would bring attention to these structural problems and design activities to realign the family.

Boundaries are important to structural theory and can be viewed from different perspectives. Therapists can examine a family's external boundary with the outside community. For example, is a family an open and flexible, or closed and rigid, system? An open family has fluid boundaries, allowing people to come and go and inviting others into the home. Children are comfortable bringing friends home. In a closed system, the family has little interaction with the outside community and, in a sense, is closed off to the external world. In this situation, a child may not be allowed to have friends over, and the family keeps to themselves.

Another way of looking at family boundaries is to assess if the space between generations is appropriate. Problematic boundaries might include a parent and child coalition; a parent confiding information to a child that is not fitting; a child taking on too much responsibility in the family; or a parent sexually abusing a child. A third approach to boundaries is how a family respects the privacy and space of each individual. What, for example, is the level of closeness? When boundaries between family members are rigid, there is little emotional connection, and members may feel distant and disengaged from one another. At the other extreme is loose boundaries, relationships are enmeshed or too close with not enough separation and - there is a lack of respect for privacy.

Structural family assessment looks for those alliances, coalitions, or triangles, discussed previously that may interfere with optimal family function. Alliances can be problematic when two or more members join together to oppress another member, who is excluded from the group. This can happen when a sibling group targets, and is cruel to, another sibling.

Alliances can also cut across boundaries and subsystems. Take, for instance, the previously mentioned example, in which an improper connection forms between a parent and a child. In this situation, the child may be given too much authority over the other siblings. This alliance could also work against the other parent, whose position in the family is weakened. A triangle occurs when parents bring a child into their problems, projecting their issues onto the child, who becomes the symptom bearer.

In all of these situations, the practitioner would play an active role in fixing misalignments and structural problems. She would communicate the problems directly, and perhaps try a strategic alignment with an oppressed family member to elevate this person's position in the family. Engaging in clear, open, and candid dialogue is an important part of structural family therapy, and the practitioner becomes an example of good communication in the sessions.

Roles and family rules are assessed as part of the family's organization and structure. For a family to run smoothly, it needs rules that everyone understands, and members should know their family roles. Sometimes rules are implicit and need to be made explicit; sometimes roles need to change when they are no longer satisfying. Both roles, and the way they're assigned, and rules should stay flexible to allow for changing family needs. Families are often in flux, and their systems must respond to life span and developmental shifts that take place, both on the larger and individual level. For example, as children become older, they might want more responsibility at home to participate in decision making. Problems occur when parents are unable to recognize these changes in their children and are not willing to give them a greater voice in family governance. Power struggles between parents and adolescents can result. Role overload is another common difficulty in today's society. With two parents working, there can be a drain on whichever parent assumes a greater responsibility for earning money and taking care of the house and children.

Sometimes family members are assigned unhealthy roles. Perhaps they're labeled the family hero, or they become the scapegoat, the symptom bearer of the family's problems. In either case, there is an overvaluing or an undervaluing of the family member, and there is unfair pressure to live up to these false stereotypes. For the person in question, it is an undue burden to always fulfill someone else's expectation, to not feel free to be oneself, with both strengths and weaknesses. The practitioner's role is to uncover these myths and allow family members to see each other more realistically.

In structural family therapy, the practitioner's goal is to make organizational and structural changes in the family and to challenge rigid, repetitive patterns that handicap a family's optimal functioning (Corsini & Wedding, 2008, p. 424). Families come for help when they are feeling stress, when they can't adapt to changes during times of family transitions. Or maybe they come because of the symptoms of a child, who has become the scapegoat. Through the active intervention of the therapist, the family undergoes realignment and restructuring to improve the outlook both for the family as a unit and each individual family member. Structural family therapy continues to be popular today and has special relevance in child welfare work.

References

Argyris, C. & Shon, S. (1974). *Theories in Practice: Increasing Professional Effectiveness*. San Francisco, CA: Jossey Bass.

Astin, J. A., Shapiro, S. L., Eisenberg, D. M., & Forys, K. (2003). Mind-body medicine: State of the science, implications for practice. *American Board of Family Medicine, 16*(2), 131–147.

Bandura, A. (1977). *Social Learning Theory*. Englewood Cliffs, N.J.: Prentice-Hall.

Beck, A. T. (1967). *Depression: Clinical, Experimental, and Theoretical Aspects*. New York: Hoeber.

Beck, A. T. (1976). *Cognitive Theory and the Emotional Disorders*. New York: International Universities Press.

Ben-Shahar, T. (2007). *Happier*. New York: McGraw-Hill.

Benson, H. (2000). *The Relaxation Response*. New: York Harper Collins Publishers.

Berzoff, J. (2012). *Falling Through the Cracks: Psychodynamic Practice with Vulnerable and Oppressed Populations*. New York: Columbia University Press.

Bregman, O. C. & White, C. M. (Eds.), (2001). *Bringing Systems Thinking to Life—Expanding the Horizons for Bowen Family System*. New York: Routledge.

Bowen, M. (1978). *Family Therapy in Clinical Practice*. Northvale, NJ: Jason Aronson.

Brown, K. W. & Ryan, R. M. (2003). The benefits of being present: Mindfulness and its role in psychological well-being. *Journal of Personality and Social Psychology, 84*(2), 822–845.

Burns, D. (1990). *Feeling Good: The New Mood Therapy*. New York: William Morris & Co.

Burton, C. M. & King, L. A. (2004). The health benefits of writing about intensely positive experiences. *Journal of Research in Personality, 38*(2), 150–163.

Bruner, J. (1990). *Acts of Meaning*. Cambridge, MA: Harvard University Press.

Cooper, M. G. & Lesser, J. G. (2011). *Clinical Social Work Practice: An Integrated Approach* (4th ed.). Boston: Allyn & Bacon.

Corsini, R. J. & Wedding, D. (2008). *Current Psychotherapies*. Pacific Grove, CA: Thomson Brook/Cole.

Dean, R. G. (1993). Constructivism: An approach to clinical practice. *Smith College Studies in Social Work, 63*(2), 127–146.

Emmons, R. A. & McCullough, M. E. (2003). Counting blessings versus burdens: An experimental investigation of gratitude and subject well-being in daily life. *Journal of Personality & Development, 69*, 209–216.

Ford, J. J., Durtschi, J. A., & Franklin, D. L. (2012). Structural therapy with a couple battling pornography addiction. *The American Journal of Family Therapy, 40*(4), 336–348.

Fishman, K. D. (June, 1991). Therapy for children. *Atlantic Monthly*, 71–94).

Fleck-Henderson, A. (1989). Personality theory and clinical social work practice. *Clinical Social Work Journal, 17*(2), 128–137.

Fredrickson, B. L. (2004). The broaden-and-build theory of positive emotions. *Philosophical transactions of the Royal Society B:Biological Sciences, 359*(1449), 1367–1378.

Hartman, A. & Laird, J. (1983). Family centered social work practice. New York: Free Press.

Heller, N. & Northcut, T. (2011). The integration of psychodynamic and cognitive behavior. In J. Berzoff, L. M. Flanagan, & P. Hertz (Eds.), *Inside Out and Outside In: Psychodynamic Clinical Theory and Psychopathology* (3rd ed., pp. 208–221). Lanham, MD: Rowman & Littlefield Publishers.

Miley, K., O'Melia, M., & DuBois, B. (2009). *Generalist Social Work Practice: An Empowerment Approach*. Boston: Allyn & Bacon.

Minuchin, S. (1974). *Family and Family Therapy*. Cambridge, MA: Harvard University Press.

Minuchin, S. & Fishman, H. C. (1981). *Family Therapy Techniques*. Cambridge, MA: Harvard University Press.

Norlin, J. M. & Chess, W. (1997). *Human Behavior and the Social Environment: A Social Systems Model* (3rd ed.). Boston: Allyn & Bacon.

Parry, A. (1991). A universe of stories. *Family Process, 30*(1), 37–54.

Payne, M. (2005). *Modern Social Work Theory*. Chicago: Lyceum Books, Inc.

Peterson, C. & Seligman, M. (2004). *Character Strengths and Virtues: A Handbook and Classification*. New York: Oxford University Press.

Saleebey, D. (1994). Culture, theory and narrative: The intersection of meanings in practice. *Social Work, 39*(4), 351–359.

Shon, D. (1983). *The Reflective Practitioner. How Professionals Think In Action*. London: Temple Smith.

Thomlinson, R. J. (1984). Something works: Evidence from practice effectiveness studies. *Social Work, 29*, 51–57.

Timberlake, E. M., Sabatino, C. A., & Martin, J. A. (1997). Advanced practitioners in clinical practice: A profile. *Social Work, 42*(4), 374–385.

Vaillant, G. (1997). *The Wisdom of the Ego.* Cambridge, MA: Harvard University Press.

Walsh, J. (2010). *Theories for Direct Social Work Practice* (2nd ed.). Pacific Grove, CA: Brooks/Cole Cengage Publishing.

Weinberger, J. (1995). Common factors aren't so common: The common factors dilemma. *Clinical Psychology: Science and Practice, 2*(1), 45–69.

White, R.W. (1963). *Ego and Reality in Psychoanalytic Theory: A Proposal Regarding Independent Ego Entities.* New York: International Universities Press.

White, M. (1995). *Re-Authoring lives: Interviews & Essays.* Adelaide, S. Australia: Dulwich Centre Publications.

White, W. & Epston, D. (1990). *Narrative Means to Therapeutic Ends.* New York: W.W. Norton.

Winnicott, D. W. (1975). *Collected Papers: From Pediatrics to Psycho-Analysis.* New York: Basic.

Woods, M. & Hollis, F. (2000). *Casework: A Psychosocial Therapy.* Boston: McGraw-Hill.

3

Practice With Serious and Life-Threatening Illness

Allen: "I'm not a heart on my sleeve kind of guy."

Setting: Inpatient Hospital

This chapter discusses one of the five video recorded mock interviews, the case of Allen, a medical patient in an urban hospital who is waiting for open heart surgery. This case example provides an opportunity to learn about medical social work practice in the context of a hospital setting. It brings attention to some of the challenges social workers face when working with clients with serious and life-threatening illness. It also looks at some ethical and practice issues that social workers confront in medical settings. Excerpts from the interviews and process recordings are included to demonstrate practice skills and theories used in intervention.

Description of Practice Area

Allen is representative of the types of patients social workers interact with daily in hospital settings. Hospital social workers help a myriad of patients from diverse backgrounds who suffer from many different kinds of illnesses and injuries. The illness or loss may be brief and the patient may be expected to make a full recovery, or it may be long term. Another patient may be dealing with a chronic condition that requires accommodations and lifestyle changes, or may be suffering with a terminal illness and given a poor prognosis. Depending on the situation, the loss has different implications and meanings for the patient. However, what every situation has in common is that life as usual has stopped and the patient is vulnerable, helpless, and in a dependent position needing assistance.

Loss and Meaning-Making

Loss often triggers the memory of past losses for clients. These losses are relived again in the present situation and may add to a patient's stress. This sometimes happens on an unconscious level and may become more conscious when the client talks to the social worker. As you will read in Allen's case, as he experiences heart problems and contemplates his own mortality, it stirs up an earlier, unresolved loss related to his father's early death from heart disease. By using psychodynamic theory, the social worker helps Allen to understand how his panic attack and fears about surgery may be related to his memory of his father's early death. This discussion brings up issues from Allen's childhood about how his family did not communicate well with each other about this significant loss.

As Allen begins to make meaning out of the impact of his father's death on his life, he is also reviewing the past to understand how to incorporate this event into his ongoing life story. Social work interventions using narrative approaches can be helpful in hospital settings. They assist patients in looking at current problems in the context of a larger life narrative that helps to understand the meaning of illness in their lives. Narrative interventions become reflective processes to cope with the impact of unexpected or negative events. Borden (1992) states:

> In telling and hearing stories, a person can come to organize and understand experience in ways that help to restore and maintain a sense of coherence and continuity. A central task in adaptation to adverse life experience, accordingly, is incorporation of the event into the ongoing life story. Failure to maintain an ordered or intelligible narrative, from this point of view, may lead to distress, dysfunction, and fragmentation. (p. 136)

In Allen's case, the social worker helped Allen to find a meaningful way to understand and convey to others what caused his panic attack.

Listening to Patients' Stories

Working with clients in medical settings is not much different from working with them in other practice settings. As discussed in the first chapter, sound clinical practice includes both relationship building and knowing how to ask questions; these are part of the collaborative process of understanding and finding solutions to problems. Helen Perlman, the founder of social casework, refers to these steps as "beginning with the caseworker's attitude of attentiveness and receptivity...being an active listener and an active inquirer" (1957, pp. 111–112). Qualities found to be important in forming relationships include being empathic, genuine, warm, caring, sincere, honest, and nonjudgmental. These qualities help the client to "begin to feel safe in revealing his story and himself...the burgeoning of relationship and the securing sense that the worker is with him" (Perlman, 1957, p. 111). Perlman continues by saying that the client needs to feel confident that the social worker knows how to be helpful, "and this becomes manifest in the ways the social worker begins to help the client tell his troubles" (1957, p. 111). Being an active inquirer has to do with how social workers ask clients questions and how they use theories in action in their interventions with clients.

In thinking about how to listen and talk with clients in hospital settings, we need to reflect on what it means to sit with someone who has suffered an extreme loss and may never be able to work again, or has just been told that he has only six months left to live. How can you really help in these situations? This is a question raised by Ram Dass and Paul Gorman

(1987), who reflect on what it means to be a helper and listen to another person's pain. They believe that to open the heart and show compassion to another in the face of pain and suffering means to be open to the experience of suffering. It means we must let go of our own thoughts and distractions to be truly present with another human being and his experience in that moment. "The more deeply we listen, the more we attune ourselves to the roots of suffering and the means to help alleviate it" (Dass & Gorman, 1987, p. 112).

What Ram Dass and Paul Gorman (1987) talk about in their book is similar to what social workers discuss when they refer to the skills of self-reflection and self-awareness. Professional social work practice requires that social workers pay attention to how their personal experiences, values, and biased assumptions may provide obstacles to listening to clients in helpful ways (CSWE, 2008). To assist clients, social workers must practice self-reflection and be self-aware to guard against imposing their own views on clients, or overreacting to clients in unprofessional ways based on their own histories.

Practicing self-reflection means paying attention to our internal dialogue when sitting in the midst of pain and suffering. What comes up for us, or what memories get triggered when confronting issues of loss? To be able to open the heart and listen with compassion to another person's suffering requires the social worker to look within and be attuned to the self. It is impossible to listen to another person's suffering if we are preoccupied with our own thoughts, unresolved conflicts, or personal experiences with loss. If we are in denial about our own vulnerability and unable to understand the struggles, doubts, fears, and pain in our lives, we cannot help others. By confronting what it means to be human in this way, only then are we able to let go of ourselves to be truly there for another person.

Meditative and Mind–Body Practices

Meditative practices are another way of tuning in to the self; social workers can use meditative techniques themselves, and they can teach them to patients as ways to manage and treat illness and to promote healing. When the body can relax fully, it has a wisdom of its own that knows how to bring itself back into balance (Kabat-Zinn, 1990). Mind–body practices are often used in combination with traditional medical protocols. They include mindfulness meditation, mantra meditation, yoga, tai chi, and qigong. Meditation can help with self-regulation, pain management, and stress management, and it can also promote self-awareness (Freeman, 2004).

Mindfulness practice is another way of looking at what it means to be fully present with another person in the moment. For many, mindfulness practice is a philosophical approach to life. It helps to keep attention grounded in the present by requiring full awareness of what is happening moment to moment. To clear the mind, one needs to rid the self of thoughts of the past or worries about the future, to notice and be open to what is possible right now. This practice can facilitate a social worker being fully present with the client, and to listen in an open and empathic way without judgment that appreciates the client's perspective. Mindfulness is also used by social workers as a form of meditative practice that can be taught to clients as a stress-management technique to help clients manage difficult situations. Mindfulness is discussed more in chapter 2 under behavioral theories. In the case of Allen, the social worker discusses mindfulness and relaxation exercises with Allen as an intervention strategy to help him manage stress before his surgery.

Another important dimension of social work in medical settings, which requires some awareness and understanding, is the relationship between the mind and body. Holistic medicine is becoming more accepted now by both the established medical community and the general public and is often a part of traditional medical care. Research has found a connection between positive emotions and good health, and has confirmed the role that one's attitude and approach to illness can have in patient recovery (Cousins, 1979; Salovey et al., 2000; Siegel, 1986, 1990, 2011; Simonton et al., 1992). This holistic approach looks at ways to employ the mind to treat the body, and involves the patient more in the healing process. Rather than being a passive recipient of care, the patient plays a central role in getting better and can be given tools to participate in his own recovery. Those working with patients are encouraged to find opportunities to use humor as another stress-management technique, as it has a secondary benefit: releasing the healing properties of positive emotions (Cousins, 1979; James, 1995).

Individual and Family Life Cycle Assessment

During the assessment process, the social worker explores the meaning of the illness for Allen in terms of life cycle and family developmental issues. According to Erik Erikson's paradigm (Erikson, 1963), Allen is in midlife, known as the stage of generativity versus stagnation or self-absorption. It is a time that emphasizes sharing one's knowledge with the next generation, also investing in young people and mentoring relationships. It can also be a time of loss when a person might have to deal with aging parents or the death of parents. This may set off deeper reflection into one's purpose in life and ultimate death, especially as midlife marks a kind of halfway point to the end of life. The person has a different appreciation for life, and it can be a wake up call that time is running out. Midlife often spurs re-evaluation—returning to old dreams, setting new priorities, looking for new challenges and goals. It sometimes motivates people to revisit the past, review and resolve unfinished business, and then reinvest in the present.

Before hospitalization, Allen appeared to balance his career, family, and hobbies moderately well, staying actively involved in all three. His heart condition causes him to stop and take a closer look at his life and contemplate the possibility of death or disability. Everything has changed for him. This experience triggers memories of past losses and unfinished business in his family-of-origin, particularly the illness and death of his father when he was young. It makes Allen profoundly aware that he wants to be there for his children, unlike his own father.

The panic attack before surgery brings Allen back to an earlier time and to unresolved grief over his father's death. It provides him with another opportunity to understand the impact of this loss on his life. In his discussion with the social worker after the panic attack, he gains insight into how his tendency to suppress emotions is unhealthy, and he begins to open up and share his feelings more. After the surgery, he intends to follow up on a referral for outpatient psychotherapy to continue to probe these issues, and deal with the crisis of illness and the transition to midlife. With a practitioner's help, he can re-evaluate his life and relationships, resolve past losses, and explore new aspects of himself as he connects with his feelings.

In addition to working with the individual client, medical social workers also work with the client's family. Social workers are trained to see problems through an ecological lens that looks at the social environment and larger systems. Psychosocial assessment involves collecting data on micro, mezzo, and macro levels to fully appreciate the client's problem in context. Illness can impact a client's identity, his family, his work, and other areas of daily life. In the interview with Allen, the social worker explores Allen's family relationships to determine if they are a source of support and can serve as a resource in his recovery and discharge plan. Social workers also assess how the family is impacted by the client's illness, and whether there are areas of conflict that require intervention as they relate to the patient's situation, his recovery, and his aftercare.

When one person in the family falls ill, it impacts the whole family system. John Rolland (1987) looks at the unfolding of illness in a developmental context that involves three levels—the illness itself, the individual, and the family. There is a continual interplay between the backdrop of individual and family life cycle tasks and the illness. In Allen's family, his two children are at the stage of forming their identities and separating from the parents as they prepare to leave home (Erikson, 1963). In terms of family development, this is referred to as "launching children and moving on" (Carter & McGoldrick, 1999). As children leave home, and the parents begin to develop adult relationships with the children, the couple refocuses its energy on each other and become closer again.

Allen's heart disease diagnosis and imminent cardiac surgery will affect both individual and family development. It is expected he will recover from open heart surgery, but he still faces a period of rehabilitation and will need to make changes in his lifestyle. Before the surgery, his panic attack was associated with talking to his doctors about "do not resuscitate" (DNR) and healthcare proxy, which forced him to come to terms with the seriousness of his situation. Rolland (1987) describes this crisis phase as the initial period of readjustment and coping, and describes tasks for the family during this early stage:

> The family needs to: create a meaning for the illness event that maximizes a preservation of a sense of mastery and competency; grieve for the loss of the pre-illness family identity; move toward a position of acceptance of permanent change while maintaining a sense of continuity between its past and future; pull together to undergo short-term crisis reorganization; and, in the face of uncertainty, develop a system flexibility toward future goals. (Rolland, 1987, p. 207)

Allen's family will need to find a way to make meaning out of his illness, pull together, and reorganize during the crisis. For a time, the illness may derail certain family members from their individual life cycle tasks, bringing them instead back into the family fold. For example, Allen's children might need to postpone moving on with their lives, because they are called upon to help their father recover. Although Allen and his wife are at the family stage of launching their children, they will have to put this task on hold until some sense of normalcy is returned to the family. This new norm will differ from that of the "pre-illness" family, and an expected period of grieving and loss will precede a return to individual and family developmental tasks.

Setting: Social Work in a Hospital Setting
How Context Shapes Practice

Social workers practice in many different settings with diverse populations. One of the core competencies states that social workers need to be able to respond to contexts that shape practice (CSWE, 2008). Understanding the importance of context stands out in the interview that was done with Allen in a hospital. Social workers employed by a hospital must be knowledgeable about the expectations and professional standards found in this organizational setting. For example, social workers are part of an interdisciplinary team and practice within the framework of a medical model. Unlike working in an agency in which social work is the primary goal, social work services are secondary to why patients go to a hospital. At times this can present ethical dilemmas for social workers when their goals may differ from other professionals with whom they interact in the hospital.

Although social work practice is shaped by medical settings, social work has also shaped medical practice. Responding to the limits of the medical model, social work has advocated for understanding psychosocial issues related to health, and emphasized treating the whole person. Patient assessment now includes a bio/psycho/social/spiritual approach that is more holistic and pays attention to how psychosocial issues impact health and recovery. Browne (2006) states this approach expands the traditional medical model of health, which focuses primarily on the biological causes of disease, by considering nonmedical determinants of illness in collaboration with the medical (p. 24). Although there is widespread support for the importance of the bio/psycho/social/spiritual model, studies suggest that psychosocial factors continue to be overlooked or missed in many medical settings (Astin et al., 2003).

Social work has also contributed to healthcare by bringing the strengths perspective to assessment. In contrast to deficits in the medical model, social workers look for patient strengths when doing assessment and help other professionals to acknowledge and find ways to use these strengths in the patient's treatment. As social workers collect data for the assessment, they ask questions, identify client assets, and share this personal information with the medical staff.

The case example with Allen gives students a window into the practice of social work in medical settings. As you watch the video, read the transcript, and review the initial short case description, notice how the social worker's practice is influenced by the hospital setting. At the outset, the social worker is called by the floor nurse to visit Allen, after he has experienced a panic attack related to fears about his open heart surgery, scheduled for the following day. You learn there had been an interdisciplinary patient care meeting with the professional medical staff, and the social worker had shared her concerns about Allen's emotional readiness for the surgery. The nurse remembered the social worker's comments at the meeting, which led her to call on the social worker after the panic attack. The social worker learns that the attack occurred shortly after the doctor discussed healthcare proxy and advance directives with Allen. From this information, you can begin to appreciate how the social worker's practice is influenced by the dynamics of the hospital environment.

There are certain challenges for social workers employed in a medical setting. To begin, a social worker must practice within the framework of the medical model, which is hierarchical and places the doctor always at the top. The more collaborative model of social work practiced in social work agencies shifts. Clients become patients in the hospital setting and assume a more dependent and passive role. Knowledge resides with the doctors who are considered experts on their patients and each one's various ailments, and therefore it is the doctors who are expected to determine the proper treatment. Patients are encouraged to follow their doctors' orders and are often less active participants in the treatment process. This is in sharp contrast to how clients and social workers talk about problems, be they health or otherwise, in more mutual ways, appreciating what each has to contribute to understanding and treating any issues that arise.

Other challenges relate to professional collaboration in a hospital or medical setting. Although there may be frequent contact between the different healthcare professionals, they may not have equal voices in the care planning process, roles may be unclear, and professional perspectives and ethics may clash (Browne, 2006, p. 36). Social workers are not always given equal respect. In fact, there may be instances when social workers are considered nuisances, especially when advocating for patients to receive necessary services out of a sense of ethical obligation. Browne (2006) believes this leads to interprofessional strain, because certain health professionals may be annoyed by patient and family behavior that does not fit neatly within hospital practice (p. 37). This could happen when a social worker encourages patients to ask more questions concerning their care, request another opinion, or advocate for more services.

Changes in the healthcare system, with emphasis on cutting costs and shorter lengths of stay in the hospital, have had a profound effect on social work services in these settings. Although case management was once the domain of social work, it is now being taken over by nurses and other professionals. In some instances, hospital social work departments are being turned over to nurse-led case management departments, in which nurses are supervising social workers (Globerman, White, & McDonald, 2003). With roles becoming more blurred and ambiguous, social work as a profession must differentiate what is special and different about what it can offer.

Although it may be true that social work has lost ground in hospital case management and discharge planning, there are new opportunities appearing as well. With the enactment of the Affordable Care Act, there is greater emphasis on the importance of patient-centered medical homes and patient-centered primary care collaboratives. Social workers should position themselves on the ground floor of this new movement. They can build relationships with primary care physicians, and prove themselves an indispensable part of the interdisciplinary team that delivers comprehensive services to patients. Using a holistic framework, social workers can also play an important role in reducing healthcare costs, by addressing patients' psychosocial issues. This can reduce or prevent the onset of serious medical problems by removing barriers that might cloud the clearest picture of patient health.

There are additional tools social workers need to learn to work in medical settings. They must be familiar with medical terminology and protocols, health insurance and healthcare policy, and medical records and documentation. They should understand the roles of the different health professionals, HIPPA, the Diagnostic and Statistical Manual of Mental Disorders (DSM), discharge planning, home care, and patients' bill of rights. And importantly, they need an understanding of how to work effectively on a multidisciplinary team. Medical social workers must be prepared to enter a different organizational culture and understand the unique challenges this presents. Once these obstacles are overcome, there are many rewards that come from working with patients who may be struggling with difficult and life-threatening illnesses or medical conditions.

Diagnosis and Intervention: Diagnosis of Panic Attack

Medical settings use the DSM to diagnose patients with psychiatric symptoms. Although required to use the DSM for reimbursement by insurance companies, social workers are sensitive to its limitations and often ambivalent about giving a patient a label. A diagnosis includes a list of symptoms but does not describe the problem in its context or look at specific developmental history, culture, or personal characteristics. In some ways, it tells you very little about the person. In contrast, social workers place more importance on the bio/psycho/social/spiritual assessment that looks at the uniqueness and strengths of each person. Although social workers must do a "diagnostic dance" in order to do their jobs, it may be possible to combine the two approaches, think diagnostically yet flexibly about their clients, and focus more on symptoms than categories (Probst, 2012).

Panic Attack and Panic Disorder

In Allen's case, it is determined that he had a panic attack, which is different from being diagnosed with a Panic Disorder. A Panic Disorder consists of recurrent panic attacks followed by either relentless concern about facing another attack, changes in behaviors in an attempt to avoid future attacks, or a combination of both of these actions for a month or longer. The DSM criteria for Panic Disorder requires that the patient experience a discrete period of intense fear or discomfort, in which four or more of 13 symptoms are manifested and reach a peak in 10 minutes. Below is a list of the 13 symptoms found in the DSM-V (APS, 2013) for Panic Disorder.

DSM-V Criteria for Panic Disorder

Discrete period of intense fear, reaching peak within 10 minutes, and involving four or more of the following symptoms:

- Palpitations, pounding heart, or accelerated heart rate
- Sweating
- Trembling or shaking
- Sensations of shortness of breath or smothering
- Feelings of choking
- Chest pain or discomfort
- Nausea or abdominal distress
- Feeling dizzy, unsteady, lightheaded, or faint
- Feelings of unreality (de-realization) or of being detached from oneself (de-personalization)

- Fear of losing control, going crazy
- Fear of dying
- Numbness or tingling sensations (paresthesias)
- Chills and hot flushes

Evidence-Based Intervention for Panic Disorder

Social workers are expected to engage in research-informed practice and practice-informed research (CSWE, 2008) and to employ evidenced-based interventions. However, there can be many ways of thinking about evidence-based practice (EBP), depending on one's professional reference. The medical and social work communities differ in their approach and use of EBP. Many professions outside of social work bring a particular point of view and technical skill set to EBP. This contrasts with a social work perspective that comes from direct practice that is client-centered, collaborative, and uses lengthy case examples to describe real people (Drisko & Grady, 2012, p. v).

In Allen's case, he is suffering from a Panic Attack. There are several empirically supported treatments (EST) for panic disorder. They include cognitive restructuring, exposure, and somatic calming and coping strategies. Following is a summary of these treatments taken from Jongsma and Timothy (2010, pp. 12–14).

Cognitive Restructuring
- Panic disorder maintained by biased, fearful thoughts and beliefs
- Cognitive restructuring (CR) helps clients identify, challenge, and change fearful thoughts
- Dialogue and homework help identify, challenge, and change fearful thoughts
- Behavioral experiments test the validity of fearful and alternative beliefs

Exposure for Panic Disorder
- Exposure to bodily sensations
- Exposure to feared activities/situations
- Uses a fear and avoidance hierarchy

Somatic Calming and Coping Strategies
- Some empirical support for applied relaxation
- Breathing retraining alone appears unnecessary
- Some train applied relaxation with diaphragmatic breathing as coping skill
- Many do not train somatic coping strategies at all
- Coping skills are not to be used to avoid feared bodily sensations—management exposure is the goal

Medical Terminology

If you were a medical social worker on the cardiac floor of a hospital, you would need to be familiar with the medical terms associated with patients suffering from heart disease. At the end of the chapter is a list of some common terms related to heart disease, and other seriously ill patients. Social workers are expected to be familiar with these terms when working in a cardiac unit. Some terms are germane to working with medical patients overall, such as healthcare proxy, advance directives, and DNR.

Case Description
History

Allen is a 58-year-old married man with two children in their twenties who are still living at home. He comes from a middle-class background, graduated from a four-year business college, and has a professional job as an accountant. His wife works as a nurse manager at a local community hospital. Allen is from an Anglo-Saxon background and comes from an old New England family that is proud of its American heritage.

Allen has a family history of heart disease. His father died of a massive heart attack at the age of 56. A week ago Allen was hospitalized for shortness of breath and chest pain. After a series of tests, he was told that he had a serious blockage and needed to remain in the hospital to prepare for open heart surgery.

Leading up to the surgery, Allen met with his team of doctors, nurses, and social worker to go over the procedure. The social worker, Carol, met with him several times to do a psychosocial assessment. This is a routine practice used to gather a patient's history, determine his psychological readiness for surgery, and anticipate what services might be needed after discharge from the hospital. The nurses also referred Allen for social work services. They felt he was denying the seriousness of his situation by often joking with them about the surgery and not expressing his true feelings.

Precipitating Event for Social Work Crisis Intervention

The day before the surgery, the cardiac surgeon stopped by Allen's room to answer any questions Allen might have for him. The doctor went over the risks of surgery again and reviewed the information on Allen's chart about healthcare proxy and advance directives.

After the doctor left the room, Allen became very anxious as he thought about what the doctor had said. Although he knew there were risks to any surgery, he had never given them much thought before now, and suddenly he grasped the reality that he could die on the operating table tomorrow. As he thought about the surgery more, his breathing became heavier, his heart started to race, and he felt like he was having a heart attack. He turned on the emergency light for the nurse, who responded to his situation quickly.

After the doctors determined Allen was having a panic attack, the nurse called his social worker, Carol, to visit him. The nurse remembered how, at the interdisciplinary care meeting the day before, the social worker had shared concerns about how Allen did not seem to acknowledge the seriousness of the surgery. Carol was worried that his defensive behavior might interfere with his emotional preparation for the surgery, and she hoped he would open up more about what he was feeling as he got closer to the actual procedure.

Although the nurse had originally thought Allen's form of denial might be a good defense and coping strategy, she now wondered how his blocked feelings might have triggered the anxiety attack. She was relieved she could reach Carol before she left for the day. Carol appreciated the call and said she would stop by to see Allen shortly. On her way to the cardiac floor, she thought of how fortunate she was to be working in a setting that appreciated and respected the services of a social worker. She truly felt a part of the medical team.

On the way to meet with Allen, the social worker reflected on her previous visits with him. She had been concerned that he did not share his feelings about the surgery, and he seemed quick to dismiss the gravity of his situation. He came across as a very private man who did not want to talk about his personal life. She thought about how he seemed to fit the stereotype of a heart patient, someone who kept a lot of feelings bottled up inside of him, not expressing them easily. He presented himself as being very independent, strong, and self-reliant. Being a busy man, he didn't want the surgery to interfere with his life, and wanted to get back to work as soon as possible. He didn't want to hear that he was going to need a longer period of recovery than he expected.

Although he said he enjoyed talking with her, Allen also told the social worker that she should spend her time with the patients who really needed her. He was fine with the surgery and just wanted it over with so he could go back to his normal life. He was anxious to get back to work and put all this behind him. Although the social worker attempted to discuss the recovery process and some of the feelings he might experience after the surgery, Allen said he was a very strong and determined man who did not let his feelings run away from him like others. He was tough and would do whatever was necessary to get back on his feet again. He didn't let things bother him and just dealt with what had to be done. He said you have to take what life gives you and not wallow in self-pity.

The purpose of Carol's current meeting with Allen was to talk with him about his anxiety and to help him prepare emotionally for surgery. She expected he would be more open to sharing his feelings after the panic attack. From her past conversations with him, she knew how much he wanted to be in control of his feelings. She thought that this panic attack must have made Allen feel out of control and hence very vulnerable. Carol hoped that their meeting would help Allen better understand and manage his feelings so that he would be ready for surgery the next morning.

First Excerpt from Transcript and Process Recording

Social work students are often required to do process recordings in their field placements. Process recordings are used in supervision to give students feedback on their interventions with clients, and to encourage their self-reflection and sensitivity to issues that may come up in the field. Students go over the process recordings with their supervisors to reflect on individual sessions. Together, they discuss what worked well, what didn't, and then explore other possible interventions that might have been more effective or taken the conversation in a different direction. As supervisors and their students review the process recording, they find ways to understand and make meaning out of their client's stories. Similarly, at the end of each excerpt from Allen's transcript and process recording, there will be further discussion of theories and practice skills used in the interventions.

In the excerpt that follows, each box is numbered to make it easier to reference during discussion. The first column in the process recording is referred to as the content, and includes verbatim what the social worker and client say in the interview. Most interviews are not recorded like the ones in this book, so it is important for the social worker to write down as much as she can remember of what was said in the session as soon as the client leaves. The sooner this is done, the more will be recovered of what transpired in the conversation. It is important to stay as close to the exact words as possible, and not summarize what the main points were. Staying true to the narrative will provide rich teaching opportunities in supervision. It is important for students to avoid changing what was said in order to dazzle the supervisor, because this prevents learning from mistakes.

The second column, observations and reflections, emphasizes the importance of the social worker being in tune with herself and her client and noticing what is happening in the moment. It includes the social worker's self-dialogue, what she is thinking and feeling about the session while sitting with the client. This is referred to as "reflection-in-action," a term defined by Donald Shon (1983) as a type of "thinking on your feet" (discussed in chapter 1). Effective helping requires the ability to reflect while "doing" practice. This column also relates to self-reflection, how the social worker notices her own reactions to what the client is sharing. It is important for social workers to be aware of personal biases that affect their interactions with clients. As part of professional practice, social workers need to monitor their personal reactions to what their clients are saying to ensure they are responding to clients' needs rather than their own (CSWE, 2008).

The third column, the analysis of intervention, looks at both theory and practice. It identifies the theories the social worker uses when she intervenes with the client, either making a statement or posing a question. As professionals, social workers must be prepared to explain their interventions with clients, the rationale behind what they are doing. Their interactions with clients are based on a body of knowledge that has been well established and developed over time, undergone the rigors of scientific research, and is cited in the professional literature. Social work is moving in the direction of relying more heavily on interventions and practice that is evidence based. This requires that the social worker use critical thinking skills to assess the options in front of her during a session, and choose an intervention that will produce the best outcomes. Analyzing the intervention after the session involves another kind of critical thinking that helps the social worker evaluate the interventions and question if others might have been more effective. Shon (1983) refers to this as "reflection-on-action."

In the following pages is an excerpt from the transcript that takes place at the beginning of the interview with Allen. The full transcript of the interview with Allen is available in the appendix. You may also watch the videotape of the interview on the CD that accompanies the casebook. During the beginning of the patient interview, Carol enters the patient's room to find him reading in his chair next to the bed. She greets him and sits in the chair next to him.

Content	Observation/Reflection	Analysis of Intervention: Theories and Practice
1. Carol: I know I was in to see you earlier today and, um, I was about to leave and the nurses called and said that they were concerned about you, that you had had a panic attack this afternoon after the doctor had been in to see you. So they asked if I would stop by and see you, and I wanted to just say hello and see how you're doing.	Patient is sitting in his chair next to his bed. I notice that he presented very differently from our previous meetings. He seems less cheery and more serious. I am wondering what the effects of his panic attack will have on our conversation now. Will he share more personal information and feelings than previously?	Practice: Communication skills, engagement and beginning interview. I paid attention to patient's nonverbal cues, body language that indicated a change in mood. Tuning in to self and client at beginning of session.
2. Allen: Thanks for coming by; yeah I guess, you know, I got a little wound up this morning. But they were really, uh, the hospital people were great. They took care of me right away.	He is acknowledging that something happened that caused him to get "wound up." I appreciate how Allen is very bright and uses language that provides insight into his experience.	Theory: Narrative. I am noticing how client uses words and language. This provides more information into his character.
3. Carol: Can you tell me what happened?	I want to know what happened from his perspective.	Theory: Narrative. I am encouraging Allen to tell his story without much interference. Practice: Communication skill of exploration.
4. Allen: You know I don't know, I mean my body kind of went haywire on me, I guess I was thinking too much, about all the things that were, that are on my mind right now. You know it was getting hard (Patient paused) to breathe and my heart was pounding and stuff, it was weird. I never really had anything like that before.	Interesting use of language—his body went "haywire" on him. This signals that he is feeling out of control. He is aware of body symptoms that include his breathing and heart rate. I wonder if he can connect what is happening in his body to what he is thinking and feeling.	Theory: Narrative I am paying attention to Allen's use of language. Behavioral theory: Mind–Body, stress theory. Allen is paying attention to what is happening in his body.
5. Carol: You never had that before, so it must have felt like you were having a heart attack all over again.	I want to acknowledge how his symptoms might have made him feel like he was having a heart attack again. In retrospect, I wish I had asked him what he thought was happening first.	Practice: Communication skills. Reflecting back feelings. I reflect back what Allen had said and then take it a step further by connecting these symptoms to his heart problems. Self-reflection, In reflecting on my intervention, I wished I had responded differently to Allen. Instead, I might have used Cognitive and Behavioral theory and said, "It sounds like your thoughts were making you very upset. Could you tell me more what you were thinking?"

(Continued)

Content	Observation/Reflection	Analysis of Intervention: Theories and Practice
6. Allen: Yeah, well, or getting there. It didn't make sense to be doing that the day before surgery.	He seemed confused and worried about what was happening to him the day before surgery.	
7. Carol: No, it must have been pretty scary.	Again, I am noticing how I was too quick to reflect on what I thought he was feeling rather than ask him.	Practice: Communication. Putting client's feelings into words. Self-reflection: I could have explored more what thoughts were making him so upset and used and explored using a cognitive/behavioral approach.
8. Allen: Yeah, it was. Yeah but as I say the hospital people jumped right in. They helped me breathe and helped me just get back in the moment. Because I guess, you know, I was thinking about the surgery, I'm thinking about the day after, all this stuff.	He agrees and begins to connect his breathing problems with his thinking about the surgery. He is aware that his mind is racing. I am impressed that the nursing staff jumped right in to help him with his breathing and staying in the moment (mindfulness).	Theory: Cognitive/Behavioral. He connects his feelings of panic to his thoughts about the surgery. Mind–Body theory. Use of breathing and meditation/relaxation exercises to manage anxiety.
9. Carol: Too much.	Supporting his feeling overwhelmed	Practice: Communication skill, offering support.
10. Allen: Yeah, I got kind of overwhelmed. I mean I've had stress before, at work, or butterflies or something like that, but this was just different.	He is beginning to open up a little more and recognizes that his symptoms were more than the usual stress reactions. I am finding it easier to talk with him. I notice that he uses the word "butterflies" as a metaphor to explain how what he was feeling with the panic was more than what he felt in past (narrative).	Theory: Behavioral theory. stress. Narrative theory: I am paying attention to the words he uses, i.e., butterflies.
11. Carol: This was a lot more. More extreme, much more scary.	Here, I am picking up on his being overwhelmed and trying to get him to acknowledge his feelings.	Practice: Communication skills, putting client's feelings into words and reflecting back feelings.
12. Allen: Yeah, they gave me some medication and that helped but you know they also helped me breathe and move and things like that.	He does not choose to pick up on his scary feelings. He prefers staying with the technical aspect of managing the situation to "move things along." He wants to get past feeling out of control. I wonder how much he will be willing to reflect on what happened.	
13. Carol: Good, excellent. You said your mind was kind of racing and thinking about a lot of things. What were you thinking about?	I am trying to help him understand the meaning of his panic attack and to make some connections between what he was thinking about and feeling overwhelmed.	Theory: Cognitive/Behavioral theory: Allen's anxiety and his feeling out of control is related to his thoughts. To manage the anxiety, Allen needs to understand the thoughts that triggered the anxiety. Practice: Communication skill, exploration, clarification, elaboration

(Continued)

Content	Observation/Reflection	Analysis of Intervention: Theories and Practice
14. Allen: Well, the surgery, the surgery is a big event, certainly to me. They try to downplay it and make you feel good about how everything's going to go, but you don't know and I don't know. I never had much more than a couple hospitalizations and nothing on this scale. Yeah, so I was thinking about that, and I met with the doctor today and a lot of stuff becomes, it becomes very much more real when he says what he has to say.	He is beginning to make the connection between his panic attack and his thoughts about the surgery. I think he is projecting when he says they try to downplay it, since I have noticed that he, in fact has downplayed the surgery up until now.	Theory: As I listen to Allen, I am interpreting his use of the defense mechanism, projection. I am thinking in terms of psychodynamic theory.
15. Carol: What did he have to say? What did he tell you?	Here I use an open-ended question.	Practice: Communication skill, exploration.
16. Allen: Well you know, they're required to go through scenarios of what could happen, what I'll feel like, and also discuss different outcomes, and do the paperwork. Whether it's a healthcare proxy, advance directives. My wife is a nurse so we kind of, she knows about that stuff. I don't really.	This discussion with the doctor signals to him the seriousness of the surgery. This is the first time he brings up his wife. I wonder how her being a nurse affects the situation for them both.	
17. Carol: So you've talked to her a little bit about it?	I wonder if Allen has talked to his wife about these choices and the surgery.	Theory: Family systems theory. This question allows me to begin to gather information about Allen's family system. Practice: Communication skill, exploration
18. Allen: Yeah, we discuss it. She's very much involved in what I'm going through, so that helps.	I would like to know more about his relationship with his wife.	
19. Carol: That does help. It seems that the doctor coming in and talking to you about what to expect, and directives, triggered something in terms of your beginning to think more realistically about what was going to happen tomorrow, and that it really was a big deal.	Here, I am summarizing what I think happened when the doctor came in to talk to him about the surgery. I am connecting how the discussion with the doctor triggered his feeling more anxious. As I reflect on what I said in this exchange, I wish I had explored his relationship with his wife more.	Theory: Cognitive/Behavioral theory: Exploring what preceded his panic attack and the triggers for his panic. Instead of this intervention, I could have asked him more about his relationship with his wife. Practice: Communication skills, summarizing, normalizing feelings, Professional self-reflection.

(Continued)

Content	Observation/Reflection	Analysis of Intervention: Theories and Practice
20. Allen: Yeah, the healthcare proxy, the point of that is that if you don't come out of this or if you come out of this incapacitated, who's going to make decisions for you. I didn't really think about that before.	He is more aware that there is a chance he may not make it through the surgery, and if he does, he could be incapacitated. As I sit with him, I am aware of feeling more of his anxiety about the surgery. I remember my friend's open heart surgery experience and how he struggled with these life-and-death issues. I am feeling more sensitive to these issues now. His use of word "incapacitated," conjures up images of not being able to function after the surgery.	Narrative Theory: I am noticing Allen's use of language and how he talks about his experience, i.e., incapacitated. Practice: Professional self-awareness. I am aware of friend's experience with open heart surgery and this is making me more sensitive to the issues.
21. Carol: Pretty scary.	I am sharing what I think he feels. It is hard for him to put feelings to his experience, so I am helping him to pick up on his feelings.	Practice: Communication skills, putting the client's feelings into words.
22. Allen: Yeah you always kind of think in terms of the next day; what I'm going to do tomorrow. But here, you've been talking around it for a week whatever or a month and then suddenly he says, "Who is going to make these decisions for you? We have to put this in writing." I hadn't really thought about that.	For Allen, putting it in writing makes it "real." He is projecting again, saying "You've been talking around it for a month." Who is the "you?" Is it the doctor, his wife, the staff, me? From my experience talking to Allen, he has been talking around it. However, he now seems ready to talk about the seriousness of the surgery. I need to help him see this on his own and not be too confrontational.	Theory: Psychodynamic, interpretation of the defense of projection. A later intervention will be to help him identify the use of this defense.
23. Carol: Yeah, and of course a lot of the doctors, this is kind of something they do every day and they don't think of it as a big deal. But for you sitting there and listening, it must have felt very different.	I am trying to stay with Allen's perception of the doctors' not understanding the impact of what they are saying to him. I am trying to be supportive of his experience and help normalize what he is feeling.	Practice: Empathizing. Communication skill, paraphrasing.
24. Allen: Yeah, I don't think they, I don't think it's the same reality to them at all. I'm sure they're trained to be sensitive about it, or maybe to be not so sensitive so that they don't spook the patient. It definitely got to me.	Again, I think he is projecting, indicating that the doctors are downplaying what they are saying so as not to "spook" him. However, he may be avoiding thinking or feeling about the surgery so as not to spook himself. I notice his use of language, "spook" which shows how scared he was by what the doctors said to him. Allen's use of language continues to be a strength for him that provides insight into his experience.	Theory: Psychodynamic, interpretation of defense of projection. Narrative theory and analysis of his use of word "spook" to explain his experience. Practice: Strengths Perspective. I am identifying one of Allen's strengths as being his use of language to understand him better.

(Continued)

Content	Observation/Reflection	Analysis of Intervention: Theories and Practice
25. Carol: What is it like to be in your shoes right now?	I want him to tell me know what he is feeling, in his own words.	Theory: Narrative. I am encouraging Allen to tell his story from "his shoes." Practice: Communication skill, Exploration, elaboration.
26. Allen: Well, right, the doctor's point of view is...the doctor's point of view and the nurse is seeing things differently and, you know, I'm the guy who's going to get cracked open tomorrow like a clam and they're going to do their thing. But that's just their environment, it's not mine, this is the place they're comfortable, but I'm thinking about my family, what my family's thinking about, thinking about how soon I can get back to work, you know, all those things.	Wow, he is telling me what he is feeling. He is expressing more of his anger with his use of language, "being cracked open like a clam." This metaphor sounds like he is going to be attacked and devoured. I also think of his being clammed up, keeping the lid on his feelings. As he talks of the place he is coming from, he is thinking about his family and work, but I am still wondering about what this all means to him.	Theory: Narrative, use of metaphor, being cracked open like a clam. This is a vivid image of what Allen is feeling, using his words to explain the experience.

Reflection of First Process Recording and Discussion of Practice Skills and Theories Used in Intervention

As Carol was sitting with Allen now, she was aware of how different this conversation was compared to the last one. She thought about his use of language when he said that he was "the one being cracked open tomorrow." This signaled to her that he better grasped the seriousness of his situation. The social worker acknowledges his use of language as a strength that provides a window into his experience. Allen is beginning to acknowledge his worries, so Carol knew she could explore them with him more now. She also wanted to ask him more about his family and his relationship with his wife. How much had Allen confided with his wife about his feelings about the surgery? Or did he need to appear strong to her also?

Communication Skills

The social worker uses various communication skills during the intervention and reflection upon the client's statements. Following is a list of communication skills, their definitions, and the box in which they were used.

Box 1

Engagement and beginning interview: Carol wants to be honest from the start and let Allen know at the beginning of the session that she was called by the nurse to see him because of the panic attack. She wants to show concern and ask how he is doing now.

Attending to nonverbal cues, body language: Allen's body language communicates to Carol that he is feeling very differently from earlier in the day. His facial expression is more serious.

Boxes 3, 13, 15, 25

Exploration of the problem: This is a way of gaining more information about a client's situation. When continuing to explore the problem, the social worker listens for underlying feelings about the situation, who else is involved, and what resources are available to help resolve it.

The social worker uses this skill to explore what happened to Allen concerning the panic attack. Exploration is a communication skill, but can also be used as an intervention strategy in narrative and psychodynamic approaches.

Boxes 5, 11

Reflecting back feelings: This is when the social worker gives a short response that acknowledges what the client is feeling. It lets the client know the social worker is listening, and may also be used when a client is having a hard time expressing his feelings. In this situation with Allen, Carol wants to emphasize how new this feeling is for him. He had never felt like this before.

Boxes 7, 11, 21

Putting the client's words into feelings: There may be times when a client has difficulty identifying the feeling he wants to express in the narrative. The social worker can help in these situations by responding to the client and using feeling words to summarize what the client has said. There are many times this happens with Allen, since he tends to intellectualize his story and has trouble expressing feelings.

Box 9

Offering support: When a client shares a story that is painful, it helps if the social worker offers encouragement. By acknowledging the difficulty of the situation, you provide support for the client and allow him to continue the story. In box 9, Carol only says "Too much." Although this is a small affirmation, it shows Allen that she also feels his struggle, that what he has gone through is too much. He responds by agreeing with Carol.

Box 11

Reflecting back feelings: Again, this is when the social worker gives a short response to the client that mirrors the feeling the social worker heard the client express. It is used to let the client know the social worker is listening. In box 11, the social worker reflects back feelings ("much more scary") to Allen, and in the next interaction, Allen agrees. This shows that Carol is connecting with Allen and understands what he is saying.

Boxes 13, 25

Exploration of the problem: This is a way of gaining more information about a client's situation. When continuing to explore the problem, the social worker listens for underlying feelings about the situation, who else is involved, and what resources are available to help resolve it.

Seeking clarification: At different times during a session, the social worker may ask a client to talk about his perception of a situation, in order to make sure she understands the client's point of view.

Elaboration: This involves asking clients to describe what they are talking about in more detail. The social worker may ask the client, "I'm not sure I understand what you mean. Can you say more about that?" The social worker may also ask the client for examples of what the client is referencing. "Can you give me an example of when you felt that way?"

Exploration, clarification, and elaboration are very similar skills that are used when the social worker is trying to understand on a deeper level what the client is saying. In box 13, the social worker wants to go back to something Allen had said at the beginning of the interview about having too much on his mind. She asks him to expound on what he was thinking about.

Box 19

Summarizing: Partway through the session, and again at the end of the interview with the client, the social worker summarizes what has been said up to that point. This helps reinforce for the client what has been discussed and ensures that the social worker and client both understand the focus of the session.

Normalizing feelings: Clients often believe that their feelings are unacceptable or abnormal. The social worker helps clients see that their feelings are a natural reaction to the given situation. In box 19, the social worker is reviewing the effects of Allen talking to the doctor about advance directives. She is also normalizing Allen's reactions by emphasizing that this was a "big deal."

Box 23

Paraphrasing: Paraphrasing is when the social worker uses her own words to repeat what she just heard the client say. This shows that the worker is listening and following the conversation. In box 23, in an empathic response, the social worker says in her own words what she just heard Allen say. Although doctors have conversations every day about advance directives, patients don't think about such things so regularly, and it was this conversation that scared Allen.

Box 23

Showing empathy: The social worker maintains a nonjudgmental stance or remains neutral. The worker need not totally understand the client's situation, but she must show that she is trying to grasp what the client is feeling or experiencing. The social worker might say, "Tell me more about your experience" or "I want to understand more about what this means from your perspective."

In box 23, the social worker shows empathy in her response, communicating that she understands how scary this experience is for Allen. She does this by paraphrasing what she heard him say, and demonstrating support for his situation.

Other Practice Skills Used

Box 1

Tuning into self and client at beginning of interview: As the social worker begins the interview with Allen, she is thinking about how Allen may be feeling after the panic attack. She is wondering how his recent experience will affect how he engages with her.

Boxes 5, 7, 19

Self-reflection: The skill of self-reflection is an important part of professional practice. Social workers are expected to engage in personal reflection and self-correction to assure continual professional development (CSWE, 2008).

Self-reflection is used several times in this excerpt and demonstrates how the social worker uses critical thinking skills and "reflection-in-action." In box 5, the social worker questions her intervention and wonders if it would have been better to ask Allen more about what he was thinking. Again, in box 7, the social worker wonders if she should have stayed with his thoughts about what was scaring him. The social worker notices that she tends to be quick to support, before exploring the client's thought processes. In box 19, the social worker uses her critical thinking skills to question her intervention and wishes she had asked Allen more about his wife here.

Box 20

Professional self-awareness: After reflecting on reactions triggered during a client session, the worker becomes more self-aware and can separate personal issues from her professional work with clients. In box 20, as the social worker listens to Allen, she is reminded of her friend's experience with open heart surgery. She is aware of her friend's experience, and then brings her focus back to Allen.

Box 24

Identifying strengths: During assessment, social workers listen for client strengths they can use to help solve certain problems. As clients talk about their situation and their stories unfold, workers identify strengths that are embedded in the narrative. Throughout the interview, the social worker appreciates how Allen uses language to describe his experience, and she sees this as a strength.

Theories Used in Interventions

In this section, I analyze the language used by both the social worker and client to identify theories in action during the interview. I attempt to link what the social worker has said in her intervention to a theory, and also to explain how her interpretations of Allen's thoughts and feelings are framed by a theoretical lens. There may be times when Allen's responses to Carol are influenced by her use of language and reflect a particular theoretical perspective that she has verbalized. It is important to notice ways in which the client and social worker are influenced by each other.

Several theories were referenced in the first excerpt, including narrative, cognitive/behavioral, psychodynamic, and family systems theories. In the following section, I explain the different theories by citing boxes in the excerpt where they are found.

Narrative Theory

Narrative theory comes up several times in the first excerpt. By paying attention to how clients use words and language to tell their story, social workers can learn a lot about clients and how they make meaning of their experiences. Allen is an excellent example of this. His choice of words, use of metaphors, and rich descriptions tell a lot about him. In the excerpt, the social worker brings a heightened awareness to the way that Allen tells his story, the language he uses, and by doing so, comes away with a deeper understanding of him.

Box 2

Allen says he got "a little wound up this morning." The social worker notices this as an initial sign that Allen was anxious and wound up tight.

Box 3

The social worker is encouraging Allen to tell his story without interfering with his narrative.

Box 4

Allen says his "body kind of went haywire" on him, which helps the social worker to understand that he was feeling out of control.

Box 10

Allen uses the metaphor of having "butterflies" to distinguish between how he was feeling during the panic attack, versus a less acute case of anxiety, a simple case of butterflies. He explains that this experience was much worse than what he has experienced with normal work stress.

Box 20

When referring to the healthcare proxy, Allen shows us by his use of the word "incapacitated" that he is fully aware of the implications of the surgery and the meaning behind the healthcare proxy.

Box 24

Allen shows how anxious he is about the discussion with the doctors by using the word "spook." He describes how the doctors are trained to talk to patients so they don't "spook" them. This implies that what the doctors have to share is very scary.

Box 25

The social worker encourages Allen to tell his story again, by asking him what it is like to be in his shoes right now.

Box 26

Allen responds that he's "the guy that is going to be cracked open tomorrow like a clam." This is a strong metaphor that provides insight into how vulnerable he feels about the surgery. The social worker understand Allen's response in two ways: (1) he may be seeing the surgery as an attack on him, and he'll be exposed and devoured, and (2) although he has kept a tight lid on his feelings, his shell is being cracked open, and he will not be able to protect himself from his overwhelming feelings.

Cognitive and Behavioral Theories

In the excerpt, the social worker also uses interventions from cognitive and behavioral theories. To understand clients' behaviors, social workers applying cognitive and behavioral approaches seek to clarify what thoughts or emotions preceded the behavioral response, and, in Allen's case, this response would be the panic attack. The first excerpt has many examples of connecting Allen's anxiety to the discussion that preceded the panic attack. It also has an example of the hospital staff using stress management techniques to help Allen control his breathing and reduce his anxiety.

Box 4

The social worker reflects on what Allen is saying and thinks in terms of stress theory and the relationship between mind and body. This happens when Allen says that his mind was going "haywire," followed by his saying that his breathing was difficult and his heart was pounding. This might help him connect how his thoughts and feelings had an impact on what was happening in his body, in other words, to make the mind–body connection for him. It may be possible for Allen to understand how his "thinking too much about what was on my mind," caused him to have trouble breathing.

Boxes 5, 7

The social worker reflects on her interventions and wishes she had used a cognitive and behavioral line of questions to link more succinctly his upsetting thoughts with the panic attack.

Box 8

Allen shows insight that his anxiety was related to how he was thinking about the surgery. He also explains how the hospital staff used behavioral techniques to help him with his breathing, and mindfulness practice to bring him back to the present moment.

Box 10

Allen acknowledges how he felt overwhelmed and how it was more than just a case of "butterflies." This continues the link he is making between mind and body.

Box 13

The social worker is reinforcing the mind–body connection by going back to how Allen had said his mind was racing and asking him to share what he was thinking about. In this way, the social worker links his racing thoughts to his anxiety and panic attack.

Box 19

The social worker summarizes what Allen has said up to this point and takes it one step further to connect the dots. The social worker says that the doctor talking to Allen about advance directives triggered thoughts and feelings that led to the panic attack.

Psychodynamic Theories

There were several instances in which the social worker's interventions were informed by psychodynamic theories. When social workers use ego psychology, they are sensitive to how clients use defenses to manage difficult situations. Defense mechanisms are unconscious processes that protect clients from overwhelming thoughts and feelings by keeping them out of their conscious awareness. These perceived threats are disowned by clients and then projected onto others. When Allen is talking about his experience, the social worker notices that he often projects what he may feel or think onto others. In the interview, there are times when the social worker helps Allen to become more conscious of what he might be defending against.

Box 14

Allen feels that the doctors are downplaying how serious the surgery is, but in fact, it has been Allen who, up to this point, has minimized the significance of the surgery. In psychodynamic theory, this could be interpreted as the defense of projection, attributing unacceptable thoughts or feelings to others.

Box 22

When Allen is speaking, the social worker reflects again on how Allen may be projecting when he says, "you've been talking around it for a week whatever or a month," and then suddenly he says, "Who is going to make these decisions for you?" The social worker feels he may be blaming the hospital staff when, in fact, it has been Allen who has been avoiding these uncomfortable conversations.

Box 24

When Allen refers to the doctors tiptoeing around how they tell patients about surgery, so as not to spook them, he may be projecting again. Instead, he may be defending against not thinking or feeling about the surgery up to now, so as not to be "spooked" himself.

Family Systems Theory

Whenever social workers engage with clients, they also realize that they are working with a family system. If one part of a system is impacted, the effects reverberate throughout the whole, and other parts of the system are affected as well. When working with patients in a hospital, social workers often work with the family and assess family relationships. In the first excerpt, there is only a beginning attempt to understand Allen's family system. This will become more important in the second excerpt.

Box 17

The social worker begins to explore Allen's communication with his wife and learns in box 18 that his wife is very involved in what he's "going through." However, the social worker doesn't yet understand the extent to which his wife is aware of the emotional implications for Allen.

Second Excerpt from Transcript and Process Recording

Content	Observation/Reflection	Analysis of Intervention: Theories and Practice
27. Carol: So you haven't been able to share some of your fears about the surgery with her?	I want to know more about his style of communication with his wife.	Theory: Family systems theory, exploring communication in family
28. Allen: No and I kind of don't think I should, I don't want her to worry, you know, because she is a nurse, she knows all the things, better than I do what could go wrong or how wrong it could go. But I'm supposed to be the strong guy.	He is showing me how he believes he needs to protect his wife from worry and appear to be strong in front of her. He believes it is weak to show his feelings to her.	Theory: Family systems theory, communication and family roles. Cognitive theory: I will want to question Allen's belief system, which he believes, as a man, he is supposed to be the strong one.
29. Carol: Oh, so you're not supposed to have feelings?	Here I am confronting his belief system, using humor. I wonder if it came off as sarcastic.	Theory: Cognitive, questioning his belief system and his irrational thoughts. Practice: Professional self-awareness.
30. Allen: Well, I can have feelings but I want to be strong for them and confident. It's just another day to the doctors, it's another day at the hospital, and I'll get through it.	I believe he is joining me in looking at the way he interacts with his family. As he is explaining his defensive behavior, he also seems to be questioning the logic behind his need to be so strong and deny his feelings in the face of surgery.	Theory: Psychodynamic, use of defense, denial.
31. Carol: And maybe the panic attack was a way of your body telling you that you can't always be the strong man, that there are times when you have to acknowledge what you are feeling and that that could be helpful to be able to work through some of this.	Although my goal is to interpret what I believe is the meaning behind what he is saying, it comes off a little like I am lecturing him. I could have worded this differently. I have to be careful not to come off as "preachy."	Theory: Psychodynamic, interpretation of panic attack being about defending against his feelings about the surgery. Cognitive, looking at the logic behind his beliefs. Narrative: meaning-making, understanding what the experience means to him. Practice: Professional self-awareness.
32. Allen: I guess that's somewhat the way I am anyway. I'm not a heart on my sleeve kind of guy or anything. You know I'm going to hold those, suppress those feelings. I try not to get too happy or too sad.	Interesting use of language again, "I'm not a heart on my sleeve kind of guy." He uses this metaphor to define who he is, being someone who suppresses his feelings. I am aware of how much I appreciate Allen's use of language and how I can use it to understand him better.	Theory: Narrative, I continue to notice how Allen uses language and metaphors to describe himself to others.
33. Carol: So that must have been very surprising to you when, all of a sudden, you were feeling so much and feeling out of control?	I am bringing him back to what happened earlier with his panic attack. I wonder if he is surprised when he is no longer able to suppress those feelings. This is out of character for him.	Practice: Communication skills, reflecting back feelings, exploring feelings, holding to focus. Empathy, wanting to understand how this must have felt to him.

(Continued)

Content	Observation/Reflection	Analysis of Intervention: Theories and Practice
34. Allen: Yeah it was like my body kind of was revolting and it wasn't in my control and I guess that sort of causes it to feed on itself. It just went fast and got out of control quick.	He uses language artfully to describe his experience. He associates his expression of anxiety as his body betraying him, revolting against him. I feel sad that he feels this way and does not see how his body is helping him to get in touch with his feelings.	Theory: Narrative, I pay attention to Allen's use of words to understand how he is feeling. Behavioral, attention to symptoms of his body being out of control. Practice: Self-awareness.

Reflection of Second Process Recording and Discussion of Practice Skills and Theories Used in Intervention

As the social worker continued with the session, reflected in this second excerpt, she wanted to make the mind–body connection with Allen. She also wanted to explore more about his family system, the relationships among family members, communication patterns, and the role Allen played in his family. Up until now, he has been in control of his feelings and has not wanted to show vulnerability with his family. Earlier, the social worker reflected on the stereotype of heart patients as those who hold back from expressing their emotions. In this excerpt, it seems Allen has worked hard to block uncomfortable emotions from others and feels the need to be strong for his family. As he says, "I'm not a heart on my sleeve kind of guy." Blocking his feelings about the surgery may have led to his anxiety attack. By the end of the second excerpt, Allen is beginning to show signs of accepting the mind–body connection and understanding how his thoughts and feelings about surgery played a role in his panic attack. As you read the process recording, try to note how the social worker uses multiple theories in her interventions and how they all contribute to her work with Allen.

Communication Skills

Box 33

Reflecting back feelings: This is when the social worker gives a short response to the client that mirrors the feeling the social worker heard the client express. It is used to let the client know the social worker is listening.

Allen has said that he is not a "heart on my sleeve kind of guy." However, he was not able be suppress his feelings during the panic attack. In box 33, the social worker is reflecting back feelings to emphasize how feeling out of control emotionally was new to him.

Box 33

Exploring underlying feelings: The social worker asks the client his feelings on the subject under discussion.

In box 33, as Carol reflects back Allen's feelings, she also poses a question and attempts to explore his underlying feelings about the panic attack, wanting him to elaborate.

Box 33

Holding to focus: Holding to focus is when the social worker helps the client stay on the topic under discussion. There may be times when, if a client is uncomfortable with the conversation, he may try to change the subject. In these cases, the worker tries to redirect the client back to the topic.

In box 33, the goal of the social worker's response is to keep Allen focused on his feelings.

Box 33

Showing empathy: The social worker maintains a nonjudgmental stance or remains neutral. The worker need not totally understand the client's situation, but she must show that she is trying to grasp what the client is feeling or experiencing.

In box 33, the social worker's response is empathic; she understands how surprised Allen was when his feelings got out of control during the panic attack.

Other Practice Skills Used
Boxes 29, 34

Professional self-awareness: After reflecting on reactions triggered during a client session, the worker becomes more self-aware and can separate personal issues from her professional work with clients.

In box 29, the social worker is aware of her style of questioning. She brings humor into the conversation in an attempt to confront Allen's defenses, specifically his need to be the strong one in his family. However, she is concerned she may have come off a little sarcastic. Humor can often be an effective way to help clients question their behavior, but the social worker must be careful that the client does not misunderstand her efforts.

In box 34, the social worker demonstrates self-awareness when she observes that she is feeling sad when Allen characterizes his body as "revolting" when he could no longer control his feelings. She wonders if she is feeling just sad for Allen or if this triggered memories of times when she has suppressed her feelings, too.

Theories Used in Intervention
Family Systems Theory
Boxes 27, 28

Although a social worker may be working with an individual client, the social worker also thinks about the client's family system and how it may contribute to an understanding of the problem at hand. This involves seeing the individual as part of a larger system, and examining how the different parts influence each other.

In box 27, at the beginning of the second excerpt, the social worker starts off by exploring communication patterns in the family. Understanding how families communicate with each other is important in family assessment. Helping families to communicate more directly and honestly with each other is an intervention strategy in family systems therapy.

In box 28, Allen tells the social worker that he doesn't think he should share his worries with his wife since he is supposed to be the "strong guy." His role in the family is to be strong and protect others from his feelings.

Cognitive Theory
Boxes 28, 29, 31

In box 28, the social worker uses a cognitive approach when she reflects on Allen's belief that he needs to be strong as the man of the family. The social worker had recently read an article about masculinity and the needs of hospitalized men that related to what she observed in her conversations with Allen. It said that men have been socialized to adopt behaviors and attitudes consistent with masculine norms of self-reliance and controlled emotions. These gender roles had a strong influence on men seeking help, and created obstacles for their accepting services (Winnett, Furman, & Enterline, 2012).

In box 29, using a cognitive intervention, the social worker questions Allen, using humor, asking if he's not supposed to have feelings. She is helping him to see that his thoughts may be based on false assumptions.

In box 31, Carol confronts Allen's cognitive distortion that he must always be strong and suppress his feelings.

Psychodynamic Theory
Boxes 30, 31

In box 30, Allen demonstrates how he tried to use the defense of denial and suppression of feelings to get through the surgery, without paying attention to his feelings. He felt he had to be strong and confident and not appear to have feelings of weakness.

In box 31 the social worker interprets Allen's defenses by saying that his body was telling him something, that there are times when it's important to acknowledge feelings. Defenses are ways that clients protect themselves from painful situations and emotions. Using psychodynamic theory, a social worker helps clients understand this process and then identify the situation and underlying feelings that they are protecting themselves from.

Narrative Theory
Boxes 31, 32, 34

In box 31 Carol confronts Allen's description of himself and use of the word "strong" to explain the role he feels he must fill for his wife.

In box 32 the social worker observes Allen's use of language again. He uses the metaphor, "not a heart on my sleeve kind of guy," to explain how he suppresses his feelings. The social worker appreciates how Allen uses language that helps her understand him better. His intellect and language skills are a source of great strength.

In box 34, the social worker notices the strong images Allen uses to explain how he felt when he lost control of his feelings. He saw the panic attack as his body "revolting" against him. This shows how he has separated his body and mind from one another, and he looks at the panic attack as a sign that his body has betrayed him.

Behavioral Theory

Box 34

In box 34, when Allen talks about his body being out of control, behavioral and mind–body theory would pay attention to these symptoms. The body often signals to us when something is wrong, and it is important to see these signs and symptoms of stress as an opportunity to address and manage the stressors.

Third Excerpt from Transcript and Process Recording

In the following is an analysis of the third excerpt from the transcript. Before this interaction, the social worker explored more about Allen's father's experience with heart disease (see appendix 2 for the full transcript). Allen seemed uncomfortable with the discussion at first. The social worker wondered if this was the time to address his father's death and its impact on him. As part of her reflection-in-action, she debated within herself whether to continue this exploration. She worried that it might just upset him more, and this could be a bad idea the day before his surgery. However, she also thought that if his father's death from a heart attack was a factor in his anxiety, talking about it could be helpful, especially if he was thinking about it on some level anyway. She decided to follow her intuition and ask more about his father's death. If Allen said he didn't want to talk about it, she would respect his wishes and stop this line of inquiry.

The social worker learned that Allen's father had his first heart attack when he was in his forties, and died 10 years later from a massive heart attack. Allen acknowledged that this was 30 years ago, before medicine had advanced to where it is today, with the technology to treat persistent heart disease. His father had changed his diet and was exercising, so no one expected he would have another heart attack. In this excerpt, Allen says that he has followed a similar track since he was diagnosed with heart problems, and is frustrated to still have a problem. The social worker asks him if he sees any similarities between his father and him. This leads him to see a connection between his thinking about his dad's death from a heart attack and then his having an anxiety attack earlier. He is fully engaged in the conversation with the social worker and seems capable of having insight about what might have caused his anxiety.

Other information learned about Allen's family of origin: Allen was 10 years old when his father had his first heart attack. No one in his family talked about it much. He was just told his father wasn't feeling very well, was in the hospital, and he noticed his mom was "acting weird." Allen didn't understand why no one was talking about it. Since he was the second oldest, he guessed his mother was talking to his older brother. He also had a younger sister and brother and when he said in the transcript, "What are you going to talk to them about?" he may have been referencing that they were too young to take part in the conversation.

As the social worker listened to Allen speak about his childhood family, she could see some parallels between how his family growing up communicated and expressed feelings with each other, and what he was describing in his own family now. From a family systems perspective, Allen was repeating a pattern that he had learned in his family, when he was younger. In this excerpt, as the social worker talks more about the similarities between his father and him, you will notice how Allen becomes very sad and teary. When he compares himself to his father, he says that he doesn't want his children to lose him.

Content	Observation/Reflection	Analysis of Intervention: Theories and Practice
35. Allen: Yeah and I thought, and I think he thought, he was probably doing what he was supposed to do, changed his diet. I think he was a smoker because I've seen pictures of him after college and stuff, he was a smoker, and I think he gave that up at that time. So he did all the things that I think he was supposed to do to the extent he could. And I'm doing the same thing and look where I am. It's a little frustrating....It was tough to lose him and I don't....(Allen becomes very sad and teary at this point.)	Allen is feeling very sad about his dad's death at this point. It is hard for him to finish what he is saying. It seems that his father's death is very much on his mind as he thinks about his surgery. I am aware of feeling very sad with him at this moment. I intuitively know that is very important to sit with the sadness and share it with him. I want to let him stay with the feeling and not interrupt his inner process. I am feeling very connected to him at this moment.	Theory: Psychodynamic, looking at how the past influences the present. Identifying patterns, intersubjective experience with Allen that tells me that something is changing as he opens up more.at this moment. Practice: Professional self-awareness.
36. Carol: Can you tell me about that?	I sit for a moment with Allen's sadness and then encourage him to put more words to what he is thinking and feeling. Allen is beginning to get more in touch with his feelings. As he shows his feelings more, I am aware of feeling more connected to him. I am feeling how sad it was for him to lose his dad. As I empathize with him. I am also aware of my own loss of parents and understand his loss.	Practice: Communication skill, opening up affect. Professional self-awareness.
37. Allen: I don't want...my family to lose me.	I am feeling Allen's profound sadness. He is having trouble finishing his sentence, and I encourage him to go on. I am aware of how hard this is for him. I am staying with him and feel the intimacy of this moment.	Practice: Professional self-awareness.

(Continued)

Content	Observation/Reflection	Analysis of Intervention: Theories and Practice
38. Carol: Of course not. It's a very sad thought. It was very sad for you.	I am reflecting back feelings and helping Allen to stay with his feelings in the moment. I am supporting his feelings.	Practice: Communication skills, reflecting back feelings.
39. Allen: So, I'm just trying to be positive and not be....	He is quick to regain control and move the discussion away from his feelings to something more positive instead. By moving on to another subject, he is defending against further expression of his sad feelings.	Theory: Psychoanalytic theory, using defenses to protect from feelings of sadness, intellectualization.
40. Carol: Can you just stay with your feelings for a minute? It seems like you're feeling a lot right now.	As I observe that Allen is defending again his feelings and moving the discussion in another direction, I interrupt him and ask him to pay attention to what he is feeling in the here and now.	Theory: Mindfulness, helping client to stay in the present and be aware of feelings. Practice: Communication skills: Understanding process and content. Processing what Allen is feeling in the present moment.
41. Allen: Yeah it's very real, you know.	He is saying that he is aware of his feelings now.	
42. Carol: It is very real.	I am reflecting back what Allen has just said.	Practice: Communication skills, reflecting back feelings.
43. Allen: I think probably I'll get through the operation OK, but they have to introduce a little doubt you know, and that kind of gets to you, you know.	Allen is connecting his anxiety to his feelings of uncertainty about the operation.	
44. Carol: And it's natural for you to be thinking of your father now, having lost him when you were a young man and you're facing surgery for a heart condition. It's natural that you would think about him.	I am normalizing Allen's thinking about his father who died of heart disease as he prepares for his own heart surgery.	Practice: Communication skills, normalizing feelings.
45. Allen: Yeah, I kind of want to do better than he did. I got a lot of stuff left to do; I got to see my kids grow up. He didn't, he didn't have that chance, and I didn't have that chance. That's what I'm trying. I guess that's what got to me this morning, you know, thinking about all that, and at the same time trying to suppress it, which probably wasn't the right thing to do.	By doing it better, Allen is saying that he wants to live and be there for his family unlike his father. He is showing more insight about how his defending against these feelings might have triggered a panic attack. Allen is also connecting his feelings to his behavior.	Theory: Psychodynamic theory, defense mechanisms. Cognitive behavioral theory, connecting thoughts/feelings/behavior.
46. Carol: It seems like that maybe you can't always suppress your feelings, that there are times when maybe it helps to express them.	Information-giving to client.	Theory: Psychodynamic, explaining defenses Practice: Communication skills, Information-giving to client.
47. Allen: Yeah it does.		

(Continued)

Content	Observation/Reflection	Analysis of Intervention: Theories and Practice
48. Carol: How are you feeling right now?	By asking this question, I want Allen to tune in to his feelings. I want him to experience what it is like to stay with his feelings as opposed to suppressing them. I am hoping that he will understand that what he fears will happen is not as scary as he thinks. In fact, the fear and panic may turn out to be worse than the feeling he is avoiding. I am aware of how I am experiencing Allen at this moment. I asked him this question because I was tuning into Allen and feeling that he seemed much calmer now.	Theory: Mindfulness, Being aware in the present. Practice: Communication skills, Reaching for feelings. Professional self-awareness.
49. Allen: I don't know, sad, kind of sad, and kind of scared.	Allen is tuning in to his feelings.	
50. Carol: Is it OK to be sad and scared?	This is a closed ended question. I might have asked instead, "What is it like to be aware of your feelings?"	Practice: Communication skills, Questioning. Self-reflection
51. Allen: Yeah I guess it's perfectly normal. I just have been trying to do my best to avoid it.	Allen says it is normal to acknowledge feelings, but it hasn't been for him. He uses a little humor in his response.	
52. Carol: To avoid the feelings?	I choose to pick up on his insight to avoid feelings.	Theory: Psychodynamic theory, Insight into defenses.
53. Allen: Yeah, I don't know how much good it does to let them out.	Here Allen is showing that he is not a firm believer in the benefit of expressing his feelings.	Theory: Psychodynamic, understanding ambivalence.
54. Carol: We're going to get a chance to see because you're feeling them right now.	By encouraging him to stay with his feelings, I want him to notice what happens.	Theory: Mindfulness, Being aware in the present moment, noticing what happens in the present.
55. Allen: But it makes everybody nervous.	I believe Allen is projecting his fear onto others. I think it makes him nervous.	Theory: Psychodynamic, Projection, defense mechanisms.
56. Carol: Who's it making nervous now?	By asking this question, I am hoping that Allen can show insight that he is the one who is nervous.	Theory: Psychodynamic, Encouraging insight into his behavior.
57. Allen: Well, just me mostly. I appreciate you being here, it's nice to have an opportunity to talk; because I can't really do this with my wife or my kids. It doesn't help them to see it. I'm supposed to be...	Allen shows that he understands that he is the one who is nervous. He is still ambivalent about letting his family see his feelings.	

(Continued)

Content	Observation/Reflection	Analysis of Intervention: Theories and Practice
58. Carol: You're the strong one again. I know you keep saying you're the strong one, but you don't always have to be strong.	There is a little resistance to his letting go of his defenses. I wish I could have worded this differently. It sounds a little "preachy" or patronizing.	Theory: Psychodynamic, resistance, defenses. Practice: Communication skill, confrontation. self-reflection.
59. Allen: No I know.		
60. Carol: Especially the day before your surgery, this is quite normal to have these feelings.	I am normalizing Allen's feelings of being scared the day before cardiac surgery.	Practice: Communication skill, normalizing feelings.
61. Allen: Well, like I say I appreciate that I can share it with you.	Allen is saying that he can share these feelings with me. There seems to be a hidden message that he is still not sure he can share these feelings with his wife or family.	

Reflection of Third Process Recording and Discussion of Practice Skills and Theories Used in Interventions

Communication Skills

Box 36

Opening up affect: Opening up affect is when the social worker encourages the client to open up more and elaborate on what he is feeling.

In box 36, the social worker pauses for a moment and sits silently with Allen in his sadness. Then she encourages him to put words to what he is feeling. She is careful not to change the subject but realizes the importance of helping him stay with his feelings.

Boxes 38, 42

Reflecting back feelings: This is when the social worker gives a short response to the client that mirrors the feeling the social worker heard the client express. It is used to let the client know the social worker is listening.

In box 38, by reflecting back feelings, the social worker is supporting Allen's feelings of sadness and helping him to stay with those feelings.

In box 42, the social worker reflects back to Allen that his feelings are indeed very real, in response to his own acknowledgment of this.

Boxes 44, 60

Normalizing feelings: Clients often believe that their feelings are unacceptable or abnormal. The social worker helps clients see that their feelings are a natural reaction to the given situation.

In box 44 the social worker is normalizing Allen's feelings by letting him know that it is natural for him to think of what happened to his dad as he prepares for his surgery.

In box 60 the social worker tells Allen it is normal for him to be feeling anxious before the surgery, and that he doesn't always have to be the strong one.

Box 46

Information-giving: Information-giving means informing the client about the social agency, the problem, and the resources for change. The social worker is knowledgeable about human development and human behavior and can help clients by sharing information that relates to a problem they are experiencing. For instance, a mother may complain that her 4-year-old daughter is misbehaving, and not understand how the birth of a new sibling has affected the older daughter.

In box 46, the social worker provides information to Allen when she explains that he can't always suppress his feelings, and then encourages him to find opportunities to express himself more freely.

Box 48

Reaching for feelings: This is when the social worker tries to understand what the client is feeling when a particular subject or issue comes up. The social worker may use this skill when she senses the client is avoiding, or is not in touch with, the feelings related to the current discussion. This may bring out strong reactions in the client, and it is important that the social worker is sensitive to what this means.

In box 48, by asking what Allen is feeling right now in the moment, the social worker wants Allen to tune in and stay with his feelings and not dismiss them or change the subject. She believes that by doing this Allen can discover that he doesn't have to be afraid and then suppress his feelings.

Box 50

Questioning: This is a way of gaining more information about a client's situation. There are many different kinds of questions, for example, open- and closed-ended questions and reflexive questions.

In box 50, the social worker asks, "Is it OK to be sad and scared?" This is in response to Allen saying he is feeling kind of sad and scared. After she says this, she wonders about using a closed-ended question. Instead, she could have asked, "What is it like to be aware of your feelings?"

Box 58

Confrontation: Confrontation is used by the social worker when there are inconsistencies between what the client has said and what is known to be true. The social worker believes it is best if the client comes to terms with this discrepancy. Workers can also use confrontation to question a client's behavior that is harmful to the client.

In box 58, in response to Allen saying he can't talk about his feelings with his family, Carol confronts this notion that he always has to be the strong one.

Other Practice Skills Used
Boxes 35, 36, 37, 48

Professional self-awareness: After reflecting on reactions triggered during a client session, the worker becomes more self-aware and can separate personal issues from her professional work with clients.

As Allen talks about his father in box 35, he says it was tough to lose him. He becomes teary and can't finish his sentence. He is feeling very emotional, and the social worker is aware of feeling connected to him in this moment they share. She reflects on her reading on intersubjectivity as a qualitative measure of change in clients, and this fits with her experience with Allen at this moment. Experiencing these moments with clients lets the social worker know that her efforts are contributing to the client's subjective experience in a beneficial way. This knowing "guides the moment to moment and week-to-week decisions about what to do next" (Arnd-Caddigan, 2011, p. 372).

In box 36, as the social worker connects with Allen more over the loss of his dad, she is also aware of the loss of her own parents. She is aware of this, and then redirects her attention back to Allen.

In box 37, the social worker is aware of the intensity of Allen's feelings. She sits with these feelings and is mindful not to fill in the gaps but gives him time to finish his sentence after teary pauses. She is aware of how much easier it is now to leave to these gaps, not to rescue clients in these moments and try to make them feel better. This was something she was more apt to do as a younger, less experienced social worker. As hard as it is to sit with his sadness, she knows that this is the best treatment for him.

In box 48, the social worker uses her own self-knowledge and experience with feelings to guide her interventions. By acknowledging, tuning in, and staying with feelings, the social worker believes clients can learn that there is nothing to fear. In fact, avoiding and suppressing feelings can cause more anxiety and be worse than the feelings that are being avoided. The social worker has learned this from her own experience and through her many years of social work practice with clients.

Box 40

Understanding process and content: An interview is made up of two parts, process and content. Process refers to what is happening in the social worker and client relationship, whether it's the result of authority issues, client resistance, or lack of attunement or connection. Process is sometimes related to strong feelings that surface in the client at a particular moment in the session. Content refers to substantive information about the client or subject being talked about. At some points in the interview, the social worker needs to move the discussion from what is being said (content) to the underlying feelings in the social worker–client relationship or to what the client is feeling (process).

In box 40, rather than concentrate on what he is saying (the content), the social worker wants Allen to process what he is feeling in the moment with her (the process). The social worker decides to bring him back to what he was feeling a moment ago when he was sad and teary, rather than let him defend against these feelings. It becomes an opportunity to let him experience and share his feelings with someone, and then watch the effects of that.

Boxes 50, 58

Self-reflection: The skill of self-reflection is an important part of professional practice. Social workers are expected to engage in personal reflection and self-correction to assure continual professional development (CSWE, 2008).

In box 50, as part of reflection-on-action, the social worker reflects on her use of a closed-ended question. In retrospect, she wishes she had asked instead, "What is it like to be aware of your feelings?"

In box 58, the social worker reflects on her sounding a little "preachy" or infantilizing in this response to the Allen. She was trying to use humor but it may have come off as sarcastic. She thinks it would have been better to say, "What makes you think that it doesn't help your family to see your feelings?" or "What makes you think your family only wants to see you as strong?"

Theories Used in Intervention

Psychodynamic Theory

Boxes 35, 39, 45, 46, 52, 53, 55, 56, 58

In box 35, the social worker uses a psychodynamic approach when she explores Allen's history. Social workers are interested in the past as it relates to the present. Carol has reason to believe that some of Allen's current anxiety relates to the childhood loss of his father from heart disease. By bringing awareness to certain unconscious fears related to his father's death at an age similar to himself, Allen may be able to better control his feelings. He can come to realize the differences between himself and his dad, and feel more confident in the advances of medical technology. This new awareness might also help Allen understand how the vulnerability he felt as a child of 10 when his father had his first heart attack, and later when his father suffered his fatal heart attack, are still affecting him today. They may have played a role in his perceived need to defend against and manage his present-day overwhelming feelings. In fact, he might have been reliving these feelings of vulnerability from childhood during his panic attack. If Allen could see this connection, he could learn that as a child, he did not know how to deal with his overwhelming emotions, especially in a family that did not talk about feelings. However, now as an adult, he can find support and learn ways to express his feelings, so they do not overwhelm him.

In box 39, as the social worker listens to Allen, she notices that he is changing the subject to avoid staying with his feelings. She interprets this as his defending against feelings of sadness, using denial.

In box 45, as Allen talks about what he feels, he realizes that he suppressed his feelings that morning, resulting in the panic attack.

In box 46, the social worker's intervention helps Allen see that he doesn't always have to defend and suppress his feelings; rather there can be times when he expresses them.

In box 52, the worker reinforces Allen's insight into his tendency to avoid feelings.

In box 53, Allen shows that he's still unsure if he should let his feelings out. He is not quite willing to let go of his defenses, and is showing ambivalence about change.

In box 55, Allen defends against letting his feelings out again, and says it makes everybody nervous when he does this.

In box 56, the social worker asks him whom it makes nervous. This helps Allen see that he is projecting his feelings onto others, when he is actually the one who is nervous.

In box 58, when Allen resists showing his feelings to his family, the social worker tries to show him empathically that he doesn't always have to be the strong one.

Behavioral Theory Using Mindfulness
Boxes 40, 48, 54

In box 40, the social worker uses mindfulness, a behavioral intervention, when she asks Allen to stay focused on his present feelings. Rather than moving on to another subject, she wants him to pay attention to what he is feeling in the here and now. By using this approach, the social worker believes that Allen can manage his feelings in the present and learn that he has nothing to fear. This lesson might help him release his rigid need to defend against feelings.

In box 48, by asking Allen what he is feeling right now, in the moment, the worker wants him to tune in and experience what it is like to stay with his feelings rather than suppress them. She believes this will lead to his being less fearful taking this approach in the future.

In box 54, the social worker encourages Allen to stay with his feelings so that he can discover for himself what happens when he does so. Mindfulness practice emphasizes being fully aware and noticing what is happening from moment to moment; it discourages against blocking or denying experience.

Cognitive-Behavioral Theories
Box 45

As Allen speaks in box 45, he is connecting his thoughts and feelings to his behavioral symptoms to learn how to identify irrational thoughts and emotions that precede anxiety.

Summary of Third Excerpt and Conclusion: Significance of Social Work Interventions

There is a noticeable change that happens in the third excerpt that indicates a progression in how Allen views himself. Change can be measured in different ways and with different theoretical explanations. Psychodynamic theory interprets that Allen is gaining insight into his defenses and learning how to be more aware of his feelings, and thus less defensive. Mindfulness practice acknowledges how Allen is learning to be present with himself and aware of his experience from moment to moment. Cognitive-behavioral theories would look at the importance of Allen learning to identify and change irrational thoughts and feelings that precede the anxiety, in order to manage these symptoms. Family systems theory would take credit for improved communication in the family. Narrative theory would document progress by noticing how Allen's life story changes and how he constructs new meaning to life events. No one theoretical perspective informs Allen's transformation; each must take its place alongside other, equally important theories in informing the social worker's interventions. Still, it's clear that something is changing within Allen as a result of time spent with the social worker after his panic attack.

Although there are times in the interview when Allen appears ambivalent and resistant to change efforts, he eventually acknowledges that suppressing his feelings was not such a good thing. The social worker encourages him to stay with his feelings in the moment, and he learns that he has nothing to fear. During the conversation about his panic attack, the social worker uses the opportunity to provide Allen with information about anxiety. Allen learns that defending against unwanted feelings doesn't make them go away. In his case, they kept building until they erupted in the form of a panic attack. This is one interpretation of anxiety and panic that is from the psychodynamic perspective. In this scenario, when a person's continued attempts to defend against overwhelming feelings fail, those feelings break through into consciousness and cause anxiety. In Allen's case, by trying to avoid addressing his feelings about the surgery, he became more anxious. His trying to control his feelings had the opposite effect and made him feel out of control.

Summary of the Remainder of the Interview with Allen

Preparing for Surgery

Later in the interview, the social worker talks with Allen about how he could prepare for the surgery using behavioral techniques. She wants to introduce Allen to mind–body practices and their role in healing. The social worker shares information about relaxation and meditation techniques and how they can reduce anxiety. She and Allen also discuss research on how having a positive attitude going into surgery can be beneficial. Before she leaves, the social worker suggests certain meditation tapes that could be helpful if he is feeling anxious.

Endings

Before she leaves the room, the social worker notices how much calmer Allen appears compared with earlier in the day. She shares this perception with him, to see if he had picked up on the change as well, and is happy to learn that he notices feeling differently. Her experience of the qualitative differences in Allen at the beginning and end of the session is an outcome measure of change as a result of treatment. This correlates with Arnd-Caddigan's (2011) findings related to intersubjective, practice-based evidence.

As the social worker leaves the room, she feels positive about the intervention and how Allen used the crisis to learn more about himself and make important changes. She enjoyed working with him and appreciated his many personal strengths and his capacity for insight and change. She looks forward to continuing her work with him following the surgery. This kind of session confirms my belief that people are highly motivated to change during a crisis, and underscores how a crisis can become a turning point in a person's life. This is one of the reasons I personally enjoyed working in medical social work.

Assessment

Please refer to the three outlines in chapter 1 on Practice for detailed descriptions of the problem-solving method, the bio/psycho/social/spiritual assessment, and the psychosocial assessment and intervention plan. Assessment is an important step in treatment and informs the intervention choices made by the social worker. As stated in chapter 1, assessment is an ongoing process that continually shifts as the social worker receives new information about the client and the client's situation. Treatment plans and interventions must be flexible to accommodate this new information.

Problem-Solving Method

This assessment follows the outline on the Problem-Solving Method found in chapter 1 and is the social worker's attempt to apply the Problem-Solving Method to Allen's case. It is written in the first person, from the social worker's perspective.

Engagement

In my first two meetings with Allen, he was very polite and welcoming. I introduced myself to him on the first day as the medical social worker assigned to the cardiac unit, and explained that I would be checking in periodically during his hospital stay. I let him know that I would stop by each day before the surgery to act as a resource and a support to him as he prepared for the surgery. From the start, Allen reassured me that he was fine, and although he appreciated the gesture and my visits with him, he felt I should spend my time with the patients who needed me more. He was friendly, but at the same time he was dismissive of my efforts to talk with him about his situation or the implications of the surgery. Any effort I made to draw out his feelings was met with resistance and a change of subject. Realizing his strong defenses, I let him take the lead in the conversations. My first goal was to work on building a relationship with Allen that eventually might allow him to open up if he needed to. We talked about the book he was reading, his interest in music, and his family. I found him to be bright and quick-witted with a wonderful sense of humor. I enjoyed talking with him, and he seemed to look forward to our visits. Although I often left the room laughing from his jokes, I was concerned that he avoided any discussion of the seriousness of his situation and the surgery.

Assessment

From my visits with Allen, I learned that he had been married for 30 years to his wife Mary who is a nurse, and that they had two children, a son Abbot, 28, and a daughter Julia, aged 26. He spoke of his family with a great deal of affection, and from all accounts, it appeared that they were a very loving and close family. This assumption was supported by the nursing staff, which reported that his family members were frequent visitors and seemed very supportive. When taking his history, I learned that he came from an old New England family whose ancestors came from England and settled in Boston in the 1700s. He was proud of having a relative who fought in the Revolutionary War. His family of origin consisted of deceased parents, an older brother, and a younger sister and brother.

Noteworthy was that his father suffered his first heart attack in his forties, when Allen was 10 years old, and died from his second massive heart attack when Allen was 20 years old. Allen's father was a lawyer who provided well for his family but worked long hours and often seemed stressed. His mother was a stay-at-home mom. As a result of his father's heart disease, Allen has made an effort to watch his diet, exercise regularly, and take time to do the things he enjoys. For employment, he works as an accountant for a nonprofit agency in Boston. In spare hours, he likes to spend time with his family and play music. During our visits, Allen avoided discussion of his feelings about the surgery. When the procedure came up, he said he was fine with it and changed the subject.

Assessment Summary

Allen is a 58-year-old white man, married with two children, who was admitted to the hospital with chest pain. After a series of tests, he was diagnosed with a serious heart blockage that required open heart surgery. Allen was easy to engage in friendly conversation but avoided any in-depth discussion of his feelings about the surgery during my regular visits with him. When the subject of the surgery came up, he would say he was fine with it and move the conversation in a different direction. The day before the surgery, Allen had a panic attack triggered by his doctor talking with him about advance directives and his healthcare proxy. Allen's anxiety attack stemmed from suppressing his feelings about the seriousness of his situation. It became a turning point in his treatment and resulted in his opening up with me about his concerns.

Planning

The initial plan was to meet with Allen to do a psychosocial assessment. The nurses also referred Allen to me out of concern that he was not dealing with the seriousness of his situation. As a result, I planned to make regular visits with Allen to see if I could help him open up about his feelings about the surgery. The patient did not initiate the treatment, and I picked up on some initial resistance. As a result, I planned to work slowly with him to build a relationship that might in turn allow him to talk more about the meaning of his illness and future surgery.

Intervention

The intervention began with my trying to establish a trusting relationship with Allen that would allow him to open up eventually and discuss his feelings about the surgery. My early meetings with him provided a foundation from which we could later build on if needed. As it turned out, I received a crisis call from his nurse, asking me to speak with him following a panic attack. The crisis intervention involved another conversation with Allen to help him understand the role of his feelings in causing his anxiety. My task was to help him gain insight into this mind–body connection. I also provided him with information about anxiety and how the symptoms he was feeling in his body were related to uncomfortable thoughts and feelings that were hard to control. He had the chance to reflect on the effect his father's early death had on him, how his family did not talk about it, and how he learned from this to keep feelings to himself. In addition, I provided him with information about stress management, relaxation exercises, meditation, and the role of positive emotions in preparing for surgery and healing.

Following the surgery, I continued to meet with Allen and helped him with his discharge plans. He was planning to join a cardiac support group to continue his recovery after leaving the hospital. He also requested a reference for a psychotherapist to help him with unresolved grief about his father's early death. I gave him the name and contact information of a clinical social worker for him to make an appointment with when he was ready. I encouraged him to call me to let me know how he was doing.

Evaluation

Although Allen did not request social work services, they were part of his treatment as a cardiac patient in the hospital. My initial goal was to establish a relationship with him and obtain a psychosocial history for the medical record that would address any concerns that might interfere with Allen's surgery or recovery. Allen did not see the purpose of my visits but used the time to enjoy our conversations. My role changed with him after his panic attack, and I quickly became more actively involved in helping him understand the meaning behind his anxiety. I helped him work through his overwhelming feelings and gave him tools for managing his anxiety. We continued to work together until his discharge. The panic attack represented a crisis in his life that motivated him to work on unresolved grief issues around his father's death and also to look at his defensive style of suppressing feelings in his life.

During the last visit, Allen and I evaluated our work together. Allen expressed appreciation for my responding so quickly to his panic attack, and recognized that our meetings had helped him understand himself and manage his feelings better. He was looking forward to starting individual therapy to continue the work he started with me. I acknowledged his many strengths and the courage he showed in confronting his fears and learning from his experiences. I was optimistic about his prognosis and expected he would continue to make progress.

Before discharge, Allen was also given a patient satisfaction survey, on which he evaluated the services he received while in the hospital.

Termination

As my work with Allen came to a close, I reflected on one of the disadvantages of working in a hospital: the short-term relationships with clients. After working closely with a client like Allen, it was often hard to say goodbye and refer him to someone else. However, I used the last visit as an opportunity to reinforce the progress he had made and prepare him for the next stage in his recovery. Allen was excited to start cardiac rehabilitation, join the cardiac support group for patients and families, and start his personal therapy. Although I felt a little sadness about letting him go, I also felt a sense of satisfaction in how well the work with Allen had gone. I wish all cases could end so successfully.

Follow-up

A month after Allen left the hospital, I called him to confirm he got an appointment with the clinical social worker I had recommended, and to inquire how his rehabilitation and support group were going. Allen said he was back to working full time, was gradually increasing his exercise in the rehabilitation program, and that he and his wife had attended two support meetings. He had made one appointment with the social worker and felt she was a good fit for him. I added my notes to his record and closed the case.

Bio/Psycho/Social/Spiritual Assessment

The ecological method uses the bio/psycho/social/spiritual approach, which looks at the relationships among many different systems that continually interact with each other. Using this approach, the social worker looks at how an individual is affected by biological, psychological, and social systems. When analyzing a client's problem, it is important to understand how the systems affect each other. Please refer to chapter 1 for the outline on Bio/Psycho/Social/Spiritual Assessment.

Applying Bio/Psycho/Social/Spiritual Assessment to the Case of Allen

Allen is a 58-year-old married white male, hospitalized for a heart blockage that necessitated open heart surgery. He has a family history of heart disease; in particular, his father died of a massive heart attack at the age of 56. Before hospitalization, Allen led a healthy lifestyle, paying attention to his diet and exercising regularly. He has no other health issues. There is no indication of any addiction to alcohol or drugs. While in the hospital, Allen had a panic attack, although there had been no prior history of an anxiety disorder. He was treated with an anti-anxiety medication.

Allen presents as a very bright, well-educated man of above-average intelligence. He demonstrates a good capacity for insight and self-reflection. He has excellent communication skills and engages effectively with others. He appears to have good self-esteem. He has healthy relationships with family members and friends, and these reflect an ability to take the perspective of another and be empathic. Allen was 20 years old when his father died. His father had his first heart attack when Allen was 10 years old, and this event had a profound effect on Allen. No one talked to him about his father's illness and its impact on him. Feelings were avoided in his family, and this led to him defending against them; it was difficult for him to acknowledge or express feelings. While in the hospital, Allen had a panic attack that related to his suppressed feelings about the surgery. The event also triggered unresolved feelings of loss around his father's early death. Allen responded well to a psychotherapeutic intervention and has agreed to continue outpatient therapy to work on the issues that surfaced during his hospitalization. He appears motivated to understand himself better and make changes in his life. He is a good candidate for insight-oriented therapy.

Socially, Allen has an excellent network of family and friends. He is happily married with two children in their twenties. He also has two brothers and one sister who live in the area, and whom he sees regularly. His family appears to be an open system with good boundaries. Allen graduated from a four-year business college and works full time as an accountant for a nonprofit company. During his leisure time, he enjoys playing music in a band. He also enjoys reading and watching movies with his family.

On a spiritual level, illness provides an opportunity for people to stop and reflect on the meaning of their lives. This was the case with Allen, who was diagnosed with heart disease and faced life-threatening surgery. His attempts to defend against thoughts of death and the consequences of his surgery triggered a panic attack, and it became clear that at this critical juncture he needed to address these issues, not avoid them. Through my intervention with Allen, he got in touch with his feelings about past and present loss. He also came to appreciate how because of these losses, he has blocked off certain experiences with himself and others. Illness gave him a chance to look at his life differently, confront issues of life and death, and develop more intimate relationships with others as he opened up to his feelings. Although we only touched on these subjects briefly, I expect that Allen will continue to reflect on the meaning of his life in ongoing outpatient treatment with a clinical social worker.

Psychosocial Assessment and Intervention Strategy

Please refer to chapter 1, which includes outlines for the Psychosocial Assessment and Intervention Plan. Applying a psychosocial assessment and intervention to Allen's case would occur as follows.

Identifying Data

Allen is a 58-year-old married white male who was hospitalized for heart problems. Allen has been married to Mary for 30 years and they have two children, a son Abbott, 28, and a daughter Julia, aged 26. The family has resided in Arlington for 30 years.

When I entered Allen's hospital room, he was sitting in a chair next to his bed reading a book, a biography on the life of Elvis Presley. Allen presents as an attractive middle-aged man of medium build, 5'7" and with gray hair. He has a pleasant and friendly demeanor. He greeted me warmly with a smile and strong hand shake.

Presenting Problem

Allen was hospitalized after suffering chest pains and going to the emergency room. He was diagnosed with having a serious blockage that required open heart surgery. The day before the operation, he experienced a panic attack after talking to his doctor about the surgery.

Current Functioning, Social Supports, Strengths

Allen has a strong family support system and many good friends. He graduated from a four-year business college and presently works full time as an accountant at a nonprofit agency. He is bright, articulate, friendly, and engages well with others using his good sense of humor. He enjoys music and plays bass guitar in a band in his leisure time. He has many supports and resources that will help him cope with the surgery. A risk factor is his tendency to defend against his feelings and not talk about his problems.

The day before surgery, Allen had a panic attack triggered by the doctor talking to him about advance directives and healthcare proxy. This made him realize the seriousness of his situation and resulted in overwhelming emotions.

Relevant Past History

Before the hospitalization, Allen had few health problems. He paid attention to his diet and exercised regularly. There is a history of heart disease in his family. His father had his first heart attack when Allen was 10 years old, and died from a massive heart attack when Allen was 20. This loss had a profound effect on his childhood. He described his family as not able to talk openly about either his father's first heart attack or second fatal one. Allen states that he learned from his family not to talk about feelings or problems but to keep everything bottled up inside.

Formulation

Allen is a 58-year-old white male, married with two children and a strong support system of family and friends. Although Allen has many strengths, a risk factor is his tendency to suppress feelings that cause him anxiety. The day before surgery, he had a panic attack that was triggered by a conversation with his surgeon. His strong defenses broke down, and he had to come to terms with his feelings. Our discussion took place after his panic attack; it provided him with an outlet to express his feelings about the surgery, better preparing him for it. This crisis was a turning point in Allen's life and has motivated him to make positive changes.

Intervention Strategy

The intervention began with me establishing a trusting relationship with Allen that I hoped would allow him to open up and discuss his feelings about the surgery. My early meetings with him provided a foundation on which we could later build as needed. As it turned out, I received a crisis call from his nurse, asking me to speak with him following a panic attack. The crisis intervention involved another conversation with Allen to help him understand the role of his feelings in causing the anxiety. My task was to help him gain insight into this mind–body connection. I also provided him with information about anxiety and how the symptoms he was feeling in his body were related to uncomfortable thoughts and emotions that were hard to control. He had the chance to reflect on the effect his father's early death had on him, how his family did not talk about it, and how he learned from this to keep feelings to himself. In addition, I gave him information about stress management, relaxation exercises, meditation, and the role of positive emotions in preparing for surgery and healing.

Following the surgery, I continued to meet with Allen and helped him with his discharge plans. He intended to join a cardiac support group to augment his recovery after leaving the hospital. He also requested a reference for a psychotherapist to help him with unresolved grief about his father's early death. I gave him the name and contact information of a clinical social worker for him to make an appointment when he was ready. I encouraged him to call me to let me know how he was doing.

Termination and Evaluation

During the last visit, Allen and I evaluated our work together. He expressed appreciation that I responded so quickly to his panic attack, and recognized that our meetings had helped him understand himself and manage his feelings better. He looked forward to starting individual therapy to continue the work he started with me. I acknowledged his many strengths and the courage he showed in confronting his fears and learning from his experiences. I was optimistic about his prognosis and expected he would continue to make progress. Before discharge, Allen was also given a patient satisfaction survey, on which he evaluated the services he received while in the hospital.

As my work with Allen came to a close, I reflected on one of the disadvantages of practicing in a hospital: the short-term relationships with clients. After collaborating with a client like Allen, it was often hard to say goodbye and refer him to someone else. However, I used the last visit as an opportunity to reinforce the progress he had made and to prepare him for the next stage in his recovery. Allen was excited to start cardiac rehabilitation, join the cardiac support group for patients and families, and begin his personal therapy. Although I felt a little sadness about letting him go, I also felt a sense of satisfaction in how well the work with Allen had gone. I wish all cases could end so successfully.

Theoretical Lens

I used psychodynamic, cognitive, behavioral, family systems, and narrative theories to understand and plan interventions with Allen. Psychodynamic theory helped me understand how Allen used defenses; I interpreted these defenses in my intervention to give him insight into their meaning and to show him how to be more aware of his feelings, and thus less defensive. Mindfulness practice taught Allen to live in the present, aware of his experience from moment to moment. Cognitive behavioral theories demonstrated to Allen the importance of learning to identify and change irrational thoughts and feelings that precede anxiety, in order to manage these symptoms. Family systems theory looked at Allen's family history and patterns of communication in his family-of-origin, and how these influenced his style of relating to his own family. This, in turn, was used to improve communication in the family. Narrative theory helped me understand how Allen used language to make meaning out of his life experiences. It also helped me document Allen's progress by noticing how his story changed and how he constructed new meaning from past life events. No one theoretical perspective informed Allen's transformation; I benefited by integrating the different theories into my interventions with Allen.

End of Chapter Resources
Questions for Students

I have included questions that can be used to supplement the text for additional student learning. They are organized around the 10 core competencies in the Council on Social Work Education (CSWE, 2008). The questions can be used for classroom or online discussion, given as written homework assignments, structured as classroom exercises, or used by students to do outside research. They can be adapted for use in hybrid or online courses.

Educational Policy 2.1.1: Identify as a Professional Social Worker and Conduct Oneself Accordingly

These skills include advocating for clients, practicing personal reflection, demonstrating professional demeanor, engaging in career-long learning, and using supervision and consultation. Professional social work practice requires that social workers pay attention to how their personal experiences, values, and assumptions provide obstacles to listening to clients in helpful ways. Many of the questions that follow will help students become more self-aware and develop competence in this area.

1. How comfortable would you have been talking about death with the patient? Have you ever talked about death with someone? What was it like for you?
2. What is your understanding of countertransference? Write down your definition of this concept. Were there any moments for you in the interview that triggered any feelings or experiences from your life? Were there times when you reacted to something that happened in the interview with Allen?
3. Were you aware of times when Allen showed his feelings during the interview? If so, how did it make you feel? How do you think the social worker handled these moments? What are some other ways you could have responded in the moment?
4. What have been your experiences in the role of a patient? How have your experiences as a patient influenced how you look at healthcare?
5. Read the material by Donald Shon on the reflective practitioner, especially on reflection-in-action and reflection-on-action. What is the difference between these two types of reflection?
6. At different points in the interview, the social worker reflected on what was the best way to proceed in her conversation with Allen. She referred to acting on her intuition on the best course of action. What role do you think intuition and practice wisdom have in clinical work?
7. What are some ways that a social worker can be an advocate for a patient in the hospital?

Educational Policy 2.1.2: Apply Social Work Ethical Principles to Guide Professional Practice

The questions that follow are to make students more aware of ethical issues that social workers confront every day in their practice.

1. Social workers often encounter ethical challenges when working in medical settings. Can you think of situations in which social workers' professional values and ethics would put them in conflict with other professionals and management of hospitals?
2. What are some ways that hospital policy could create an ethical dilemma for social workers?
3. There may be instances when social workers are considered nuisances in a hospital setting, especially when advocating for patients to receive services based on a sense of ethical obligation. How could this lead to interprofessional strain?

Educational Policy 2.1.3: Apply Critical Thinking to Inform and Communicate Professional Judgments

Critical thinking is an important skill in social work practice, and students are expected to demonstrate this competency before graduation. These exercises promote the ability of students to become critical thinkers in practice.

1. Death is often a taboo subject. Although the social worker talked about the patient's father's death and its impact on him, she never talked directly to the patient about his death or the possibility that he may die from the surgery. Do you think the social work should have explored his death during the interview? What are the pros and cons of talking about Allen's death directly with him? Were there any opportunities in the interview when it could have been explored? If so, explain when?

2. Allen used denial as a defense against his feelings about the surgery. When is denial appropriate and protective of a client and when is it not? Give some examples.

3. The literature on grief work often refers to the term "unfinished business." What does unfinished business mean in clinical work? Do you think Allen had any unfinished business that he needed to work on? Explain your answer.

4. What did you think of how the social worker used mind–body techniques with the patient? Do you think Allen was responsive to these ideas? Can you imagine a situation when a patient might not respond as well?

5. In the interview Allen shared that he kept his feelings inside and that he needed to be strong for his family. What factors might have contributed to his need to play this role in his family? Explore gender roles, socialization of boys in this culture, and family communication patterns.

6. Read the full transcript of this interview, located in appendix 2. At the end of the interview, the social worker reassured the patient that she was sure he would be fine. Is this something the social worker should have done? Share your thoughts about this. What would you have done?

Educational Policy 2.1.4: Engage Diversity and Difference in Practice

These questions are designed to teach students about engaging cultural diversity and understanding difference in practice.

1. What does it mean for a social worker to be culturally competent? What is the importance of cultural sensitivity in working with patients in a medical setting? How was it important in this case?

2. Read the article by Congress (2004) cited at the end of this chapter on "Cultural and ethical issues in working with culturally diverse patients: The use of the Culturagram to promote culturally competent practice in healthcare settings." Evaluate this assessment tool that is recommended for healthcare professionals. What are the strengths

and weaknesses of this tool? Do you think it will help advance healthcare professionals' understanding of culturally diverse patients and their families?

3. Hospitals often employ translators to help communicate with patients from diverse cultures whose primary language is not English. Contact your local hospital to inquire about the types and range of diversity they experience in their patient population. Next, ask if they have translators to help communicate with these patients.

4. Allen's ethnicity was English, his ancestors coming to America from England in the colonial era. How do you think Allen's cultural background influenced how he coped with his illness? Do you think ethnicity plays a role in how people cope with illness? How would the interview be different if Allen were a Latino man? Explain your answer.

Educational Policy 2.1.5: Advance Human Rights and Social and Economic Justice

Students are expected to address human rights and social justice issues as needed in their practice. These questions are to help students think in terms of social and economic justice and become more competent in this area.

1. Watch the movie Sicko, a documentary on healthcare in America by Michael Moore. How do you understand Michael Moore's analysis of this country's healthcare delivery system? What are some of the social and economic justice issues presented in the documentary?

2. How do race and ethnicity factor into access to and quality of healthcare services?

3. What are some healthcare disparities?

4. How do social and physical conditions in poor neighborhoods affect health?

5. What is the role of public health services in promoting social and economic justice? Can you give some examples?

Educational Policy 2.1.6: Engage in Research-Informed Practice and Practice-Informed Research

Research assignments encourage students to engage in research-informed practice and practice-informed research. This helps students to practice and become more competent in this competency as defined by the CSWE.

1. What does evidence-based treatment (EBT) and empirically supported treatment (EST) mean?

2. Describe three empirically supported treatment interventions for clients with panic disorder.

3. Research the effect of positive emotions and laughter on healing. Find two sources that you can share with your peers in class. Include the source and a paragraph summary of each one.

4. Research the area of alternative medicine. What are some types of alternative medicine used with patients?

5. Research how mindfulness meditation is used in clinical work.

6. There are many examples of disparities in health based on race, gender, ethnicity, or sexual orientation. Research an area of interest related to discrimination in healthcare or inequality of health services. For example, you could choose discrimination to gays/lesbians by healthcare providers or the high level of AIDS among African Americans.

7. Research the history of social work in healthcare settings. Prepare a PowerPoint presentation for the class and include five sources that you used.

8. Read the research cited in this chapter on the role of gender and hospital care (Winnett, Furman, & Enterline, 2012). Based on what you learn from the article, create your own small-scale study on the impact of gender on care. Locate men who are willing to volunteer to be interviewed about their experiences, and construct an interview schedule to carry out the research. Report your findings to the class.

9. Explain objectivity and subjectivity in terms of doing research. Have the class divide into two sides of the argument on whether research can be objective or if all research is subjective.

10. Watch the movie Sicko, a documentary on healthcare in America by Michael Moore. What is your evaluation of Michael Moore's research and analysis of this country's healthcare delivery system? Identify any points in the documentary where you observe bias.

Educational Policy 2.1.7: Apply Knowledge of Human Behavior and the Social Environment

These questions will help students apply theories critically to assess and evaluate work and interventions with clients.

1. Integrative therapy is when the social worker uses intervention strategies from different theoretical perspectives in an interview with a client. What are the advantages and disadvantages of using techniques from different theoretical backgrounds during a session as opposed to staying with one theoretical approach?

2. Give examples of when the social worker used different theories in her interventions with Allen and your evaluation of how they were applied. Were there times when you would have you used a different approach? Include psychodynamic, narrative, cognitive and behavioral, and family systems theories.

3. Look at each of the theories used in the interventions with Allen. What assumptions are made by each theory and how do they differ in how they look at human behavior? Include psychodynamic, narrative, cognitive and behavioral, and family systems theories.

4. Write up a case vignette with some basic client information, including a description of the client, the identified problem, and history of the problem. Practice a role-play with another student in class in which you try interventions from different theories, including psychodynamic, narrative, cognitive and behavioral, and family systems theories.

5. Allen is in midlife. What life cycle stage is he in? What do you think it means for Allen to have a life-threatening experience at this time in his life?

6. What family life stage is Allen's family in? How do you think Allen's illness affects the family and family developmental issues?

Educational Policy 2.1.8: Engage in Policy Practice to Advance Social and Economic Well-Being and Deliver Effective Social Work Services

These questions are to encourage students to look at the role of policy in social work practice.

1. Discuss what social workers are doing now to change the way healthcare is delivered. Give some examples. Include some legislative efforts by the National Association of Social Workers to advocate for better healthcare for everyone.

2. Review in class Health Insurance Portability and Accountability Act (HIPPA) regulations and rules governing confidentiality in medical settings.

3. Review the Affordable Care Act and how it addresses issues of social and economic justice. Are there areas that need to be addressed in this law to ensure equal access to healthcare for everyone?

4. How does universal care differ from the Affordable Healthcare Act?

Educational Policy 2.1.9: Respond to Contexts That Shape Practice

Social workers practice in many different settings and may need to familiarize themselves with the particular skills required in these settings. These questions help students to appreciate how context shapes practice and develop competencies in this area.

1. What are some of the different settings in which medical social workers are employed? Name five different settings and describe the role of the social worker in these settings. What specialized skills are needed in these different settings?

2. Explain what an interdisciplinary or team meeting is in a medical setting. Who attends these meetings and what is the purpose of them? What is the social worker's role in these meetings?

3. How would you define holistic health? Describe some holistic health approaches to working with patients? What is the role of social work in holistic care?

4. What does illness mean to you? What are your thoughts on how attitude and emotions affect health? How does being a consumer of health services change your view of healthcare?

5. What does case management mean in a healthcare setting? What are the differences between nurses and social workers doing case management?

6. Interview a medical social worker in a medical setting to learn more about his or her role.

7. Have four students role-play an interdisciplinary meeting that includes a doctor, an inpatient nurse, a nurse from a home care agency, and a social worker. Explore what the role of the medical social worker would be in this meeting.

8. Different types of documentation are used to record patient information in the medical record. Practice writing a note that would go into the patient record based on the videotaped interview with Allen. How much of the interview would be shared in the medical record? What is important to include and what does not have to be included?

9. Have a medical social worker from a stress management/behavioral health clinic visit the class to discuss the role of meditation, relaxation, visualization, and other behavioral strategies to help patients manage stress and/or treat illness.

Educational Policy 2.1.10(a)–(d): Engage, Assess, Intervene, and Evaluate with Individuals, Families, Groups, Organizations, and Communities

These questions are intended to give students practice engaging, assessing, intervening, and evaluating clients.

1. What are some situations in which a social worker may use meditation and relaxation exercises with a client?

2. Ask students to bring a meditation or relaxation exercise they can share with the class. Practice doing a meditation or relaxation exercise in class and process the experience with students.

3. Watch the videotaped interview together as a class. Stop the interview at significant points to highlight any learning objectives you have outlined. Also, look for moments when you observe other options for interventions and have the students role-play them.

4. Process and content are two parts of an interview that a social worker pays attention to when meeting with a client. Content is when the social worker pays attention to the substance of what the client is saying. Process is when the social worker notices the dynamic of the client–social worker relationship, or when the social worker notices and brings attention to something the client is feeling during the session. There were several times during the interview when the social worker tuned in to what the client was feeling and processed these feelings during the meeting. Point out the times when this happened and comment on them. What effect did this have on Allen and how the interview progressed?

5. When reflecting on the three different assessments at the end of the chapter, what were the differences between them? Did you prefer one over another, and if so, explain your answer.

6. Identify communication and interviewing skills used in the videotaped interview with Allen that you want to highlight. Have students role-play these interviewing skills to demonstrate their competencies in these areas.

Interviewing Skills Used in the Case of Allen

Following is a list of interviewing skills the social worker used with Allen. They are listed in order of when they appeared. Although others social workers may refer to these interactions differently, or define the skills in others ways, this is one way of looking at them.

Become familiar with these interviewing skills and practice them with other students in role-plays.

Engagement and Beginning of Interview

At the beginning of the first meeting with the client, the social worker welcomes the client, tries to make the client comfortable, and tunes in to her own and the client's initial feelings about the first meeting.

Attending to Nonverbal Cues, Body Language

The social worker shows that she is listening through her body language, such as eye contact, facial expressions, nodding, and leaning forward. These nonverbal skills help the client elaborate and feel comfortable sharing personal information. The social worker also pays attention to the client's nonverbal cues, body language, and facial expressions. These communications might indicate a change in mood, whether the client is engaged with the social worker or seems distracted, and so on.

Exploration of the Problem

This is a way of gaining more information about a client's situation. When continuing to explore the problem, the social worker listens for underlying feelings about the situation, who else is involved, and what resources are available to help resolve it.

Reflecting Back Feelings

This is when the social worker gives a short response back to the client that mirrors the feeling that the social worker heard the client express. It is used to let the client know the social worker is listening.

Putting Client's Words into Feelings

There may be times when a client has difficulty identifying the feeling he wants to express in the narrative. The social worker can help in these situations by responding to the client and using feeling words to summarize what the client has said.

Offering Support

When a client shares a story that is painful, it helps when the social worker offers encouragement. By acknowledging the difficulty of the situation, you provide support for the client and allow him to continue the story.

Seeking Clarification

Periodically, the social worker may ask the client to talk about his perception of a situation in order to make sure she understands the client's point of view.

Elaboration

Elaboration involves asking clients to describe what they are talking about in more detail. The social worker may ask the client, "I'm not sure I understand what you mean. Can you say more about that?" The social worker may also ask for examples of what the client is referencing. "Can you give me an example of when you felt that way?" (Exploration, clarification, and elaboration are similar skills used when the social worker is trying to understand on a deeper level what the client is saying.)

Summarizing

Part way through the session, and again at the end of the interview with the client, the social worker summarizes what has been said up to that point. This helps to reinforce for the client what has been discussed and ensures that the social worker and client both understand the focus of the session.

Normalizing Feelings

Clients often believe that their feelings are unacceptable or abnormal. The social worker helps clients see that their feelings are a natural reaction to the given situation.

Paraphrasing

Paraphrasing is when the social worker uses her own words to repeat back to the client what she just heard the client say. This shows that the worker is listening and following the conversation.

Showing Empathy

The social worker maintains a nonjudgmental stance or remains neutral. The worker need not totally understand the client's situation, but she must show that she is trying to grasp what the client is feeling or experiencing. The social worker might say, "Tell me more about what your experience was" or "I want to understand more about what this means from your perspective."

Exploring Underlying Feelings

The social worker asks the client his feelings on the subject under discussion.

Holding to Focus

Holding to focus is when the social worker helps a client stay on the topic under discussion. There may be times when, if a client is uncomfortable with the subject matter, he may try to change the subject. In these cases, the social worker redirects the client back to the topic.

Opening up Affect

Opening up affect is when the social worker encourages the client to open up more and elaborate on what he is feeling.

Providing Information

Providing information, sometimes referred to as "information-giving," means informing the client about the social agency, the problem, and the resources for change. The social worker is knowledgeable about human development and human behavior and can help a client by sharing information about a problem the client is experiencing. For instance, a mother may complain that her four-year-old daughter is misbehaving, and not understand how the birth of a new sibling has affected the daughter.

Reaching for Feelings

This is when the social worker tries to understand what the client is feeling when a particular subject or issue comes up. The social worker may use this skill when she senses that the client is avoiding, or is not in touch with, the feelings related to the current discussion. This may bring out strong reactions in the client, and it is important that the social worker is sensitive to what this means to the client.

Questioning

Questioning is a way of gaining more information about a client's situation. There are many different kinds of questions, for example, open- and closed-ended questions and reflexive questions.

Confrontation

Confrontation is used by the social worker when there are inconsistencies between what the client has said and what is known to be true. The social worker believes it's best if the client comes to terms with this discrepancy. A worker can also use confrontation to question a client's behavior that is harmful to the client.

Medical Terms and Definitions for Cardiac Patients

Advance Directives

These are written documents completed by an individual that specify treatment preferences for healthcare decision making, particularly about end-of-life care and whether to use life-sustaining treatment. Advance directives provide an avenue for individuals to make known their wishes about end-of-life treatment (Browne, 2006).

Angina Pectoris

"Strangling of the chest." A temporary imbalance between the coronary arteries' ability to supply oxygen and the cardiac muscle's demand for oxygen. No permanent damage of heart muscle (Ignatavicius & Workman, 2006).

Aortic/Mitral Valve Replacement

Prosthetic (synthetic) or biological (tissue) valves are used. Clients must receive oral anticoagulation therapy because of the risk for clots. The older the client, the longer the valve will last because there is less calcium in the blood to break it down (Ignatavicius & Workman, 2006).

Asystole

Flatlined; cannot shock this patient because there is no electrical activity of the heart. Can do compressions and medications to get the heart pumping again (Ignatavicius & Workman, 2006).

Arrhythmia

An absence of cardiac rhythm (Ignatavicius & Workman, 2006).

Atrial Fibrillation

The most common dysrhythmia; multiple rapid impulses from many points in the atria of the heart (Ignatavicius & Workman, 2006).

Atrial Flutter

A dysrhythmia; rapid atrial depolarization at a rate of 250 to 350 times per minute. If untreated, results in a block (Ignatavicius & Workman, 2006).

Atrial Septal Defect

A congenital (from birth) heart defect that enables blood flow between the left and right atria. Normally the two are separated (Ignatavicius & Workman, 2006).

Bradycardia

If the rate of the heart is less than 60 beats per minute (Ignatavicius & Workman, 2006).

Cardiogenic Shock

Class IV heart failure; necrosis of more than 40% of the left ventricle has occurred (Ignatavicius & Workman, 2006).

Cardiomyopathy

Abnormalities in the structure and function of the heart (Ignatavicius & Workman, 2006).

Cardioversion

A synchronized counter shock that may be performed in emergencies to correct heart rhythms resistant to medications (Ignatavicius & Workman, 2006).

Congestive Heart Failure

A general term for the inadequacy of the heart to pump blood throughout the body. Causes insufficient oxygen and nutrients to the body tissues (Ignatavicius & Workman, 2006).

Coronary Artery Bypass Graft

This is performed if the cause of a dysrhythmia is coronary artery insufficiency that is unresponsive to medical therapy (Ignatavicius & Workman, 2006).

Coronary Artery Disease

This is a broad term that includes stable angina pectoris and acute coronary syndromes. It affects the arteries that provide blood, oxygen, and nutrients to the myocardium (Ignatavicius & Workman, 2006).

Do Not Resuscitate

Cardiopulmonary resuscitation is the most common end-of-life discussion. When patients are hospitalized with a potentially terminal or irreversible illness, they may choose "do not resuscitate" orders, usually upon admission to a long-term care facility, home healthcare, in-patient or home hospice, or palliative care. These are physician's notes in a patient's medical records that alert providers not to attempt cardiopulmonary resuscitation (Mizrahi & Davis, 2008).

Dysrhythmia

Abnormal rhythms of the heart's electrical system. A disturbance in cardiac rhythm (Ignatavicius & Workman, 2006).

Electrocardiogram

Also known as electrocardiogram or ECG, provides a graphic representation, or picture, of cardiac electrical activity (Ignatavicius & Workman, 2006).

End-Stage Heart Disease

A heart disease of any origin that has progressed to an end stage or advanced form of the disease. The patient is sick and likely disabled and unable to function at even limited levels of activity (http://www.uihealthcare.org/2column.aspx?id=236411).

Healthcare Proxy

The most common advance directive (along with a living will). This is durable power of attorney for healthcare (Browne & Gehlert, 2006).

Heart Transplant

For people with cardiomyopathies; must meet the following criteria:

1. Life expectancy less than 1 year
2. Age generally less than 65 years
3. New York Heart Association class III or IV
4. Normal or only slightly increased pulmonary vascular resistance
5. Absence of active infection
6. Stable psychosocial status
7. No evidence of drug or alcohol abuse (Ignatavicius & Workman, 2006).

Hypertension

Blood pressure greater than 140/90 (normal is 120/80). In most people it can be effectively controlled with lifestyle modification and/or medication (Ignatavicius & Workman, 2006).

Idiopathic

From an unknown cause (Ignatavicius & Workman, 2006).

Increased Lipids

Seen in atherosclerosis (thickening of the arteries). The elevated lipids include cholesterol and triglycerides. Total cholesterol levels should be less than 200 mg/dL (Ignatavicius & Workman, 2006).

Infarction

Necrosis, or cell death, occurs when severe ischemia is prolonged and irreversible damage to tissue results (Ignatavicius & Workman, 2006).

Ischemic

Ischemia occurs when insufficient oxygen is supplied to meet the requirements of the myocardium (Ignatavicius & Workman, 2006).

Interdisciplinary Approach

The interdisciplinary approach links social work to other disciplines within complex domains of practice. Contrasted with multidisciplinary practice, in which social workers practice alongside other disciplines and professions, all of whom pursue their own intervention aims, interdisciplinary requires a blending and combining of those practices in pursuit of a common set of outcomes. Interdisciplinary requires collaboration, the integration of knowledge and action, and the formation of a common agenda of practice (Davis & Mizrahi, 2008).

Left Ventricular Assistive Device

Clients with end-stage heart failure who are ineligible for transplantation may have improved survival rates with a left ventricular assistive device compared with medical support alone (Ignatavicius & Workman, 2006).

Medical Record and Documentation

Social workers who work in medical settings will be expected to document in the patient's medical record. Each patient has a medical record that contains the pertinent information about the patient's care from each team member who works with the patient. This may include the physician, nurses, social workers, clinical psychologists, physical therapists, speech therapists, occupational therapists, recreational therapists, nutritional therapists, and so on. Social workers help other members of the team understand the patient better by sharing information about the patient's psychosocial history, levels of family support, issues of loss and adaptation, and plans for discharge.

New York Heart Association Scale

Stage 1: Clients with cardiac disease but without resulting limitations of physical activities. Ordinal physical activity does not cause undue fatigue, palpitation, dyspnea, or angina pain.

Stage 2: Clients with cardiac disease resulting in slight limitation of physical activity. They are comfortable at rest. Ordinary physical activity results in fatigue, palpitation, dyspnea, or angina pain.

Stage 3: Clients with cardiac disease resulting in marked limitation of physical activity. They are comfortable at rest. Less than ordinary physical activity causes fatigue, palpitation, dyspnea, or angina pain.

Stage 4: Clients with cardiac disease resulting in inability to carry out any physical activity without discomfort. Symptoms of cardiac insufficiency or of the anginal syndrome may be present, even at rest. If any physical activity is undertaken, discomfort is increased (Ignatavicius & Workman, 2006).

Peripheral Vascular Disease

Includes disorders that alter the natural flow of blood through the arteries and veins of the peripheral circulation. Affects lower extremities more than upper extremities (Ignatavicius & Workman, 2006).

Tachycardia

If the rate of the heart is greater than 100 beats per minute (Ignatavicius & Workman, 2006).

Ventricular Fibrillation

Life-threatening dysrhythmia; the result of electrical chaos in the ventricles. No recognizable deflections on an electrocardiogram. Emergency cardioversion (Ignatavicius & Workman, 2006).

Ventricular Tachycardia

Life-threatening dysrhythmia; occurs with repetitive firing of an irritable ventricular ectopic focus. This is usually at a rate of 140 to 180 beats per minute, or more. If the patient has a pulse, administer oxygen, and give an electrocardiogram. If there is not a pulse, give emergency cardioversion (Ignatavicius & Workman, 2006).

References

American Psychiatric Association. (2013). *Diagnostic and Statistical Manual of Mental Disorders* (5th ed.). Washington, DC: American Psychiatric Association.

Arnd-Caddigan, M. (2011). Toward a broader definition of evidence-informed practice: Intersubjective evidence. *Families in Society: The Journal of Contemporary Social Sciences, 92*(4), 372–376.

Astin, J. A., Shapiro, S. L., Eisenberg, D. M., & Forys, K. (2003). Mind-body medicine: State of the science, implications for practice. *American Board of Family Medicine, 16*(2), 131–147.

Borden, W. (1992). Narrative perspectives in psychosocial intervention following adverse life events. *Social Work, 37*(2), 135–141.

Browne, T. A. (2006). Social work roles and healthcare settings. In S. Gehlert & T. A. Browne (Eds.), *Handbook of Health Social Work* (pp. 23–42). Hoboken, NJ: Wiley.

Carter, B. & McGoldrick, M. (Eds). (1999). *The Changing Family Life Cycle: A Framework for Family Therapy* (3rd ed). Boston: Allyn & Bacon.

Congress, E. (2004). Cultural and ethical issues in working with culturally diverse patients: The use of the Culturagram to promote culturally competent practice in health care settings. *Social Work in Health Care, 39*(3/4), 249–262.

Council on Social Work Education. (2008). *Educational Policy and Accreditation Standards*. Alexandria, VA: Council on Social Work Education.

Cousins, N. (1979). *Anatomy of an Illness, as Perceived by the Patient*. New York: W.W. Norton & Co.

Dass, R. & Gorman, P. (1987). *How Can I Help? Stories and Reflections on Service*. New York: Alfred A. Knopf.

Drisko, J. W. & Grady, M. D. (2012). *Evidence-Based Practice in Clinical Social Work*. New York: Springer.

Erikson, E. H. (1963). *Childhood and Society*. New York: Norton.

Freeman, L. W. (2004). *Mosby's Complementary & Alternative Medicine: A Research- Based Approach*. St. Louis: Mosby.

Globerman, L, White, J., & McDonald, G. (2003). Social work in restructuring hospitals: Program management five years later. *Social Work in Health Care, 27*(4), 274–283.

Ignatavicius, D. & Workman, L. (2006). *Medical Surgical Nursing: Critical Thinking for Collaborative Care*. St. Louis: Saunders.

James, D. H. (1995). Humor: A holistic nursing intervention. *Holistic Nursing, 13*(3), 239–247.

Jongsma Jr. A. & Timothy, B. (2010). *Evidence-Based Treatment Planning for Panic Disorder*. Hoboken, NJ: Wiley.

Kabat-Zinn, J. (1990). *Full Catastrophe Living: Using the Wisdom of Your Body and Mind to Face Stress, Pain, and Illness*. New York: Delacorte.

Mizrahi, T. & Davis, L. E. (2008). *Encyclopedia of social work*. New York: Oxford.

Perlman, H. (1957.). *Social Casework: A Problem-Solving Process*. Chicago: The University of Chicago.

Probst, B. (2012). Diagnosing, diagnosis, and the DSM in clinical social work. *Families in Society: The Journal of Contemporary Social Services, 93*(4), 255–263.

Rolland, J. S. (1987). Chronic illness and the family life cycle. *Family Process, 26*, 203–221.

Shon, D. (1983). *The Reflective Practitioner. How Professionals Think in Action*. London: Temple Smith.

Siegel, B. S. (2011). *Book of miracles: Inspiring True Stories of Healing, Gratitude and Love*. Novato, CA: New World Library.

Salovey, P., Rothman, A., Detweiler, J., & Stewart, W. J. (2000). Emotional states and physical health. *American Psychologist, 55*(1), 110–121.

Siegel, B. S. (1990). *Peace, Love and Healing: Body mind Communication & the Path to Self-Healing: An Exploration*. New York: Harper & Row.

Siegel, B. S. (1986). *Love, Medicine and Miracles: Lessons Learned about Self-Healing from a Surgeon's Experience with Exceptional Patients*. New York: Harper & Row.

Simonton, C. O., Creighton, J., Simonton, S. M., & Matthews, M. (1992). *Getting Well Again: The Bestselling Classic about the Simontons' Revolutionary Lifesaving Self-Awareness Techniques*. New York: Bantam Books.

Winnett, R., Furman, R., & Enterline, M. (2012). Men at risk: Considering masculinity during hospital-based social work intervention. *Social Work in Health Care, 51*, 312–326.

4

Practice with At-Risk Populations: The Elderly and Public Assistance

Betty: "If I don't get money here, I'll be out on the street."

Setting: Public Assistance Office

Clients' lives and identities are shaped by many factors, including how they perceive themselves as different from others. As a consequence of this, clients often experience discrimination, are marginalized by society, feel alienated, and possess less power and limited access to resources. There are many ways clients may stand out as different: class, age, color, culture, ethnicity, race, religion, gender, sexual orientation, immigration status, disability, mental or physical health, and appearance.

Description of Practice Area

The case of Betty engages diversity and difference in practice in two important areas, which are aging and poverty. Negative attitudes and stereotypes about older people and the poor are pervasive in American society. Discriminatory practices exist in employment, also mental and physical healthcare; basic fair treatment is too often discarded. Women are often singled out based on age and gender and do not receive the same care as younger patients in terms of access to services, types of services received, and in length and quality of treatment (Garner & Young, 1993, pp. 224-225).

This chapter will cover discriminatory practices addressed by social work related to class, race, age, gender, and disability. It also will discuss social and economic justice issues in contemporary American culture and the role of social policy to redistribute wealth and create more equality. To cover these topics sufficiently, the chapter will be longer than the others, since it gets to the heart of social work.

The Role of Individualism in American Society

American society, unlike most other industrialized nations, believes that economic success or failure is the responsibility of the individual alone (Bellah et al., 1996). In this "culture of individualism," independence and self-reliance are valued above all else. Even during hard times, Americans generally subscribe to the philosophy of social Darwinism and believe it is up to the individual to survive or perish. They do not look for structural discrepancies to explain poverty; they see the root of the problem in the individual. Today, American society has great income disparities, and this increasing inequity coincides with reductions in government spending on public support programs. For example, government expenditures on public housing continue to fall while spending on prisons increases (Wacquant, 2009). At a time when we need a larger safety net for our most vulnerable citizens, government policies have reduced the reach of social programs. Instead, rates of criminalization have increased, and our poorest citizens are disproportionately represented in the country's prison systems.

The gap between the haves and the have-nots is ever widening, a phenomenon that goes deeper than a simple "failure" of the individual. Since the 1970s, average American wages have suffered dramatic reductions while per capita domestic product steadily increased. Unfortunately, gains were not shared equally, and many Americans' incomes went down. This was not true of other countries, like Japan and Germany, which also had highly developed technologies but shared their increased GDP with all segments of society (Thurow, 1992). Robert Reich (1991) describes a three-tier class system to explain how Americans are divided: the "overclass," an elite group that has accumulated most of the wealth and enjoys the luxuries it provides them; the "underclass," that struggles to meet basic needs and lives in bleak and often violent neighborhoods; and the "anxious class," that sees itself sinking and fears joining the "underclass." The shrinking middle class, holding on to its belief in individualism, does not blame the elite for its success, but instead blames the "underclass," who it looks down on (Bellah et al., 1996). Indeed, we have come to a time in our history marked by unprecedented income inequality.

Those who have gained the most are the top 1%, which accumulates continued wealth and values money above civic engagement. As social workers look to understand increasing inequities, many others still explain poverty in terms of individual failings rather than real factors in the lives of everyday people: downsizing, the diminished need for an unskilled work force, technological advances, information systems and the global market, and structural issues in our economy. Despite these realities, our politics still try to explain the class divide as fueled by deficits in the individual, or weak personal and family values, reflected in out-of-wedlock children and divorce. We complain that big government spends money recklessly on public programs. These attitudes of "neocapitalism" have undermined an American sense of community at every level, and "threatens our sense of solidarity with others" at a time when it is needed most (Bellah, Madsen, Sullivan, Swidler, & Tipton, 1996, p. xxx).

We are facing a national moral crisis that compares to the morass of the 1850s leading up to the Civil War. Lincoln said that slavery was wrong and that it contradicted fundamental human principles and a belief in freedom. It's possible to apply Lincoln's words about a "house divided" by slavery to economic issues: A house divided by class cannot stand either. "We believe the degree of class difference today is wrong in the same way that Lincoln believed slavery was wrong: it deprives millions of people of the ability to participate fully in society and to realize themselves as individuals. This is the festering secret that Americans would rather not face" (Bellah et al., 1996, pp. xxxiv–xxxv).

I believe that a true mark of a humanitarian society is how it treats its most vulnerable members. At the present time in America, we would certainly receive low marks in this area. Those who have accumulated great wealth face a moral choice. Those of us who are concerned can only hope that our country will somehow, collectively, make the right choice, moving from a narrow, self-centered, individual view of welfare to a broader communal belief in the importance of caring for others.

> If the members of the overclass can overcome their own anxieties they may realize that they will gain far more self-respect in belonging to an establishment than to an oligarchy. They may come to see that civic engagement—a concern for the common good, a belief that we are all members of the same body—will not only contribute to the good of the larger society but will contribute to the salvation of their souls as well. Only some larger engagement can overcome the devastating cultural and psychological narcissism of our current overclass. A return to civic membership, to commitments to community and solidarity, on the part of the overclass would be good not only for society as a whole but also for its individual members. (Bellah et al., 1996, p. xxxi)

Poverty and Social Welfare Policies

Poverty among the elderly is more widespread than in any other age group and is very high among significant subgroups, such as minorities and women (Report of the Villers Foundation, 1987). The feminization of poverty refers to the fact that women as a group are more likely to be poor, since women of all races earn less than men. Poor elderly women are likely to suffer long-term poverty and have fewer chances to increase their incomes. Despite a pervasive myth to the contrary, the elderly do not have a safety net to protect them from poverty (Report of the Villers Foundation, 1987).

Public assistance programs are intended to help the poor, but they often do little to alleviate the roots of poverty. A pervasive antiwelfare sentiment in American society isn't helping. In surveys about welfare recipients, respondents believed that the recipients were undeserving and that African-Americans were lazy (Gilens, 1999, p. 90; Pallitto, 2010, p. 165). These two deeply held beliefs are most influential in generating antiwelfare attitudes, and, in combination, produced stronger hostility to welfare (Pallitto, 2010, p. 165). Stereotypes about black people on welfare have some basis in real statistics, but to focus on race as the main issue obscures the larger issue of class. Racial discrimination is a function of class, and class transcends race in how it separates people (Hochschild, 1995).

This strong, national antiwelfare sentiment creates a kind of built-in obstacle for those trying to complete applications for assistance. Karen Gustafson (2011) believes that welfare policies, rather than supporting poor families, are intended to deter welfare use by making it difficult for people to apply and receive aid. In a process known as "churning," the federal government increased the amount of paperwork required to determine eligibility, under the welfare reforms enacted by President Richard Nixon in the 1970s. Many of the interviewees receiving benefits and profiled in Gustafson's book recounted onerous paperwork that made it confusing for them to navigate the system. In the video-recorded mock interview that follows with Betty, she shares this same frustration. She talks about having to return to the office three times, and how she was once kept waiting as long as three hours.

Although our views on social welfare often revolve around public assistance, that's only part of the story. Richard Titmuss (1965) has outlined another more comprehensive way to view welfare, one that shows how all classes of society enjoy benefits from the spectrum of social welfare policy. Titmuss, a well-known British social policy analyst, identified a three-tier system. What we think of as the social welfare system, comprising Temporary Assistance for Needy Families (TANF), food stamps, and other programs, is only one part. The other two tiers, the fiscal welfare system (e.g., numerous federal tax deductions, child care tax credits) and occupational welfare (e.g., bonuses, health insurance, pensions), although not acknowledged as such, are also welfare programs that benefit middle and upper class society.

Although Titmuss' analysis was done 50 years ago, we still need reminding of its insights and relevance today (Abramovitz, 2001; Mann, 2008). Based on a review of new data, the welfare programs Titmuss identified in his three-tier system continue to serve the interests of middle class families, wealthy households, and large corporations (Abramovitz, 2001). Instead of benefiting certain segments of the population, the goal of social policy should be to distribute wealth and services fairly across all segments of society.

History of Public Assistance Programs

There was a brief moment in the early 1960s when President Lyndon Johnson declared a "war on poverty." This sparked a welfare-rights movement led by disadvantaged families that supported the notion that the poorest Americans had a right to government assistance and a minimum standard of living (Chappell, 2010; Gustafson, 2011). The Johnson era ushered in legislation for civil rights, medical care, education, housing, and job training for the poor. It also set up the Office of Economic Opportunity (OEO) to jumpstart urban renewal, community development, drug-abuse rehabilitation, alternative programs for juvenile delinquents, and countless other solutions for wide-reaching social problems. As well intentioned as these initiatives were, unfortunately, they did little to change the structural causes of poverty (Murray, 1984).

After the Johnson era, the interest in ending poverty reversed and began trending in the opposite direction, particularly following the election of President Richard Nixon. In contrast to Johnson's war on poverty and its resulting social policies, we are now facing a time of shrinking social programs that do little to help the poor. Herbert Gans (1995) refers to this period in opposite terms, referring to the "war against the poor" characterized by antipoverty policy. Those who are in power and possess wealth justify their actions by blaming, stereotyping, and stigmatizing the poor (Gans, 1995).

President Nixon was a strong critic of welfare and spoke out against Johnson's "Great Society" in his 1968 campaign. Once in office, the Nixon administration was quick to dismantle earlier legislation including, for example, the OEO (Murray, 1984). Later, during

Ronald Reagan's presidency, there were more massive cuts to social programs, part of a conservative agenda that began an historic shift in social welfare policy (Abramovitz, 2001). Since passage of the 1988 Family Support Act, the federal government has been relinquishing responsibility for poor families (Chappell, 2010). This trend continued under President Bill Clinton with the passage of federal welfare reform legislation, known as the Personal Responsibility and Work Reconciliation Act of 1996. At that time, welfare as it previously existed was abolished and replaced by TANF.

While emphasizing a work requirement, TANF reduced welfare rolls, but these reforms did little to get poor mothers out of poverty. Instead, it only created a surplus of low-income wage jobs that ultimately served to drive everyone's wages down (Brush, 2011). This shift occurred alongside an ongoing tendency to blame the poor for their problems and focus on their bad behaviors. With the enactment of TANF also came a belief that poor people had to be policed. We have moved away from our image as a country that believed government should care for its most vulnerable to one that believes it is more important to investigate welfare fraud and police poor people (Brush, 2011; Chappell, 2010; Gustafson, 2011).

What accounts for such strong sentiments against welfare recipients and the poor? On an individual level, psychodynamic theory may explain these hypercritical attitudes as a projection of one's own vulnerability, which is preferred to be forgotten or downplayed. In other words, blaming people on public assistance for their problems is a way of projecting one's own dependent needs onto the poor. On a societal level, a social constructivist and narrative approach would look at how the dominant group in society controls knowledge and power and uses both to oppress and subordinate others. This same dominant group often controls the media and thereby helps to perpetuate discriminatory beliefs and has a strong influence on public policy. If we could stop our continued exposure to biased media depictions of devalued groups, many Americans might be challenged to empathize with the poor and endorse policies that would create "more equal and just conditions" (Johnson et al., 2009, p. 474).

Despite this period of diminishing social welfare policy, one activist rights group called Survivor's Inc. has resurrected the battle to improve the lives of poor women in the Boston area. Survivors Inc. is a group of low-income women who organize and educate around issues of poverty, welfare, and low-income survival. It is one small example of a local grassroots effort that seeks to eliminate social and economic injustice—and the difference its members can make. The organization offers training in areas such as writing, advocacy, computer skills, speaking, and leadership to help empower low-income women to be heard and gain access to resources. They do outreach with welfare offices and publish a newspaper, Survival News.

Criminalization of Poverty

There is a long tradition of treating the poor as criminals in both England and America. This attitude traces its origins, in part, to the ideologies of social Darwinism and Calvinism that blamed poor individuals for their situations, rather than looking at the inherent inequalities of capitalism (Spencer-Wood & Matthews, 2011). Prevailing English laws that made vagrancy a crime were brought to the colonies. The able-bodied poor were put in prisons and poorhouses and required to perform hard labor. Barbara Ehrenreich (2009) believes this practice continues today in cities where the police arrest poor people for crimes of begging, loitering, and sleeping in streets.

Criminalization of poverty is a term used to explain the current fervent interest in going after welfare fraud. Government welfare policies treat the poor as a "criminal class" (Karen Gustafson, 2011, p. 644). They emphasize punishment for any welfare cheating, which adds "the stigma of criminality" to the already existing stigma of poverty. Rather than showing concern for the well-being of low-income families, current welfare policies are more interested in prosecuting poor people who have been typecast as criminals.

As part of the 1996 federal welfare reforms, states were expected to be "tough on welfare" and were required to implement measures to control welfare fraud. Gustafson (2011) provides numerous examples of "criminalizing policies and practices" that stigmatize and seek to control the poor: surveillance, fingerprinting, "fugitive felon provisions," criminal prosecution of welfare fraud instead of civil administrative remedies, and excluding welfare recipients who engaged in illicit behavior in the past from eligibility. Gustafson (2011) also highlights the growing intersection between the welfare and criminal justice systems, referring to collaborative practices and shared information systems. Aggressive and increasing investigations of welfare fraud involve both the welfare offices and the criminal justice systems. Welfare recipients found guilty of fraud pay a high price that includes steep monetary penalties and permanent criminal records.

Poverty and Healthcare Policy

There is a strong relationship between poverty and poor health for people of all ages (Berkman & Syme, 1976). This is especially true for older women who generally have less money than younger women and men, and are more likely to have deteriorating health issues. So while a poor older woman's need for healthcare increases, her ability to obtain and pay for that care decreases (Belgrave, 1993, p. 195). Since life spans have increased, older women find themselves without adequate finances to pay for healthcare. Jorgensen (1993) believes that social security benefits for older adults and especially for women barely keep them above the poverty level. One of the greatest challenges facing older adults is affordability and availability of healthcare (Jorgensen, 1993, p. 201).

Aging individuals with disabilities face other challenges, especially in the right to self-direct, and retain control over their own lives (Ruggiano, 2012). Social workers and other healthcare professionals need to consider this subgroup of older adults who perhaps learned to manage their disabilities at an early age and want to stay independent in directing their care. This group mastered self-advocacy early on, and may have negative reactions when relegated to the role of patient within health and aging systems (Ruggiano, 2012). There is an opportunity that, as this group ages, they can teach other older adults about their rights and their obligation to become better advocates for their own healthcare.

Health policy usually exhibits classism, ageism, and sexism. Older women experience greater discrimination in healthcare based on these factors (Belgrave, 1993). Healthcare policy does not adequately protect older women who are more vulnerable and need more care (Belgrave, 1993; Jorgensen, 1993). Although Medicare coverage for people aged 65 and older technically provides them with health insurance, "access to health care and the quality of health care that is received are affected by the ability to pay co-payments and other out-of-pocket costs" (Belgrave, 1993, p. 193; Neugarten, 1983). Although there are insurance plans to supplement Medicare and cover these extra expenses, lower-income elderly women often can't afford them. Medicaid is a public welfare program to help the poor with healthcare, but older women may not be eligible and may be required to spend down "into poverty" to receive this assistance (Muller, 1990). This results in many older women going without necessary medical treatment because they can't afford it.

When looking at the gaps in healthcare under Medicare and the problems with Medicaid eligibility, it is not hard to understand how the potential for some form of national health insurance comes up as a remedy. Arthur Flemming, former Secretary of the Department of Health, Education, and Welfare and a former Commissioner on Aging, when interviewed by Bernice Neugarten, responded that older persons would do better under a national health insurance program than Medicare (Neugarten, 1983). Flemming points to additional Medicare weaknesses such as lack of benefits covering eye care, dental work, and prescription drugs.

Mental health and substance abuse treatments for older adults are often inadequate and are further examples of age discrimination. Flemming (Neugarten, 1983) in particular contends that the mental health needs of the elderly are not met and result from institutional ageism. Mental health professionals have tended either to show complete apathy or to turn their backs on providing services to older adults. The rationale is that, with limited resources, using funds on children and younger adults is a better investment. Also, with the media attention on Alzheimer's disease and dementia, there is an assumption that old people are or will be demented (Kimmel, 1988) and not able to benefit from the services.

As the population of older adults increases, especially with the Baby Boom generation reaching retirement age, experts predict growing numbers of individuals with alcohol- and drug-related problems (Consensus Panel Members, Center for Substance Abuse, 2001). Although alcohol and drug use generally decreases with age, these issues are expected to be important health problems for the current cohort of aging adults. Related issues that might crop up and require support include elder abuse, neglect, and homelessness. Overall, this will demand greater societal and professional awareness of and empathy for the problem, multidisciplinary collaboration, cultural competence, effective treatments protocols, and professional training (Imbody & Vandsburger, 2011).

To deal with ageism and age-related health issues effectively, we need to look at the role of education. Often, educational curricula about aging are overlooked or given little attention in schools (Kimmel, 1988; Neugarten, 1983). However, when students take courses in adult development and aging, the results are positive, showing that their attitudes about older adults improve (Boswell, 2012; Cottle & Glover, 2007). Studies also confirm that there is a significant relationship between education about aging and interest in pursuing a career with older adults (Boswell, 2012; Cummings et al., 2003; Harris & Dollinger, 2001).

The problem of ageism in mental health services does not occur just in America. It is well documented in England as well. Due to increasing isolation and fewer social supports related to aging, there is a recognized need for more outreach and education about healthy lifestyles for the older population in England, who often struggle with undiagnosed depression (Davies, 2011; Parish, 2009). Despite the prevalence of mental health problems in people over 65, access to services is still identified as a key issue (Parish, 2009). Another barrier to properly treating older patients is the false assumption that mental health services for the elderly are only about dementia, ignoring other severe and enduring clinical issues (Collier, 2005).

Age Discrimination in the Workplace

We live in an aging society in which older adults make up a larger percentage of the world's population than ever before. Advances in medical science are allowing people to live longer, and this "age-quake or silver tsunami will transform society and the global workforce" (Brownell & Kelly, 2013, xi) in new ways. The following passage from Patricia Brownell and James Kelly's text (2013) reminds us that we must respond to mistreatment of older workers. Their book on ageism in the workforce can guide employers, managers, researchers, and policy makers to understand the implications of an older workforce and to advocate for policy that is sensitive to the human rights of our aging population.

> Worker, workforce managers, work environments, and organizational cultures have not yet accommodated to these transformative socio-demographic changes. As a result, intentional and unintentional ageist practices pervade the contemporary work-force. The aging of the workforce has generated a growing body of policy responses and these require a new understanding of the roles of older adults in the workforce. Employers and managers will also have to devise new remedies to change ageist values and prevent mistreatment of older workers (Brownell & Kelly, 2013, xi–xii).

Age discrimination in the workplace can begin as early as 50, when certain workers are forced out of long-held positions in preference for younger, cheaper workers, or as a result of downsizing. Many of the unemployed in their 50s and 60s find it challenging to get hiring managers to take them seriously when new positions become available. With the current economic crisis, some older Americans must work longer as they witness their retirement funds decreasing in value and realize they can no longer afford to stop working. However, age discrimination makes it difficult for them to find, or keep, jobs.

Ageism was recognized as a social problem and addressed by Congress when it enacted the Age Discrimination in Employment Act (ADEA) in 1967. The intent of ADEA was to promote hiring practices based on ability rather than age, to prohibit arbitrary age dis-crimination, and to help employers and workers resolve workplace issues related to age. Many argue that the ADEA has been ineffective in protecting the civil and economic rights of older people (Powell, 2010; Rothenberg & Gardner, 2011). Of the 16,134 cases brought to court and resolved in 2007 for age discrimination, only 1% was successfully mediated in favor of the employee (Rothenberg & Gardner, 2011). In spite of ADEA, a majority of older adults still report experiencing age-based discrimination during their careers (Ory et al., 2003).

Ageism and age-related abuse in the workplace deny basic human rights to older adults "through the use of negative stereotypes, bullying and economic oppression" (Powell, 2010, p. 657). Attitudes and behaviors toward older workers reflect significant bias when compared to younger employees regarding competence, attractiveness, and behavior (Kite et al., 2005). Studies have found harmful stereotypes of older workers, who are described as senile, slow, unproductive, hard to train, resistant to change, and less flexible (Lahey, 2005; Roscigno et al., 2007; Raushenbach et al., 2012; Weiss & Maurer, 2004). Older adults are more likely than younger workers to be forced into retirement (Chan & Stevens, 2004).

Ageism is pervasive in American society and linked to social and economic exclusion, and discriminatory practices in all forms of healthcare. With the Baby Boom generation aging, there will be more pressure to tackle the problem of ageism, and this has implications for age-related social policy. Existing policies have proved ineffective in solving age discrimination. Since all of us will become old whether we like it or not, we must come to terms with what it means to age. Asian cultures that respect their elders' wisdom and value close relationships with them are examples of different, more humane ways to treat older adults (Gupta & Pillai, 2002). It may be time to let go of our attachment to individualism and capitalism, and embrace a sense of community that cares for all members of society.

Setting: Public Assistance Office

The mention of public assistance usually conjures the image of an impersonal bureaucracy with an abundance of complicated rules and overworked employees awash in piles of paperwork. As you read excerpts from this transcript, notice how the language of the worker reflects this bureaucratic picture. The conversation between Ann and Betty takes you the reader into this organizational maze, which can be a nightmare to some clients.

Karen Gustafson (2009) has identified a trend in our welfare system toward more bureaucracy, starting in the 1970s under the welfare reforms of President Nixon. Where before social workers visited the homes of welfare recipients, now those workers were replaced by office caseworkers who processed routine paperwork. In a phenomenon referred to earlier as "churning," the federal government imposed stricter verification requirements and increased paperwork on welfare clients. Many eligible low-income families who could not keep up with the paperwork were denied benefits (Casey & Mannix, 1989).

This is true in Betty's case. She is overwhelmed by the demands placed on her for documentation and confused with the application process. Her worker realizes this and suggests assigning her to an advocate to help her navigate the complicated system.

Case Description

Situation

Betty is a 70-year-old woman applying for benefits at the local public assistance office in Boston, Massachusetts. This is her third time visiting the office, and she is angry and frustrated with the lack of help she has received. She describes the workers as "snippy" and feels they have treated her poorly, making her wait as long as three hours. Now, she is demanding to see a supervisor.

Precipitating Event for Social Work Intervention

Betty is facing eviction because she can't pay her rent. She has worked as a babysitter, but recently her hours were reduced because, as the children got older, the family didn't need her as much. Employed only part time, Betty cannot afford to pay living expenses on her present salary. She has always worked for herself taking care of children, and her employers never paid into social security for her.

First Excerpt from Transcript and Process Recording

The first excerpt represents the beginning of the interview and includes the introduction, the beginning stage of engagement, and the problem definition. As Ann, the social worker, tries to assess the situation, she collects data by asking questions and clarifying the problem. Early in the interview, the worker is sensitive to issues of diversity and is sad to see how someone of Betty's advancing age has to worry about being evicted and thrown out in the street. As she listens to Betty's story, Ann shows empathy for her situation.

There are many moments in the interview when Ann practices the skill of self-reflection. She is aware of her inner dialogue and personal reactions to Betty's story. She finds it difficult to hear how much her client struggles to make ends meet. During the beginning phase of the work, Ann listens to Betty ventilate and voice her frustration about the office staff mistreating her, having her babysitting hours cut, and concerns that the "mean" landlord will kick her out on the street.

Two theories are identified in the first excerpt, psychodynamic and narrative. The psychodynamic approach employs ego-sustaining interventions, including ventilation and sustainment. Ventilation encourages the client to express feelings about a problem for relief. Sustainment promotes a positive client–worker relationship. By paying attention to language and how Betty tells her story, the worker uses a narrative approach, which provides her with more depth and meaning to understand Betty's experience. Her use of words like "evicted," and being "out on the street," gives us insight into how desperate Betty feels.

Content	Observation/Reflection	Analysis of Intervention: Theories and Practice
1. Ann: Hi Betty, I'm Ann. I'm one of the directors here. You're having a problem I guess? What's the matter?	I notice that Betty is very upset and agitated.	Practice: Engagement. Communication skills. Introduction and problem definition.
2. Betty: Oh yeah, I've been...well it's my third day coming here. I mean I came in two days ago and I wanted some help, because I can't...I'm gonna get evicted probably and I can't pay the rent and I asked a worker for some help...and so she said I had	I understand how frustrated and angry Betty is as I listen to her experience. This is the part of the job I hate, when I can see how much clients struggle to get the help they deserve, especially for someone at her age. It shouldn't be so	Theory: Psychodynamic ventilation. Narrative: Betty's language, "nasty and snippy workers," reflects how poorly treated she feels. Also use of word "boss" implying bureaucracy and hierarchy, issues of power.

(Continued)

Content	Observation/Reflection	Analysis of Intervention: Theories and Practice
to get a letter from the woman who hired me because I you know I do part-time work as a babysitter and I have to get a letter from that woman and I have to get a letter from my landlord...and so I went home and I got the letter, I didn't want to, but I did...and I came back yesterday and I gave the letter to a worker and the worker was very snippy she was really nasty, she didn't treat me right so I said I wanna see another worker so I'm here today and I wanna I've been waiting for two hours and I wanna you know...are you the boss?	hard for them. It's good that she can vent some of her frustration with me.	Practice: Self-reflection, sensitivity to diversity (aging).
3. Ann: Yes I am...I'm the boss. Now, when you came three days ago did you actually do the application form already?	It's important for her to know that I am the boss and will take charge of the situation.	Practice: Communication skills, clarification of role and questioning.
4. Betty: No I just told her that I wanted some money, and I needed money.		
5. Ann: So no application was ever taken from you?	I am wondering if an application was even started.	Practice: Communication skill, clarification of problem.
6. Betty: Well she talked to me for a little bit then she told me, yeah, she put something in her computer, I don't know what she was sitting at her computer.	It's hard for clients to understand the process.	
7. Ann: So you don't know if you have an application filed at this time?	I'll check this later. Let me start at the beginning with her and figure out what she's eligible for.	Practice: Communication skill, clarification of problem.
8. Betty: No I don't.		
9. Ann: Are you currently getting food stamps?		Practice: Data collection.
10. Betty: No, no, no.		
11. Ann: Or any benefits?		Practice: Data collection.
12. Betty: No, no, no.		
13. Ann: So how have you been getting along every day?	I can imagine that each day is hard for her to get by on what little she has.	Practice: Data collection. Communications skills, questioning, open-ended question.
14. Betty: Well I've been having a hard time. I've been...you know I work part time like I said, you know, so I get some money from babysitting but my rent, my rent is...		
15. Ann: Are you paying full rent or do you have a subsidized rent?		Practice: Data Collection. Communications skill, questioning.

(Continued)

Content	Observation/Reflection	Analysis of Intervention: Theories and Practice
16. Betty: No, no, no. I'm supposed to pay full rent and I was able to do it when I worked full time, but now she cut my hours because, you know, the kid she does, you know, the kid's bigger now the kid doesn't need me so much and so she cut my hours. So I don't have that much money and the landlord said he would evict me if I didn't pay the rent.	I can see how very upset and desperate she is about her situation.	Theory: Psychodynamic, ventilation. Practice: Communication skill, listening empathically.
17. Ann: Ok, Ok, and how many months in arrears are you in the rent? What do you owe the landlord now?		Practice: Data Collection. Communications skill, questioning.
18. Betty: I owe him for two months.		
18(a). Ann: Two months.		
19. Betty: He's not very nice. He's nasty too he says he's gonna kick me out if I don't pay the rent and I'm gonna be on the street.	She must be living with such fear of what's going to happen to her.	Theory: Psychodynamic, ventilation. Narrative, Betty's words show us how her desperate her situation is; she refers to landlord as "nasty," "going to kick her out," and she'll be "on the street." Practice: Communication skill, listening empathically.
20. Ann: Oh OK. Well let's not worry about that right now today, because today we have to take care of getting you applied you have to apply today if that hasn't already happened. Now do you have any dependents living with you?	Let's not go there right now. I need to get the basic information to complete this application.	Practice: Data collection. Communications skills, holding to focus, questioning.
21. Betty: No, no, no, no. I don't.		
22. Ann: So it's just you?		Practice: Data collection. Communications skills, clarification, questioning.
23. Betty: I don't have any family. If I don't get money here I'll be out on the street.	How sad to feel there's no one she can depend on and to worry about being on the streets.	
24. Ann: Oh OK, and you've never applied for social security because you were working.		Practice: Communication, clarification.
25. Betty: Well I couldn't get social security because I was doing babysitting and babysitters can't get social security.		
26. Ann: OK, and you don't have any disability that you know of?		Practice: Data collection. Communication skill, questioning.
27. Betty: No, no, no. I don't think so.		
28. Ann: Up until babysitting you've been working all along?		Practice: Data collection. Communication skill, clarification.

Reflection of First Process Recording and Discussion of Practice Skills and Theories Used in Intervention

Communication Skills

The social worker uses various communication skills during the intervention and reflection upon the client's statements. Below is a list of communication skills, their definitions, and the box in which they were used.

Box 1

Introduction: At the beginning of the first meeting with the client, the social worker welcomes the client, tries to make the client comfortable, and tunes in to her own and the client's initial feelings about the first meeting.

Beginning stage of engagement: Engagement is the initial step in the problem-solving method and involves building a relationship and an alliance with the client and defining the problem.

In box 1, Ann introduces herself to Betty and engages her in defining the problem.

Box 1

Problem definition: This is a collaborative process between the social worker and the client; they come to an agreement about what the problem is and what they will work on together.

In box 1, Ann asks Betty directly what the problem is and begins the process of exploring the issues.

Box 3

Clarification of role: The social worker helps the client understand what services the agency offers, and what her role as social worker will be. There are times when the client needs reminding that the work is collaborative; it is the social worker's job to facilitate not direct the process.

In box 3, Ann clarifies to Betty that she is the boss. This is important to Betty, because she is frustrated with how other workers have treated her. This gives Betty more confidence that Ann has the power to help her.

Boxes 3, 13, 15, 17, 20, 22, 26

Questioning: This is a way of gaining more information about a client's situation. There are many different kinds of questions, for example, open- and closed-ended questions and reflexive questions. Questioning is often used in assessment as part of data collection.

In box 3, Ann begins to question Betty to understand whether she has completed the application form for assistance.

In box 13, Ann asks an open-ended question to understand how Betty has been getting along without any assistance. In Box 15, Ann asks a closed-ended question to find out whether Betty pays full or subsidized rent.

In boxes 17, 20, 22, and 26, Ann continues to collect data by asking questions about how much money Betty owes her landlord and whether there are dependents living with her. She also asks Betty whether she has any disabilities.

Boxes 5, 7, 22, 24, 28

Clarification of problem: When sitting with a client, the social worker gathers details that further explain the nature of the problem. This is an ongoing process in which the worker collects new information and keeps an open mind to alternative interpretations and perceptions.

In boxes 5 and 7, Ann does not understand whether Betty has filled out an application based on her last answers; Ann's trying to get to the bottom of that. In Boxes 22 and 24, Ann clarifies that Betty lives alone and has never applied for social security. In Box 28, Ann clarifies that Betty has been babysitting all along up to now.

Boxes 16, 19

Showing empathy: The social worker maintains a nonjudgmental stance or remains neutral. The worker need not totally understand the client's situation, but she must show that she is trying to grasp what the client is feeling or experiencing. The social worker might say, "Tell me more about what your experience was" or "I want to understand more about what this means from your perspective."

In boxes 16 and 19, Ann listens empathically as Betty shares how difficult life has become since the family she babysits for has cut her hours. Betty is worried about being on the streets because she can't pay her rent, and Ann is sensitive to the fear this causes her.

Box 20

Holding to focus: This is when the social worker helps the client stay on the topic under discussion. There may be times when, if a client is uncomfortable with the conversation, he may try to change the subject. This could also happen if a client goes off on a tangent or gets distracted. In these cases, the worker tries to redirect the client back to the topic.

In box 20, Ann wants to focus on collecting the information she needs to determine eligibility, so she moves the discussion away from Betty's fear of getting kicked out on the street to the questions she needs to ask for the application.

Other Practice Skills Used

Box 2

Self-reflection: The skill of self-reflection is an important part of professional practice. Social workers are expected to engage in personal reflection and self-correction to assure continual professional development (CSWE, 2008). Practitioners need to understand themselves on a deep level that includes deciphering their values, reactions to others, the influence of family-of-origin patterns, and basic assumptions about culture and difference. It requires setting aside time to ponder the meaning of clinical work—how our personal experiences and biases may trigger reactions to clients that are unwarranted. We learn a lot about ourselves from doing practice; sometimes, we need outside help to sort out what issues that arise during our work.

In box 2, as Ann listens to Betty, she reflects on how she hates to hear how much clients are struggling to get by and wishes their lives were easier.

Box 2

Sensitivity to diversity: Social workers must show openness and sensitivity to every client's culture and ethnicity. There are many other ways clients are diverse: class, age, color, race, religion, gender, sexual orientation, immigration status, disability, mental or physical health, and appearance. Although social workers engage clients around diversity and appreciate difference in people's lives, society may marginalize and discriminate others based on difference. It is important to acknowledge the impact of this oppression on people's lives.

In box 2, Ann is aware of Betty's advancing age and how this puts her more at risk.

Boxes 9, 11, 13, 15, 17, 20, 22, 26, 28

Data collection: In the data collection stage, the social worker explores the problem in more depth. This involves getting information from multiple sources about the client's life and situation, and about the social systems that may impact the problem. Sources might include client records, bio/psycho/social history, self-assessment tools, and other professionals who have worked with the client. Also, through interviewing the client, the worker elicits information about the client, her perception of the problem, her social network, and her strengths. The social worker may construct a genogram or eco-map with the client in order to better understand the family history and social network. In the boxes described below, Ann is collecting data for use in Betty's application to determine eligibility for benefits.

In boxes 9, 11, and 13, Ann tries to learn if Betty already receives any benefits and to understand how she has been getting along.

In boxes 15, 17, 20, and 22, Ann wants to know if Betty pays full rent or is subsidized, how much she is behind in her rent, and whether she has dependents living with her.

In boxes 26 and 28, Ann asks whether Betty has any disabilities, and whether she has been working up until now.

Theories Used in Intervention
Psychodynamic Theory
Boxes 2, 16, 17, 19

Ventilation: Ventilation is one of the ego-sustaining interventions that encourages the client to express feelings about a problem for relief.

In the following boxes, Betty shows how upset and anxious she is about her situation and finds an outlet for venting those feelings with the worker.

In box 2, Betty conveys frustration and anger about her experience applying for assistance.

In box 16, Betty uses ventilation when she explains that because her employers cut her babysitting hours, she doesn't earn enough money to pay her rent, and she is afraid she will be evicted.

In boxes 17 and 19, Betty is ventilating about her landlord who is nasty and is going to kick her out of her apartment if she doesn't pay her rent.

Narrative Theory

Box 2

Betty describes workers as "nasty" and "snippy" to reflect how poorly treated she felt. Her words show frustration with the system, how she is kept waiting for hours, goes from one worker to another, and is sent away to get documentation. You feel how powerless Betty feels. She wants to see the boss, implying a sense of hierarchy, and hopes that this person will rectify the situation. This language reminds the worker of how impersonal and disempowering bureaucracy is.

Box 19

Betty's choice of words shows how desperate her situation is. We understand better how "nasty" her landlord is when she says he's going to "kick" her out, and then picturing her "on the street."

Second Excerpt from Transcript and Process Recording

The second excerpt stands out for two challenging moments, value conflicts that surface between the client and worker. It starts in box 29 when Betty refers to "these welfare cheats who sit on their butts all day…they're sitting on their butts all day and I'm not getting anything." She refers to liberals and the government helping others, including illegal immigrants, but not their "own people," like Betty. Ann finds herself in an ethical dilemma. Although Betty is her client, Ann needs to confront these stereotypes and derogatory statements about the other clients in the office applying for assistance. Ann understands Betty's frustration and shame about having to ask for help. At the same time she must stop Betty from taking her anger out on people who are also poor and disenfranchised. She provides Betty with information and helps her to see another perspective.

The second challenging moment starts in box 37 when Betty notices a policeman in the office looking at her and becomes agitated by his presence. She is worried that he will arrest her or, worse, shoot her, and defends herself to the worker saying she is not a criminal. In her narrative, Betty brings up the notion of criminalization of the poor by saying, "they treat the poor like criminals." Ann reassures Betty, spelling out the reason for the police. Ann also tries to contain Betty's emotional reaction by asking her to relax while she explains the situation.

There are three theories used in the second excerpt: psychodynamic, cognitive, and narrative. The psychodynamic approach makes sense of Betty's projective identification in her attack on other clients asking for assistance. It helps the social worker understand the shame that Betty must feel as a vulnerable, poor, older person asking for money. Betty is a proud, independent woman who has supported herself up until now by babysitting. Her fear of what the police will do, even shoot her, may be projections of her anger. Betty uses ventilation to express her resentment for welfare cheats, people sitting on their butts; and for the system, the government and liberals who give immigrants assistance but not her.

The worker also uses cognitive theory and cognitive restructuring to challenge Betty's false assumptions about welfare recipients and the need for police in the office. Narrative theory continues to provide the worker with insight into Betty's experience and what things mean to her. Her derogatory words about welfare clients show Ann the shame Betty feels now that she is the one asking for help. Similarly, the words Betty uses when she reacts to the police illustrate how she feels like a criminal by applying for assistance.

Content	Observation/Reflection	Analysis of Intervention: Theories and Practice
29. Betty: I've been working all my life. I'm not like one of these welfare cheats who sit on their butts all day. I've been working you know those other people in the office you know they're here for welfare they're sitting on their butts all day and I'm not getting anything.	It looks like Betty believes in the welfare stereotype of lazy cheats sitting on their butts, having a free ride.	Theory: Psychodynamic, ventilation. Narrative theory, use of words like "welfare cheats," sitting on their butts" to refer to welfare recipients.
30. Ann: Well, I know and I see your frustration but you know everyone's here because maybe the other people out there sitting or they may have been working at some point and came into hard times like yourself because that's what happens. I think when you come into the office a lot of people have the feeling that you know they're not getting treated right because they bring a lot of shame with it because they have to come here, but that's what the system is for. So, I don't know why your worker didn't describe or explain to you the application process and I'm very frustrated like you right now because we don't even know if you've applied but what we will do is once we find out about your application process we'll go back to the day you first came in to apply and that will be your start date we'll get any money owed to you back those days, alright.	It drives me crazy that clients like Betty buy into the stereotype of people on welfare. I can't let her get away with saying this. I need to confront her biases. She must be feeling shame about being here. It seems like she is projecting her disgust about applying for assistance on to clients in the office.	Theory: Psychodynamic, defense of projective identification. Cognitive theory, cognitive restructuring, challenging assumptions about welfare recipients. Practice: Self-reflectiion. Communication skill, reflecting back feelings, confrontation and challenging moment, acknowledging value conflict, helping client to see another perspective, reassuring client.
31. Betty: Well, what kind of money will you give me?	Now we have to deal with the hard reality of how little I can offer.	
32. Ann: Ok, so depending on what you're eligible for you have to be, you know, hit the requirements for the federal guidelines for social security so you have to be over that age, and if you have any other disability, other than that if you have no dependents, there is no money available for you unfortunately.	Sometimes I feel like such a bureaucrat and end up in the position of telling people what they're not entitled to get instead of giving needed assistance.	Theory: Narrative, words used reflect images of bureaucracy, such as eligible, requirements, federal guidelines. Practice: Self-reflection. Communication skills, information-giving.

(Continued)

Content	Observation/Reflection	Analysis of Intervention: Theories and Practice
33. Betty: Well, the government gives all this money to the liberals I don't know why I can't get some. I mean they get it all and they don't do anything for their own people	Here we go again. I wish she would stop talking about liberals and welfare cheats. I'm aware of reacting to her stereotypes again. I need to focus on understanding what it means for her to be in this office. It seems like she is projecting again.	Theory: Psychodynamic, ventilation, defense of projection. Narrative, Betty's language shows how unfairly treated she feels. Practice: Self-reflection.
34. Ann: I know I know.	It's hard for her to ask for help.	Practice: Communication skill, showing empathy.
35. Betty: I mean I'm a citizen and those people are just coming in illegally and getting all this money and why can't the government help its own people.	How can I get her off of dwelling on others getting assistance and focus on getting her help?	Theory: Narrative, Betty's language continues to reflect how unfair she feels the system is. Psychodynamic, ventilation, defense of projection.
36. Ann: I know you're frustrated about that but there are certain programs where certain people qualify for certain things and the government doesn't let anybody go hungry.	This sounds a little bureaucratic and impersonal. Also, it's not really true—I do see people not getting help and going hungry. I want to convey that I understand her frustration, won't let her go hungry.	Theory: Narrative, words like certain programs, government and eligibility continue to reflect impersonal, bureaucratic images. Practice: Communication skills, empathy, reassuring client, information-giving.
37. Betty: Why is the policeman looking at me? Is he gonna arrest me? I'm not a criminal.	Betty appears more agitated, her voice is louder and her gestures are more aggressive.	Theory: Narrative, words such as policeman, criminal equate welfare with crime.
38. Ann: Oh, I know Betty you're not.	How sad that so many clients are made to feel like criminals for asking for assistance.	Communication skill: Reassuring client.
39. Betty: So, why then, why do I need a prisoner....why do I need a policeman?	She is becoming more upset and having trouble speaking.	Theory: Narrative, use of words, like prisoner, policeman continue association of welfare with criminal justice system.
40. Ann: Ok I just want you to relax just a minute, so I can explain to you why the officer is nearby. The officer is nearby because first of all your voice is raised and your escalated and they don't know if you're gonna strike at me or anything.	Betty is attracting attention because of her loud, angry voice and gestures. I need to help her calm down and de-escalate the situation.	Theory: Cognitive, cognitive restructuring, helping Betty to understand police presence. Communication skill: giving client feedback, challenging moment, containment, information-giving.

(Continued)

Content	Observation/Reflection	Analysis of Intervention: Theories and Practice
41. Betty: Oh so you think I'm gonna throw like my cane?	Her cane may look like a weapon to the policeman. I bet she would like to throw her cane now, but I don't feel any threat from her.	Theory: Psychodynamic, ventilation.
42. Ann: Well, some people do get mad enough and do throw their canes at me.	She needs to understand that the cane can be used to attack a worker.	Theory: Cognitive. Practice: Communication skills, information-giving.
43. Betty: Well I can see why, I can see why.	She identifies with some clients' frustration and anger.	Theory: Psychodynamic, ventilation.
44. Ann: Well it is and there's a very.... it's a very frustrating situation, this process is terrible to navigate especially to navigate alone, you go from one person to the next, you don't understand why your worker's changed, there's no explanation...it's a bureaucratic nightmare but people do need assistance and we're going to get you what you need today...so that today you go forward knowing where you are in the process and what benefits are available to you...the officer is gonna stand by unfortunately because of situations and the time that we're in with the government and people with difficult times...they are armed, they're armed officers and they are scheduled to be here.	This has been so hard for her to be here. She seems very proud and she doesn't like being in the position of asking for help. This application process is so difficult for clients to understand. Being shuffled around from one person to another makes it worse. The officer triggers her feeling like a criminal, stealing money from the government. What a system.	Theory: Psychodynamic, ego sustaining. Cognitive, cognitive restructuring, confronting assumptions. Narrative, use of words bureaucratic nightmare, process, benefits, navigate refer to welfare as bureaucracy. Practice: Showing empathy, reassuring client, clarification of role of officer.
45. Betty: Well they can shoot me.	She is afraid of the policeman. I wish we didn't need to have police in the office. It can be frightening for clients and scare others away.	Theory: Psychodynamic, ventilation. Narrative, Betty uses words like shoot, prisoner, criminal to show how vulnerable she is feeling.
46. Ann: Well I don't think they're gonna shoot you. Betty now c'mon unless you act up. Let's see what's gonna happen, but no, our officers don't pull their guns or anything else, but they are here in case any situation gets out of control, and we're also what you call the city police as well.	I wonder if she would like to shoot someone. She is angry about being in this position.	Theory: Cognitive, cognitive restructuring, confronting false assumptions. Psychodynamic: defense of projection. Narrative, continue use of words that are metaphors for crime: shoot, officers, guns, outs of control, city police. Practice: Communication skill, reassuring client, information-giving.

(Continued)

Content	Observation/Reflection	Analysis of Intervention: Theories and Practice
47. Betty: Well they treat the poor like criminals don't they?	She's right here. We don't treat poor people well. It reminds me of readings in graduate school on criminalization of welfare.	Theory: Psychodynamic, ventilation. Narrative, use of word criminal to describe how a poor person feels. Practice: Self-reflection.
48. Ann: Well I think sometimes people feel like that when they come here they do, but sometimes the workers feel unsafe with some of the clients that come in that are facing extraordinary time or are off medicine and they can sometimes act out and be very aggressive and because of the numbers that come through here we have to keep officers in the building, so they're not gonna go away and they're not here to you know cause you any problems but let's see what we can do for you today to get you moved on because I mean I feel your frustration but you don't know who your worker was three days ago, can you recall who your worker was.	She seems to be calming down. I want to refocus her and concentrate on getting her assistance.	Theory: Cognitive, explaining system to Betty. Practice: Communication skill, empathy, information-giving, helping client see another perspective, reassuring client, holding to focus.

Reflection of Second Process Recording and Discussion of Practice Skills and Theories Used in Intervention

Communication Skills

Box 30

Reflecting back feelings: This is when the social worker gives a short response back to the client that mirrors the feeling the worker heard the client express. It is used to let the client know the worker is listening. In box 30, the worker reflects back to Betty her feelings of frustration about waiting so long at the office without getting help. Betty feels she has worked hard all her life and deserves better treatment.

Box 30

Confrontation: Confrontation is used by the social worker when there are inconsistencies between what the client has said and what is known to be true. The social worker believes it's best if the client comes to terms with this, faces the discrepancy in light of the facts. Workers can use confrontation to question a client's behavior that is harmful to the client. Also, a worker may confront a client's false assumptions or biases. In box 30, Ann challenges Betty's false and derogatory statements about welfare recipients "being cheats" and "on their butts all day."

Boxes 30, 40

Challenging moment: There may be times during an interview that are uncomfortable for both the social worker and the client. At these times, the social worker needs to contain both her feelings and the client's feelings. The social worker sits with these feelings and tries to understand them with the client. This can be hard to do, and many beginning social workers want to apologize or avoid pursuing uncomfortable subjects.

In box 30, Ann is challenged when Betty makes derogatory comments about welfare clients. She is confronted with a value conflict that she must address with Betty. In box 40, Betty gets upset about the policeman looking at her, and Ann is challenged to get the situation under control to prevent Betty from becoming more agitated.

Boxes 30, 48

Helping client to see another perspective: When clients can only see the problem from their own point of view, the social worker's task is to expand their understanding or perception of the problem. This may include discussing how other people think about or see the issue at hand.

In box 30, Ann helps Betty see that the clients in the welfare office are struggling and have come upon hard times, like her. In box 48, Ann explains to Betty why they need a police officer in the office. Instead of seeing the officer as threatening and out to arrest the clients, Ann presents another perspective to Betty: that the officer is there to protect the workers from clients who become aggressive.

Boxes 30, 36, 38, 44, 46, 48

Reassuring client: At times, the social worker needs to allay a client's anxiety by supporting her efforts to change or accept new resources.

In box 30, Ann reassures Betty that she is going to find out about her application. Ann tells her that she will make sure Betty gets the money owed her, starting from the first day she came in to the office.

In box 36, Ann reassures Betty that she will receive aid, and that the government will not let anyone go hungry. In boxes 38, 46, and 48, Ann reassures Betty that she is not a criminal, and that the policeman will not arrest her and certainly not shoot her. In box 44, Ann lets Betty know that she will help her get what she needs before she leaves that day.

Boxes 32, 36, 40, 42, 46, 48

Information-giving: Information-giving means informing the client about the social agency, the problem, and the resources for change. In Boxes 32 and 36, Ann explains to Betty the eligibility requirements for public assistance.

In boxes 40, 42, 46, and 48, Ann helps Betty understand the reason for the police officer, and that sometimes clients get mad enough to throw their canes at her. She points out that the officer will not give Betty any trouble unless she acts up. The officer is only present because sometimes clients get aggressive and threaten workers.

Boxes 34, 36, 44, 48

Showing empathy: The social worker maintains a non-judgmental stance or remains neutral. The worker need not totally understand the client's situation, but she must show that she is trying to grasp what the client is feeling or experiencing.

In boxes 34, 36, 44 and 48, Ann shows empathy for Betty's situation and her frustration with the slow process of getting assistance. She appreciates what it must be like for Betty to navigate such a complicated system and realizes it's akin to a "bureaucratic nightmare" for Betty.

Box 40

Giving client feedback: This is when the social worker finds an opportunity to provide the client with information about his behavior and its effect on him or on other people. It can prove difficult, because the client may not want to hear or accept what the social worker is saying.

In box 40, Ann gives Betty feedback about how she is drawing the policeman's attention to her. She is making Betty aware of her behavior. When Betty raises her voice and escalates the situation, the policeman may wonder if she is going to strike Ann with her cane.

Box 40

Containment: There are two types of containment situations, one in which the social worker contains herself from speaking or acting, and another when the worker contains the client from spinning out of control. In the first case, as a client begins to tell his story, the worker may have an urge to "help" before he completes the whole story. If the worker can contain herself and not speak too soon, the client can finish the story and express feelings without interruption. In the second case, when a client begins to get out of control or expresses too much emotion, the worker will intervene to calm the client down. In box 40, Ann tries to contain Betty's behavior and calm her. She asks Betty to relax for a minute while she explains why the policeman is looking at her.

Box 44

Clarification of role: The social worker helps the client understand what services the agency offers and what her role as social worker will be. In box 44, the worker clarifies the role of the police officer to help reassure Betty that he poses no threat to her.

Box 48

Holding to focus: This is when the social worker helps the client to stay on the topic under discussion. In box 48, Ann wants to move the conversation away from concern about the policeman and back to focusing on how to expedite Betty's application.

Other Practice Skills Used

Boxes 30, 32, 33, 47

Self-reflection: The skill of self-reflection is an important part of professional practice. Social workers are expected to engage in personal reflection and self-correction to assure continual professional development (CSWE, 2008).

In boxes 30 and 33, Ann is aware that she is annoyed with Betty's false assumptions about people applying for assistance. This goes against Ann's personal and professional values. She knows she has to speak up about Betty's prejudicial remarks.

In box 32, Ann sees a conflict when she has to play the role of bureaucrat and sometimes deny people benefits, especially when the rules seem unjust.

In box 47, as she listens to Betty's comment about how the poor are treated like criminals, Ann reflects on the truth of this statement. It reminds her of readings she did on this subject in graduate school.

Theories Used in Intervention
Psychodynamic Theory
Boxes 29, 33, 35

Ventilation: Ventilation is one of the ego sustaining interventions that encourages the client to express feelings about a problem for relief.

In boxes 29, 33 and 35, Betty vents her anger about the welfare system. She feels she has worked all her life, unlike "welfare cheats" who sit "on their butts all day," and should be treated better. She doesn't understand why she can't get some money.

Boxes 30, 41, 45, 47

Projection: This defense mechanism unconsciously protects an individual from unacceptable thoughts or feelings by making him believe that it's another person having those thoughts.

In box 30, Ann interprets Betty's reaction to people on welfare as projection. Ann reflects that part of Betty feels disgusted with herself for needing assistance, and she carries shame about asking for help. She projects her vulnerability and disgust onto the other clients.

In box 41, Ann identifies projection again when Betty questions Ann about whether she thinks Betty will throw her cane. Ann wonders if Betty is defending against an actual wish to throw her cane out of anger and frustration at her treatment.

In box 45, it's possible Betty is projecting her own wish to shoot someone, and in box 47, she may be using projection to defend against feeling like a criminal for asking for assistance.

Box 44

Sustainment: This takes place within the client-worker relationship and includes activities by the social worker to show interest, understanding, acceptance, and confidence in the client.

In box 44, Ann uses sustainment by expressing empathy and support for Betty's situation. Ann validates Betty's feelings of frustration and is sincere when she tells Betty that she will get what she needs.

Cognitive Theory
Boxes 30, 40, 42, 44, 48

Cognitive restructuring: This describes interventions aimed at helping clients change their belief systems. In boxes 30 and 40, Ann uses cognitive restructuring to challenge Betty's false assumptions about welfare clients and why it's necessary to have a policeman in the office.

In boxes 42, 44 and 48, Ann educates Betty about how some clients become aggressive and do throw canes at her. She uses reason and cognitive processes to help Betty understand more clearly the need for a policeman.

Narrative Theory
Boxes 29, 32, 33, 35, 37, 39, 44, 45, 47

Narrative theory explains how Betty is feeling through her use of metaphors and language. The second excerpt is full of dramatic examples and descriptive words that show how Betty links welfare to an unfair system. She also makes a strong connection between welfare and the criminal justice system. The term "criminalization of poverty" appears in the professional literature to explain the trend for public assistance offices to get tough on welfare recipients and go after fraud. In the following examples, I concentrate on Betty's language, and her emphasis on the unfairness of welfare and its connection to the criminal justice system.

In box 29, Betty refers to "welfare cheats" who sit on "their butts all day." She continues to show her anger at the unfairness of the system in box 33 by saying the government gives all the "money to the liberals." She implies they give money to immigrants and none to "their own people." In box 35, Betty says again that the government gives money to illegal immigrants.

In box 37, Betty asks if the policeman is going to arrest her and protests that she is not a criminal. She refers somewhat inexplicably to a "prisoner" in Box 39 and then says again, "why do I need a policeman?" In box 45, Betty says, "they can shoot me," and in box 47, she says, "they treat the poor like criminals, don't they?"

Ann's narrative is also important. When Ann speaks, her language reflects that of a bureaucrat. In box 32, she uses words such as "eligible," "requirements," and "federal guidelines." She explains how if Betty doesn't qualify on paper for assistance, there may be no money available, unfortunately.

In box 36, Ann refers to programs that only certain people qualify for. In box 44, Ann mentions navigating a "bureaucratic nightmare" and continues to talk about the process and the potential benefits.

Third Excerpt from Transcript and Process Recording

In the third excerpt, Ann keeps collecting data for her assessment of Betty's eligibility for public assistance, as well as her need for a referral and advocacy. When Betty is anxious about how little money she can expect from welfare, and afraid of being on the streets, Ann explores other resources with her. It becomes apparent to Ann that Betty will need an advocate to help navigate the maze of agencies and bureaucracies that complicate access to services.

Content	Observation/Reflection	Analysis of Intervention: Theories and Practice
49. Betty: I don't know what her name was.		
50. Ann: You don't.		
51. Betty: She was so snippy I don't even wanna know.	I know some of the workers are not empathic.	Theory: Psychodynamic, ventilation. Narrative, use of word "snippy" to describe her experience with workers.
52. Ann: Ok, well, have you brought the paper work today that you need...have you brought the landlord's letter?	I hope she brought the documentation I need.	Theory: Narrative, paperwork. Practice: Data collection. Communication skill, questioning.
53. Betty: Yeah I brought it.	Oh, good. I wonder if she's ready to be assigned a new worker to finish the application.	
54. Ann: So if I bring you out now and we start you out with a new worker, do you think that that would be OK?	Let's give it a try. I'm feeling impatient because I have a meeting to go to soon.	Practice: Assessment, self-reflection. Communication skill, questioning.
55. Betty: Well if she treats me right, OK yeah.	I appreciate her standing up for her rights, but it also shows she still angry.	Theory: Psychodynamic, ventilation.
56. Ann: Alright so I'm gonna go out now and your wait will not be any longer.	Let's see who I can find to help Betty who would be more empathic.	Practice: Communication skill, reassuring client.
57. Betty: Well what kind, what kind of help can I get?	I don't think she's ready to let go of me yet. She's pulling me in with this question. Maybe I need to spend a little more time with her.	Theory: Psychodynamic, ego sustaining, positive transference and wants to depend on worker more. Practice: Assessment.
58. Ann: Ok, so what you'd be eligible for is the maximum that we could give you if you fit into where I think you do in this program would be three hundred and three dollars a month.	This is always the hard part. I hate telling clients how little they can expect. I don't think she's going to like what I have to tell her.	Theory: Narrative, eligible, maximum, program. Practice: Self-reflection. Communication skills, information-giving.
59. Betty: Three hundred and three dollars...I can't even pay my rent with that.	She looks surprised and disappointed.	
60. Ann: I know, I know.	I thought she wouldn't be happy with this amount. I wish I could give more. I know how hard it is to live on such a meager amount.	Practice: Communication skills, empathy, offering support.
61. Betty: My rent is seven hundred. What am I supposed to do? I'm gonna be on the street.	I can see her fear about being on the street coming back again.	Theory: Narrative, metaphor of being on the street.
62. Ann: Have you applied or gone to...at this point you need to go to all your other resources...you have to go in the directions of trying to find subsidized housing, elderly housing?	I am feeling some of her desperation and need to explore other resources. These cases are never easy.	Practice: Data collection, brokering. Communication skills, questioning, referral.

(Continued)

Content	Observation/Reflection	Analysis of Intervention: Theories and Practice
63. Betty: Ok, well how do I do that?	She has a strong will and wants to take charge.	Practice: Assessment, acknowledging strengths.
64. Ann: Ok, so we have a bunch of resources out in the lobby for housing. Your worker can also direct you over to the local nearest place that can help you with the systems. There are also other Boston agencies. How did you get here, did you get here by subway or did you drive?	I need to find her an experienced worker who can connect her to other resources. I wonder if this can feel overwhelming to Betty.	Theory: Narrative, Ann's language, resources in lobby, direct you, systems, agencies. Practice: Data collection, Communication skills, information-giving, referral, questioning.
65. Betty: Oh no, I don't have a car.		
66. Ann: You don't have a car?		Practice: Data collection. Communication skill, questioning.
67. Betty: I walk.		
68. Ann: Ok, you walked, so then you're within walking distance from where you live so then are you familiar with the bus line since you do you know how to walk places.	I wonder if she would know how to get to all the agencies I need to send her to.	Practice: Data Collection, Communication skill, questioning.
69. Betty: Yeah.		
70. Ann: Ok, so if we gave you the proper bus lines of where you needed to go and told you what directions you need can you get there, or do you think I could offer you an advocacy group that could assist with someone like yourself?	I think she's going to need an advocate. She seems overwhelmed with all this information. It can be a lot to take in, especially for someone of her age.	Practice: Data collection, assessment, advocacy. Communication skill, referral.
71. Betty: Yeah I could use...I don't understand all this stuff I could use someone who knows.	I'm glad she will accept help from an advocate. This is another strength.	Practice: Assessment, acknowledging strengths.
72. Ann: Ok, so have you worked with an advocate before?	I doubt she knows what an advocate is.	Practice: Data collection. Communication skill: Questioning.
73. Betty: What's an advocate?		
74. Ann: An advocate is a person that is knowledgeable in each of the areas you need—housing, monetary, food, and also I mean I that you don't...well they are also there to help people that are noncitizens but I know that you've said you've been a citizen of the US all along....and they know what programs are available to you, they know how to navigate the system which can be difficult. You're still gonna have to wait Betty. I'm sorry the zip codes that our office covers that are in our office are huge. They have poverty, high poverty areas so when you come into our office there's only x amount of workers and they have x amount of a case load, so when you come in the wait can sometimes be up to three hours.	I hate telling her that she has to be patient and maybe wait up to three hours to get help. What's wrong with this country when we make it so hard for someone like Betty to get help? However, I need to prepare her for this reality.	Theory: Narrative, language of bureaucracy, hard to navigate, programs, zip codes, wait, huge office. Cognitive, educating Betty about an advocate and preparing her for long waits. Practice: Self-reflection. Communication skill, information-giving, empathy.
75. Betty: Oh my God.	It seems to be sinking in—how long she could wait.	

Reflection of Third Process Recording and Discussion of Practice Skills and Theories Used in Intervention

In this section, Ann is more empathic and seems to establish a strong alliance with Betty. Some of the communication skills she uses to form a bond with Betty are: reassuring client, listening empathically, offering support, identifying strengths, and advocating for client resources.

Communication Skills

Boxes 52, 62, 65, 68, 72

Questioning: This is a way of gaining more information about a client's situation. There are many different kinds of questions, for example, open- and closed-ended questions and reflexive questions. In this excerpt, Ann uses it for data collection and for her assessment of Betty's eligibility for benefits.

In box 52, Ann asks Betty if she brought the paperwork from the landlord about her rent. In boxes 62, 65, and 68, Ann's questions are designed to explore if Betty has applied for other resources, whether she has a car, and whether she can use the bus system. Realizing that Betty needs help to sort everything out, Ann asks Betty in box 72 if she has ever worked with an advocate before.

Box 56

Reassuring client: At times, the social worker needs to allay a client's anxiety by supporting her efforts to change or accept new resources. In box 56, Ann reassures Betty that she won't have to wait any longer to get another worker to help her today.

Boxes 58, 64, 74

Information-giving: Information-giving means informing the client about the social agency, the problem, and the resources for change.

In box 58, Ann provides Betty with information about the maximum amount of money she can expect to get. When Betty is upset about this figure, Ann then tells her about other resources in box 64. To help Betty navigate these other systems, Ann educates Betty in box 74 about how an advocate could help her gain access to further assistance.

Boxes 60, 74

Showing empathy: The social worker maintains a nonjudgmental stance or remains neutral. The worker need not totally understand the client's situation, but she must show that she is trying to grasp what the client is feeling or experiencing.

In box 60, Ann shows Betty she is aware that the small allowance she can offer is not enough to pay her rent. In box 74, Ann is empathic when she apologizes for the long waits in the office. She says to Betty that she is sorry Betty has to wait so long.

Box 60

Offering support: When a client shares a story that is painful, it helps when the social worker offers encouragement. By acknowledging the difficulty of the situation, you provide support for the client and allow him to continue the story. In box 60, Ann offers support by acknowledging that she understands how the money Betty is eligible for is not enough to cover rent.

Boxes 62, 64, 70

Referral: This is when a client needs additional resources outside of the agency in which she's receiving services. With the client's permission, the worker makes the referral in order to help the client access other avenues for help.

In boxes 62 and 64, Ann identifies other useful resources that she can refer Betty to. In box 70, Ann realizes how overwhelmed Betty is and recommends an advocate to help her navigate through the maze of agencies and services available.

Other Practice Skills Used

Boxes 52, 62, 64, 66, 68, 70, 72

Data collection: In the data collection stage, the social worker explores the problem in more depth. This involves getting information from multiple sources about the client's life and situation, and about the social systems that may impact the problem. In the third excerpt, Ann asks a lot of questions to gather the data needed to determine Betty's eligibility for public assistance, and to assess whether she requires an advocate.

In box 52, Ann asks Betty if she brought the necessary paperwork from the landlord.

In box 62, she wants to know if Betty has help from any other agencies that could provide, for example, subsidized or elderly housing.

In boxes 64, 66, 68, and 70, Ann gathers information about whether Betty drives or uses public transportation to get places. This is important, because certain offices may be hard to reach by bus. In box 68, Ann asks if Betty thinks she can get to places on her own, or if she needs an advocate.

In box 72, Ann wants to know if Betty has ever worked with an advocate before. This will help Ann know what she needs to explain to Betty about these services.

Boxes 54, 58, 74

Self-reflection: Social workers are expected to engage in personal reflection and self-correction to assure continual professional development (CSWE, 2008).

In box 54, Ann becomes aware of her impatience and wants to assign another worker to Betty so she can go to her next meeting. Later, she realizes that Betty is not ready for another worker, and she needs to spend more time with her.

In box 58, Ann reflects on how she hates to tell clients how little they can expect from public assistance. When clients hear what they will get, they usually become upset and worried about how they will manage on such a small stipend.

In box 74, Ann becomes aware again of certain things she dislikes about her job, such as preparing clients for long waits that seem dehumanizing and disrespectful.

Box 70

Advocacy: This is a macro practice skill that involves social action with or on behalf of clients. It includes obtaining services or resources for clients that they otherwise could not access. Advocacy also works to influence and change social policy that negatively impacts client systems.

In box 70, Ann realizes that Betty needs an advocate to help her obtain additional resources. She wants to refer Betty to someone who ensures she gets all the help she can. Ann cannot play this role in her managerial position in Public Assistance. However, she recognizes the important role advocacy plays in social work, especially with a vulnerable client like Betty.

Boxes 54, 57, 70, 71

Assessment: Assessment is a multidimensional concept that can be approached in many ways using different theoretical lenses. It is an active and ongoing process between the client and social worker using relevant theories and knowledge to help make meaning out of the client's situation. Assessment leads to an understanding of the problem, what causes it, and the solutions, and it has implications for intervention.

In box 54, Ann assesses whether Betty is ready to move on to another worker, and in box 57, she picks up that Betty needs to stay with her a little longer. She interprets Betty asking her another question as a way to keep her there, implying Betty was not ready to get referred to someone new.

In box 70, Ann tries to determine whether Betty is capable of following directions and using the bus system to get to other agencies, or if she needs an advocate. Betty lets her know, in box 71, that she could use someone who understands "all this stuff."

Boxes 63, 71

Identifying strengths: During assessment, social workers listen for client strengths they can use to help solve certain problems. As clients talk about their situation and their stories unfold, workers identify strengths that are embedded in the narrative. By focusing on positive attributes and characteristics, workers shift the focus away from deficits to inquiring about and affirming strengths.

In box 63, Ann recognizes that Betty has a strong will, is independent, and wants to take charge. When Betty hears about other resources, she asks how she can access them.

In box 71, Ann interprets Betty's willingness to accept the services of an advocate as a strength. Betty is not resistant to having another person help her, and realizes that she needs this assistance to obtain more resources.

Theories Used in Intervention

Psychodynamic Theory

Boxes 51, 55

Ventilation: Ventilation is one of the ego sustaining interventions that encourages the client to express feelings about a problem for relief. In box 51, Betty vents to Ann about how the last worker was snippy with her and, in box 55, she again discharges some of her anger by saying that she will accept another worker only if she treats her right.

Box 57

Sustainment: This takes place within the client-worker relationship and includes activities by the social worker to show interest, understanding, acceptance, and confidence in the client. In this third excerpt, Ann appears more empathic, and you can see the beginning of a working alliance. In box 57, Betty begins to show a positive transference to Ann. Betty is cooperating and depending on Ann more by asking what kind of help can she get.

Narrative Theory
Boxes 51, 52, 58, 61, 63, 70, 74

Betty uses words and language to express her feelings of frustration and vulnerability. She uses the word "snippy" in box 51 to describe the worker she was assigned to during her last visit. In box 61, Betty lets you know how desperate she feels by saying again that she's afraid she'll be on the streets. This is a strong metaphor for her feelings of vulnerability.

Ann's language contains descriptive words associated with bureaucracy; however, she is showing more empathy and concedes how hard the system sometimes is to understand. In box 70, Ann identifies Betty's need for an advocate. Her continued bureaucratic language reflects the context in which she works.

In box 52, Ann refers to paperwork and, in Box 58, she uses words such as "eligible," "maximum," and "program." In box 63, she talks about "resources out in the lobby," "systems," and "agencies." In box 74, Ann explains how hard it is to navigate the system and refers to programs, zip codes, huge offices, high poverty areas, and long waits.

Cognitive Theory

Cognitive therapy helps clients interpret events and construct reality in new ways, and engage in more effective problem-solving and decision-making behavior. By explaining the welfare system to Betty at the end of the third excerpt, Ann is trying to adjust Betty's thinking and expectations about her experience at the welfare office. This will help Betty be better prepared the next time.

Box 74

In box 74, Ann provides Betty with information about how the welfare office works and prepares her for more long waits in the future. She also engages in problem solving when she informs Betty about advocates and recommends that as an option.

Fourth Excerpt from Transcript and Process Recording

In the fourth excerpt, a stronger alliance is building between Ann and Betty. The conversation and data collection are done in a more collaborative way. An example is when Ann aligns with Betty by acknowledging how "stupid" the system can be and supports Betty's frustration with getting help.

Ann actively explores other avenues for helping Betty and may be feeling some of Betty's anxiety about being on the street. There is a possibility that Ann is overwhelmed by Betty's situation and compelled by a sense of urgency to help her. This is referred to as parallel process in clinical supervision. It happens when a worker is caught up with what the client is experiencing and unconsciously plays out similar feelings. For example, Ann could feel pressure to help Betty in the same way Betty is anxious about being on the street. This can be observed in how the worker interacts with the client or how the worker talks about the client in supervision. When it occurs, the supervisor can call attention to the tendency and help the social worker gain insight about it.

What also stands out in the fourth excerpt is the discussion about welfare fraud and further criminalization of poverty.

Content	Observation/Reflection	Analysis of Intervention: Theories and Practice
76. Ann: And I know it's very challenging and it's very difficult for you but if you don't put the time in at the application process then you're never gonna get your assistance. So what you need to do is grow as much patience as you can handle, sit tight, and have a worker give you all the information and follow through with what you need to bring. What you need to bring is critical, and if you don't bring it in hand, mail it. Do you have access to mail or a post office nearby so you don't have to sit for three hours?	It's a value conflict for me helping clients adapt to an unfair system.	Theory: Psychodynamic, ego sustaining. Narrative, words of bureaucracy, challenging, difficult, application process, patience, information, sit for three hours. Practice: Self-reflection. Communication skill, information-giving, empathy.
77. Betty: Yeah, yeah.	She's getting it. She seems less angry and more willing to work with me.	Practice: Assessment.
78. Ann: Ok, so what we're gonna do today …		
79. Betty: But they're gonna lose it though, because I know they always lose things.	She's not very trusting, but probably for good reason. She's had a hard life.	Theory: Psychodynamic, issues of trust. Practice: Assessment.
80. Ann: I know I know but we have to get something resolved for you today. You're gonna have to be turned on to an advocate, you're gonna have to follow through with an appointment with the advocate, you're gonna have to take some time to explain to them what's happening to you…that there's no more babysitting, that you're behind on your rent, no more hours at all…are you able to work at all?	This is too hard for her to do on her own. She's going to need the advocate we talked about to help her navigate through the system.	Theory: Cognitive, rehearsal. Practice: Assessment, data collection. Communication skill: information-giving, questioning.
81. Betty: I can still work.	Here's another strength. I can tell she's a hard worker and still wants to work.	Practice: Identifying strengths.

(Continued)

Content	Observation/Reflection	Analysis of Intervention: Theories and Practice
82. Ann: Have you got any skills? What are your skills?	What did I just say? I sound judgmental. I'm glad I rephrased my question. I wonder if that affected Betty.	Practice: Assessment, data collection, self-reflection. Communication skill: questioning about strengths.
83. Betty: Babysitting, I've been taking care of children all my life. I'm good at that, yeah.	Her skills used for babysitting are strengths for her.	Practice: Identifying strengths.
84. Ann: Ok, Ok. Have you ever registered with any of the child care agencies of the state?		Theory: Cognitive, brainstorming. Practice: Data collection.
85. Betty: No.		
86. Ann: Ok, so that's another avenue you wanna go up you wanna investigate OK, because we run some we give vouchers out to day care…and it could be that you could assist in some of the day cares that are offered state wide because they need the help, because while you're on assistance they require certain clients to want to have work, you know there'll be a work requirement to get your money.	I wonder if she can still handle the demands of babysitting. She seems vulnerable but that could be the effect of being in this office and feeling frustrated.	Theory, narrative, language of bureaucracy, investigate, vouchers, assistance, work requirements. Practice: Communication skills, information-giving.
87. Betty: Really.		
88. Ann: Oh yeah.		
89. Betty: You mean that lousy three hundred and three dollars.	I understand her sarcasm. She's still angry.	Theory: narrative, use of "lousy," to refer to meager amount of money to expect.
90. Ann: Well the three hundred and two dollars, the three hundred and three dollars Betty is used for someone who is elderly or disabled, so they're usually exempt from work and they're also required to apply for social security and any of the benefits that ever would have been you know awarded to them.	I'm being a little defensive. I wish I had just agreed with her. Sometimes I have conflicting loyalties, between clients and agency.	Theory: Narrative, impersonal, language of bureaucracy, exempt, apply, required, benefits, awarded. Practice: Self-reflection, value conflict re: allegiance to client or agency. Communication skill: Information-giving.
91. Betty: Well, my boss never put in any money on social security and I never did either.	I see this so often where people work under the table. They don't realize how this will hurt them later.	
92. Ann: Oh OK, so you haven't been paying taxes?	It doesn't look like she has social security benefits. I shouldn't have worded it this way. I sound a little judgmental and threatening.	Practice: Self-reflection. Communication skill: seeking clarification.
93. Betty: So I'm not gonna get social security?		

(Continued)

Content	Observation/Reflection	Analysis of Intervention: Theories and Practice
94. Ann: Oh OK, so you're not eligible for social security, so but what's gonna happen is you still have to go and apply, they're still gonna, the screen we're linked to a computer system state wide into that computer system...so what's gonna have to happen is you're gonna have to go to the social security office, you're gonna have to file an application and it's gonna come back denied but that next application process is what will guarantee you to be able to get you into our program	I feel sad to explain that she won't be getting social security. However, she still has to apply. No wonder it's so difficult to understand the system. It's not meant to be easy to get assistance. If you can make it through all these hurdles, you might get a few dollars. There's got to be a better way. I'm frustrated with the system too.	Theory: Cognitive, rehearsal. Narrative, words of bureaucracy, apply, screen, linked to computer, file, application, denied, program. Practice: Self-reflection. Communication skill, information-giving.
95. Betty: That's pretty stupid isn't it?	She's right. I'm glad Betty can let off steam about how stupid this bureaucracy is.	Theory: Psychodynamic, ventilation. Narrative, use of word stupid.
96. Ann: It is isn't it?	By aligning with Betty against the agency, I have put myself in an awkward position showing my conflicting loyalties. I wonder if I should have worded this differently.	Practice: Self-reflection. Communication skills, empathy, being authentic and genuine.
97. Betty: That's really stupid.		Theory: Psychodynamic, ventilation.
98. Ann: It's a bureaucratic...that's correct...the bureaucratic system seems to have a lot of those roads that lead nowhere, and we share the same computer so you would think that we would know already that you're not getting a benefit...but unfortunately for us the state managed federal programs so what happens is each state has a management system to help manage their programs...so say if you were living in New Jersey on a yacht you may not get three oh three it may be a different amount in that state it could be lower it could be higher...so the program that since you have no dependents the program that you're eligible for or that you would be eligible for would be a program in Massachusetts where Massachusetts gives out three oh three is the maximum benefit, OK?	Now I am explaining how the system works in a more diplomatic way. I can still acknowledge how cumbersome and frustrating it is. I hope this will help us work together better. I want her to feel I am for her, not against her.	Theory: Psychodynamic, ego sustaining. Narrative, descriptive and critical language about bureaucracy, system, roads lead nowhere, not getting a benefit, management system. Practice: Communication skills, information-giving, empathy.
99. Betty: Can I get food stamps?	I'm glad she asked about food stamps. It illustrates her strength and ability to seek needed resources.	Practice: Assessment, identifying strengths.

(Continued)

Content	Observation/Reflection	Analysis of Intervention: Theories and Practice
100. Ann: You'd be eligible for food stamps, yes.		Practice: Communication skills, information-giving,
101. Betty: OK.	I feel like we have a good flow going between us. I think she is beginning to trust me.	.
102. Ann: And also what they'll do is they'll screen you for an expedited...do you have any food at the home now?	I prefer being able to tell clients what they're entitled to versus what they can't have.	Theory: Narrative, use of jargon, "expedited." Practice: Self-reflection. Communication skill, questioning.
103. Betty: Not much.		
104. Ann: Ok, so you have been OK...so with expedited we will get all you need.		
105. Betty: What's expedited?	I get so use to our lingo that I forget clients don't understand what these words mean. I realize I need to be clearer. I am glad she asked.	Practice: Self-reflection identifying strengths, client knows to ask what this means.
106. Ann: expedited means a very quick, you'll have benefits this month. You'll get a flat rate which may not be your rate of preference it'll just be a flat rate		Theory: Narrative, use of jargon, "expedited," "flat rate." Practice: Communication skill, information-giving.
107. Betty: So you say this month, but how soon this month?		
108. Ann: Very soon this month depending on where your social security number ends. You could have it actually when you're expedited you could have it as soon as tomorrow after eleven o'clock in the morning, OK?	At least there is something she can depend on soon to help.	Practice: Communication skills, information-giving, reassuring client.
109. Betty: OK, OK, OK.	She seems to be listening and understanding.	
110. Ann: Now that money will have to last you until you're approved or denied on your applications...so you wanna stretch that out so you only get the food stamp money once a month on a card OK...when you get a cash program the money is divided monthly, you get two checks so you don't spend it all at once...you're gonna get some money and two weeks later you're gonna get the rest of the money half and half...but your food stamp money you have to manage it yourself and you have to be a good manager and you can only buy food products with the money.	I don't think this will be a problem for Betty, because she seems like she is used to making ends meet. However, she needs to understand how it works.	Practice: Communication skill, information-giving.
111. Betty: I see some people buy liquor with food stamps. Why can they buy liquor?	I know this is a common stereotype.	Theory: Psychodynamic, ventilation.

(Continued)

Content	Observation/Reflection	Analysis of Intervention: Theories and Practice
112. Ann: They can buy liquor and those places that are selling liquor to them, uuhh, are being investigated...so it may look like that to you and I know that people have these prejudice against all different people using their cards...as a matter a fact a very funny story is I went into my bank the other day to my bank machine and there was a man in there with three or four of those cards that didn't belong to him with codes written down taking money off of it, because you know what Betty, people sell them for drugs.	Maybe I can inject a personal story that acknowledges her concerns.	Theory: Cognitive restructuring, challenging assumptions. Narrative, images of welfare fraud, investigation, prejudice, welfare people on drugs. Practice: Communication skills, information-giving, being authentic and genuine.
113. Betty: That policeman should go get it.	I notice that Betty is using some humor here.	Theory: Psychodynamic, ventilation. Narrative, association with policeman again.
114. Ann: I know, he should've but he can't...there is a squad, we have a fraud department and many many calls they are just as well overworked but the fraud department we have a 1-800 number for fraud...and anyone that knows that that's happening and the vendor if they're caught selling liquor on their debit card and a lot of times what people mistake as being sold on the food card is it's the same card show for whether food or cash, so do you have a bank card?		Theory: Narrative, words associated with welfare fraud, squad, fraud department. Practice: Communication skills, clarification, information-giving.
115. Betty: no no.		
116. Ann: OK, if you ever had a bank card when you go into a store to use your debit card they'll say on the store do you wanna do debit or credit, when you take your debit card and you go to use it at a food store or a liquor store they're asking if your debit if it's for food or cash...he could've been taking money out for cash and spending it on his own liquor even though it looks like it's being if someone were to video him in the corner it looks like he's used it as a food card...the cards are used for both but when you pick food only the food store deducts the money off the food side, you're able to go into a cash machine and get cash if you're getting the three oh three and food stamps...two hundred dollars would be allotted for your food and when you go to a grocery store you pick food when you use the card and it deducts whatever you bought your produce and your meats and whatever and then if you were using your card for cash then you can just use it to buy whatever but they're not supposed to obviously we don't promote that you use the cash the card at all for liquor, cigarettes, or anything of that nature, or gambling but you know people in desperate times will do desperate things, drug addicts will sell the rest of their money and go without food in order to get drugs, it's a terrible situation.	This is a common misunderstanding when clients use debit cards.	Theory: Narrative, words describe times, desperate times, people do desperate things. Practice: Communication skills, clarification, information-giving.
117. Betty: It's a terrible, terrible world.	This explanation taps into her feeling terrible too.	Theory: Psychodynamic, ventilation. Narrative, describes world as terrible.

Reflection of Fourth Process Recording and Discussion of Practice Skills and Theories Used in Intervention

Communication Skills

Boxes 76, 80, 86, 90, 94, 98, 100, 106, 108, 110, 112, 114, 116

Information-giving: This means informing the client about the social agency, the problem, and the resources for change.

In box 76, Ann gives Betty information about how to complete her application and get assistance. Again in box 80, Ann instructs Betty on what she needs to do to get an advocate.

In box 86, Ann offers information to Betty on registering with state child care agencies that could assist her in getting more babysitting jobs.

In box 90, Ann tells Betty about how the $303 is used by the elderly and disabled who, although exempt from work, still have to apply for social security. Then in box 94, Ann explains to Betty that, even though she is not eligible for social security, she has to apply and then be denied as part of the application for assistance.

Ann continues to give Betty information in box 98 about the frustration of navigating through the bureaucracy. In box 100, Ann informs Betty that she is eligible for food stamps.

By answering Betty's question, in Box 106, Ann explains what expedited means. In box 108, Ann lets Betty know that she could begin getting food stamps as early as the next day. In box 110, 112, 114, and 116, she explains to Betty how the food stamp and debit systems work.

Boxes 76, 96, 98

Showing empathy: The social worker maintains a nonjudgmental stance or remains neutral. The worker need not totally understand the client's situation, but she must show that she is trying to grasp what the client is feeling or experiencing.

In box 76, Ann shows empathy by recognizing how difficult Betty's situation is. By agreeing with Betty that the system is stupid in box 96, Ann shows empathy for the extra work Betty must go through to apply for social security. Ann continues to support Betty empathically in box 98 by understanding how cumbersome it is to apply for assistance.

Box 80

Questioning: This is a way of gaining more information about a client's situation. There are many different kinds of questions, for example, open- and closed-ended questions and reflexive questions. Questioning is often used in assessment as part of data collection. In box 80, Ann asks Betty if she can still work; this is part of Ann's data collection and assessment process.

Boxes 92, 114, 116

Seeking clarification: At different times during a session, the social worker may ask the client to talk about her perception of a situation in order to make sure she understands the client's point of view. This is also useful when the worker wants to check what she heard the client say, so as not to make the wrong assumption.

In box 92, the social worker asks Betty directly if she has been paying taxes. She doesn't want to assume that Betty hasn't paid taxes because her employer didn't pay into social security. In boxes 114 and 116, Ann clarifies for Betty how the debit card can be used for food or cash.

Boxes 98, 112

Being authentic and genuine: This refers to the worker being sincere and honestly expressing what she feels in a natural, personal way. These qualities help build positive relationships with clients. In box 98, the worker openly responds to Betty's question about the system being stupid and supports Betty's position. By sharing a personal story with Betty, Ann is also being authentic and genuine in box 112.

Box 108

Reassuring client: At times, the social worker needs to allay a client's anxiety by supporting her efforts to change or accept new resources. In box 108, Ann reassures Betty by letting her know that she could receive food stamps as early as the next day.

Other Practice Skills Used
Boxes 76, 90, 92, 94, 96, 105

Self-reflection: The skill of self-reflection is an important part of professional practice. Social workers are expected to engage in personal reflection and self-correction to assure continual professional development (CSWE, 2008).

In box 76, Ann reflects on how she finds herself in a value conflict advising clients how to adapt to an unfair system. As she listens to herself ask Betty to be patient and willing to wait three hours, she thinks she should look for another job. She stays, though, because she knows she can advocate for clients like Betty. In some small way, she can make a difference to some of the most vulnerable clients.

In box 90, Ann engages in self-reflection and wonders if she is being defensive when she reacts to Betty's sarcastic remark in box 89 about the "lousy $303." Sometimes Ann finds that she is in a value conflict, caught between conflicting loyalties to client and agency.

In box 92, Ann worries that she may have sounded too judgmental when she asked Betty about paying taxes. Upon reflection, she wishes she had worded the question differently. She wondered if, at some level, she might resent that certain people get around paying taxes. In Betty's case, her boss did her a disservice by not paying into social security for her.

Related to social security, in box 94, Ann is frustrated she has to tell Betty to apply for social security, only to get denied, before she can get public assistance. Ann is irritated with a public assistance program that makes clients jump through so many hoops to get so little money.

In box 96, Ann agrees with Betty that the system is stupid and then wonders if she should have worded this differently. By describing the system as stupid, Ann is attacking her employer, which highlights her conflicting loyalties.

In box 105, Ann reflects on using jargon that Betty couldn't understand. She was glad that Betty asked what expedited meant. Ann is aware of sometimes getting caught up with the impersonal language of the office.

Boxes 77, 79, 80, 82

Assessment: Assessment is a multidimensional concept that can be approached in many ways using different theoretical lenses. It is an active and ongoing process between the client and social worker using relevant theories and knowledge to help make meaning out of the client's situation. Assessment leads to an understanding of the problem, what causes it, and the solutions, and it has implications for intervention.

In box 77, Ann notices how Betty is listening to her and closely following the conversation. As she assesses their working relationship, she sees it changing, with Betty cooperating more.

However, in box 79, she witnesses Betty's continued mistrust when she refers to her papers getting lost if she mails them. This helps confirm Ann's earlier assessment that Betty needs an advocate.

In box 82, Ann is also making an assessment when she tries to get a handle on Betty's skills.

Boxes 81, 83, 99, 105

Identifying strengths: During assessment, social workers listen for client strengths they can use to help solve certain problems. As clients talk about their situation and their stories unfold, workers identify strengths that are embedded in the narrative. By focusing on positive attributes and characteristics, workers shift the focus away from deficits to inquiring about and affirming strengths.

In box 81, Ann identifies one of Betty's strengths: that she is a hard worker and still wants to work. In box 83, Betty lets Ann know that babysitting is one of her skills and that she has taken care of children all of her life. When Betty asks if she can get food stamps in box 99, Ann identifies this as another strength. By asking about services that she could be eligible for, Betty is seeking out needed resources. In a similar way, in box 105, Betty is assertive in asking what expedited means.

Boxes 80, 84

Data collection: This involves getting information from multiple sources about the client's life and situation, and about the social systems that may impact the problem. In Box 80, Ann asks Betty if she is still able to work. This information will affect her assessment and intervention strategy. Related to this question, in box 84, Ann inquires whether Betty has registered with any child care agencies.

Theories Used in Intervention

Psychodynamic Theory

Boxes 76, 79, 95, 98, 111

Sustainment: This takes place within the client–worker relationship and includes activities by the social worker to show interest, understanding, acceptance, and confidence in the client.

In box 76, Ann is sensitive to how Betty's situation is challenging and frustrating. She also advises Betty to be patient and supply all of the information needed to complete the application so she can get assistance. Ann seems genuinely interested in helping Betty, and Betty picks up on it and agrees.

In box 98, Ann continues to show understanding about the difficulties of the welfare system, and how so many roads seemingly lead nowhere. Ann's remarks serve to support Betty and build the relationship.

Box 79

Trust: Trust is a psychodynamic concept that looks at the types of relationships people form with others. When a client is overly suspicious about people's motives, these feelings might relate back to insecure attachments with parents in childhood that make the client mistrustful in the present. A lack of trust could also be related to early disappointments with caregivers, which made the client feel he couldn't depend on others or that others were out to hurt him. Parent–child relationships based on warmth, mutuality, consistency, and support help children form strong identities and develop a sense of trust in relationships. On the other hand, children from homes that lack these qualities and instead harbor instability, anger, frustration, abandonment, and loss, will form insecure attachments and be distrustful of others.

In box 76, Betty is distrustful about sending her papers in the mail, because she is sure they will be lost.

Boxes 95, 111, 113, 117

Ventilation: Ventilation is one of the ego-sustaining interventions that encourages the client to express feelings about a problem for relief.

In box 95, Betty vents about how stupid the system is for making her apply for social security and get denied before she can receive assistance. Since the computers are linked between Public Assistance and Social Security, she thinks there should be an easier way to approach the process.

In box 111, Betty is annoyed about how some people buy liquor with food stamps, expressing a common stereotype. In box 113, Betty uses humor and sarcasm to vent her feelings when she tells Ann that the police should get those people taking money from debit cards to buy drugs.

In box 117, Betty lets off steam by saying, "It's a terrible, terrible world," ending the fourth excerpt. It is interesting to note that Betty uses the word terrible right after Ann said, "it's a terrible situation," referring to drug addicts going without food in order to get drugs. This shows how Betty is following Ann's lead, and how they are forming a strong alliance.

Narrative Theory

In the fourth excerpt, there are many references to bureaucracy with words that are linked to rules and conjure up an impersonal image of what a bureaucracy means. They will be discussed in the following identified boxes.

Box 76

In box 76, Ann uses office terminology and language to advise Betty on what she needs to do to get assistance. To work in a bureaucracy, whether you like it or not, you must use certain words and phrases: application process, difficult, assistance, patience, sit tight, get all the information, follow through.

Boxes 86, 90

This continues in box 86 with words like investigate, vouchers, assistance, work requirements. In box 90, Ann's impersonal use of language includes the words exempt, apply, required, benefits, awarded.

Boxes 94, 98

In box 94, Ann mentions: apply, screen, linked to computer, file, application, denied, program. Her descriptive and critical language about bureaucracy comes through in box 98 when Ann refers to "roads that lead nowhere," "not getting a benefit," and a "management system to help manage their programs."

Boxes 102, 106

In Box 102, Ann uses jargon, the term "expedited," when talking with Betty. This is another technical, impersonal word that Betty doesn't understand. In Box 106, Ann explains what the jargon means and then goes on to use another technical term, "flat rate."

Box 112

In box 112, when describing welfare fraud, Ann talks about investigations, prejudice, and welfare people on drugs.

Boxes 114, 116

The language intensifies in box 114 and 116 when Ann uses the words squad, fraud, and the fraud department, which brings the conversations back to welfare and the criminal justice system. In box 116, Ann tries to explain certain behavior by saying that in desperate times, people do desperate things. This is in contrast to criminalizing poor people's behavior.

Box 89

Compared to Ann, Betty's language is much more direct and emotional. In box 89, Betty uses the word "lousy" to refer to the meager amount of money she would get from welfare.

Boxes 95, 96, 97

In boxes 95 and 97, Betty uses the word "stupid" to describe some of the welfare system policies. In box 97, she says "really stupid" to emphasize her frustration. After Ann agrees with Betty in box 96 that some of the policies are stupid, this gives Betty more steam to increase her attack on welfare. She now feels comfortable saying it is "really" stupid.

Cognitive Theory

Boxes 80, 94

Rehearsal: This is a strategy in cognitive therapy to help clients prepare for a challenging or difficult situation. The social worker instructs the client on what to say and do, and they may role-play the situation in advance to build the client's confidence.

In boxes 80 and 94, Ann plays an active, directive role using cognitive approaches. In the first situation, she goes through the steps Betty must follow to get an advocate and maximize the services available to her. It is as if she is rehearsing with Betty what she needs to do to get things resolved. In box 94, Ann coaches Betty through the steps to apply and then get denied for social security. This rehearsal helps Betty prepare to apply for public assistance.

Box 84

Brainstorming: Brainstorming is another technique used in cognitive therapy for improved problem solving. Clients are prompted to create as many solutions to a problem as possible. Once the client has created an exhaustive list of ideas, he evaluates each one with the social worker to determine which seems the best choice at the time.

In box 84, in an effort to exhaust all options for helping Betty work again, Ann asks Betty if she is registered with any of child care agencies. This resource could help Betty get another babysitting job.

Box 112

Cognitive restructuring is used to describe interventions aimed at helping clients change their belief systems. In box 112, Ann challenges Betty's false assumptions about welfare recipients buying alcohol with food stamps.

Fifth Excerpt from Transcript and Process Recording

In the fifth excerpt, Ann directs Betty away from talking about other clients and back to the urgency of her own situation and the need to get her benefits. Ann moves the discussion from food stamps (in the fourth excerpt) to questions about heating assistance and subsidized housing. The relationship between Ann and Betty becomes even stronger in this excerpt. Ann demonstrates her genuine interest in helping Betty obtain resources to cover her basic needs so she has a roof over her head, a place to sleep, heat, and something to eat. Ann also helps Betty to see another perspective and coaches her on how to act and communicate with others when she is in the office.

Content	Observation/Reflection	Analysis of Intervention: Theories and Practice
118. Ann: It is but you have to worry about Betty right now. You have no roof over your head right now you're in fear of losing your unit, right.	Let's get back to Betty's situation. It's easy to go off on a tangent about how terrible the world is.	Practice: Communication skills, holding to focus.
119. Betty: Yes, yes.		
119. Ann: And we need to get you heat assistance because it's getting cold you're gonna need heat OK.		Practice: Communication skills, information-giving.
120. Betty: Yeah.		
122. Ann: Who pays for your utilities right now? Are you paying them or are they in with the landlord?		Practice: Data collection. Communication skill, questioning.
123. Betty: They're in with the landlord.		

(Continued)

Content	Observation/Reflection	Analysis of Intervention: Theories and Practice
124. Ann: Ok, so you need to make sure that they are, next place we get you if you go into subsidized, certain subsidies pay for your utilities certain don't...so this is why you need an advocate to help navigate for you, you have to know all the questions to ask...how long have you lived where you're living?	There is so much involved. She really needs an advocate to navigate through all the different agencies.	Theory: Cognitive, problem-solving, coaching. Practice: Communication skills, information-giving, offering support.
125. Betty: Oh I've lived there for years.		
126. Ann: And so why do you think the landlord would not give you a little bit of grace period to pay him?		Practice: Data collection. Communication skill, questioning.
127. Betty: Well, he's gotten nasty....I guess you know he lost his job so I guess he's in trouble too.	She seems sensitive to his situation too. She's able to take the perspective of another which is also a strength.	Practice: Assessment, identifying strengths.
128. Ann: Ok.		
129. Betty: So you know he's not, he used to be nice but he's not as nice anymore	Betty shows understanding for her landlord.	
130. Ann: Ok, so are there any other units in the building...does he take any subsidized units do you know, are any of your neighbors on subsidy?		Practice: Data collection. Communication skill, questioning.
11. Betty: No, I don't know...I don't talk to...		
132. Ann: Oh, you don't talk to them?	She seems very isolated.	Practice: Assessment.
133. Betty: No I don't even talk to my neighbors I don't know.	She must feel lonely at times in her living situation.	
134. Ann: Alright, well we have to get you together today so that when you leave here you feel like you've...your application has been taken, know whether or not you're getting food stamps, OK.		Theory: Psychodynamic, ego sustaining. Practice: Communication skills, reassuring client, offering support.
135. Betty: Yeah, OK.	She's following me and I think we are working well together now.	
136. Ann: So your frustration level goes down...now I'm telling you Betty you're gonna come back here another time and you're gonna be as equally frustrated, OK?...you have to try to keep your comments about your black people and all that...everybody here needs assistance, OK?...the workers are tired they have no right to treat you in a way that's disrespectful...you don't know what your benefits are but you also can't come in with any attitudes of prejudices towards the workers OK.	I think she may be more open to this feedback now. She needs to be treated respectfully but also has to treat the staff and other clients with respect as well.	Theory: Cognitive, coaching. Practice: Communication skills, giving feedback, information-giving, helping client to see another perspective.

(Continued)

Content	Observation/Reflection	Analysis of Intervention: Theories and Practice
137. Betty: Yeah, OK.	I am aware of how she feels very different now from when I first sat down with her. I think she feels more listened to and that someone wants to help her.	Theory: Psychodynamic, intersubjective, tuned in to changes in how she is present with me.
138. Ann: They have a lot of people in need right now so we have to all take care of each other and it's tough at times out there, alright?	I may be a little preachy, but I want to impress on her how she has to be sensitive to other clients who are struggling like her.	Practice: Self-reflection. Communication skills, giving feedback, helping client see another perspective.
139. Betty: Well you know you're pretty nice for a boss...I don't expect a boss would be nice.	I guess I got through to her. I'm glad she's not as angry and knows that we want to help. I feel a good working alliance with her. I like being told I'm nice. Maybe it's my narcissism, but this job is hard and it helps to be acknowledged by clients at times.	Theory: Psychodynamic, Intersubjective, she demonstrates in words and body language that we are tuned in to each other. Practice: Self-reflection.
140. Ann: Well you know there's a lot of us. We all work really hard in here and we all have the same goal. We're all here to help people like yourself, not here to be mean, and I'm not gonna lie some of my workers have an attitude they're tired and they're cranky, they treat people sometimes they desensitize and it happens to all of us some days I'm not on my greatest game either, but the common goal is that everybody get the benefits they need as quickly and as accurately as possible	I hope I'm not being too defensive or scolding her.	Theory: Cognitive, cognitive restructuring, confronting assumptions, Narrative, words to describe workers, cranky, desensitize, not on my greatest game. Practice: Self-reflection. Communication skills, clarification of role, helping client see another perspective.
141. Betty: Yeah.		
142. Ann: And alright, I want you leaving here understanding what you're getting. I don't want you coming in next week, and if I'm not here, saying I was back four days now and still left not knowing if I've applied, not knowing if I have food stamps, OK.	I am being a little directive, but I want to empower her to have the information she needs to follow-up when she comes in next.	Practice: Self-reflection, Empowering client. Practice: Communication skills, information-giving.
143. Betty: OK.		
144. Ann: So, I want you to step it up a little., I want you to ask the questions and demand it of your worker and I'm gonna give you assign you a worker now so that you feel comfortable when you've left here that you know what you've applied for and you know what you have to bring back, OK, alright.		Theory: Cognitive, coaching. Practice: Communication skills, information-giving.
145. Betty: OK, I and I won't have to wait that long.		

Content	Observation/Reflection	Analysis of Intervention: Theories and Practice
146. Ann: You may still have to wait Betty now I've told you that earlier, and I know you're tired and you've been here but there may still be a wait…if it gets to be over an hour and you're uncomfortable, I want you to go back up to the desk and tell them you've been waiting over an hour, and see if your worker can come down and speak with you, and let you know how long the wait is, alright?	I wish I had said this differently and left off the "I've told you that earlier." I guess I am tired now too, but I also need to prepare her that she may still have to wait a long time.	Practice: Self-reflection, Empowerment. Communication skill, information-giving.
147. Betty: OK, OK.		
148. Ann: Do you think we can agree to that?	I hope this didn't sound demeaning to her. How could I have said this differently?	Practice: Self-reflection.
149. Betty: OK, OK.	She seems OK. This seems like a good place to stop with her and refer to another worker. I think she is ready now.	Practice: Assessment.
150. Ann: Alright great, thank you.	I feel we made a lot of progress from when we started to now. Her body language, tone of voice and attitude are signs to me that she has made progress in our session. I now feel ready to refer her to another worker.	Practice: Evaluation, Intersubjective evidence.

Reflection of Fifth Process Recording and Discussion of Practice Skills and Theories Used in Intervention

Communication Skills

Box 118

Holding to focus: This is when the social worker helps the client stay on the topic under discussion. In box 120, Ann is refocusing Betty on her needs rather than going off on a tangent talking about how people use their debit cards and what a terrible world it is. Ann wants to move her application along and make sure she has a roof over her head.

Boxes 120, 124, 142, 146

Information-giving: Information-giving means informing the client about the social agency, the problem, and the resources for change.

In box 120, Ann explains to Betty that she needs to apply for heating assistance to assist with her bills. Ann continues in box 124 by giving Betty information on subsidized housing and explaining why she needs an advocate to help her navigate through the various agency systems.

In box 142, Ann realizes she has given Betty a lot of information and wants to make sure Betty comprehends everything. In box 146, Ann tells Betty what to expect the next time she comes to the office and how she should ask to speak to her worker if she's been waiting more than an hour.

Boxes 122, 126, 130

Questioning: This is a way of gaining more information about a client's situation. There are many different kinds of questions, for example, open- and closed-ended questions and reflexive questions. Questioning is often used in assessment as part of data collection.

In boxes 122, 126, and 130, Ann collects information about Betty's living situation as part of the assessment process to determine eligibility for services. She asks Betty if she or her landlord pays the utilities, and if her landlord has any subsidized units. Ann also questions Betty about whether she thinks her landlord would give her a grace period if she can't pay her rent.

Boxes 124, 134

Offering support: When a client shares a story that is painful, it helps when the social worker offers encouragement. By acknowledging the difficulty of the situation, you provide support for the client and allow him to continue the story.

In boxes 124 and 134, it is clear that Ann is offering support to Betty. Her questions demonstrate her genuine interest in understanding Betty's situation so she can link Betty to appropriate services and provide the most help possible. She explains again that she wants to refer Betty to an advocate for additional support in obtaining the resources she needs.

Box 134

Reassuring client: At times, the social worker needs to allay a client's anxiety by supporting her efforts to change or accept new resources. In box 134, Ann reassures Betty that, by the time she leaves, her application will have been initiated, and she will know whether she will get food stamps or not.

Boxes 136, 138

Giving feedback: This is when the social worker finds an opportunity to provide the client with information about his behavior and its effect on him or on other people. It can prove difficult, because the client may not want to hear or accept what the social worker is saying.

In boxes 136 and 138, Ann gives Betty feedback about how her behavior and disparaging language about black people in the office is inappropriate. She also tells Betty that she can't show disrespect to either the clients or the workers. Ann further advises Betty that in tough times, it's crucial that people take care of each other, not treat each other poorly.

Boxes 136, 138, 140

Helping client to see another perspective: When clients can only see the problem from their own point of view, the social worker's task is to expand their understanding or perception of the problem. This may include discussing how other people think about or see the issue at hand.

In box 136, Ann tells Betty that everyone in the office needs assistance, like her, and she can't take her frustration out on black clients. She wants Betty to understand that the workers may be tired, and Betty should not hold a grudge against them, while also acknowledging that the workers should not act disrespectful of her either.

In box 138, Ann wants Betty to recognize that it's a tough time, and many people are in need. In box 140, she again tries to show Betty the perspective of the worker. She says to Betty that "we all work really hard in here" and that the goal is to help people, not to be mean. Ann explains that the workers may be cranky and seem insensitive at times, but it's because they are tired or having a bad day, and this can happen to anyone.

Box 140

Clarification of role: The social worker helps the client understand what services the agency offers, and what her role as social worker will be. There are times when the client needs reminding that the work is collaborative; it is the social worker's job to facilitate and not direct the process.

In box 140, Betty clarifies the worker's role by explaining that her workers all have the same goal to support clients, and they are not there to be mean. They want to help people get the benefits they need as quickly as possible.

Other Practice Skills Used
Boxes 122, 126, 130

Data collection: In the data collection stage, the social worker explores the problem in more depth. This involves getting information from multiple sources about the client's life and situation, and about the social systems that may impact the problem.

In boxes 122, 126, and 130, Ann asks Betty questions about her housing situation and landlord to collect more data in her assessment process. She is exploring different areas to get the information she needs to determine Betty's eligibility for benefits.

Box 127

Identifying strengths: During assessment, social workers listen for client strengths they can use to help solve certain problems. As clients talk about their situation and their stories unfold, workers identify strengths that are embedded in the narrative. By focusing on positive attributes and characteristics, workers shift the focus away from deficits to inquiring about and affirming strengths.

In box 127, as Betty speaks about her landlord, Ann notices that Betty shows some understanding for his situation as well. Ann identifies Betty's awareness that her landlord's nasty behavior could be related to losing his job as a strength, which demonstrates Betty's capacity for empathy.

Boxes 132, 149

Assessment: Assessment is an active and ongoing process between the client and social worker using relevant theories and knowledge to make meaning out of the client's situation.

Assessment leads to an understanding of the problem, what causes it, and the solutions, and it has implications for intervention.

In box 132, when Ann asks Betty if she talks to her neighbors, she is assessing the extent of Betty's social support system. When Ann learns that Betty has no contact with them, she is cognizant that Betty is very isolated in her living situation.

In box 149, Ann determines that Betty is in a good place to stop. She has assessed from their conversation that Betty is ready to be referred to another worker who will help her from this point on. Ann is tuned in to Betty and has noticed her shift in mood and feels confident that Betty will cooperate with the next worker.

Boxes 138, 139, 140, 142, 146, 148

Self-reflection: The skill of self-reflection is an important part of professional practice. Social workers are expected to engage in personal reflection and self-correction to assure continual professional development (CSWE, 2008).

Betty challenges Ann to self-reflect several times during this excerpt. In box 138, Ann is worried that she might sound a little "preachy" as she tries to impress on Betty how tough it is out there for people, and wants Betty to be more sensitive to other clients.

In box 139, she is reassured when Betty says that she's "pretty nice for a boss." Ann is aware that she's glad Betty isn't mad at her and likes being appreciated by her. Since Betty was open to her remarks in box 138, Ann decides to continue defending the workers but then wonders if she has lingered on the point too long.

In box 142, Ann is aware of being directive with Betty, wanting to make sure she understands what she's getting before she leaves the office, so she doesn't come back in four days not knowing.

In box 146, Ann reflects on how she may have talked down to Betty when she said, "I've told you that earlier." Ann is aware she's tired and wished she hadn't said that. When she told Betty she knew she was tired, Ann may have been projecting how she felt.

Again, in box 148, Ann wonders if she came across as overly directive and demeaning to Betty when she said, "Do you think we can agree on that?" Sometimes she thinks the work environment creates unnecessary power struggles between clients and workers, and she falls into them without meaning to. She doesn't like being in a position of authority over others.

Box 142

Empowering clients: This is providing clients with information and skills to take action on their own behalf, advocate for their rights, and gain access to needed resources.

In box 142, although Ann is directive with Betty, her goal is to empower Betty to leave the office knowing that she has applied for assistance and whether or not she is eligible for food stamps. This is key information for Betty to have when she returns to the office and will help her speak up for herself. In addition to linking Betty to services, Ann wants to inform Betty of her standing, knowing it will give her power over her situation.

Theories Used in Intervention

Cognitive Theory Using Coaching and Cognitive Restructuring

Boxes 124, 136, 144

Coaching: This is an intervention used in cognitive therapy that helps a client take a different approach to a problem or to an interaction with another person or group.

In box 124, Ann coaches Betty to look into subsidized housing that pays for utilities and to be aware that some do not.

In box 136, Ann advises Betty again, this time about how to behave in the office and how to communicate with and about others. Ann tells Betty that next time, she can't be disrespectful to clients or workers by making prejudicial remarks.

In box 144, Ann coaches Betty to step it up a little and ask questions of her worker. She is teaching her ways to be more assertive.

Box 140

Cognitive restructuring: This describes interventions aimed at helping clients change their belief systems.

In box 140, Ann challenges Betty's assumptions that the workers are mean and says they all have the same goal to help people. Although some workers may act cranky because they are tired or having a bad day, their main interest is getting clients the benefits they need.

Psychodynamic Theory

Boxes 137, 139

Intersubjectivity: Intersubjectivity is a term used in psychodynamic theory to refer to worker sensitivity and awareness of the client's experience. A worker who has achieved this level of relatedness with a client will have an easier time reading the client, in essence is aligned and attuned with what the client feels. As a worker notices changes in a client's mood and general well-being, the worker can use this information as a way to measure client progress.

After Ann tells Betty she can't show disrespect to others in the office, Betty agrees in box 137. She listens and appears open to Ann's feedback. There is a noticeable change in Betty's demeanor compared to the beginning of the interview. Betty is present with Ann in a qualitatively different way that shows they are working well together and have achieved a level of relatedness. At some point in the conversation, Betty picked up that Ann cares about her situation and sincerely wants to help her. Ann is attuned to how Betty feels and can read her. She feels this shift in Betty's mood from early anger, frustration, and irritability to one of cooperation and appreciation, reflected in her saying to Ann, in box 139, that, "You know you're pretty nice for a boss." Betty is demonstrating in words and body language that she and Ann are tuned in to each other.

Narrative Theory

Box 140

In box 140, Ann uses the words "cranky" and "desensitize," and also the expression, "not on my greatest game" to describe the workers who may appear mean to Betty. Cranky is a strong word that has a harsh sound and is often used stereotypically to describe older adults. It has a negative connotation and applies to someone who is unhappy and responds irritably to others. "Not on my greatest game" is a sports metaphor implies that a person is just having a bad day and his performance is not typical.

Summary of Excerpt 5 and Conclusion: Significance of Social Work Interventions in Public Assistance

In the last excerpt, Ann is holding Betty's focus to the important task of getting her assistance and continues to explore other avenues, like fuel assistance and subsidized housing. She learns that Betty has no contact with her neighbors and realizes how isolated Betty is in her living situation. Ann wants to make sure that Betty knows what has been done when she leaves the office and coaches her on how to assert her needs on her next visit. Ann has a breakthrough with Betty when she tells her that she's "pretty nice for a boss." Ann's work with Betty exemplifies a successful intervention.

Assessment

Please refer to chapter 1 for outlines on the problem-solving method, psychosocial assessment and intervention plan, and the bio/psycho/social/spiritual assessment.

Problem-Solving Method

Below is the social worker's attempt to apply the problem-solving method to Betty's case. It is written in the first person from the social worker's perspective.

Engagement

My engagement with Betty began when another worker asked me to see her, because Betty was angry about how the office staff was treating her. We were off to a rough start. I recognized Betty's need to ventilate and find an outlet to express her desperate feelings and her fear of being out on the street. This was Betty's third day coming to the office, and she complained that she was kept waiting for long hours without getting any help. Betty was visibly upset and agitated and had difficulty finding the words to tell her story in a coherent way. I tried to engage her right off with questions about whether she had started an application and what benefits she might be eligible for. Since she felt that no one had paid attention or really listened to her, I tried to show her that I was concerned about her situation and wanted to ask the right questions to get her benefits. It took Betty a while to feel comfortable with me and trust that I would help.

Betty needed assistance, and my goal was to de-escalate the situation and contain some of Betty's emotion so she could be referred to a worker. Our mutual goal was to get her the help she needed and complete her application for benefits.

Assessment

Betty is an older adult, in her mid-70s, who is applying for assistance because she's not earning enough money to pay her rent. This is her third trip to the office, and she is frustrated and angry about her treatment and the lack of help she's getting. She walks with a slight limp and with the assistance of a cane. From my conversation with Betty, I learned that she had been working full time as a babysitter until recently when her hours were cut. She is receiving pressure from her landlord about back rent owed him. She described her landlord as "nasty" and fears he will kick her out on the street.

Betty has always worked as a babysitter and would like to continue if she can find another babysitting job. She is not eligible for social security benefits, because her employers never paid into it for her. She doesn't receive food stamps, heating assistance, or subsidized housing. I identify many strengths in Betty, including determination and persistence, a strong work ethic, and an ability to advocate for herself. She has a capacity for empathy demonstrated by her sensitivity to her landlord being out of work.

It seems that Betty has little support and is isolated in her social environment. She has no family to rely on, and she says she doesn't talk to her neighbors. Betty comes across as a proud woman and finds it difficult to have to ask for assistance. She projects some of her shame onto the clients in the office, whom she refers to as "welfare cheats who sit on their butts all day." Some of the risks factors in working with Betty are: her advancing age, possible health issues, her living situation, a lack of social support, financial worries, and isolation. She will need an advocate to help her navigate through the many different agencies and resources for help.

Planning

The initial plan was for me to meet with Betty briefly to contain some of her anger toward the office staff. I also needed to assess whether I could de-escalate the situation enough to assign Betty to another worker to help with her application, or determine if she posed a threat to staff. Once I sat with Betty and experienced how agitated and distressed she was, I realized she was not a danger to anyone. My plan then became to spend more time with her so she could vent her frustration and build trust in our ability to help her. When I felt Betty was ready, I would refer her to another staff member and make sure she was comfortable with that new worker. The plan was to get her a monthly allowance, food stamps, heating assistance, and subsidized housing that included utilities, and to have her registered with child care agencies. To help Betty link to these resources, she would be assigned an advocate.

Intervention

The intervention began with my listening to Betty's situation to show empathy and understanding. An important part of the intervention was building a working relationship with her and gaining her trust so I could then transfer this good will to another worker. The goal was to prepare her for the next step, so she could cooperate with staff to complete her application for assistance.

My questions in the interview were aimed at establishing her eligibility for benefits. I took on the role of educator and coach. I challenged her false assumptions and prejudice about other clients and staff, and gave her another perspective. I educated her about her position as a client in the office and what she could expect. I coached her about what to do if she had waited more than hour, how she could behave in a way that was both appropriate and assertive.

When I assessed that she was ready, I referred Betty to another worker, as well as to an advocate to link her to the many additional services.

Evaluation

At the end of my meeting with Betty, I noticed a significant difference in her mood and cooperation with me. Compared to our rough start and her extreme agitation, she was now calm and accepting of the help we could offer her. We had built an alliance and trust that could be transferred to the next worker. She understood her role and what was expected of her, as well as the next steps in getting help. We came to an agreement at the end, and she was ready for me to assign her a worker. The initial goal of preparing Betty for referral was achieved, making it a successful intervention with positive outcomes.

Termination

My work with Betty was expected to be brief. Once Betty was cooperating and ready for referral to other staff, we terminated our work together. Although our relationship is ending, I hope her experience with me was beneficial and that she will go forward feeling more positive about human service workers who want to help her, in spite of some of the bureaucratic obstacles. I enjoyed getting to know Betty and appreciated understanding the suffering behind her anger. It confirmed my belief that there are always reasons behind clients' anger when they come into the office.

Follow-up

I realize that follow-up is almost impossible with such heavy caseloads and new clients arriving every day. However, I referred Betty to a worker near my office, so I can check on Betty's progress. In my administrative role, I don't often get time with clients, and I'm conscious of how much I miss the personal client contact. Having had a chance to get to know Betty, I will follow up on her case. This will also be important feedback on how the office is managed.

Psychosocial Assessment and Intervention Strategy

The following is an example of psychosocial assessment and intervention. It is applied to Betty's case and told in the first person, in the voice of the worker.

Identifying Data

Betty is an older woman in her mid-70s, single and with no family, who has come to the Public Assistance Office for financial help. She works as a babysitter, but recently her hours were cut and she does not earn enough to pay her rent. She lives in an apartment building but does not speak to other residents and appears to be isolated.

Presenting Problem

Betty was referred to me because she was becoming loud and threatening to staff. She was angry after waiting so long and agitated at how, after three trips to the office, she still could not get any help. She was also worried that her landlord might put her out on the streets. In her desperate situation, she had become disrespectful to other clients and staff, and her loud and angry voice brought attention to her. Staff was worried she might hit them with her cane.

Current Functioning, Social Supports, Strengths

Betty is struggling to make ends meet on her limited budget and is behind in her rent. Until recently, she worked full-time as a babysitter, but her hours were cut because the children are older. This has made it hard for her to pay her bills. She appears to have little social support, no family, and no connection to people in her apartment building or neighborhood. She has problems with her mobility and walks with the assistance of a cane.

Betty has many strengths that she can use to her benefit including her determination and persistence in getting assistance in spite of obstacles, a strong work ethic, and an ability to advocate for herself. She has demonstrated incredible independence and resilience in managing her finances on her own until now with limited means. She has empathy shown by her sensitivity to her landlord, who although described as "nasty," she also understands might be struggling because he's out of work.

Some of the risks factors that Betty faces are: her advancing age, possible health issues and difficulty walking, her poor living situation, a lack of social support, financial worries, and isolation.

Relevant Past History

I do not know much about Betty's history except that she has always worked as a babysitter. Unfortunately, her employers have not paid into social security for her, so she has no access to these benefits. She has stayed independent and self-sufficient until recently when her hours babysitting were decreased. She is a proud woman who has worked hard all her life and doesn't like asking for help. At some point, walking became difficult for her, requiring her to use a cane to get around. She speaks of having no family and seems to have little social support.

Formulation

Betty is an older, single woman in her mid-70s. She has no family, little social support, and is struggling financially to pay her bills. She is earning less money babysitting since her hours were cut recently, and this makes her anxious about not meeting her rent obligations. She also worries that her landlord will throw her out on the street.

On her third visit to the Public Assistance Office, she became angry, loud, agitated, and threatening to staff over her long wait and frustration about getting help. She was referred to me to assess the danger to staff and to de-escalate the situation. I was able to contain her emotions and build a relationship with her that allowed me to refer her safely to another worker to complete her application for assistance. In addition to her financial allotment, she needs help applying for food stamps, fuel assistance, and subsidized housing. She would benefit from the assistance of an advocate to help her navigate through the many agencies and resources for help.

Intervention Strategy

My plan was to meet with Betty to establish a relationship, if possible, and contain some of her emotion so she can be referred to another worker to complete her application for assistance and receive benefits. My involvement was brief, and when I felt she was ready to cooperate, I referred her to other staff. During my intervention, I asked her questions to collect information and determine her eligibility for different programs. I also coached and educated her on her behavior and how she needed to communicate differently to others in the office. I helped her understand the process of getting help and appropriate ways for her to be assertive.

Termination and Evaluation

I evaluated the treatment by noticing any change in Betty's demeanor and mood from the start of our meeting to the point at which I referred her to another worker. I hope she will contain some of her emotion and cooperate with staff. I also referred her to an advocate to help her apply for food stamps, fuel assistance, and subsidized housing.

Theoretical Lens

In working with Betty, I used psychodynamic, cognitive, and narrative theories. Psychodynamic theories helped me to know the importance of empathy in building a relationship with Betty. Ego-sustaining interventions stress the importance of personal characteristics, that the worker must be understanding and genuine, and demonstrate a sincere desire to help the client. I demonstrated ego sustaining interventions when I showed patience and let Betty vent some of her frustration with the welfare office. By applying psychodynamic theory, I could understand how Betty was using the defense of projection to displace her shame about applying for assistance onto the other clients in the office. Through intersubjective knowledge, and being attuned to Betty, I was able to assess when she was ready for referral to another worker. I also used this knowledge as evidence of our progress.

Cognitive theories were useful in providing strategies to deal with some of Betty's thought processes. I used cognitive restructuring to confront Betty's prejudices and false assumptions about other clients and my staff. I used education to teach her more appropriate behavior when she was in the office, and what to expect as she goes forward with her application. I also coached her on how to stay involved and assertive in the process of applying for benefits.

Narrative theory helped me understand how both Betty and I used language and words differently in our work together. Betty's words and phrases conjured strong images based on her feelings, her prejudices, and her ideas about welfare and bureaucracy. My language reflected the culture in which I work and included many references to bureaucracy and office lingo. Although the words were sometimes impersonal, I hope I was able to convey, nevertheless, a sense of caring for Betty.

Bio/Psycho/Social/Spiritual Assessment

The ecological method uses the Bio/Psycho/Social/Spiritual approach, studying the complex relationships between multiple systems that continually interact with each other. Using this approach, the social worker looks at how an individual is affected by biological, psychological, and social systems. When understanding a client's problem, it is important to understand how each system affects the other. Here, the worker (writing in the first person) applies the Bio/Psycho/Social/Spiritual Assessment to the case of Betty.

Biological Assessment

Betty is an older, single, Caucasian woman in her mid-70s who has come to the Public Assistance Office for financial help. Little is known about her health, except that she has limited mobility and depends on a cane to walk. It appears she has been in relatively good health and has worked full-time until recently. She also feels capable of continuing her work. Although she appears irritable in her disposition, this could be the result of frustration in her financial situation.

Psychological Assessment

Betty appears alert, oriented, intelligent, and does not appear to have any cognitive impairment. She pays close attention to and understands what I say. I believe she has capacity for insight and problem solving. Her issues communicating effectively in the office could be related to how desperate she feels. She seems to have good self-esteem by acknowledging her skills as a babysitter. However, she also seems shameful about her predicament and having to apply for help. Her emotions were out of control briefly in the office, but after talking with me for a short time, she was able to contain them. She appears to have a strong will that is reflected in her determination and persistence at the welfare office and history of self-reliance.

Betty used projection when she verbally attacked people on welfare, and this defense reflected her own feelings of vulnerability, her discomfort at being in this dependent position and needing help. Once the worker explained that everyone in the office was having a hard time, she became more understanding. She showed empathy for her landlord who was out of work and understood that this was, perhaps, the reason he was acting "nasty" with her.

Betty's reality testing is good; she is realistic and can understand what to expect as she completes her application. She demonstrates solid problem-solving skills and judgment by knowing to apply for assistance when she couldn't pay her rent. She is open to other options for assistance and the help of an advocate.

Social Assessment

Betty has no family and few social supports. It is not known if she has any friends, but she does not talk to the neighbors in her apartment building. Overall, she appears isolated and without a social network. Her principal activity seems to be her work. This has become a stressor lately, since her hours were cut as the children got older. She would still like to work full-time.

Up until now, she has not received help from public agencies. Going forward, in addition to applying for public assistance, she will be linked to several other agencies to receive food stamps, heating assistance, Medicaid, and subsidized housing. She will also work with an advocate to help her obtain these resources.

Because Betty is an older, single, poor woman, this makes her more vulnerable to and at risk for discrimination. It is important that she have an advocate to help overcome any obstacles in her path.

Spiritual Assessment

It is hard to assess Betty's engagement with spiritual issues. At this point, Betty is wrestling with more pressing concerns: how she is going to meet her basic needs and survive financially. It's possible that she doesn't have the opportunity now to delve into the larger issues of purpose and meaning in life, connection to something larger than herself. One can imagine that it might benefit Betty to explore these areas more when she resolves her current financial problems and has time to reflect on the meaning of her life and prepares for death. Regardless, Betty has a good energy level and sees her potential to keep working. Overall, one could say she is a good "spirit."

End of Chapter Resourcess

Questions for Students

I have included questions to supplement the text for additional student learning. They are organized around the ten core competencies in the Council on Social Work Education (CSWE, 2008). The questions can be used for classroom or online discussion, given as written homework assignments, structured as classroom exercises, or used by students to do outside research. They can also be adapted for use in hybrid or online courses.

Educational Policy 2.1.1: Identify as a Professional Social Worker and Conduct Oneself Accordingly

1. In the interview with Betty, the worker brought up referring Betty to an advocate. Describe the role of an advocate and describe situations in which a client would benefit from these services.
2. In the video-recorded interview with Betty, the social worker, Ann, played the role of an advocate, exploring services and benefits that Betty might be eligible for. How well do you think Ann modeled these skills? What did you like, and what would you do differently?
3. After a class discussion on the skill of advocacy, write up your own role-play with a client who needs assistance gaining access to services. The class will break up into groups of three. One student will play the client, one the social worker, and the third student will

be the observer. The observer's job is to give feedback to the student who is in the role of social worker about her advocacy skills. Students will take turns playing the role of social worker. Each role-play should last about five minutes.

4. After completing exercise 3, students should write a reflective paper on their role-play and their knowledge of advocacy skills. In the paper, students can reflect on the skills they demonstrated, what they liked about the role-play, what went well, what they would do differently, and what they learned from the classroom experience.

5. There was a moment in the interview when Ann aligned herself with Betty by acknowledging how stupid the system can be. Was this appropriate? Do you think the worker violated any boundary issues?

6. Several times during the process recording, the social worker engaged in personal reflection. What role does this play in clinical work? Were there moments in the interview when you personally might have overreacted to something said or when Betty's comments triggered a response in you?

7. Comment on Ann's professional demeanor: her behavior, appearance, and communication. Were there any moments in which you were uncomfortable with her professionalism?

Educational Policy 2.1.2: Apply Social Work Ethical Principles to Guide Professional Practice

The questions below are to make students more aware of ethical issues that social workers confront every day in their practice.

1. When Ann acknowledged that the lack of coordination between the offices of social security and public assistance was stupid, was this statement a violation of professional social work values?

2. Were there any ethical issues raised for you in the interview with Betty?

3. How did the social worker deal with Betty's prejudicial and discriminatory comments about people on public assistance? What would you have done in this situation? Have you ever experienced a moment like this with a client and, if so, how did you handle it?

4. Do you think the worker was right in addressing Betty's prejudicial remarks in the meeting or should she have ignored them? Did it represent an ethical dilemma?

5. When watching the video, were you aware of having any feelings of counter-transference toward Betty regarding her prejudice? If yes, how would you handle these feelings? Do you think you would be able to work with Betty?

6. Ethical dilemmas can occur when a social worker feels conflicting loyalties between her responsibility to the client and to the agency. Did you notice any times in the interview when this happened? How would you address these issues?

7. What are some other work settings where social workers may find themselves caught up in conflicting loyalties between the client and the employer?

8. What are your personal values about people on public assistance? Are there some groups you think should be excluded or dealt with more punitively?

Educational Policy 2.1.3: Apply Critical Thinking to Inform and Communicate Professional Judgments

Critical thinking is an important skill in social work practice, and students are expected to demonstrate this competency before graduation. These exercises promote students becoming critical thinkers in practice.

1. After reading Gustafson's article, "The Criminalization of Poverty" (full citation found under references), explain how the welfare system and the criminal justice system in the United States are connected and work together on some cases.
2. Read Titmuss's article, "The role of Redistribution in Social Policy," and Abramovitz's article, "Everyone Is Still on Welfare: The Role of Redistribution in Social Policy" (full citations under references). What are their major arguments? How do you view their assessment of who is on welfare?
3. Betty was an older, poor white woman applying for assistance. How does this fit with the stereotype of people on public assistance? Do you think her experience would be different if she were a black, older woman in the same situation?
4. How does the current social, economic, and political context in the United States affect citizens' attitudes about public assistance?
5. How do the media influence the general public's opinion of people on welfare? Give three examples by referring to newspapers, journals, movies, and television shows.
6. In Box 86 in the process recording, the social worker gives information to Betty about registering with state child care agencies that could help her get babysitting jobs. At the same time, the social worker wonders if Betty is still up for handling the demands of babysitting. How would you evaluate whether Betty is able to work with children or if she is too vulnerable?
7. In the last stage of Erik Erikson's psychosocial theory, he refers to how the resolution of this crisis can either result in a sense of integrity or its opposite, despair (Erikson, 1982). How do you think Betty is navigating her way through this last stage?

Educational Policy 2.1.4: Engage Diversity and Difference in Practice

These questions are designed to teach students about engaging cultural diversity and understanding difference in practice.

1. Were there any issues of diversity and difference in Betty's case? If so, what were they, and how well were they addressed by the worker? What is the importance of acknowledging and engaging diversity and difference in practice?
2. What are ten stereotypes about older adults? What are the actual facts that can counter these biases? Are you aware of any prejudicial attitudes you have about older people?
3. What are ten stereotypes or derogatory statements used to describe people on public assistance? Are you aware of holding any biases again the poor? If so, can you understand where these views come from?

4. What are some ways that older adults are discriminated against? Explain your answer with supporting evidence from research.
5. What does the term, "the culture of poverty," mean? Include the sources you used to come up with this definition.
6. Many young social workers do not want to work with older adults. What are your thoughts and feelings about working with this age group?

Educational Policy 2.1.5: Advance Human Rights and Social and Economic Justice

Students are expected to address human-rights and social-justice issues when they come up in their practice. These questions are to help students think in terms of social and economic justice and become more competent in this area.

1. What were some of the human-rights and social- and economic-justice issues raised in the interview with Betty?
2. What would a welfare system look like that was based on real distributive justice, rather than the current one that rewards power and privilege?
3. How do the prevalent values in American society on individualism and social Darwinism affect people's attitudes about public assistance?
4. Identify a social and economic justice issue that is related to age or class and find a way to engage this issue in practice to advance the rights of this group. For example, you could get involved in an activity with a welfare-rights organization.
5. When Betty says that they treat the poor like criminals, what does she mean? What is the evidence for this? What are your views on this subject?

Educational Policy 2.1.6: Engage in Research-Informed Practice and Practice-Informed Research

1. Research cultural differences in how older people are treated. Compare how older adults are treated in America society with five other cultures.
2. Research immigrant rights to find out what public-assistance programs immigrants are eligible to receive. Are there any programs that exist for immigrants?
3. Research the differences in welfare policy in the United States and England. What are some of the differences?
4. Read the research literature on best practices when working with older adults who have substance abuse problems. Write a two-page summary of what you found.
5. Answer the question, "To what extent do older adults receive mental health services?" Consult the research literature on the subject to answer this question.

Educational Policy 2.1.7: Apply Knowledge of Human Behavior and the Social Environment

These questions will help students critically apply theories to assess, intervene, and evaluate work with clients.

1. In applying lifespan issues to Betty, how would you describe her situation in terms of development? As an older adult, what are the issues that challenge her, and what are the tasks she must address at this life stage?
2. Identify the theories used in working with Betty and explain how they were applied. Were there other theories you would have used to help you understand Betty or intervene in her situation?
3. Explain what projection means. Did you notice any moments in the interview when Betty used this defense? How can this term help explain how society blames people on public assistance for their problems?
4. At one point in the interview, Ann commented to Betty that some people feel shameful coming to the welfare office. What did she mean? How do you interpret the shame that some people feel when applying for public assistance?
5. How do you understand the general attitude of the public toward poor people? How can the defense of projection explain the tendency to blame the poor for their problems and not want to help them?

Educational Policy 2.1.8: Engage in Policy Practice to Advance Social and Economic Well-Being and to Deliver Effective Social Work Services

These questions are to encourage students to look at the role of policy in social work practice.

1. Read material on the 1996 federal welfare reform legislation, referred to as the Personal Responsibility and Work Opportunity Reconciliation Act of 1996. How did this government policy lead to the treatment of the poor as criminals?
2. What does the "social construction" of welfare fraud mean?
3. How can welfare law be changed to ensure that welfare recipients enjoy basic constitutional protections?
4. Describe ways in which welfare policies are infused with race, class, and gender bias.
5. During the 1980s, President Ronald Reagan popularized the term, "welfare queen." This expression for welfare recipients came from Reagan's exaggerated account of two publicized women convicted of welfare fraud. How did federal welfare policy and programs change with Reagan's emphasis on welfare fraud?
6. In response to the vilification of welfare recipients and attention to welfare fraud, welfare-rights advocates brought attention to corporate welfare and abuses by pharmacies and doctors. What were some of these abuses? How do they compare to those of welfare recipients? Give examples of corporate welfare and other crimes by the middle and upper class that cost the government more than welfare programs.
7. Would older people be in a better position on Medicare or on a national health insurance program? What are some of the weaknesses of Medicare? What services are omitted in Medicare?
8. How has the Age Discrimination in Employment Act of 1967 failed to protect older workers?

9. Talk to someone who works in the legislative branch of your local chapter of NASW. Learn about a social policy that is currently being proposed or amended in the state legislature and supported by social workers. Bring the information to class and discuss ways in which students can become involved in supporting this legislation.

Educational Policy 2.1.9: Respond to Contexts That Shape Practice

Social workers practice in many different settings and may need to familiarize themselves with the particular skills required in these settings. These questions help students to appreciate how context shapes practice and to develop competencies in this area.

1. What does organizational culture mean? How would you apply this concept to a public assistance office? How would you describe the organizational culture of a welfare office? Describe 10 characteristics of its culture.
2. What could be some effects of having a police officer stationed in a public assistance office?
3. Visit a public assistance office for part of a day and take notes on your observations, including the physical space and appearance, working conditions, volume of clients, emotional atmosphere, etc. Write up a three-page paper and describe your experience and observations.
4. Burnout is psychological and emotional exhaustion related to job stress. This can be caused by lack of supervisory support, lack of staff and resources, and constant bureaucratic constraints. How do you think burnout could affect a worker's personal and professional life? What are some ways to prevent burnout?
5. In the interview, Betty referred to some of the workers as mean and "snippy." What could cause public assistance workers to be insensitive to the needs of their clients? How would you remedy this situation?

Educational Policy 2.1.10(a)-(d): Engage, Assess, Intervene, and Evaluate with Individuals, Families, Groups, Organizations, and Communities

These questions are intended to give students practice engaging, assessing, intervening, and evaluating clients.

1. Betty was initially frustrated and angry during the interview with Ann. How well did Ann engage Betty? Do you think Betty felt heard by Ann? Explain your answer.
2. Did the worker's style of relating to Betty show empathy? Give an example. Were there times when Ann did not seem empathic? If yes, give an example.
3. Put yourself in the role of Betty. Write a one-page paper in the first person, describing what Betty is feeling. To do this, you must put yourself in Betty's shoes for a few moments.
4. How well do you think Ann helped Betty to feel less angry and frustrated? Is there anything the worker could have done differently to help Betty feel less stressed?

5. What does intersubjective evidence mean? How could it be used to evaluate Betty's progress from the beginning to the end of the meeting with Ann?
6. If, while working with Betty, you noticed she had a drinking problem, how would you address it? How would that change your approach to Betty?

Interviewing Skills Used in the Case of Betty

Below is a list of interviewing skills the social worker used in the session with Betty. They are listed in order of when they appeared in the interview. Although others may refer to these interactions differently or define the skills in others ways, this is one way of looking at them. Become familiar with these interviewing skills and practice them with other students in role-plays.

Introduction

At the beginning of the first meeting with the client, the social worker welcomes the client, tries to make the client comfortable, and tunes in to her own and the client's initial feelings about the first meeting.

Problem Definition

Problem definition is a collaborative process between the social worker and the client; they come to an agreement of what the problem is and what they will work on together.

Clarification of Role

The social worker helps the client understand what services the agency offers and what her role as social worker will be. There are times when the client needs reminding that the work is collaborative; it is the social worker's job to facilitate and not direct the process.

Questioning

Questioning is a way of gaining more information about a client's situation. There are many different kinds of questions, for example, open- and closed-ended questions and reflexive questions. It is often used in assessment as part of data collection.

Clarification of Problem

When sitting with a client, the social worker gathers details that further explain the nature of the problem. This is an ongoing process in which the social worker collects new information and keeps an open mind to alternative interpretations and perceptions.

Holding to Focus

Holding to focus is when the social worker helps the client stay on the topic under discussion. There may be times when, if a client is uncomfortable with the conversation, he may try to change the subject. This could also happen if a client goes off on a tangent or gets distracted. In these cases, the social worker tries to redirect the client back to the topic.

Reflecting Back Feelings

This is when the social worker gives a short response back to the client that mirrors the feeling the worker heard the client express. It is used to let the client know the worker is listening.

Confrontation

Confrontation is used by the social worker when there are inconsistencies between what the client has said and what is known to be true. The social worker believes it's best if the client comes to terms with this, faces the discrepancy in light of the facts. Workers can use confrontation to question a client's behavior that is harmful to the client. Also, a worker may confront a client's false assumptions or biases.

Challenging Moment

There may be times during an interview that are uncomfortable for both the social worker and the client. At these times, the social worker needs to contain both her feelings and the client's feelings. The social worker sits with these feelings and tries to understand them with the client. This can be hard to do, and many beginning social workers want to apologize or avoid pursuing uncomfortable subjects.

Showing Empathy

The social worker maintains a non-judgmental stance or remains neutral. The worker need not totally grasp the client's situation, but she must show that she is trying to understand what the client is feeling or experiencing. The social worker might say, "Tell me more about what your experience was" or "I want to understand more about what this means from your perspective."

Reassuring Client

At times, the social worker needs to allay a client's anxiety by supporting their efforts to change or accept new resources.

Information-Giving

Information-giving means informing the client about the social agency, the problem, and the resources for change. The social worker is knowledgeable about human development and human behavior and can help clients by sharing information that relates to a problem they are experiencing. For instance, a mother may complain that her 4-year-old daughter is misbehaving and not understand how the birth of a new sibling has affected the daughter.

Giving Client Feedback

There may be times when the social worker finds an opportunity to provide the client with information about his behavior and its effect on him and on other people. It can prove difficult, because the client may not want to hear or accept what the social worker is saying.

Containment

There are two types of containment situations, one in which the social worker contains herself from speaking or acting, and another when the worker contains the client from spinning out of control. In the first case, when the client begins to tell his story, the worker may have an urge to "help" before he completes the whole story. If the worker can contain herself and not speak too soon, the client can finish his story and express feelings without interruption. In the second case, when a client begins to get out of control or expresses too much emotion, the worker will intervene to calm the client down.

Helping Client to See Another Perspective

When clients can only see the problem from their own point of view, the social worker's task is to expand their understanding or perception of the problem. This may include discussing how other people think about or see the problem.

Offering Support

When a client shares a story that is painful, it helps when the social worker offers encouragement. By acknowledging the difficulty of the situation, you provide support for the client and allow him to continue the story.

Referral

Referral is when a client needs additional resources outside of the agency in which she's receiving services. With the client's permission, the worker makes the referral in order to help the client access other avenues for help.

Seeking Clarification

At different times during a session, the social worker may ask the client to talk about her perception of a situation in order to make sure she understands the client's point of view. This is also useful when the worker wants to check what she heard the client say so as not to make the wrong assumption.

Being Authentic and Genuine

Being authentic and genuine refers to the worker being sincere and honestly expressing what she feels, in a natural, personal way. These qualities help build positive relationships with clients.

Terms and Definitions for a Public Assistance Client

Advocacy

Advocacy is a macro practice skill that involves social action with or on behalf of clients. It includes obtaining services or resources for clients that they otherwise could not access. Advocacy also works to influence and change social policy that negatively impacts client systems. Advocates assist clients by making recommendations, finding the services they need, and ensuring they receive the services to which they are entitled.

Burnout

Burnout refers to psychological and emotional exhaustion caused by job-related stress that results in a social worker feeling emotionally depleted and unable to perform his or her duties. There are signs that can help you identify burnout. They include: becoming irritable and showing a lack of sensitivity to clients; feeling unable to separate from a client's situation; bringing problems home and spending a lot of time thinking and talking about them; taking client problems personally; losing initiative or interest in work; complaining or using derogatory language about clients; blaming clients for their problems; drinking to forget about work problems, and; becoming pessimistic about people's ability to change. This phenomenon can stem from heavy caseloads, poor supervisory support, boundary problems, a weak culture of work, or personal problems affecting work.

Diversity

Diversity is most commonly used to refer to differences between cultural groups, but it also can describe differences in terms of ethnicity, race, class, religion, sexuality, age, health, disability, and gender.

Department of Transitional Assistance

The Department of Transitional Assistance (DTA) is located within the State of Massachusetts Executive Office of Health and Human Services. Its mission is to assist low-income individuals and families to meet their basic needs, increase their incomes, and improve their quality of life. The DTA serves one out of every eight people in the Commonwealth—including working families, children, elders, and people with disabilities. The services include food and nutritional assistance, cash assistance, and employment supports. Please note that I referenced the DTA, a welfare program in Massachusetts, because Betty's case takes place in Massachusetts. What most state welfare programs have in common is the emphasis on temporary assistance, discouraging recipients from becoming dependent on the system. http://www.mass.gov/eohhs/gov/departments/dta/

Duty Worker

This is an intake welfare counselor who refers clients to appropriate resources they need and determines client eligibility for specific programs.

EBT Card

This is a Supplemental Nutrition Assistance Program (SNAP) Electronic Benefit Transfer (EBT) card, which works like a debit card with a PIN number when checking out at grocery stores. The client is allowed to use the EBT card to buy food, such as breads, cereals, fruits, vegetables, meats, fish, and poultry, as well as seeds and plants that produce food for the household to eat. In some areas, restaurants are authorized to accept benefits from qualified homeless, elderly, or disabled people in exchange for low-cost meals. Households cannot use SNAP benefits to buy alcohol, cigarettes, or tobacco. Also, EBT cannot get used for nonfood items such as: pet foods, soaps, paper products, household products, vitamins and medicines, grooming supplies, cosmetics, food eaten in-store, hot foods, energy drinks classified as supplements, or live animals. Junk food such as soft drinks, candy, cookies, snack crackers, and ice cream are food items and are therefore eligible items.

Eligibility Requirement

The TAFDC is based on both income standards for the parent of a child under age 18 and household size. It is adjusted annually as prescribed by Massachusetts budget. SNAP is also based on income and household size, but it is adjusted annually as prescribed by the United States Department of Agriculture/Food and Nutrition Service.

Empowerment

Empowerment entails providing clients with information and skills to take action on their own behalf, advocate for their rights, and gain access to needed resources. It involves helping clients have confidence in their ability to control their lives.

Food Stamps

Food stamps are a type of government assistance to help low-income households buy food. Food stamps can be used to buy almost any food item in any store where one usually shops for food. The SNAP in Massachusetts replaced the original Food Stamps Program. Starting in the late 1980s, the changeover began from paper stamps to the more portable EBT card.

National Association of Social Workers

The National Association of Social Workers (NASW) is the largest professional organization of social workers in the world with 145,000 members. The goal of the NASW is to "enhance the professional growth and development of its members, to create and maintain professional standards, and to advance sound social policies." http://www.naswdc.org

National Association of Social Workers Code of Ethics

The Code of Ethics was approved by the NASW Delegate Assembly in 1996 and is a guide to the everyday professional conduct of social workers. The Code has four sections, which are the Preamble, Purpose of NASW Code of Ethics, Ethical Principles, and Ethical Standards. The Preamble is a summary of the mission and core values of the field of Social Work. The Purpose is an overview of the Code's main functions and a brief guide for dealing with ethical problems in social work. The Ethical Principles section presents broad ethical principles based on social work core values. Ethical Standards sites specific ethical standards to guide social worker conduct. The NASW Code of Ethics is available in paperback or on the NASW's website. http://www.naswdc.org

Social Welfare Policy

Social welfare policy refers to programs that confront social problems, such as poverty, child abuse, and substandard housing. It is influenced by the socio-political culture and political ideologies of the government in power at the time (e.g., liberalism and conservatism).

SNAP

The Supplemental Nutrition Assistance Program (SNAP), formerly the Food Stamps Program, provides assistance to low-income families with children, elders, the disabled, and the temporarily unemployed, as well as to the working poor with limited income.

SSI

Supplemental Security Income (SSI) is a federal program that provides monthly cash payments to people in need. SSI is for people who are 65 or older and in financial need as well as for blind or disabled people of any age, including children. The money is provided for basic needs, such as food, shelter, and clothing. Some clients may qualify for food stamps. To qualify, clients must have little or no income and few resources. They also must live in the United States or the Northern Mariana Islands. If they are not U.S. citizens, but are residents, they may still be able to get SSI.

TAFDC

The Transitional Aid to Families with Dependent Children (TAFDC) is a government program the DTA oversees that gives cash and medical assistance to needy families with dependent children, including pregnant women, to help them meet the basic needs of their children. This is also sometimes referred to simply as "welfare."

References

Abramovitz, M. (2001). Everyone is still on welfare: The role of redistribution in social policy. *Social Work, 46*(4), 297–308.

Bellah, R. N., Madsen, R., Sullivan, W. M., Swidler, A., & Tipton, S. M. (1996). *Habits of the Heart: Individualism and Commitment in American Life.* Berkeley, CA: University of California Press.

Berkman, L. F. & Syme, S. L. (1976). Social class, susceptibility, and sickness. *American Journal of Epidemiology, 104*(1), 1–8.

Boswell, S. S. (2012). Old people are cranky: Helping professional trainees' knowledge, attitudes, aging anxiety, and interest in working with older adults. *Educational Gerontology, 38*(7), 465–472.

Belgrave, L. L. (1993). Discrimination against older women in health care. *Journal of Women and Aging, 5*(3–4), 181–199.

Brush, L. (2011). Poverty, battered women and work in US public policy. New York: Oxford University Press.

Brownell, B. & Kelly, J. J. (2013). *Ageism and Mistreatment of Older Workers.* New York: Springer.

Casey, T. J. & Mannix, M. R. (1989). Quality control in public assistance: Victimizing the poor through one-sided accountability. *Social Welfare Policy and Law, 22,* 1381–1385.

Chan, S. & Stevens, A. H. (2004). How does job loss affect the timing of retirement? *Contributions to Economic Analysis & Policy, 3*(1), ISSN (online) 1538-0645.

Chappell, M. (2010). *The War on Welfare: Family, Poverty, and Politics in Modern America.* Philadelphia: University of Pennsylvania Press.

Collier, E. (2005). Latent age discrimination in mental health care. *Mental Health Care Practice, 8*(6), 42–45.

Consensus Panel Members, Center for Substance Abuse. (2001). *Substance Abuse Among Older Adults.* Rockville, MD: U.S. Department of Health and Human Services.

Cottle, N. R. & Glover, R. J. (2007). Combating ageism: Change in student knowledge and attitudes regarding aging. *Educational Gerontology, 33,* 501–512.

Council on Social Work Education. (2008). *Educational Policy and Accreditation Standards.* Alexandria, VA: Council on Social Work Education.

Cummings, S. M., Galambos, C., & DeCoster, V. A. (2003). Predictors of MSW employment in geronotological practice. *Educational Gerontology, 29*, 1–18.

Davies, N. (2011). Reducing inequities in health care provision for older adults. *Nursing Standard, 25*(41), 49–55.

Ehrenreich, B. (2009, August 8). Is it now a crime to be poor? *The New York Times*, p. WK9.

Erikson, E. H. (1982). *The Life Cycle Completed*. New York: W.W. Norton & Co.

Gans, H. J. (1995). *The War against the Poor: The Underclass and Anti-Poverty*. New York: Basic Books.

Gupta, R. & Pillai, V. (2002). Cultural influences on perceptions of caregiver burden among Asian Indians and Pakistanis. *The Southwest Journal, 17*(1/2), 65–74.

Garner, J. D. & Young, A. A. (1993). *Women and Healthy Aging: Living Productively in Spite of It All*. Binghampton, NY: Haworth Press.

Gilens, M. (1999). *Why Americans Hate Welfare: Race, Media, and Politics of Antipoverty Policy*. Chicago: University of Chicago Press.

Gustafson, K. (2009). The criminalization of poverty. *The Journal of Criminal Law and Criminology, 99*(3), 643–715.

Gustafson, K. (2011). *Cheating Welfare: Public Assistance and the Criminalization of Poverty*. New York: New York University Press.

Harris, I. A. & Dollinger, S. (2001). Participation in a course on aging: Knowledge, attitudes, and anxiety about aging in oneself and others. *Educational Gerontology, 27*, 657–667.

Hochschild, J. L. (1995). *Facing up the American Dream: Race, Class, and the Soul of the Nation*. Princeton, NJ: Princeton University Press.

Imbody, B. & Vandsburger, E. (2011). Elder abuse and neglect: Assessment tools, interventions, and recommendations for effective service provision. *Educational Gerontology, 37*(7), 634–650.

Johnson, J. D., Olivo, N., Gibson, N., Reed, W., & Asburn-Nardo, L. (2009). Priming the media stereotypes reduces support for social welfare policies: The mediating role of empathy. *Personality and Social Psychology Bulletin, 35*(4), 463–476.

Jorgensen, A. A. B. (1993). Public policy, health care and older women. In J. D. Garner & A. A. Young (Eds.), *Women and Healthy Aging: Living Productively in Spite of It All*. Binghampton, NY: Haworth Press.

Kimmel, D. C. (1988). Ageism, psychology, and public policy. *American Psychologist, 43*(3), 175–178.

Kite, M. E. A., Stockdale, G. D., Whitley Jr., B. E., & Johnson, B. T. (2005). Attitudes towards younger and older adults: An applied meta-analytic review. *Journal of Social Forces, 61*(2), 241–266.

Lahey, J. (2005). *Do older workers face discrimination?* Retrieved from http://www.bc.edu/centers/crr/

Mann, K. (2008). Remembering and rethinking the social divisions of welfare: 50 years on. *Journal of Social Policy, 38*(1), 1–18.

Muller, C. F. (1990). *Health Care and Gender*. New York: Russell Sage.

Murray, C. (1984). *Losing Ground: American Social Policy 1950-1980*. New York: Basic Books.

Neugarten, B. (1983). Health care, Medicare, and health policy for older people. *American Psychologist, 38*(3), 311–315.

Ory, M., Hoffman, M. K., Sanner, B., & Mockenhaupt, R. (2003). Challenging aging stereotypes: Strategies for creating a more active society. *American Journal of Preventive Medicine, 25*, 164–171.

Pallitto, R. (2010). The public secrets of welfare. *The Journal of Progressive Human Services, 21*, 154–178.

Parish, C. (2009). Access is the key. *Mental Health Practice, 12*(9), 3.

Powell, M. (2010). Ageism and abuse in the workplace: A new frontier. *Journal of Gerontological Social Work, 53*, 654–658.

Rauschenbach, C., Goritz, A. S., & Hertel, G. (2012). Age stereotypes about emotional resilience at work. *Educational Gerontology, 38*(8), 511–519.

Reich, R. (1991). *The Work of Nations: Preparing Ourselves for the 21st Century Capitalism*. New York: Knopf.

Report of the Villers Foundation. (1987). *On the Other Side of Easy Street: Myths and Facts about the Economics of Old Age*. Washington, DC: Villers Foundation.

Roscigno, V. J., Mong, S., Byron, R., & Tester, G. (2007). Age discrimination, social closure, and employment. *Social Forces, 86*(1), 313–334.

Rothenberg, J. Z. & Gardner, D. S. (2011). Protecting older workers: The failure of the age discrimination in employment act of 1967. *Journal of Sociology and Social Welfare, 38*(1), 9–30.

Ruggiano, N. (2012). Consumer direction in long-term care policy: Overcoming barriers to promoting older adults' opportunity for self-direction. *Journal of Gerontological Social Work, 55*, 146–159.

Spencer-Wood, S. M. & Matthews, C. N. (2011). Impoverishment, criminalization, and the culture of poverty. *Historical Archaeology, 45*(3), 1–10.

Syme, S., Berkman, L., & Berkman, L. F. (1990). Social class, susceptibility, and sickness. In P. Conrad & R. Kern (Eds.), *The Sociology of Health and Illness: Critical Perspectives*. New York: St. Martins.

Thurow, L. (1992). *Head to Head: The Coming Economic Battle among Japan, Europe, and America*. New York: Warner.

Titmuss, R. M. (1965). The role of re-distribution in social policy. *Social Security Bulletin, 39*, 14–20.

Wacquant, L. (2009). *Punishing the Poor: The Neoliberal Government of Social Insecurity*. Durham, NC: Duke University Press.

Weiss, E. M. & Maurer, T. J. (2004). Age discrimination in personnel decisions: A reexamination. *Journal of Applied Social Psychology, 34*(8), 1551–1582.

5

Practice with Children: Issues of Childhood Leukemia and Divorce

Emily: "Will they be scared of me, thinking they might catch it?"

Setting: Outpatient Hospital Clinic

Description of Practice Area
Practice with Children

Social work practice with children uses a multisystemic approach that involves engaging the child, parents, school, medical community, and other groups, such as friends and church. Social workers need to integrate knowledge from many areas when doing assessments on children. They must pay particular attention to different perspectives on development, including whether the child has reached normal developmental milestones for her age. Life span developmental theories, psychodynamic theory, and cognitive theories are additional knowledge sources that illuminate children's cognitive and emotional development. Family systems theories are also important to understand a child's problems in the context of family life.

Emily is an 11-year-old child who has just been diagnosed with Leukemia. At the same time, she is struggling with a painful family situation that occurred five months ago when her father separated from her mother and left the family home. With this information you can begin to imagine how these events might impact her life in developmental, cognitive, and emotional ways. As you listen to the video-recorded interview between the social worker and Emily and read the process recording in each of the five excerpts, you will observe the multi-systemic approach in action and also appreciate the theories and practice skills that are used to help her. The social worker's interventions with Emily will include collaborating with various systems: her family, other members on the medical team, the school, and community resources.

Developmental Theory

Social workers use developmental theory to understand clients. Development occurs throughout the lifecycle from birth to death and explains changes taking place in the individual on different levels—biological, psychological, social, and spiritual. Both individuals and families go through a series of stages as part of development. In this chapter, we will concentrate on Emily and look at childhood development. The next chapter will include an interview with Emily's mother and will discuss the family from a developmental perspective.

Erik Erikson (1963, 1968) developed a psychosocial theory to explain development throughout the life span. His approach is often referred to as the "Eight Stages of Man," because it describes eight stages of human development. Each stage is characterized by a developmental crisis that the individual must cope with and master to make a successful transition to the next stage. If the crisis is not resolved, the individual will struggle with successive stages. Since Emily is between childhood and adolescence, I will cover development starting with school-age children, and then through the preteen years to adolescence. This spans two of Erikson's life stages: stage 4, or middle children, which occurs between the ages of 6 and 12, and is referred to as "industry versus inferiority"; and stage 5, which occurs during the adolescent years. Because Emily is 11 years old, she technically falls under stage 4. However, since she will enter her adolescent years quite soon, I also will discuss this stage.

Children start school at age 5 and are exposed to the wider world with new demands on them. As they venture out into this new social environment, between the ages of 5 and 8, they still experience the fears and fantasies of early childhood that make them susceptible to worries. They need their parents to act as a security blanket, a place of refuge to maintain "a cocoon of safety and order—a place of bedtime rituals and regular meals and things kept where they belong" (Taffel, 1991, p. 40). During this period of middle childhood, referred to as "latency" in psychodynamic terms or "industry versus inferiority" by Erikson (1963, 1968), children are industrious. They want to be productive, learn as much as they can, and acquire skills. School is important to them, as are their relationships to parents and teachers.

Between the ages of 10 and 12, as they become preteens, children often appear to embody "Jekyll and Hyde." This means a child might change from "a moody, sloppy, obstructionist kid who thinks parents are geeks, nerds, and dorks to a waif who wants to sit in a parent's lap and hear a favorite storybook tale read aloud" (Taffel, 1991, p. 40). During this stage, children expect their parents to represent a combination of "chum and cop" and are testing their parent's capacity both for holding them and "reining" them in when necessary (Taffel, 1991). Wanting to stay in their parent's laps may indicate some ambivalence about moving from childhood to adolescence and having more responsibility.

As children push for more independence during adolescence, they don't want the parents to let go completely. They strive to find their own unique identities (Erikson, 1968), but they still need to feel connected to parents. They yearn for freedom and autonomy, but they also want to know their parents will still care for and protect them; they want parents to remain a strong presence is their lives despite "protestation to the contrary" (Taffel, 1991, p. 70). Adolescents rebel knowing that their parents are still at the helm and provide what

Taffel refers to as an "empathic envelope." Taffel (1991) explains what makes for successful families and the role of the family therapist to help them:

> The most successful families are those who know how to connect with their kids, how to create for them and their children an "empathic envelope," a kind of psychic container or nest in which children feel they are being held, secure as much as possible from external threat and the extremes of their own impulses. It is the therapist's job not only to help parents strengthen this envelope, but to model for them in therapeutic work how to connect differently with children of different ages. Far from limiting freedom, a strong empathic envelope encourages the parent-child bond, allowing children and parents to live without the terrible anxiety that the container is flimsy, and that one day they will all suddenly find themselves alone and drifting in space. (p. 70)

Another defining characteristic of adolescence is how kids form relationship with friends. At this stage, they are more aware of their social environment, especially their peers whose company they now prefer to parents. As this shift takes place, the family does not play the same central role in an adolescent's life, but it is still important and provides the "empathic envelope," a sense of security and feeling loved that allows this exploration. Simultaneously, adolescents have increasing cognitive abilities, which means they can understand more abstract concepts and show deeper insight.

Lifecycle changes affect a child's relationship with his parents from early to late childhood to adolescence and then on to early adulthood. During childhood, kids tend to idealize their parents who are their role models. This is reflected in ways they imitate what they observe their parents doing. For the most part, in healthy families, children like their parents and want their approval. Then, adolescence arrives at age twelve or thirteen, and parents notice a change—their children no longer want to spend as much time with them and become argumentative and critical of them. As adolescents move into the next developmental stage, early adulthood, in their early 20s, they go through another reappraisal process and begin to see their parents more realistically, with both positive and negative characteristics.

As you listen to Emily in the interview, notice how she reflects aspects of the older child and preteen but is also transitioning into adolescence. School is important to her and has formed a critical part of her identity, giving her positive self-esteem. She excels in her studies, and her teachers recognize her as an excellent student. Friends are becoming valuable to her as well, and during the interview with the social worker, Emily says she is worried about how her illness will affect these peer relationships. She misses her friends and wants them to visit her to "take her mind off things." She is still attached to her parents but distressed about their separation. Emily feels close to both her parents and wants her dad back home with her. She tells the worker in the interview that she likes waking up in the morning and seeing both her parents. This is Emily's way of saying she still needs her parents to provide her with a strong "container" to keep her safe and care for her during her illness.

Although Emily appears quite mature and articulate in the interview, there are signs that the stresses in her life, the leukemia and her parent's separation, may be affecting her development and causing some regression, with a partial retreat into wishful thinking and fantasy. She needs her parents more than ever, not less. She wants them to support her and not fight with each other, especially in front of her. She worries about her family and is less secure about their role in her life, making it harder for her to transition to the next stage. Although her parent's fighting could hasten her move into adolescence and its associated period of disillusionment, this does not appear to have happened yet. She has a mixture of childlike thought processes, reflected in her impossible wishes, talk of a fortune-teller, and the fantasy of reuniting her parents. She wants her parents "to maintain the cocoon of safety and order" with the rituals that are important to her; for example, she wants to wake up in the morning and find both her parents. At the same time, there is the beginning of abstract thinking and a capacity for insight. This is demonstrated when she says that if her parents stop fighting, it will help her get better. She also shows that she can reflect deeply about what is happening and how it affects her on multiple levels. She is resilient, and when confronted with making changes in her lifestyle due to chemotherapy, she is able to adapt.

Emily's leukemia diagnosis might present challenges for her psychosocial develop-ment and interfere with the tasks associated with this life stage: having educational goals, nurturing a health body image, creating identity, becoming more independent, and building family and peer relationships. If Emily loses her hair as part of chemotherapy, it will have a profound effect on her body image. Studies have found a negative relationship between cancer and body image (Carpentier & Fortenberry, 2010; Pendley et al., 1997). Negotiating a healthy body image is a critical part of adolescence, and a diagnosis of cancer can make it more difficult to achieve (Bellizzi et al., 2012). Helping Emily cope with the changes that occur to her body during chemotherapy will be an important part of her work with Gloria, the social worker. It has implications for the future, because "a poor body image can lead to poor self-esteem and may affect the ability to form healthy peer and intimate relationships during young adulthood" (Davison & McCabe, 2006, p. 15).

Resiliency

Resiliency refers to one's ability to overcome hardships and thrive in spite of obstacles. A child's exposure to certain risk factors does not always predict a specific outcome (Schriver, 2011, p. 119). His personal characteristics might play a role in resiliency, though. Examples include: social competence (flexibility, empathy, communication skills, sense of humor, relationship skills, adaptability); problem-solving skills (thinking abstractly and reflectively, and exploring alternative solutions); autonomy (sense of identity and self-efficacy, ability to exert some control over the environment and act independently); and a sense of purpose and future (DuBois & Miley, 2010, pp. 377–378).

Studies of childhood cancer survivors suggest the possibility that some are resilient. In retrospect, they attribute their favorable adult experiences to having had cancer as a child (Zebrack et al., 2012). Positive outcomes after a traumatic event, such as childhood cancer, are related to the survivors perceiving benefits from the episode (Chester & Parry, 2005; Orbach et al., 2005; Woodgate, 1999). These children interpret their battles against cancer in constructive ways and find meaning in illness (Barakat et al., 2006). In a study of childhood cancer survivors between the ages of 14 and 25, more than half saw themselves as having more concern for others, an ability to cope with traumatic events, a sense of identity, and spiritual well-being (Zebrack et al., 2012). In another study of cancer survivors between the ages of 11 and 19, the participants identified four or more positive outcomes they associated with having had cancer, after at least one year post treatment (Barakat et al., 2006). It appears that a cancer history has shaped and continues to shape people's sense of themselves and the world around them (Zebrack et al., 2012).

Research on resilience has important implications for interventions with children with childhood cancers. By understanding the factors that contribute to resilience, social workers can promote these characteristics in children and perhaps prevent certain negative consequences often associated with childhood cancer. These ideas will also affect Emily, who has just received a diagnosis of leukemia and will be starting chemotherapy.

Play and Expressive Therapies with Children

Play and expressive therapies are traditionally used with children and adolescents. They date back to the earliest days of the social work profession and were used by Jane Addams in the settlement houses in the late 1800s (Brieland, 1990; Koerin, 2003). These techniques continue to prove helpful today for a number of reasons. Younger children can communicate better through play and other expressive modalities. Both children and adolescents may find that these alternative outlets for showing their feelings are more effective than just talking. Through the use of play therapy, children can vent or contain their emotions and work through their problems with a trained practitioner who understands the meaning of their play. Older children can eventually connect the metaphors in play to their lives and verbalize what they are learning about themselves.

Play therapy can be directive or nondirective, depending on the orientation of the practitioner. Virgina Axline published one of the first books on play therapy that uses a client-centered, nondirective approach. The child has the freedom to be himself without facing criticism or pressure to change. A nondirective style gives the child "the opportunity to experience growth under the most favorable conditions," and the child "begins to realize the power within himself to be an individual in his own right, to think for himself, to make his own decisions, to become psychologically more mature, and, by doing this, to realize selfhood" (Axline, 1947, p. 16).

Play therapy is a kind of talk for children in which they express themselves through metaphors and symbols. Play is a window into a better view of the child's life and gives meaning to her experiences. It provides the social worker with valuable insights about the child and her progress throughout the course of treatment. The worker must watch and listen to the child's use of metaphors and symbols in play to understand her reality, fears, struggles, and coping styles. If you are working with children, you need a room supplied with some essential toys and materials, such as dolls, a dollhouse and figures, vehicles, stuffed animals, blocks, puppets, clay, crayons, cards, paint, chess or checkers, and a doctor's kit. In the case of Emily, a preadolescent, she would not be inclined to play with dolls and puppets, but she may be willing to draw and model clay.

Play therapy is catered to each individual case with specific goals, and it is important to remember that what is helpful with one child may not be with another. A worker can use play therapy for several purposes with children, including: ventilation; binding anxiety; working through certain issues; for communication purposes; in the service of regression; for the development of skills; and toward the modification of lifestyle (Burns, 1970). Play therapy in a hospital context is often used more to bind or contain anxiety than to interpret (Adamo & DeFalco, 2012). As children express feelings that upset them, they may become so nervous that it can be damaging (Burns, 1970). In these instances, it helps to give them something to reduce the anxiety, like clay to sculpt, or cards to play.

Adamo and DeFalco (2012) illustrate this point with an example from their work in a hospital with a 7-year-old boy over the course of a year up until his death. One of the ongoing themes in the boy's drawings was of a house, which he named after the therapist. The house was a metaphor for a container and symbolized how the practitioner helped to contain the boy's emotions. The drawings of the house also reflected the child's changing physical state. As his medical condition deteriorated, the house also transformed from a small red dot to a "rickety house" to a "fairly solid house" in the final days, perhaps showing how he felt "sufficiently welcomed and contained" (Adamo & DeFalco, 2012, p. 102).

Interventions using expressive therapies can draw on a variety of disciplines: the graphic arts; music; poetry and other forms of creative writing; movement and dance; drama, theater and improvisation; horticulture; interaction with animals; and mind-body practices such as meditation, yoga, and tai chi (Peck et al., 2005; Rosaen & Benn, 2006; Wall, 2005). There are numerous social work articles describing effective art-based interventions with children. A selection of these articles describe art therapy and writing with deaf children (Cohene & Cohene, 1990); art in existential family therapy (Alford & Lantz, 1995); drawing with street children (DiCarlo et al., 2000); art with children in crisis (Klingman et al., 1987); music with children (Lefevre, 2004); music and art with traumatized children (Davis, 2010); and poetry in school social work (Maki & Mazza, 2004). Empirical studies have confirmed the efficacy of holistic arts-based group work with children in foster care (Coholic et al., 2009) and cultural arts programs with at-risk youth (Rapp-Paglicci et al., 2006).

One innovative and experiential intervention receiving considerable attention is Animal Assisted Therapy (AAT), a new approach that employs animals as part of intervention. Pet Partners, formerly Delta Society, is a national organization that uses animals to help people. In 1990, Pet Partners established its Therapy Animal Program, which trains volunteers and their pets for work with children, adults, seniors, and families struggling with mental health issues and loss. The organization also offers animal programs in hospitals, nursing homes, rehabilitation centers, schools, and other facilities. Pet Partners' national network links volunteers with facilities in their own communities that request visiting pets and respond to community crises. For example, during the tragic shootings at the elementary school in Newtown, Connecticut in December 2012, Pet Partners' staff worked closely with the therapy animal teams and representatives who reside in Connecticut to offer local services. Social workers use a wide range of animals for AAT, including dogs, cats, birds, rabbits, and horses. The animals facilitate the development of trust, positive communication, and emotional growth and learning (Fine, 2006). The targeted use of horses has shown some promise with at-risk children and adolescents (Trotter et al., 2008) and youth who have experienced family violence (Schultz et al., 2007).

As part of a three-year project to examine all aspects of pediatric cancer treatment and recovery, Sargent, a children's cancer charity in England, began an international initiative that encouraged children to tell their stories through photography (www.clicsargent.org.uk). Starting in 2005, the grant provided money for children to buy disposable cameras that were used to document what it was like to live with cancer. Children around the world were first asked to capture their personal experiences in hospitals and, later, returning to school. This project shows how expressive therapies can help children cope with serious illness; it had a secondary benefit of educating the public about issues surrounding childhood cancer.

Divorce and Children

In this chapter, we concentrate on the impact that Emily's parents' separation has on her. The next chapter covers an interview with Emily's mother and includes material on family systems and a developmental perspective for understanding the family lifecycle.

Rising divorce rates (Johnson et al., 2004) have important implications for the well-being of children of divorced parents who experience a significant disruption in their young lives. Many conflicting studies exist on the social, emotional, and psychological costs of divorce on children and potential long-term effects. Some studies have shown that a lack of family cohesion due to parental separation, divorce, or transiency causes adjustment problems in children (Amato, 2005; Bank et al., 1993; Grych & Fincham, 1990; Guidubaldi et al., 1983; Huffman, 2013; Shifflet & Cummings, 1999; Troxel & Matthews, 2004). Another study (Bernstein et al., 2012) found that divorce was not associated with higher rates of depression or low self-esteem in young adults, and was potentially related to empathy and an increased ability to take the perspective of others. However, this same study (Bernstein et al., 2012) showed that young adults in divorced families had a fear of abandonment after divorce, a sentiment often associated with later attachment insecurity.

There are certain critical factors to consider when understanding the impact of divorce on children: the ages of children at the time of the divorce; the child's temperament and personality; the amount of conflict and fighting between the parents; and outside support from family members, friends, and other groups. When studying the relative importance of genetics versus the environment on children's problem behaviors, research has found that environmental influences better explain the behavior of children whose parents have divorced (Button et al., 2005; Compas et al., 2001; Huizink et al., 2007; Robbers et al., 2012). The frequency, intensity, and style of parental conflict and fighting may mediate and moderate children's behavioral reactions to divorce (Compas et al., 2001).

The results of these studies have implications for Emily and how her parents handle their separation and divorce. Emily shares concern about her parents' fighting and asks the social worker to help them stop, especially in front of her. If the parents can decrease their level of conflict with each other, this would make a difference for her. Since Emily will receive services from the medical social worker in the outpatient clinic for the next two years, the worker will play a key role in assisting the family with these issues. Social work intervention with the parents can help them communicate better with each other and fight less. It can also address how to cooperate on parenting issues, especially related to Emily's special needs during her cancer treatment.

It's considered most difficult for children between the ages of 6 and 11 to cope with divorce, because they are old enough to feel pain but too young to understand or control their emotional reactions. Adolescents may feel forced into adulthood, have difficulty coping with family changes, and experience pressure to choose between their parents. External social support systems can act as buffers against some of the alienation kids may feel, which could explain why children and adolescents tend to seek help from people outside their family during divorce (Adams, 1982; Wallerstein & Kelly, 1980).

Children often think that their parents will get back together, denying the possibility of divorce. Sometimes they will do everything in their power to try to mend the rift. When social workers observe this happening, it is important to discourage these thoughts and help kids come to terms with the divorce. This might include having the parents participate in some of the treatment to confront the child's normal flight into wishful thinking and fantasy. In Emily's case, she talks about her wish for her parents to get back together. She tells the social worker that she tries to keep them from fighting by distracting them with questions off topic. With the onset of leukemia, she may think that her illness will bring her parents back together.

An important determinant of children's adjustment to divorce is the quality of the parent/child relationship. A healthy involvement with both parents is important. Parents need to talk directly and honestly with the children about the separation, the divorce, and what the future will look like in terms that the child will comprehend. Parents also need to communicate well with each other and agree on how to discipline and raise the children. Divorce education programs for parents can help build protective behaviors that improve children's adjustment over time (Kelly & Emery, 2003). Current research includes policy recommendations to help make divorce less anxiety-provoking and more understandable to children:

> Psychoeducational materials directed at divorcing parents, for example, may help impart the ongoing, diplomatic, and developmentally appropriate conversations with their children about the reasons for and implications of the divorce. These conversations may help to attenuate children's fear of abandonment and other problematic beliefs fostering distress in future relationships. Given our nation's high rate of marital dissolution, this should be an important social and political goal. (Bernstein et al., 2012, p. 726)

Practice with Leukemia and Childhood Cancer

Medical advances in the last 30 years have led to early detection and treatment of childhood cancers that have resulted in higher survival rates. For example, the five-year survival rate of pediatric cancer is about 80%, resulting in a growing population of childhood cancer survivors (Cruz-Arrieta & Weinshank, 2008). What once was a fatal illness is now a chronic condition and calls for more psychosocial services. This requires new paradigms for helping children and their families cope with the effects of cancer treatment and chronic illness in their lives (Clarke et al., 2005). It also means that schools must be prepared for children to return after treatment (Franklin et al., 2009; Germain, 2006; Ross & Scarvalone, 1982). Emily will meet regularly with a social worker in the hospital outpatient clinic, and the worker will follow her case throughout her lengthy treatment. This worker will also coordinate Emily's care with other members of the multidisciplinary medical team and with Emily's school.

Addressing psychosocial issues as part of the treatment of childhood cancer has received attention in recent years (Hicks, 2001; Ljungman et al., 2003; Mitchell et al., 2006; Waters et al., 2003). Patients often come to the hospital with psychosocial issues that existed before they became ill (Cruz-Arrieta & Weinshank, 2008). Social workers need to address these issues, because they can weaken a patient's immune system and ability to fight disease. Longstanding psychosocial issues can also compromise a child's capacity to cope with the additional stress of illness. This is true for Emily, who in addition to being diagnosed with leukemia, is also dealing with her parents' separation and possible divorce. To effectively treat her cancer using a holistic approach, the team, of which the social worker is an integral part, must tackle any pressing psychosocial needs that might interfere with optimal recovery. This will be discussed in more detail later in the chapter, under a section on diagnosis and treatment of childhood leukemia.

Studies have found that children with cancer might develop psychological problems during their treatment, as indicated by both parents' and teachers' responses (Earle & Eiser, 2007; Gerali et al., 2011). In regard to children diagnosed with leukemia, they appeared to have more significant issues at the beginning of treatment, but showed a slight improvement in psychological functioning over the next six months (Gerali, 2011). In addition to individual counseling, children benefit from psychoeducational groups at the time of diagnosis or shortly after. Using a cognitive-behavioral approach, these groups offer emotional support, improve coping skills, and enhance adaptation to illness. Positive outcomes corresponded to psychoeducational group intervention for children with cancer that focused on: information-giving, teaching relaxation exercises, and instilling social competence and positive thinking (Maurice-Stam et al., 2009). These groups also provide a forum in which children with cancer can share stories and gain support from their peers, an added benefit.

Setting: Social Work in an Outpatient Hospital Clinic

Please refer to chapter 3 for additional information about social work in a medical setting. Rather than repeat information already discussed, I would like to concentrate on some of the nuances of Emily's case that relate to collaborating with other healthcare professionals. In particular, I want to emphasize the tendency of social workers to undervalue their knowledge and skills in medical settings in which social work is not the primary focus. This may result, in part, from the hierarchies embedded in the organizational culture of medical settings. However, I believe it may also stem from a lack of confidence that social workers have about their role in medical environments and their feeling of being undervalued by other healthcare professionals.

When I first entered social work in the 1970s, hospital social work held a more prominent position than is does today, and this was reflected in the organizational structure of hospitals. At that time, case management was under the direction of hospital social work departments that were larger and staffed better. Social workers played a vital role in addressing psychosocial issues with patients and working with families and other members of the multidisciplinary team on patient planning. These days, many hospitals employ fewer social workers. This is partly due to cost-cutting measures in the 1990s, when psychosocial services were considered too expensive and less essential than other services (Kazak et al., 2003). Social workers who remained in hospitals often had their roles diminished. Case management, once the purview of social workers, was taken over by nursing professionals, with social workers instead reporting to these new nurse managers.

When these changes began to take hold, the social work profession did not speak up loudly enough to protest the cutting of hospital social work programs. We did not advocate for the importance of psychosocial care and our unique perspective on multidisciplinary healthcare teams. We gave up the battle without much of a fight. However, with the potential for big shifts in the future of healthcare delivery, we have another opportunity as social workers to reclaim our role in healthcare. We can demonstrate how our services reduce healthcare costs by addressing patient psychosocial issues that contribute to poor health.

In the case of Emily, I highlight moments in the interview when Gloria relinquishes some of her power and defers to the doctor and other members of the medical team to explain Emily's illness to her. Although it is true that doctors are the first to give a patient diagnosis, further discussion about it can continue with other members of the medical team, social workers included. I draw attention to examples of Gloria deferring to doctors and nurses, because I think it illustrates how social workers need more confidence in their value in the hospital setting. A social worker's special skill-set, of building relationships and communicating with others, makes her ideally-suited to talk to an 11-year-old about her illness, sometimes more so than doctors. Not only can Gloria use language Emily understands, she also has the time to explore with Emily the meaning of this information. She can help Emily ask practical questions that she's perhaps not comfortable asking the doctor.

As you read the process recordings, you will notice several instances when Gloria seems unsure about how much to explain to Emily about her diagnosis and treatment. I wonder if she was afraid of stepping on the doctor's toes or if she didn't feel confident in how best to do this. Gloria seems quick to rely on the experts to explain what is wrong with Emily and what she should expect for treatment. In the beginning of the interview, Gloria asks Emily if she can help her with any of the questions she has. In box 23, Gloria asks Emily if it would help to have someone explain her diagnosis a little better, and in box 25, Gloria says the doctors should be the ones to explain how they want to treat the leukemia. At the end, in box 145, Gloria says "I think it would be helpful to speak with the medical team so that they can come back in the room and really explain in a way that would be helpful to you what exactly the diagnosis is, how they plan on treating it, what the side effects will be, so that you feel better and clearer about what to look forward to." In this last statement, Gloria implies that the doctors can clarify these details for Emily better than she can.

Diagnosis and Intervention: Diagnosis of Childhood Leukemia

In this section, I will explore areas that a medical social worker would cover with an 11-year-old child recently diagnosed with leukemia. As mentioned earlier, practice with children is multisystematic, and when working in a medical setting, collaboration with other team members and a multidisciplinary approach are essential. In addition to coordinating with the medical team, the social worker may intervene with the family system that is impacted by the child's illness, and she will also work with the school system to prepare them for the child's return. In sessions with the child, the worker would address her concerns and questions about the diagnosis and explore the meaning of the illness in her life. The worker would discuss how leukemia might affect the child's lifestyle, her school schedule, her relationships with peers and family, as well as the effects of chemotherapy on hair loss and body image. Overall, the social worker serves as an important advocate for the child and family, available for emotional support, problem solving, counseling, and education. She can also provide child and family with valuable resources about leukemia and make community referrals for additional services.

In this interview, Emily is worried about hair loss, one of the side effects of chemotherapy. For a young girl approaching puberty and already concerned about her appearance and what her friends think about her, these issues will become magnified when she begins to lose her hair. The treatment may cause children to look and feel different at a time when they have a strong need to conform and appear similar to their friends (Davison & McCabe, 2006; McCollum, 1975). The medical social worker's job is to prepare Emily for the changes she can expect to see in her body and physical stamina that are associated with chemotherapy, and to help her cope with these side effects.

Friends are important at this stage of life. Emily shows us this by making several references to her friends in her meeting with Gloria. She wonders how to tell her friends about her illness, what they will think of her once they find out, especially when she loses her hair, and whether they will fear that they can catch this disease from her. She's particularly unsure of how to tell her friends about her illness. She is concerned about this, because she needs her friends now and wishes they would visit her to help her get "her mind off of things." Gloria reassures Emily that she can help with this, especially advising her how to tell her friends about the illness and all the changes that go with it.

The medical social worker will also address school issues with Emily and the effect of long absences due to her medical treatments. Returning to school is vital for children, especially in elementary school, because of the important role it plays in their life and also because it confirms that the child is better and is coping, even mastering stress (Ross & Scarvalone, 1982). Since she is an excellent student, Emily receives a lot of recognition from teachers for her school work, and she is proud of her studies. She builds positive self-esteem through her high academic standing and her abilities. It will be difficult for her to lose this source of support at a time when she feels the full impact of her treatment and begins to lose hair.

Although returning to school may create some anxiety for Emily, it is something she thinks about and looks forward to with some anticipation.

In helping Emily prepare for school, the worker will need to discuss with her how other students might react to her change in appearance. Certain students might be frightened by Emily's illness and avoid or isolate her due to a lack of understanding. Other children may tease or be mean to her for looking different. How this plays out will depend on the child's previous status in the peer group, her self-confidence, and her sense of self-worth (McCollum, 1975, p. 101). Emily seems resilient, and has good self-esteem and relationships with friends already; still, she worries about how her friends will react after she undergoes treatments for leukemia. Changes in appearance, weight, strength, activity, and well-being "require physical and emotional adjustment and threaten the child's developing self-image and ability to compete successfully with classmates" (Travis, 1976, p. 338). These are all important areas that Gloria, Emily's social worker, will explore and support her in. Gloria will also collaborate with the school social worker to facilitate a healthy return to classes for Emily.

Another area of loss that the social worker will address with Emily is changes in her lifestyle. The treatment may restrict what she can do and prohibit her from engaging in some activities she has enjoyed in the past, like soccer and modeling. Gloria will explore these limitations with Emily, understand her reactions, and help her find ways to adapt. Gloria may refer Emily to an online support community for adolescents to give her access to other young people coping with similar issues. These virtual groups provide information and emotional comfort through advice and empathizing; they enhance health outcomes and quality of life for young people with cancer by providing age-specific knowledge and fulfilling peer-support needs (Love et al., 2012, p. 558).

Hospital social workers also look at the impact of illness on siblings in the family and may ask to meet with them. Depending on the age, siblings could resent the amount of attention their sister or brother is receiving, and be upset about the absence of the parents and the added responsibilities this absence thrusts onto them. Studies have found that role overload, when well children in the family take on more responsibilities, is a stressor among siblings of children with cancer (Hamama et al., 2008). Also, with the attention focused on the child who is ill, parents may not take the time to explain to siblings exactly what the problem is and what the implications are for the family. This lack of information might confuse and scare other children in the family. Hospital social workers play an important role in reaching out to siblings so they understand the cancer. Finally, social workers also engage the parents to help them cope with the impact of their child's illness on them, their relationship, and the family.

In Emily's case, she is also dealing with her parent's separation and has the added burden of feeling sad about this. She worries about their fighting and hopes they won't fight in front of her at the hospital or during her treatment. Emily feels she will do better if they don't fight during this period. With Gloria's help, Emily will find a way to explain this to her parents, and Gloria also plans to work with the parents on this issue. Illness impacts the whole family, and as you can see, interventions are targeted at different parts of the family unit.

Although Emily is expected to recover and continue her life as a leukemia survivor, having a serious illness will likely open up discussions about her vulnerability and the possibility of death. Emily may have concerns about dying but be afraid to bring up the subject. The social worker will need to listen for cues from Emily that she wants to talk about her mortality and what it means to her. This could also raise spiritual issues, and the social worker must be prepared to address these areas as they come up and not avoid them. That means the social worker must be comfortable with discussions about death, dying, and spirituality.

Case Description

Emily is a previously healthy 11-year-old girl recently diagnosed with acute lymphoblastic leukemia. Emily lives with her mother, Lisa, and her 17-year-old brother, Joseph, who is a senior in high school and will leave for college next year. They live in a small home in western Massachusetts. Emily's father, Robert, has lived in New York City for the last five months since he separated from his wife, Lisa. The parents are fighting constantly and filing for divorce. Since the parent's separation, Emily and her brother have traveled to New York City every other weekend to see their father.

Emily attends sixth grade at the local middle school where she excels academically. She is an active member of her soccer team, participates in cheerleading, plays the piano, and models on the weekends. In spite of her busy schedule, she manages to spend quality time with friends who are an important source of support.

Medical History

Emily fell recently while playing soccer after school. She did not sustain significant injuries other than scrapes on her knees. The next evening, she developed fatigue, fever, and a slight cough. The following morning, her mother brought Emily to her pediatrician's office, where she was told to go to the emergency room at the local hospital. Further evaluation at Metropolitan Children's Hospital confirmed a diagnosis of acute lymphoblastic leukemia. She and her mother Lisa met with staff in the outpatient clinic to talk about the diagnosis and plan for treatment. They were told Emily would require chemotherapy over a period of two years and that one of the side effects was hair loss.

In the video-recorded interview, Emily is meeting with a medical social worker in the outpatient pediatric clinic at the Metropolitan Children's Hospital, where she will soon begin chemotherapy treatment. The role of the social worker, Gloria, is to help Emily talk about her illness, answer her questions, and explore how she can support Emily during her treatment. In the meeting, they talk about the illness, the effects of chemotherapy and hair loss, Emily's family, her parents' separation, her school, and her friends. Emily asks Gloria to help her figure out how to tell friends about her illness, and how to get her parents to stop fighting.

First Excerpt from Transcript and Process Recording

Content	Observation/Reflection	Analysis of Intervention: Theories and Practice
1. Gloria: Hi Emily. How are you doing?		Practice: Communication skill, introduction.
2. Emily: Good. How are you?		
3. Gloria: Good. Do you know who I am?		Practice: Communication skill, clarification of role.
4. Emily: No.		
5. Gloria: OK. I met with your Mom a couple of minutes ago. I'm Gloria. I'm one of the social workers here in the hospital. I work with kids that are usually first diagnosed. And I come into the room or wherever the kids are and I introduce myself and we talk a little bit about some things that might be going on for you, for your family, any questions that you may have. I understand that you just heard yesterday that you have leukemia, is that true?	Emily is a very pretty, young girl with beautiful, long blond hair. She seems bright, alert, and attentive. I am wondering how she is reacting to such a devastating diagnosis.	Practice: Communication skill, introduction, clarification of role, exploration of the problem.
6. Emily: Yeah.		
7. Gloria: So I wanted to come in and check in how you're doing and any questions that you may have that I might be able to answer for you. How are you doing?	Emily seems like she's still in shock and hasn't had time to take it all in. She seems very calm on the outside.	Practice: Communication skill, exploration of the problem.
8. Emily: I'm doing OK. I'm just a little nervous.	I guess on the inside she is feeling nervous. I wonder what, in particular, she is nervous about.	Theories: Narrative, use of word nervous to explain how she is doing.
9. Gloria: What's making you nervous?		Practice: Communication skill, elaboration.
10. Emily: I don't know a lot of things like how my friends are going to react, and if I can visit my dad or not, because he lives in New York. I think he's coming in a couple weeks but I'm not sure.	It will be important to explore more about her family system.	Theory: Family systems.
11. Gloria: Does your Dad know?		Theory: Family systems. Practice: Communication skill, questioning.
12. Emily: Yeah he knows, my Mom talked to him.		Theory: Family systems.
13. Gloria: Have you spoken with your Dad?		Theory: Family systems. Practice: Communication skill, continued exploration of the problem.

(Continued)

Content	Observation/Reflection	Analysis of Intervention: Theories and Practice
14. Emily: No. Not yet.		
15. Gloria: What about your friends? Have you told them yet?		Practice: Data Collection. Communication skill, continued exploration of the problem
16. Emily: No. They think that I'm sick but they don't know what.		
17. Gloria: How do you feel about your friends knowing?		Practice: Communication skill, reaching for feelings.
18. Emily: I don't know. I think it will be better because I know they'll also help me so that's good.	She is very articulate for an eleven year old.	
19. Gloria: That's great. Anything else that you are concerned about or worried about?		Practice: Communication skill, continued exploration of the problem.
20. Emily: I'm concerned because I haven't really heard of this much. And so I don't know how they'll treat it or what I'm going to go through.	I am glad she's asking practical questions.	Theory: Narrative, use of word concerned again.
21. Gloria: What do you think this is about? What do you think leukemia is in your mind?		Practice: Communication skill, elaboration.
22. Emily: At first I didn't know what it was. I knew it was a kind of cancer but I didn't know exactly what it was. They explained it to me that it was cancer of the blood. I don't know. Does it mean like there's something in my blood or something like that? I don't really know much about it besides that.	I can understand how she would be confused about what cancer of the blood is. I'm aware of how much education children need and how we can't assume they know what this means.	
23. Gloria: OK. Would it be helpful to have someone explain it a little better and answer some of your questions?	It looks like I am dodging the bullet here. I guess I always assume the doctors can explain this better.	Practice: Self-reflection. Communication skill, questioning, referral.
24. Emily: Yeah.		
25. Gloria: Well I can explain it a little bit what it is and some of the things the doctors are probably going to try to do, but I think it's better to have your doctors come in and give you a better explanation of what they think would be helpful to treat your leukemia. Leukemia is basically a disease in your blood where the cells in your blood are just not working OK. They're basically working too fast and we need to quiet them down so that they can reproduce at a normal rate. And the doctors need to give you medicine to make sure that happens. Have they told you for how long they need to give you medicine?	I'm not sure why I also refer to the doctors on this issue, since I can probably explain it better in simple terms that she can understand. I need to feel more confident in this area. I plan to bring this issue up in my next supervision.	Theory: Cognitive, clarifying what leukemia is. Practice: Self-reflection. Communication skill, providing information, questioning.

(Continued)

Content	Observation/Reflection	Analysis of Intervention: Theories and Practice
26. Emily: They said not too long, but pretty long, just that I should wait through, that it will go by fast.	Doctors also minimize the time it will take to complete the treatment. For children, time moves at a slow pace.	
27. Gloria: Have they talked to you about the medicine and the side effects and things?		Practice: Communication skill, continued exploration of the problem.
28. Emily: Well, they talk about one side effect where I would lose my hair. I don't know about that, I'm kind of nervous about that.	This must be an awful thought for someone of her age who is so sensitive to body issues and wants to be like everyone else.	Theories: Psychodynamic, developmental theory; narrative, use of word nervous.
29. Gloria: Yeah, tell me more about that.		Practice: Communication skill, elaboration.
30. Emily: I do some modeling on the weekends so I'll be nervous I will not be as pretty. Will my hair not grow back far enough and will it look bad?	Wow, this will impact her modeling as well as other activities she might have done. I am sad she has to go through this.	Theory: Narrative, use of word nervous again.
31. Gloria: Sure that's hard, hard to imagine isn't it. What have you thought about, that you might want to do about this?		Theories: Cognitive, problem-solving. Practice: Communication skill, empathy.
32. Emily: Well, I probably won't want to go back to school for a little while even though I'll miss it but, yeah.	It sounds like she may not want to go to school until her hair grows back. I will have to address this with her later.	

Reflection of First Process Recording and Discussion of Practice Skills and Theories Used in Intervention

As Gloria listened to Emily, she was sensitive to how the news of her leukemia diagnosis was impacting her. At first, Emily didn't seem to show much feeling, and Gloria thought she might still be in a state of shock, trying to comprehend what it all meant. In the first excerpt, Emily is just beginning to form questions and reflect on how the treatment will alter her life, especially the loss of her hair. Many of her concerns revolve around side effects, her family, and her friends.

In this excerpt and the ones that follow, Gloria shows a tremendous amount of empathy for Emily and is very engaging. She conveys her empathy both verbally and nonverbally. Her facial expressions show a range of emotions and also demonstrate her warmth, compassion, and the authenticity of her concern. Gloria is also expressive with her hands in a way that brings Emily into the conversation. Her tone of voice is soft and tender, showing sensitivity to each subject they discuss. She also leans in toward Emily several times during the interview, which confirms her focused attention on what Emily is telling her.

Communication Skills

The social worker uses various communication skills during her conversation with Emily. Below is a list of these skills, their definitions, and the box in which they were used.

Boxes 1, 5

Introductions: At the beginning of the first meeting with the client, the social worker welcomes the client, tries to make the client comfortable, and tunes in to her own and the client's initial feelings about the first meeting. In box 1, Gloria, greets Emily and asks how she is doing. In box 5, Gloria introduces herself and explains her role to Emily.

Boxes 3, 5

Clarification of role: The social worker helps the client understand what services the agency offers, and what her role as social worker will be. There are times when the client needs reminding that the work is collaborative; it is the social worker's job to facilitate and not direct the process. In box 3, Gloria asks if Emily knows who she is, and in box 5, she clarifies her role to Emily. She explains that she works with children when they are first diagnosed with leukemia, tries to understand what is going on for them, and answers any questions they may have.

Boxes 5, 7

Exploration of the problem: This is a way of gaining more information about a client's situation. When continuing to explore the problem, the social worker listens for underlying feelings about the situation, who else is involved, and what resources are available to help resolve it.

In box 5, Gloria begins to explore the problem by asking Emily if she learned about her leukemia diagnosis yesterday. In box 7, Gloria explains that she wanted to check in to see how Emily was doing and to ask if Emily had any questions for her. She ends by asking Emily how she is doing.

Boxes 9, 21, 29

Elaboration: Elaboration involves asking clients to describe what they are talking about in more detail. The social worker may ask the client, "I'm not sure I understand what you mean. Can you say more about that?" Or the worker may ask for examples of what the client is referencing: "Can you give me an example of when you felt that way?" Also, a social worker can encourage clients to continue telling their stories through nonverbal communication that shows interest, such as leaning forward or a simple nod of the head.

In box 9, after Emily says that she is nervous, Gloria asks what makes her nervous. In box 21, Gloria wants Emily to elaborate on how she understands leukemia in her own mind. In box 29, when Emily says that she is nervous about losing her hair as a side effect of chemotherapy, Gloria again seeks elaboration, and asks Emily to tell her more about that.

Boxes 13, 19, 27

Continued exploration of the problem: When continuing to explore the problem, the social worker listens for underlying feelings about the situation, who else is involved, and what resources are available to help resolve it. In box 13, after Emily explains that her mother told her dad about the diagnosis, Gloria asked Emily if she had spoken with her dad yet. In box 19, Gloria continues to explore the problem by checking if Emily is concerned or worried about anything else. In box 27, Gloria asks Emily if she has talked to the doctors about the medicine and possible side effects, another example of exploration.

Boxes 11, 23, 25

Questioning: This is a way of gaining more information about a client's situation. There are many different kinds of questions, for example, open- and closed-ended questions and reflexive questions. Questioning is often used in assessment as part of data collection.

In box 11, Gloria asks Emily if her dad knows about her diagnosis. In box 23, after Gloria realizes that Emily needs more information about her illness and treatment, she asks Emily if it would be helpful to have someone explain it better and answer some of her questions. In box 25, after Gloria describes in her own words what leukemia is and what medicine is required, she asks Emily if the doctors told her how long she will need to take the medicine.

Box 17

Reaching for feelings: This is when the social worker tries to understand what the client is feeling when a particular subject or issue comes up. The social worker may use this skill when she senses that the client is avoiding, or is not in touch with, the feelings related to the current discussion. This may bring out strong reactions in the client, and it is important that the social worker is sensitive to what this means to the client. In box 17, Gloria reaches for feelings when she asks Emily how she feels about her friends knowing about her illness.

Box 23

Referral: This is when a client needs additional resources outside of the agency in which she's receiving services. With the client's permission, the worker makes the referral in order to help the client access other avenues for help. In box 23, Gloria wants to refer Emily to the doctors, because she feels they will do a better job of explaining leukemia to her. She asks Emily if she wants a referral to someone who can answer her questions.

Box 31

Showing empathy: The social worker maintains a non-judgmental stance or remains neutral. The worker need not totally understand the client's situation, but she must show that she is trying to grasp what the client is feeling or experiencing. The social worker might say, "Tell me more about what your experience was" or "I want to understand more about what this means from your perspective." In box 31, Gloria empathizes with Emily by saying it must be hard to imagine losing your hair.

Other Practice Skills Used
Boxes 23, 25

Self-reflection: The skill of self-reflection is an important part of professional practice. Social workers are expected to engage in personal reflection and self-correction to assure continual professional development (CSWE, 2008).

In box 23, Gloria reflects on why she defers to someone else to explain leukemia to Emily. She feels she is shirking her responsibility and not showing confidence in her ability to help children understand illness. In box 25, she continues to question why she doesn't feel she can adequately explain Emily's illness to her and wants to work on this issue in supervision.

Theories Used in Intervention

In this section, I analyze the language and strategies used by both social worker and client to identify theories in action during the interview. I attempt to link what the social worker has said in her intervention to a theory, and also to explain how the worker thinks about Emily's responses using a particular theoretical framework. There may be times when Emily's words are influenced by what Gloria has just said. It is important to notice ways in which the client and social worker are influenced by each other.

There were several theories referenced in the first excerpt, including narrative, cognitive, psychodynamic, and family systems theories. Below, I will explain the different theories by citing boxes in the excerpt where they are found.

Narrative Theory
Boxes 8, 20, 28, 30

By studying how Emily and Gloria talk with each other in the first excerpt, you can see that much of the language is used to describe leukemia using words and phrases like "cancer of the blood," "blood cells," "side effects," and "losing hair." The words "know" and "don't know" reveal how much Emily doesn't understand about her illness. Also her family and friends are subjects that appear a lot. In the boxes identified below as using narrative, I concentrate on words that provide insight into how Emily is feeling.

In box 8, when asked about how she is doing, Emily responds that she is a little nervous.

In box 20, Gloria wonders if there is anything else she is concerned about, and Emily says that she hasn't really heard much about leukemia, how they'll treat it, or what she'll go through. You can begin to appreciate all the questions she is generating in her head.

In box 28, when asked if she knows about the side effects of the medicine, Emily tells Gloria how nervous she is about one of the side effects—losing her hair. For a preteen who would normally be preoccupied with body image, this represents an especially critical subject for Gloria to explore more with her.

In box 30, Gloria asks Emily to elaborate on what makes her nervous about losing her hair, and Emily responds that she does modeling on the weekends and is nervous she won't look as pretty. She wonders if it will make her look bad. When Gloria hears this, she realizes how hair loss will affect Emily, and the important role physical appearance plays in her life.

Psychodynamic Theory

Box 28

In box 28, the social worker draws on psychodynamic theory, specifically developmental theory and lifecycle stages. Emily is a preteen; she is at a stage when she is conscious of her body and any physical changes that are a part of normal development. Girls at this age want to look like their peers and do not want to stand out or appear different. It makes sense that Emily is worried about losing her hair. The social worker can appreciate the effect this will have on Emily's body image and self-esteem, and knows it's important that they discuss this subject.

Cognitive Theory

Boxes 25, 31

An important part of cognitive interventions is challenging false belief systems and using problem solving, as evidenced in the two boxes below.

In box 25, Gloria clarifies the meaning of leukemia to dispel any faulty beliefs or assumptions Emily might have formed, or to challenge any false statements she has heard about it.

In box 31, Gloria responds to Emily's concerns about losing her hair and asks, after empathizing with her, what Emily wants to do about it. This is framed as a problem-solving question that uses brainstorming to look at options.

Family Systems Theory

Boxes 10, 11, 12, 14

In boxes 10 through 14, Gloria collects information about Emily's family system. Gloria both explores this area and listens to what Emily is sharing about her family, gathering information for assessment as she goes. Gloria learns that Emily's father lives in New York, that her mother told her dad about the diagnosis, and that Emily has not spoken with her dad herself since then.

Second Excerpt from Transcript and Process Recording

In the second excerpt, we learn more about Emily's strengths and resiliency. Although she will have the challenge of attending a new school, she is confident her friends will stick by her. She appears to have good relationships with her peers and likes hanging out with them. She is also active in a number of activities in and outside of school. When the subject of whether she can continue these activities first comes up, Emily says she's not sure what she would do if she couldn't continue them. But, when Gloria asks Emily what she could do to get through it, Emily responds that she would find something less active that she could handle better. Gloria engages Emily in problem solving, and Emily shows she has great resources and skills to find other options as needed.

Gloria continues to ask questions and collect data for her assessment of Emily. She is learning more about Emily's development—her strong attachment to friends, her academic successes, and her range of extracurricular activities and skills. Using Erikson's psychosocial theory, Emily is in stage 4, "industry versus inferiority," and she seems to have mastered the tasks of the stage. She is a good student, she keeps busy with numerous hobbies and interests, and she has solid peer relationships.

Content	Observations/Reflections	Analysis of Intervention: Theories and Practice
33. Gloria: Yeah, your mom tells me that you're an excellent student and your very active in school so I would think that not going back to school would not feel so great for you, would it? Yeah.	Being a good student is a strength but it will be hard for her to miss school and not feel support from teachers and friends.	Practice: Identifying strengths. Communication skill, empathy, problem definition.
34. Emily: I just hope it doesn't affect, because since I'm going to a new school, it's middle school, 6th grade, it's kind of hard to make new friends. I don't know if this will affect it too much.	It will be hard for her to start a new school at this time.	
35. Gloria: Yeah, yeah what about your old friends from school; will they be coming to this school too?	I wish I had stayed with her feelings more and explored her fears of going to a new school, especially with the challenges of treatment for Leukemia.	Theory: Cognitive, problem solving. Practice: Self-reflection, data collection. Communication skill, exploration of problem.
36. Emily: Yeah, yeah that's good; none of them went to a separate school, so I know they'll stick by me.	Interesting use of word, "stick" by her. It gives me the image of how close her relationships are. I think of the expression—"stick by each other through thick and thin."	Theory: Narrative, use of word "stick" by her.
37. Gloria: Do you have a best friend?	This was a closed-ended question. I wonder if I should have said, "Tell me about your friends?"	Practice: Self-reflection, assessment. Communication skills, questioning.
38. Emily: Actually, my closest friends are all my best friends; I don't have one.	She's getting to the age when girls start to have a group of friends they do things with.	
39. Gloria: Yeah? Can you name a few?		Practice: Self-reflection, assessment. Communication skills, questioning.
40. Emily: Jenny, and Susan. Those are the two that I most hang out with. One of my friends really likes gymnastics so she can't really come over as much but she's still one of my best friends.	It looks like she has good friends that will be a support system for her. It makes it real for me when the child can give me their names.	Theory: Psychodynamic, attachment theory. Practice: assessment.

(Continued)

Content	Observations/Reflections	Analysis of Intervention: Theories and Practice
41. Gloria: Oh that's wonderful. I'm glad that you have that. What else do you like to do during the weekends or when you're at school other than hanging out with your friends?		Theory: Narrative. Practice: Data collection, assessment, identifying strengths. Communication skills, questioning
42. Emily: I like the sports that I play like soccer, and how I play the cello; that's fun to do.	I can see she has a lot of strengths that will help her through this.	Theory: Psychodynamic, developmental theory. Practice: Assessment, identifying strengths.
43. Gloria: That's awesome, that's great. So do you think that going through the leukemia will affect you in those areas?		Practice: Assessment, Communication skills, offering support, questioning,
44. Emily: I hope not. I don't think it will much, but I hope it really doesn't because I like all those activities.	She is gradually going to have to come to terms with how her life will have to change. This is still so new to her.	
45. Gloria: How do you think that would feel if that affected you in that area?		Theories: Cognitive, problem solving, coping skills. Practice: Assessment. Communication skills, exploration of the problem
46. Emily: I would feel really bad, I would, I'm not sure how I would go through that.	I feel sad she is going to have to go through this too. There is so much she will have to face over the next two years.	
47. Gloria: Yeah, what do you think would help you get through that? What would be important?		Theories: Cognitive, problem solving and brainstorming. Practice: Communication skills, questioning.
48. Emily: If I could find something else that I would be better at.	Wow, I can't believe I just heard her say this. It almost seems too good to be true. If I were Emily, I would probably be crying my eyes out. What an adaptable and resourceful child she is. However, maybe everything hasn't sunk in yet.	Theories: Psychodynamic, developmental theory. Practice: Assessment, identifying strengths, resiliency.
49. Gloria: What else would interest you?		Theory: Cognitive, problem solving and brainstorming. Practice: Communication skills, questioning.
50. Emily: Well if I couldn't do soccer maybe I could do something like, I don't know, something less active like, I don't know.	She's not someone who gives up easily. She is very resilient. I think she is going to make it through this situation OK.	Practice: Assessment, resiliency.

Reflection of Second Process Recording and Discussion of Practice Skills and Theories Used in Intervention

Communication Skills

Box 33

Seeking client feedback: When seeking client feedback, the social worker asks for the client's perception of a particular situation, the client-worker relationship, or the helping process. It is often used in assessment as part of data collection.

In box 33, Gloria says, "Not going back to school would not feel so great for you, would it?" By adding, "would it?" at the end, Gloria is seeking Emily's feedback.

Box 33

Showing empathy: The social worker maintains a non-judgmental stance or remains neutral. The worker need not totally understand the client's situation, but she must show that she is trying to grasp what the client is feeling or experiencing. The worker might say, "Tell me more about what your experience was" or "I want to understand more about what this means from your perspective."

In box 33, Gloria shows empathy by communicating that she recognizes how hard it will be for Emily to miss school and not have this support. She puts herself in Emily's shoes by acknowledging that not returning to school won't feel so great.

Box 33

Problem definition: This refers to a collaborative process between the social worker and the client; they come to an agreement about what the problem is and what they will work on together. In box 33, Gloria collaborates with Emily to define a problem she'll face: not attending school during her chemotherapy.

Boxes 35, 45

Exploration of the problem: This is a way of gaining more information about a client's situation. When continuing to explore the problem, the social worker listens for underlying feelings about the situation, who else is involved, and what resources are available to help resolve it.

In box 35, Gloria talks with Emily about going to a new school and asks if Emily's friends will switch to the same school.

In box 45, Gloria explores with Emily what it would be like if Emily couldn't do some of her after-school activities because of the effects of chemotherapy.

Boxes 37, 39, 41, 43, 47, 49

Questioning: This is a way of gaining more information about a client's situation. There are many different kinds of questions, for example, open- and closed-ended questions and reflexive questions. Questioning is often used in assessment as part of data collection.

In box 37, Gloria inquires if Emily has a best friend; she wants to look at the degree of closeness Emily has in her relationships. In box 39, Gloria asks Emily if she can name a few of her friends. She uses this question to assess the extent and quality of Emily's friendships.

In box 41, Gloria wonders how Emily fills her time, and asks what else she likes to do during the weekends, or when she's at school or with her friends.

In box 43, Gloria asks Emily if leukemia will affect her ability to continue some of her activities.

In box 47, Gloria wants to know what will help Emily overcome the difficulty of having to stop some of her former activities. This question is used for problem-solving purposes.

In box 49, Gloria continues to question Emily about what else she could do with her time. This question also is used to help Emily with problem solving.

Box 43

Offering support: When a client shares a story that is painful, it helps when the social worker offers encouragement. By acknowledging the difficulty of the situation, you provide support for the client and allow him to continue the story. In box 43, Gloria offers support to Emily by saying, "That's awesome, that's great," referring to all the activities she enjoys doing.

Other Practice Skills Used
Boxes 33, 37, 39, 40, 43, 45, 48, 50

Assessment: Assessment is the process of understanding the client and his problem based on the information gathered. It is done in a holistic way that highlights the importance of context in the construction of meaning, and it is a collaborative activity that happens in tandem with the client. Assessment also includes identifying strengths and resilience.

In box 39, Gloria wants to make sure Emily has friends by asking her some of their names. She uses this question to assess the extent and quality of Emily's friendships.

In box 40, Gloria learns that Emily has a good network of friends that she can name. It makes it real when she gives their names.

In box 43, Gloria tries to assess how Emily will deal with having to stop certain activities she enjoys due to chemotherapy. To find out, Gloria asks, "So do you think that going through the leukemia will affect you in those areas?"

In box 45, Gloria explores the problem more for her assessment and asks, "How do you think that would feel if that affected you in that area?" Gloria wants to know how Emily will cope with discontinuing the activities she enjoys because of her illness.

In box 50, Gloria listens to Emily answer her question about what she would do if she couldn't play soccer. Emily answers that maybe she could do something less active. Gloria uses this response in her assessment of Emily's resiliency.

Boxes 33, 41, 48, 50

Identifying strengths: During assessment, social workers listen for client strengths they can use to help solve certain problems. As clients talk about their situation and their stories unfold, workers identify strengths that are embedded in the narrative. By focusing on positive attributes and characteristics, workers shift the focus away from deficits to inquiring about and affirming strengths.

In box 33, Gloria identifies Emily's academic successes as strengths for her.

In box 41, Gloria acknowledges that it's wonderful Emily has such good friends, and by doing so, shows Emily that this is an asset.

In box 42, Gloria recognizes other strengths that Emily has, for example that she likes sports and plays soccer and enjoys the cello.

In box 48, Emily responds to the question about how she would handle stopping certain activities by saying that she would find something else she could do better. As Gloria listens to this response, she identifies Emily's ability to adapt to solve problems and assesses that Emily has excellent ego functioning.

In box 50, resiliency is identified as another strength.

Boxes 48, 50

Resiliency: This refers to a person's ability to overcome hardships and thrive in spite of obstacles. In box 48, Gloria identifies Emily as resilient, because she is flexible in the face of difficulty. Although Emily won't be able to continue some activities she loves to do, she decides to find things she can do better that are less active.

Boxes 35, 41

Data collection: In the data collection stage, the social worker explores the problem in more depth. This involves getting information from multiple sources about the client's life and situation, and about the social systems that may impact the problem.

In box 35, Gloria asks a question to learn more about Emily's friends and whether they will attend the same new school with her. Gloria also thinks that by posing this question, it will help Emily realize that she has resources to make the transition to the new school.

In box 41, Gloria continues to inquire about what Emily likes to do at school, on weekends, and with her friends as part of collecting data for assessment.

Boxes 35, 37

Self-reflection: The skill of self-reflection is an important part of professional practice. Social workers are expected to engage in personal reflection and self-correction to assure continual professional development (CSWE, 2008).

In box 35, Gloria reflects on her intervention. She wishes she had followed up on Emily's feelings about attending a new school instead of asking about her friends. She wonders if she didn't follow up because of her own experiences starting a new school when her family moved to a new city.

In box 37, Gloria reflects on her use of a closed-ended question and wished she had asked instead, "Tell me about your friends?"

Theories Used in Intervention

Cognitive Theory

Boxes 35, 45, 47, 49

In box 35, Gloria aims her questions at problem solving when Emily shows concern about going to a new school. Gloria asks Emily whether her friends from the previous school will also attend the new one. This intervention is to make Emily aware of existing support systems that will help her adjust to the new school.

In box 45, the problem solving continues. Gloria explores how it will feel if Emily cannot resume her usual activities because of the leukemia. She asks this question to help Emily think about solutions with her.

In box 47, Gloria responds to Emily saying she will miss some of her activities by asking another problem-solving question. This encourages Emily to think about ways she could cope with certain limitations. Gloria asks Emily to think about what might help her get through it. In the next box, Emily demonstrates her resilience by responding that she will find something else that she can be better at.

In box 49, Gloria asks Emily what else would interest her. Emily collaborates with Gloria and responds by saying something less active. This shows that Emily can take a practical approach to problem solving.

Narrative Theory

Boxes 36, 40, 41

In box 36, Gloria notices that Emily uses the word "stick" to describe how her friends will stand by her when she switches to a new school with them. The word "stick" conjures an image of close relationships and shows the attachment Emily feels with her peers.

In box 40, Emily talks about how she "hangs out" with her friends. The use of this expression gives Gloria insight into the quality of Emily's relationships. When children are comfortable with their friends, they are more apt to just "hang out" together.

In box 41, Gloria uses Emily's phrase of "hanging out" to connect more with her by using her language.

Psychodynamic Theory

Boxes 40, 42, 48

Attachment theory: Attachment refers to the quality and style of relatedness between people and is part of psychodynamic theory. It's a developmental concept that looks at how people form relationships in the present based on how they related to caregivers during infancy and childhood.

In box 40, Gloria assesses that Emily has a good network of friends that she "hangs out" with and feels close to. It appears she is secure in her relationships and attaches to her friends in appropriate ways for an 11 year old, as reflected in developmental and attachment theories.

In box 42, Emily tells Gloria that she likes sports and plays soccer, and also enjoys the cello. This paints the picture of a preteen who has reached normal developmental milestones.

Emily also fits into Erikson's stage 4 of "industry vs. inferiority." She is involved in numerous activities, is productive and industrious, and has mastered many skills. Up until now, she has developed well compared to others her age.

In box 48, Gloria reflects on Emily's response that if she couldn't play sports she would find something else that was more manageable. She assesses that Emily has excellent ego functioning demonstrated by her flexibility and adaptability when dealing with problems.

Third Excerpt from Transcript and Process Recording

In the third excerpt, Gloria starts to explore family issues, and Emily explains that her parents have been separated for five months and will probably get a divorce. Emily expresses her sadness about this and wishes her parents were back together again. She liked seeing both of her parents in the morning. In box 61, Gloria asks, "What do you think would be most important for you right now?" Emily makes two wishes in boxes 62 and 64: She wishes her friends would know about her leukemia and that her parents would get back together. The act of making wishes shows how Emily is between two worlds. In one, she is still a child and wants to believe in fantasy and magic; in the other, she is more independent and has to leave the make-believe world behind to become an adolescent. Emily is beginning to have to face the "real world" with its harsh realities—parents who are separated and a serious illness.

In part of the interview, Emily talks about how she tries to make her parents fight less. She does this by distracting them, doing little things like asking them questions off topic. As Emily talks about her role in the family, you can think about how to apply family systems theory to her story, for example, triangulation.

Content	Observations/Reflections	Analysis of Intervention: Theories and Practice
51. Gloria: OK; that's fine. Tell me about your family a little bit.		Theory: Family systems theory. Practice: Data Collection. Communication skills, questioning.
52. Emily: My parents left each other about 5 months ago.		Theory: Narrative, use of expression, "left each other."
53. Gloria: Really?	I don't want to say much here. I want to encourage her to say more on her own.	Practice: Communication skills, nonverbal attending and listening skills.
54. Emily: And so that was hard at first. I have an older brother, he's going into college and so I'll miss him but he hasn't gone to college yet, so he'll still be able to come by.		Theory: Psychodynamic, family development; family systems; narrative (hard). Practice: Data collection.

(Continued)

Content	Observations/Reflections	Analysis of Intervention: Theories and Practice
55. Gloria: That's great, so your parents, are they divorced right now?	It may be helpful to have her brother around for a little longer to support her, especially with her parent's separation.	Practice: Data collection. Communication skills, continued exploration of problem.
56. Emily: Not yet, but they're probably going to get a divorce.		
57. Gloria: And this happened 5 months ago, that's very recent. How was that for you?	I wonder what role the parent's fighting and separation played in precipitating her illness?	Theory: Behavioral, mind/body. Practice: Assessment. Communication skill, exploring underlying feelings.
58. Emily: I felt bad because I liked my parents together; I like being able to see them in the morning.		Theory: Narrative, "felt bad;" psychodynamic, attachment and loss.
59. Gloria: I'm sure, and now your dad moved away, that's hard isn't it? Do you wish your dad was here?	I wish I had asked an open-ended question here instead, e.g., "What is it like not to have your dad home?"	Theory: Family systems. Practice: Self-reflection. Communication skills, offering support, putting client's words into feelings
60. Emily: Mmhmm.		
61. Gloria: I'm sure you do; this is hard isn't it, to have to deal with so many different things at the same time? So here you are, sick with leukemia and now you can't see your dad, many worries. So this is very difficult, and I understand your dad is away and you're dealing with this leukemia now. What do you think would be most important for you right now?	It must be so hard for her to deal with her parent's separation at the same time as her health issues.	Practice: Communication skills: Supporting client, empathy, putting client's words into feelings, goal-setting.
62. Emily: Well I wish my friends would know, like, I really want them to know sooner so they can come and visit me, so I can have something to do and get my mind off of it.	I wonder if she's struggling with how to tell her friends. She really wants their support. I also hear her saying that she wants to forget about this problem or put it out of her mind. But, I wonder which problem she is referring to, the leukemia or her parent's divorce or the worry about how to tell her friends about her illness?	Theory: Psychodynamic, defenses, importance of peers at this stage; narrative (wish).
63. Gloria: Yeah what about in terms of your dad, what would you like him to do? And your mom.	Oops, I changed the subject here. I need to be more aware of when I do this. I wish I had explored the underlying feelings behind her last statement and explored what she wants to get her mind off of in particular.	Practice: Self-reflection. Communication skills, goal-setting.

(Continued)

Content	Observations/Reflections	Analysis of Intervention: Theories and Practice
64. Emily: I wish my parents would get together, I mean that would lift a huge load.	This is a common fantasy for children her age—to want her parents to get back together. I notice that she is expressing more feelings as she talks about wanting her parents back together.	Theory: Psychodynamic, family systems, narrative (wishes).
65. Gloria: I'm sure. Are you feeling this need to keep them together somehow?		Theory: Family systems, psychodynamic.
66. Emily: Kind of, I've been trying to make it so they fight less because well my parents don't really want to see each other that much, but when they do they usually fight.	This is so typical of children her age to get in the middle of their parents to try to get them to stop. Again, I am aware of how Emily shows more affect when she's talking about her parent's fighting. It seems like she has more feelings about her parent's separation than the leukemia.	Theory: Family systems, psychodynamic.
67. Gloria: How do you try to stop them from fighting?	I want to acknowledge and have her recognize the role she is playing in the family getting in the middle of her parent's fights.	Theory: Family systems. Communication skills, questioning.
68. Emily: Well I try and distract them from what they're doing, but sometimes they keep me out of it, um but yeah I try to distract them by doing other things, asking them questions off topic.	It's typical for children to get in the middle to distract her parents from fighting.	Theory: Family systems, triangulating to stop parents fighting; narrative (distract, off topic).
69. Gloria: So when they're together it sounds like they're not in a good space, that they fight and they argue? And here you are in the hospital going through this. It sounds like somehow your parents are going to have to be together here in the hospital for you. How do you think that's going to go?		Theory: Family systems. Communication skill, paraphrasing, exploration of the problem, empathy.
70. Emily: I hope they don't fight.		Theory: Narrative (hope).
71. Gloria: What would that be like for you, here you are feeling sick and your parents arguing?	I can imagine that it would be difficult for her to concentrate on getting better if she is worrying about her fighting.	Theory: Family systems; Psychodynamic, reflection of situation. Practice: Communication skill, exploration of problem.
72. Emily: It'd make me very upset.		Theory: Narrative (upset).
73. Gloria: I'm sure it will. What do you think your parents need to know or need to understand so it becomes less overwhelming for you to go through this?	I can see it is going to important to work with her parents on this issue.	Theory: Cognitive, problem solving. Practice: Communication skills, empathy, questioning.

(Continued)

Content	Observations/Reflections	Analysis of Intervention: Theories and Practice
74. Emily: That if they would stop fighting it would help like a lot, it wouldn't make me feel so bad.	How great that she can articulate so clearly what she needs her parents to do.	Theory: Narrative (so bad).
75. Gloria: Right, right, in terms of you getting sick, do you have any thoughts about why this happened to you? Or why now?	I've done it again, changed the subject. This is a good question to ask but not now. What made me change the subject? What was it about her saying that if her parents stopped fighting it wouldn't make her feel "so bad." My parents divorced when I was about the same age as she is now.	Practice: Self-reflection. Communication skill, questioning.
76. Emily: I don't really know, like, how I got it or anything. I felt fine before the soccer game where I cut myself.	I wonder if she thinks the cut at the soccer game caused leukemia?	Theory: Psychodynamic, primitive thinking.
77. Gloria: Right, right; do you think that this is something that might bring your parents together to look for you in a way of helping you get through this somehow?	Back on track again, following up on the family issues. However, I hope I didn't make her think that she could get her parent's marriage back together by caring for her.	Theory: Behavioral. Practice: Communication skill, questioning.
78. Emily: I hope, that would be really nice.		Theory: Narrative (hope).
79. Gloria: Is that your hope? Yea, yea; what do you think they need to hear from you to understand that this is your hope?	I am picking up and using her word of hope twice here. I guess that shows how much I hope for this for her too.	Theory: Narrative, Gloria picks up on her "hope," and uses her word. Cognitive: Problem solving, communication. Practice: Communication skill, exploration of problem.
80. Emily: That if they stop fighting it would make them feel better, and then it would help a lot more; it would help me because I know they both care about me. I guess if I told them that they would understand more.	Well said, Emily. I am amazed at how well she can articulate what she needs.	Theory: Narrative, Emily uses words like stop fighting that are connected to feel better, help a lot, care about me, understand more. Psychodynamic, cognitive development. Practice: Assessment
81. Gloria: Have you ever tried telling them that? That you need them to stop fighting? What do you think would happen if you ever told them?	I wonder if she has ever asked them to stop fighting.	Theory: Family systems. Practice: Assessment. Communication skills, questioning.
82. Emily: I think they would understand, I've never really felt the courage to say it.		Theory: Narrative (courage).
83. Gloria: What makes you feel afraid of telling them?	This is a good open-ended question. I am curious about what her fears are.	Theory: Psychodynamic, understanding fears. Practice: Assessment. Communication skill, questioning.
84. Emily: I don't know, just because they seem so like wanting to argue, I thought maybe they would just say they needed to.	It sounds like she thinks it would be useless to ask her parents to stop. It's interesting that she says her parents need to fight.	

At the end of the third excerpt, when asked what she would like her parents to know, Emily responds, "That if they would stop fighting, it would help like a lot, it wouldn't make me feel so bad." Emily shows insight by understanding that her parents' behavior would make a difference in how she feels. However, Emily doesn't have the courage to tell them on her own. In the next excerpt, Gloria explains that her role is to help Emily tell her parents what she needs from them.

Reflection of Third Process Recording and Discussion of Practice Skills and Theories Used in Intervention

Communication Skills

Boxes 51, 67, 73, 75, 77, 81, 83

Questioning: This is a way of gaining more information about a client's situation. There are many different kinds of questions, for example, open- and closed-ended questions and reflexive questions. Questioning is often used in assessment as part of data collection.

In box 51, Gloria asks Emily to tell her about her family.

In box 67, after Emily shares that she tries to get her parents to stop fighting. Gloria asks how she does it.

In box 73, Gloria wants to know what Emily would like her parents to know to make it less overwhelming when she goes through her treatment.

In box 75, Gloria asks Emily if she understands how this happened to her—getting leukemia. This is an important question to ask children to challenge any irrational thoughts or magical thinking about how they became ill. Depending on age, children have different ideas about this. For example they might blame themselves, feeling that they did something wrong and the illness is a punishment. Younger children may associate bad thoughts with bad consequences, which is a form of magical thinking. By encouraging kids to talk about any such ideas, it can lessen their worries, guilt, and self-blame.

In box 77, Gloria redirects the conversation and asks Emily if she thinks her parents, by helping her through this, might get back together. This is an interesting but complicated question. One could interpret it as asking whether Emily's parents might argue less to help her get through treatment, or a child might think that maybe her parents will reunite more permanently as a result of the experience.

In box 81, Gloria wants to know if Emily has ever told her parents that she needs them to stop fighting. She asks Emily what she thinks would happen if she shared this information with them.

In box 83, after Emily tells Gloria that she is afraid to tell her parents to stop fighting, Gloria asks Emily what makes her afraid.

Box 53

Nonverbal attending and listening skills: The social worker shows that she is listening through her body language, such as eye contact, facial expressions, nodding, and leaning forward. These nonverbal skills help the client elaborate and feel comfortable sharing personal information.

In box 53, Gloria says very little when Emily shares that her parents left each other five months ago; by doing so, she is signaling Emily to continue her story. Gloria's attending skills express interest and concern for Emily and show that Gloria is paying attention.

Boxes 55, 69, 71, 79

Continued exploration of the problem: When continuing to explore the problem, the social worker listens for underlying feelings about the situation, who else is involved, and what resources are available to help resolve it.

In box 55, Gloria continues to explore the problem of Emily parents' separation by asking if they are divorced.

In box 69, Gloria asks more questions about Emily's parents' fighting, and what it would be like for Emily if they argued in the hospital.

In box 71, Gloria inquires again, in a slightly different way, how Emily would feel if she were sick and her parents were fighting.

In box 79, Gloria continues to explore this issue and asks Emily what she'd like her parents to know about what she needs from them now.

Box 57

Exploring underlying feelings: The social worker asks the client about her feelings on the subject under discussion. In box 57, Gloria wants to understand the effect of the separation on Emily. By asking Emily how it was for her, Gloria explores Emily's underlying feelings.

Boxes 59, 61

Offering support: When a client shares a story that is painful, it helps when the social worker offers encouragement. By acknowledging the difficulty of the situation, you provide support for the client and allow him to continue the story.

In box 59, after Emily says she wishes she could see both her parents in the morning, Gloria offers her support by saying, "I'm sure," and acknowledging how it must be hard for her.

In box 61, Gloria comforts Emily by recognizing the great difficulty of receiving a leukemia diagnosis and not having her dad around.

Boxes 59, 61

Putting client's words into feelings: There may be times when a client has difficulty identifying the feeling that he wants to express in the narrative. The social worker can help in these situations by responding to the client and using feeling words to summarize what the client has said.

In box 59, Gloria responds to what Emily has said by suggesting how she must feel. She says to Emily that it must be hard since her dad moved away and asks her if she wishes her dad were still around.

In box 61, Gloria notices that Emily looks sad and helps out by saying what she guesses Emily is feeling.

Boxes 61, 63

Goal setting: Goal setting is a collaborative process whereby the social worker and client come to a mutual understanding of what they want to accomplish.

In box 61, Gloria asks Emily what is most important for her. This shows a collaborative process between Gloria and Emily to determine what Emily wants to work on.

In box 63, Gloria explores Emily's family goals, what Emily would like help with concerning her mom and dad.

Boxes 61, 69, 73

Showing empathy: The social worker maintains a non-judgmental stance or remains neutral. The worker need not totally understand the client's situation, but she must show that she is trying to grasp what the client is feeling or experiencing. The social worker may say, "Tell me more about what your experience was" or "I want to understand more about what this means from your perspective."

In box 61, Gloria puts herself in Emily's shoes and summarizes what it must be like to deal with so many issues at the same time—having leukemia and not being able to see her dad. Gloria's empathic response communicates that she is trying to understand how Emily feels.

In box 69, Gloria shows empathy by imagining Emily's predicament, going through leukemia treatment and having her parents together in the hospital fighting.

In box 73, Gloria indicates that she understands how it will upset Emily to have her parents fighting when she is feeling sick in the hospital.

Box 69

Paraphrasing: This is when the social worker uses her own words to repeat what she just heard the client say. This shows the client that the worker is listening and following the conversation.

In box 69, Gloria begins by paraphrasing what she heard Emily say about her parents arguing and fighting.

Other Practice Skills Used
Boxes 51, 54, 55

Data collection: In the data collection stage, the social worker explores the problem in more depth. This involves getting information from multiple sources about the client's life and situation, and about the social systems that may impact the problem.

In box 51, when Gloria asks Emily about her family, she is collecting data for her family assessment.

In box 54, Gloria learns that Emily has an older brother who is a senior in high school and will leave for college next year. This is important information that relates to developmental transitions in Emily's family and has implication for Emily. Emily will have to deal with both her father and brother leaving her.

In box 55, Gloria asks Emily if her parents are divorced to learn more about the family's status.

Boxes 57, 80

Assessment: Assessment is a multidimensional concept that can be approached in many ways using different theoretical lenses. It is an active and ongoing process between the client and social worker using relevant theories and knowledge to help make meaning out of the client's situation. Assessment leads to an understanding of the problem, what causes it, and the solutions, and it has implications for intervention.

In box 57, Gloria assesses the impact of the parents' separation on Emily by asking Emily how she felt about it.

In box 80, Gloria listens attentively as Emily speaks about what she needs her parents to change to help her. This helps Gloria assess how the parents' fighting affects Emily and plan family intervention.

Boxes 59, 63, 75

Self-reflection: The skill of self-reflection is an important part of professional practice. Social workers are expected to engage in personal reflection and self-correction to assure continual professional development (CSWE, 2008).

In box 59, Gloria realizes she asked a closed-ended question and reflects that it would have been better to ask, "What is it like for you not having your dad here now?"

In box 63, Gloria wonders why she didn't stay with what Emily had just shared and reflects on her tendency to change the conversation prematurely. If she could do it again, she would explore what, in particular, Emily had wanted to get off her mind. Or, she could have brainstormed with Emily how to tell her friends about the illness.

In box 75, Gloria is aware that she changed the subject again. Emily had just said it would help if her parents stopped fighting, and then Gloria abruptly asked her if she had any thoughts about why she got sick. In this instance, Gloria reflects on whether she switched topics because she had experienced her own parents fighting a lot when she was close to Emily's age.

Theories Used in Intervention

Below, I identify theories used in the third excerpt, paying attention to the verbal and non-verbal language between Gloria and Emily, and to Gloria's interventions. I have included examples of family systems, narrative, psychodynamic, behavioral, and cognitive theories. Throughout the interview, Gloria is empathic and gives off a sense of warmth and genuineness in her interactions with Emily. Although I do not specifically refer to these moments as ego sustaining interventions from psychodynamic theory, I do believe they qualify as such, as I believe this intervention is consistent throughout the entire interview. Gloria is establishing a strong, caring relationship with Emily that will encourage Emily to trust Gloria, to open up, and to share her worries. This relationship will provide support for Emily and give her someone to depend on during struggles with family issues and her illness over the next two years.

Family Systems Theory
Boxes 51, 54, 59, 64, 65, 66, 67, 68, 71, 81

In box 51, Gloria asks Emily about her family and collects information she will use in a family assessment.

In box 54, Gloria learns that Emily's brother will leave for college soon and considers the impact this will have on the family system. Emily's dad has left home and now her brother will also be leaving.

In box 59, Gloria explores the impact of the father's departure and asks Emily if she wishes her dad were here. Gloria's question is aimed at gathering more details about family relationships and the level of intimacy in the family.

In box 64, Emily talks about how she wishes her parents would get back together. Gloria wonders how this plays out in family dynamics and how Emily interacts with her parents based on this wish.

In box 65, Gloria considers Emily's role in the family concerning the parents' fighting and separation. She asks Emily if she feels a need to keep her parents together.

In box 66, Emily explains how she gets in the middle of her parents' conflicts by trying to make them fight less.

In box 67, Gloria's question is aimed at learning how Emily tries to stop her parents from fighting. Gloria wants to learn more about the family structure and the presence of any alliances or triangles.

In box 68, as Gloria listens to Emily describe trying to distract her parents from fighting, she begins to see a pattern of Emily triangulating with her parents.

In box 71, Gloria attempts to understand how Emily will feel if her parents fight when she is sick. She is exploring the impact of the family system on Emily's treatment.

In box 81, Gloria assesses how Emily's family communicates with each other. She wants to know if Emily has tried to tell her parents how she feels when they fight.

Narrative Theory
Boxes 52, 54, 58, 62, 64, 70, 72, 74, 78, 79, 80, 82

In box 52, Emily says her parents left each other, and Gloria picks up on her use of language. By phrasing it this way, Emily may be implying that her parents aren't leaving her.

In box 54, Gloria notices that Emily uses the word "hard" when she talks about her parents having trouble. In the same breath, Emily talks about her brother going to college and how she will "miss" him. Both events are important—it is hard her parents have separated, and she will miss her brother when he leaves for college.

In box 58, Gloria observes Emily's use of the phrase "felt bad" to explain how she experiences her parents' separation. Words such as "hard" and "felt bad" are windows into understanding what Emily is feeling.

In box 62, Gloria notes that Emily "wishes" for certain things. For example, she wishes her friends would visit her to get her mind off all the problems. This in contrast to phrases such as "hard," "felt bad," and "miss," which reflect more her present experience.

In box 64, Emily wishes her parents would get back together, and explains that this would lift a "huge load" off her. Emily uses "wish" again to communicate what she needs. Her reference to a "huge load" also helps Gloria understand the enormity of her problems.

In box 70, Emily uses the word "hope" to reiterate her need to have her parents stop fighting.

In box 72, Emily says she would feel "very upset" after Gloria asks how she would respond if she were sick and had to see her parents arguing. This is consistent with the other words Emily uses to describe the effect of her parents' fighting on her.

In box 74, Emily tells Gloria she wants her parents to stop fighting, that then she wouldn't "feel so bad." Many of the words and expressions Emily chooses paint the picture of a sad child whose life is "hard" and who is carrying a "heavy load."

In box 78, Emily reverts back to "hope" again after Gloria suggests that her parents might come together to help her. Emily responds that she "hopes" so, and it will be "really nice." Emily goes back and forth between "wishing" and "hoping" on the one hand, and the hard reality of her current life on the other. As seen in this box, Gloria brings hope to Emily. In the fifth excerpt, Gloria works collaboratively with Emily to set goals and plan interventions to improve the situation.

In box 79, Gloria picks up on Emily having "hope," and uses the word herself. Gloria asks Emily if she hopes her parents will reunite to care for her.

In box 80, Emily agrees and associates "feeling better" with her parents not fighting.

In box 82, Emily explains that she doesn't have the "courage" to tell her parents that she needs them to stop fighting. Since she appears to have a good relationship with each of her parents individually, it is interesting she needs "courage" to tell them how she feels.

Psychodynamic Theory
Boxes 54, 58, 62, 64, 65, 66, 71, 76, 80, 83

In box 54, Gloria is sensitive to what it means for a family to have a child leave for college. Although all families are different and react in their own ways, it remains a critical time with its own set of unique challenges and tasks. Emily's family will have to cope with a son leaving for college, Emily undergoing treatment for leukemia, and the parents separating, all around the same time. These issues will complicate the normal crisis associated with this family developmental stage, making the transition to the next stage more difficult.

In box 58, Emily says she feels bad about her parents separating. She liked seeing them together, and she liked seeing them both in the morning. Gloria uses psychodynamic theory to understand Emily's strong attachment to her parents and her sense of loss now that they are apart. She longs for the family she once had.

In box 62, Emily wishes her friends would visit her so she could get her mind off things. This could be interpreted as Emily needing to defend against the many losses she faces and needing a distraction to put her worries out of her mind. Developmentally, this also demonstrates the importance of her friends at this stage in life.

In box 64, Gloria is reminded of how children regress into fantasy and magical thinking when experiencing traumatic situations. It is natural for Emily to wish her life were better, to wish for a fairy godmother who could wave her magical wand to make the problems disappear.

In box 65, Gloria asks Emily if she feels the need to keep her family together. She reflects on how Emily is perhaps motivated to keep her parents together to avoid the pain and loss of the separation.

In box 66, Emily admits that she tries to get her parents to fight less. As Emily talks about her parents' separation, she shows more affect in the interview, revealing how deeply she feels this loss.

In box 71, Gloria uses person-situation reflection with Emily, asking her to imagine being sick with her parents fighting. Emily is aware of her feelings and responds that it would make her very upset.

In box 76, Emily doesn't understand how she got leukemia but refers to getting a cut at the soccer game. It might be important to challenge any magical thinking that the cut caused her leukemia. Since she felt fine before the soccer game, she may think the cut and the leukemia are connected.

In box 80, Gloria observes how articulate and insightful Emily is and believes this reflects her higher level of cognitive development for someone her age.

In box 83, Gloria explores Emily's fears about telling her parents to stop fighting. She wonders if Emily's fears are rational or if they are imagined and based on unconscious and primitive thinking.

Behavioral Theory
Boxes 57, 77

In box 57, Gloria reflects on mind/body connections when she listens to Emily talk about the timing of her parents' separation and the onset of her illness. She wonders about the role of stress on weakening Emily's immune system, making her more susceptible to leukemia.

In box 77, Gloria wonders if Emily's illness might bring her parents together to help her. If the parents notice Emily feels better when they're not fighting, this might reduce the regularity and intensity of their fights. This is a behavioral intervention aimed at the parents to change specific behaviors; it requires an understanding of cause and effect, and of the relationship between behavior and its consequences. Positive outcomes, or the reward of Emily feeling better, would reinforce the benefits of the parents fighting less.

Cognitive Theory
Box 73

In box 73, Gloria applies a problem-solving intervention when she asks Emily what her parents need to understand to make the situation less overwhelming for her. She encourages Emily to join with her to find a solution to her parents' fighting. This intervention uses a cognitive approach.

Fourth Excerpt from Transcript and Process Recording

The topics of school and friends are themes in the fourth excerpt. Emily describes going to a new school where there will be more children and teachers. She begins the excerpt viewing this in a positive light. Then Gloria starts to probe how Emily will experience returning to school after her treatment, and Emily shares worries about how her friends will react. "Will they be scared of me...thinking they might catch it?" Emily confides in Gloria that she is concerned about how her friends will act and whether they will accept her or not. Notice how many times the word "scary" is used in this excerpt. This gives insight into how Emily is feeling inside. She is worrying about a lot of things now, losing her hair, and how her friends will react to her.

Content	Observation/Reflection	Analysis of Intervention: Theories and Practice
85. Emily: Especially going into a new school, so many more kids. It's a lot easier.		
86. Gloria: Of course, what about your teachers?		Practice: Data collection. Communication skill: questioning.
87. Emily: They're nice, they're very helpful, it's kind of cool having several teachers because they help me in several different ways.	School is an important support system for her.	Theory: Narrative, uses words like nice, cool, help to describe her teachers. Practice: Assessment
88. Gloria: That's great, how do you feel about going back to school when you finally feel well enough to go back?		Practice: Assessment. Communication skill: exploration of problem.
89. Emily: I really don't know how people are going to react. Will they be scared of me? Thinking they might catch it after I'm done, something like that?	Does she really think they could catch leukemia? When she says they may be scared of her, I wonder if she is projecting her own feelings of being scared?	Theory: Narrative (react, scared, catch it), psychodynamic, projection.
90. Gloria: Of course of course how differently do you think you're going to look? When you go back to school?	I wished I had explored her fear that she thinks they may catch leukemia from her. I wonder if she thinks this could happen? I could have used cognitive restructuring to challenge this faulty belief.	Theory: Psychodynamic, developmental theory, body image issues. Practice: Communication skills, questioning.
91. Emily: I don't know.	This is probably something she doesn't want to think about. Should I probe more in this area?	
92. Gloria: Well, you mentioned losing your hair.	It is hard for me to explore this with her, but I know it will be important for her to understand and deal with.	Practice: Communication skill, continued exploration of problem.
93. Emily: Yeah.		

(Continued)

Content	Observation/Reflection	Analysis of Intervention: Theories and Practice
94. Gloria: How do you imagine yourself looking without your hair?	I may be pushing her too much. Maybe she is not ready to confront this yet. This is something I want to bring up in supervision next time to check my timing.	Practice: Self-reflection. Communication skill: confrontation.
95. Emily: Kind of scary.	Here she is using scary to explain how she is feeling.	
96. Gloria: Scary, does that make you feel afraid?		Theory: Narrative, Gloria picks up on her words again and uses them to reflect back what she is feeling. Practice: Communication skills, reflecting back feelings, clarification.
97. Emily: Yeah.	She usually is very articulate, but she is having problems talking about losing her hair, showing how scared she is.	
98. Gloria: Yeah what do you think that would be like, telling your friends, or going back to school?	I think this will be tough for. She may need to first deal with her own feelings about it.	Practice: Communication skills, continued exploration of the problem.
99. Emily: Well I don't how they would act, I'm scared about how they'll act or if they'll accept me anymore.	Since friends are so important at this time in her life, the fear of rejection must be scary. I also wonder if she is projecting again and she is also saying that she may have trouble accepting herself without hair.	Theory: Narrative (scared, accept).
100. Gloria: What about your teachers, do you think they'll accept you or not?	I guess I am asking this because I think she will say yes. This could help her feel she may get support from the adults at school, her teachers.	Theory: Narrative, Gloria uses Emily's words again to connect their conversation.
101. Emily: I think because they're more adult, they might, but I'm not sure. I'm not sure.	This must be rough if she can be sure if her teachers would support her. Is she less trusting of adults because of what's happening with her parents? Maybe she feels she can't depend on adults as much as before.	Theory: Psychodynamic, trust issues. Practice: Assessment.

Reflection of Fourth Process Recording and Discussion of Practice Skills and Theories Used in Intervention

Communication Skills

Boxes 86

Questioning: This is a way of gaining more information about a client's situation. There are many different kinds of questions, for example, open- and closed-ended questions and reflexive questions. Questioning is often used in assessment as part of data collection.

In box 86, Gloria questions Emily about her teachers at the new school she has just started. In collecting data for assessment, Gloria wants to know about her social support systems, including the resources at the school.

Box 88

Exploration of the problem: This is a way of gaining more information about a client's situation. When continuing to explore the problem, the social worker listens for underlying feelings about the situation, who else is involved, and what resources are available to help resolve it.

In box 88, Gloria asks Emily how she will feel going back to school after her treatment. Gloria is exploring Emily's underlying feelings about how this will affect her.

Boxes 90, 92, 98

Continued exploration of the problem: When continuing to explore the problem, the social worker listens for underlying feelings about the situation, who else is involved, and what resources are available to help resolve it.

In box 90, Gloria continues to explore Emily's fears about how other children will react to her, especially how she looks, since body image and appearance are so important for her age group.

In box 92, Gloria keeps exploring Emily's anxiety about returning to school and specifically asks about hair loss.

In box 98, Gloria proceeds with similar questions, inquiring how Emily will feel telling her friends about the illness and going back to school. Both school and friends are important to Emily at this stage in life, so Gloria wants to address these subjects with her.

In box 100, Gloria moves on to teachers as she further explores school issues with Emily. Here, she asks Emily if she thinks her teachers will accept her.

Box 94

Challenging moments: There may be times during an interview that are uncomfortable for both the social worker and the client. At these times, the social worker needs to contain both her feelings and the client's feelings. The social worker sits with these feelings and tries to understand them with the client. This can be hard to do, and many beginning social workers want to apologize or avoid pursuing uncomfortable subjects.

In box 94, Gloria asks Emily a challenging question about how she imagines she will look without hair. Afterward, Gloria wonders if it were too early to delve into this subject, since Emily is already dealing with so much. However, she doesn't want to avoid the subject either, especially if it is on Emily's mind already. In this case, it is better to address what Emily is thinking and feeling directly, than to skirt the issue.

Box 96

Reflecting back feelings: This is when the social worker gives a short response back to the client that mirrors the feeling the worker heard the client express. It is used to let the client know the worker is listening.

In box 96, Gloria reflects back what she hears Emily say, repeating that it's scary, and asks Emily if she is afraid. You could also interpret this as Gloria exploring Emily's underlying feelings about losing her hair during chemotherapy.

Other Practice Skills Used

Box 86

Data collection: In the data collection stage, the social worker explores the problem in more depth. This involves getting information from multiple sources about the client's life and situation, and about the social systems that may impact the problem.

In box 86, Gloria wants to know about Emily's social support system, including the resources at the school. Since Emily will eventually return there after her treatment, the school environment could impact how she copes with her illness.

Boxes 87, 88, 101

Assessment: Assessment is the process of understanding the client and his problem based on the information gathered. It is done in a holistic way that highlights the importance of context in the construction of meaning, and it is a collaborative activity that is done in tandem with the client. Some of the areas that are explored include the client's developmental history, present family, family-of-origin, school, work, medical and psychiatric history, culture, ethnicity, religion, friendship and support network, strengths, community involvement, and significant events and people that have influenced the individual over time.

In box 87, Gloria listens to Emily talk about attending a new school and how she thinks teachers will treat her. School and friends are important at Emily's stage of development, so these are critical topics to address in assessment.

In box 88, Gloria's assessment continues when she asks Emily what it will be like to return to school when she feels better.

In box 101, Emily says she thinks the teachers will accept her, because they are adults, but she is not sure. Gloria uses this in her assessment and wonders if Emily has any trust issues with adults, especially after her parents' separation.

Box 94

Self-reflection: The skill of self-reflection is an important part of professional practice. Social workers are expected to engage in personal reflection and self-correction to assure continual professional development (CSWE, 2008).

In box 94, Gloria asks Emily how she imagines she will look without hair. Afterward, she wonders if she pushed Emily into an uncomfortable area. She is not sure if she should confront such an issue with Emily at this early stage and decides she will ask her supervisor about her judgment.

Theories Used in Intervention

Narrative Theory

Boxes 87, 89, 95, 96, 99, 100

In box 87, Gloria notices how Emily uses the words "nice" and "cool" to describe her teachers at the new school. She starts off this excerpt with positive feelings about school.

In box 89, Emily wonders how people at school will "react" to her, and if they will be "scared," thinking they will catch "it." Emily's words show that she is scared and that she may have some confusion about how she got leukemia. It is worth noting that Emily refers to leukemia as "it," perhaps signaling how difficult it is to say the actual word.

In box 95, Emily uses the word "scary" to describe how she thinks she will look without hair.

In box 96, Gloria picks up on Emily's use of the word "scary," referring to how she would look without hair, and repeats it back to Emily. She then asks Emily if it makes her afraid, digging deeper into Emily's feelings on the subject.

In box 99, Emily is "scared" about how her friends will react to her and if they will "accept me anymore." Her phrasing implies that her friends accept her now, but she questions if that will change once they see her without hair. This reinforces the importance of appearance at this age, and how it affects acceptance from the peer group.

In box 100, Gloria uses Emily's word, "accept," only this time Gloria refers to Emily's teachers. Frequently, Gloria uses Emily's language and words when she talks with her. This may help to create a stronger connection.

Psychodynamic Theory

Boxes 89, 90, 99, 101

Projection: This defense mechanism unconsciously protects an individual from unacceptable thoughts or feelings by making him believe that it's another person having those thoughts.

In box 89, when Emily wonders if others at school may react to her illness with fear, she may be projecting her own feelings.

In box 90, Gloria uses psychodynamic theory to reflect on developmental issues and ego functioning. In box 89, Emily demonstrated primitive thinking when she hypothesized that schoolmates may worry they can "catch" leukemia. This is probably a question Emily has as well even though it is irrational. Gloria asks Emily in box 90 how she thinks she will look after treatment. She explores this subject because she knows how important body image is for someone Emily's age.

In box 99, when Emily says she is scared about how her friends will react to her without hair, she may be projecting her own fears onto friends.

In box 101, Emily raises trust issues regarding her teachers. Although she thinks they will accept her, because they are adults, she is not sure. As a result of her parents' separation, she might feel she can't depend on the adults in her life as much.

Fifth Excerpt from Transcript and Process Recording

Before the beginning of the fifth excerpt, Emily and Gloria have a short discussion about Emily's academic workload. Although she expects a little more work in the new school, Emily feels she can handle it.

The fifth excerpt starts with a discussion of school, where Emily wants to maintain her high grades. Emily is an excellent student and her success in the classroom has contributed to her positive self-esteem. It is important for her to feel that school will continue to serve as a support.

This excerpt concentrates on Gloria helping Emily get through her illness, especially telling her friends about the leukemia and working with her parents about fighting less. Emily is worrying about a lot of things now, losing her hair, how her friends will react to her, and about her parents fighting and getting divorced. The part of Emily who is still a little girl has two wishes: that her friends would know about her illness and her parents would stop fighting. Her short flight into fantasy and magical thinking in this excerpt has her wishing for a fortune-teller who could reveal how her friends would react to her without hair.

By the end of the fifth excerpt, Gloria and Emily have defined the problems to work on, and have established goals and a plan for achieving them.

Content	Observation/Reflection	Analysis of Intervention: Theories and Practice
102. Emily: I want to continue getting good grades and just continue my life like I never had it.	I can understand her wanting to deny and pretend this never happened.	Theory: Psychodynamic, defenses.
103. Gloria: That's excellent, that sounds very optimistic of you. What do you think is going to help you get through this experience?	**I want to support her positive thinking.**	Theory: Cognitive, self-instruction, positive psychology, problem solving. Communication skills: exploration of problem.
104. Emily: If my parents stop fighting and if my friends stick with me.	It sounds so easy. I only wish it were.	Theory: Narrative (stick by her).

(Continued)

Content	Observation/Reflection	Analysis of Intervention: Theories and Practice
105. Gloria: How will you know that your friends will stick by you?	I am aware of using Emily's use of language and words to connect to how she makes meaning of her experience.	Theory: Narrative, Gloria continues to use Emily's language in their conversation to relate better to her experience. Cognitive, problem solving. Practice: Communication skill, continued exploration of problem.
106. Emily: I don't know.	I guess that was a hard question for her.	
107. Gloria: Yeah, so they don't know yet, your friends.		Practice: Communication skills, continued exploration of problem.
108. Emily: No they don't know yet.	This must be a worry for her, knowing how to tell them and then how they will react.	
109. Gloria: Have you thought about how you might want to tell them?		Theory: Cognitive, problem solving. Practice: Communication skill, continued exploration of problem.
110. Emily: Yeah, I don't know if I'll just find the right words now, like if I'll have to think about it now, or if I'll just do it right if I just tell them; I'm not sure how I'm going to.	It looks like she is putting demands on herself to know how to tell them in the right way. I wonder if she tends to be a little hard on herself and expects to be perfect. She wants to do it right.	Theory: Narrative, use of words right, twice. Cognitive, confront her belief that there is only one way and she has to do it right. Practice: Assessment.
111. Gloria: Who do you feel really the need to tell right now? Do you feel like you want to tell all of your friends? Some of your friends?		Theory: Cognitive, problem solving. Practice: Communication skills, continued exploration of problem.
112. Emily: All of my friends.	She doesn't differentiate between friends but wants to address this issue of telling to all friends. There is a little tendency to think in terms of absolutes, all or nothing.	Theory: Cognitive, all or nothing thinking.
113. Gloria: All of your friends. How do you usually communicate with them?		Theory: Cognitive, problem solving. Practice: Communication skills, continued exploration of problem.
114. Emily: Well usually I see them at school but since I'm not going to school, I'll probably call them or email them on the Internet.	This sounds like a good task for us to start with. Let's see how she feels about it.	
115. Gloria: How do you feel about us working on a way of telling your friends, if that would make you feel better?		Practice: Goal setting. Communication skills, seeking client feedback.

(Continued)

Content	Observation/Reflection	Analysis of Intervention: Theories and Practice
116. Emily: Yeah that would help.		
117. Gloria: You think that would help? Because you know that's something that I do; sometimes I work with the kids on ways that they can tell their friends at school or preparing them for going back to school, because it can be a very scary process or it can make you nervous going back and not knowing how people are going to react and just feeling a little nervous. And that's something that I do with a lot of kids here in the hospital, when they're ready to go back to school or before then, you know telling your teachers, telling friends, family, and things like that. It sounds like you're a little bit concerned about that. Would that work for you if we worked on that?	This might help to know more about my role and how I can help her in practical ways.	Theory: Cognitive, communication skills, problem solving. Narrative, Gloria uses Emily's word of scary again. Practice: Communication skills, clarification of role, information-giving, asking for client feedback.
118. Emily: Yeah.		
119. Gloria: That's great, what else do you think would help you right now, something you feel you need help with right now?		Theory: Problem solving Practice: Goal setting. Communication skills, questioning.
120. Emily: Um, I need help with knowing how they're going to treat it, and I need help with knowing, like I wish some fortune teller or someone would tell me how everyone will react when they find out.	I wonder if she means she really wants to know her fortune about how she will recover from leukemia.	Psychodynamic, magical thinking, fortune teller. Narrative, use of phrase fortune teller, wishes— part of her regression to fantasy and magical thinking.
121. Gloria: Right, right; well you know that we can't tell how everybody will react to that.		Theory: Cognitive, helping her have a realistic appraisal. Practice: Communication, providing information, giving client feedback.
122. Emily: Yeah.		
123. Gloria: And sometimes people react in a certain way because they don't have the right information, about leukemia, or about what exactly is going on. And sometimes, in my experience working with kids, they feel like they have to tell the whole world. I don't have hair because I'm going through leukemia, or because this is happening. And one of the things I tell kids is that you can decide who you want to tell, how much you want to tell, because this is your personal experience, and you choose how much of that you want to share. It's really something we can definitely work on, and also I think it would be helpful to speak with the medical team so that they can come back in the room and really explain in a way that would be helpful to you what exactly the diagnosis is, how they plan on treating it, what the side effects will be, so that you feel better and clearer about what to look forward to?	She's dealing with so much. I want to make this easier for her and not make her feel so overwhelmed with the need to tell everyone about her leukemia. I think it would help if she could break the problem up into smaller pieces to make it more manageable.	Theory: Cognitive, confronting all or nothing thinking, problem solving. Practice: Communication skill: Information-giving, referral.

(Continued)

Content	Observation/Reflection	Analysis of Intervention: Theories and Practice
124. Emily: Yes, definitely.		
125. Gloria: I think that sounds like it might help, what do you think?		Practice: Communication skills, asking for client's feedback.
126. Emily: Mmhmm.		
127. Gloria: Good, good and lastly it sounds like working with your parents might be a good way of helping you relieve some of the anxiety around being here and helping you feel comfortable as you go through this, because obviously having your parents both understand this and be on your side is going to help you get through this. I can certainly work with your parents on that, work with you, work with your family on it. How does that sound?	I think it will be helpful for her to know that I can talk to her parents also to relieve some of her stress about their fighting.	Practice: Setting goals, work with individual and family. Communication skills, asking for client's feedback.
128. Emily: That sounds good.		
129. Gloria: Yeah, great; how about if I come back maybe tomorrow and we can do, I don't know, some arts and crafts or something to pass the time and we can talk a little bit more about how you're doing and how things are going?	It might be helpful to use some play therapy with her. We have done a lot of talking today. Play therapy might be another outlet for her to express her feelings.	Theory: Psychodynamic: non-directive play therapy. Communication skills, next steps.
130. Emily: That would be really good.	I'm glad she wants to continue working together. From the sound of it and her reaction here, she genuinely is asking for help and wants to address her worries.	Theory: Narrative, really good.
131. Gloria: That works? Awesome. Good to talk to you.	This is a good place to stop. We certainly covered a lot of territory for one meeting. She seems very open to our working together. I am feeling good about our beginning relationship and look forward to seeing her tomorrow.	Practice: Communication skills, endings

Toward the end of the fifth excerpt, Gloria clarifies her role and lets Emily know that she can help her cope with some of her fears. They set goals for their work together, and Emily seems relieved that Gloria will support her through the difficult challenges ahead. Gloria plans to see Emily the next day, when she will use both individual and family interventions to achieve the goals they made collaboratively.

Reflection of Fifth Process Recording and Discussion of Practice Skills and Theories Used in Intervention

Communication Skills

Box 103

Exploration of the problem: This is a way of gaining more information about a client's situation. When continuing to explore the problem, the social worker listens for underlying feelings about the situation, who else is involved, and what resources are available to help resolve it.

In box 103, Gloria explores Emily's illness more and asks her an open-ended question about what she thinks will help her through it.

Boxes 105, 107, 109, 111, 113

Continued exploration of the problem: When continuing to explore the problem, the social worker listens for underlying feelings about the situation, who else is involved, and what resources are available to help resolve it.

In box 105, Gloria probes further into the problem of how Emily's friends will react to her illness by asking Emily how she will know they will stick by her. This question helps Gloria understand what qualities Emily deems important for her friendships.

In box 107, Gloria continues to explore whether Emily's friends know about her illness.

In box 109, as Gloria discusses with Emily the difficulty of telling her friends about the leukemia, she asks Emily if she has thought about a way to approach it.

In box 111, Gloria keeps exploring this issue with Emily, asking who she wants to tell now, and whether she wants to tell some or all her friends.

In box 113, Gloria gets into the specifics of how Emily usually communicates with friends. Her questions are meant to help Emily imagine how she could tell her friends about the illness. Gloria is engaging Emily in problem solving.

Boxes 115, 117, 125, 127

Seeking client feedback: When seeking client feedback, the social worker asks for the client's perception of a particular situation, the client-worker relationship, or the helping process.

In box 115, Gloria asks Emily if she would like them to work together to find a way to tell her friends about her illness. She is looking for Emily's feedback, so she knows this is an important goal for them to tackle.

In box 117, after Gloria explains her role to Emily, she asks Emily if they could work on some of the school issues they had discussed. By doing so, Gloria engages Emily in a collaborative process of setting goals.

In box 125, Gloria inquires if Emily would like to talk more with the doctors about her illness and treatment. Gloria does not assume what is best for Emily; instead she lets Emily respond directly about what she needs.

In box 127, Gloria asks Emily's permission to work with her parents on certain problems she and Emily had identified related to their fighting. Gloria wants Emily's feedback before going forward.

Box 117

Clarification of role: The social worker helps the client understand what services the agency offers and what her role as social worker will be. There are times when the client needs reminding that the work is collaborative; it is the social worker's job to facilitate, not direct the process.

In box 117, Gloria clarifies her role by explaining to Emily that she helps children, like Emily, prepare for their return to school. She lets Emily know that she can assist in telling her teachers, the other children, friends, family, etc.

Boxes 117, 121, 123

Information-giving: Information-giving means informing the client about the social agency, the problem, and the resources for change.

In box 117, as Gloria clarifies her role, she also provides information about some of the problems she can help Emily with.

In box 121, Gloria wants Emily to understand it is impossible to know how everyone will react to her illness. This is in response to Emily's wish that a fortune-teller could predict the future so she wouldn't feel so nervous.

In box 123, Gloria explains that Emily doesn't have to tell everyone about her leukemia; Emily can decide who to tell and how much she is comfortable sharing with them. Gloria wants Emily to feel she can take control of the process and that Gloria will help her with it.

Box 117

Normalizing feelings: Clients often believe that their feelings are unacceptable or abnormal. The social worker helps the client see that her feelings are a natural reaction to the given situation.

In box 117, Gloria helps Emily understand that it is normal for her to be scared about going back to school, especially not knowing how others will react to her. Gloria explains that she helps many children with this problem and talks with their teachers, kids at school, friends, and others.

Box 119

Questioning: This is a way of gaining more information about a client's situation. There are many different kinds of questions, for example, open- and closed-ended questions and reflexive questions. Questioning is often used in assessment as part of data collection.

In box 119, Gloria asks Emily what else she needs help with to make sure she has explored the problem sufficiently to identify what is most important to work on.

Box 121

Giving client feedback: This is when the social worker finds an opportunity to provide the client with information about his behavior and its effect on him or on other people. It can prove difficult, because the client may not want to hear or accept what the social worker is saying.

In box 121, Gloria confronts Emily's fantasy of wanting a fortune-teller to foresee how her friends will react to her illness. She helps Emily face reality that there is no way to tell how everyone will react.

Box 123

Referral: This is when a client needs additional resources outside of the agency in which she's receiving services. With the client's permission, the worker makes the referral in order to help the client access other avenues for help.

In box 123, Gloria talks to Emily about referring her to the doctors so they can provide her with more information about her diagnosis and treatment.

Box 129

Next steps: This is a phrase used when the client and the worker decide what they will work on next, and what actions they can take.

In box 129, Gloria lets Emily know what the next steps are. She tells Emily she will see her the next day, when they can talk more while doing something together, like arts and crafts.

Box 131

Endings: This is when the social worker prepares the client for the end of the session.

In box 131, Gloria feels they are at an optimal stopping point. She believes the first meeting with Emily went well, and she is confident that they will have a good working relationship.

Other Practice Skills Used
Boxes 103, 110

Identifying strengths: During assessment, social workers listen for client strengths they can use to help solve certain problems. As clients talk about their situation and their stories unfold, workers identify strengths that are embedded in the narrative. By focusing on positive attributes and characteristics, workers shift the focus away from deficits to inquiring about and affirming strengths.

In box 103, Gloria identifies strengths in Emily based on her sentiments in box 102, that she "wants to continue getting good grades like she never had it." This shows determination and a strong will to overcome obstacles. Gloria responds to Emily by saying "That's excellent," acknowledging these strengths.

In box 110, as Gloria listens to Emily, she notices that Emily is putting pressure on herself to find the "right" words to tell her friends and to do it "right." Gloria wonders if Emily has a tendency to be a perfectionist and expects too much from herself. This is something Gloria will pay attention to in her assessment of Emily. Gloria already knows that Emily excels at school and will explore if she sets exceedingly high standards for herself in this area too.

Boxes 123, 127

Self-reflection: The skill of self-reflection is an important part of professional practice. Social workers are expected to engage in personal reflection and self-correction to assure continual professional development (CSWE, 2008). Practitioners need to understand themselves on a deep level that includes deciphering their values, reactions to others, the influence of family-of-origin patterns, and basic assumptions about culture and difference.

In box 123, Gloria reflects on how she deferred to the doctors again at the end of the session, almost as if she felt she didn't succeed in helping Emily understand her illness and its treatment. She wants to talk to her supervisor about her lack of confidence. She thinks part of the problem is that she buys into the notion that the doctor will fix everything and make it right, and she wishes this could be true for Emily. Maybe this reflects some of her own magical thinking.

In box 127, Gloria wonders what it will be like to work with Emily's parents. Because Gloria often has a strong alliance with the child, she finds she needs to contain her anger at the parents when they aren't supporting the child. In Emily's case, the parents' fighting makes Emily anxious, and the parents need to understand and stop this behavior in front of her.

Boxes 123, 127

Goal setting: Goal setting is a collaborative process whereby the social worker and client come to a mutual understanding of what they want to accomplish.

In boxes 123 and 127, Gloria and Emily set goals for their work together that include finding a way to tell her friends about her illness and working with her parents about fighting less. In both boxes, Gloria asks for Emily's feedback to make sure these are goals she wants to address.

Theories Used in Intervention

The fifth and last excerpt leans heavily on cognitive theory and problem solving to help Emily define and begin to solve the problems associated with her illness and treatment. Gloria uses cognitive interventions to confront some of Emily's all-or-nothing thinking and to challenge certain unrealistic fantasies, for example, to have a fortune-teller predict how her friends will react to her illness.

Psychodynamic Theory
Boxes 102, 105, 120, 129

In box 102, Gloria understands how Emily may sometimes need to defend against the ugly reality of her leukemia and deny it. Gloria appreciates how defense mechanisms help protect clients from overwhelming issues when they need a break.

In box 105, Gloria asks Emily a question that requires deeper reflection on her situation. When she notices that Emily struggles to respond, Gloria realizes that the question was too hard and beyond Emily's capabilities. Emily is only 11 years old and can't yet use abstract and higher levels of reasoning and thought.

In box 120, as Gloria listens to Emily talk about her wishes, she relates the discussion to Emily's need to regress into early childhood and magical thinking. Her flight into fantasy plays out in her wish to have a fortune-teller predict how her friends will react to the news of her leukemia.

In box 129, before Gloria ends the interview, she discusses meeting with Emily the next day and explains that they can do arts and crafts together while they talk. Gloria will use principles of psychodynamic theory to design an approach to play therapy with Emily. Since Emily is 11 years old, her interests might tend toward drawing or modeling clay, compared to what younger children would use in play. Whatever Emily chooses, the activity will serve as an outlet for her to release anxiety and unconscious conflicts. Gloria will stay attentive to how Emily uses metaphors and other symbols when she draws or models with clay.

Cognitive Theory
Boxes 103, 109, 110, 111, 112, 113, 117, 119, 121, 123

In box 103, Gloria uses a problem-solving approach by asking Emily to think about what will get her through this experience.

In box 109, Gloria engages Emily again in the problem-solving method by inquiring how she might want to tell her friends about her illness. She continues to involve Emily in finding solutions to her problems and does not just tell her what to do.

In box 110, while Gloria listens to Emily, she wonders how she can challenge Emily's assumption that there is only one right way to tell her friends.

In box 111, Gloria works collaboratively with Emily to figure out how to approach telling her friends, and whether she wants to start with all of her friends or just some of them.

In box 112, Emily responds that she wants to tell "all" of her friends about her illness. Gloria ponders this "all-or-nothing" thinking and whether Emily would benefit, instead, by starting with some of her closest friends.

In box 113, Gloria gathers specific information to help solve the problem of how to tell Emily's friends that she has leukemia.

In box 117, Gloria explains to Emily how she can help solve some of the problems they have discussed in the interview. For example, Gloria can use communication skills to coach Emily in ways she can talk to her friends. She lets Emily know that she can speak to Emily's teachers and friends as well to prepare them for her return to school.

In box 119, before Gloria ends the interview, she asks Emily if there is anything else she needs help with as they continue to problem solve.

In box 121, Gloria challenges Emily's belief that she can know how everyone will react to her illness ahead of time. She is helping Emily move away from false assumptions and fantasy to deal with reality.

In box 123, Gloria confronts Emily's all-or-nothing thinking that she has to tell everyone about her leukemia all at once, and helps Emily understand that she can choose who to share this information with and how much to share. She wants Emily to feel she can take more control over the process.

Narrative Theory
Boxes 104, 105, 110, 117, 120

In box 104, Gloria notices Emily's use of the expression "stick with me" to explain her hope that her friends will not abandon her at this critical time. The expression conjures an image of

Emily and her friends held close together, making it hard to separate them. This is what Emily needs now—to be held close by her friends.

In box 105, Gloria picks up on the importance of this particular expression and asks Emily how she will know if her friends will "stick" by her.

In box 110, Gloria observes that Emily uses the word "right" twice: She explains her need to find the "right" words and to tell her friends about her illness in the "right" way. Gloria wonders if Emily puts too much pressure on herself to perfect how she describes problems to her friends, and if she believes she is responsible for their reactions.

In box 117, Gloria uses Emily's word "scary" to acknowledge her anxiety about returning to school.

In box 120, Emily wishes to know the future and to have a fortune-teller tell her ahead of time how her friends will react to her having leukemia. Gloria pays attention to Emily's words and language, which provide insight into how Emily thinks and feels about her situation.

Assessments

Assessment is the process of understanding the client and his problem in a holistic way based on the information gathered. It highlights the importance of context in the construction of meaning, and it is a collaborative activity done in tandem with the client. Please refer to chapter 1 for outlines on the problem-solving method, psychosocial assessment and intervention plan, and the bio/psycho/social/spiritual assessment.

Problem-Solving Method

This assessment follows the problem-solving method outline found in chapter 1. It is the social worker's attempt to apply the problem-solving method to Emily's case. It is written in the first person, from the social worker's perspective.

Engagement

I met with Emily for the first time in the outpatient clinic, shortly after her diagnosis of childhood leukemia. At our initial meeting, Emily came across as quite bright, a pretty 11-year-old girl with fair skin and beautiful, long blond hair. She was attentive during the interview and disclosed early that she was a little nervous. We quickly got into what was on her mind and engaged well throughout the session. At times, she didn't seem to show many feelings, but this changed, especially when she talked about her parents' fighting and separation five months ago. She was comfortable opening up to me. She also wanted help with some of the overwhelming problems in her life related to both her leukemia and her parents' separation. We made a good connection, and I plan to meet with her again tomorrow.

Assessment

Emily is an 11-year-old girl just diagnosed with leukemia. She and her mother, who accompanied her, were referred to the cancer outpatient clinic after tests in the emergency room confirmed abnormalities in Emily's blood. At the first meeting, I learned that she lives in western Massachusetts with her mother and brother. Five months ago, her father separated from her mother and is now living in New York. The separation came after a long period of the parents arguing and fighting with each other. Emily's brother is a senior in high school. He will be leaving for college next year, and Emily will miss him. Emily and her brother visit their father in New York every other weekend.

Emily is proud that she is an excellent student and appears to enjoy school. She is in the sixth grade, and has just started a new school where there are more students and teachers. She has many friends who are important to her, and she gets together with them often. She is active in soccer, plays the cello, and models on weekends.

The first interview explored the meaning of leukemia in Emily's life. One of her primary concerns was how her friends would react to the news. She was worried about how to tell them and whether they would accept her once they knew. Several times, it appeared she wanted to regress to early childhood and magical thinking. This surfaced when she wished a fortune-teller could predict how everyone would react to her after treatment. She was scared about losing her hair during chemotherapy, how she would look, and going back to school. Physical appearance is critical for someone of Emily's age, and this will be an important issue to help Emily cope with.

Another major stressor for Emily is her parents' separation. She misses waking up in the morning with both parents at home with her. She wanted her parents to stop fighting, especially during her treatment, and stated that this would help her feel better. She described times when she tried to stop her parents from arguing by distracting them, reflecting a tendency to get in the middle and triangulate with her parents.

Emily presented as a resilient child who could adapt to difficult situations. When confronted with having to stop sports and other activities, she responded that she would find something better to do that was less active. She appeared to have a positive attachment with her parents, although this may be changing as a result of the parents' separation and feeling less secure about the future. Her peer relationships seem normal for her age, and she is close with her brother. Developmentally, she is in middle childhood but will soon enter adolescence. Her thinking vacillates between these two stages—from abstract with moments of insight to the more primitive thinking of childhood, perhaps as a result of the changes and loss currently taking place in her life.

Assessment Summary

Emily is a bright, articulate, resilient, 11-year-old girl who was recently diagnosed with childhood leukemia. She lives with her mother and older brother in western Massachusetts. Her parents separated five months ago, and her father lives in New York where Emily and her brother visit every other weekend. Emily is struggling to prepare herself for the effects of her leukemia treatment and worries about how her friends will react, especially when she loses her hair. In addition to dealing with leukemia and chemotherapy, she is upset about the changes in her family and misses her father. Emily and I engaged well in our first meeting and set goals for our work together. She appreciated having someone to talk to about her leukemia and her family problems.

Planning

Collaboratively, Emily and I defined the problems and established goals for our work. Emily wanted help with how to tell her friends about her illness and how to prepare for her return to school. She was scared of losing her hair, what she would look like, and how others would react to her, identifying this as another problem to address. Emily also needed help to get her parents to stop fighting, especially at the hospital during her treatments. Emily and I agreed that I would work with her individually and also with her parents doing family sessions. We set up a meeting for the next day.

Intervention

The intervention began in the first meeting when I engaged Emily in a therapeutic relationship, one in which she could trust me, open up, and share her concerns about her leukemia diagnosis. In our initial discussion, Emily talked candidly about the various worries and fears she faced—telling her friends, losing her hair, how she will look, how others will react to her, going back to school, and her parents' separation. I used ego-sustaining techniques by showing empathy and support and building a caring relationship with Emily. Cognitive interventions included working together with Emily on problem solving, and cognitive restructuring to challenge some of her false assumptions. I kept aware of how Emily used language during the interview and mirrored some of her words to form a stronger alliance and connection with her.

Termination

As we approached the end of the interview, I summarized what I heard Emily say she was worried about and needed help with. I explained my role in working with other children who shared many of her concerns. I let her know that we would find a way to tell her friends about her illness and, in addition, that I would work with the school to prepare them for her return. I relieved some of Emily's fears about her parents fighting and let her know I would meet with them to discuss how they can get along better to support her. Our first interview ended well with a plan to meet again the next day.

Evaluation

Emily and I engaged well in the first meeting and are beginning to establish a strong, caring relationship. She was receptive to social work intervention and opened up to share her worries with me. Emily was attentive and articulated well what she needed help with. By the end of the first meeting, Emily and I had defined the problems she was dealing with, established goals, and planned for our future meetings. From her responses, Emily demonstrated appreciation and relief and wants to continue to meet.

Follow-up

Emily and I will schedule appointments at different intervals over the next two years while she is receiving treatment for leukemia. During our work together, I also will coordinate her care with the medical team, school, and family. I have referred Emily to a monthly support group with other children her age and expect this will serve as a valuable resource for her. It will be another place where she can discuss her fears about losing her hair as a result of che-motherapy; only this time, she can talk with her peers who understand from her perspective what it really means and how to get through it.

Psychosocial Assessment and Intervention Strategy

Please refer to chapter 1, which includes outlines for the psychosocial assessment and inter-vention plan. This is one example of applying a psychosocial assessment and intervention to Emily's case and is written in the social worker's voice.

Identifying Data

Emily is an 11-year-old girl who has just been diagnosed with leukemia. She has long blond hair and is of normal height and weight. She appears bright and alert, although somewhat nervous. She is in the sixth grade and has just started middle school. She lives in western Massachusetts with her mother and older brother. Her parents separated five months ago, and her father resides in New York now. Emily and her brother visit him every other weekend.

Presenting Problem

Emily was referred to the outpatient children's oncology department from the emergency room where the results from blood tests showed the possibility of leukemia. Specialists con-firmed the diagnosis and met with Emily and her mother to convey this information and arrange treatment. The plan was for her to be hospitalized immediately to begin treatment. While in the outpatient department, I met with Emily to assess her psychosocial needs going forward.

Current Functioning, Social Supports, and Strengths

Emily is a bright, articulate 11-year-old who has achieved major developmental milestones for someone her age. She demonstrates many strengths and appears to have a good support system. She is an excellent student who excels in her studies. She has good relationships with her teachers and peers, including several close friends that she gets together with. She plays soccer, plays the cello, and models on the weekends.

Emily's leukemia diagnosis will present many challenges for her. The side effects of treatment will include fatigue and loss of hair. She will not have the energy to engage in rigor-ous sport activities, and losing her hair will affect modeling. However, Emily appears resilient and adaptable and says she will just find better things to do that aren't as active.

It seems that Emily has good relationships with both her parents and her brother, although the family is undergoing stress and major transitions that are problems for Emily and may complicate her treatment. Her parents separated five months ago, and Emily is upset about the level of conflict in their relationship and not seeing both parents each morning. She is anxious about how to tell her friends that she is ill and about her parents fighting during her treatment.

Relevant Past History

Prior to her leukemia diagnosis, Emily had few health problems. She did well in school, played sports, and was involved in extracurricular activities. Family life was disrupted five months ago when her father separated from her mother and went to live in New York. This has created inner turmoil for Emily who is upset about the separation and the resulting changes in her family.

Formulation

Emily is a pretty, bright, articulate, and resilient 11-year-old girl who has been diagnosed with leukemia. Her parents separated five months ago, and Emily lives in western Massachusetts with her mother and older brother. There are multiple stressors in Emily's life that include her recent diagnosis, lengthy treatment and side effects, her parents' separation, and fear of how to tell her friends about her illness and whether they will still accept her. She is also concerned about going back to school and how everyone will react to her losing her hair. Emily is open to social work intervention, and during our first meeting we established goals and a plan for working together to address the identified problems. Emily is motivated to tackle the issues and engaged well with me.

Intervention

Intervention began in the initial meeting with Emily, shortly after she was told she had leukemia. I listened empathically as Emily shared her concerns about the effects of the illness on her relationships with friends, how she will look after losing her hair from chemotherapy, going back to school, and her parents. She engaged fully with me as she discussed her worries and was receptive to our working together. I used ego sustaining techniques in this first meeting by being genuine and warm, listening attentively, and showing empathy in an effort to build a strong, trusting relationship that will underpin our future work. I helped her to understand leukemia and confront some of her irrational beliefs about how she got the illness and if her friends could catch it. We defined the problems she wanted to work on and started the problem-solving process.

Termination and Evaluation

Our first meeting came to a natural ending point and signified an excellent start to our early relationship and work together. She was receptive to talking about her illness and what it meant to her. Before we stopped, I summarized what I heard Emily say she was worried about and we established goals for our future meetings. Emily seemed reassured to have someone to help her manage her fears about having leukemia. She is looking forward to our next appointment.

I expect that I will follow Emily's case over the long duration of her treatment, which could last two years. I will schedule outpatient sessions with her when she returns to the clinic for appointments and will visit her whenever she is hospitalized. I will monitor her progress with the medical team, her parents, the school, and in conversations with her directly.

Theoretical Lens

I integrated several theories in my meeting with Emily. I used psychodynamic ego sustaining skills to build an empathic relationship with her from the start. I also depended on psychodynamic child development theories to help me understand some of her lifecycle issues and defense mechanisms. Narrative theory gave me an appreciation for how she told her story and the language and words she used to describe her fears. I used cognitive theories to confront certain cognitive distortions, and we began to address her worries by problem solving. In combination, the various theories gave me insight into Emily's situation and helped me plan intervention.

Bio/Psycho/Social/Spiritual Assessment

This approach looks at the functioning of an individual's biological, psychological, social, and spiritual systems. I will follow the outline in chapter 1. As with the other sections, it is written in the first person, from the social worker's perspective.

Applying Bio/Psycho/Social/Spiritual Assessments to Case of Emily

Emily is an 11-year-old girl who has reached normal developmental milestones for someone her age. Until now, she was healthy and active in school and extracurricular activities. She has just received a leukemia diagnosis in the children's oncology department of a Boston hospital. She will receive chemotherapy over a period of two years and is expected to suffer fatigue and hair loss, typical side effects from her treatment.

Emily is a bright, articulate 11-year-old girl with above-average intelligence. Because she stands between middle childhood and adolescence, her cognitive abilities vacillate between concrete and abstract thinking. She demonstrates an early capacity for insight and for reflecting on her situation. For example, she felt clearly that she would do better during treatment if her parents stopped fighting. She has good communication skills for someone her age and engaged well with me during our first meeting. She appears to have good self-esteem and her excellent standing at school contributes to this.

She has a healthy relationship with each of her parents and her brother but is distressed about her parents' separation five months ago. It upsets her to see her parents fighting, and she has a tendency to get in the middle of their conflict and triangulate. She feels support from her brother, but she will miss him when he leaves for college after this last year in high school.

Emily's illness and the effects of chemotherapy will present challenging psychological problems for someone her age: It will affect her body image, self-esteem, and peer relationships. Friends are important to her, as is physical appearance and wanting to look like her peers. Emily is scared about losing her hair. She is worried about how her friends and others will react and if they will reject her when she looks different.

In spite of Emily's obstacles, she is resilient and adaptable to adversity. When confronted with having to stop sports, she responded that she would find something she's better at doing that is less active. Also, she is motivated to work on her problems and engaged well with me during our first meeting. We identified treatment goals related to losing her hair, telling friends about her illness, preparing for her return to school, and getting her parents to stop fighting during her hospitalization.

Socially, Emily seems to have an excellent network of friends that she gets together with regularly. She has a good relationship with her parents individually but is upset about their separation and misses her father, whom she now only sees every other weekend. She gets along well with her older brother, but she anticipates missing him when he goes to college next fall. She is in the sixth grade and has just started a new school. She is proud of her academic abilities and is recognized as a stellar student.

During future meetings, I plan to explore Emily's church affiliations and spirituality. These two areas can play a greater role in some children's experiences in middle childhood and lead to resiliency (Haight & Taylor, 2007, 88–89). Illness can cause a person to reflect on life's meaning, and this, in turn, can help to overcome adversity and build inner strengths. As Emily confronts the meaning of illness in her life, there may be times when discussing spirituality will help her to cope better with her situation.

End of Chapter Resources

Questions for Students

I have included questions to supplement the text for additional student learning. They are organized around the ten core competencies in the Council on Social Work Education (CSWE, 2008). The questions can be used for classroom or online discussion, given as written homework assignments, structured as classroom exercises, or used by students to do outside research. They can also be adapted for use in hybrid or online courses.

Educational Policy 2.1.1—Identify as a Professional Social Worker and Conduct Oneself Accordingly

1. How would you address issues of confidentiality when working with a child and the parents? Was confidentiality addressed in the first interview with Emily? If not, should it have been?
2. Were there moments in the interview when the social worker, Gloria, used the skill of reflection to understand her own reactions to Emily and her situation?
3. How well did Gloria explain her role to Emily? Would you have done anything differently? Explain your answer.
4. In what ways might Gloria advocate for Emily? Imagine some situations where Gloria could act as an advocate for Emily or her family. Include three situations and explain how the skill of advocacy would be used.
5. Describe how Gloria was present in the interview with Emily in terms of nonverbal cues, for example, facial expressions, hand gestures, eye contact, body posture.
6. How would you evaluate Gloria's demeanor in terms of behavior, appearance, and communication (verbal, nonverbal, tone of voice)? How would you rate her level of professionalism?
7. How well did Gloria attend to issues of role and boundaries with Emily? Were there any times when she didn't maintain appropriate boundaries? If so, when?
8. Gloria deferred to the doctors several times as better able to explain Emily's illness and treatment to her. What are your thoughts about Gloria having greater confidence in the doctors to do this rather than her? Are there ways Gloria actually might do the better job?

9. There may be times when it is painful to work with very ill or dying children. As you reflect on this, is it a practice area that interests you?

10. Have you had personal experience with a very ill or dying child? If so, how did this experience affect you and your interest in working with children?

Educational Policy 2.1.2—Apply Social Work Ethical Principles to Guide Professional Practice

The questions below are to make students more aware of ethical issues that social workers confront every day in their practice.

1. As you watched the interview, were there any ethical issues that surfaced? If so, what were they and how would you address them?

2. Did the interview trigger any personal issues for you? Were there moments when your personal values would have interfered with your ability to work with Emily or her family?

3. Imagine you were asked to speak with Emily's parents after an incident during a chemotherapy treatment. Emily's nurse called you to say she had just asked the parents to leave the room, because they were raising their voices in front of her. Emily was noticeably upset. How would you handle this situation? Role-play the situation with the social worker addressing the parents, and again with the social worker talking to Emily after the incident.

4. During a meeting with Emily, she tells you she doesn't want to have any more treatments. They make her sick, and she's losing her hair. She feels that life isn't worth living any more—her home life "sucks," her parents won't stop fighting, her friends aren't visiting her and don't seem as close to her. She doesn't think there is anything worth fighting for anymore. How would you handle this? Would you share this information with anyone else? How would you address issues of confidentiality?

5. Imagine you learn that during one of Emily's chemotherapy sessions the wrong dose was administered to her, and she became very ill as a result. Staff are keeping it quiet and don't want the family to know. They are afraid of being sued. It looks like Emily will pull through, but she has suffered a setback. She will have to wait longer before she receives her next treatment. How would you handle this situation?

6. Let's hypothesize that Emily's parents are Christian Scientists. They don't believe in invasive medical treatment and putting chemicals in her body. They refuse further treatment for Emily and have her discharged from the hospital, against medical advice. What would you do?

7. You are working with a child whom the doctors have said has no chance of survival without life supports. There is very little brain activity, indicating that she would have severe mental impairment. The family can't accept this and want the doctors to keep her alive for as long as possible, hoping a miracle will happen. You have been asked to meet with the family to help them accept the situation and agree to terminate life supports. However, based on your personal religious beliefs, you do not agree with this course of action. How do you resolve this ethical dilemma, and what do you say to the doctors?

8. Who has the right to decide when and when not to use life supports? Under what conditions do you think they should be used? Considering healthcare costs and limited resources, are there any situations when they should be denied to a patient or family? Who should make this decision?

9. You are attending a school meeting to discuss Emily's learning plan at school. When you walk into the office, you hear the secretary talking about Emily with others and sharing information that you had told Emily's teacher in confidence. How do you address this issue?

Educational Policy 2.1.3—Apply Critical Thinking to Inform and Communicate Professional Judgments

Critical thinking is an important skill in social work practice and students are expected to demonstrate this competency before graduation. These exercises promote students becoming critical thinkers in practice.

1. How do life span developmental theories address issues of diversity and culture? Do you think all children develop according to the same principles, regardless of culture? Explain your answer.

2. How do you think illness affects the development of a child or adolescent's identity? How could having leukemia shape Emily's life and identity? Looking ahead, how could being a survivor of childhood cancer affect Emily's identity as a young adult?

3. At what age do you think children should have a right to make decisions about their own medical treatment?

4. All members of the multidisciplinary medical team are professionals and must abide by the same rules of confidentiality. With this in mind, is it ever appropriate that certain information should be privileged and not shared in a group meeting? Could there be a situation when keeping information from others would negatively impact treatment?

5. Imagine you are the practitioner working with Emily. She has told you that some of the girls are teasing her at school for losing her hair. What is your role? Do you work with Emily on strategies to deal with the girls, or do you address this issue at the school?

6. Since you are a medical social worker helping Emily cope with leukemia, should you also be talking to her about her parents' divorce?

7. Once a doctor has shared a leukemia diagnosis with a patient and her family, what should be the social worker's role in answering questions about her medical condition and treatment in the future?

8. Since Emily is an 11-year-old child, how much should the social worker collaborate with her on treatment as opposed to choosing goals that she thinks is best, based on her experience? What did Gloria do? Give examples.

Educational Policy 2.1.4—Engage Diversity and Difference in Practice

These questions are designed to teach students about engaging cultural diversity and understanding difference in practice.

1. What are some ways in which Emily is different? Try putting yourself in Emily's shoes, and write a one-page paper in the first person, expressing how Emily might feel after her diagnosis.
2. How would you engage someone of Emily's age in treatment? Explain the interventions you would use.
3. Children who experience serious illness feel different from their peers. How might Emily feel different? What are some ways the social worker could minimize this? Explain the social worker's role with Emily, her friends, and the school.
4. How is childhood cancer portrayed in the media? How does the general public approach children who may look different due to illness, for example, losing their hair?
5. The social worker, Gloria, is a different ethnicity than Emily? How could this impact the treatment or relationship she has with Emily? How might this difference come up in their work together?
6. Teachers can interfere with a child's return to school after chemotherapy by treating her differently and setting up dual standards that further isolate the child from classmates. Explain what this statement means and provide some examples of how this could isolate the child. How would you remedy this situation?
7. In box 94 of the transcript, the social worker asks Emily how she imagines she will look without hair. After she asks this question, she reflects on whether she is pushing Emily too soon into an uncomfortable area. She wonders if she should have waited and decides she will ask her supervisor about her judgment in this area. What are your thoughts about Gloria bringing this up in the first interview?

Educational Policy 2.1.5—Advance Human Rights and Social and Economic Justice

Students are expected to address human-rights and social-justice issues when they come up in their practice. These questions are to help students think in terms of social and economic justice and become more competent in this area.

1. Since Emily is 11 years old, she is a minor, and her parents make decisions about her care. What are the rights of children who are seriously ill? Do they have a right to refuse chemotherapy? Is there any area in which they have control over their treatment?
2. Can a parent keep information about a diagnosis from a child of 11? What is the child's right to know?
3. Do children have the same rights regarding confidentiality as adults?
4. If a child's parents neglected following up on appointments for the child, is there anyone who could intervene on behalf of the child? What would the process be?
5. What are the rights of children to receive medical treatment if they were brought into the country illegally and do not have medical insurance?
6. What are children's rights regarding visitation arrangements that are made during the legal proceedings for a divorce?

Educational Policy 2.1.6—Engaging in Research-Informed Practice and Practice-Informed Research

1. Research child development from different cultural perspectives. Choose a culture other than your own that you are interested in learning more about. Explore how they understand and have different expectations for children at different ages. Do they approach childhood as a series of stages as we do? If so, what are they? How are they similar or different from our stages?

2. Research best practices for psychosocial interventions for children with cancer. Find five research articles from scholarly journals and summarize each one. Include the full citation for each one, following APA format.

3. Interview a social worker who works in pediatric oncology at a local hospital. From her experience working in the field, ask her about any questions she has formed that she would like to research. What would be her research question?

4. Research the use and efficacy of alternative treatments for childhood leukemia. Are there any treatments, in particular, that have been found to be useful in combination with traditional medicine?

5. Research the use of expressive therapies with children with cancer. Discuss any that you think would be helpful in Emily's treatment.

6. What are the best practices for telling children about divorce?

Educational Policy 2.1.7—Applying Knowledge of Human Behavior and the Social Environment

These questions will help students learn how to apply theories critically to assess, intervene, and evaluate work with clients.

1. After reading the literature on child development, apply it to Emily. What are some of the tasks and challenges for 11-year-old children? How would you assess Emily's development compared with the theory? What are the developmental milestones for her age group and has Emily reached them?

2. Explain how developmental theory is used in work with children? How does it help Gloria understand Emily better and choose appropriate interventions?

3. How would you apply a family developmental perspective to Emily's family? What are some of the challenges in Emily's family, and how could they affect the family's development?

4. What does triangulation mean in structural family therapy? Were there any times in the interview when Emily described this happening? If so, when, and how does this example fit your definition of triangulation?

5. Read the literature on risk and resiliency. What are the some of the risk factors for Emily that surfaced in the first meeting? Based on resiliency theory, what are some of the characteristics that promote resiliency in children? Does Emily demonstrate any of these attributes?

6. Read the literature on adult survivors of childhood cancer. What are some of the effects of surviving childhood cancer? What are some of the benefits and consequences? Are siblings of cancer survivors impacted in the same way?
7. How does a child's age affect how she understands and copes with divorce? Apply developmental theory and the literature on divorce and children to an 11-year-old girl, as in the case of Emily. Are there different implications for girls and boys?
8. How do you understand what makes children act unkindly to another child who appears weak or different, as in the case of a child returning to school after losing her hair due to cancer treatment?

Educational Policy 2.1.8—Engage in Policy Practice to Advance Social and Economic Well-Being and to Deliver Effective Social Work Services

These questions are to encourage students to look at the role of policy in social work practice.

1. After watching the video and reading the transcript of Emily's interview, can you identify any policy issues that relate to her situation?
2. How do HIPPA regulations address the rights of children?
3. Are there school policies for children who have long class absences due to illness? Contact the administration of a local middle school and ask if there is a policy related to children returning to school after an illness.
4. Are there any special provisions for children under the Affordable Care Act? Do all children have equal access to medical treatment, regardless of cost?
5. Are there any policies that parents getting a divorce should follow that relate to their parenting? For example, are they mandated to take a course that will enhance their parenting skills after the divorce, so that the transition will be less damaging on the children? If you were to design a policy for parents getting divorced, what would you include? Do you think there should be a course for children also?

Educational Policy 2.1.9—Respond to Contexts That Shape Practices

Social workers practice in many different settings and may need to familiarize themselves with the particular skills required in each setting. These questions help students to appreciate how context shapes practice and to develop competencies in this area.

1. How does working in an outpatient hospital clinic affect the way a social worker practices?
2. What is the purpose of multidisciplinary meetings in an outpatient oncology clinic for children? Who might attend these meetings? Do all members of the team have the same status and authority? What are some issues the social worker would address in this type of meeting?
3. What role does confidentiality play in sharing information at multidisciplinary meetings? Is there anything that would be privileged and excluded?

4. A hospital social worker interacts with a number of systems both in and outside the hospital. Discuss these different systems and their roles in medical social work.

5. What are some of the effects of working with children who are seriously ill and dying? Are there resources available to help workers cope with losses they witness? What are some ways that social workers and other healthcare providers might protect themselves from burnout?

6. What is the role of school social workers in helping a child with cancer return to school after a long absence? Describe some of the interventions a school social worker might use to facilitate the child's return to school, acceptance by peers, and adjustment to the transition?

Educational Policy 2.1.10(a)-(d)—Engage, Assess, Intervene, and Evaluate with Individuals, Families, Groups, Organizations, and Communities

These questions are intended to give students practice engaging, assessing, intervening, and evaluating clients.

1. How well did the worker engage Emily in the interview? Explain your answer and give examples.

2. What issues were discussed in the first interview with Emily? Was there anything not addressed that should have been? Explain your answer.

3. What goals did Emily and Gloria established in their first meeting?

4. What is the role of confidentiality in work with children? Was it discussed with Emily? If not, do you think it should have been? How would you explain confidentiality to Emily?

5. How well did Gloria do explaining leukemia to Emily? How would you describe it to Emily?

6. In what ways would Gloria get involved with Emily's school and teachers? Explain how Gloria could help prepare both Emily and the school for her return.

7. How do you think Emily will handle losing her hair? What factors affect how she copes with this stressor and change in her appearance? How can the social worker help prepare her for this?

8. When Emily visits the outpatient clinic for her second chemotherapy treatment, she tells you about an incident at school. She explains that a couple of girls in her class are teasing her because she's losing her hair. They do it when there are no adults around. She's afraid to say anything to the teachers, because the girls will give her a hard time for it later. She asks your advice about what to do. How do you help her? What are some strategies for dealing with bullying and harassment?

9. What strengths do you identify in Emily? How can you use these strengths to help her cope with cancer?

10. Having watched Emily in the interview, how do you understand her reaction to the diagnosis? Were there times when she seemed to show more emotion? If so, when were those moments? What was she most worried about? Was she open to Gloria helping her?

Interviewing Skills Used in Case of Emily

They are listed in the order in which they appeared.

Introduction

At the beginning of the first meeting with the client, the social worker welcomes the client, tries to make the client comfortable and tunes in to her own and the client's initial feelings about the first meeting.

Clarification of Role of Social Work

The social worker helps the client understand what services the agency offers and what her role as social worker will be. There are times when the client needs reminding that the work is collaborative; it is the social worker's job to facilitate and not direct the process.

Exploration of the Problem

This is a way of gaining more information about a client's situation. When continuing to explore the problem, the social worker listens for underlying feelings about the situation, who else is involved, and what resources are available to help resolve it.

Elaboration

Elaboration involves asking clients to describe what they are talking about in more detail. The social worker may ask the client, "I'm not sure I understand what you mean. Can you say more about that?" Or the worker may ask for examples of what the client is referencing: "Can you give me an example of when you felt that way?" Also, a social worker can encourage clients to continue telling their stories through nonverbal communication that shows interest, such as leaning forward or a simple nod of the head.

Questioning

This is a way of gaining more information about a client's situation. There are many different kinds of questions, for example, open- and closed-ended questions and reflexive questions. Questioning is often used in assessment as part of data collection.

Continued Exploration of the Problem

When continuing to explore the problem, the social worker listens for underlying feelings about the situation, who else is involved, and what resources are available to help resolve it.

Reaching for Feelings

This is when the social worker tries to understand what the client is feeling when a particular subject or issue comes up. The social worker may use this skill when she senses the client is avoiding, or is not in touch with, the feelings related to the current discussion. This may bring out strong reactions in the client, and it is important that the social worker is sensitive to what this means to the client.

Referral

This is when a client needs additional resources outside of the agency in which she's receiving services. With the client's permission, the worker makes the referral in order to help the client access other avenues for help.

Information-Giving

Information-giving means informing the client about the social agency, the problem, and the resources for change. The social worker is knowledgeable about human development and human behavior and can help clients by sharing information that relates to a problem they are experiencing. For instance, a mother may complain that her 4-year-old daughter is misbehaving and not understand how the birth of a new sibling has affected the daughter.

Showing Empathy

The social worker maintains a nonjudgmental stance or remains neutral. The worker need not totally understand the client's situation, but she must show that she is trying to grasp what the client is feeling or experiencing. The social worker might say, "Tell me more about what your experience was" or "I want to understand more about what this means from your perspective."

Problem Definition

This refers to a collaborative process between the social worker and the client, through which they come to an agreement about what the problem is and what they will work on together.

Nonverbal Attending Skills

The social worker shows that she is listening through her body language, such as eye contact, facial expressions, nodding, and leaning forward. These nonverbal skills help the client elaborate and feel comfortable sharing personal information.

Exploring Underlying Feelings

The social worker asks the client about her feelings on the subject under discussion.

Offering Support

When a client shares a story that is painful, it helps when the social worker offers encouragement. By acknowledging the difficulty of the situation, you provide support for the client and allow him to continue the story.

Putting Client's Words in Feelings

There may be times when a client has difficulty identifying the feeling that he wants to express in the narrative. The social worker can help in these situations by responding to the client and using feeling words to summarize what the client has said.

Goal Setting

Goal setting is a collaborative process whereby the social worker and client come to a mutual understanding of what they want to accomplish.

Challenging Moment

There may be times during an interview that are uncomfortable for both the social worker and the client. At these times, the social worker needs to contain both her feelings and the client's feelings. The social worker sits with these feelings and tries to understand them with the client. This can be hard to do, and many beginning social workers want to apologize or avoid pursuing uncomfortable subjects.

Reflecting Back Feelings

This is when the social worker gives a short response back to the client that mirrors the feeling the worker heard the client express. It is used to let the client know the worker is listening.

Seeking Client Feedback

When seeking client feedback, the social worker asks for the client's perception of a particular situation, the client-worker relationship, or the helping process.

Normalizing Feelings

Clients often believe that their feelings are unacceptable or abnormal. The social worker helps the client see that her feelings are a natural reaction to the given situation.

Giving Client Feedback

This is when the social worker finds an opportunity to provide the client with information about his behavior and its effect on him or on other people. It can prove difficult, because the client may not want to hear or accept what the social worker is saying.

Next Steps

This is a phrase used when the client and the worker decide what they will work on next, and what actions they can take.

Endings

This is when the social worker prepares the client for the end of the session.

Terms and Definitions for Child Leukemia Patient

Acute Leukemia

Acute leukemia is characterized by a rapid increase in the number of immature blood cells. This increase causes crowding and means the bone marrow cannot produce healthy blood cells. Immediate treatment is required in acute leukemia due to the rapid progression and accumulation of the malignant cells, which then spill over into the bloodstream and spread to other organs of the body. Acute forms of leukemia are the most common forms of leukemia in children. In lymphoblastic or lymphocytic leukemia, the cancerous change takes place in a type of marrow cell that normally goes on to form lymphocytes, which are infection-fighting immune system cells. Most lymphocytic leukemias involve a specific subtype of lymphocyte, the B cell.

Chronic Leukemia

Chronic leukemia is characterized by the excessive build-up of relatively mature, but still abnormal, white blood cells. The cells are produced at a much higher rate than normal, resulting in too many abnormal white blood cells, but this typically takes months or years to progress. Whereas acute leukemia must be treated immediately, chronic forms are sometimes monitored for a time before treatment to ensure maximum effectiveness of therapy. Chronic leukemia mostly occurs in older people but can theoretically occur in any age group.

Chemotherapy

Chemotherapy is the general term for any treatment involving the use of chemical agents to stop cancer cells from growing. Chemotherapy can eliminate cancer cells at sites great distances from the original cancer. As a result, chemotherapy is considered a systemic treatment. More than half of all people diagnosed with cancer receive chemotherapy. For millions of people, chemotherapy treats their cancer effectively, enabling them to enjoy full, productive lives. http://www.chemotherapy.com/

Confidentiality

Confidentiality refers to the safeguarding of information shared between the social worker and the client that helps to build trust. In the beginning interview, it is important to clarify confidentiality and its limits to the client. The worker should explain that what is said during a session will remain private and only get shared if someone is put in danger. Reassuring clients about confidentiality allows them to express themselves more freely, knowing it is done in a safe environment where their privacy is protected. The worker may say to the client, "What is said here will stay here, unless you or someone else is in danger." If a client is involved in a legal case, the worker will want to explore additional limits of confidentiality.

Family Development

Similar to child and adult development, family development also has predictable stages, although they are not identical for every family. Understanding the family lifecycle helps social workers identify problems that may surface in a family that are related to these stages. Each stage involves a transition and has tasks the family must accomplish before graduating to the next stage. Some families negotiate the stages more easily than others, and some families may struggle with one stage more than others, for example, families with adolescents. Carter and McGoldrick (1999) describe the stages as: leaving home; single young adults; the joining of families through marriage; the young couple; families with young children; families with adolescents; launching children and moving on; families in later life.

Resiliency

Resiliency refers to one's ability to overcome hardships and thrive in spite of obstacles. A child's exposure to certain risk factors does not always predict a specific outcome (Schriver, 2011, p. 119). His personal characteristics might play a role in resiliency, though. Examples include: social competence (flexibility, empathy, communication skills, sense of humor, relationship skills, adaptability); problem-solving skills (thinking abstractly and reflectively, and exploring alternative solutions); autonomy (sense of identity and self-efficacy, ability to exert some control over the environment and act independently); and a sense of purpose and future (DuBois & Miley, 2010, 377–378).

Taking a Family System Perspective

Although a social worker may be working with an individual client, the social worker also thinks about the client's family system and how it may contribute to an understanding of the problem at hand. This involves seeing the individual as part of a larger system and examining how the different parts influence each other.

Triangulation

In structural family therapy, triangulation refers to the process of a two-person system pulling in a third person to relieve tension in the relationship. This can happen in multiple ways. A triangle can occur when parents bring a child into their dispute, projecting their issues onto the child, who becomes the symptom bearer. Sometimes children may act out to refocus attention on themselves and take the couple away from their own problems. Other times, a child who is uncomfortable with his parents fighting might interrupt the fighting to distract the couple. These are all examples of how a family manages conflict.

References

Adamo, S. & DeFalco, R. (2012). The role of play in psychotherapy of a child suffering from cancer. *Psychoanalytic Social Work, 19*, 101–120.

Adams, D. J. (1982). *A comparison of confidence and degree of contentment in parental role of custodial and noncustodial stepmothers.* (Unpublished doctoral dissertation). Florida State University: Tallahasse, FL.

Alford, K. A. and Lantz, J. (1995). Art in existential psychotherapy with couples and families. *Contemporary Family Therapy, 17*(3), 331–342.

Amato, P. (2005). The impact of family formation change on the cognitive, social, and emotional well-being of the next generation. *Future of Children, 15*(2), 75–96.

Axline, V. (1947). *Play Therapy.* Cambridge, MA: Houghton Mifflin.

Bank, L. M., Forgatch, G., & Fetrow, R. (1993). Parenting practices of single mothers: Mediators of negative contextual factors. *Journal of Marriage and the Family, 55*(2), 371–384.

Barakat, L. P., Alderfer, M. A., & Kazak, A. E. (2006). Posttraumatic growth in adolescent survivors of cancer and their mothers and fathers. *Journal of Pediatric Psychology, 31*(4), 413–419.

Bellizzi, K., Smith, A., Schmidt, S., Keegan, T., Zebrack, B., Lynch, C., et al; Adolescent and Young Adult Health Outcomes and Patient Experience (AYA HOPE) Study Collaborative Group. (Oct, 2012). Positive and negative psychosocial impact of being diagnosed with cancer as an adolescent or young adult. *Cancer, 118*(20), 5155–5162.

Bernstein, R., Keltner, D., & Heidemarie, L. (2012). Parental divorce and romantic attachment in young adulthood: Important role of problematic beliefs. *Marriage and Family Review, 48*(8), 711–731.

Brieland. D. (1990). The Hull House tradition and the contemporary social worker: Was Jane Adams really a social worker? *Social Work*, 35(2), 134–138.

Burns, B. S. (1970). The use of play techniques in the treatment of children. *Child Welfare*, 49(1), 37–41.

Button, T. M., Scourfield, J., Martin, N., Purcell, S., & McGuffin, P. (2005). Family dysfunction interacts with genes in the causation of antisocial symptoms. *Behavioral Genetics*, 35, 115–120.

Carpentier, M. Y. & Fortenberry, J. D. (2010). Romantic and sexual relationships, body image, and fertility in adolescent and young adult testicular cancer survivors. *Journal of Adolescent Health*, 47, 115–125.

Carter, B. & McGoldrick, M. (1999). *The Expanded Family Life Cycle*. Boston: Allyn & Bacon.

Chester, M. & Parry, C. (2005). Thematic evidence of psychosocial thriving in survivors of childhood cancer. *Qualitative Health Research*, 15(8), 1055–1073.

Clarke, W., Clarke, S., & Sloper, P. (2005). Survey of psychosocial support provided by UK pediatric oncology centers. *Arch Dis Child*, 90(8), 796–800.

Cohene, S. & Cohene, L. S. (1990). Art therapy and writing with deaf children. *Journal of Independent Social Work*, 4(2), 21–46.

Coholic, D. Lougheed, S., & Lebreton, J. (2009). The helpfulness of holistic art-based group work with children living in foster care. *Social Work with Groups*, 32, 29–46.

Compas, B. E., Connor-Smith, J. K., Salzman, H., Harding-Thomsen, A., & Wadsworth, M. E. (2001). Coping with stress during childhood and adolescence: Problems, progress, and potential in theory and research, *Psychological Bulletin*, 127, 87–127.

Council on Social Work Education. (2008). *Educational Policy and Accreditation Standards*. Alexandria, VA: Council on Social Work Education.

Cruz-Arrieta, E. & Weinshank, L. (2008). Multidisciplinary approach to psychosocial care: The Stephen D. Hassenfeld Model. *Primary Psychiatry*, 15(7), 63–67.

Davis, K. M. (2010). Music and the expressive arts with children experiencing trauma. *Journal of Creativity in Mental Health*, 5(2), 125–133.

Davison, T. E. & McCabe, M. P. (2006). Adolescent body image and psychosocial functioning. *Journal of Social Psychology*, 146, 15–30.

Delta Society (n.d.). *Animal assisted activities/therapy: At a glance*. Retrieved from http://www.deltasociety.org/Page.aspx?pid=317

DiCarlo, M. A., Gibbons, J. L., Kaminsky, D. C., Wright, J. D., & Stiles, D. A. (2000). Street children's drawings: Windows into their life circumstances and aspirations. *International SocialWork*, 43, 107–120.

DuBois, B. & Miley, K. (2010). *Social Work: An Empowering Profession*. Boston: Allyn & Bacon.

Earle, E. A. & Eiser, C. (2007). Children's behavior following diagnosis of acute lymphoblastic leukemia: A qualitative longitudinal study. *Clinical Child Psychology Psychiatry*, 12(2), 281–293.

Erikson, E. H. (1963). *Childhood and Society*. New York: W.W. Norton & Co.

Erikson, E. H. (1968). *Identity: Youth and Crisis*. New York: W.W. Norton & Co.

Fine, A. H. (2006). *Handbook on Animal Assisted Therapy: Theoretical Foundations and Guidelines for Practice* (2nd ed.). San Diego: Academic Press.

Franklin, C., Kim, J. S., & Tripodi, S. J. (2009). A meta-analysis of published school social work practice studies: 1990–2007. *Research in Social Work Practice*, 19(6), 667–677.

Gerali, M., Servitzoglou, M., Paikopoulou, D., Theodosopoulou, H., Madianos, M., & Vasilatou-Kosmidis, H. (2011). Psychological problems in children with cancer in the initial period of treatment, *Cancer Nursing*, 34(4), 269–276.

Germain, C. B. (2006). An ecological perspective on social work in the schools. In R. Constable, C. R., Massat, S. McDonald, & J. P. Flynn (Eds.), *School Social Work: Practice, Policy, and Research* (pp. 28–39). Chicago: Lyceum Books.

Grych, J. H. & Fincham, F. D. (1990). Marital conflict and children's adjustment: A cognitive contextual framework. *Psychological Bulletin*, 108, 267–290.

Guidubaldi, J., Cleminshaw, H. K., Perry, J. D., & McLoughlin, C. S. (1983). The impact of parental divorce on children: Report of a nationwide NASP study. *School Psychology Review*, 12, 300–323.

Hamama, L. Rouen, T., & Rahav, G. (2008). Self-control, self-efficacy, role overload, and stress responses among siblings of children with cancer. *Health & Social Work*, 33(2), 121–132.

Haight, W. L. & Taylor, E. H. (2007). *Human Behavior for Social Work Practice*. Chicago: Lyceum Books.

Hicks, L. R. (2001). Psychosocial practice trends in pediatric oncology. *Journal of Pediatric Oncology Nursing*, *18*(4), 143–153.

Huffman, A. M. (2013). Students at risk due to a lack of family cohesion: A rising need for social workers in the schools. *The Clearing House: A Journal of Educational Strategies, Issues and Ideas*, *86*(1), 37–42.

Huizink, A. C., Van den Berg, M., Van der Ende, J., & Verhulst, F. C. (2007). Longitudinal genetic analysis of internalizing and externalizing problem behavior in adopted biologically related and unrelated sibling pairs. *Twin Research in Human Genetics*, *33*, 55–65.

Johnson, L. J., Pugach, M. C., & Hawkins, A. (2004). School-family collaboration: A partnership. *Focus on Exceptional Children*, *36*(5), 1.

Kazak, A. E., Cant, M. C., Jensen, M. M., McSherry, M., et al. (2003). Identifying psychosocial risk indicative of subsequent resource list in families of newly diagnosed pediatric oncology patients. *Journal of Clinical Oncology*, *21*(17), 3220–3225.

Kelly, J. B. & Emery, R. E. (2003). Children's adjustment following divorce: Risk and resilience perspectives. *Family Relations*, *52*(4), 352–362.

Klingman, A., Koenigsfeld, E., & Markman, D. (1987). Art activity with children following disaster: A preventative-oriented crisis intervention model. *The Arts in Psychotherapy*, *14*, 153–166.

Koerin, B. (2003). The settlement house tradition: Current trends and future concerns. *Journal of Sociology and Social Welfare*, *30*(2), 53–68.

Lefevre, M. (2004). Playing with sound: The therapeutic use of music in direct work with children. *Child and Family Social Work*, *9*(4), 333–345.

Ljungman, G., McGrath, P. I., Cooper, E. (2003). Psychosocial needs of families with a child with cancer. *Journal of Pediatric Hematology Oncology*, *25*(3), 223–231.

Love, B., Crook, B., Thompson, C. M., Zaitchik, M. A., Knapp, J., Lefebvre, L., et al. (2012). Exploring psychosocial support online: A content analysis of messages in an adolescent and young adult cancer community. *Cyberpsychology, Behavior, and Social Networking*, *15*(10), 555–559.

Maki, M. F., & Mazza, N. (2004). The use of poetry therapy interventions in working with elementary school children. *Journal of School Social Work*, *13*, 74–83.

Maurice-Stam, H., Silberbusch, L. M., Last, B. F., & Grootenhuis, M. A. (2009). Evaluation of a psycho-educational group intervention for children treated for cancer: A descriptive pilot study. *Psycho-Oncology*, *18*, 762–766.

McCollum, A. T. (1975). *Coping with Prolonged Health Impairment in Your Child*. Boston: Little Brown & Co.

Mitchell, W., Clark, S., & Sloper, P. (2006). Care and support needs of children and young people with cancer and their parents. *Psycho-Oncology*, *15*(9), 805–816.

Orbach, T., Parry, C., Chester, M., Fritz, J., & Repetto, P. (2005). Parent-child relationships and quality of life: Resilience among childhood cancer survivors. *Family Relations*, *54*(2), 171–183.

Peck, H. L., Kehle, T. J., Bray, M. A., & Theodore, L. (2005). Yoga as an intervention for children with attention problems. *School Psychology Review*, *34*, 415–424.

Pendley, J. S., Dahlquist, L. M., & Dreyer, Z. (1997). Body image and psychological adjustment in adolescent cancer survivors. *Journal of Pediatric Psychology*, *22*, 29–43.

Rapp-Paglicci, L. A., Ersing, R., & Rowe, W. (2006). The effects of cultural arts programs on at risk youth: Are there more than anecdotes and promises. *Journal of Social Service Research*, *33*(2), 51–56.

Robbers, S., van Oort, F., Huizink, A., Verhulst, F., van Beijsterveldt, C., Boomsma, D., & Bartels, M. (2012). Childhood problem behavior and parental divorce: Evidence for gene-environment interaction, *Psychiatric Epidemiology*, *47*, 1539–1548.

Rosaen, C. & Benn, R. (2006). The experience of transcendental meditation in middle school students: A qualitative report. *Explore*, *2*, 422–425.

Ross, J. W. & Scarvalone, S. A. (1982). Facilitating the pediatric cancer patient's return to school. *Social Work*, *27*(3), 256–261.

Schultz, P. N., Remick-Barlow, G. A., & Robbins, L. (2007). Equine-assisted psychotherapy: A mental health promotion/intervention modality for children who have experienced intra-family violence. *Health and Social Care in the Community*, *16*(3), 265–271.

Schriver, J. (2011). *Human Behavior and the Social Environment*. Boston: Allyn & Bacon.

Shifflet, K. & Cummings, E. M. (1999). A program for educating parents about the effects of divorce and conflict on children: An initial evaluation. *Family Relations*, *48*(1), 79–89.

Taffel, R. (July/August, 1991). Bringing up baby: How to talk with kids. *Networker*, 39–70.

Travis, G. (1976). *Chronic Illness in Children*. Stamford, CA: Stamford University Press.

Trotter, K. S., Chandler, C. K., Goodwin-Bond, D., & Casey, J. (2008). A comparative study of the efficacy of group equine assisted counseling with at-risk children and adolescents. *Journal of Creativity in Mental Health*, 3(3), 254–284.

Troxel, W. M. & Matthews, K. A. (2004). What are the costs of marital conflict dissolution to children's physical health? *Clinical Child and Family Psychology Review*, 7(1), 29–57.

Wall, R. B. (2005). Tai Chi and mindfulness-based stress reduction in a Boston public middle school. *Journal of Pediatric Health Care*, 19(4), 230–237.

Wallerstein, J. S. & Kelly, J. M. (1980). Effects of divorce on the visiting father-child relationship. *American Journal of Psychiatry*, 30, 1534–1539.

Waters, E. B., Wake, M. A., Hesketh, K. D., Ashley, D. M., & Smibert, E. (2003). Health related quality of life of children with acute lymphoblastic leukemia: comparisons and correlations between parent and clinical reports. *International Journal of Cancer*, 103(4), 514–517.

Woodgate, R. I. (1999). Conceptual understanding of resilience in the adolescent with cancer, part 1. *Journal of Pediatric Oncology Nursing*, 16(1), 35–43.

Zebrack, B. J., Stuber, M. L., Meeske, K. A., Phipps, S., Krull, K. R., Liu, Q., et al. (2012). Perceived positive impact of cancer among long-term survivors of childhood cancer: A report from the childhood cancer survivor study. *Psycho-Oncology*, 21, 630–639.

6

Practice with Families: Parenting a Child with Leukemia

Lisa: "I'm going to crack, but not today."
Setting: Outpatient Hospital Clinic

Description of Practice Area
Practice with Families

The interview with Lisa describes the story of one family dealing with a child's diagnosis of acute lymphoblastic leukemia (ALL). Lisa is the mother of 11-year-old Emily, whose interview was featured in chapter 5. Although care is focused on Emily in the outpatient clinic, her treatment will be less effective if family issues are not addressed. A child's illness is sometimes referred to as a family phenomenon (Broome et al., 1998; Kazak, 1997; Lavee & Mey-Dan, 2003), and the experience of undergoing lengthy, intensive treatment impacts the whole family unit (McGrath, 2000).

During the interview with Lisa, the social worker listens for issues that she will want to address with the family, such as shock and feelings of distress about Emily's diagnosis; an understanding of leukemia and the options for treatment; the effect of that treatment on the family; communication with hospital and clinic staff; parental stress and conflict; family developmental problems; and how the illness affects siblings.

Social workers integrate knowledge from both practice-based and theoretical sources when doing family assessments in medical settings. They must assess the patient and her family in terms of family life cycle and lifespan developmental theories, noticing any disruptions caused by the child's life-threatening illness. In Lisa's family, the worker will also need to look at the effect of separation and divorce on development. As you read the process recordings, you'll see the social worker makes assessments and uses interventions from multiple theoretical perspectives that include: psychodynamic, family systems, cognitive, behavioral, and narrative.

Family Life Cycle

Erik Erikson was one of the early psychodynamic writers who took a life cycle approach to individual development. I referred to his work in chapter 5 when discussing Emily's developmental issues. Others have built on his work and outlined tasks for families at different stages in their development (Carter & McGoldrick, 1999; Duvall, 1977; Hill, 1970; Solomon, 1973). A family life cycle perspective gives practitioners a framework that describes the different stages families undergo as they move through time. Although development is a continuous process, looking at family stages can highlight particular experiences that many families have in common at certain critical moments in the life cycle. Acknowledging individual and family developmental issues is an important part of assessment and can provide insight into factors contributing to family problems.

In describing the traditional middle-class family, Carter and McGoldrick (1999) outline eight life cycle stages. They are: leaving home; single young adults; the joining of families through marriage; the young couple; families with young children; families with adolescents; launching children and moving on; and families in later life. Social workers should not apply these stages to client systems arbitrarily. Rather, the stages are meant as reference points, and, when used in a flexible way, they can clarify various family crises. In particular, using a family developmental framework can shed light on stress that occurs during family transitions from one stage to the next, and can help the worker target therapeutic interventions; this, in turn, means family members can reorganize and continue their development (Carter & McGoldrick, 1999). When applying this theory, it is important to consider issues of diversity and culture to understand variance in how families develop.

There are forces throughout the family life cycle that either pull a family together or push them apart, and families fluctuate between periods of closeness and disengagement (Combrinck-Graham, 1985). For example, families come together around the birth of a child and separate more during the launching of a young adult. Chronic illness can force a family back together and disrupt normal individual and family development. The family must accommodate the demands of the illness, which is in the forefront of its consciousness (Rolland, 1987). The timing of the illness may be out of phase with the family's natural momentum, and each family member may have to give up outside interests in order to cope with what's happening. Families can emerge from this crisis with a strengthened sense of mastery or a sense of failure and helplessness that will leave its mark on family belief systems (Rolland, 1987, p. 494).

The family unit needs to be dynamic and resourceful to maintain stability and to adapt to the stresses of both normal transitions and the additional crises brought on by chronic illness and divorce (Newby, 1996). When illness coincides with the developmental task of separation in the family, as in young adulthood, this can keep the young person from leaving home (Papadopoulos, 1995). This might further "derail" the family from its successful transition to the next stage, and in such cases, there is a danger that the family will become stuck in more dependent relationships with one another that threaten autonomy and individuation

(Penn, 1983). This can also happen to an adolescent with a serious illness whose emancipation from the family is delayed and becomes "frozen"; likewise, the parents in this situation who had perhaps started to give the adolescent more independence might have to accept increased involvement in caretaking again (Rolland, 1987).

John Rolland (1989, p. 433) studies the interface of illness and individual and family life cycles and emphasizes the importance of protecting individual family members. During chronic illness, a family should strive to deal head-on with developmental demands created by the illness and not expect family members to sacrifice their own or the family's development. Rolland suggests (1989, p. 454) that it is crucial to inquire how the illness has affected the family system: What life plans has the family or individual postponed as a result of the diagnosis? Whose plans are most or least affected? When and under what conditions will they resume developmental tasks? These questions keep the family aware of the need to resume normal life cycle agendas as soon as possible and not let the illness interfere with these pressing needs.

One goal of working with a child and family during illness is to keep the family on its developmental course; once there is a remission and less of an emergency, the family should pick up normal developmental tasks as much as is feasible (Veach et al., 2002). Practitioners can promote better developmental outcomes by openly addressing these issues in the problem-solving process to enhance developmental adaptation. One example is Ester Shapiro's approach (2002), which recognizes stressors, highlights strengths, and normalizes the family's strategies for stability through times of developmental stress. Shapiro worked with an adolescent, 13-year-old girl with chronic illness. She used the girl's transition to a new school as a naturally occurring opportunity to coach the child and parents through this change with greater clarity; her intervention promoted a more flexible, developmentally-adaptive interdependence that recognized the child's health needs and her maturation. It is important not to lose sight of developmental issues when working with ill children and to look for opportunities to support these natural transitions.

Separation and divorce impact child development, disrupt the family life cycle (much like family illness), and have serious consequences. Normal life cycle tasks are interrupted and altered by divorce, becoming more complex. When a child approaches a new stage, the worker must interpret what's happening based on the requirements of the stage itself, and the effects of the divorce (Peck & Manocherian, 1989, p. 335). Parenting a child with leukemia puts many pressures on a healthy marital relationship, and if the couple enters the situation with deep conflict, as in Lisa's case, it could become an even greater crisis for the family.

From a psychodynamic perspective, in healthy families, the parents' relationship serves as a container for the children that protects them from both inner and outer threats and facilitates their healthy psychological growth. It's a kind of holding environment, which gives children an emotional refuge from the outside world. It also provides kids some self-protection from the internal drives and impulses that appear as normal defenses as personality forms. When parents separate or divorce, it can destabilize the child's development by removing the needed container and leaving the child overwhelmed by immature ego structures and feelings (Piemont, 2009, p. 99).

Piemont (2009) recommends initiating couple's therapy at the earliest sign of marital discord as the first step in preventing psychological problems in the children of divorce. If workers can help couples recognize marital fighting as a problem, they can also educate the parents on how their conflict impacts their children. An understanding of the effects of divorce on children can help parents manage their hostilities in an effort to maintain a safe holding environment for their children (Piemont, 2009, p. 114).

Developmental Issues For Lisa's Children

During assessment of Lisa's family, the social worker notes that one child is 11, a preadolescent, and another is 17, in the midst of adolescence. Families at this stage must adopt greater flexibility to allow children independence, and parents, in turn, are expected to refocus on marital and career issues. However, this stage is complicated for this particular family by the added stress of a child with leukemia and parents who are separated and planning to divorce. Gloria, the medical social worker in the case, appreciates how Emily and her brother will have challenges negotiating the tasks of adolescence as a result of both Emily's illness and the parents' separation. Gloria is also sensitive to the parents' stress. They are pulling apart at a time when their daughter needs their security and protection. The couple must face their daughter's leukemia and manage the conflict in their relationship in order to encourage and comfort her, and they do not have each other to fall back on for emotional support.

Emily's illness may also impact her and her brother's psychosocial development, and this may further burden Lisa. The varying side effects of treatment can have a dramatic effect on the developmental level of a child and cause regression to an earlier stage (McGrath, 2001). In Emily's case, her transition to adolescence may be delayed due to her increasing dependence on her parents during treatment. This can prove challenging for parents, with children putting more demands on them at a time when the parents are already feeling vulnerable because of the child's illness. Leukemia also poses unique challenges, as parents must strike a fine balance between autonomy and protection for the sick child due to the risk of infection. In a qualitative study of 16 families coping with leukemia, the parents talked about how they struggle to decide when to allow the child to do previously normal activities and when to impose restrictions due to the child's physical condition (McGrath, 2001).

Emily's brother is expected to go away to college within the year, but he might feel reluctant to leave if he thinks his family needs him to help with his sister. He might have heightened concerns about the impact of his father leaving home on his mother and sister. Additionally, it's possible he won't get help with his college applications as a result of his parents concentrating on Emily's illness. He may find his parents less available to support him with this important transition. These issues will need to be discussed openly in the family.

The developmental approach is relevant to Lisa's case and can help guide the social worker's intervention with the family, paying attention to both individual and family developmental tasks. Gloria can look for opportunities to promote resilience and successful adaptation, such as Emily starting in a new school. It will also be important to provide resources for Lisa's son as he applies to college and makes a transition out of the home.

Effects of Having a Child with Leukemia

Parents react with shock and alarm when they are told their child has leukemia (Magni et al., 1988). In the qualitative study of 16 families with kids battling ALL, mentioned earlier (McGrath, 2001), parents spoke about their need to restore a sense of normalcy to the family after receiving the diagnosis. However, they felt challenged to do so because of many obstacles: interruptions to work and education; disruptions in family life; the stress of hospitalizations; and sometimes even relocating the family closer to treatment centers. Parents soon learn that returning to normalcy is impossible; they almost have to create a "new" normal. One parent shared the hope "…to be as normal as possible, even though it is not quite normal anymore" (McGrath, 2001, p. 232). The demands of the children's treatments resulted in the parents feeling strongly that their lives were on hold.

Family illness creates the need for changes and flexibility in family roles that can cause conflict for parents. For example, in one study, parents indicated that where they were used to making important decisions together, now it was often left to one parent alone while the other was at the hospital; the study found that trust was a key relationship factor to deal with these situations (McGrath, 2001). Mothers talked about the innate conflict in needing to be at the hospital with the ill child and also caring for the siblings at home. Fathers spoke about taking on more domestic roles and responsibility for household chores; they also described role conflict in meeting the demands of home, hospital, and work and felt guilt when they couldn't fulfill all their responsibilities at work (McGrath, 2001). There appears to be a need for a workplace policy that gives fathers of children with serious illness a more flexible work schedule and options for funded leaves of absence (Nicholas et al., 2009).

Although one would expect negative consequences on the marital relationship, the literature shows mixed results and indicates that the impact of having a child with ALL changes over time and that certain couples find their relationship strengthened. Some research has observed parents of children with cancer more distressed than those in the comparison group (Cornman, 1993; Fife et al., 1987); others had no significant difference (Wittrock et al., 1994). One study found marital distress in one fourth of parents two months after diagnosis (Dahlquist et al., 1993). Parents in other studies described a more positive attitude toward their spouses and increased marital cohesion (Greenberg & Meadows, 1991). Although parents acknowledged the strain on their marriage and concern about the breakup of the relationship, some parents still felt the experience brought them closer together (McGrath, 2001). However, in terms of sexual relationships, research has found that marriages are often negatively impacted (Hughes & Lieberman, 1990; Lavee & Mey-Dan, 2003; Thoma et al., 1993).

In studying the pattern of change in these marital relationships over time, it appears that they deteriorate in the first year and after four or more years, but positive outcomes are reported among parents whose children were ill at the two- and three-year mark (Lavee & Mey-Dan, 2003). This indicates that parents are more satisfied with their relationship when meeting the demands of a sick child in the second and third years, perhaps sharing strong emotions and responsibilities, before the situation becomes a deep burden. This changes when the illness extends over the longer term, and parents reach a point of exhaustion that adversely impacts the relationship. The period following diagnosis and that of prolonged treatment both have negative consequences, but when treatment ends or there is a remission, the family may be relieved to return to normal, and the parents may feel strengthened following a stretch of disruption (Brown et al., 1992). With this in mind, psychosocial interventions are especially important at the time of diagnosis and during the first year, and in cases where the treatment continues beyond three years.

To cope with difficult emotions, some parents provided a balance for each other, so that when one was discouraged, the other would be more positive (McGrath, 2001). They also described the importance of having a sense of humor, not getting upset about little things, and talking openly with each other during difficult times (McGrath, 2001). Trust in the marital relationship, belief in their partners, and flexibility in roles were portrayed as essential ingredients for enduring the experience (McGrath, 2001).

Conceptual Framework for Parenting a Child with Leukemia

Based on qualitative interviews with 23 parents of children with ALL (Kars et al., 2008), researchers coined the term "being there" to characterize the overall parental response to the perceived vulnerability of the child. The parents describe the response as being triggered by an existential crisis at the time of diagnosis and the thought of their child suffering from illness and the ensuing treatment. The concept of "being there" is a way to explain the underlying force that enables parents to provide ongoing care to their ill child despite the personal costs to them; it is at the heart of their parenthood and the core of their existence (Kars et al., 2008, pp. 1586–1587). This idea also has implications for how parents are involved in their child's care while at the hospital, which I discuss again later.

The notion of "being there" has two purposes: protection and preservation (Kars et al., 2008). Protection means keeping the child safe from adverse consequences related to the illness and its treatment in order to improve his well-being. It might involve preventing harm that others could inflict. Parents understand that medical staff do not always put their child first and may even make mistakes. In these cases, parents stress the importance of staying alert to safeguard their child's interests. Preservation refers to how parents can help their child cope better with the illness and treatment. For example, when children feel the burden of treatment is too much and want to stop, the parents' presence supports the child and makes it a joint process, and this sense of doing it together increases the child's cooperation (Kars et al., 2008).

Family Beliefs about Illness and Role of Positive Emotions

Beliefs shape how families interpret and respond to chronic and life-threatening illness. The degree to which a family has a flexible belief system about illness can make the difference between experiencing loss with a sense of mastery and competency or a sense of failure and helplessness. Flexibility and adaptability are the key variables for optimal family functioning during a chronic or serious illness (Rolland, 1987, p. 499). The conviction that a family has some control and can affect the outcome of an illness also helps them to get through the crisis with a greater sense of proficiency. These beliefs lead family members to become active participants in their care versus passive recipients in the healthcare process.

Related to the critical role of family belief systems, research on optimism has found it is related to better health outcomes and positive coping with family illness (Curbow et al., 1993; Fitzgerald et al., 1989; Fotiadou et al., 2008; Fournier et al., 2002; Greenberg et al., 2004; LaMontagne et al., 2003; McIntosh et al., 2004). In an exploratory study of the emotional health of parents with children fighting cancer, the parents showed relatively low levels of optimism, psychological well-being, and subjective health perceptions when compared with a control group (Fotiadou et al., 2008). This has implications for healthcare providers to provide families with hope, while not denying the seriousness of an illness.

Although optimism is usually thought of as a long-term concept and geared to the future, another study focused on the role of hope in the short term to help parents cope with childhood leukemia (Salmon et al., 2012). In this qualitative study, which interviewed 53 parents at nine pediatric centers in England, parents needed hope to function effectively in the midst of despair, and they all wanted their oncologists to help them be hopeful in the present. Parents made frequent reference to a desire to "keep positive," and they linked a positive attitude to an ability to act and think effectively during the child's treatment. One father in the study urged the oncologists to "offer crumbs of hope." Another parent was quoted saying, "That's one of the biggest things, we've got to keep positive…because if you don't, you know what happens to the rest of your family…You've got to try and keep positive but it's not really easy…because you feel as if you're in a black hole" (Salmon et al., 2012, p. 400).

The study concluded that parents needed to have hope, and this did not mean they were in denial of their children's long-term prognosis. They just had to put these fears aside, avoid information about the long term, and focus on the short term. Instead of worrying about a cure, they described dealing with the illness in "little bits," and "just dealing with the now." According to the study's authors, the parents looked for signs that "the illness was not as bad as it might be, and milestones associated with treatment came to define parents' perspective, so they typically described taking life 'day by day' or 'a week or a fortnight at a time.' Parents struggled to keep this perspective and it could take time to learn" (Salmon et al., 2012, pp. 400–401).

Parents of children with cancer reported peace of mind when they could trust the oncologist (Mack et al., 2009). They appreciated that the oncologists had a plan for the future, but they didn't always want the doctor to share every detail with them; the parents wanted to keep their focus on hope in the short term, taking life one day at a time (Salmon et al., 2012). These parents weren't necessarily denying death; rather they needed to engage with their child's cancer in a life-affirming way (Eliott & Olver, 2002, 2007). Having a sense of hope in the short term allowed the parents to keep going and to function on a daily basis. It is important for healthcare providers to understand this need and join with parents to maintain a positive, hopeful approach.

Setting: Social Work in an Outpatient Hospital Clinic

Please refer to chapter 3 for general information about social work in a medical setting. In this section, I concentrate on some of the issues related to this case, especially the parents' relationship, its effect on Emily, and its implications for Emily's brother. From the interview with Lisa, we know that there are already problems in the marital relationship. The stress of having a child with leukemia will present additional challenges for the parents. Emily will need her parents' support to battle this illness, and any parental issues must be addressed if they interfere with or create obstacles for Emily. In the previous chapter, Emily also verbalized that she needed her parents to stop fighting to get better, and this will help guide the social worker's role with the parents.

Parents' Relationship

Conflict in the marital relationship can greatly impact a child facing serious, life-threatening illness. As described earlier, parents serve as a container for their children, protecting them from both inner and outer threats and facilitating their healthy psychological growth. When parents separate or divorce, this can destabilize a child's development by removing the needed container, leaving the child without an emotional refuge or protection from the outside world (Piemont, 2009). If a child is struggling with a serious illness like ALL, not having the full support of the parents due to marital discord can leave the child more vulnerable and without a safe haven to insulate her from overwhelming experiences during treatment.

Parents are responsible for maintaining a stable atmosphere for the family, especially during times of crisis, as in the case of a child falling ill. Having a strong, healthy marital relationship as a foundation increases the well-being of all family members and promotes psychological adjustment and adaptation to family illness. This is in contrast to what we learn from Lisa, Emily's mother, who describes her family as under enormous stress, with her and her husband having recently separated. In this case, the couple will need extra services in order to preserve family stability and support both children during Emily's leukemia treatment.

In the interview with Gloria, Lisa recounts an unhappy marriage that led to her husband moving out of the home five months ago. When Lisa told her husband about Emily's diagnosis, he began to attack her for how she was handling the situation and said that the doctors were jumping to conclusions. Lisa feels that she will have to answer for whatever happens to Emily, since she brought Emily to the hospital, made decisions about treatment, and signed consent forms. She believes that no matter how she handles Emily's care, it will never be good enough for her husband and feels stuck in a "lose–lose" situation. It is easier for her husband to stand by and second-guess somebody else's decision than to actually make the decision himself. Although she describes him as a great father, she says he is challenging as a husband.

Since Lisa's husband has moved to New York, she will be a single parent at home with her two children. Without her husband to depend on for ongoing, daily family needs, and with the added burden of a sick child, Lisa will be at risk for emotional and physical exhaustion. As Gloria listens to Lisa in the interview, she is assessing whether Lisa requires psychosocial supports to help her carry out her family responsibilities.

Gloria will also want to address the marital issues that impact Emily, in particular the couple's fighting in front of her, which Emily has identified as stressful. Gloria needs to enlist the parents' support for Emily and help them to understand how their fights will impact her, especially during treatment. It is likely the parents will need a referral for more intensive couple's therapy to deal with deeper marital issues and the extra pressure of having a child with ALL. The goal is to reinforce the couple's ego functioning and more mature defenses to make them better parents and reduce the psychological and emotional risks on their children.

Sibling Issues

Siblings of a child with life-threatening illness are a vulnerable group and often feel left out or abandoned as a result of the amount of time parents spend with the sick child during treatment (Carr-Gregg & White, 1987; McGrath, 2001). Studies have found that siblings are at risk for both emotional and behavioral problems (Barbarin et al., 1995; Bendor, 1990; Cohen et al., 1994; Fife et al., 1987). Parents carry the burden and frustration of being away from their well children and being unavailable for some of the most important routines of morning and night (McGrath, 2001).

Lisa tells Gloria she needs help explaining Emily's diagnosis to her son. At the time of their interview, she reports that her son is at home with friends and "in the dark." He will be waiting for her when she comes home, and she is unsure how to communicate the news to him. Lisa describes herself as numb and still in shock and is troubled over how to handle the diagnosis and talk to both her children about leukemia. As part of her role, Gloria will need to provide Lisa with information about the illness and help her find a way to talk openly with her family about what the diagnosis means for them.

Diagnosis and Intervention: Effect of Emily's Diagnosis of Leukemia on Family

In this section, I cover communication issues surrounding diagnosis and treatment on various levels. I concentrate on how the patient and family are delivered the news of acute lymphoblastic leukemia (ALL) and the role social work can play in helping the family digest this information. I also deal with family reactions to the diagnosis and explore how certain families use defense mechanisms to handle feelings of sadness, anger, and helplessness over the situation. Finally, I discuss the importance of open and ongoing communication between the medical staff and the family, and among family members.

Diagnosis of Acute Lymphoblastic Leukemia

In children under the age of 15, leukemia is the most common form of cancer and ALL is the largest diagnostic group, making up 80% of all cases (Souhami & Tobias, 1995). Whereas in the 1950s children with ALL were expected to die in about a year, 60% to 80% of all newly diagnosed children today will survive (Robinson et al., 1991). However, cure does not come without a cost. Success is achieved after a long, invasive, and difficult treatment process that can last two or three years and requires lengthy hospitalizations (Emanuel et al., 1990; Henderson et al., 1992). Treatment depends on aggressive chemotherapy regimens given in blocks to allow bone marrow recovery. Despite treatment taking place in phases, side effects are common and aren't always easy to endure, especially hair loss.

Shortly after parents are told their child has leukemia, they are forced to make critical decisions about participating in clinical trials at a time when they are still dealing with the trauma of the diagnosis. Hospital staff struggle with how to relay information to parents in straightforward and simple terms that do not put further demands on them. Although parents often consent to treatment, it is not clear whether they are prepared for or understand what they are consenting to. The literature on childhood leukemia indicates a need to improve the informed consent process (Cousino et al., 2011; Hazen et al., 2010). To achieve this goal, one medical team at Children's Hospital in Cleveland, Ohio made a DVD that parents could take home that guided them through the informed consent process. In the study that followed, 92% of parents reported that the video made it easier to understand information that their child's physician later provided, 83% said it helped them think of questions to ask the physician, and 67% indicated that the video made them feel more comfortable overall asking questions of the physician (Hazen et al., 2010).

Another intervention tailored to improving positive physician behaviors and communication strategies with parents was found effective in improving the informed consent process (Cousino et al., 2011). In this study, physicians volunteered to attend a training program that would help them develop better relationship and communication skills to use with parents to describe a child's diagnosis and treatment. This approach led to the parents becoming more knowledgeable about what they were consenting to.

Parents Being Given a Diagnosis of Acute Lymphoblastic Leukemia

Parents react with shock and alarm when they are told their child has ALL (Magni et al., 1988). It causes psychological stress, especially at the time of diagnosis (Kars et al., 2008), and parents describe the first two and a half weeks after receiving the news as an especially difficult time (McGrath, 2001). Crisis reactions include shock, disbelief, despair, sorrow, and anger (Kars et al., 2008; McGrath, 2002; Patistea et al., 2000). In one study, even those parents coping well reported that they were "only just managing;" they felt forced to make decisions and change normal family routines while emotionally distraught (McGrath, 2001). In the early stages, when parents are feeling the extreme strain of the shock, there also is a transitory risk that they'll use discipline as a way to relieve frustration (McGrath, 2001).

Some doctors find themselves in a value conflict with parents when they believe it is their professional responsibility to tell a child about his diagnosis, and the parents object. The doctor may think the child is developmentally and cognitively ready to deal with the information, but the parents still disagree. This could stem from cultural differences wherein nondisclosure of life-threatening illness is acceptable, or from a family's desire to protect their child. The decision regarding the best way to tell a child has many challenges. It's beneficial if the doctor is sensitive to the family's cultural background and guides the family toward an appreciation of the adverse consequences of not telling the child. Being truthful allows the doctor to discuss hope, address questions and fears the child or adolescent may have, and help the whole family cope best with the challenges ahead (Gupta et al., 2008). Honesty also builds a more trusting relationship between the child and the doctor that will be important during the long treatment.

The manner in which the family and patient are given this information has significant implications for the partnership between the family and the medical team. Lisa found the entire process of learning about her daughter's leukemia traumatic. In the interview, Lisa describes it as insensitive, confusing, and chaotic. She felt she was left in the dark for a long time, shuttled from her pediatrician's office to an emergency room and then again to an out-patient oncology clinic with little information. She complains about waiting for hours with residents and interns flowing in and out, responding to lots of questions, but receiving no answers to her own concerns. When doctors finally had something to tell her, she explains to the social worker that they descended on her with the news and told her that Emily would need to stay in the hospital to begin treatment immediately.

Lisa is angry at how the news was delivered, and is still unclear about what is wrong with Emily and what the next steps are. She feels she has received conflicting messages and is confused by the medical terminology, particularly the part about inserting a port into Emily's body. She is struggling with how to organize the information and deal with her son who is home with friends and "in the dark." In addition, she needs to relay the details to her husband who has a different opinion about the whole diagnosis. Talking to her husband about Emily's illness is complicated because of their marital problems and history of poor communication. Lisa consented to Emily's treatment, but she's unsure what she consented to, and now has to answer to her husband.

Communication between Parents and Medical Staff

With today's emphasis on evidence-based practice and improved treatment outcomes, there is reason for medical staff to pay attention to parents' feelings about how their children are treated. Studies have found that a reduction in children's symptoms and improved health is associated with parents' satisfaction with the quality of care, and that when parents are content, there is also an improved adherence to the therapeutic regimen (Ammentorp et al., 2006; Hall et al., 1988, Matziou et al., 2011). Staff attitudes, parents' involvement in their child's care, trusting relationships between the family and staff, and adequate sharing of information with parents and children were all linked to parental satisfaction (Matziou et al., 2011). However, the same study also reported a need to improve communication between children, their parents, and healthcare providers and to encourage greater parental involvement to optimize hospital care of ill children.

Lisa's experience demonstrates poor communication between the medical staff and Lisa around her daughter's care. The social worker will need to help improve this communication, especially since Emily is a minor, and Lisa must give consent for her treatment. She and her husband will have to discuss the different options with the doctors, Emily, and each other to make an informed choice that is best for their daughter. The parents will have to put aside their differences and come together to care for Emily. They need to show her they are united when it comes to making the right decisions for her. It is important for Emily to feel secure that her parents are handling her treatment well to take this worry away from her, so she can put all her positive energies into healing.

Returning to the concept of "being there," discussed earlier, it is easy to understand how conflicts between healthcare providers and parents can surface. The primary interest of parents is that their child receives the best treatment, and their criticisms of the medical team often revolve around a perceived lack of attention to the child's distress (Kazak et al., 1995). Parents need to be present for their children, and their involvement influences their evaluation of the medical care and affects how they act toward the professional staff. Parents believe they know their child best and want healthcare providers to use this knowledge and develop a partnership with them to deliver the best services for the child (Falk-Rafael, 2001; Kars et al., 2008). If the medical staff can value what parents have to offer and form an alliance with them, this will improve the child's care, relieve parent's stress, and improve health outcomes. By mirroring this notion of "being there," modeling their care, in part, after the parents, healthcare providers can relieve some of the burdens parents feel they need to assume (Kars et al., 2008).

Families in Lisa's situation are usually seeking more information about the leukemia, its treatment, and what doctors will expect of them regarding physical care for their children. With the emphasis of care shifting from exclusively inpatient to include more outpatient treatment when possible, parents will take on a greater role managing medications, everyday treatment needs, and emergency situations (Abum & Gott, 2011). Education, discharge planning, and collaboration between the medical team and the family will become increasingly important in the future. A review of 22 articles in the literature on this subject found a lack of research on best practices for educating parents and planning hospital discharge, and no specific studies that looked at parental perceptions of these issues (Abum & Gott, 2011).

Linking families to support services, information, and resources is a crucial function of social work in hospital settings. In the interview with Lisa, she says she needs more details about the disease, treatment options, and also resources and support services for her family. Gloria, her social worker, begins to fulfill this need in the first meeting by sharing with Lisa some of the information she seeks about different treatment protocols, financial help, tutoring and counseling for Emily, and services for Lisa's son to help him with the college application process.

Projection and Displacement: Use of Defense Mechanisms

In high-conflict couples, there is a tendency to blame using splitting and projection as a defense (Piemont, 2009). In projection, a person attributes his unacceptable thoughts and feelings to someone else; splitting is the tendency to see people as either "all good," or "all bad." Although these defenses may apply to Lisa and her husband, they may also appear when Lisa communicates with healthcare providers, as a defense to deal with her anxiety and anger about Emily's illness.

Displacement is a psychodynamic term that describes another unconscious defense mechanism. It happens when a person redirects feelings from their original source to a separate object that is deemed safe or acceptable. This can occur when families feel over-whelmed and helpless in coping with a life-threatening illness and become angry with the doctors. Since it is difficult to be angry at the illness, the situation, or the person who is sick, a family member may displace this anger onto medical staff. In Lisa's interview with the social worker, she is quite angry and critical of how the medical staff has treated her. Although partially warranted, her anger may also be excessive and represent defensive behavior. Lisa's husband might also use this defense. Lisa brings this up in the interview and describes him as someone who likes to blame others; when talking to him on the phone about Emily's diag-nosis, her husband reacted by saying that she was making poor decisions and that the doctors were jumping to conclusions.

To minimize projection, displacement, and other defensive behaviors in these situa-tions, it is important for healthcare providers to sit with families and explore their feelings of helplessness and anger about their child's illness. Although physicians and nurses may not have the time to attend to families around their emotional needs, this is where social workers can step in and facilitate improved working relationships and collaboration between families and the medical team.

Communication among Family Members

Communication about the illness among family members is also essential. Death and serious illness cannot be controlled, but the practitioner can help the family talk about these issues openly with each other. She can encourage family members to express feelings about the illness without censoring themselves, and without the expectation that others in the family will rescue or feel the need to fix them (Brown, 1989, p. 472). A more dif-ferentiated family is able to do this by listening to each other's feelings without overreact-ing emotionally. In Lisa's family, as the process recording will show, she and her husband fight a lot. They are less differentiated and unable to accept each other's separate points of view. From a psychodynamic perspective, when this happens in high-conflict couples, it means they have primitive object relations and tend to use splitting and projective pro-cesses, making it difficult to tolerate difference, ambivalence, and disagreements (Cohen & Levite, 2012). This appears to be happening in Lisa's marital relationship. The social worker will need to teach the couple better ways to communicate that include openness, respect for difference, and less fighting, especially in front of Emily during her treatment. It is likely that Gloria will also refer them to couples therapy to address these issues in more depth.

Case Description

Lisa finds herself in the outpatient clinic of the pediatric oncology department after a series of events that she describes as a "blur." She is angry and frustrated with the care she has received so far: Medical staff has kept her waiting; different residents and interns have asked the same questions as the person before; and then suddenly the diagnosis of leukemia "descended" upon her. Overall, she is unhappy with the process of trying to discover what is wrong with her daughter. She vents with the social worker about how unclear everything is, about getting conflicting and contradictory messages. Lisa also complains to her about the leukemia treatment, which she sees as "intrusive," "horrific," and using "toxins" that are poisonous.

Lisa struggles with how to talk to Emily about her diagnosis and treatment, how to tell her son about it, and how to handle her husband who is angry. She finds her husband challenging, and no matter what she does, it will never be good enough for him. During her recent phone conversation with her husband, he blamed Lisa for handling the situation poorly and criticized the doctors for jumping to conclusions. Lisa says he has his own ideas about the problem and what should be done.

When Lisa reached out to her friends, she felt they had "extreme" reactions; they were either so upset she actually had to care for them, or they pulled away to give her space. In any case, she wasn't feeling support from her husband or her friends. She describes herself as "numb" and says that she will deal with her own feelings later. Right now, she feels she needs to focus on the children, and her own issues can wait. However, she imagines that in the future she is going to crack.

Lisa shows displeasure in the interview about a lot of things—the diagnosis of leukemia and what it means, the medical team, her husband, her friends, and even the social worker. At different moments during the interview with Gloria, the social worker, Lisa displays anger toward her by saying their conversation was a waste of her time. Gloria works hard to engage Lisa in these moments and does not take it personally but rather continues to offer emotional support. Although sometimes uncomfortable with Lisa's anger, Gloria listens for what may lie hidden behind it to identify what Lisa needs during these challenging points in the interview. Gloria discovers that Lisa is looking for more information, and as Gloria provides her with this, she finally shows appreciation for Gloria's help.

Toward the end of the interview, Lisa begins to express sadness and also show insight about her feelings. When asked what she'll find most difficult to witness as Emily goes through chemotherapy, Lisa becomes despondent and says, "Not being able to help her." Although she has always succeeded in solving problems in the past, Lisa realizes she has no control over getting rid of her daughter's leukemia. Observing Lisa's feelings of helplessness, Gloria astutely responds by asking her what she "can" have control over. This question helps Lisa begin to brainstorm how to help her daughter get through this illness; for example, she wants to find a way to get Emily's friends involved.

It is important for parents to feel that they have a role to play in their child's care and that the medical staff appreciates their knowledge on their child. When Gloria asks Lisa what the healthcare team should know to best provide for her daughter in the hospital, it shows Lisa that she can contribute to Emily's care. Lisa shares some ideas with Gloria on useful approaches to take with her daughter; for example, she says it will be vital to get Emily involved with other children going through the same experience and to keep her active by engaging various interests and hobbies. Lisa's response reinforces the belief that parents should engage with the medical team treating their children. A parent's knowledge about her child can improve the delivery of care and also help the parent feel valued.

Although Lisa at first shows some ambivalence about Gloria's intervention, she is thankful at the end of the interview. Lisa asks if she could have the opportunity "to catch up" with Gloria, after she has had time to digest all the new information. Lisa's request to meet with Gloria again shows the importance of social work intervention at the very beginning of the child's diagnosis and treatment.

Recommendations for Social Work Practice

I return often to the findings of a qualitative study that included interviews with 16 parents who had children battling ALL. This particular study provides a rich perspective for social work practice in medical settings on how to support families during this crisis. Families need to hear from the social worker that what they are experiencing is normal under their circumstances. They also need reassurance that they are not alone in how they experience the intensity of their feelings in response to extremely difficult and challenging conditions. Most of all, families need the emotional and practical support of the social worker. The following list of eight suggestions for social work interventions are based on this study (McGrath, 2001, pp. 236–237):

- Affirming the reality: telling families that the disruption they feel in family life is normal and to be expected.
- Redefining "normalcy: explaining that maintaining family life as normal is impossible and how they need to redefine normalcy from the perspective of dealing with illness.
- Fostering contact with other families: finding support with other families in the same situation through contact, groups, or newsletters.
- Providing information: providing families with material on social and emotional experiences they are likely to experience.
- Offering practical assistance: finding resources to help with the demands of maintaining a family during treatment, such as child care, domestic help, travel, parking.
- Taking time-out: supporting families to take time out from the intense medical situation whenever possible.
- Naming the stage: helping families understand the different stages of treatment and to recognize the maintenance stage when they can return home for lengthier intervals.
- Finding community-based services: locating community-based medical services to reduce the impact of being away from home for long periods of time.

Although emotional and social supports are crucial for the parents of a child with leukemia, these are often found lacking and even adversely affected by illness. Studies have found that social support is more limited in families with a sick child than in families with a healthy child (Mastroyannopoulou et al., 1997). This is an area for social workers to explore with parents to identify where support systems are lacking and to locate additional resources that will help parents manage the stress of caring for their child.

First Excerpt from Transcript and Process Recording

In the first excerpt from the transcript, Gloria introduces herself and explains her role to Lisa. From the start, Lisa reacts with sarcasm, criticism, and anger, which sets the tone for much of the interview. Once she describes her experience and explains how she was given her daughter's leukemia diagnosis, her anger seems justified. Notice how Lisa uses language in this excerpt—her style of relating, exaggerated and dramatic speech, and words repeated several times for emphasis. There are also moments when she uses defense mechanisms to protect herself from the harsh reality of her daughter's illness. The social worker does a good job staying tuned in to what Lisa is feeling by showing empathy and not reacting to her anger.

Content	Observation/Reflection	Analysis of Intervention: Theories and Practice
1. SW: Hi Lisa, how are you doing?		
2. Mother: Um, I would say I've had better days.		
3. SW: I'm sure you have. I'm Gloria. I'm one of the psychosocial clinicians here in the hospital, and, um, I wanted to come in and introduce some of the services that we offer for our newly diagnosed families.	What made me say I was a psychosocial clinician instead of a social worker? Sometimes I worry that people may react negatively to being a social worker. I am glad NASW is working on the image campaign for our profession, and I need to play my part in telling my clients I am a social worker.	Practice: Communication skills, introductions, clarification of role.
4. Mother: I guess that's what we are, isn't it?	Maybe how I introduced my role sounded too impersonal. Am I feeling defensive, or should I be picking up on her anger?	Practice: Self-reflection.
5. SW: Yeah, I understand that you were diagnosed yesterday. Is that fair?	I wonder why I said is that fair; maybe I was feeling her sarcastic remark wasn't fair.	
6. Mother: I guess so, yeah.		
7. SW: Would you like to tell me how you arrived here? Sort of how did this all happen?		Practice: Communication skills, exploration of the problem.

(Continued)

Content	Observation/Reflection	Analysis of Intervention: Theories and Practice
8. Mother: I would have to say it's, a lot of it is just a blur. I mean everything was normal. We were at my daughter's soccer game, and um, she fell down and she hurt herself and she got a small cut. And then, you know, we bandaged it up and then went home, and then the next night she was not feeling well. She was feeling kind of sick and coughing and kind of weak. And I thought well, you know, maybe she was just coming down with something. And then the next morning she wasn't any better and I thought, you know, better safe than sorry, I'll take her to the pediatrician, and so I did. The pediatrician decided to take some tests, some blood tests. And when the blood work came back, she didn't even talk to us. She just had somebody at the desk tell us to go, that we needed to go over to Children's Hospital, and so we did. And then I didn't know what to tell my daughter. We were just there waiting, waiting, and waiting. You know all these residents and interns, and god knows who they are, kept flowing in and out and asking the exact same questions as the person before, and nobody had any answers. They just had questions, questions, and questions. Then, finally, they all came, descended on us, and they said to us that she had leukemia. I still don't even, like, I can't even grasp that, like what? So, now the plan appears to be that she's going to have to stay and have some treatment, and I don't really understand what that is either. So, that's my day.	She is very upset and angry with the staff about how she has been treated. I can understand how this has been a horrible ordeal. It is interesting how she seems to use dramatic and exaggerated language by repeating words three times to get her point across and using such phrases as "descended upon us," to explain how the staff told her that Emily had leukemia..	Theory: Narrative, uses word "waiting" and word "question" three times to emphasize her frustration with care. Uses word "descended" upon us to explain how she was given her daughter's diagnosis.
9. SW: Not a very good day.		Practice: Communication skills, empathy.
10. Mother: No.		
11. SW: So, just to see if I understand this, you are at your pediatrician's office, she just rushes you to the emergency room, and, suddenly, you're told that your daughter has leukemia, and shock, something that you didn't expect.		Practice: Communication skills, summarizing.
12. Mother: No, I still don't get it.		
13. SW: The day before you had a normal day and lives, and, today, you're here in the hospital and don't really know sort of the plan ahead. I'm sorry that you're in this situation. That's unfortunately not a situation that parents want to be in. How is your daughter doing?		Practice: Communication skills, empathy, questioning.

(Continued)

Content	Observation/Reflection	Analysis of Intervention: Theories and Practice
14. Mother: She goes back and forth. Sometimes she seems to be fine, maybe not thinking about it, maybe it's not on her mind. Then, other times, she is really just so upset, but she doesn't know how to articulate what she's experiencing because she's only 11 years old. How can she reflect on what the long-term implications are when she's not even thinking abstractly yet? She's just sort of just goes about her day and does the best she can, so I guess that's how will do this as well.	I wonder if she works in education or counseling. It's interesting she referred to her daughter not being old enough to reflect or think abstractly. Not many of my parents use these terms.	Theory: Psychodynamic, defenses, intellectualizing.
15. SW: So what have you been told, in terms of treatment and how long she will be in the hospital?		Practice: Communication skills, seeking clarification.
16. Mother: I have to say that's where I am kind of angry, because I am very unhappy with the process of learning about not only what is wrong but what will be done about it. It's unclear; there are conflicting messages, you know, one person says one thing, mainly nobody knows. All these people just keep coming in and asking questions and examining her and really being very intrusive, I think, about her physically. At one point, I did hear, although I don't know because other things contradict, but, what I did hear was that there would be this surgical procedure, which just sounds horrific, where they'll insert this port into her body. And it would be a direct access into one of the major artery's in order to allow for continuous administration of this chemical, toxin, which is intended to harm the cancer and will, of course, also harm her. You just think there has got to be a better way than putting something into a child and then poisoning it.	She is doing a lot of the talking, but maybe I need to let her vent some of her anger, helplessness, and frustration with the situation. She also seems to be displacing her anger about her daughter's illness onto the staff. She is very bright and articulate but somewhat intellectual in her presentation. On another level, I am wondering with how the staff did handle telling the mother and Emily about the diagnosis. This is an important subject that I will bring up at the next multidisciplinary meeting.	Theory: Psychodynamic, ventilation, displacement. Narrative, words, such as unclear, conflicting messages, intrusive, contradict, horrific, toxin, poisoning, to describe how unhappy she is with the process of learning about the diagnosis and treatment.
17. SW: Have they spoken to the different ways of accessing her, that it doesn't necessarily have to just be a port? It could be a central line or a PICC line.		Practice: Communication skill, information-giving.
18. Mother: No.		
19. SW: OK, because that's another thing that we can discuss with the medical team, because if it makes you feel a little bit uncomfortable about her having that foreign object implanted in her. There are other ways. Usually, the medical team tends to feel better about the port, but there are other ways if that would make you feel better, sort of getting more information about the other procedures.	I feel a need to give her information rather than explore her feelings more. I wonder if I am a little afraid of her anger and want to please her.	Theory: Narrative, words used, foreign object, implanted, to reflect mother's feelings about procedures. Practice: Self-reflection. Communication skill, offering support, information-giving.

(Continued)

Content	Observation/Reflection	Analysis of Intervention: Theories and Practice
20. Mother: I think it would be helpful to just sort of be able to understand the pros and cons of various procedures. I mean, there's a piece of me that is there and then there's another part that's like, I don't want to think about this.	I can understand her need to defend against this horrible news about her daughter's cancer.	Theory: Psychodynamic, defenses, denial.

As Gloria begins to assess Lisa and the family, she learns how Lisa and Emily got bounced from the pediatrician's office, to the emergency room, to the outpatient oncology clinic, an awful process. Lisa is unhappy about how she learned what was wrong with Emily and unclear on the treatment and next steps due to confusing and conflicting messages. Gloria normalizes some of Lisa's feelings and offers some initial information about treatment options for Emily.

Reflection of First Process Recording and Discussion of Practice Skills and Theories Used in Intervention

Communication Skills

The social worker uses various communication and practice skills during her intervention, and reflects on the client's statements in the moment as the interview progresses. Below is a list of communication skills, their definitions, and the boxes in which they were used.

Box 3

Introductions: At the beginning of the first meeting with the client, the social worker welcomes the client, tries to make the client comfortable, and tunes in to her own and the client's initial feelings about the first meeting.

In box 3, Gloria introduces her to Lisa by saying that she is a psychosocial clinician in the hospital and that she wants to introduce some of the services offered for newly diagnosed families. It is interesting that she chose not to identify herself as a social worker. One explanation is that she believes Lisa would respond better to the term psychosocial clinician.

Box 3

Clarification of role: The social worker helps the client understand what services the agency offers and what her role as social worker will be. There are times when the client needs reminding that the work is collaborative; it is the social worker's job to facilitate and not direct the process.

In box 3, Gloria explains her role to Lisa and what services she provides to families. Rather than personalizing the intervention to Lisa, she refers to "services that we offer for our newly diagnosed families." Gloria reflects on how her introduction perhaps sounded too impersonal and wishes she had explained it differently.

Box 7

Exploration of the problem: This is a way of gaining more information about a client's situation. When continuing to explore the problem, the social worker listens for underlying feelings about the situation, who else is involved, and what resources are available to help resolve it.

In box 7, Gloria begins to explore the problem and asks Lisa how she arrived at the outpatient clinic.

Boxes 9, 13

Empathy: The social worker maintains a nonjudgmental stance or remains neutral. The worker need not totally understand the client's situation, but she must show that she is trying to grasp what the client is feeling or experiencing. The social worker might say, "Tell me more about what your experience was" or "I want to understand more about what this means from your perspective."

In box 9, Gloria shows empathy when she says "Not a very good day" to describe what she heard Lisa share about her day.

In box 13, Gloria is sensitive to how the medical staff has treated Lisa and tells her she is sorry that she is in this situation. Gloria shows empathy in her tone of voice, body gestures, and facial expressions.

Box 11

Summarizing: Part way through the session, and again at the end of the interview with the client, the social worker summarizes what has been said up to that point. This helps reinforce for the client what has been discussed and ensures that the worker and client both understand the focus of the session.

In box 11, Gloria summarizes what she heard Lisa tell her about the process of getting to the outpatient oncology clinic and learning that her daughter had leukemia. This shows Lisa that she is listening to her.

Box 13

Questioning: This is a way of gaining more information about a client's situation. There are many different kinds of questions, for example, open- and closed-ended questions and reflexive questions. Questioning is often used in assessment as part of data collection.

In box 13, Gloria begins to question Lisa about her impression of how her daughter is doing.

Box 15

Seeking clarification: At different times during a session, the social worker may ask the client to talk about her perception of a situation in order to make sure she understands the client's point of view. This is also useful when the worker wants to check what she heard the client say, so as not to make the wrong assumption.

In box 15, Gloria wants to clarify what Lisa has been told about her daughter's treatment and how long it will take. This is important to understand so she doesn't make assumptions about what Lisa knows.

Boxes 17, 19

Information-giving: Information-giving means informing the client about the social agency, the problem, and the resources for change. The social worker is knowledgeable about human development and human behavior and can help clients by sharing information that relates to a problem they are experiencing. For instance, a mother may complain that her 4-year-old daughter is misbehaving and not understand how the birth of a new sibling has affected the daughter.

In box 17, when Lisa expresses concern about her daughter having a surgical procedure to install a port for chemotherapy, Gloria responds with information about other options.

In box 19, Gloria continues to explain alternative ways for Emily to receive chemotherapy.

Box 19

Offering support: When a client shares a story that is painful, it helps when the social worker offers encouragement. By acknowledging the difficulty of the situation, you provide support for the client and allow him to continue the story.

In box 19, Gloria offers support to Lisa who is upset about how the chemotherapy will be administered and provides her with information about other options.

Other Practice Skills Used

Boxes 4, 19

Self-reflection: The skill of self-reflection is an important part of professional practice. Social workers are expected to engage in personal reflection and self-correction to assure continual professional development (EP 2.1.1).

In box 4, Gloria reflects on how she introduced her services to Lisa and wishes she had taken a more personal approach, rather than using the first person plural.

In box 19, Gloria considers her decision to give Lisa information and worries that she did so to appease her and avoid talking more directly about Lisa's anger.

Theories Used in Intervention

In this section, I identify theories used in action during the interview. I attempt to link what the social worker has said in her intervention to a theory, and also to explain how her interpretation of Lisa's thoughts and feelings are framed by a theoretical lens. There may be times when Gloria's responses to Lisa mimic Lisa's use of language; it is important to notice ways in which the client and social worker influence each other.

I discuss two theories from the first excerpt, narrative and psychodynamic. In the following, I refer to the boxes where they occur and explain how each theory was applied.

Narrative Theory
Boxes 8, 16, 19

In box 8, Gloria describes her experience by saying that it's all a "blur," getting bounced from the pediatrician's office, to the emergency room, to the outpatient oncology clinic. She uses the word "waiting" three times to emphasize how annoyed she was with how long it took for the doctor to see Emily. She also repeats the word "question" three times to convey a sense of frustration with the flow of doctors coming in and out, asking the same questions. Lisa chooses the word "descended" to explain what it was like when the doctors came to tell her the diagnosis, and this signifies that Lisa felt overwhelmed and attacked.

In box 16, while Lisa vents anger about how she has been treated and informed about her daughter's diagnosis, she uses evocative language to describe the experience. Gloria notes specific words and phrases that give her insight into Lisa's feelings, including: unclear, conflicting messages, intrusive, contradict, horrific, toxin, poisoning.

In box 19, Gloria shows Lisa that she understands her concerns about chemotherapy and uses words such as "foreign object" and "implanted" to reflect Lisa's feeling that chemotherapy is intrusive.

Psychodynamic Theory
Boxes 14, 16, 20

In box 14, Gloria notices Lisa's language when she talks about her daughter's cognitive level, and interprets this as Lisa using intellectualization, a defense mechanism to protect her from overwhelming feelings.

In box 16, Gloria sees Lisa's reactions as her need to vent feelings of anger and helplessness brought on by the situation. Gloria also wonders if Lisa is displacing some of her anger at the diagnosis and situation onto the medical staff.

In box 20, Gloria hears Lisa admit that part of her doesn't want to think about the problem. This is Lisa's way of saying she would like to deny what's happened and not have to deal with the illness.

Second Excerpt from Transcript and Process Recording

In the second excerpt, Gloria begins by asking questions to collect more information on Lisa's situation, wanting to understand the larger context of the problem. Gloria learns about the family, and Lisa opens up about her marital conflicts and how she is separated from her husband. She explains to Gloria that he is angry with her and very critical of how she is handling Emily's treatment. Lisa uses the word "tense" four times consecutively to explain the situation with her husband. She also tells Gloria that she is putting off dealing with her feelings but knows that sometime in the future she is going to crack. In this excerpt, Gloria's explores the problem, and her responses continue to show empathy and sensitivity to Lisa's struggles; she normalizes what Lisa is feeling, and both reassure and support her.

Content	Observation/Reflection	Analysis of Intervention: Theories and Practice
21. SW: How, when, why; how is this all happening? Of course, of course. Where are you now in terms of sort of the logistics of all of this? You were just at your pediatrician's office, emergency room, hospital. I'm assuming you have a life outside of here.	Let's see if I can get the bigger picture of what else is going in her life.	Practice: Data collection. Communication skill, understanding the larger context.
22. Mother: Safe to say, I'm really struggling with how to organize everything. My son is with some friends right now and they're in the dark. I haven't shared and it's because I don't know what to say. I don't even, I don't know how to tell myself that this has happened, so how I can explain it to someone else is just beyond me. So there's that, and then there's my husband, and then that's another, uh, what a mess.	She's beginning to show how overwhelmed and helpless she is feeling. She seems like someone who likes to be in control but now she is struggling to keep it together.	Theory: Narrative, uses words and phrases, like struggling, how to organize to reflect her need to gain control. Also refers to son being in the "dark" which is also describes how she feels. She ends by saying, "It's a mess." Practice: Assessment.
23. SW: Right.	I want to encourage her to keep talking without interruption. She needs me to show that I am listening and understanding what she is going through.	Practice: Communication skill, nonverbal attending and listening skills.
24. Mother: He has his own ideas about how this needs to be handled, and, you know, I didn't grasp what it is that we're doing, never mind second guessing what is being done. In other words, he has ideas that physicians are, you know, jumping to conclusions, and that it's, um, something I failed to do is to get additional opinions before rushing in and getting the treatment here. And yet I don't know how on earth I was supposed to get an additional opinion when I went from the pediatrician's office to the emergency room, but that's just how he is. And now the decisions that we make, if there is ever a problem with Emily, it would be on my head, because I'm the one who had to bring her and I'm the one who had to sign the consent and I'm the one who had to make the decisions. And I think it's a lot easier to stand by and second guess somebody's decisions in an emergency than it is to actually have to make the decisions. And to be with Emily and later with her brother. So, I mean, I don't mean to bad mouth him. He means to be a good father, and he is a great father. A husband ... very, very challenging. And so here I am trying to deal, it's a lose–lose no matter how I handle this. It will never be good enough.	It sounds like there is a chain reaction here with her husband blaming her for her decisions, and, then, she in turn, has been critical of her experience with the hospital and staff. It looks like the conflict between Lisa and her husband is only the tip of the iceberg. It will be important to learn more about the family dynamics, especially as it impacts on Emily. It sounds like feels she can never be "good enough" for her husband. I wonder if the children feel like this too.	Theory: Psychodynamic, defense mechanisms; family systems theory. Narrative, uses words like, grasp, second guessing, jumping to conclusions, challenging, lose–lose and phrase, never be good enough to describe communication with husband and then ends with the phrase, don't mean to bad mouth him, to mitigate her criticism of him. Practice: Assessment.

(Continued)

Content	Observation/Reflection	Analysis of Intervention: Theories and Practice
25. SW: You know, I don't know if this helps in anyway, but this is something that a lot of our parents struggle with.	There are many parents who disagree on how to manage their child's treatment, but I sense this situation may be more complicated.	Practice: Communication skills, reassuring client, normalizing feelings.
26. Mother: They do?		
27. SW: Yes it's very common for this to happen where couples tend to have different opinions where we see families really struggle with making medical decisions. This is very difficult to do. Here you are in this position, attempting to make the best decision you can possibly make with the information that you know at the time. And the medical team usually tells you time is of the essence, and you're feeling overwhelmed just by having received the news, feeling emotionally really shocked and all of these different things that go through your mind and having on top of that to really make decisions that will affect you daughter and there's only so much that can be asked of you and you're doing the best you can.	She needs support to know that she is doing the best she can.	Practice: Communication skill, information-giving, putting client's feelings into words, empathy, supporting client.
28. Mother: That's the truth.	She needed to hear that.	
29. SW: Has he been in, your husband?		Practice: Communication skill, exploration of the problem.
30. Mother: No		
31. SW: Where is he?		Practice: Communication skill, continued exploration of the problem.
32. Mother: He moved to New York; he had a job change, and there's a lot of conflict around that between the two of us. And so when he decided to take the position that he was offered in New York City we both agreed that it would probably be best that he go. So, he sees the kids every other week, and since this happened he's been on the phone with me and it's been very, very, very, very tense. He just, you know, rather than deal with the problem, rather than help me, he needs to blame someone. He's very angry. I would imagine I'll be angry eventually, but, at the moment, I'm just not there yet. He's angry at the physicians, he's angry at me, mainly angry at me, and then I have to deal with his anger at the physicians, and I just, that's something I don't need on top of all the rest of this.	It's interesting that she says she's not angry yet like her husband, because she was very angry at the beginning of the interview.	Theory: Narrative, uses "very" four times to show how tense it is; family systems theory; psychodynamic, defenses. Practice: Assessment.

(Continued)

Content	Observation/Reflection	Analysis of Intervention: Theories and Practice
33. SW: Of course not; you're needing support right now, to get through this. What about you, in terms of your feelings about all of this and having your daughter affected by all of this?	Maybe I can begin to ask her more about her feelings now. It is easier for me to explore sad feelings than angry ones.	Practice: Self-reflection: Communication skills, exploring underlying feelings, showing empathy.
34. Mother: When very bad things happen I tend to not be aware of what I'm feeling, I just know, I go numb, and I contend with it later, especially when my children are around. I just focus on them and what they need and that helps me actually to deal with myself because I'm not dealing with myself just yet. And so I would imagine sometime in the future I'm going to crack, but not today.	It sounds like she isolates herself from her feelings to protect herself from overwhelming stimuli. To deal with a crisis, she needs to focus on her children first. I sensed this in the beginning in the way she seemed to be intellectualizing about the treatment.	Theory: Psychodynamic, defenses, isolation of feeling—goes numb to defend against feeling. Narrative, terms like numb and going to crack to describe how she is putting off dealing with her feelings now.
35. SW: Right. It's that inner strength that you need to be strong to get through with this. Have you told anyone else what is happening? Do you have any support systems around?		Practice: Data collection, assessment, identifying strengths. Communication skills, acknowledging strengths, questioning.
36. Mother: Well, yea, I've told a couple of my friends. It's funny though, you know, when I share with them their reactions are so extreme that I almost wish I hadn't said anything because they kind of overreact and I don't, and then I feel like I need to take care of them and help them come to some understanding and in some ways that can be a little bit helpful but mainly I just feel like I don't have, and then I feel like maybe they're pulling away from me because they don't know how to help me and so they figure the best thing to do is just give me some space and in some ways that's true but in other ways it would be really nice if they could help.	I can understand what she is saying. I hear this from many parents that their friends aren't as supportive as they would like. It seems the other parents are frightened by the news and don't want to think this could happen to their children. They may be pulling away due to their own discomfort with loss. I suppose it could be like a type of denial: if they aren't around the person, they can pretend it is not happening.	Theory: Psychodynamic, refer to other parents' defensive behaviors. Narrative, word "funny" to describe friends' extreme overreactions, pulling away from her, giving her space.
37. SW: Sure, sure, and I can't begin to tell you how many of our parents struggle with those same concerns.		Practice: Communication skills, normalizing feelings.
38. Mother: Really?	It does help to normalize client's feelings, so they don't feel so alone, or that they think there is something wrong with them.	

(Continued)

Content	Observation/Reflection	Analysis of Intervention: Theories and Practice
39. SW: It's very natural for all of these things you talk about to be happening right now.		Practice: Communication skills, Normalizing feelings, reassuring client.
40. Mother: It doesn't feel natural.	It's hard to understand since she has never been through this before. It will be helpful to have her join a parent's group of children with leukemia.	
41. SW: It's part of the process I guess, and as horrible as that feels and seems, it's some of the natural things that our families do struggle with. And that's why we want to be able to provide some type of support to help families to cope with all of this, because we understand that this is a very difficult time.		Theory: Cognitive, problem-solving. Practice: Normalizing feelings, offering support.

At the end of the second excerpt, Gloria normalizes Lisa's feelings by saying that parents often disagree about their child's treatment and that many parents also struggle with their friends pulling away from them, either because they don't know how to support them or overreact. Although Lisa feels it's not natural, Gloria reassures her that it is part of what she is going through, and explains that this is why she is there to help her cope through this difficult time.

Reflection of Second Process Recording and Discussion of Practice Skills and Theories Used in Intervention

Communication Skills

Box 21

Understanding the larger context: The social worker needs to explore the client's family, social system, and larger environment to better understand the problem and its context.

Box 23

Nonverbal and attending skills: The social worker shows that she is listening through her body language, such as eye contact, facial expressions, nodding, and leaning forward. These nonverbal skills help the client elaborate and feel comfortable sharing personal information.

In box 23, Gloria keeps her response to a minimum to encourage Lisa to continue her story without interruption. Gloria shows Lisa that she is listening through nonverbal signs: eye contact, facial expressions, and body gestures.

Boxes 25, 39

Reassuring client: At times, the social worker needs to allay a client's anxiety by supporting her efforts to change or accept new resources.

In box 25, Gloria reassures Lisa that many parents disagree and struggle with the same issues that she has described.

In box 39, Gloria normalizes Lisa's experiences and feelings, which also serves to reassure her.

Boxes 25, 37, 39, 41

Normalizing feelings: Clients often believe that their feelings are unacceptable or abnormal. The social worker helps the client see that her feelings are a natural reaction to the given situation.

In box 25, Gloria normalizes what Lisa is going through by explaining to her that many parents experience conflict with their partners and disagree about their child's treatment.

In box 37, Gloria tells Lisa that she's not alone in her struggles to connect with friends after Emily's diagnosis, in order to normalize the experience for Lisa.

In box 39, after Lisa seems surprised to hear this, Gloria again tells her how natural it is for her to have all the feelings she has described.

In box 41, Gloria returns again to the experience that Lisa has related about her friends pulling away from her. Gloria explains that this, though difficult, is a natural part of the process. She tells Lisa that it's one important reason the clinic offer services to her, because it's not easy.

Box 27

Information-giving: Information-giving means informing the client about the social agency, the problem, and the resources for change. The social worker is knowledgeable about human development and human behavior and can help clients by sharing information that relates to a problem they are experiencing.

In box 27, Gloria provides information to Lisa about how couples tend to have different opinions about medical decisions.

Boxes 27, 33

Empathy: In box 27, Gloria empathizes with Lisa by acknowledging how difficult it is to get pressured by the doctors to make decisions quickly, while at the same time feeling overwhelmed and in shock. Gloria tells Lisa there is only so much others can ask of her, and she is doing the best she can. In box 33, Gloria responds empathically to Lisa by agreeing that she doesn't need her husband to give her added problems. Gloria says Lisa is the one who needs support now.

Boxes 27, 41

Offering support: When a client shares a story that is painful, it helps when the social worker offers encouragement. By acknowledging the difficulty of the situation, you provide support for the client and allow him to continue the story.

In box 27, Gloria offers support to Lisa when she tells Lisa she is doing the best she can.

In box 41, Gloria explains that the clinic wants to provide support to families, particularly since many people may pull away during this tough time, as Lisa has described her friends doing.

Box 29

Exploration of the problem: This is a way of gaining more information about a client's situation. When continuing to explore the problem, the social worker listens for underlying feelings about the situation, who else is involved, and what resources are available to help resolve it.

In box 29, Gloria explores the problem of Lisa's husband being critical and asks Lisa if he has visited the hospital yet to see Emily. Gloria wonders about the husband's level of involvement so far, especially given his anger at Lisa, who is doing her best under tricky circumstances.

Box 31

Continued exploration of the problem: When continuing to explore the problem, the social worker listens for underlying feelings about the situation, who else is involved, and what resources are available to help resolve it.

In box 31, Gloria makes further inquiries about where Lisa's husband is, and wonders what role he will play in Emily's treatment.

Box 33

Exploring underlying feelings: The social worker asks the client her feelings on the subject under discussion.

In box 33, after Lisa talks about her husband's anger, Gloria wants to understand Lisa's underlying feelings about what is happening. She senses a change in Lisa's mood and uses this as an opportunity to broach the subject further.

Box 35

Acknowledging strengths: Acknowledging strengths can help clients improve their self-esteem and give them more confidence to take action on their own behalf. It empowers them by providing them with hope and a sense that they have the capacity and resources within themselves to improve their lives and overcome obstacles. When clients feel overwhelmed by difficulties, they may not recognize their positive traits, so the worker pointing them out can bolster the client's self-confidence.

In box 35, Gloria recognizes Lisa's ability to put her own feelings aside while she focuses attention on her children's needs. By doing this, Gloria says it gives Lisa the inner strength to get through hardship.

Other Practice Skills Used

Boxes 21, 35

Data collection: In the data collection stage, the social worker explores the problem in more depth. This involves getting information from multiple sources about the client's life and situation, and about the social systems that may impact the problem.

In box 21, Gloria begins to ask Lisa about the larger context, and wants to understand more about Lisa's life outside of the hospital and her daughter's illness.

In box 35, Gloria continues to collect information for her assessment by asking Lisa about her support systems.

Boxes 22, 24, 32, 35

Assessment: Assessment is the process of understanding the client and his problem based on the information gathered. It is done in a holistic way that highlights the importance of context in the construction of meaning, and it is a collaborative activity that is done in tandem with the client.

In box 22, Gloria listens to Lisa and assesses how she is managing. She learns how overwhelmed and disorganized Lisa feels. Gloria sees her as someone who likes to be in control and appreciates how helpless Lisa must feel with news of her daughter's illness.

In box 24, Gloria assesses what Lisa is saying about her husband and how he reacts to Emily's diagnosis and to Lisa. A picture of an unhealthy marital relationship is emerging. Lisa describes her husband as always criticizing her, and she feels she is never good enough. Gloria also thinks she sees a defensive chain reaction occurring, in terms of displacement and projection. She wonders if Lisa's husband starts it by blaming and venting his anger onto Lisa, who in turns does the same with the medical staff.

In box 32, Gloria continues to assess the family dynamics. Lisa describes her husband as angry with the doctors but even angrier with her, and says that he needs to blame someone. She uses the word "tense" four times consecutively to explain what it is like to talk to her husband over the phone about Emily's diagnosis. She doesn't feel she can deal with his stress on top of everything else. Gloria wonders if this pattern of his blaming her for problems contributed to their separation.

Box 35

Identifying strengths: During assessment, social workers listen for client strengths they can use to help solve certain problems. As clients talk about their situation and their stories unfold, workers identify strengths that are embedded in the narrative. By focusing on positive attributes and characteristics, workers shift the focus away from deficits to inquiring about and affirming strengths.

In box 35, Gloria identifies one of Lisa's strengths as being able to focus attention on her children first and putting her own needs and feelings aside until she has the time to deal with them.

Box 33

Self-reflection: The skill of self-reflection is an important part of professional practice. Social workers are expected to engage in personal reflection and self-correction to assure continual professional development (EP 2.1.1). In box 33, as Gloria picks up that Lisa is unhappy, she begins to explore this more and realizes it is easier for Lisa to discuss sad rather than angry feelings.

Theories Used in Intervention

Narrative Theory

Boxes 22, 24, 32, 34, 36

In box 22, Lisa uses words and phrases that describe how overwhelmed and helpless she feels, such as, "in the dark" and "what a mess." When Lisa says she is "struggling" to organize everything, Gloria pictures that Lisa is a woman who is used to being organized and in control and is uncomfortable that she has lost this control.

In box 24, Lisa explains how her husband's role is to "stand-by" during an emergency and "second guess" what she has done. He criticizes the doctors for "jumping to conclusions," tells Lisa she has "failed" to get other opinions before "rushing in," and that it will be on "her head" if anything happens to Emily. Lisa feels she is in a "lose–lose situation" and that no matter how she handles it, nothing will ever be "good enough." The language she uses to describe her husband paints a disturbing picture of a man who finds it easier to blame and to attack others than to take responsibility for his family.

In box 32, Lisa uses the word "tense" four times in a row to describe the phone calls between her and her husband. She uses the word "angry" six times in box 32 to describe her husband's feelings. He would rather "blame' her than "help" her, and she doesn't need this "on top of all the rest." Lisa is saying she needs his support, not his blame and anger, which makes everything tenser.

In box 34, Lisa helps Gloria understand her frailty by using the word "numb" to explain what it's like to put off her feelings; she expects that sometime in the future she will "crack." It wouldn't take much to crack her outer shell and expose her vulnerability.

In box 36, it is interesting that Lisa uses the word "funny" to describe friends who over-reacted to the news of Emily's illness, making Lisa feel the need to take care of them. Gloria reflects on how "funny" is used in a tragic/comic way, since it has a level of absurdity to it. Lisa describes other friends as "pulling away" and giving her "space," to emphasize the lack of support.

Psychodynamic Theory

Boxes 24, 32, 34, 36

In box 24, Gloria hears about Lisa's husband's defensive behavior and sees a pattern of his using projection and displacement. It looks like her husband blames Lisa for the problems and takes his anger out on her, and Lisa, in turn, displaces some of her anger at her husband and the situation onto the medical staff.

In box 32, Lisa talks about her husband's use of defense mechanisms when she says he needs to blame someone. Gloria interprets his anger at physicians or at Lisa as the defense of displacement—he tends to direct his anger at others rather than deal with its true source, which is the situation or his daughter's illness.

In box 34, Lisa describes herself as "numb" and uses the defense of isolation to separate herself from her overwhelming emotions during this crisis. When she says that she imagines that in the future she will crack, she reveals how helpless she is feeling and how her defenses are necessary at the moment.

In box 36, Lisa tells Gloria that some of her friends have pulled away during this time of need. Gloria wonders if they are defending against their own vulnerable feelings about having a child with leukemia. By keeping at a distance, these parents don't have to acknowledge how it makes them feel.

Family Systems Theory

Boxes 24, 32

In box 24, Lisa describes a family pattern in which her husband projects problems in their relationship onto her. He also tends to displace his anger onto Lisa, especially about his daughter's leukemia diagnosis. It appears that Lisa takes the lion's share of responsibility in the family, and her husband, from a distance, second guesses and criticizes whatever decision she makes.

In box 32, Gloria learns more about Lisa's husband taking a job in New York City and how they decided it was best for them to separate. Lisa describes a conflicted relationship that is characterized by blame, anger, and criticisms.

Cognitive Theory

Box 41

In box 41, Gloria explains how families often feel unsupported during their child's diagnosis and treatment and normalizes Lisa's experience. She lets Lisa know that, for this reason, the clinic provides support services to help families get through this difficult time.

Third Excerpt from Transcript and Process Recording

The third excerpt starts off with Lisa displacing her anger onto Gloria. Lisa questions Gloria's motives, saying the hospital has just given her someone to gripe to, and this is a waste of her time. Lisa says that she doesn't need help with her feelings; she needs information to figure out the best way to help her daughter. This is a challenging moment for Gloria, but she responds well and is not defensive. Instead, in this excerpt, she gives Lisa the details she wants and provides her with valuable guidance and resources.

Content	Observation/Reflection	Analysis of Intervention: Theories and Practice
42. Mother: I feel like in some ways, you know, it's very nice that you're coming in and chatting with me, and I appreciate your time. But, at the same time, what is the point of…I feel like in some ways the hospital is kind of giving me you so I can gripe about how I'm feeling, but what I'm feeling is that I don't have good information, and I don't have a coordinated treatment team, and I don't have an idea of what is going to happen, and I don't have clear good information to make good decisions. And you're a social worker and that's lovely and you can help me with my feelings, but the thing that helps me with my feelings most is good information. So this is kind of, not to be rude to you, but a waste of my time in some respects, because I need to figure out the best way to help my daughter.	It seems like when we get closer to her more vulnerable feelings, she defends against them with her anger again. Although it can be hard to hear this, I know it's important not to react or get defensive in return, but to understand what she is feeling. This is an area I have to keep working on. I hope it doesn't show that I am too uncomfortable with what she is saying.	Theory: Psychodynamic, venting, defenses, displacement. Narrative: uses phrases like chatting with me, gripe about things, rude to you, waste of her time, to show how cynical and angry she is with the hospital and social worker. Practice: Self-reflection, assessment. Communication skill, challenging moment.
43. SW: That is excellent that you tell me. Because that's part of what we do today, to sort of understand what it is that would be beneficial to you. And what you're telling me is that gathering more information and helping understanding how to help your daughter would be beneficial to you. And that's something I can work with you around. I work closely, very closely with the medical team, and any concerns that families bring up, that families feel the medical team needs to help them understand, or that we need to collaborate better with the medical team, I tend to facilitate those discussions with the medical team. Sometimes families request, I don't know, weekly meetings with the medical team on the floor, and I would facilitate that where I would be present, the family would be there, the medical team would be there.	It's interesting I respond with "excellent." That is not what I am really feeling. I am obviously uncomfortable with her anger, but I don't want to show it. I want her to be free to express what she is feeling. She wants information, so this is what I will offer her. I think I may be going overboard telling her what I can give her, maybe to appease her anger. I wish I could have openly addressed her anger and acknowledged it to her at this moment, rather than avoid it. This is an example when I am focusing on the content, rather than processing our interactions. I always find it easier to work with the children. I need to keep working on these issues in supervision.	Practice: Self-reflection. Communication skills, information-giving.

(Continued)

Content	Observation/Reflection	Analysis of Intervention: Theories and Practice
44. Mother: You know can I ask you? The medical team, speaking of that, you know in some ways I'm not interested in working with a team, I'm interested in working with the person who ultimately will help me make the decisions. And I feel like all these people floating in and out and asking questions and intruding and examining my daughter for their own interest, for their own curiosity, for their own training purposes. What is that all about? I want to work with a person or some people who actually have something to offer, rather than people who need her as an opportunity to expand their training.	I guess she needs to vent her anger some more, but I wish I could have the courage to bring it out in the open. However, she may need to release her feelings more, and if I interpret her defenses, this may make her more angry or shut down. I think I will let it be.	Practice: Self-reflection.
45. SW: Right, right. When I speak of the medical team, it's usually the resident, the attending on the floor, and the fellow, and that would include me as a social worker. We also have resource specialists who are people who can help families with financial needs, transportation needs, any of those things that are beneficial at some point.	I am trying to pull everything out of my pockets to give her to make her happy. Maybe this is what she needs now. I don't think I am avoiding talking about her anger directly. However, at some point, I should bring it up and normalize feelings of anger about being in this situation.	Practice: Self-reflection. Communication skill, information-giving.
46. Mother: When you say financial needs, what do you mean?	Oh, boy, it looks like I opened up a can of worms. I didn't want to cover this today. She has enough to deal with.	
47. SW: I mean some families sometimes need financial assistance, and we have different agencies throughout the nation that can help families that are going through different cancer diagnoses with financial assistance while they're in the hospital.		Practice: Communication skills, information-giving.
48. Mother: Oh, so I wouldn't be applying for public assistance or something.		
49. SW: Not necessarily, but, if any point that becomes something that you feel is needed for your family, we have resource specialists that can help you with that process.		Practice: Communication skills, information-giving.
50. Mother: Oh my god. So, in other words, in addition to my daughter being ill, there's a good chance that we will come into financial ruin.	I don't feel like I can say anything right with her. She's a bomb waiting to explode. I need to clarify what I meant and reassure her again. She can be overly dramatic and jump to conclusions.	Theory: Narrative, financial ruin, another example of mom being dramatic and overreacting.

(Continued)

Content	Observation/Reflection	Analysis of Intervention: Theories and Practice
51. SW: Um, that's not necessarily what I mean by that. What I mean by that is that if at any point you feel that it would be helpful for your family to apply for those benefits, we have people on the team that could help you with that process. It's just a way of you feeling like, if there is something that I need, at least there will be someone out there that I can go to that could help me with this process, so that on top of feeling overwhelmed about everything that's going on right now I don't have to go outside of the hospital or different places looking for someone who can help me with these resource needs that I may have at some point.		Practice: Communication skill, clarification of problem, reassuring client.
52. Mother: What about my daughter's academics. She's a very committed student, I mean we're talking, I mean it's unclear to me tragically, I have no idea what exactly this entails in terms of time, but it seems at least a few weeks, which is really a big chunk of time when there are only 180 days in a school year.	Her use of the word tragically provides insight in how she experiences her daughter's illness as a tragedy.	Theory: Narrative, tragically.
53. SW: Right, right, what are your concerns in terms of school for her?		Practice: Communication skill, exploration of problem.
54. Mother: That she's not going. That she'll, you know, fall very behind.		
55. SW: Right, right. Well I can tell you that here in the hospital we also have assistance for that. Some of the kids, while they're receiving their inpatient treatment, we can facilitate tutoring services where we work closely with the school that they're attending, so that the school can send the materials and work with the tutor. That is at no cost for you, it's facilitated by the town where she is going to school, and that tutor will come in to the hospital and work with her, of course depending on how well she feels. And you and the tutor can coordinate what that looks like. And one thing that happens sometimes is that when kids leave the hospital and they're receiving outpatient treatment, some days they don't feel well enough to go to school and some decide to go back to school half days, and some go back full time. Some families keep the tutor so the child can receive tutoring those days that they're not going to school, so that they don't feel like they're completely behind either. So that's something that helps, too.	I am giving her a lot of information now but this what she needs now. Information and knowledge help her to feel more in control.	Practice: Communication skills, information-giving, empowering client, reassuring client.
56. Mother: Well, that's a lot.	I think she felt reassured that there are resources to prevent her daughter from falling behind in school.	

(Continued)

Content	Observation/Reflection	Analysis of Intervention: Theories and Practice
57. SW: Yes and I'm sorry if I'm bombarding you with too much information.	It's interesting that I used the word bombarding here. I wonder if it is a Freudian slip that may suggest that I unconsciously would like to bombard her. I have been uncomfortable with her anger and reactions at times during the interview.	Theory: Narrative, use of word bombarding; psychodynamic, slip of the tongue. Practice: Self-reflection, Communication skills, showing empathy.
58. Mother: No that's alright, I guess I wanted information. Not sure what I'm supposed to do with it yet.	Perhaps the information helps her feel more in control.	
59. SW: What would you say are your major concerns right now?		Practice: Communication skill, prioritizing problem.
60. Mother: Well um, how to be most helpful to Emily and to my son. I can only imagine what this is like for him. You know he's planning to go to college soon and, you know, it's a tough time and he's applying and we we're in the process of writing his essays and I can't imagine what this is like for him to, you know, in some ways losing me. I'm a big resource for him in this process. It's always a challenge to balance your time, my time, between the two children, and so, in this case, he's sort of left out.	We have had a chance to talk about her son, but I am glad this has come up. Siblings are often ignored during this process.	Theory: Family systems, effect of illness on siblings. Practice: Data collection.
61. SW: Left out, right, and you know, that's unfortunately something that we see a lot, with siblings, where they experience that loss of their families, and feel left out. And so for that reason we tend to try to facilitate services for siblings as well so the parents don't feel like they're not providing any type of care for their other children.		Theory: Cognitive, problem-solving, information for siblings. Practice: Communication skill, information-giving.
62. Mother: What does that mean, services?		
63. SW: That means that we do have other clinicians on the team that could work closely with your child that could identify what his needs are right now. If he needs help in writing college essays, or if he needs help applying to different colleges, or different things that you may not be able to assist him right now, we have clinicians on the team that could help him with that. We really here in the hospital try to do whatever we can to try to alleviate some of the stress that the families go through.	I need to explain more specifically what we can offer her son. The more detailed information I can give her, the better she feels. She is hungry for this information, and in a sense, I am giving her something that she can take in. It may be interpreted as my feeding her, in this case, symbolically with knowledge. It's another way of caring for her and showing my support.	Theory: Psychodynamic, ego sustaining. Practice: Assessment. Communication skill, information-giving.

(Continued)

Content	Observation/Reflection	Analysis of Intervention: Theories and Practice
64. Mother: That's amazing, thank you.	I'm glad she can begin to see how our services can help. She responds well to getting more information that will be useful.	

What stands out in the third excerpt is the importance of providing Lisa with "good information." Gloria responds to Lisa's requests and fills her in about the medical team, financial and transportation needs, tutoring services to help her daughter keep up with school work, and resources to support her son through the college application process. This excerpt ends very differently from how it started, with Lisa showing appreciation for what Gloria has to offer after all; Lisa says to Gloria at the end, "That's amazing, thank you." Because Gloria listened to what Lisa needed and didn't react defensively to the attack on her services, she changed Lisa's feelings.

Reflection of Third Process Recording and Discussion of Practice Skills and Theories Used in Intervention

Communication Skills

Box 42

Challenging moment: There may be times during an interview that are uncomfortable for both the social worker and the client. At these times, the social worker needs to contain both her feelings and the client's feelings. The social worker sits with these feelings and tries to understand them with the client. This can be hard to do, and many beginning social workers want to apologize or avoid pursuing uncomfortable subjects.

In box 42, Gloria experiences a challenging moment when Lisa directs her anger at Gloria and questions her motives, saying the hospital just provides someone she can gripe to. She also tells Gloria she doesn't need to share her feelings and that it's a waste of her time. Instead, Lisa wants good information to figure out how to help her daughter. Gloria responds professionally and doesn't react defensively to Lisa; instead she provides Lisa with the advice she needs.

Boxes 43, 45, 47, 49, 55, 61, 63

Information-giving: Information-giving means informing the client about the social agency, the problem, and the resources for change. The social worker is knowledgeable about human development and human behavior and can help clients by sharing information that relates to a problem they are experiencing.

In box 43, in response to Lisa saying their conversation is a waste of time, Gloria lets Lisa know that she has medical information and resources that might prove beneficial for her and her family.

In box 45, Gloria explains who will be on Lisa's daughter's medical team. This is after Lisa accuses people of floating in and out to examine Emily for their own training purposes. Gloria also informs Lisa about specialists who can provide her with information on financial, transportation, and other needs she may have.

In box 47, Gloria clarifies for Lisa her previous reference to financial needs and explains that there are resources for financial assistance if medical expenses become problematic.

In box 49, Gloria continues to clear up what she means about financial assistance and also explains that specialists are available to help only as issues arise.

In box 55, Gloria provides information to Lisa about tutoring and other resources that will allow her daughter to keep up in school while at the hospital.

In box 61, Gloria introduces the subject of resources for siblings and lets Lisa know that they often feel left out.

In box 63, Gloria tells Lisa what specific help her son could expect in terms of applying for college and writing college essays.

Box 51

Clarification of problem: When sitting with a client, the social worker gathers details that further explain the nature of the problem. This is an ongoing process in which the worker collects new information and keeps an open mind to alternative interpretations and perceptions.

In box 51, Gloria realizes that Lisa is jumping to conclusions about why she brought up financial assistance. She clarifies that this resource is available in-hospital, and if at any time in the future Lisa felt she needed financial help, she wouldn't have to go outside the hospital looking for it.

Boxes 51, 55

Reassuring client: At times, the social worker needs to allay a client's anxiety by supporting her efforts to change or accept new resources.

In box 51, Gloria reassures Lisa that she wasn't implying she would be in financial ruin, and clarifies what she meant about financial assistance.

In box 55, by giving Lisa information about tutoring and different options for Emily going back to school, Gloria reassures Lisa that there are resources to help her daughter keep up with her studies during her leukemia treatment.

Box 53

Exploration of the problem: This is a way of gaining more information about a client's situation. When continuing to explore the problem, the social worker listens for underlying feelings about the situation, who else is involved, and what resources are available to help resolve it.

In box 53, Gloria picks up on Lisa's question about academics and asks Lisa what her concerns are regarding Emily and school.

Box 55

Empowering clients: Providing clients with information and skills to take action on their own behalf, advocate for their rights, and gain access to needed resources.

In box 55, Gloria realizes that information is what Lisa needs and that this knowledge empowers her to take more control over the situation and feel competent.

Box 57

Showing empathy: The social worker maintains a non-judgmental stance or remains neutral. The worker need not totally understand the client's situation, but she must show that she is trying to grasp what the client is feeling or experiencing. The social worker might say, "Tell me more about what your experience was" or "I want to understand more about what this means from your perspective."

In box 57, Gloria responds to Lisa by saying that she must feel bombarded with information. In this interaction, Gloria puts herself in Lisa's shoes and imagines what it must be like to receive so much advice.

Box 59

Prioritizing problems: After the social worker and client have explored the problem(s) the client wants help with, they might need to prioritize what to work on first.

In box 59, Gloria asks Lisa about her major concerns. This is an attempt to determine which problems are most important to work on first.

Other Practice Skills Used
Boxes 42, 43, 44, 45

Self-reflection: The skill of self-reflection is an important part of professional practice. Social workers are expected to engage in personal reflection and self-correction to assure continual professional development (CSWE, 2008).

In box 42, Gloria reflects on how difficult it is when Lisa's anger is directed at her. She is aware she should work more on this issue with her supervisor. She also knows it is crucial not to react defensively, but to understand what Lisa is feeling and what she needs.

In box 43, Gloria continues to reflect on her discomfort with Lisa's ill temper. She wonders if she should encourage Lisa to process her feelings of anger in the moment or simply stay with the content of what she is asking for. Gloria chooses to give Lisa information, but makes a mental note to discuss this issue more in supervision.

In box 44, Gloria decides it is best to let Lisa vent her angry feelings and not interpret or process the anger in this initial interview.

In box 45, Gloria realizes it was best to follow her intuition with Lisa and not process her anger yet. She comes to understand that what Lisa really needs in this interview is as much information as she can absorb. In later meetings, if anger is still an issue, Gloria can address it with her. Dealing with her daughter's diagnosis and what it will mean for the family, along with learning information about resources, is enough for Lisa to handle in one day. Gloria wants to make sure she gains Lisa's trust and they start to build a relationship that will encourage Lisa to keep coming back.

Box 60

Data collection: In the data collection stage, the social worker explores the problem in more depth. This involves getting information from multiple sources about the client's life and situation, and about the social systems that may impact the problem.

In box 60, Gloria begins to collect information about Lisa's son to learn how Emily's illness might impact him. She reflects on how the well siblings are often ignored and feel abandoned.

Theories Used in Intervention

Psychodynamic Theory

Boxes 42, 57, 63

In box 42, Lisa vents her anger about the lack of help she is getting from the clinic staff. In this interaction, Lisa displaces her anger onto Gloria when she claims that talking to her is a waste of time. Lisa says it's "lovely" that Gloria wants to help with her feelings, but what she really needs is good information.

In box 57, Gloria reflects on her own use of the word "bombarding" and wonders if it is a slip of the tongue, providing insight into her unconscious feelings about Lisa's anger at her. Does she have a subliminal fantasy of wanting to bombard Lisa in retaliation for her earlier assaults? It's interesting to stay aware of this, and she knows she would never act on her impulses.

In box 63, Gloria explains more specifically to Lisa what services are available for her son. Gloria looks at Lisa's needs symbolically from a psychodynamic perspective. She interprets that Lisa is hungry for this information, and Gloria compares it to a kind of food she is giving Lisa to sustain her during this difficult time.

Narrative Theory

Boxes 42, 50, 52, 57

In box 42, Lisa shows how cynical and frustrated she is with descriptive words, phrases, and language such as: chatting, gripe, rude, waste of her time. She says, "It's lovely you can help me with my feelings," but she uses the word "lovely" in an ironic way, since she rejects Gloria's attempts to help in this way. Lisa does this again when she says she doesn't want to "be rude" to Gloria, but then she turns around and does just that, saying the session is "a waste of time."

In box 50, Lisa is overly dramatic and exaggerates when she references going into "financial ruin." This is in response to Gloria sharing information about financial assistance that exists if she needs it in the future.

In box 52, as Lisa talks about her daughter's academics, she uses the word "tragically," which provides Gloria with insight on how Lisa sees her daughter's illness as a tragedy.

In box 57, Gloria is cognizant that she used the word "bombarding" to describe how she is giving Lisa a lot of information at once.

Family Systems Theory

Box 60

In box 60, Gloria listens as Lisa worries about her son and how she will be less available to him at an important time when he is applying to colleges. Lisa tells Gloria she is a big resource for him, and she will struggle balancing time with both children. Gloria uses family systems theory to understand the impact of illness and life cycle development on the family. She is getting the picture of a mother who is devoted to her children and can take their perspective in times of crisis.

Cognitive Theory

Box 61

In box 61, Gloria uses cognitive strategies to problem solve with Lisa by identifying resources to help her son with college applications and other supports so he can share his feelings about Emily's illness and the meaning it will have for him.

Fourth Excerpt from Transcript and Process Recording

At the start of the fourth excerpt, Gloria asks Lisa what she anticipates Emily will find most difficult. They discuss the stress of Emily losing her hair, feeling sick, and losing weight. When Gloria asks Lisa what will be most difficult for her to witness, Lisa begins to show her vulnerability and expresses sadness that she can't help her daughter. As a mother, she could make most problems go away, but this is something she can't control.

As you read through the process recording, notice how many times Gloria seeks feedback from Lisa. As a result of Lisa's anger with Gloria in the last excerpt, when Lisa told her their conversation was a waste of time, Gloria is sensitive to Lisa's reactions. She uses a communication skill referred to as "seeking client feedback" to get Lisa's perception of a particular situation and general feedback about the process.

Content	Observation/Reflection	Analysis of Intervention: Theories and Practice
65. SW: Sure, sure. In terms of Emily, what do you anticipate will be difficult for her as she goes through this process?		Practice: Assessment. Communication skill: exploration of the problem.
66. Mother: You know I don't know what the process really involves, but you know it's physically painful; obviously that's not going to be a picnic for her. She's very resilient. You know if things are kept relatively normal for her, you know if people don't treat her like she's a fragile ornament or something, you know, and maintain a sense of humor and normality, I think she will probably do OK. I think, you know not feeling well and losing her hair, oh my god, those will be big, big, big challenges.	This is helpful information for us to have. She knows her daughter well. I wonder what role religion and spirituality play in Lisa's life.	Theory: Narrative, picnic, resilient, fragile ornament, sense of humor, normality, uses "big" three times to describe challenges. She uses "God" here and a few other times in the interview.

(Continued)

Content	Observation/Reflection	Analysis of Intervention: Theories and Practice
67. SW: Right, right. How important is her hair would you say?		Practice: Communication skill, seeking client feedback.
68. Mother: Her hair, and I mean she's not especially vain or anything, but you know, a little girl, her hair...		
69. SW: She's eleven.	I know it will be a big deal for an eleven year old.	
70. Mother: It's a big deal, and she's got a nice head of hair! It is important to her. She has a lot of interests that have to do with being physical. And that's one of my worries in addition to school. She plays the cello, and she plays soccer, and she does modeling on the weekend. She's a very active little person.		Theory: Narrative, uses adjectives like big and very to make a point. Also refers to daughter as active, little person.
71. SW: Very active.	It's better I say little here and let her continue.	Practice: Communication skill, Nonverbal attending and listening skills.
72. Mother: Being sick and being physically changed, and, God knows, she'll probably lose weight. I just can't even imagine what that's going to be like for her, or me.	It's so hard to look at what the reality will look like for Emily. Lisa's getting in touch with her feelings more. She referred to God several times in the interview. I wonder if she is religious or if she is using just references to God as an expression. I find that parents turn to religion when confronted with their child's serious illness.	Narrative, uses God again.
73. SW: What do you anticipate will be most difficult for you as you witness that change?		Practice: Communication skill, reaching for feelings.
74. Mother: Not being able to help her.	That must be hard for a mother. She's very insightful here and showing her feelings now.	
75. SW: Not being able to help her. (Pause) I can understand that. That's very difficult.	I can relate to what she is saying more now as she gets in touch with her feelings. I am glad she is finally able to express her sadness.	Practice: Communication skill, reflecting back feelings, empathy.

(Continued)

Content	Observation/Reflection	Analysis of Intervention: Theories and Practice
76. Mother: Most things you can make go away, but this doesn't sound like something I can have any control over at all.	I find it easier to sit with her and feel more connected when she expresses her feelings of sadness. She shows insight about how she doesn't have control over Emily's illness. She can't make it go away. It's hard to lose control when something awful is happening to your child.	
77. SW: Yeah, absolutely. What do you think you can have control over?	It's important for her to feel she can have control over something.	Theory: Cognitive, problem-solving, helping her to gain control and mastery. Practice: Communication skill, seeking client feedback.
78. Mother: Well, I can try to import some of the nicer aspects of her life to the hospital setting, you know, like make sure that she maintains connection with her father, try to reduce her understanding of the conflict that we're experiencing. I know that's been a challenge for her over the years to know that her father and I don't get along as well as we'd like too. I think bringing her friends, although I don't know how her friends' families will feel about that, but to the extent that I can get them to remain actively involved with her, and remain her friends. I think that's going to be enormously important to her to not just be abandoned. To lose so much, it seems like this whole is about one loss after another loss; her physicality, her athleticism, her school, her friends, loss of her hair. Yeah that will be challenging.	At times, she seems to use dramatic and exaggerated language. She has some good, concrete suggestions for what she can do to help Emily. I need to acknowledge this strength and use this information to help her gain more control.	Theory: Cognitive, problem-solving; Narrative, use adjectives, nicer (aspects), actively (involved), enormously (important), abandoned. Practice: Assessment, identifying strengths.
79. SW: Absolutely, and it seems like you're very in tune, exactly right on target with the things that she may experience at this time.	She seems to know her daughter well.	Theory: Psychodynamic, attunement. Practice: Communication skill, acknowledging strengths.
80. Mother: I think I'd prefer not to be in tune. It just seems like a very big challenge.	I guess to be in tune means to be sensitive to her physical and emotional pain. It's not easy to be in tune with your daughter's pain and losses.	Theory: Narrative, use of adjectives again, very, big (challenge).
81. SW: Yes, yes. What do you anticipate would be helpful for her, that we could provide for her here in the hospital?	I think it will be important to help her feel she has control over this and is the expert on what Emily needs.	Practice: Communication skill, seeking client feedback.

(Continued)

Content	Observation/Reflection	Analysis of Intervention: Theories and Practice
82. Mother: Well I think if she has long stretches of time where she is just left to sit by herself and watch TV or something that would be awful, and so, you know, if there are groups of other girls who are going through similar things it would be really important for her, you know can she get involved with other girls, other boys, other children. Can she be kept busy, you know, she's an active person, to just sit and stare at the wall for hours on end would be just terrible for her.	I think she likes to be able to help us understand what Emily needs, and this can help her feel that she is doing something to help her daughter. Parents need to feel that they have some control and power in this otherwise helpless situation.	
83. SW: Right, right; well let me tell you a little bit about what we can offer for her here in the hospital. First of all, I think that given the many losses you've mentioned that she's gone through, I think it would definitely be beneficial for her to be in some type of psychotherapy, and I don't know what you're feelings are around that.		Practice: Assessment. Communication skill, information-giving, seeking client feedback.
84. Mother: I'm not sure; I don't know. I've always been suspicious of people trying to get into my daughter's head. I don't really go for that.	It's interesting how she responded. I wonder if she's had counseling before, or if it has been suggested in the past.	Practice: Assessment.
85. SW: OK, OK, and we also have groups like you mentioned where she can be with other girls who are going through leukemia, similar experiences, similar age range, where she can express herself, and it doesn't necessarily have to be psychotherapy. It could be someone who could come in and just sit with her and do different craft projects and talk about how she is feeling without it necessarily being framed as psychotherapy.	Psychotherapy scares parents. I need to reframe this so it sounds less intimidating to her.	Theory: Psychodynamic, play therapy; cognitive, support group. Practice: Communication skills, reframing, information-giving.
86. Mother: She would love that.		
87. SW: If that would be something you would prefer. I think finding some way of helping her talk about how she is feeling, talk about the difficulties of going through this, might be beneficial. Also, her father, how often he will come in? Where are we in terms of that arrangement? Will he be part of this process?		Theory: Psychodynamic, play therapy; Family systems. Communication skills, information-giving, questioning.
88. Mother: I'm not sure. He's a very good father and I think he will do his best. I think in this kind of situation this is not his strength; this is not his strength. He will, I don't know, time will tell I suppose.	It sounds like Lisa doesn't think her husband will be involved in coming to the hospital often.	Theory: Family systems; Narrative, repeats this is not his strength twice for emphasis.
89. SW: I feel like I've given you some information. I don't know how you're feeling about what we've talked about so far.		Practice: Communication skill, seeking client feedback.

(Continued)

Content	Observation/Reflection	Analysis of Intervention: Theories and Practice
90. Mother: I'm feeling good; no I'm not, that's a lie. I'm feeling a little more reassured that there are a lot of resources although vague about what exactly the form they'll take and at the same time I feel like I've taken in as much as I can take in at the moment. I don't know if you have some written materials, or if I can have the opportunity to catch up with you again when I have some more clarity, on what my questions might be, and a chance to digest.	Although there is still a tinge of criticism in her response, it seems that she is feeling better than when we started. She has more information, which is empowering. She has seemed ambivalent about my talking with her, but I can see that she is also saying here that she wants to meet again. This is a good sign and shows she is beginning to trust me and accept my help.	Theory: Narrative, words, lie, vague, catch up, clarity, digest.
91. SW: Absolutely, absolutely. That's definitely possible. It's often the experience of some of our parents that they feel like the first few days they are just bombarded with so much information that there is only so much that they can take at once. I can certainly come by at another time and we can go over some written materials. I can maybe stop by and leave them for you to take a look at them when you have some time and we can certainly talk about the resources available; things like that that might be helpful for you. Do you have any questions for me so far?	Here I go again with the word bombarded. I wonder how I am feeling about her and our first meeting. She's not a particularly easy person to talk to, and I'm never quite sure when she's going to explode.	Theory: Narrative, I use bombarded again, and also repeat "absolutely" twice. Practice: Communication skills, normalizing feelings, next steps, seeking client feedback.
92. Mother: Well I think we've gone over most of them at this point.		
93. SW: Great, great; it was a pleasure meeting you. And I look forward to working with you closely.	I notice that I am repeating words like I found Lisa doing.	Practice: Communication skill, endings.
94. Mother: Thank you.		

Reflection of Fourth Process Recording and Discussion of Practice Skills and Theories Used in Intervention

Although the fourth excerpt starts with Lisa feeling sad that she can't help her daughter, Gloria's questions allow her to see another perspective. Their discussion reveals ways that Lisa can play an important role by collaborating with the medical staff about the best approach to take with Emily. Gloria helps Lisa regain a sense of control and mastery over the situation and feel competent. She also talks about interventions that could help Emily during her treatments. By the end of the interview, Lisa feels more reassured and asks if she can meet with Gloria again once she has digested all of the new the information.

Communication Skills

Box 65

Exploration of the problem: This is a way of gaining more information about a client's situation. When continuing to explore the problem, the social worker listens for underlying feelings about the situation, who else is involved, and what resources are available to help resolve it.

In box 65, Gloria explores the problem of Emily's treatment and wants to know what she'll find difficult. This is part of Gloria's prioritizing the problems and assessing what interventions Emily needs first.

Boxes 67, 77, 81, 83, 89, 91

Seeking client feedback: When seeking client feedback, the social worker asks for the client's perception of a particular situation, the client-worker relationship, or the helping process.

In box 67, Gloria knows that Emily will lose her hair during treatment for leukemia and asks Lisa how important Emily's hair is to her. She is seeking Lisa's feedback on this subject and wants to understand from the mother's perspective how Emily will take this.

In box 77, Gloria asks Lisa what she thinks she can have control over, understanding her frustration as a parent who can't make the leukemia go away for her daughter. Gloria recognizes that Lisa needs to feel she can control something to help her master the situation and feel competent again.

In box 81, Gloria inquires what they, at the hospital, could provide to help Emily. By seeking Lisa's knowledge, Gloria sends her a message that her information about her daughter is critical and that the medical team can use it to provide better care for Emily.

In box 83, Gloria recommends psychotherapy for Emily, and asks Lisa for her feedback on this.

In box 89, Gloria seeks Lisa's feedback about all of the information she has given her so far. This is especially important for Gloria to assess since Lisa had felt the session was a waste of time earlier in the interview.

In box 91, Gloria asks Lisa if she has any questions before she ends their first meeting. She is aware that she's checking in more with Lisa during this excerpt, perhaps as a result of Lisa's anger earlier in the interview.

Box 71

Nonverbal attending and listening skills: The social worker shows that she is listening through her body language, such as eye contact, facial expressions, nodding, and leaning forward. These nonverbal skills help the client elaborate and feel comfortable sharing personal information.

In box 71, Gloria intentionally says very little but listens to Lisa attentively and encourages her to continue sharing her concerns about the effects of chemotherapy. She notices that Lisa's mood has shifted from anger to sadness as she talks about the impact of treatment on her daughter. By not interrupting Lisa, Gloria allows her to access her feelings of sadness more.

Box 73

Reaching for feelings: This is when the social worker tries to understand what the client is feeling when a particular subject or issue comes up. The social worker may use this skill when she senses that the client is avoiding, or is not in touch with, the feelings related to the current discussion. This may bring out strong reactions in the client, and it is important that the social worker is sensitive to what this means to the client.

In box 73, Gloria asks Lisa what changes she'll have the most difficulty seeing in her daughter as a result of treatment. With this question, Gloria is reaching for Lisa's feelings; she notices that Lisa shows some sadness and invites her to delve into these feelings more.

Box 75

Reflecting back feelings: This is when the social worker gives a short response back to the client that mirrors the feeling the worker heard the client express. It is used to let the client know the worker is listening.

In box 75, Gloria repeats what she heard Lisa say and acknowledges the great difficulty she faces not being able to help her daughter. Gloria pauses in her response, taking her time, and this gives Lisa permission to sit with her feelings.

Box 75

Showing empathy: The social worker maintains a nonjudgmental stance or remains neutral. The worker need not totally understand the client's situation, but she must show that she is trying to grasp what the client is feeling or experiencing. The social worker might say, "Tell me more about what your experience was" or "I want to understand more about what this means from your perspective."

In box 75, Gloria shows empathy for Lisa's situation when she recognizes how hard it will be that Lisa can't prevent the changes that occur to her daughter from chemotherapy.

Box 79

Acknowledging strengths: Acknowledging strengths can help clients improve their self-esteem and give them more confidence to take action on their own behalf. It empowers them by providing them with hope and a sense that they have the capacity and resources within themselves to improve their lives and overcome obstacles. When clients feel overwhelmed by difficulties, they may not recognize their positive traits, so the worker pointing them out can bolster the client's self-confidence.

In Box 79, Gloria acknowledges one of Lisa's strengths when she tells her she's very in tune with her daughter and what she may experience because of her illness. Acknowledging strengths helps empower clients.

Boxes 83, 85, 87

Information-giving: Information-giving means informing the client about the social agency, the problem, and the resources for change. The social worker is knowledgeable about human development and human behavior and can help clients by sharing information that relates to a problem they are experiencing.

In box 83, Gloria tells Lisa that, given the losses Emily will experience, she might benefit from some form of psychotherapy.

In box 85, Gloria recommends that Emily participate in a group for girls her age who are going through the same treatments, where she could express herself. Gloria also proposes having someone visit Emily to do arts and crafts, and to talk with Emily about how she is doing.

In box 87, Gloria tells Lisa that it would be beneficial for her daughter to have someone to talk to.

Box 85

Reframing: Reframing helps clients see themselves, their problems, and other people from a different perspective, generally in a more positive way.

In box 85, Gloria reframes psychotherapy for Lisa to make it more acceptable. She explains that someone could sit with her daughter and do different craft projects and talk. Packaging therapy differently made it tolerable to Lisa, who said her daughter would love that.

Box 91

Normalizing feelings: Clients often believe that their feelings are unacceptable or abnormal. The social worker helps the client see that her feelings are a natural reaction to the given situation.

In box 91, Gloria normalizes Lisa's feelings by saying that many parents need a few days to digest the information they receive after diagnosis. Gloria offers to go over what she has covered with Lisa again sometime, and also agrees to get some written material for Lisa to read.

Box 91

Next steps: This is a phrase used when the client and the worker decide what they will work on next, and what actions they can take.

In box 91, Gloria goes over the next steps and explains that she will stop by with some written materials that they can review and to discuss other resources.

Box 93

Endings: This is when the social worker prepares the client for the end of the session. In box 93, Gloria prepares Lisa for the end of the interview by asking her if she has any more questions and going over the next steps. She tells Lisa that it was a pleasure to meet her and that she looks forward to working with her closely. The ending is congenial with the expectation of meeting again soon. Lisa thanks Gloria for her help.

Other Practice Skills Used
Boxes 65, 78, 83, 84

Assessment: Assessment is the process of understanding the client and his problem based on the information gathered. It is done in a holistic way that highlights the importance of context in the construction of meaning, and it is a collaborative activity that is done in tandem with the client.

In box 65, to assess what Emily will need during treatment, Gloria asks Lisa what she anticipates will be most difficult for her daughter.

In box 83, Gloria gives her assessment to Lisa: She believes Emily would benefit from some form of psychotherapy, based on the number of losses she will experience.

In box 84, Gloria wonders what to make of Lisa's response to her question about psychotherapy for Emily. Her assessment is that Lisa is suspicious of therapy, and Gloria thinks she could have had a bad counseling experience in the past, or had it recommended to her before.

Box 78

Identifying strengths: During assessment, social workers listen for client strengths they can use to help solve certain problems. As clients talk about their situation and their stories unfold, workers identify strengths that are embedded in the narrative. By focusing on positive attributes and characteristics, workers shift the focus away from deficits to inquiring about and affirming strengths.

In box 78, as Gloria listens to Lisa talk about what she can do to help her daughter, she realizes that Lisa has some excellent concrete suggestions, especially bringing Emily's friends to visit. She identifies Lisa's ability to hit on practical ideas as a strength that could play an important role during treatment and also facilitate her feeling more in control.

Theories Used in Intervention

Narrative Theory

Boxes 66, 70, 72, 80, 88, 90, 91

In box 66, Lisa says it won't be a "picnic" for Emily to receive chemotherapy, but she describes her daughter as "resilient." In recommending how to approach Emily, Lisa encourages keeping things relatively "normal," not treating her like a "fragile ornament," and maintaining a "sense of humor." She uses the adjective "big" three times and says "oh my God" when referring to the challenge of Emily losing her hair. Lisa's words and language provide insight on her coping strategies and how she stays strong in the face of adversity.

In box 70, Lisa says it a "big deal" for Emily to lose her hair, especially since she has a "nice head of hair." It is interesting that Lisa refers to Emily as an "active, little person." Seeing her daughter as "little" may reflect her wish to protect her young child from the effects of chemotherapy.

In box 72, Lisa again references "God." Gloria is curious if this is just an expression or if religion has meaning for her. She will listen for other comments about religion or spirituality and use them as an opportunity to explore this area with Lisa.

In box 80, Lisa uses a string of adjectives to make a point about the scale of what Emily faces: a "very big challenge."

In box 88, when asked about her husband's involvement in Emily's care, Lisa repeats twice that, "this is not his strength." Based on Lisa's way of talking about her husband, Gloria does not feel optimistic that he will visit his daughter often and share responsibilities with Lisa.

In box 90, in response to Gloria's question about how she's doing, Lisa says, "I'm feeling good," and then quickly withdraws those words, admitting that's a "lie." She is still critical that certain information she's received is "vague," but she shows interest in meeting with Gloria again to "catch up" and gain more "clarity," once she has had a chance to "digest" everything. Her use of the word "digest" fits with the concept of information as a metaphor for food. In this context, Gloria has given her enough to eat at this sitting, and now she needs time to digest or process it.

In box 91, Gloria uses the word "bombarded" again to explain how much information she has given to Lisa. Gloria is sensitive about how Lisa might interpret this word and wonders if she still feels uncomfortable from Lisa's previous anger. Gloria feels that Lisa is not a particularly easy client; like a bomb, she could go off at any time. However, Gloria empathizes with her situation, feels they have made a lot of progress in this meeting, and does want to continue working with her.

Cognitive Theory

Boxes 77, 78

In box 77, Gloria uses the problem-solving method to help Lisa think of ways to have some control over the situation to feel less helpless and more competent.

In box 78, Lisa responds to Gloria's problem-solving question with a flurry of ideas for what she could do to make a difference. For example, Lisa says she could make sure that Emily maintains contact with her father and friends, and she could try to reduce her conflicts with her husband. Lisa continues to use dramatic language when she says that Emily's friends are "enormously" important to her, and she can't feel "abandoned."

Cognitive-Behavioral Theory

Box 85

In box 85, Gloria refers to a support group for girls Emily's age who are also struggling with leukemia. The group's goal is to provide the girls with encouragement and problem-solving strategies to deal with the problems associated with chemotherapy. The group is based on cognitive and behavioral theories.

Psychodynamic Theory

Boxes 79, 85, 87

In box 79, Gloria uses psychodynamic language when she says that Lisa is "in tune" with her daughter. The notion of attunement refers to a close mother–child relationship in early childhood wherein the mother or significant caregiver is tuned in to and responds to what the child is feeling and needing in the moment.

In box 85, Gloria avoids saying it's psychotherapy, but she talks about a psychodynamic, nondirective play therapy, which could help Emily express her feelings. Gloria calls it simply craft projects and talking, making it more acceptable to Lisa.

In box 87, Gloria continues to emphasize the benefits of play therapy as a means for Emily to express her emotions.

Family Systems Theory
Boxes 87, 88
In box 87, Gloria asks questions about Emily's father to ascertain how often he will visit her, what the arrangements will be, and how he will take part in the process. She wants to assess family functioning, especially under the stress of illness, to determine the parents' roles and how they will share responsibility for the children during Emily's treatment.

In box 88, Lisa responds to Gloria's question about her husband with a comment that this kind of situation is not his strength. She thinks he will do his best and ends by saying that time will tell. Gloria has growing concerns about how much Emily's father will be involved in a supportive and constructive way.

Assessment

Assessment is the process of understanding the client and his problem in a holistic way based on the information gathered. It highlights the importance of context in the construction of meaning, and it is a collaborative activity done in tandem with the client. Following are examples of applying different assessment outlines to Lisa's case.

Problem-Solving Method
This assessment follows the problem-solving method outline found in chapter 1. It is the social worker's attempt to apply the problem-solving method to Lisa's case. It is written in the first person, from the social worker's perspective.

Engagement
I met with Lisa for the first time in the outpatient clinic, shortly after her daughter was diagnosed with acute lymphoblastic leukemia. At our initial meeting, I found Lisa easy to engage with. She came across as an attractive, intelligent, articulate woman whose speech was dramatic at times. She described herself as numb, which might mean she's still in shock over news of her daughter's diagnosis, and says that she will probably crack sometime in the future when she begins to deal with what is happening. She vacillated in her attitudes toward me: Either she was receptive and communicated openly about her experiences, or she expressed anger and frustration with different medical staff for their ill treatment and for how I was wasting her time. She also shared irritation with her husband, who she separated from five months earlier, and who is critical of how she handled the situation with their daughter. By the end of the interview, after I provided information about treatment options for Emily and other resources for her family, Lisa was receptive to social work intervention.

Assessment
Lisa is a recently separated woman in her 40s who has two children, an 11-year-old daughter recently diagnosed with leukemia, and a 17-year-old son who is a senior in high school and

applying to colleges. She and her two children live in western Massachusetts, and her husband lives in New York, where Emily and her brother visit every other weekend. The marital separation came after a long period of Lisa and her husband arguing and fighting with each other. She told her husband over the phone about Emily's diagnosis, and he is in denial; he complains about Lisa mishandling the situation and believes the doctors are jumping to conclusions. If Emily has any problems because of the decisions she makes, Lisa feels that it will be on her head.

In my interview with her, Lisa demonstrated a range of feelings: shock and what she described as being numb; anger and frustration with healthcare providers; sadness that she can't take this problem away from her daughter; worry about her son at home and how to tell him the news; annoyance with her husband who is angry at her handling of Emily's care; and finally reassurance and appreciation for the information I gave her during the interview. She told me she is not dealing with her feelings, because she needs to put her children's needs first, but knows that she will crack sometime in the future. Although she has told a few friends about Emily's diagnosis, she found they reacted by either becoming overly emotional or distancing themselves and pulling away to give her space.

During the interview, I noticed a tendency for Lisa to intellectualize to deal with her feelings about the situation. She also used colorful and descriptive language, with a style of relating that was more exaggerated and dramatic to get her point across. For example, in the very beginning of our meeting, she used the words "waiting" and "questions" three times consecutively to describe her experience with the medical team. Later, she referred to interactions with her husband as "very, very, very, very tense;" this provides insight about her conflicted relationship with her husband. Although she tends to be dramatic, she also seems high functioning, someone who takes charge and is quite capable of handling problems.

Lisa is off to a difficult start with the medical team, which hasn't communicated well with her about Emily's diagnosis and has left her confused and with a lot of questions about her daughter's treatment. Since a good relationship and partnership between the staff and Lisa is significant for effective treatment outcomes, we will need to address these issues early to reverse the direction it has started to go in. The goal is that, with healthy collaboration between the doctors and the family, everyone is working together for Emily's best interests. It is possible that some of Lisa's anger is a projection of her own feelings of anger and helplessness over her daughter's illness. As she vents these feelings with me, some of this will dissipate. However, it will remain important for the doctors and staff to communicate better and heed Lisa's questions and her need for more detailed information.

There are many significant stressors on Lisa: her daughter's diagnosis of leukemia and its ensuing need for lengthy treatments over a two-year period; a marriage that has recently ended in separation and is characterized by frequent fights and arguments; an older sibling at home who doesn't know about Emily's diagnosis yet and who is in transition, applying to colleges; a daughter who will need considerable support to cope with the side effects of chemotherapy and adapt to illness; and her own feelings about her daughter's illness, including helplessness that she can't make this problem go away for her daughter.

Assessment Summary

Lisa is a bright, articulate, single parent who lives in western Massachusetts with her two children. She and her husband separated five months ago, and he now lives in New York; their relationship was conflicted, with a lot of fighting and arguing. She was recently told that her daughter has acute lymphoblastic leukemia and will need lengthy treatment over a two-year period. Lisa is confronted with many emotional and physical challenges. She must deal with her daughter's illness and needs, as well as her husband's denial and confrontational style of questioning her decisions. She must explain Lisa's diagnosis to her son, who meanwhile needs help applying to colleges. And finally, she must come to terms with her own feelings about her daughter's life-threatening illness and the loss of her marriage at a time when she needs more emotional support.

Planning

Lisa has multiple psychosocial needs that must be addressed. To begin with, she is desperate for more information and resources to understand Lisa's diagnosis and what the treatment options are. This presents an opportunity for the medical team to make up for its previous poor communication and work with Lisa and her daughter so they better grasp the diagnosis and treatment. Lisa has asked for help talking with Emily and her brother about the illness and how it will impact their life over the next couple of years. Marital issues should be tackled when they impact Emily's treatment, especially if the couple fights in front of her and if they disagree about treatment choices. Lisa will need additional supports to manage the demands on her as a single parent with a hospitalized child and another child at home, complicated by additional marital stressors.

Intervention

The intervention began in our first meeting when I worked to gain Lisa's trust in my ability to help her. Although she was unsure of what I had to offer, by the end of the interview she was appreciative of the role I could play with the family during Emily's treatment and the information I gave her. I will continue to meet with her, advise her about services, answer questions about Emily's care as they surface, and be available for emotional support. Because Emily's education is important, I will connect her to tutors while in the hospital so she can keep up with her studies. Lisa's son cannot be ignored; he will need resources to help him with the college application process. I will also explore any financial concerns Lisa has as the mother of a child with leukemia, which requires a lengthy treatment. Periodically, I will meet with Lisa and her husband to ensure they are conveying a strong alliance to support Emily and to prevent adverse reactions that could occur with their fighting and quarreling in front of her.

Another important intervention will be facilitating better communication between the medical staff and the family to encourage a strong partnership that will lead to better treatment outcomes for Emily. I will work with Emily's doctors to help them understand Lisa's feelings, family situation, and psychosocial needs and to help them take a different approach with her in future meetings. I plan to set up a family conference as soon as possible to get these problems resolved and put everything on the right track, so that going forward, Lisa won't have this stressor and can feel more confident in her daughter's care.

Termination

At the end of our first meeting, I felt confident in the early relationship I was able to establish with Lisa. After venting frustrations about her experiences with the clinic, the hospital staff, and her husband, Lisa was open to working on some of the problems that came up during the interview. Before she left, she said that she would like to meet again once she had digested the information I had shared with her. I feel sure that she will follow-up with me on some of the issues we began to address in our initial session.

The ending of our first meeting is the beginning of a relationship that will span over the two years of her daughter's treatment.

Follow-up

I have left it so that Lisa can reach out to me when she is ready. I am confident that she will take advantage of my services. She is a high-functioning woman who I expect will take full advantage of the resources I have to offer. I will also touch base with her soon to set up a treatment conference between her and the principal medical staff who will be managing her daughter's care.

Psychosocial Assessment and Intervention Strategy

Please refer to chapter 1, which includes an outline for the psychosocial assessment and intervention plan. This is one example of applying a psychosocial assessment and intervention to Lisa's case and is written in the social worker's voice.

Identifying Data

Lisa is an attractive, articulate, and bright woman in her 40s whose daughter was diagnosed with acute lymphoblastic leukemia in the pediatric oncology clinic. She is a single mother living in western Massachusetts with her two children, the 11-year-old daughter and a 17-year-old son. She separated five months ago from her husband who now lives in New York. She appears angry and frustrated with how the medical staff has treated her and her daughter, and how they were told about the diagnosis. During the interview, she described herself as being numb and needing to attend to her children's needs first, saying that she will crack sometime in the future. Her speech and demeanor came across as dramatic and exaggerated at times. However, she also seemed competent and able to take charge of problems, especially when given information and resources.

Presenting Problem

Lisa accompanied her daughter Emily to the outpatient pediatric oncology department after first getting shuffled around from her pediatrician's office to the emergency room and then finally to the clinic. Once in the clinic, results from blood tests confirmed that her daughter had acute lymphoblastic leukemia. The plan was for Emily to be hospitalized immediately to begin treatment.

While in the outpatient department, I met with Lisa to assess her and her family's psychosocial needs related to the daughter's diagnosis. A problem that surfaced quickly was her anger at the medical staff for how she and her daughter were treated and first told the diagnosis. She was confused about the details of the illness and needed more information about the treatment options. She was also struggling to communicate with her husband. Lisa told her husband of the daughter's diagnosis in a phone conversation that ended with the husband accusing her of making poor decisions about her daughter's care. In addition, she shared not knowing how to tell her son about his sister's diagnosis; he was at home and still in the dark.

Current Functioning, Social Supports, and Strengths

Lisa is an attractive, bright, and articulate single parent in her 40s recently separated from her husband and dealing with her daughter's sudden diagnosis of lymphoblastic leukemia. Lisa demonstrates many strengths: She is intelligent and can convey her needs to others; she can advocate for herself and her daughter concerning how the medical staff treats them; she shows some insight about her tendency to ignore her own feelings while attending to her children; she appears competent and wants to master her problems; she is devoted to her kids; and she is willing to accept social work intervention. However, she's also at risk due to her recent separation and the overwhelming demands of parenting a daughter with a life-threatening illness alone and dealing with a conflicted marital relationship.

Lisa seeks more information about Emily's leukemia diagnosis and treatment options. She is faced with the challenge of discussing Emily's illness and medical protocols with her husband, who disagrees with her decisions and is critical of her choices. She is struggling with how to tell her son about Emily's diagnosis and how to support him as he applies to and prepares for college. She also worries about the impact of treatment on Emily: how she will cope and adapt to her illness; how she will manage pain and deal with losing her hair during chemotherapy; how she will keep up with her studies while in the hospital; and how she will continue her friendships that are very important to her. Lisa admits she needs advice on how to talk to Emily about these stressors and support her during this difficult time. She feels sad and helpless that she can't protect Emily as she always has in the past. She has concerns about the potential financial burden associated with her daughter's illness, and constant transportation to the city for treatments.

Lisa appears to have a good relationship with both her children. She has friends, but so far they have not given her the support she needs, either because they are too emotional about the situation or they are distancing themselves from her, perhaps out of fear and discomfort about leukemia. There is little known at this time about Lisa's work history, extended family, or community supports, but these are important areas for exploration in future meetings.

Relevant Past History

Lisa has struggled this past year due to ongoing fighting with her husband that led to marital separation five months ago. She now lives with her two children in western Massachusetts, assuming most of the responsibility for their care, while her husband resides in New York. She comes across as a high-functioning and competent parent who has managed to take charge of family problems, as demonstrated with the present crisis. She has friends in town, many of whom are the parents of her children's friends. She is an attentive mother who supports her children in their school and extracurricular activities. At this early stage, there is little known about her work history, family-of-origin relationships, hobbies, group affiliations, or other interests.

Formulation

Lisa is an attractive, bright, and articulate single mother of two children; her daughter was recently diagnosed with acute lymphoblastic leukemia. She shoulders most of the daily responsibilities for her children since her husband moved to New York five months ago at the time of their separation. She demonstrates many strengths: She is able to share anger and frustration about how medical staff have treated her and her daughter; she can advocate for her daughter and assert her needs for more information and better care; she is competent and wants to be better informed about leukemia to take charge of her daughter's illness; and she is motivated to improve her situation through social work intervention. She also has challenges ahead as she deals with the many stresses of a life-threatening illness, its impact on both her children, her marital conflict, the extra responsibilities of a sick child who requires more care, and her own emotional needs. Both individual and couple's counseling are recommended.

Intervention Strategy

I recommend individual counseling for Lisa with an emphasis in the beginning on providing her with information and resources about leukemia and the options for treatment. Next, I plan to coordinate with her daughter's medical team to help them understand Lisa's dissatisfaction with her treatment thus far, particularly the way she was told about her daughter's diagnosis. To facilitate better communication and an effective partnership between Lisa and the team, I will arrange a conference with the family and significant members of the medical staff taking charge of Emily's case; the goal is to answer Lisa's questions, ensure she has the information she needs, and build stronger and more trusting relationships.

I will meet with Lisa individually to address identified psychosocial needs, helping her to: find a way to talk to her children about the illness; vent and use healthy outlets for expressing her anger and frustration with the situation; connect her daughter to tutoring services to keep up with her studies while in the hospital; locate resources to help her son with college applications; explore financial needs related to the stress of her daughter's lengthy treatment; recommend a community support group for parents of children with acute lymphoblastic leukemia; and explore other resources in the extended family and community. I will also plan conjoint sessions with Lisa and her husband to engage them in ways to support Emily during her treatment and reduce their fighting, especially around her. I expect I'll refer them to outpatient couples' therapy to deal with their marital issues in more depth. My interventions with Lisa and the family will span over the two years of her treatment.

Termination and Evaluation

My ongoing interventions with Lisa and her family will end when Emily's treatment for leukemia stops, in approximately two years. After that, she will be followed intermittently by the outpatient clinic for five years, and I will continue to meet with the family during this time. Follow-up is important, since the literature indicates that stressors and psychosocial adjustment in the aftermath of leukemia treatment can persist for several years. When the active treatment ends, along with our frequent visits, I will refer Lisa to outpatient treatment in her community as a preventive measure. When the active phase of our work together finishes, I will ask the family to fill out a survey where they can anonymously evaluate the social work services they received. This feedback can improve the quality of our interventions with children and their families coping with serious illness.

Theoretical Lens

In making my assessment and formulation of the problem, I used multiple theories that included individual and family lifespan developmental theories, psychodynamic theories, cognitive and behavioral theories, and narrative theory.

Bio/Psycho/Social/Spiritual Assessment

This approach looks at the functioning of an individual's biological, psychological, social, and spiritual systems. I will apply the outline in chapter 1 to Lisa's case. As with the other sections, it is written in the first person, from the social worker's perspective.

Applying Bio/Psycho/Social/Spiritual Assessment to the Case of Lisa

Lisa is in her 40s, a single mother of two children. She is of average height and weight, and despite the stress of her daughter's recent diagnosis of acute lymphoblastic leukemia, she still appears energetic. She also seems healthy, though there is no immediate information on her medical history. She is an active parent who assumes most of the daily care of her two children, taking them to school and extracurricular activities.

Lisa is a bright, articulate woman with above-average intelligence. She is in middle adulthood, with an 11-year-old daughter in 6th grade and a 17-year-old son in high school, who soon will leave home for college. Her life stage issues and the family's normal developmental transitions are complicated by the crises of her marital separation and her daughter's life-threatening illness. Instead of her children becoming more autonomous, they need more of her attention to cope with these new family stressors; instead of refocusing on her marital relationship, she is losing this important source of support. These issues put her at greater risk for emotional problems.

Lisa's cognitive abilities appear strong; she was quick to learn and pick up information that I shared during our first meeting. She was also alert and attentive during our conversation, and had a capacity for abstract thought, insight, and problem solving. Although she was angry and frustrated in her dealings with the medical staff, the issues seemed to revolve around the staff not clarifying information properly and not spending enough time with her. She communicated effectively with me and was able to articulate what made her upset and what she needed help with. I noticed she had a tendency to use colorful and exaggerated language and was sometimes overly dramatic during our conversation. This could be part of her personality or a response to stress.

At our first meeting, Lisa demonstrated many assets. She is competent, and wants to exert some control over the process of helping her daughter adapt and recover from leukemia. She is self-confident and shows high self-esteem despite her many losses and her husband's frequent criticisms. She struggles with her relationship with her husband whom she is separated from; she describes him as challenging and someone who will second-guess any decision she makes. Although she characterizes him as full of anger and blame, she doesn't seem to internalize his projections or accept his attempts to put her down. Instead, she talks about having to deal with his problems on top of everything else; she doesn't belittle herself because of his attacking behavior.

Lisa had a tendency to intellectualize during our meeting, but she acknowledged she was ignoring her own feelings in order to attend to the needs of her children first. She is fragile, given the enormity of the stressors on her, and admitted she will probably crack sometime in the future. In the interview, she did express angry feelings, but she also showed sadness when she imagined the difficulty of watching her daughter go through painful treatments with awful side effects without the ability to protect her. Her ill temper at the staff and at me was possibly a projection of her anger and frustration with the situation onto others.

Lisa exhibits good ego functioning in a number of areas. She has an ability to take the other's perspective and be empathic, demonstrated in her relationship with her children. During our session, she also seemed to have good reality testing and understood fully the seriousness of her daughter's illness. She articulated the problems she expects to encounter as a result of the diagnosis and wants information and resources to help her cope and adapt to the stressors on her. She is trying to make informed decisions and wants to see all options for her daughter's treatment. She expressed she needed time to digest all of the information, showing that she is thoughtful about decisions and not impulsive.

There is missing information for a thorough social assessment of Lisa. Our first interview dealt more with the crisis of her daughter's diagnosis. I did not have time to explore family and other social supports in sufficient depth. I do know that she and her husband separated five months ago and that their relationship is one of high conflict, characterized by frequent fights and arguments. However, she appears to have a close relationship with her two children, a daughter who is 11 and diagnosed with leukemia, and a son who is 17, a senior in high school and applying to colleges.

Lisa has told some of her friends about Emily's illness but does not feel supported by them. She described a few friends who overreacted to the news and became very emotional. Others distanced themselves from her and could be uncomfortable dealing with a life-threatening illness.

At this time, I do not have information about Lisa's family-of-origin or extended family relationships. I will also need to explore other areas of social and community support, work and educational history, and religious and other affiliations. In terms of economic status, I would conjecture that Lisa is middle class, but new financial stresses may crop up as a result of the marital separation and Emily's lengthy treatment.

Spiritually, Lisa is going through an existential crisis and may struggle to understand why this is all happening to her now—her daughter's diagnosis of leukemia and her separation from her husband. She will be challenged to put her daughter's illness into a perspective that makes sense to her. It will be important for me to explore these issues of loss and reflect on how she makes meaning out of these experiences. I will listen for times when she raises these concerns and initiate a dialogue that explores her beliefs about a higher consciousness or being. Does she feel connected to something larger than herself? Does she have a religious affiliation, and what role does spirituality occupy in her life? What or who does she turn to for inspiration or hope during difficult times like these? Sometimes when terrible things happen, it tests one's faith. Is this happening to Lisa?

Midlife brings its own set of doubts, and similar to the identity crisis of adolescence, a person at this stage often wrestles with questions like, "What is the purpose of my life?" and "What do I want to do with the rest of my days?" As a person approaches the second half of life, he also starts to wonder about death and if there is anything more. It's a time to review life up to this point, reflect on its meaning, and focus on what is important going forward, especially since time may be running out. In midlife, as children get older, there is also a quest to redefine one's role in the family, but this becomes complicated for Lisa, because she must face the possible death of her child due to leukemia. In my work with Lisa, I will look for opportunities and moments to have these essential conversations to help her with any unresolved spiritual issues.

End of Chapter Resources
Questions for Students

I have included these questions to supplement the text for additional student learning. They are organized around the ten core competencies in the Council on Social Work Education (CSWE, 2008). The questions can be used for classroom or online discussion, given as written homework assignments, structured as classroom exercises, or used by students to do outside research. They can also be adapted for use in hybrid or online courses.

Educational Policy 2.1.1—Identify as a Professional Social Worker and Conduct Oneself Accordingly

1. In the beginning of the interview the social worker introduces herself as one of the psychosocial clinicians in the hospital instead of as a social worker. What do you make of this? What is the difference between these two introductions? Are there any implications or consequences for starting out this way? What do you think are her reasons for doing this?

2. Go the website of the National Association of Social Work (NASW) and read about the profession's image campaign. What are your thoughts about the image of social work in the general public and media? What can you do to promote a positive image of social work?

3. What is countertransference? Are there any times in the interview when you noticed this happening? Explain your answer. How would you handle these situations?

4. What role did self-reflection play in the interview with Lisa? How important is self-reflection and self-awareness in social work? What can social workers do to incorporate this into their professional practice?

5. How would you evaluate Gloria in terms of conducting herself as a professional social worker?

6. At different times in the interview, during reflection, Gloria identified concerns she wanted to address with her supervisor. What were these issues and how do you understand them?

Educational Policy 2.1.2—Apply Social Work Ethical Principles to Guide Professional Practice

The questions below are to make students more aware of ethical issues that social workers confront every day in their practice.

1. At different times during the interview, Lisa refers to "God." Locate these instances and explain what you think her references to God mean.
2. Is it unethical for a social worker to discuss religion and issues of spirituality with clients? Under what circumstances is it appropriate, or inappropriate?
3. If a client does not bring up religion or spirituality, is this a subject that a social worker should explore? If so, when and how? Explain your answer.
4. What is the role of confidentiality when a social worker is working with both a child and the parents? If a child shares something that she doesn't want the parents to know, what would you do? Think of a situation when you might tell a parent and another when you wouldn't. How would you make these decisions?
5. Would there be a conflict of interest in working with both the parents and Emily? Can you think of a situation when it could be a conflict?
6. Social workers in medical settings often feel conflicting loyalties between the patient and the administration where they work. Describe a situation when this could happen and how you would resolve it.
7. What are the ethical issues and consequences of a family not understanding what they consent to regarding clinical trials for their child's leukemia? How can they be resolved?
8. A couple has a 7-year-old daughter who is a cancer patient at a renowned Children's Hospital. They have been told that their daughter's cancer is spreading and there is only a small hope of recovery. The pediatric oncologist suggests a research protocol for an experimental drug but it has little chance of improving her life. The parents don't have much education, are Hispanic, and have always agreed with their doctors' recommendations. Is the couple able to make an informed consent? Does the chance for recovery take precedence over informed consent?
9. Continuing with the hypothetical situation in question 8, does informed consent include a responsibility to explain the treatment to the child? What are the child's rights if she refuses?

Educational Policy 2.1.3—Apply Critical Thinking to Inform and Communicate Professional Judgments

Critical thinking is an important skill in social work practice, and students are expected to demonstrate this competency before graduation. These exercises will encourage students to become critical thinkers in practice.

1. In the transcript, you learn that Lisa's husband is critical of the decisions she has made regarding Emily's treatment. If two parents disagree about their child's care, what happens? Does it make any difference if the parents are separated or divorced? Do you need both parents to consent to treatment to administer chemotherapy?

2. Gloria, the social worker, reflected at one point on whether to process Lisa's anger in the first meeting or focus on giving her information. What would you have done? How important is it to address Lisa's anger and how could it impact treatment? What do you think is behind Lisa's anger?

3. What is the interplay between mental health and physical health? What are the positive and negative implications for making this connection?

4. In the case of Lisa's family, Emily wants her parents to get back together. We learned in the last chapter that Emily sometimes gets in the middle of her parents' arguments by distracting them to stop their fights. Emily has said that she hopes her parents will reunite over her illness. What are your thoughts about the role of Emily's illness in the family dynamics?

5. Having positive relationships between healthcare providers and patients improves treatment outcomes. What are the ingredients for a healthy partnership between both parties? What is the role of social work in fostering this relationship?

6. Gloria has met with Lisa, Emily's mother, and is forming an opinion about Lisa's husband from what Lisa tells her. What is the danger of making assumptions about the dad and could this bias Gloria if the father attends a session? What are your recommendations for working with the family system? Is it possible to stay neutral and not take sides?

Educational Policy 2.1.4—Engage Diversity and Difference in Practice

These questions are designed to teach students about engaging cultural diversity and understanding difference in practice.

1. How do your cultural background and those of your clients influence assessment and intervention?

2. There are many cultures in which nondisclosure of a life-threatening illness to family members is acceptable. How would an American doctor handle a situation in which a family member asks him not to tell the patient about his diagnosis if this request conflicts with the doctor's professional and personal values?

3. In the past, white Americans have dominated the social work taking place in healthcare settings. How has this history influenced the principles and values upon which medical social work was built? Has this changed at all today?

4. What is the role of medical social work to address provider biases against lower socioeconomic groups and different ethnicities? What are some examples of confronting these issues in the medical setting?

5. How do you think having medical personnel from different racial, ethnic, and socioeconomic backgrounds affects medical care?

6. Explain how people's healthcare beliefs are affected by ethnic and racial backgrounds. Provide examples from two different cultures.

7. What is the importance of having language translators employed by hospitals? Survey hospitals in your area to inquire if these services are available.

8. How pressing is it to have bilingual social workers who can communicate with an increasingly multicultural patient population?

9. To what extent are healthcare providers trained in cultural competence and knowledge about various ethnicities? Interview a doctor, nurse, and social worker about diversity training in their fields and compare the differences.

Educational Policy 2.1.5—Advance Human Rights and Social and Economic Justice

Students are expected to address human-rights and social-justice issues when they come up in their practice. These questions are to help students think in terms of social and economic justice and become more competent in this area.

1. Should a physician always truthfully disclose a patient's diagnosis even if the extended family disagree and believe that full disclosure could emotionally harm the patient? There are many cultures in which not telling family members of a life-threatening illness is acceptable. How would a doctor handle this situation? What is justice in this case?

2. Read Gupta et al. (2008), "When disclosing a serious illness to a minor conflicts with family values" (full citation in the reference section). If you were the physician in this case, how would you handle the family?

3. How does Gloria empower Lisa during the interview? Describe some moments when this happened and explain how social work can empower patients and their families in medical settings.

4. What is a patient advocate? Would these services help Lisa? Explain your answer.

5. What are health disparities? Explain what this term means and provide examples of health disparities.

6. What is NASW, the professional organization of social workers, doing to address health disparities? Find a way you could engage in social action to address health disparities in your local chapter of NASW.

Educational Policy 2.1.6—Engage in Research-Informed Practice and Practice-Informed Research

Research assignments encourage students to engage in research-informed practice and practice-informed research. This helps students become more competent in this area.

1. Research the effect of a serious, life-threatening illness on siblings in the family. Summarize information from three scholarly articles and include the full citation of each article using APA format.

2. Research family belief systems and illness, and analyze how these beliefs can impact a family's involvement in treatment. For example, one person might believe illness is a matter of fate; another might feel that it's under his own control. How could these different ideas influence treatment outcomes and patient behaviors?

3. The United States is the only industrialized country in the western world that does not have a national insurance program. There have been many attempts to pass legislation for universal healthcare and a one-payer system, but they have failed. Research the history of these attempts up to the present.

4. Research health disparities based on race, ethnicity, and socioeconomics as they relate to treatment of childhood cancer.

5. Research alternative medical approaches to treatment of childhood leukemia and summarize three articles that you have found on the subject, citing your sources using APA format.

6. Sometimes confronting issues of death forces families to think about loss, which encourages them to see life with a greater appreciation for the relationships they have, and what they feel is most important. Research the literature on the impact of life-threatening illness on people's lives.

Educational Policy 2.1.7—Apply Knowledge of Human Behavior and the Social Environment

These questions will help students critically apply theories to assess, intervene, and evaluate work with clients.

1. Explain how the social worker, Gloria, uses the theory on individual life cycle and family development in her assessment of Lisa's family.

2. There are times in the interview with Lisa when the social worker identifies defense mechanisms. Which defense mechanisms do Lisa and her husband use and how do you understand what they mean?

3. Narrative theory looks at how people use language to story their experiences. Describe Lisa's style of communicating and the way she uses language and words to tell her story.

4. Were there times when Gloria picked up on Lisa's language and used it during the interview? Describe moments when this happened. What purpose does it serve to use client's words when talking with them in a session?

5. What does the term "locus of control" mean, and how can it affect how a patient looks at her illness and participates in treatment?

6. What does "ego sustaining" mean in psychodynamic theory? How would you apply this term to Gloria's interventions with Lisa?

7. During the conversation with Lisa, Gloria remarks that Lisa is in tune with her daughter's needs. What does it mean for a mother to be attuned to her child? What theory talks about "attunement" and mother-child relationships? Explain this concept in terms of the theory.

Educational Policy 2.1.8—Engage in Policy Practice to Advance Social and Economic Well-Being and to Deliver Effective Social Work Services

These questions are to encourage students to look at the role of policy in social work practice.

1. Many parents may experience financial impacts from their child's lengthy leukemia treatment. What programs are available to help parents with the financial burden of their child's care?
2. Are there any special provisions for children with serious and chronic illness in the Affordable Care Act?
3. What does informed consent mean?
4. Medicare and Medicaid federal healthcare policies are increasingly complex and changing. Explain what these policies are and what makes it important for social workers to know about them when working in the field of medical social work.
5. What are the eligibility requirements for Medicaid in your state?
6. Are children who are disabled or who suffer from long-term chronic illness have any benefits under social security? If so, what are they?

Educational Policy 2.1.9—Respond to Contexts That Shape Practice

Social workers practice in many different settings and may need to familiarize themselves with the particular skills required in each setting. These questions help students to appreciate how context shapes practice and to develop competencies in this area.

1. Throughout the interview Lisa has expressed her anger and frustration with how the medical staff has treated her and how she was told about Emily's diagnosis. What role can the social worker play in improving communication between Lisa and the doctors?,
2. Although the medical doctor is the professional with the authority to diagnose, how can social workers communicate with the patient and families about illness and treatment after the diagnosis has been given? Could any problems occur when the social worker gets involved with sharing medical information?
3. In boxes 66 and 78, Lisa begins to tell Gloria about the best approach to take with her daughter while in the hospital. What is the role of families in collaborating with the medical team and sharing this information? How can it be used?
4. What are some examples of professional challenges or clashes that can occur in medical settings between different disciplines? What are some of the fundamental differences between the disciplines?
5. Explain some different roles that social workers can have in healthcare settings?
6. What are the differences and similarities between clinical healthcare social workers and those who work on an administrative or policy level?
7. What is public health social work? What do public health social workers do? What are the various roles of a public health social worker? What other disciplines work in the field of public health?

8. Hospital chaplains are often called upon to address a patient's religious or spiritual needs. Are they the only ones qualified to have these discussions with patients? What is a social worker's role in discussing these concerns with patients when they come up?

9. Interview a social worker in a pediatric oncology clinic. Learn about this area of practice and how social workers deal with personal feelings about working with very ill children, some of whom will die.

Educational Policy 2.1.10(a)-(d)—Engage, Assess, Intervene, and Evaluate with Individuals, Families, Groups, Organizations, and Communities

These questions are intended to give students practice with engaging, assessing, intervening, and evaluating clients.

1. How would you rate how the social worker opened the session with Lisa and introduced herself?

2. When Gloria explained to Lisa that she wanted to introduce some of the services the hospital offered for newly diagnosed families, Lisa responded, "I guess that's what we are, aren't we?" What do you make of Lisa's reaction? What are some other ways Gloria could have clarified her role that Lisa might have responded to better?

3. There were several times when Gloria used the interviewing skill of normalizing feelings to support Lisa. When did she use this skill and how did Lisa respond to what Gloria shared.

4. What is your opinion of Gloria's attending and listening skills? How did she use body language, facial expressions, and gestures to show that she was listening to Lisa? Were there any times when you were uncomfortable or felt she used nonverbal attending skills too much?

5. Gloria mentioned several services to Lisa when she was providing her with information during the interview. What were they? What services would you refer Lisa to during her daughter's treatment?

6. How might Emily's illness affect Lisa's son? What interventions could Gloria provide for Lisa's son?

7. In the interview, Lisa explains to Gloria the best approach to take with her daughter while she's in the hospital. Do families always know what is best for their children? How do social workers assess the validity of parent's knowledge about their children and use it in their interventions?

8. What are some of the strengths that Gloria identifies in Lisa and acknowledges in the interview? Were there any others that you noticed in the first interview?

9. Gloria talks about Lisa being "in tune" with her daughter's needs. Is there any danger that Lisa could over-identify with her daughter's experience or project her vulnerability onto Emily? How would you assess if this were happening and how would you intervene?

Interviewing Skills Used in the Case of Lisa

Following is a list of interviewing skills used in the interview with Lisa in the order in which they appeared in the transcript.

Introductions

At the beginning of the first meeting with the client, the social worker welcomes the client, tries to make the client comfortable, and tunes in to her own and the client's initial feelings about the first meeting.

Information-Giving

Information-giving means informing the client about the social agency, the problem, and the resources for change. The social worker is knowledgeable about human development and human behavior and can help clients by sharing information that relates to a problem they are experiencing.

Exploration of the Problem

This is a way of gaining more information about a client's situation. When continuing to explore the problem, the social worker listens for underlying feelings about the situation, who else is involved, and what resources are available to help resolve it.

Showing Empathy

The social worker maintains a nonjudgmental stance or remains neutral. The worker need not totally understand the client's situation, but she must show that she is trying to grasp what the client is feeling or experiencing. The social worker might say, "Tell me more about what your experience was" or "I want to understand more about what this means from your perspective."

Summarizing

Part way through the session, and again at the end of the interview with the client, the social worker summarizes what has been said up to that point. This helps reinforce for the client what has been discussed, and ensures that the worker and client both understand the focus of the session.

Questioning

This is a way of gaining more information about a client's situation. There are many different kinds of questions, for example, open- and closed-ended questions and reflexive questions. Questioning is often used in assessment as part of data collection.

Seeking Clarification

At different times during a session, the social worker may ask the client to talk about her perception of a situation in order to make sure she understands the client's point of view. This is also useful when the worker wants to check what she heard the client say, so as not to make the wrong assumption.

Offering Support

When a client shares a story that is painful, it helps when the social worker offers encouragement. By acknowledging the difficulty of the situation, you provide support for the client and allow him to continue the story.

Understanding the Larger Context

The social worker needs to explore the client's family, social system, and larger environment to better understand the problem and its context.

Nonverbal Attending and Listening Skills

The social worker shows that she is listening through her body language, such as eye contact, facial expressions, nodding, and leaning forward. These nonverbal skills help the client elaborate and feel comfortable sharing personal information.

Reassuring Client

At times, the social worker needs to allay a client's anxiety by supporting her efforts to change or accept new resources.

Normalizing Feelings

Clients often believe that their feelings are unacceptable or abnormal. The social worker helps the client see that her feelings are a natural reaction to the given situation.

Putting client's feelings into words: There may be times when a client has difficulty identifying the feeling he wants to express in the narrative. The social worker can help in these situations by responding to the client and using feeling words to summarize what the client has said.

Challenging Moments

There may be times during an interview that are uncomfortable for both the social worker and the client. At these times, the social worker needs to contain both her feelings and the client's feelings. The social worker sits with these feelings and tries to understand them with the client. This can be hard to do, and many beginning social workers want to apologize or avoid pursuing uncomfortable subjects.

Continued Exploration of the Problem

When continuing to explore the problem, the social worker listens for underlying feelings about the situation, who else is involved, and what resources are available to help resolve it.

Exploring underlying feelings: The social worker asks the client her feelings on the subject under discussion.

Acknowledging Strengths

Acknowledging strengths can help clients improve their self-esteem and give them more confidence to take action on their own behalf. It empowers them by providing them with hope and a sense that they have the capacity and resources within themselves to improve their lives and overcome obstacles. When clients feel overwhelmed by difficulties, they may not recognize their positive traits, so the worker pointing them out can bolster the client's self-confidence.

Clarification of the Problem
When sitting with a client, the social worker gathers details that further explain the nature of the problem. This is an ongoing process in which the worker collects new information and keeps an open mind to alternative interpretations and perceptions.

Empowering Client
Providing clients with information and skills to take action on their own behalf, advocate for their rights, and gain access to needed resources.

Prioritizing problems: After the social worker and client have explored the problem(s) the client wants help with, they may need to prioritize what they work on first.

Seeking Client Feedback
When seeking client feedback, the social worker asks for the client's perception of a particular situation, the client–worker relationship, or the helping process.

Reaching for Feelings
This is when the social worker tries to understand what the client is feeling when a particular subject or issue comes up. The social worker may use this skill when she senses that the client is avoiding, or is not in touch with, the feelings related to the current discussion. This may bring out strong reactions in the client, and it is important that the social worker is sensitive to what this means to the client.

Reflecting Back Feelings
This is when the social worker gives a short response back to the client that mirrors the feeling the worker heard the client express. It is used to let the client know the worker is listening.

Reframing
Reframing helps clients see themselves, their problems, and other people from a different perspective, generally in a more positive way.

Next Steps
This is a phrase used when the client and the worker decide what they will work on next, and what actions they can take.

Endings
This is when the social worker prepares the client for the end of the session.

Terms and Definitions

Acute Leukemia

Acute leukemia is characterized by a rapid increase in the number of immature blood cells. This increase causes crowding and means the bone marrow cannot produce healthy blood cells. Immediate treatment is required in acute leukemia due to the rapid progression and accumulation of the malignant cells, which then spill over into the bloodstream and spread to other organs of the body. Acute forms of leukemia are the most common forms of leukemia in children. In lymphoblastic or lymphocytic leukemia, the cancerous change takes place in a type of marrow cell that normally goes on to form lymphocytes, which are infection-fighting immune system cells. Most lymphocytic leukemias involve a specific subtype of lymphocyte, the B cell.

Central Line

Also known as the central venous catheter; a long, thin, flexible tube used to give medicines, fluids, nutrients, or blood products over a long period of time, usually several weeks or more; often inserted in the arm or chest through the skin into a large vein until it reaches another large vein near the heart.

Chemotherapy

Chemotherapy is the general term for any treatment involving the use of chemical agents to stop cancer cells from growing. Chemotherapy can eliminate cancer cells at sites great distances from the original cancer. As a result, chemotherapy is considered a systemic treatment. More than half of all people diagnosed with cancer receive chemotherapy. For millions of people, chemotherapy helps treat their cancer effectively, enabling them to enjoy full, productive lives. http://www.chemotherapy.com/

Chronic Leukemia

Chronic leukemia is characterized by the excessive build-up of relatively mature, but still abnormal, white blood cells. The cells are produced at a much higher rate than normal, resulting in too many abnormal white blood cells, but this typically takes months or years to progress. Whereas acute leukemia must be treated immediately, chronic forms are sometimes monitored for a time before treatment to ensure maximum effectiveness of therapy. Chronic leukemia mostly occurs in older people but can theoretically occur in any age group.

Confidentiality

Confidentiality refers to the safeguarding of the information shared between the social worker and the client that helps to build trust. In the beginning interview, it is important to clarify confidentiality and its limits to the client. The worker should explain that what is said during a session will remain private and only get shared if someone is put in danger. Reassuring clients about confidentiality allows them to express themselves more freely, knowing it is done in a safe environment where their privacy is protected. The worker may say to the client, "What is said here will stay here, unless you or someone else is in danger." If a client is involved in a legal case, the worker will want to explore additional limits of confidentiality.

Defense Mechanism

In psychodynamic theory, defense mechanisms are unconscious and automatic processes that serve to protect people from unwanted or threatening thoughts or feelings.

Denial

This defense mechanism is a refusal to recognize the existence of an anxiety-producing thought, emotion, or conflict.

Displacement

This is another defense mechanism that happens when a person redirects feelings from their original source to an object that is felt to be safe or acceptable. It can happen when families feel overwhelmed and helpless in coping with a life-threatening illness and become angry with the doctors. Since it is difficult to get angry at the illness, the situation, or the person who is sick, a family member may displace this anger onto medical staff.

Family Development

Similar to child and adult development, family development also has predictable stages, although they are not identical for every family and are influenced by racial and ethnic diversity. Understanding the family life cycle helps social workers identify problems that may surface in a family that relate to these stages. Each stage involves a transition and has tasks the family must accomplish before going to the next stage. Some families negotiate the stages more easily than others, and some families may struggle with one stage more than others, for example, families with adolescents. These stages are complicated by divorce, separation, and family illness. Carter & McGoldrick (1999) describe the stages as: leaving home; single young adults; the joining of families through marriage; the young couple; families with young children; families with adolescents; launching children and moving on; families in later life.

Intellectualization

This is a defense mechanism that occurs when a person avoids talking or thinking about feelings, and instead uses more abstract and higher forms of speech, devoid of emotions.

PICC Line

Also known as a peripherally inserted central catheter; a long, slender, small, flexible tube inserted into a peripheral vein, typically in the upper arm, and advanced until the catheter tip terminates in a large vein in the chest near the heart to obtain intravenous access; used for treatments including chemotherapy, nutrition, and prolonged IV antibiotic treatment.

Port

This is the location on the skin where a subcutaneously implanted medical reservoir is inserted into the body.

Projection

This defense mechanism attributes unacceptable thoughts and feelings to another person. For example, if a wife is angry with her husband and uncomfortable sharing this, she believes her husband is angry with her and thus avoids dealing with the feeling herself. She may, in fact, tell others he is angry with her and blame him for these feelings.

Taking a Family System Perspective

Although a social worker may be working with an individual client, the social worker also thinks about the client's family system and how it may contribute to an understanding of the problem at hand. This involves seeing the individual as part of a larger system and examining how the different parts influences each other.

Ventilation

Ventilation is one of the ego sustaining interventions that encourages the client to express feelings about a problem for relief.

References

Abum, G. & Gott, M. (2011). Education given to parents of children newly diagnosed with acute lymphoblastic leukemia: A narrative review. *Journal of Pediatric Oncology Nursing, 28*(5), 300–305.

Ammentorp, J., Mainz, J., & Sabroe, S. (2006). Determinants of priorities and satisfaction in pediatric care. *Pediatric Nursing, 32*, 333–340.

Barbarin, O. A., Sargent, J. R., Carpenter, P. J., Sahler, O. J., Roghman, K. J., Mulhern, R. K., et al. (1995). Sibling adaptation to childhood cancer collaborative study: Parental views of pre- and postdiagnosis adjustment of siblings of children with cancer. *Journal of Psychosocial Oncology, 13*(3), 1–20.

Bendor, S. J. (1990). Anxiety and isolation in siblings of pediatric cancer patients: The need for prevention. *Social Work, 14*(3), 17–35.

Broome, M. E., Knafl, K., Pridham, K., & Freeham, S. (Eds.). (1998). *Children and Families in Health and Illness.* Thousand Oaks, CA: Sage Publications.

Brown, F. H. (1989). The impact of death and serious illness on the family life cycle. In B. Carter & M. McGoldrick (Eds.), *The Changing Family Life Cycle: A Framework for Family Therapy* (2nd ed., pp. 457–482). Boston: Allyn & Bacon.

Brown, R. T., Kaslow, N. J., Hazzard, A. P., Madan-Swain, A., Sexson, S. B., Lambert, R., et al. (1992). Psychiatric and family functioning in children with leukemia and their parents. *Journal of the American Academy of Child and Adolescent Psychiatry, 3*, 495–502.

Carr-Gregg, M. & White, L. (1987). Siblings of pediatric cancer patients: A population at risk. *Medical and Pediatric Oncology, 15*, 62–68.

Carter, B. & McGoldrick, M. (Eds.). (1999). *The Changing Family Life Cycle: A Framework for Family Therapy* (3rd ed.). Boston: Allyn & Bacon.

Cohen, D. S., Friedrich, W. N., Jaworski, T. M., Copeland, D., & Pendergrass, T. (1994). Pediatric cancer: Predicting sibling adjustment. *Journal of Clinical Psychology, 50*(3), 303–319.

Cohen, O. & Levite, Z. (2012). High conflict divorced couples: combining systemic and psychodynamic perspectives. *Journal of Family Therapy, 34*, 287–402.

Combrinck-Graham, L. (1985). A developmental model for family systems. *Family Process, 24*, 39–50.

Cornman, B. J. (1993). Marital conflict: Differential effects on the family members. *Oncology Nursing Forum, 20*, 1539–1566.

Council on Social Work Education. (2008). *Educational Policy and Accreditation Standards.* Alexandria, VA: Council on Social Work Education.

Cousino, M., Hazen, R., Yamokoski, A., Miller, V., Zyzanski, S., Drotar, D., et al; Multi-site Intervention Study to Improve Consent Research Team. (2011). Parent participation and physician-parent communication during informed consent in childhood leukemia. (2011). *Pediatrics, 126*(6), 1544–1551.

Curbow, B., Somerfield, M. R., Baker, F., Wingard, J. R., & Legro, M. W. (1993). Personal changes, dispositional optimism and psychological adjustment to bone marrow transplantation. *Journal of Behavioral Medicine, 16*, 423–466.

Dahlquist, L. M., Czyzewski, D. I., Copeland, K. G., Jones, C. L., Taub, E., & Vaughan, J. K. (1993). Parents with children newly diagnosed with cancer: Anxiety, coping, and marital distress. *Journal of Pediatric Psychology, 18*, 365–376.

Duvall, E. M. (1977). *Marriage and Family Development* (5th ed.). Philadelphia: Lippincott.

Eliott, J. & Olver, I. (2002). The discursive properties of "hope": A qualitative analysis of cancer patients' speech. *Qualitative Health Research, 12*, 173–193.

Eliott, E. M. & Olver, I. (2007). Hope and hoping in the talk of dying cancer patients. *Social Science Medicine, 64*, 138–149.

Fife, B., Norton, J., & Groom, G. (1987). The family's adaptation to childhood leukemia. *Social Science Medicine, 24*, 159–168.

Emanuel, R., Colloms, A., Mendelsohn, A., Muller, H., & Tersta, R. (1990). Psychotherapy with hospitalized children with leukemia: Is it possible? *Journal of Child Psychotherapy, 16*, 21–37.

Falk-Rafael, A. R. (2001). Empowerment as a process of evolving consciousness: A model of empowered caring. *Advanced Nursing Science, 24*, 1–16.

Fitzgerald, T. F., Tennen, H., Affleck, G., & Prantsky, G. S. (1989). The relative importance of dispositional optimism and control appraisals in quality of life after coronary artery bypass surgery. *Journal of Behavioral Medicine, 16*, 25–43.

Fotiadou, M., Barlow, J. H., Powell, L. A., & Langton, H. (2008). Optimism and psychological well-being among parents of children with cancer: An exploratory study. *Psycho-Oncology, 17*, 401–409.

Fournier, M., de Ridder, D., & Benning, J. (2002). Optimism and adaptation to chronic disease: The role of optimism in relation to self-care options of type I diabetes mellitus, rheumatoid arthritis and multiple sclerosis. *British Journal of Health Psychology, 7*, 409–432.

Greenberg, H. S. & Meadows, A. T. (1991). Psychodsocial impact of cancer survival on school-age children and their parents. *Journal of Psychosocial Oncology, 9*(4), 43–56.

Greenberg, J. S., Seltzer, M. M., Krauss, M. W., Chou, R. J. A., & Hong, J. (2004). The effect of quality of relationship between mothers and adult children with schizophrenia, autism or Down syndrome on maternal well-being: The mediating role of optimism. *American Journal of Orthopsychiatry, 74*(1), 14–25.

Gupta, V. B., Willert, J., Pian, M., & Stein, M. T. (2008). When disclosing a serious diagnosis to a minor conflicts with family values. *Journal of Developmental and Behavioral Pediatrics, 29*(3), 231–233.

Hall, J. A., Roter, D. L., & Katz, N. R. (1988). Meta-analysis of correlates of provider behavior in medical encounters. *Medical Care, 26*, 657–675.

Hazen, R. A., Eder, M., Drotar, D., Zyzanski, S., Reynolds, A., Reynolds, C., et al. (2010). A feasibility trial of a video intervention to improved informed consent for parents of children with leukemia. *Pediatric Blood Cancer, 55*, 113–118.

Henderson, J., Goldacre, M., Fairweather, J., & Marcovitch, H. (1992). Conditions accounting for substantial time spent in hospital in children aged 1–14. *Archives of Disease in Childhood, 67*, 83–86.

Hill, R. (1970). *Family Development in Three Generations*. Cambridge, MA: Schenkman.

Hughes, P. M. & Lieberman, S. (1990). Troubled parents: Vulnerability and stress in childhood cancer. *British Journal of Medical Psychology, 65*(1), 53–64.

Kars, M. C., Duijnstee, M., Pool, A., van Delden, J., & Grypdonck, M. (2008). Being there: Parenting the child with acute lymphoblastic leukemia. *Journal of Clinical Nursing, 10*, 1553–1562.

Kazak, A. E., Boyer, B. A., Brophy, P., Johnson, K., Scher, C. D., Covelman, K., et al. (1995). Parental perceptions of procedure-related distress and family adaptation in childhood leukemia. *Child Health Care, 24*, 143–158.

Kazak, A. E. (1997). A contextual family systems approach to pediatric psychology: Introduction to the special issue. *Journal of Pediatric Psychology, 22*, 141–148.

LaMontagne, L. L., Hepworth, J. T., Salisbury, M. H., & Riley, L. P. (2003). Optimism, Anxiety, and coping in parents of children hospitalized for spinal surgery. *Applied Nursing Research, 16*(4), 228–235.

Lavee, Y. & Mey-Dan, M. (2003). Patterns of change in marital relationships among parents of children with cancer. *Health and Social Work, 28*(4), 255–263.

Mack, J. W., Wolfe, J., Cook, E. F., Grier, H. E., Cleary, P. D., & Weeks, J. C. (2009). Peace of mind and sense of purpose as core existential issues among parents with children with cancer. *Arch Pediatric Adolescent Medicine, 163*, 519–524.

Magni, G., Silvestro, A., Tamiello, M. Zanesco, L., & Cerli, M. (1988). An integrated approach to the assessment of family adjustment in acute lymphocytic leukemia in children. *Acta Paedictrica Scandinavica, 75*, 639–642.

Mastroyannopoulou, K., Stallard, P., Lewis, M., & Lenten, S. (1997). The impact of childhood non-malignant life threatening illness on parents: Gender differences and predictors of parental adjustment. *Journal of Child Psychol Psychiatry, 38*(7), 823–829.

Matziou, V., Boutopoulou, B., Chrysotomou, A., Vlachioti, E. Mantziou, T., & Petsios, K. (2011). Parents' satisfaction concerning their child's hospital care. *Japan Journal of Nursing Science, 8*, 163–173.

McGrath, P. (2000). *Confronting Icarus: Psycho-Social Perspectives in Haematological Malignancies.* Aldershot, Hampshire, UK: Ashgate.

McGrath, P. (2001). Findings on the impact of treatment for childhood acute lymphoblastic leukemia on family relationships. *Child and Family Social Work, 6*, 229–237.

McGrath, P. (2002). Beginning treatment for childhood acute lymphoblastic leukemia: Insights from the parents' perspectives. *Oncology Nursing Forum, 29.* 988–996.

McIntosh, B. J., Stern, M., & Ferguson, K. S. (2004). Optimism, coping and psychological distress: Maternal reactions to NICU hospitalization. *Child Health Care, 33*(1), 59–76.

Newby, N. M. (1996). Chronic illness and the family life cycle. *Journal of Advanced Nursing, 23*, 786–791.

Nicholas, D. B., Gearing, R. E., McNeill, T., Fung, K., Lucchetta, S., & Selkirk, E. (2009). Experiences and resistance strategies utilized by fathers of children with cancer. *Social Work in Health Care, 48*, 260–275.

Papadopoulos, L. (1995). The impact of illness on the family and the family's impact on illness. *Counseling Psychology Quarterly, 8*(1), 27–37.

Patistea, E., Makrodimitri, P., & Panteli, V. (2000). Greek parents' reactions, difficulties, and resources in childhood leukemia at time of diagnosis. *European Journal of Cancer Care, 9*, 86–96.

Peck, J. S. & Manocherian, J. (1989). Divorce in the changing family life cycle. In B. Carter & M. McGoldrick (Eds.), *The Changing Family Life Cycle: A Framework for Family Therapy* (2nd ed.). (pp. 335–370). Boston: Allyn & Bacon.

Penn, P. (1983). Coalitions and binding interactions in families with chronic illness. *Family Systems Medicine, 1*, 16–25.

Piemont, L. (2009). The epigenesist of psychopathology in children of divorce. *Modern Psychoanalysis, 34*(1), 97–115.

Robinson, L., Mertens, A. & Neglia, J. (1991). Epidemiology and etiology of childhood cancer. In D. Fernback & J. Vietti (Eds.), *Clinical Pediatric Oncology* (pp. 49–68). St. Louis: Mosby.

Rolland, J. (1989). Chronic illness and the family life cycle. In B. Carter & M. McGoldrick (Eds.), *The Changing Family Life Cycle: A Framework for Family Therapy* (2nd ed.). (pp. 433–456). Boston: Allyn & Bacon.

Rolland, J. (1987). Family illness paradigms: Evolution and significance. *Family Systems Medicine, 5*(4), 482–503.

Salmon, P., Hill, J., Ward, J., Gravenhorst, K., Eden, T., & Young, B. (2012). Faith and protection: The construction of hope by parents of children with leukemia and their oncologists. *The Oncologist, 17*, 398–404.

Shapiro, E. (2002). Chronic illness as a family process: A social-developmental approach to promoting resilience. *JCLP/In Session: Psychotherapy in Practice, 58*(11), 1375–1384.

Souhami, R. & Tobias, J. (1995). *Cancer and Its Management* (2nd ed.). Cambridge, MA: Blackwell Science.

Solomon, M. (1973). A developmental conceptual premise for family therapy. *Family Process, 12*, 179–188.

Thoma, M. F., Hockenbery-Eaton, M., & Kemp, V. (1993). Life changes events and coping behaviors in families of children with cancer. *Journal of Pediatric Oncology Nursing, 10*, 105–111.

Veach, T. A., Nicholas, D. R., & Barton, M. A. (2002). *Cancer and the Family Life Cycle: A Practitioner's Guide.* New York: Brunner-Routledge.

Wittrock, D. A., Larson, L. S., & Sandgren, A. K. (1994). When a child is diagnosed with cancer: Parental coping, psychological adjustment, and relationships with medical personnel. *Journal of Psychological Oncology, 12*(3), 17–32.

7

Practice with Domestic Violence

Nicole: "I'm scared for my life and want to be around for my kids."

Setting: Domestic Violence Shelter

This chapter discusses the case of Nicole, a 25-year-old, single, African-American woman with two young children, who is seeking refuge from her fiancé who has become more threatening to her lately. Nicole describes her fiancé as controlling, jealous, possessive, and both verbally and physically abusive. The turning point for her came when he threatened to kill her if he saw her with a study partner from school. Scared for herself and her children, she decided it was time to leave her boyfriend and go to a domestic shelter recommended by a close friend in whom she had confided.

This case provides rich learning opportunities for practice in the areas of domestic violence, cultural competence and intimate partner violence (IPV), and IPV screening. It allows for a discussion of the characteristics often associated with domestic violence relationships, as well as the resources available to help victims. The literature in this field is extensive, and I have only grazed the surface. I encourage those who want to learn more to visit the website of the Centers for Disease Control and Prevention, National Center for Injury Prevention and Control.

Description of Practice Area

Nicole's case touches on the subject of violence against women and looks at this problem through the lens of gender, race, ethnicity, culture, poverty, and mental health. I cover the importance of screening for intimate partner violence (IPV), and include several interventions appropriate for work with survivors of domestic violence.

Intimate Partner Violence

Intimate partner violence (IPV) is physical violence, sexual violence, threats of physical or sexual violence, or psychological abuse by a current or former partner as defined in the National Intimate Partner and Sexual Violence Survey (NISVS) (Black et al., 2011). The survey, published by the Centers for Disease Control and Prevention, also compiles significant statistics that highlight the seriousness and prevalence of domestic violence in American society. For example, one in three women in the United States have experienced physical violence, rape, and/or stalking by an intimate partner at some point in their lives; one in four women have faced severe physical violence; and overall, there are 12 million victims of IPV each year.

The survey further reveals that IPV starts at an early age: 22.4% of victims first encounter IPV between the ages of 11 and 17, and 47.1% between the ages of 18 and 24 (Black, 2011). In another study, factors that made women more prone to intimate partner violence were economic hardship, maternal economic dependence, and traditional gender beliefs. One in five mothers in this particular study had already been abused when their children were only 3 years old; of those, 26% were Hispanic and 35% were foreign born (Golden et al., 2013), showing a strong link between IPV and ethnicity.

Intimate partner violence might start early for some women, but it can also have life-long health consequences. Researchers have connected IPV with issues related to women's mental health (depression, anxiety, post-traumatic stress disorder [PTSD], suicidal thoughts, and suicidal behavior), physical health (injuries, asthma, diabetes, heart disease, complex pain syndromes), and sexual and reproductive health (unintended pregnancies, pregnancy complications, gynecological disorders, unsafe abortions, and sexually transmitted infections or HIV) (Black, 2011). Many abused women suffer from shame and guilt (Vatner & Bjorkly, 2008) and experience a sense of hopelessness, depression, and loss of control over their lives (Goodwin et al., 2003). Affected women often express concern about their lack of financial resources (Haj-Yahia & Cohen, 2008) and continued unemployment (Goodwin et al., 2003).

Indeed, intimate partner abuse appears to have severe repercussions for women's economic stability. Many victims experience anxiety about their financial security; they have low self-esteem and little belief in their ability to sustain a career (Davies et al., 2008). Economic abuse is also a tactic wielded by abusive partners. In an exploratory study with 120 IPV survivors, 94% dealt with some form of economic abuse; approximately 79% came up against issues of economic control, financially exploitative behaviors, and employment sabotage by their partners (Postmus et al., 2012). The additional burden of economic abuse severely impairs a woman's efforts to separate from the abusive partner and be independent and has implications for practice and policy. Social work advocates working in the field of domestic violence need to offer financial tools to help women become self-sufficient, and policy makers need to create legal strategies that will curtail economic abuse.

Work with Domestic Violence and Relationship Characteristics

Social workers practice in a wide range of clinical settings, such as schools, child welfare agencies, courts, drug and rehabilitation centers, and outpatient mental health clinics, where they may encounter women and children who are victims of domestic abuse. However, many families who are at risk for violence may not be identified or receive appropriate interventions because they are not routinely screened for domestic violence. It is important for social workers to know how to recognize these potentially dangerous situations in order to provide the appropriate referrals and resources for assistance. Regular screening for domestic violence will help to pinpoint women in relationships that may put them and their children most at risk.

It is estimated that one half to two thirds of women in abusive relationships seek out couple's therapy. Even so, they often do not receive needed treatment to address the abuse, again because the problem is not properly identified. A national survey of couple's therapists found that only 4% followed established guidelines for domestic violence screening that would normally include separate interviews and questionnaires for the couple involved (Schacht et al., 2009). Some practitioners may actually use couple's therapy in cases in which it would be counterindicated if they realized there was evidence of violence, whereas other interventions would be more appropriate to address the abuse.

Understanding relationship characteristics has implications for intervention with women who are domestic violence victims. One study outlined four specific types of domestic violence that can be differentiated by partner dynamics: Coercive Controlling Violence, Violent Resistance, Situational Couple Violence, and Separation-Instigated Violence (Johnson & Kelly, 2008). The first pattern, Coercive Controlling Violence, occurs most frequently and is seen in situations with men who exert power and control in the relationship. The second type, Violent Resistance, describes relationships in which the partner responds to violence with violence. Situational Couple Violence refers to isolated times when arguments escalate between a couple and result in violence. The fourth, Separation-Instigated Violence, happens after a separation or divorce; in this case, it is unexpected, there is no prior history of violence, and it is limited to one or two incidents.

Because Coercive Controlling Violence is most common and also describes Nicole's situation in this chapter's case study, I will describe it in more detail. Men who fall into this category often use nonviolent control measures with their partners at first, and then move on to violence, which escalates over time. Control issues are often an important predictor of continued or increased violence in this group of men (Kelly & Johnson, 2008, p. 483). Women whose partners exert power and control in the relationship experience intimidation, threats, isolation, and emotional and physical abuse, often followed by their partners minimizing, denying, or blaming them for such behavior. They report that the psychological abuse has a greater impact on them than the physical; the emotional tolls are fear and anxiety, low self-esteem, depression, nightmares, flashbacks, and hyperarousal (Kelly & Johnson, 2008, p. 483). In a qualitative study of 30 women who had each survived a brutal attack that almost resulted in homicide, the women described their partners as having used stalking, extreme jealousy, social isolation, physical limitations, or threats of violence as means to control them (Nicolaidis et al., 2003, p. 790).

This chapter's client, Nicole, is in a relationship with a man who fits the Coercive and Controlling Violence pattern. Nicole appears anxious in the interview as she describes how her fiancé has become more controlling and threatening. At the beginning of the relationship, she found him charming, as had her family. Over time, his true character appeared to her, although it remained hidden from her family, who still looked up to him. Nicole has come to the domestic violence shelter after a scary argument with her fiancé; he threatened to kill her if she went back to school to work with her study partner, who happened to be male. This was the precipitating event. It helped Nicole know that it was time to leave and get help by admitting herself and her children to the shelter.

Contrary to the commonly held belief that women do not leave abusive situations, research has found that substantial numbers of women do quit abusive partners (Black et al., 2011; McDonald & Dickerson, 2013). A qualitative study of 21 women of various ages, ethnicities, and backgrounds who had left violent relationships found they were living successful, productive, and meaningful lives five or more years after the relationship (McDonald & Dickerson, 2013). From interviews with the women, six themes emerged that encapsulate some of the strategies they used to move on: developing and maintaining self-reliance; learning how to work out problems in a relationship; creating a safe and supportive environment; challenging societal roles and expectations; nurturing the self; and protecting the children (McDonald & Dickerson, 2013, p. 388). The study also found that these women fostered and strongly protected their independence, and they lived with a sense of purpose. Having survived violence, they continued to have difficulty establishing trust and ceding control of their lives to others.

One promising and creative intervention strategy to empower female survivors of domestic violence toward financial security is equine assisted career therapy (EACT). The aim of this program is to help IPV survivors reach career goals through personal development rather than simply offering them a list of job opportunities (Froeschle, 2009, p. 183). It's a type of animal-assisted therapy that uses horses to help clients develop trust and gain mastery over their lives (Macauley & Gutierrez, 2004). Women victims of domestic abuse face career challenges related to low self-esteem and self-efficacy, believing they have no control over their lives, and underdeveloped problem-solving abilities. Equine assisted career therapy enables clients to deal with these obstacles by allowing them to work one-on-one with trained horses and be in charge. The therapy is meant to encourage feelings of empowerment, trust, and self-efficacy; banish feelings of fear and anxiety; and bring confidence in setting appropriate career goals (Froeschle, 2009, p. 185). It offers career counselors an effective, alternative method for domestic violence survivors who need to overcome fear to progress with their career aspirations (Froeschle, 2009, p. 188).

Intimate Partner Violence Screening

Although approximately 35% of all women who go to the emergency room are there for symptoms related to battering, the problem is only identified in 5% of cases (Randall, 1990). The Joint Commission on Accreditation of Health Care Organizations (JCAHO, 1992) has recommended that accredited emergency rooms should have education, policies, and procedures to deal with the problem of domestic violence, but it is not known how often screening takes place and whether cases of domestic violence are all that well documented. This is a critical topic for emergency room social workers to address, since they have the knowledge and skills to identify battered women, intervene on their behalf, and refer them to the appropriate community resources. Boes (2007, p. 320) states, "It should be the role of the ER Social Worker and the main function of the Social Work Department to coordinate and ensure that the ER protocols to identify and treat victims of abuse are effectively utilized."

Statistics show that intimate partner violence (IPV) is a serious threat to women's health and well-being, affecting the lives of 28.8% of women in the United States physically, sexually, or psychologically (Black et al., 2011). But although this kind of violence is a prevalent and urgent health problem, women whose partners abuse them rarely disclose their experiences in health settings (Hegarty & Taft, 2001). Effective prevention and treatment of domestic violence depends on practitioners in healthcare settings successfully identifying these cases as a first step. This requires that medical staff directly involved with patient care is trained to know what to look for and how to implement screening tools. The American Medical Association has supported routine violence screening in healthcare settings since 1984 (AMA, 1984). The Institute of Medicine's Clinical Prevention Services Women Consensus Report also advised universal screening for violence as part of women's preventative services (Institute of Medicine, 2011). This latter recommendation was adopted by the US Department of Health and Human Services, which means that hospitals should offer IPV screening and counseling as part of their basic care for all women.

Applying these recommendations, and making sure IPV screening becomes a standard of good practice, requires careful monitoring and ongoing research with attention given to lessons learned about implementation (Institute of Medicine, 2011; McCaw, 2011; Nelson et al., 2012). Although screening and counseling literature is important, its value depends on practitioners using it routinely. To date, research on the benefits of IPV screening has been insufficient; there's little information available to explain why certain interventions work or fail, how to use screening tools effectively and offer counseling, and how to respond to gaps in providing services once the problem is identified (Decker et al., 2012). Although there is evidence that IPV screening materials have improved since they were first introduced, it is still not clear how often they are implemented and, when used, how successful they are in improving women's health and well-being. For IPV screening to work clinicians using the tool must have knowledge about the IPV problem; understand how screening can help patients who are domestic violence victims; and see a role for themselves putting the screening policy into action (Decker et al., 2012).

Kaiser Permanente, a large health organization in the United States, has an integrated system designed to make use of its entire healthcare environment and assimilate IPV screening into daily, routine care (McCaw, 2011). McCaw describes that the key component of this systems approach is ensuring an effective clinical response to IPV, regardless of where the client receives care. Support staff who regularly do intake and referral ask patients about domestic violence in a sensitive manner to encourage disclosure and know how to respond to abuse when identified. On-site behavioral health workers assess the mental health of patients and begin safety planning as needed. These workers, in turn, are linked to domestic violence agencies in the community for crisis intervention and ongoing advocacy support services. The leadership at each medical center maintains statistics on IPV identification and referral rates, and they communicate their findings quarterly to all hospital and clinic departments (McCaw, 2011).

In another example, social workers in the emergency department of an Australian hospital enacted a domestic violence screening protocol and studied its effectiveness three months after its start. Emergency department staff was trained in an easy-to-use screening tool that asked all women over the age of 16 three questions: Has a partner or significant other made you feel afraid; hurt you physically or thrown objects; or constantly humiliated or put you down (Power, Bahnisch & McCarthy, 2011). The women were asked these questions while alone, without their families or partners present, and when identified, were provided with resources to help them. Results of the study found a dramatic increase in the number of women referred to social workers for domestic and family violence; in the three-month period, there were 32 extra referrals when compared to the previous three-month period, an increase of 213% (p. 545). The study confirmed a pivotal role for social workers in terms of implementation, staff support, referral, and continuity and development of domestic violence screening (pp. 551–552).

Cultural Competence and Intimate Partner Violence

Health officials now recognize that intimate partner abuse is a serious and potentially life-threatening health problem, but there is scant research that looks at the role of race in formulating services for women who are victims of this kind of violence (Cho & Kim, 2012). Survey studies on African Americans, Asian-Pacific Islanders (API), and American Indian/ Alaska Natives have shown significantly higher rates of domestic violence when compared to data on their white counterparts (Tjaden & Thoennes, 2000). However, because many of these studies combine mixed-race respondents into one group, it is difficult to understand specific distinctions between racial and ethnic populations. For the most part, research on domestic violence has failed to look at the disparities that exist between categories of people of color; certain subsets, such as Asian-American women, have been almost entirely ignored. African-American communities are often reported to have high rates of domestic violence, but these numbers might gain perspective from comprehensive research on other racial groups (Hampton et al., 2005).

Violence against women cuts across race, ethnicity, age, socioeconomic status, religion, sexual orientation, and geographic boundaries. Although no population is immune from this problem, it has had a detrimental effect on African-American communities, where women appear to suffer from more severe injuries than other racial and ethnic groups (Bent-Goodley, 2009). It's important, though, to understand these findings in their proper context, looking at issues of class, poverty, and the long-term effects of racism and race-inspired violence against African-American people. West (2005), in explaining the prevalence of violence among African Americans, brings attention to certain factors affecting domestic abuse that "trump" race—poverty, unemployment, and recent migrations.

Until recently, African-American women have underreported domestic violence for a variety of reasons. In one survey, some African-American women believed that speaking out invited more surveillance of their communities and was associated with community betrayal; others felt they had to protect themselves and their communities from stereotypes, in a kind of self-imposed "gag order" to stay silent about IPV (West, 2005). Some women may keep quiet because they don't see their abuse as traumatic, depending on the circumstances of their lives and their past experiences, namely, if they've already been victims of racism, sexism, and early childhood abuse (Bent-Goodley et al., 2010). Also, African-American women may have witnessed violent and traumatic events growing up in their communities (West, 2005), so they might not recognize the seriousness of their abusive relationships.

Again, critics have faulted national domestic violence studies for not capturing accurate statistics on the prevalence of domestic violence in racial and ethnic groups (Cho & Kim, 2012; Kim et al., 2010; Tjaden & Thoennes, 2000). For example, community domestic violence surveys and police reports show more pervasive abuse among Asian-Pacific Island women than do national studies. Kim et al. (2010) explain that this discrepancy stems from cultural beliefs that prevent women from reporting abuse. Western culture emphasizes the central role of the individual, but cultural expectations in other traditions are often quite different. Abused women in API families carry shame that they were not good mothers or wives and deserve the punishment; also these women do not want to malign the abuser's reputation and, instead choose to protect the reputation and dignity of their families out of a need to "save face" (Kim et al., pp. 107–108).

Current research does bear out that minority victims of domestic violence receive fewer IPV services than their white counterparts. In particular, when compared to white victims, racial minorities seem to depend more on informal helping systems and personal social networks than on formal systems and community services (Cho & Kim, 2012). One study on the informal helping networks for women in the African-American community found they included advice giving, financial aid, and assistance with child care and housing, but not emotional supports, because the community perceived IPV as normal and not deserving of attention (Morrison et al., 2006). African-American women have also identified the black church as a source of reassurance, but even this can come with problems; some have reported that pastors are sexist and encourage women to stay with the abuser (Potter, 2007).

Victims from oppressed groups may refrain from using community domestic violence services out of distrust, and because they see them as agents of oppression (Brice-Baker, 1994). Many minority women have come up against discriminatory practices in healthcare, for example, health professionals who are disinterested, judgmental, and disrespectful, and this makes the women less likely to try to find outside help (Bent-Goodley, 2007). Other reasons for not seeking services could include a lack of knowledge about what's available, language obstacles, and a perceived insensitivity to cultural issues (Leong & Lau, 2001; Sue et al., 1991). There is a need for IPV services that are culturally competent, which can in turn uncover the barriers that different racial and ethnic groups face in accessing appropriate resources (Cho & Kim, 2012; Lockart & Danis, 2010).

Culturally competent IPV interventions with African-American women should emphasize the important role of family, religion, and spirituality (Bent-Goodley et al., 2010). From slavery through the Civil Rights movement to the present day, African Americans have found the church a great source of strength, comfort, and refuge (Brice-Baker, 1994; Gillum, 2009). As a result, it seems natural for African-American women to turn to the church for help when dealing with IPV. Black women in unhealthy relationships are more likely to identify prayer and spirituality as significant ways to cope with and heal from their abusive situations (Gillum, 2008, 2009). An ethnographic study of 21 African-American survivors of IPV described how these women used spirituality to recover from their abuse (Taylor, 2004). Based on these studies, service providers working with African-American IPV victims need to include spiritual components in their programs and reach out to the black church in their community for assistance.

Although traditionally black women have relied on their church and pastors for help with abusive relationships, some did not feel supported and instead felt blamed for the problem. These women were encouraged to stay in the relationship and were treated in a paternalistic, sexist way (Gillum, 2008; Potter, 2007). Despite these stories, under the right circumstances the black church can help address domestic abuse and become a positive force in the community to break the cycle of violence. Gillum (2009, p. 7) provides many practical suggestions for how the church can contribute to this transformation. It can educate and train clergy and lay leaders on IPV to raise awareness and facilitate healthy responses; provide instrumental support for women who want to end abusive relationships, like food, clothing, shelter, transportation, employment counseling, child care, and financial assistance; offer spiritual counseling; refer women to trusted community resources; create support groups; and design services for the perpetrators of abuse as well.

Intimate partner violence and spirituality can intersect in important ways for the African-American male perpetrator of abuse. Indeed, IPV services must go beyond just treating the victim if we are to stop the problem. Multiple factors contribute to an understanding of why men become abusive; among them are the complexities of racism and oppression, rap music's use of violent lyrics and images, and desensitization to violence as a result of past experiences of injustice (Hubbert, 2011). Using spirituality in a holistic treatment strategy with abusive African-American men should appeal to them if they are seeking ways to make their spirit whole again.

Hubbert (2011, p. 135) states that, "To transform abusive behavior, research must explore spirituality as the concept of involving personal experiences, frameworks of meaning, purpose, fulfillment of the relationship with self, others, and ultimate reality with the sense of the sacred and divine." This approach to social work practice with African-American men who are abusers will empower individuals and the black community to confront IPV. According to Hubbert, "This can provide the perpetuator with a connection to something higher than one's self and a source of accountability for one's behavior. It can cause the perpetuator to look introspectively at his or her actions, and if they do not line up with the precepts of that higher spiritual authority, then it could be the catalyst for a change in behavior" (2011, p. 136).

There are promising implications here for work with all men, but African-American men in particular, who are often raised with a deep appreciation for the role of religion and spirituality in their lives. An emphasis on spirituality opens up clinical discussions about meaning and purpose in life, our values and how we treat one another. It focuses on what really matters, the importance of relationships and our humanity. It strikes at the core of what religion is about and attempts to bind humanity by the spirit that exists within all of us.

Setting: Domestic Violence Shelter

Domestic violence shelters provide temporary assistance to women and their children during crisis and act as a safety net for women while they get back on their feet and start a new life. They are considered the primary resource for survivors of partner abuse. There are approximately 2,000 community-based shelter programs in the United States, and they offer emergency shelter to 300,000 women and children each year (National Coalition Against Domestic Violence, 2008). These shelters are a safe refuge, protecting abused women from immediate danger. They also provide women with additional services, everything from counseling and support groups to legal, career, financial, and housing assistance. A prime time for positive intervention with victims of abuse is when they are residents of a domestic violence shelter (Johnson & Ziotnick, 2009). Those who do stay in shelters are often more vulnerable and so receive more services than women who do not (Grossman & Lundy, 2011).

Although domestic shelters can provide critical help to women affected by IPV, not all victims seek out shelter. There are many reasons for this. In one study, researchers found that a large proportion of abused women were not knowledgeable about domestic violence services (Fugate et al., 2005). In another, cultural barriers were cited to explain why ethnic minority women did not accept assistance from shelters (West, 2004). And although domestic violence shelters are usually sensitive to culture and provide language services, the staff highlighted in yet another study found it difficult to describe the needs of ethnic minorities and how culture could impact victim experiences (Eisbart, 2011). Shelters would benefit from putting more effort into this subset of their services to improve the care they provide for diverse populations.

Religion and spirituality are other factors that influence whether an abused woman uses a domestic violence shelter or not. Survivors with a more pronounced sense of spirituality were more likely to use faith-based resources than shelters, but these resources did not adequately address intimate partner abuse (Fowler et al., 2011). As mentioned earlier, many pastors in the black church, although a source of support, can also present obstacles for victims when they encourage these women to stay with the abuser (Potter, 2007). One way to increase usage of domestic violence shelters might be to integrate spirituality into the services offered. In a qualitative study of 22 survivors residing in a domestic violence shelter, the women were asked whether spirituality services should be available; they overwhelmingly agreed (Fowler & Rountree, 2009). "Overall, spirituality was viewed by the women survivors as a salient dimension in their lives that provides strength, influences outcomes, and assists in the regulation of positive behavioral responses" (p. 1247).

Although women in domestic violence shelters are in a safe environment, they also soon realize that being homeless (apart from the shelter) has its own set of stresses and challenges. One study found that women did not use their time well while staying at an emergency shelter and spent significant amounts of each day sleeping or resting, in passive recreation, and socializing with other residents (McNulty et al., 2009). It may be easy to criticize these women for such poor use of time, but it is important to understand their unique circumstances and the difficult housing, economic, work, and other personal transitions that they face. Their increased time sleeping or resting may stem from the emotional trauma and depression that itself resulted from their abuse. These women might need greater socialization with other residents because of a common safety policy that does not allow family or friends to know the location of the shelter. And limited exercise could simply be a byproduct of spending more time inside to feel protected from the abuser.

To help this group of women better use their time, the study emphasized the importance of understanding the restrictions on these women due to their living situation and experiences (McNulty et al., p. 189). The study authors also suggested that homeless mothers could benefit from the resources of an occupational therapist. This kind of support person could help them gain insight into how they were spending their time and evaluate how their current routines served (or hindered) their stress management and well-being, which in turn could improve the quality of their lives (McNulty et al., p. 189).

Motivational interviewing has also proved effective with clients who are ambivalent about change. It is often associated with substance abuse treatment, but recently has shown some promise as a strategy for working with women in domestic violence shelters as well. Motivational interviewing engages the client collaboratively, uses reflective listening and empathy, and seeks to enhance the client's motivation to change through use of "change talk" (Walsh, 2014). In an experimental study of 20 women receiving services at a domestic violence shelter, 10 took part in regular counseling, whereas the other 10 women in the experimental group worked with shelter staff trained in motivational interviewing. The study found significant differences between the two groups; the women who experienced motivational interviewing had a greater belief in their ability to end the violence and avoid abusive relationships in the future (Hughes & Rasmussen, 2010).

A new program for sheltered, battered women with post-traumatic stress disorder (PTSD), referred to as HOPE, is a short-term cognitive-behavioral treatment designed to overcome PTSD through empowerment (Johnson & Ziotnick, 2009). It takes the approach that PTSD should be addressed in the context of any issues a woman is currently facing in the shelter, including safety concerns, loss of an intimate relationship, lack of social support, and worry about her children. HOPE focuses on stabilization and safety by teaching women skills to manage their PTSD symptoms, because those symptoms often prevent them from accessing crucial community resources and therefore protecting themselves and their children (Johnson & Ziotnick, 2009, p. 234). The treatment sets the stage for future changes and hopefully prevents PTSD relapse. Although the intervention is planned for women while they are shelter residents, the program is expanding to include additional sessions after the women leave to reinforce newly acquired skills.

Case Description

Nicole is an attractive, well-groomed, intelligent, single 25-year-old African-American woman with two young children. She has come to the Safe Haven Domestic Violence Shelter for protection from an abusive relationship with her fiancé. The precipitating event was an argument between them in which he threatened to kill her if he saw her again at school with her male study partner. He had never said anything like this before, and his words stood out in a defining way that pushed her to get help. In this first meeting, she shares how this threat on her life made her feel "really" scared.

In the first excerpt, the social worker Carol introduces herself and her role to Nicole and wants to find out how Nicole is doing, since she was just admitted to the shelter two hours previously. Nicole keeps good eye contact, and is attentive, responsive, and engaging with Carol. At the outset, Nicole appears sad, has a flat affect, and speaks in a monotone voice. Although she seems uncertain in the beginning as to why she is at the shelter, this soon changes as Nicole opens up about her story of abuse. Notice her becoming more animated and at times agitated when she talks about unfair and abusive treatment she's experienced. As you watch the video, be aware of moments when Nicole nods in agreement with Carol and shows anger at her fiancé's efforts to limit her activity and keep her home. In defiance to this, she says that she's only 25 and too young to stay home all the time. Very early on, Nicole demonstrates strong character, resilience, and many ego strengths. For example, she questions what her fiancé says to her, resists his attempts to control her, and is taking action to make a better life for herself and her children.

First Excerpt from Transcript and Process Recording

Content	Observation/Reflection	Analysis of Intervention: Theories and Practice
1. Carol: Hi Nicole. My name is Carol Dorr and I'm the intake coordinator here at Safe Haven. I wanted to welcome you here and see how you're doing. I understand you've been here two hours now. I wanted to touch base with you to see how you're doing.	Nicole appears well dressed and groomed. She seems anxious as we begin the interview. Coming to a domestic violence shelter looks like a new situation for her and must be difficult.	Practice: Engagement. Communication skills: Introduction, reaching for feelings.
2. Nicole: Right now, I'm doing alright. I'm a little worried right now and I don't really know what I'm doing here. I guess I'm doing alright.	I see this reaction a lot. After taking this big step, she may be questioning being here. She may feel the need to minimize or deny the seriousness of the problem at first.	Theory: Psychodynamic, defense mechanisms
3. Carol: Tell me a little bit about how you came here today. What was happening before you came?	She is keeping good eye contact.	Theory: Narrative, inviting her to tell her story. Communication skills: Exploration of the problem.
4. Nicole: It's a long story, but, right before I came here, I had an argument with my fiancé. He said something that really scared me. He's never said it before, but I thought it was time to come here and get help.	She seems unsure of herself and has a sad affect as she begins to tell her story with a somewhat monotone voice. I wonder what he said that really scared her. Whatever it was, it seemed to be a turning point for her to leave the relationship. It was significant and made her realize she had to get help.	Theory: Narrative, telling a story with something new in it.
5. Carol: Can you tell me more about what he was saying to you?		Theory: Narrative, encouraging her to tell her story. Communication skills: Continued exploration of the problem

(Continued)

Content	Observation/Reflection	Analysis of Intervention: Theories and Practice
6. Nicole: Today he told me he was mad. I was studying at the library, because I'm in school, with a study partner who was a male. I told him he was only a study partner. I have no other dealings with him. We need study partners, and he became very upset when I told him I was with my study partner. He told me he would kill me if I ever went back to school to study with my study partner. He doesn't even want me in school anyways.	This sounds like a familiar pattern with an abusive partner who is jealous and controlling. As she talks about this incident, she seems more agitated.	Theory: Psychodynamic theory, object relations, insecure attachment
7. Carol: How come?	I think I was too quick to follow up on her last statement about his not wanting her in school. I jumped right over her saying he would kill her. I think it would have been better to explore his threat to kill her and his violence history. Is this just a threat or is it real? Does he have access to weapons or other means to seriously hurt her? Is there something I am afraid of exploring here?	Practice: Self-reflection. Communication skills: Questioning
8. Nicole: I don't know why. He said there's no reason for me to be in school and that he'll take care of me. He said there's no reason to go back to school because I have two kids.	As Nicole says this, she seems to show with her facial expressions and nonverbal behavior that what he is saying is not right. This also fits with the pattern of abusive men who want to keep their partners dependent on them and restrict any effort to be more autonomous and independent.	Theory: Psychodynamic, object relations, attachment
9. Carol: How old are your children?	I am torn here. I want to know more about her children, but I also want to ask her what she thinks about what he tells her about school.	Theory: Family systems. Practice: Data collection, self-reflection. Communication skills: Questioning.
10. Nicole: My older son is not his, but he's 4, and my daughter's three, and she is his. He wants me to stay home, but I'm tired of staying home. I'm young. I'm only 25. I don't want to stay in the house all the time. When we first got together it wasn't like that, and now he gets angry when I want to do better things for myself.	I hear so many strengths in how she questions the relationship and his attempts to control her. She has a strong voice and can assert her needs. She doesn't want to stay in the house all the time.	Theory: Family systems. Psychodynamic, ego strengths. Practice: Assessment, identifying strengths.

(Continued)

Content	Observation/Reflection	Analysis of Intervention: Theories and Practice
11. Carol: Has he threatened you before?		Practice: Communication skills, Continued exploration of the problem.
12. Nicole: He's never told me he would kill me, but in the past he's hit me. He's pulled my hair. I don't know what I did to deserve this.	This is an important distinction (between saying he would kill her now and hitting her in the past) and helps to understand what made her seek help now. It sounds like the situation is getting worse. It's good she didn't wait any longer, and this demonstrates her strength to seek help now. This is a good sign that she is questioning the abuse. She seems really sad when she says she doesn't know what she did to deserve this.	Theory: Cognitive, identifying distinctions that supports motivation to change. Psychodynamic, ego psychology, projection. Practice: Assessment, identifying strengths.

Post-Excerpt Comments

In the first excerpt, although Nicole begins with uncertainty about why she's at the shelter, it quickly becomes clear why she has come. She identifies the moment when she realized her relationship was dangerous, enough so that she had to leave for her safety. Her fiancé said something he had never said before, and it scared her. He threatened to kill her if he saw her at school again with her male study partner. Nicole's instinct to leave the fiancé shows good judgment and demonstrates many ego strengths. She displays insight into how this is an unhealthy relationship with unreasonable demands on her to stay home. At the end of the excerpt Nicole says she doesn't know what she did "to deserve this," but at the same time, it appears she can almost answer her own question; that, in fact, she does not deserve to be treated in this way.

Reflection of First Process Recording and Discussion of Practice Skills and Theories Used in Intervention
Communication Skills

The social worker uses various communication skills during the intervention and reflection upon the client's statements. Follwoing is a list of these skills, their definitions, and the boxes in which they were used.

Box 1
Introduction: At the beginning of the first meeting with the client, the social worker welcomes the client, tries to make the client comfortable, and tunes in to her own and the client's initial feelings about the first meeting.

In box 1, Carol introduces herself and her role to Nicole. She observes that Nicole is anxious and checks in with her to ask how she's doing.

Box 1

Reaching for feelings: This is when the social worker tries to understand what the client is feeling when a particular subject or issue comes up. The social worker may use this skill when she senses that the client is avoiding, or is not in touch with, the feelings related to the current discussion. This may bring out strong reactions in the client, and it is important that the social worker is sensitive to what this means to the client.

In box 1, Carol tunes in to what Nicole is feeling at the very beginning of the interview and picks up that she may be anxious. She addresses this by asking Nicole directly what she is feeling.

Box 3

Exploration of the problem: This is a way of gaining more information about a client's situation. When continuing to explore the problem, the social worker listens for underlying feelings about the situation, who else is involved, and what resources are available to help resolve it.

In box 3, Carol explores the problem that brought Nicole to the shelter. She asks Nicole what was happening before she came for help.

Boxes 5, 11

Continued exploration of the problem: When continuing to explore the problem, the social worker listens for underlying feelings about the situation, who else is involved, and what resources are available to help resolve it.

In box 5, Carol follows up on what Nicole has started to tell her about the argument with her fiancé in which he verbalized something that scared her. She asks Nicole what her fiancé said that made her realize she had to get help.

In box 11, Carol returns to the event that scared Nicole and precipitated her coming to the shelter. She asks Nicole if her fiancé had ever threatened her before.

Boxes 7, 9

Questioning: Questioning is a way of gaining more information about a client's situation. There are many different kinds of questions, for example, open- and closed-ended questions and reflexive questions. Questioning is often used in assessment as part of data collection.

In box 7, Carol asks Nicole why her fiancé doesn't want her attending school. By posing this question, she hopes to learn what Nicole thinks her fiancé's reasons are for keeping her from school, and if she understands what the true motivation might be.

In box 9, Carol chooses to ask Nicole about the ages of her children, because Nicole referenced them at the end of box 8. After she asks this question, Carol wonders if this was the best line of inquiry. It might have been better to explore what Nicole thought about her fiancé's statement that she had no reason to go to school because she had children.

Other Practice Skills Used

Box 1

Engagement: Engagement is the initial step in the problem-solving method and involves building a relationship and an alliance with the client and defining the problem.

In box 1, Carol engages with Nicole by welcoming her to the shelter and showing concern for her. She acknowledges that Nicole has been at the shelter for two hours and wonders what her experiences have been so far.

Boxes 7, 9

Self-reflection: The skill of self-reflection is an important part of professional practice. Social workers are expected to engage in personal reflection and self-correction to assure continual professional development (CSWE, 2008). Practitioners need to understand themselves on a deep level that includes deciphering their values, reactions to others, the influence of family-of-origin patterns, and basic assumptions about culture and difference. It requires setting aside time to ponder the meaning of clinical work—how our personal experiences and biases may trigger reactions to clients that are unwarranted. We learn a lot about ourselves from doing practice; sometimes, we need outside help to sort out issues that arise during our work.

In box 7, Carol questions how she responded to Nicole. She wonders what made her skip over the most important part of what Nicole had just said, about her fiancé's threat to kill her if her saw her at school with her male study pattern. Carol realizes she needs to understand why she didn't explore the threat at this moment in the interview, especially because it was the event that triggered Nicole's coming to the shelter.

In box 9, Carol reflects on her response to what Nicole had just said in box 8. She is aware that there are different paths a conversation can take based on what you choose to pay attention to, and this directs where the discussion will go next. In box 9, Carol hoped to get more information on Nicole's children, but she also wanted to know what Nicole thought about her fiancé restricting her from attending school. She keeps this in the back of her mind and will go back to it at some point in the interview.

Box 9

Data collection: In the data collection stage, the social worker explores the problem in more depth. This involves getting information from multiple sources about the client's life and situation, and about the social systems that may impact the problem. Sources might include client records, bio/psycho/social history, self-assessment tools, and other professionals who have worked with the client.

In box 9, Carol begins to obtain information about Nicole's children and learns that she has two kids, a son who is 4 and a daughter who is 3.

Boxes 10, 12

Assessment: Assessment is a multidimensional concept that can be approached in many ways using different theoretical lenses. It is an active and ongoing process between the client and social worker using relevant theories and knowledge to help make meaning out of the client's situation. Assessment leads to an understanding of the problem, what causes it, the solutions, and it has implications for intervention.

Identifying strengths: During assessment, social workers listen for client strengths they can use to help solve certain problems. As clients talk about their situation and their stories unfold, workers identify strengths that are embedded in the narrative. By focusing on positive attributes and characteristics, workers shift the focus away from deficits to inquiring about and affirming strengths.

In box 10, as Carol listens to Nicole, she identifies strengths in the way Nicole tells her story that demonstrate a high level of ego functioning. In this passage, Nicole describes how her fiancé wants her to stay home all the time, but that she is tired of doing this. She says she is only 25 and wants to do better things for herself and her children. In relaying this message, she is assertive, exhibiting more affect and anger about her fiancé's attempt to limit and control her. This reaction shows good judgment and a strong sense of identity.

In box 12, Carol again recognizes Nicole's ability to question her fiancé's actions. When Nicole laments that she doesn't know what she did to deserve his abusive treatment, she seems to be really saying that she didn't do anything wrong. There is a rational and self-confident part of her that understands it is her boyfriend whose behavior is inappropriate, not hers.

Theories Used in Intervention

Psychodynamic Theory

Boxes 2, 10

In box 2, Carol notices Nicole's uncertainty about why she came to the shelter, and interprets this as a tendency to minimize or deny the problem. Denial is a defense mechanism in ego psychology that negates an important aspect of reality until the person is ready to deal with the threat.

In box 10, Nicole demonstrates many ego strengths and good ego functioning, for example, awareness of her external world, appropriate thought processes, and good judgment. She is able to assess her situation accurately and realize it is wrong for her fiancé to try to keep her at home all the time and prevent her from doing things to better her life.

Narrative Theory

Boxes 3, 4, 5

In box 3, Carol invites Nicole to tell her story by asking what brought her to the shelter. Carol says as little as possible, using an open-ended question, to encourage Nicole to talk about her situation freely with as little interruption or influence as possible. Carol wants to understand how Nicole makes meaning of her experience and interprets her relationship with an abusive partner.

In box 4, it is interesting that Nicole begins by saying, "It's a long story," framing her response using a narrative lens. The social worker is invited to listen to her story. Describing experiences through story and particular moments that emphasize the event engages the listener through the use of language and a plot. Nicole starts to build the story, and the social worker is drawn in and wants to learn more. When Nicole recounts, "He said something that really scared me," Carol is curious and asks Nicole what it was that frightened her.

Box 5 is a continuation of the story that began in the previous box. Carol wants to know more about the story—particularly what Nicole's fiancé said that really scared her. Carol encourages Nicole to proceed with her story by inquiring about this.

Family Systems Theory
Boxes 9, 10
In box 9, Carol asks questions about the ages of Nicole's children to collect data for her assessment of the family. The life cycle needs of families with young children are important factors to consider in domestic abuse cases, since many women feel isolated and more dependent on their partners with kids of preschool age.

In box 10, Nicole explains that she has two children, a son who is 4 that she had with another man, and a 3-year-old daughter fathered by her fiancé. The family system appears to be closed and rigid; her fiancé wants to isolate her at home to keep her from attending school or going out with friends. He is jealous of her outside relationships and tries to control her with both physical and verbal threats. Although his goal is to keep Nicole dependent on him in an enmeshed relationship, she is beginning to realize this is an unhealthy situation and wants to separate from him.

Cognitive Theory
Box 12
In box 12, Nicole talks about times when her fiancé hit her and pulled her hair. When she says she doesn't know what she did to deserve this, she seems to be making a point that she didn't deserve to be treated this way. This is an example of her making a cognitive distinction between deserving and not deserving to be abused, the assumption being the latter. When looking at abusive behavior from a rational point of view, it is clear that no one deserves to be harmed in this way.

Second Excerpt from Transcript and Process Recording
Pre-Excerpt Comments
Nicole often speaks in story form, an engaging style of narrative that pulls Carol in, so that she herself can feel what Nicole has gone through in this battering relationship. In box 14, Nicole shares more about the abuse she's experienced at the hands of her fiancé and seems comfortable opening up with Carol, who supports her. As the conversation between them continues, Nicole's stories build her case, explain her reasons for leaving her fiancé, and clearly justify her actions. However, her family still loves him and can't see through the show he puts on for them, and she is scared she won't get their support to break off the engagement.

Throughout the second excerpt Carol uses ego-sustaining interventions by showing support and empathy, offering reassurance and information, acknowledging strengths, and normalizing Nicole's feelings. Nicole is vulnerable and seems appreciative of Carol's sensitivity to her situation. Several times, Nicole nods in agreement with Carol's positive feedback to her. Carol engages well with Nicole and is developing trust in the relationship.

Content	Observation/Reflection	Analysis of Intervention: Theories and Practice
13. Carol: You haven't done anything to deserve this. This is frequently what a lot of women who have been abused feel. That they must have done something to cause the abuse, but that's not true. It's not your fault. Can you tell me a little bit about how long it's been going on or when it got started?	I notice that Nicole nods her head in agreement with what I say and knows intuitively that she didn't cause the abuse.	Theory: Psychodynamic, ego sustaining. Cognitive, cognitive restructuring, confronting assumptions. Communication skills: Reassuring client, information-giving, normalizing feelings, continued exploration of the problem.
14. Nicole: At first he wanted to go through my phone and say I was with other guys, but I was with him every day. The one minute I go to the corner store he tells me I was talking to guys at the corner store. It's not my fault guys are in front of the store. One day he thought I was out with some guys when I was out with my friends and he slapped me. I was crying and I told him I was going to leave him. He told me I would never leave him and he slapped me in my face. That was the first time. I can't take it anymore. I can't continue to go through that.	Here she expresses how her fiancé is overly jealous for no reason. She knows his behavior is irrational and doesn't make any sense. This is common for abusive men to be overly jealous and imagine things. She's upset, can't take it anymore, and seems to be at a turning point.	Theory: Narrative Theory; Psychodynamic, ventilation; Cognitive theory.
15. Carol: Of course not. I'm glad you decided to call us. It sounds like you've been suffering in this relationship for quite a while now.	She has been through a lot with this man. She is scared for a reason. I hope she is ready to make a permanent change and not feel the need to go back to him. It sounds like she is ready to leave him.	Theory: Psychodynamic, sustainment. Communication skills: Empathy, offering support, reflecting back feelings
16. Nicole: Yeah. I'm just really scared to leave him right now, because my family knows we're engaged and I don't know how we're going to break this off. Everyone loves him. He puts on a show like he's so nice for everyone else. That's who he was when I first met him, but I don't know what's going on.	She looks worried about her family's reaction as she says this. This happens all too often, when families build up an attachment to the boyfriend, having no idea of how abusive the situation is. This makes it even harder for the women to leave without the family support that is so important.	Theory: Psychodynamic, Ventilation; Family systems.

(Continued)

Content	Observation/Reflection	Analysis of Intervention: Theories and Practice
17. Carol: This is frequently a pattern with abusers. They can be very charming on the outside and very abusing at home. Your describing of him being controlling and possessive is also common to abusers. He seems to be really fitting into this pattern.		Theory: Cognitive, education; Psychodynamic, false self. Practice: Communication skills: information-giving, normalizing feelings.
18. Nicole: He always degrades me. He tells me that I'm fat and I don't do anything. That's why I went back to school, but that's not even good enough for him. I just want to do good for me and my kids. I want to see us have a good life. I really want to stay with him, because I want the proper environment for my children. I don't want men in and out of their lives but I can't do it anymore.	She is agitated again as she talks about her fiancé's behavior. Her speech is more pressured. She shows good ego strengths and resilience, going back to school and wanting a better life for her and her children. Although she wants to stay with him, it seems she won't at any cost to her.	Theory: Psychodynamic, ventilation, assessing ego functions, projection. Practice: Assessment, identifying ego strengths.
19. Carol: It seems that you have many strengths. I'm impressed you're going back to school, in spite of the pressures from him, and continuing to want to do what's good for you and your family and your children. And that's very important. What often happens is the abusers try to put down their partners so the partners feel weak and helpless and dependent. You have a real strength because you're trying to get out of that relationship and better yourself to support your family. That's really wonderful	She nods her head in agreement again and appreciates the support I am giving her. I am encouraged she will be able to change her life and get out of this relationship.	Theory: Psychodynamic, sustainment, assessing ego functioning. Cognitive, education. Practice: Communication skills: offering support, acknowledging strengths, normalizing feelings, giving client feedback
20. Nicole: I love my kids		
21. Carol: I can see that you must be a very good mother.	I can tell she is a loving mother and this will be a motivator for her to get out of this abusive relationship.	Psychodynamic: Sustainment; Communication skills: Offering support, acknowledging strengths.
22. Nicole: Yes		
23. Carol: How are the children doing? Have they been hit by him or abused by him or observed your being hit?		Theory: Family systems. Practice: Data collection. Communication skills: continued exploration of the problem.
24. Nicole: I don't think they've ever observed me being hit, but I can't say they've never heard him screaming at me. They live with us. I hope not. My older son, sometimes I feel he's even meaner to him, his name is Terrell. Sometimes I feel he treats Terrell so mean.	She seems upset with how her fiancé is treating her son. I wonder how much the children have observed. It is often more than parents know.	Theory: Family systems

Post-Excerpt Comments

At the end of the second excerpt, Nicole describes her concerns for her children. She has stayed with her fiancé because she doesn't want to expose them to different men coming in and out of their lives. Although she doesn't think her children have witnessed his physical abuse, she realizes that they have probably heard her fiancé screaming at her. In box 24, Nicole finishes by saying that she is worried that her fiancé is "mean" to her son, Terrell, who is not his son. At some point it will be important to understand what it means when Nicole says her fiancé treats her son "so mean." This has implications for the involvement of protective services for the children.

Refelection of Second Process Recording and Discussion of Practice Skills and Theories Used in Intervention

Communication Skills

Box 13

Reassuring client: At times, the social worker needs to allay the client's anxiety by supporting her efforts to change or accept new resources.

In box 13, Carol reassures Nicole that she has done nothing to deserve her fiancé's abusive behavior. Although violent men may try to blame certain actions on their victims, it is not usually the victim's fault.

Boxes 13, 17

Information-giving: Information-giving means informing the client about the social agency, the problem, and the resources for change. The social worker is knowledgeable about human development and human behavior and can help clients by sharing information that relates to a problem they are experiencing. For instance, a mother may complain that her 4-year-old daughter is misbehaving and not understand how the birth of a new sibling has affected the older daughter.

In box 13, Carol tells Nicole about a common pattern of abusive relationships, in which the victims are often blamed for problems and wrongly take responsibility for the abuse when it is not their fault.

In box 17, after listening to Nicole's experiences with her fiancé, Carol helps Nicole to understand another pattern of domestic violence, when the abuser tries to charm the family into thinking he is someone he is not. Carol explains that this is often an attempt to isolate the victim from getting family support to leave the relationship.

Boxes 13, 17, 19

Normalizing feelings: Clients often believe that their feelings are unacceptable or abnormal. The social worker helps the client see that her feelings are a natural reaction to the given situation.

In box 13, Carol reassures Nicole that the abuse is not her fault by explaining the patterns of abusive relationships to normalize her feelings.

Again in boxes 17 and 19, Carol describes common patterns of abuse to normalize what Nicole feels. In box 17, Carol talks about how it is typical for the batterer to charm a woman's family to prevent them from supporting the victim's attempts to leave the relationship. In box 19, Carol explains how the abusive partner often degrades a woman, making her feel weak and helpless in an effort to keep her dependent on him.

Box 15

Showing empathy: The social worker maintains a nonjudgmental stance or remains neutral. The worker need not totally understand the client's situation, but she must show that she is trying to grasp what the client is feeling or experiencing. The social worker might say, "Tell me more about what your experience was" or "I want to understand more about what this means from your perspective."

In box 15, Carol shows empathy for Nicole by telling her that she must have been suffering in this relationship for a while, and that she understands why Nicole can't go through this anymore.

Boxes 15, 19, 21

Offering support: When a client shares a story that is painful, it helps when the social worker offers encouragement. By acknowledging the difficulty of the situation, you provide support for the client and allow him to continue the story.

In boxes 15, 19, and 21 Carol offers support to Nicole for what she has been through in this relationship and shows that she understands Nicole's need to leave. Carol does this in box 19 by saying she is impressed with Nicole's efforts to make a better life for herself and her children. Nicole nods her head in agreement as Carol says this and seems to appreciate her encouragement. In box 21, Carol offers emotional support by observing that Nicole must be a very good mother, to which Nicole responds in box 22 by saying, "yes."

Box 15

Reflecting back feelings: This is when the social worker gives a short response back to the client that mirrors the feeling the worker heard the client express. It is used to let the client know the worker is listening.

In box 15, Carol reflects back to Nicole what she heard her say about her experiences with abuse and acknowledges how much she has suffered in this relationship.

Boxes 19, 21

Acknowledging strengths: The social worker focuses on the client's positive attributes and characteristics, shifting the focus away from deficits to inquiring about and affirming strengths. Acknowledging clients' strengths can also serve to empower clients. It can help to improve their self-esteem and give them more confidence in themselves to take action on their own behalf. It provides them with hope and communicates to them that they have capacity and resources within themselves to improve their lives and overcome obstacles.

In box 19, Carol begins by telling Nicole that she has exhibited many strengths, including going back to school in spite of her fiancé's attempts to block her from improving her life. Carol also points out how courageous she has been by doing what is best for her and her family and not submitting to her fiancé's pressures.

In box 21, Carol acknowledges that Nicole must be a good mother based on Nicole's genuine concern for her children.

Box 19

Giving client feedback: This is when the social worker finds an opportunity to provide the client with information about his behavior and its effect on him or on other people. It can prove difficult, because the client may not want to hear or accept what the social worker is saying.

In box 19, Carol gives Nicole feedback that she is impressed with her going back to school to improve her life in spite of her fiancé's attempts to stop her. She also lets Nicole know how she appreciates her efforts to resist her fiancé's roadblocks and how she instead continues to do what is best for her and her children.

Box 23

Continued exploration of the problem: When continuing to explore the problem, the social worker listens for underlying feelings about the situation, who else is involved, and what resources are available to help resolve it.

In box 23, Carol probes the children's experience of abuse by asking Nicole how they are doing. She explores whether the children have been hit or have observed her being hit by the fiancé. This is vital information that will determine whether there is a need for protective services for the children.

Theories Used in Intervention

Psychodynamic Theory

Boxes 13, 14, 15, 16, 17, 18, 19, 21

In boxes 13, 15, 19, and 21, Carol continues to build the relationship with Nicole by using ego-sustaining techniques to support her. Carol reassures Nicole that the abuse is not her fault and normalizes Nicole's feelings by providing information about the typical patterns and strategies abusive men use to control and exert power over women. Carol also finds opportunities to emphasize Nicole's strong ego strengths that will allow her to escape an abusive relationship and make a better life for her and her family.

In boxes 14, 16, and 18, Nicole talks about incidents when her fiancé degraded her, exhibiting behavior that was both controlling and abusive. Sharing these experiences provides Nicole with an outlet to ventilate and express her outrage at how she has been treated. She also conveys anger at how her fiancé has manipulated her family into thinking he is charming, and she worries that this tactic will make it harder to garner support from her family to leave him.

In box 17, Carol interprets the fiancé's attempts to charm Nicole's family and put on a show for them as examples of his "false self." This refers to a person going out of his way to please and compliment others to get them to like him.

In box 18, Carol listens to Nicole speak of times when her fiancé made degrading comments to her, and thinks about what this means in terms of his ego development. From what she is learning from the interview with Nicole, it appears that he is functioning at a much lower level than Nicole. He seems to have a faulty perception of his external world, poor judgment and impulse control, low self-esteem, immature defense mechanisms, and interpersonal deficits. Often batterers project their poor image of themselves onto their victims. Because Nicole has a more solid identity and sense of self, she rejects his verbal attacks and knows there is no basis for his criticisms. In box 19, Carol acknowledges Nicole's ego strengths, demonstrated by her going back to school, leaving an abusive situation, and wanting a better life for her and her children.

Cognitive Theory
Boxes 13, 14, 17, 18, 19

In box 13, Carol uses cognitive theory to confront the fiancé's false accusations and attempts to blame Nicole for the abuse. Nicole did nothing to deserve the abuse. When Nicole relates instances when her fiancé was overly jealous in box 14, imagining her talking or being with other men, Carol understands how these are examples of cognitive distortions and faulty assumptions. She plans to help Nicole re-examine these statements from a realistic and rational perspective.

Some cognitive interventions use education and skills training to provide clients with information to help them understand and cope with problems they are facing. In box 17, Carol explains to Nicole that her fiancé fits the pattern of many abusive men who charm their partners' families to make it more difficult for victims to leave.

In box 18 Nicole complains about how her fiancé degrades her, saying she doesn't "do anything." He doesn't recognize her return to school as worthwhile; nothing she does seems good enough for him. Nicole is questioning her fiancé's verbal attacks with Carol and beginning to see that they are not rational. In box 19, Carol points out to Nicole that she has many strengths, for example not submitting to her fiancé's attempts to control her. She is proving her fiancé wrong by actively making changes to improve her life.

Narrative Theory
Box 14

Nicole consistently uses stories to talk about her abusive relationship, which Carol sees again in box 14, when Nicole references incidents when her fiancé was overly jealous and lashed out at her. It is easy to engage and listen to Nicole's stories, which pull you in, make you want to hear more, and help you understand her lived experience better.

Third Excerpt from Transcript and Process Recording

Pre-Excerpt Comments

The third excerpt starts out with Carol supporting Nicole's decision to leave the abusive relationship that puts her children at risk. Carol is cognizant of the need to make a referral to Child Protective Services that will provide additional resources for Nicole and her family. She will discuss this with Nicole at their next meeting so as to not overwhelm her with too much information in one day. In this excerpt Nicole discloses the "worst moment" she encountered with her fiancé. She talks about how it made her "really, really scared."

Content	Observation/Reflection	Analysis of Intervention: Theories and Practice
25. Carol: That's another good reason for your leaving. For yourself and your children, because you don't want them to have to be victims of his anger and his abuse. I think that's good that you came here. In terms of the history of the abuse, can you tell me a moment that was the worst that you had?	I notice Nicole becomes teary here. Her wish to protect her children is strong and will reinforce her need to leave. Carol is aware that she will need to talk to Nicole soon about the importance of involving Child Protective Services as another resource to help her separate from the abuse. When I ask Nicole about her worst moment, I am eliciting another story to understand her experience with more depth.	Practice: Data collection; Assessment, identifying need for referral to child protective services, identifying strengths. Communication skills: Elaboration.
26. Nicole: I was in the shower one day and he came in the house. I was in the best mood ever, and I get out of the shower and said, "Hi honey, how are you today?" He said, "Where have you been today." I said, "Sweetheart, I called and you didn't answer the phone. I was in the shower." He said, "I just called and you didn't answer," and I said, "I was in the shower." He started to hit me and my head hit the tub. It was crazy and I was really scared, but the kids weren't home.	It's hard to hear the stories but it helps to reinforce the need to leave. Although I might like to avoid the details, I know this is important for her to do. Her emotions get re-ignited in the telling of the story and this makes the abuse and threat to her and her children very real.	Theory: Narrative, telling the story of her abuse. Psychodynamic, ventilation. Cognitive, appraisal. Practice: Self-reflection.
27. Carol: You must have been very scared.		Theory: Psychodynamic, sustainment. Communication Skills: Empathy, reflecting back feelings.

(Continued)

Content	Observation/Reflection	Analysis of Intervention: Theories and Practice
28. Nicole: I was really, really scared.	She must be re-living the experience as she shares the story.	Theory: Psychodynamic, ventilation.
29. Carol: Have you ever needed to go to the hospital?		Practice: Data collection. Communication skills: Continued exploration of the problem.
30. Nicole: No, I never went to the hospital. I made up excuses for my bruises and handled it myself by putting ice on the bruises and sun glasses.	She's made a habit of hiding the abuse from others. This may represent some shame she feels about what happened.	Theory: Psychodynamic, defense of denial.
31. Carol: It must be horrible.	She's been through a lot.	Theory: Psychodynamic: Sustainment. Communication skill, Empathy, being authentic and genuine.
32. Nicole: It is really bad.	As she talks about the abuse, she becomes stronger in her assessment of how bad the situation is. This will help her be more determined to get out of the relationship.	Theory: Psychodynamic: Ventilation.

Post-Excerpt Comments

In the third excerpt, Nicole tells Carol the circumstances around her "worst moment" of abuse and recreates the dialogue she had with her fiancé to describe what happened. She explains that she greeted him warmly as she got out of the shower, saying, "Hi honey," and then referred to him as "sweetheart." He responded by asking her where she had been and then proceeded to strike her, causing her to fall and hit her head on the tub. Nicole shows a lot of emotion as she tells the story. Re-living this moment in the interview with Carol builds her case against her fiancé and makes her more determined than ever to leave him.

Reflection of Third Process Recording and Discussion of Practice Skills and Theories Used in Intervention

Communication Skills

Box 25

Elaboration: Elaboration involves asking clients to describe what they are talking about in more detail. The social worker may ask the client, "I'm not sure I understand what you mean. Can you say more about that?" The social worker may also ask the client for examples of what the client is referencing. "Can you give me an example of when you felt that way?" Also, a social worker can encourage clients to continue telling their story through nonverbal communication that shows interest, for example, leaning forward or a simple nod of the head.

In box 25, Carol asks Nicole to tell her about her worst moment with her fiancé. By asking this pointed question, Carol hopes Nicole will re-tell a specific incident with rich description and details, providing more insight into the relationship.

Boxes 27, 31

Showing empathy: The social worker maintains a nonjudgmental stance or remains neutral. The worker need not totally understand the client's situation, but she must show that she is trying to grasp what the client is feeling or experiencing. The social worker might say, "Tell me more about what your experience was" or "I want to understand more about what this means from your perspective."

In box 27, Carol shows empathy after Nicole shares the story of her worst experience of abuse with her fiancé. She tries to put herself in Nicole's shoes and says that it must have been very scary. Carol does this again in box 31 when she responds to Nicole's descriptions of putting ice on her bruises and wearing sunglasses to hide the abuse from others.

Box 27

Reflecting back feelings: This is when the social worker gives a short response back to the client that mirrors the feeling the worker heard the client express. It is used to let the client know the worker is listening.

When Carol reflects back (box 27) what she heard Nicole say about being very scared, Nicole agrees and says, "I was really, really scared."

Box 29

Continued exploration of the problem: When continuing to explore the problem, the social worker listens for underlying feelings about the situation, who else is involved, and what resources are available to help resolve it.

In box 29, Carol asks if Nicole has ever gone to the hospital because of an injury resulting from an altercation with her fiancé. Here, she is continuing to explore the problem in more depth.

Box 31

Being authentic and genuine: This refers to the worker being sincere and honestly expressing what she is feeling, in a natural, personal way. These qualities help build positive relationships with clients.

In box 31, after listening to how Nicole has to cover up signs of her abuse, Carol feels how horrible this must be and communicates this sentiment to Nicole in an authentic and genuine way. Sitting with a client like Nicole, who has suffered physical and emotional abuse, brings out Carol's own sense of spirituality and humanness and her overwhelming concern for how people are treated.

Other Practice Skills Used
Boxes 25, 29

Data collection: In the data collection stage, the social worker explores the problem in more depth. This involves getting information from multiple sources about the client's life and situation, and about the social systems that may impact the problem. Sources might include client records, bio/psycho/social history, self-assessment tools, and other professionals who have worked with the client.

In box 25, Carol asks Nicole to tell her about the worst situation she has experienced with her fiancé. Nicole's response will provide valuable information for assessing the level of violence in the relationship. Carol then follows up with another question in box 29 to explore whether Nicole has ever needed to go to the hospital for injuries sustained after an abusive incident.

Box 25

Identifying strengths: During assessment, social workers listen for client strengths they can use to help solve certain problems. As clients talk about their situation and their stories unfold, workers identify strengths that are embedded in the narrative. By focusing on positive attributes and characteristics, workers shift the focus away from deficits to inquiring about and affirming strengths.

In box 25, Carol identifies and acknowledges Nicole's good judgment in coming to the shelter to get help. Nicole is no longer willing to be subject to her fiancé's jealousy, angry rages, and abuse.

Box 26

Self-reflection: The skill of self-reflection is an important part of professional practice. Social workers are expected to engage in personal reflection and self-correction to assure continual professional development (CSWE, 2008).

In box 26, Carol recognizes that it is hard for her to hear the horrific details in Nicole's stories of abuse. On the other hand, she also realizes the important role such details can play in helping her assess the danger and the need for protection, and also for understanding the meaning of the abuse.

Theories Used in Intervention

Narrative Theory

Box 26

In box 26, Nicole narrates her worst experience of abuse from her fiancé. She engages Carol as she talks about the episode, using dialogue between her and her fiancé from the actual event. Carol appreciates Nicole's use of a story to describe what happened because it engages her more emotionally, making the incident real and vivid.

Psychodynamic Theory

Boxes 27, 31

Sustainment: This takes place within the client–worker relationship and includes activities by the social worker to show interest, understanding, acceptance, and confidence in the client.

In boxes 27 and 31, Carol uses sustainment in her responses to Nicole's stories of physical abuse. She shows empathy in a genuine and authentic way, demonstrating the types of characteristics that build trust in the worker–client relationship.

Box 30

Denial: This defense mechanism is a refusal to recognize the existence of an anxiety-producing thought, emotion, or conflict.

In box 30, Nicole reveals how she tries to deny and minimize the abuse by hiding her symptoms from others.

Boxes 26, 28, 32

Ventilation is one of the ego-sustaining interventions that encourages the client to express feelings about a problem for relief.

In boxes 26, 28, and 32, Nicole is able to express her feelings and talk about her abuse, and it becomes a cathartic experience that gives her some relief. In telling her story, she shares how crazy it was and how scared it made her in box 26; how "really, really scared" she was in box 28; and how it was "really bad" in box 32.

Cognitive Theory

Box 26

In box 26, Nicole talks about the worst situation she experienced with her abusive fiancé. As she tells Carol the story, she says how it was "crazy." This indicates Nicole has good cognitive and reasoning ability because of her appropriate appraisal of the situation and her boyfriend.

Fourth Excerpt from Transcript and Process Recording

Pre-Excerpt Comments

In the fourth excerpt, Nicole shows more resolution about her decision to leave her fiancé. This becomes especially apparent after Carol begins the excerpt asking Nicole how she is feeling at this point in the interview. She responds unequivocally, "I want out." This reveals a striking progression in the interview from Nicole's indecision and not knowing why she was at the shelter in the first excerpt to her strong determination to leave the abusive relationship seen in this fourth excerpt.

Content	Observation/Reflection	Analysis of Intervention: Theories and Practice
33. Carol: How are you feeling right now as you're talking about it?	I wonder if she is aware of her growing determination to leave the relationship as she talks to me now. My asking this question is to help her take stock of what is going on inside her now.	Communication skills: Opening up affect, focusing on the process.
34. Nicole: I want out. I feel like it has to end at some point, if for anyone I guess for my kids. I'm scared for my life and want to be around for my kids.	This intervention worked. She can see for herself what she wants at this point in the interview.	Practice: Assessment, identifying strengths.

(Continued)

Content	Observation/Reflection	Analysis of Intervention: Theories and Practice
35. Carol: You mentioned he's charming to your family, and your family likes him. Is that right?		Theory: Family systems. Communication skills: Clarification of problem
36. Nicole: Yes. They love him.		
37. Carol: They don't know about any of the abuse?		Theory: Family systems. Communication skills: clarification of problem
38. Nicole: No.		
39. Carol: Have you shared this with anyone?	I fear she has been keeping a big secret. I wonder if this relates to believing she is responsible for the abuse and feeling shame about it.	Communication skills: Continued exploration of the problem.
40. Nicole: The only person I shared it with was my best friend. Her name is Chevon, and she's actually the one who told me about this place. She can't stand him and she knows he's been hitting me for a very long time. She wants me to leave him alone. She says I can do better. I tell her the things he says and she says they are not true.	This is a good sign that she has a good friend who can see the problem and help her to take another perspective. This friend who cares for her welfare is in contrast with her fiancé, who is abusive. She has the capacity to be in a healthy, caring relationship.	Theory: Psychodynamic: ego psychology and functions and object relations. Cognitive, cognitive restructuring.
41. Carol: It's important to be in a better environment where you feel cared about. That's partly why you are here and I hope you feel safe here.		Theory: Psychodynamic, sustainment, object relations. Communication skills: reassuring client, offering support, advocacy.
42. Nicole: I hope so too.	She seems less anxious now.	

Post-Excerpt Comments

Nicole makes it clear by the end of the fourth excerpt that she wants a better environment for her and her children. Although she may not have support from her family, she does have it from her best friend Chevon, who knows the truth, wants Nicole to get out of the abusive relationship, and was the one who directed her to the shelter.

Reflection of Fourth Process Recording and Discussion of Practice Skills and Theories Used in Intervention

Communication Skills

Box 33

Opening up affect: Opening up affect is when the social worker encourages the client to open up more and elaborate on what he is feeling.

In box 33, by asking Nicole how she is feeling at this point in the interview, Carol encourages Nicole to open up and elaborate on what she's thinking in that moment. Nicole has told her stories of abuse with increasing indignation, and Carol hopes that Nicole's response will show more determination to leave her fiancé. This is exactly what happens in the next box.

Box 33

Focusing on the process: At some points in the interview, the social worker needs to move the discussion from what is being said (content) to the underlying feelings in the social worker–client relationship (process).

In box 33, Carol asks a question to move the discussion from the content to the process, from talking about the abuse to understanding Nicole's feelings about it while sharing her experiences. Carol wants to know how Nicole makes meaning out of what she is saying. By focusing on what Nicole is feeling in the interview at that moment, Carol hopes to get a sense of whether Nicole is ready to leave the relationship. How is she processing what is being talked about? In the next box, Carol gets her answer when Nicole responds with strong resolve that "I want out."

Boxes 35, 37

Clarification of problem: When sitting with a client, the social worker gathers details that further explain the nature of the problem. This is an ongoing process in which the worker collects new information and keeps an open mind to alternative interpretations and perceptions.

In box 35, Carol wants to clarify the problem of how Nicole's family sees her fiancé, and asks if she's right in believing that he has charmed them into liking him. Nicole confirms this in the next box, responding that they love him. Carol does this again in box 37 when she asks Nicole if her family knows about the abuse.

Box 39

Continued exploration of the problem: When continuing to explore the problem, the social worker listens for underlying feelings about the situation, who else is involved, and what resources are available to help resolve it.

In box 39, Carol continues to explore how much Nicole has shared with others about the abuse and asks Nicole if she has told anyone. She soon learns that Nicole's best friend, Chevon, is the only person who knows, and that Chevon was the one who directed her to the shelter.

Box 41

Reassuring client: At times, the social worker needs to allay a client's anxiety by supporting her efforts to change or accept new resources.

Carol reassures Nicole in box 41 that she is in a better place at the shelter where she can feel safe and cared about.

Box 41

Offering support: When a client shares a story that is painful, it helps when the social worker offers encouragement. By acknowledging the difficulty of the situation, you provide support for the client and allow him to continue the story.

In box 41, Carol supports Nicole's decision to remain at the shelter where she is in a protected environment away from the abuse.

Box 41

Advocacy: This is a macro practice skill that involves social action with or on behalf of clients. It includes obtaining services or resources for clients that they otherwise could not access. Advocacy also works to influence and change social policy that negatively impacts client systems.

In box 41, Carol advocates for Nicole staying in the shelter where she can receive services and continue to make changes to start a new life.

Other Practice Skills Used
Box 34

Identifying strengths: During assessment, social workers listen for client strengths they can use to help solve certain problems. As clients talk about their situation and their stories unfold, workers identify strengths that are embedded in the narrative. By focusing on positive attributes and characteristics, workers shift the focus away from deficits to inquiring about and affirming strengths.

In box 34, when Nicole makes it clear that she wants out of the abusive relationship, Carol again identifies her strength and courage to separate from an unhealthy situation. Nicole's determination reflects her solid sense of self and good judgment.

Theories Used in Intervention
Family Systems Theory
Boxes 35, 37

In boxes 35 and 37, Carol asks Nicole questions about the family, their opinion of her fiancé, and how much they know about the abuse. She learns that Nicole hasn't divulged anything about the violence to her family. This leads Carol to believe that Nicole comes from a closed family system where there are family secrets and poor communication.

Cognitive Theory
Box 40

Cognitive restructuring is used to describe interventions aimed at helping clients change their belief systems.

In box 40, Carol learns that Nicole told her friend Chevon some of the insulting things that her fiancé had said about her, and Chevon helped Nicole understand they were not true. This is an example of cognitive restructuring, when a client's belief systems are challenged and altered.

Psychodynamic Theory
Box 40

In box 40, Nicole displays both healthy ego functioning and object relations when she tells Carol about her relationship with her best friend Chevon. She trusts her friend enough to share instances when she has been verbally and physically abused. Nicole feels supported by this friend, who helps her to question what her fiancé says about her, and she acts on Chevon's recommendation to go to the shelter. By taking in the perspective of the other, Nicole is able to assess her situation more accurately and make a rational choice based on sound judgment to leave her fiancé.

Box 41

Sustainment: This takes place within the client–worker relationship and includes activities by the social worker to show interest, understanding, acceptance, and confidence in the client.

In box 41, Carol uses ego-sustaining techniques to support Nicole. The client–worker relationship that Carol is building with Nicole throughout the interview conveys interest, empathy, acceptance, and confidence, characteristics that help clients increase their self-esteem and make positive changes in their lives.

Fifth Excerpt from Transcript and Process Recording
Pre-Excerpt Comments

The fifth and last excerpt has an empowerment theme. Carol explains to Nicole what to expect while she is staying at the shelter and outlines some of the resources that she can take advantage of to rebuild her life. Nicole shows special interest in continuing her education and obtaining financial assistance to make a healthy break from her abusive partner, on whom she was economically dependent.

Content	Observation/Reflection	Analysis of Intervention: Theories and Practice
43. Carol: Safe Haven is a place for women who have experienced abuse, like yourself. There are presently eight other families here with children as well. There are a few rules that are important for you to understand while you are here. It's very important that no one knows where you are right now and that no one knows the address. That is for your safety and the safety of the other women here.	I notice that Nicole nods at times when I am speaking. This shows that she is listening to what I say. She is very engaged in the conversation and keeps good eye contact.	Theory: Cognitive, education. Communication skills: Clarification of role of social work, information-giving, referral, empowerment.

(Continued)

Content	Observation/Reflection	Analysis of Intervention: Theories and Practice
You'll have a social worker assigned tomorrow and she'll go over more of this with you. I'd like to show you around in a few minutes to let you see some of the other offices and resources here. We do have a department that helps with legal issues. We have another one with finding homes. There are many different resources here. We do have an evening meeting every night for the mothers to get together to discuss their experiences and provide support for each other. There are a lot of services to help you get a new start and rebuild your life and get out of the abuse.		
44. Nicole: Will I still be able to go to school?	This demonstrates the importance of school to her.	
45. Carol: Absolutely. As a matter of fact, we may be able to find some scholarship money for you and financial help.	She'd be a good candidate for scholarship money to continue school.	Communication skills: Clarification of role of social work. Information-giving, advocacy.
46. Nicole: That would really help because he was paying for a lot of the things I have. That was another concern I had.	Financial dependence on the abuser keeps many women in an unhealthy relationship. Maybe I can advocate for her to get some scholarship money.	
47. Carol: Anything else? Any other questions you have before we stop and I show you around the home?		Communication skills: Seeking client feedback.
48. Nicole: No, I think I'm all set. I don't have any questions.		
49. Carol: Well, I'm really glad you came here, and I really feel we can work well together and get you a new life.		Theory: Psychodynamic, sustainment. Communication skills: Collaboration, empowerment.
50. Nicole: Thank you.		

Post-Excerpt Comments

At the close of the interview, Carol feels optimistic about Nicole's future and confident that she can follow through with steps to break off her engagement with her fiancé and start a new life. It was easy for Carol to talk with Nicole, since she engaged well in the therapeutic process and opened up to share her experiences; she also demonstrated good interpersonal skills, trust in others, and resilience. Carol felt privileged to sit with Nicole, a feeling she often has with other women like Nicole who have experienced terrible abuse and shown tremendous courage and inner strength to start a better life. Carol sat for a moment after Nicole left to reflect on her interview with Nicole and marvel at the wonders of the human spirit.

Reflection of Fourth Process Recording and Discussion of Practice Skills and Theories Used in Intervention

Communication Skills

Boxes 43, 45

Clarification of the role of social worker: The social worker helps the client understand what services the agency offers and what her role as social worker will be. There are times when the client needs reminding that the work is collaborative; it is the social worker's job to facilitate and not direct the process.

In boxes 43 and 45, Carol explains to Nicole that she will be assigned a social worker who will orient her to the shelter and its rules, and refer her to the many resources that will help her start a new life, free of abuse. Carol lets Nicole know that her social worker will be her advocate and look into scholarship money for her to continue school.

Boxes 43, 45

Information-giving: Information-giving means informing the client about the social agency, the problem, and the resources for change.

In boxes 43 and 45, Carol reviews some of the shelter's rules, including one that requires women not to divulge the address of the shelter to anyone, in order to protect the safety of residents. Carol also provides information about resources available to Nicole, for example, counseling, financial support, legal services, and housing advice.

Box 43

Referral: This is when a client needs additional resources outside of the agency in which she's receiving services. With the client's permission, the worker makes the referral in order to help the client access other avenues for assistance.

Carol explains in box 43 that Nicole will be referred to a social worker who will link her to essential resources for re-establishing her life.

Boxes 43, 49

Empowerment: Empowerment is providing clients with information and skills to take action on their own behalf, advocate for their rights, and gain access to needed resources. It involves helping clients have confidence in their ability to control their lives.

In boxes 43 and 49, Carol empowers Nicole by informing her about the resources available at the shelter to help her take charge of her life again.

Box 45

Advocacy: This is a macro practice skill that involves social action with or on behalf of clients. It includes obtaining services or resources for clients that they otherwise could not access. Advocacy also works to influence and change social policy that negatively impacts client systems.

Carol is impressed with Nicole's drive to continue her studies and knows that education will allow her to improve her life and support her children. She feels strongly that making a financial investment in Nicole will pay off, and she wants to advocate for her to get scholarship money for school.

Box 47

Seeking client feedback: When seeking client feedback, the social worker asks for the client's perception of a particular situation, the client–worker relationship, or the helping process.

Before the interview ends, Carol asks Nicole if she has any other questions before she shows her around the shelter. From past experience, Carol knows this is important, because clients often leave a session and later wish they had brought something up that needed attention.

Box 49

Collaboration: Collaboration is when the social worker and client work together to define the problem, set goals, and plan possible intervention strategies.

In box 49, Carol tells Nicole that she is really glad she came to the shelter for help and that the interview went well. She believes there will be a good collaboration between Nicole and the shelter staff that will lead to a better life for Nicole.

Theories Used in Intervention

Cognitive Theory

Box 43

In box 43, as part of cognitive interventions, Carol provides Nicole with knowledge about the shelter, its rules, its resources, and what to expect. She orients Nicole to her new environment and to the staff that will help her evaluate her life, past, present, and future, and challenge the way she thinks about herself and her relationships.

Psychodynamic Theory

Box 49

In box 49, Carol uses sustainment in her intervention with Nicole by supporting her decision to come to the shelter and giving her hope about a new life.

Assessment

Assessment is the process of understanding the client and his problem in a holistic way based on the information gathered. It highlights the importance of context in the construction of meaning, and it is a collaborative activity done in tandem with the client. Following are examples of applying different assessment outlines to Nicole's case.

Problem-Solving Method

The problem-solving method looks at the different phases of the helping process, including engagement, assessment, planning, intervention, evaluation, termination, and follow-up.

Although the method describes discrete phases, each stage is really ongoing and continuous. Please refer to chapter 1 on Practice for a recap on the problem-solving method.

Engagement

I met with Nicole for the first time at the Safe Haven Shelter, approximately two hours after she arrived with her two children, a son who is 4, and a daughter who is 3. The daughter is her fiancé's child, but the son is not. Nicole came after an argument with her fiancé that scared her. He said he would kill her if he saw her again with her male study partner at the library, and it was the first time he'd spoken that way. She seemed anxious as she began to talk about the argument and how her fiancé had become increasingly jealous, controlling, and abusive in the relationship. The situation was so bad that she was now scared for her life. Nicole opened up to me quite easily about her concerns and engaged fully in the interview. She was neatly dressed, alert, articulate, motivated to seek help, and she demonstrated many strengths as her story unfolded.

Assessment

Nicole is a single, 25-year-old, African-American woman, and a survivor of emotional and physical abuse. She was admitted to the shelter with her two young children, ages 3 and 4, after an argument with her fiancé in which he threatened to kill her if he saw her again with another student at school. The abuse she experienced in her relationship with the fiancé is referred to as Coercive Controlling Violence. This type of violence is characterized by power and control issues; the abusive partner usually intimidates, threatens, isolates, and blames the woman for the problems in the relationship. Although these tactics are meant to make the victim dependent on her partner, they did not work with Nicole, an assertive, confident woman with many ego strengths who now questions her fiancé's behavior.

Nicole decided to go back to school to make a better life for herself and her kids, but it created more stress and made things worse with her fiancé. He didn't support her education, interpreted it as an effort on her part to be more independent, and only found more reasons to be jealous. When he didn't succeed in stopping her from attending school, he tried to wield more power and control over her by threatening to kill her.

Although the relationship with the fiancé started out fine, it became increasingly more abusive, both verbally and physically, and now Nicole is scared for her life. She explained how at first he would to go through her phone to look at her calls, assuming she was out with other guys. When she ran errands to the corner store, he would accuse her of talking to guys in front of the store. One day, after he wrongly insinuated she had been out with other men, she said she was going to leave him. He lashed out at her by slapping her face and telling her this wouldn't happen.

In addition to this physical violence, there was verbal and emotional abuse, times when the fiancé would tell Nicole she was fat and make other disparaging remarks. At first, she endured these verbal assaults, believing she wanted to stay with him for the sake of the children, not wanting men in and out of their lives. She has never observed the fiancé hitting her children, and she doesn't think they have seen her physically abused by him, but she realizes they have heard him screaming at her. Also, she is worried about her older son, Terrell, who is not the fiancé's son, and to whom she believes the fiancé is mean.

Nicole described to me the worst situation she had experienced in the relationship. She was in the shower, and her fiancé came in, angry with her for not answering her phone, and started to hit her, causing her to fall and bump her head on the tub. She was very scared and described the situation as being "crazy," but was relieved the kids weren't home. She hid the bruises and abuse from others and never went to the hospital. She made up excuses for any physical signs of abuse and handled it by using ice and wearing sunglasses. It is likely she carries some feelings of shame about her situation.

She has one friend, Chevon, who has been very supportive to her and gave her the number for the shelter. Chevon dislikes Nicole's fiancé, knows about the physical and emotional abuse, and wants Nicole to leave him. She bolsters Nicole's self-esteem by discrediting any negative comments the fiancé makes about Nicole. Because the fiancé puts on a show for Nicole's family, though, they have been charmed into thinking he is a great guy. She doesn't know how to break off the engagement because her family loves him. However, she is determined to get out of the relationship after his threat to kill her. She's scared for her life and wants to be around for her kids.

Nicole appears to be a bright, strong, determined woman with many ego strengths. Although her fiancé has tried to control her with physical, verbal, and emotional abuse, she has proved resilient and sought assistance at the shelter. Throughout the interview, she was very engaging and showed good interpersonal skills in opening up, sharing her story, and trusting me with her information. She showed much love and concern for her children, whom she wants to protect and make a better life for. She sees education as one way to do this, and she communicated her strong desire to continue school. I am optimistic about her taking full advantage of the shelter's resources to improve her life and leave the abusive relationship.

Because the children have been exposed to her being verbally and emotionally abused, at a minimum, Child Protective Services will need to be involved. This is another resource outside of the shelter that can provide additional services for her and her family.

Assessment Summary

Nicole is a bright, articulate, well-dressed and groomed, single, 25-year-old, African-American woman with two young children. She was admitted to the shelter after her fiancé threatened to kill her if he saw her again at school with another male student. She is a survivor in the true sense, demonstrating resilience and many ego strengths that will help her to find success starting a new life. She shows a capacity for questioning her fiancé's faulty assumptions and distortions about her, evaluating her external environment, and using solid judgment. Her concerns for her children and wanting them to have a better life are further proof that she is a good mother. She has excellent interpersonal skills, responded well to the interviewer, and will likely use the resources of the shelter well. Child Protective Services will need to get involved and will become another source of support.

Planning

The shelter will refer Nicole to an in-house social worker who will serve as her advocate and connect her with the resources needed to start a new life. Collaboratively, they will establish goals for their work together. The social worker will also make a referral to protective services, after first explaining the reasons to Nicole. One of the priorities will be to help Nicole continue school, an aspiration that she has and one that will contribute to her economic independence and her ability to provide for her children. Nicole will also be referred for financial, legal, and housing assistance, and for outside counseling. I believe Nicole shows great promise. She has a capacity for insight, for acting on a better understanding about her life, and for jumpstarting the big changes she needs to make.

Intervention

The intervention began in the first meeting when I engaged Nicole in a therapeutic relationship, one in which she felt cared about and could open up and trust enough to share her story of abuse. In our initial discussion, Nicole demonstrated good interpersonal skills and participated nicely, maintaining good eye contact. She talked candidly about the various incidents of abuse and how she was very scared for her life. She often spoke in a captivating narrative story format. She appreciated our conversation, which came at a critical point for her, and she showed a readiness to leave the abusive relationship.

I used ego-sustaining techniques by showing empathy and providing a holding environment for Nicole to feel safe and supported in the relationship. From a psychodynamic perspective, she displayed good ego strengths and ego functioning, reflected in her excellent sense of self, identity, resilience, and determination. Cognitive interventions included education and explaining to Nicole the patterns of abusive relationships. She exhibited fine cognitive abilities, as well; she was able to assess and evaluate her abusive relationship, identify her fiancé's cognitive distortions and faulty assumptions about her, and apply problem-solving skills.

Termination

As we approached the end of the interview, I let Nicole know how glad I was that she had come to the shelter. I believed she would gain the help she needed from being here. The conversation ended well, with Nicole more determined to leave the abusive relationship and more knowledgeable about the resources available to her at the shelter. Afterward, I showed her around the shelter. She was appreciative of our meeting and looked forward to working on her issues in a supportive environment.

Evaluation

Nicole and I engaged well in the first meeting, and I am confident that she will work proactively with the social worker assigned to her. She is motivated to use the resources of the shelter and was receptive to ongoing work regarding the abuse she has suffered. Nicole was attentive during the interview and articulated her problems in the abusive relationship and her hopes for the future. By the end of the meeting, Nicole was ready to be shown around the shelter and start her recovery. She will benefit from the services available to her, and I anticipate she will have excellent outcomes.

Follow-up

I will refer Nicole to a social worker who will work with her on her personal goals while at the shelter. I will follow-up with this social worker to check how Nicole is doing at different intervals and to make sure the referral is made to Child Protective Services. I also will encourage Nicole's social worker to help her apply for scholarship funds to continue her education, and I will personally advocate for her receiving this assistance. Because I believe Nicole has such promise, I plan to monitor her progress to make sure she maximizes her use of the services available to her. I enjoyed my interview with Nicole and appreciated her many strengths, and I look forward to watching her start a new life.

Psychosocial Assessment and Intervention Strategy

Please refer to chapter 1, which includes outlines for the psychosocial assessment and intervention plan. This is one example of applying a psychosocial assessment and intervention to Nicole's case and is written in the social worker's voice.

Identifying Data

Nicole is a single, 25-year-old, African-American woman with two young children who came to the shelter after being threatened by her fiancé. She is bright, alert, articulate, and well-dressed and groomed. She began the interview somewhat nervous but was very engaging, maintained good eye contact, and seemed motivated to get help. She was referred by a good friend who encouraged her to come and gave her the shelter's phone number.

Presenting Problem

Nicole arrived at the shelter after an argument with her fiancé in which he threatened to kill her if he saw her again with her male study partner at school. Nicole has suffered episodes of physical, emotional, and verbal abuse. She has been the subject of degrading remarks and been hit on numerous occasions during her partner's jealous rages. Her fiancé also tries to control her from going out with others.

Current Functioning, Social Supports, and Strengths

Nicole is a bright, articulate 25-year-old woman who demonstrated good ego strengths and ego functioning in her first meeting with me. She participated actively in the interview and had excellent interpersonal skills, seen in her ability to open up and trust another person. During our conversation she showed a capacity for insight into her abusive relationship and reflected on some of her fiancé's irrational thinking, faulty assumptions, and distortions about their relationship. She expressed concern and love for her children, whom she wants to protect and create a better life for. She asserted her wish to continue school and is motivated to take full advantage of the resources at the shelter.

In the initial interview, she spoke of a best friend, Chevon, whom she has confided in about the abuse and who has been helping Nicole muster the courage to leave the relationship. Chevon gave Nicole the shelter's phone number and encouraged her to call. Nicole is uncertain about how much support her family will give her to break off the engagement, because they have been charmed by her fiancé and they seem infatuated with him. Despite having limited outside support except for her best friend, Nicole will use the resources and people at the shelter to make changes in her life.

Relevant Past History

At this time, I have minimal knowledge about Nicole's history beyond the stories of her fiancé's abuse and the scant information she provided about her family and best friend. Her next meeting with her individual social worker will cover a more extensive psychosocial history to learn more about her development, her family, other friends, work, religion, school, relationship history, and her interests and hobbies.

Concerning the incidents of abuse, she shared how she has been physically attacked as a result of her fiancé's jealous rages, isolated from others and kept from going out, screamed at, and told disparaging things about herself. Her children have heard the screaming, but she doesn't believe they have witnessed or been the object of the fiancé's abuse. However, she is concerned that her fiancé is mean to her older son, who is 4 and not his biological child. Her fiancé is the father of her 3-year-old daughter.

Formulation

Nicole is an intelligent, alert, single, well-dressed and groomed, 25-year-old African-American woman with two young children, ages 3 and 4, who came to the shelter after being threatened by her fiancé. The first interview revealed several incidents of physical, emotional, and verbal abuse that has increased over time and culminated in her seeking help. The event that precipitated her visiting the shelter was when her fiancé threatened to kill her if he saw her again at school with her male study partner. He had never threatened this before, and she took it seriously, as it really scared her. She is motivated to get help and use the resources of the shelter to make a better life for her and her two children. Because this is a domestic violence situation in the presence of young children, the case will also be referred to protective services.

Intervention

Intervention began in the initial meeting with Nicole, shortly after she arrived at the shelter with her two children. I listened empathically as Nicole shared her stories of abuse and her concerns for herself and her children. She engaged fully with me as she discussed her experiences and was receptive to ongoing work with a social worker and referral to needed resources. I used ego-sustaining techniques in this first meeting by being genuine and warm, listening attentively, and showing empathy in an effort to build a strong, trusting relationship that will underpin future work. I helped Nicole understand the patterns of abusive relationships and confront some of her fiancé's irrational beliefs and faulty assumptions about her. I explained the rules of the shelter, and how her individual social worker would help her access the many resources available to her there. Once she is assigned a social worker, that worker will explain to Nicole the importance of involving protective services for her children and how this will be yet another helpful support structure for them.

Termination and Evaluation

The initial interview ended well, and it signified an excellent start to Nicole leaving an abusive relationship. She seemed appreciative to be in a safe place and have this opportunity to change her life. Nicole was fully engaged in our meeting and open to talking about her personal situation and experiences of abuse. Toward the end of the interview, I let her know that I would refer her to another social worker at the shelter who would help her access needed resources. Before we stopped, I asked if Nicole had any further questions before showing her around. She is motivated to address her personal issues while at the shelter, and with her many assets, I expect she will make good progress and create a better life for her and her children.

Theoretical Lens

I integrated several theories in my meeting with Nicole. I used psychodynamic ego-sustaining skills to build an empathic relationship with her from the start. I also depended on psychodynamic developmental theories to help me assess her ego strengths and ego functioning. Narrative theory gave me an appreciation for her use of stories in our interview, which was done in a way that encouraged me to listen closely, always wanting to know more. I used cognitive theories to educate Nicole about common patterns of abusive relationships and to confront her fiancé's cognitive distortions, false beliefs, and incorrect assumptions. In combination, the various theories gave me insight into Nicole's situation and informed my interventions. They also helped me feel confident about her future success, and I shared what I learned about Nicole with her individual social worker.

Bio/Psycho/Social/Spiritual Assessment

This approach looks at the functioning of an individual's biological, psychological, social, and spiritual systems. I will follow the outline in chapter 1. As with the other sections, it is written in the first person, from the social worker's perspective.

Applying Bio/Psycho/Social/Spiritual Assessment to Case of Nicole

Nicole is a 25-year-old African-American woman who has been the victim of physical and emotional abuse. Although appearing healthy, except for being overweight, she has suffered from physical altercations with her fiancé that left her with bruises. She states that the injuries were never serious enough to require hospital care, but she did apply ice to reduce the swelling and had to wear sunglasses to hide the marks. Nicole had two normal pregnancies resulting in a son who is 4 and a daughter who is 3. She demonstrates a healthy concern for her children who have witnessed verbal abuse. As a result of her case involving domestic violence in the presence of young children, it will be referred to Child Protective Services to prevent future abuse and to provide additional social services as needed.

A bright, attractive, young woman, Nicole is alert and well oriented to person, place, and time. She is engaging, articulate, and appears to be of average to above-average intelligence. Developmentally, she is in early adulthood, a time when she is still forming her identity and establishing intimate relationships. Her interest in continuing her education is part of her search for identity, but at the same time she is struggling with an unhealthy relationship that is abusive. She has good ego strengths and ego functioning, as reflected in her ability to realistically assess and evaluate her external environment. She also questions her fiancé's irrational thinking and behavior, and shows good judgment. She has a capacity for insight and is quick to understand how her relationship with her fiancé fits into the abusive pattern described to her during the intake interview. I observed excellent communication skills during our meeting; she kept eye contact, listened attentively, and responded appropriately.

Nicole's experiences, and the effects of emotional abuse from her fiancé, will present challenging psychological problems for someone her age with a young family. It is likely she will show signs of PTSD that can be addressed in her individual counseling. Also, she will face financial, housing, and legal roadblocks as she starts her new life without the abusive partner she was dependent on. In spite of these obstacles, Nicole is resilient and will likely be able to adapt to adversity. She has a strong will and determination to succeed.

There is limited information on her social environment after only one meeting. Nicole has two children, a 3-year-old daughter fathered by her fiancé, and a 4-year-old son, who is from another man. She has a best friend, Chevon, whom she has confided in about the abuse and was the one who encouraged her to leave the fiancé and get help at the shelter. Nicole is uncertain if she will get family support to end the relationship with her fiancé, because they have been charmed by his public behavior and fooled into thinking he is someone he is not. However, having stellar interpersonal skills, Nicole will form positive relationships with the staff and other residents at the shelter who can serve as additional resources for her. She attends school and hopes to continue her studies with assistance. Her social worker at the shelter can refer Nicole to financial, housing, and legal services. She will also refer Nicole to Child Protective Services, a state agency whose goal is to strengthen families and prevent abuse.

Nicole appears to have an irrepressible spirit that has not been stifled by the abuse. She is scared but this has not stopped her from questioning her fiancé's beliefs about her and his willingness to resort to physical force. Her counseling at the shelter can address any spiritual concerns she may have following the abuse. It is possible that the violence has challenged her faith and beliefs about humanity. Alternately, it's possible her faith is an important source of strength that can help her make it through this difficult time. The social worker will ask her about the role of religion and spirituality in her life and be open to continuing the discussion if Nicole responds to this line of questioning. A traumatic relationship like the one Nicole had with her fiancé often stirs up life's big questions and a search for meaning. It is important for social workers not to avoid this critical subject.

End of Chapter Resources
Questions for Students

I have included questions to supplement the text for additional student learning. They are organized around the 10 core competencies in the Council on Social Work Education (CSWE, 2008). The questions can be used for classroom or online discussion, given as written homework assignments, structured as classroom exercises, or used by students to do outside research. They can also be adapted for use in hybrid or online courses.

Educational Policy 2.1.1: Identify as a Professional Social Worker and Conduct Oneself Accordingly

These skills include advocating for clients, practicing personal reflection, demonstrating professional demeanor, engaging in career-long learning, and using supervision and consultation. Professional social work practice requires that social workers pay attention to how their personal experiences, values, and assumptions provide obstacles to listening to clients in helpful ways. Many of the questions that follow will help students become more self-aware and develop competence in this area.

1. How well did Carol introduce herself and define her role and purpose for meeting with Nicole? Is there anything you would have done differently?
2. Were you aware of any personal reactions or feelings that surfaced when watching the interview between Nicole and Carol? How comfortable do you think are working in the field of domestic violence?
3. Were there any times when Carol's personal experiences, values, and assumptions came through in the interview? Are you aware of anything within yourself that would get in the way of being fully present with Nicole and able to listen to her story if you were in Carol's place?
4. What role did self-awareness play in Carol's work with Nicole? Look back at the process recording and find any moments when she reflected on her interaction with Nicole.
5. Imagine you are a social worker working in the domestic violence field. Explore opportunities for continuing education for your professional development. What programs are available to you through the National Association of Social Workers or other professional organizations?

Educational Policy 2.1.2: Apply Social Work Ethical Principles to Guide Professional Practice

The questions that follow are to make students more aware of ethical issues that social workers confront every day in practice.

1. Were there any ethical issues that surfaced for you in the interview with Nicole? If so, what were they?
2. Carol did not call Child Protective Services after the initial intake. She planned to include this recommendation in her referral to the shelter social worker who would follow the case and start working with Nicole the next day. Do you agree or disagree with this decision?
3. If you were working with a woman like Nicole and you learned that she had gone against the rules and told a friend the address of the shelter, would you tell your supervisor, particularly if you knew this was grounds for your client being asked to leave the shelter?
4. Imagine one of the women at the shelter discloses to you that she observed another mother at the shelter hitting her young child. She tells you this in confidence and says you must never tell anyone that she was the source for this information. How do you respond, and do you bring it up with the mother accused of this?
5. You notice another social worker exhibiting poor boundaries with one of the mothers at the shelter. The worker seems to spend a lot of time with this woman compared to her other clients and frequently brings her up in meetings, advocating for additional services for her. How would you handle this?
6. Would you be willing to work with a batterer who you knew had caused serious injury to his partner? Would this raise any ethical issues for you and how would you resolve them?
7. How would you react if a woman you were working with at the shelter decided to return to an abusive relationship? Would you try to convince her to stay at the shelter and continue receiving services, or let her go?

Educational Policy 2.1.3: Apply Critical Thinking to Inform and Communicate Professional Judgments

Critical thinking is an important skill in social work practice, and students are expected to demonstrate this competency before graduation. These exercises will encourage students to become critical thinkers in practice.

1. When is conjoint treatment of domestic violence appropriate and when would it be counterindicated? Refer to the literature on the subject before answering the question.
2. What criteria must be met to determine whether or not there is evidence of maltreatment in referrals to Child Protective Services? Based on what you know from Carol's interview with Nicole, are there grounds for reporting the case to Child Protective Services? If so, what are they?
3. If maltreatment is not substantiated in the case of Nicole's children, could the family still receive support from Child Protective Services? Would there be any benefit to this?
4. Do you believe Nicole's experience with domestic violence is typical for cases of partner abuse? What are your beliefs and assumptions on the subject and how were these opinions formed? Reflect on personal experiences that have influenced your way of thinking on this subject.
5. How do the media portray domestic violence? How does this contribute to how the general public responds to people who are victims of violence? Provide some examples.
6. What do you think allows some women to leave abusive situations while others stay? Are there ways of predicting successful outcomes in advance?
7. What does blaming the victim mean? Do you think this happens with women who have experienced partner abuse? If so, what are some ways in which abused women may be blamed for their situation and what could you do to change this misperception?

Educational Policy 2.1.4: Engage Diversity and Difference in Practice

These questions are designed to teach students about engaging cultural diversity and understanding difference in practice.

1. How do you understand violence against women in terms of gender, race, ethnicity, culture, and poverty? How do these factors intersect with one another?
2. How important is it to understand cultural influences when dealing with cases of domestic violence? Provide an example to support your opinion.
3. What is the prevalence of domestic violence in different racial and cultural groups? How do you understand discrepancies that exist between the various groups?
4. What role does spirituality and the church play in the lives of African-American women who have been victims of domestic violence?
5. Are there variations in how different ethnic and racial groups utilize domestic violence services? Explain your answer. If so, what are the obstacles for some groups and how would you address them?

Educational Policy 2.1.5: Advance Human Rights and Social and Economic Justice

Students are expected to address human rights and social justice issues as needed in their practice. These questions are to help students think in terms of social and economic justice and become more competent in this area.

1. Violence against women is a human rights issue that connects to problems of social and economic injustice. Explain this statement and what social workers are doing to address these issues. Identify human rights and social justice issues as they relate to victims of domestic violence.
2. What are some of the myths about domestic violence and battered women that perpetuate violence again women? What can be done to counteract these stereotypes and false assumptions?
3. Identify groups and organizations on the local and national level that advocate for the rights of domestic violence victims.
4. What were some of the findings and recommendations made by the Institute of Medicine in 2011 concerning clinical prevention services for abused women? (Full citation in bibliography.)
5. What is the history of domestic violence shelters? When and where was the first sheltered opened and how did this movement get started?

Educational Policy 2.1.6: Engage in Research-Informed Practice and Practice-Informed Research

Research assignments encourage students to engage in research-informed practice and practice-informed research. These questions will help students practice this competency.

1. Research the prevalence of violence against women and children in American society today as compared to 20 years ago. Do you notice any trends, and if so, how do you understand them?
2. What are some problems encountered when gathering statistics on battered women?
3. What are some of the factors that affect increased rates of domestic violence in American society?
4. Review the literature on domestic violence, race, and ethnicity. What specific differences exist between rates of domestic violence in different ethnic and racial groups?
5. What is the relationship, if any, between alcohol and violence?
6. Research best practices in IPV screening and program implementation. Review the literature to determine what is known about the success of implementing IPV interventions to improve women's health.
7. Research the literature to find resources on violence assessment screening tools that could be used in a hospital emergency department to identify a patient's risk for violence.
8. Research treatment programs for batterers and their outcomes. How successful are these programs in reducing future violence? Are there programs that have been found effective?

9. Although there is more literature on violence against women, what are the statistics on violence against men by their women partners? How are the characteristics of these abusive relationships the same or different?

Educational Policy 2.1.7: Apply Knowledge of Human Behavior and the Social Environment

These questions will help students apply theories critically to assess and evaluate work and interventions with clients.

1. Using different theoretical lenses, how would you understand the problem of violence in society? Include psychodynamic, cognitive, behavioral, family systems, and narrative perspectives.
2. Following up on the last question, which theory or theories make the most sense to you and help you best understand this problem?
3. Review the literature on the problem of domestic violence. From your reading, what are the factors that contribute to spousal abuse?
4. What is "battered women syndrome?"
5. What are some reasons why battered women stay with their abusers?
6. What are the traits and characteristics of an abusive perpetrator?
7. What does the "cycle of abuse" mean?" Describe strategies for intervening and stopping the cycle from repeating.
8. After reading the article on conjoint treatment of intimate partner violence (LaTaillade et al., 2006), describe in your own words a cognitive-behavioral approach to treating domestic violence.

Educational Policy 2.1.8: Engage in Policy Practice to Advance Social and Economic Well-Being and to Deliver Effective Social Work Services

These questions are to encourage students to look at the role of policy in social work practice.

1. Interview a social worker at a domestic violence shelter about its policies and the rationale for them. How effective are the policies, and does the social worker have any suggestions for improving them?
2. What changes, if any, in current police and court practices are needed to improve intervention services for abused women and provide better protection for victims of domestic violence?
3. What is being done at your local NASW office to deliver more effective services for abused women? Interview a staff person at your local chapter on the issue.
4. Imagine you are working with a domestic violence situation in your field placement. Are there policies to address student safety in field placements in your social work program field manual? Read through your school's field manual to see if social work safety is discussed.

5. What training is offered at your field practicum on safety issues for social workers? Is there a policy on worker safety at the agency? If so, bring it to class and compare it with policies from other agencies.

6. What are the NASW standards on workplace safety for social workers? What has your local chapter of NASW done to promote legislation in your state to address workplace safety issues for social workers?

7. What is a restraining order? What protections does it offer? What are the consequences of someone violating a restraining order?

Educational Policy 2.1.9: Respond to Contexts That Shape Practice

Social workers practice in many different settings and may need to familiarize themselves with the particular skills required in each one. These questions help students to appreciate how context shapes practice and to develop competencies in this area.

1. Imagine you are the supervisor for a new social worker at a domestic violence shelter. You have noticed that she seems invested in her clients leaving their abusive partners. It appears she is upset that one specific client is planning to leave the shelter and return to the batterer. How would you help her cope with this situation and suggest ways she could discuss it with the client before she leaves?

2. Explain what IPV screening means and describe best practices for IPV screening implementation in hospital emergency departments.

3. Interview a social worker at a domestic violence shelter to learn more about this area of practice. What do you think would be the most challenging aspect of this type of social work?

4. Are there different philosophies behind domestic violence shelters in terms of their approach to abused women? Compare two different shelters to see if you notice disparities.

5. A doctor in the primary care setting where you work refers a patient to you because of concerns about domestic violence. When the woman comes to talk to you, she minimizes the problems. What would you do?

6. What does empowerment mean and how does it relate to partner abuse? What are strategies for empowering women in a domestic violence shelter?

Educational Policy 2.1.10(a)–(d): Engage, Assess, Intervene, and Evaluate with Individuals, Families, Groups, Organizations, and Communities

These questions are intended to give students practice engaging, assessing, intervening, and evaluating clients.

1. The beginning of an interview often sets the tone for the rest of the session with a client. How did the beginning of the interview go with Nicole? How well did Carol engage Nicole and make her feel comfortable?

2. Many battered women worry that others will judge them and are embarrassed about their situation. Were there any times in the interview when you noticed this with Nicole? If so, how did Carol handle those moments? Were there times when Carol was judgmental?

3. What role does confidentiality play in work with abused women who are living in a domestic violence shelter? How would you explain confidentiality and its limits to your clients?

4. What are some counseling strategies for working with women who have been in abusive relationships? Find a journal article or chapter in a book that uses an approach that you like and cite the source.

5. Imagine you are working with a client who has a history of violence. During his meeting with you, he appears agitated and has made threatening comments about his girlfriend who he believes has been flirting with other men. Although you try to reason with him, he raises his voice and says, "I better not see her giving other men those sexy looks again, or else." When you ask what he means by this, he doesn't answer and says he needs to leave. What do you do?

6. Past violence is the best predictor of future violence. Did Carol ask Nicole questions about her fiancé's past or current violent behaviors? What is your opinion of Nicole's risk for future violence in this relationship?

7. What would you include in a risk assessment for violence?

8. Many families react negatively when told they are being referred to Child Protective Services. How would you bring up the issue and talk to Nicole about filing a report to Child Protective Services? Are there approaches that might help her respond more favorably?

Interviewing Skills Used in the Case of Nicole

Following is a list of interviewing skills the social worker used with Nicole. They are listed in the order in which they appeared. Although others social workers may refer to these interactions differently, or define the skills in others ways, this is one way of looking at them.

Become familiar with these interviewing skills and practice them with other students in role-plays.

Engagement and Beginning of Interview

At the beginning of the first meeting with the client, the social worker welcomes the client, tries to make the client comfortable, and tunes in to her own and the client's initial feelings about the first meeting.

Reaching for Feelings

This is when the social worker tries to understand what the client is feeling when a particular subject or issue comes up. The social worker may use this skill when she senses that the client is avoiding, or is not in touch with, the feelings related to the current discussion. This may bring out strong reactions in the client, and it is important that the social worker is sensitive to what this means to the client.

Exploration of the Problem

This is a way of gaining more information about a client's situation. When continuing to explore the problem, the social worker listens for underlying feelings about the situation, who else is involved, and what resources are available to help resolve it.

Continued Exploration of the Problem

When continuing to explore the problem, the social worker listens for underlying feelings about the situation, who else is involved, and what resources are available to help resolve it.

Questioning

This is a way of gaining more information about a client's situation. There are many different kinds of questions, for example, open- and closed-ended questions and reflexive questions. Questioning is often used in assessment as part of data collection.

Reassuring Client

At times, the social worker needs to allay a client's anxiety by supporting her efforts to change or accept new resources.

Information-Giving

Information-giving means informing the client about the social agency, the problem, and the resources for change. The social worker is knowledgeable about human development and human behavior and can help clients by sharing information that relates to a problem they are experiencing. For instance, a mother may complain that her 4-year-old daughter is misbehaving and not understand how the birth of a new sibling has affected the older daughter.

Normalizing Feelings

Clients often believe that their feelings are unacceptable or abnormal. The social worker helps the client see that her feelings are a natural reaction to the given situation.

Showing Empathy

The social worker maintains a nonjudgmental stance or remains neutral. The worker need not totally understand the client's situation, but she must show that she is trying to grasp what the client is feeling or experiencing. The social worker might say, "Tell me more about what your experience was" or "I want to understand more about what this means from your perspective."

Offering Support

When a client shares a story that is painful, it helps when the social worker offer encouragement. By acknowledging the difficulty of the situation, you provide support for the client and allow him to continue the story.

Reflecting Back Feelings

This is when the social worker gives a short response back to the client that mirrors the feeling the worker heard the client express. It is used to let the client know the worker is listening.

Acknowledging Strengths

Acknowledging strengths can help clients improve their self-esteem and give them more confidence to take action on their own behalf. It empowers them by providing them with hope and a sense that they have the capacity and resources within themselves to improve their lives and overcome obstacles. When clients feel overwhelmed by difficulties, they may not recognize their positive traits, so the worker pointing them out can bolster the client's self-confidence.

Giving Client Feedback

This is when the social worker finds an opportunity to provide the client with information about his behavior and its effect on him or on other people. It can prove difficult, because the client may not want to hear or accept what the social worker is saying.

Elaboration

Elaboration involves asking clients to describe what they are talking about in more detail. The social worker may ask the client, "I'm not sure I understand what you mean. Can you say more about that?" The social worker may also ask the client for examples of what the client is referencing. "Can you give me an example of when you felt that way?" Also, a social worker can encourage clients to continue telling their story through nonverbal communication that shows interest, that is, leaning forward or a simple nod of the head.

Being Authentic and Genuine

This refers to the worker being sincere and honestly expressing what she is feeling, in a natural, personal way. These qualities help build positive relationships with clients.

Opening up Affect

Opening up affect is when the social worker encourages the client to open up more and elaborate on what he is feeling.

Focusing on the Process

At some points in the interview, the social worker needs to move the discussion from what is being said (content) to the underlying feelings in the social worker–client relationship (process).

Clarification of Problem

When sitting with a client, the social worker gathers details that further explain the nature of the problem. This is an ongoing process in which the worker collects new information and keeps an open mind to alternative interpretations and perceptions.

Advocacy

This is a macro practice skill that involves social action with or on behalf of clients. It includes obtaining services or resources for clients that they otherwise could not access. Advocacy also works to influence and change social policy that negatively impacts client systems.

Clarification of the Role of Social Worker

The social worker helps the client understand what services the agency offers and what will be her role as social worker. There are times when the client needs reminding that the work is collaborative; it is the social worker's job to facilitate and not direct the process.

Referral

This is when a client needs additional resources outside of the agency in which she's receiving services. With the client's permission, the worker makes the referral in order to help the client access other avenues for assistance.

Empowerment

Providing clients with information and skills to take action on their own behalf, advocate for their rights, and gain access to needed resources. It involves helping clients have confidence in their ability to control their lives.

Seeking Client Feedback

When seeking client feedback, the social worker asks for the client's perception of a particular situation, the client–worker relationship, or the helping process.

Collaboration

Collaboration is when the social worker and client work together to define the problem, set goals, and plan possible intervention strategies.

Terms and Definitions

Child Abuse Prevention and Treatment Act (CAPTA)

This act was passed by the federal legislature in 1974 to address child abuse and neglect and delineates roles for both federal and state government in its implementation. States are mandated to have systems in place for reporting, investigation, prosecuting, and intervening in cases of child abuse. Although CAPTA establishes minimum standards, states determine specific rules about what constitutes abuse and neglect, who must report, and when cases are referred to law enforcement. The federal government provides funding to states in the form of grants for education and prevention programs, as well as support for research, evaluation, technical expertise, and data collection.

Child Protective Services (CPS)

Child Protective Services is the name of a governmental agency responsible for protecting children from child abuse or neglect; it responds to reports made on children under the age of 18. Some states use other names for this agency that put more emphasis on a family-centered approach to services, for example, Department of Children and Families. Child Protective Services workers assess family functioning, identify strengths and risks in the home, and develop a plan to address any problems found in order to make it safe for children to live with the parent or caretaker.

Defense Mechanism

This is an unconscious, automatic response that protects a person from a threat by keeping it out of the person's awareness. It is a coping technique that protects the person from overwhelming stimuli and anxiety until the person is ready to deal with the situation.

Domestic Violence Shelter

A domestic violence shelter is a place of temporary refuge and support for women who are leaving violent or abusive situations and need a safe place to stay while reorganizing their lives. Shelters offer many resources to help women get out of abusive relationships, for example, counseling, advocacy, housing, legal aid, financial assistance, and family support. Because the addresses of shelters are kept confidential for safety reasons, women are instructed not to reveal where they are staying to friends or family when they are admitted.

Equine Assisted Therapy

This is a type of animal-assisted therapy that uses horses to help clients overcome life challenges using a bio/psycho/social/spiritual perspective. It has proved effective with female survivors of domestic violence to attain career goals by dealing with low self-esteem, insecurity, problem solving, anxiety about economic future, and self-efficacy (Froeschle, 2009)

Intimate Partner Violence (IPV)

Intimate partner violence is a serious, preventable public health problem that affects millions of Americans. It describes physical, sexual, or psychological harm by a current or former partner or spouse. This type of violence can occur among heterosexual or same-sex couples and does not require sexual intimacy http://www.cdc.gov/violenceprevention/intimatepartnerviolence/index.html.

Motivational Interviewing

This style of interviewing has become popular in the last 20 years and has shown success with clients ambivalent about change. It engages the client collaboratively, uses reflective listening and empathy, and seeks to enhance the client's motivation to change through use of "change talk" (Walsh, 2014).

Post-Traumatic Stress Disorder (PTSD)

Post-traumatic stress disorder develops after a terrifying ordeal that involved physical harm or the threat of physical harm. The person who develops PTSD may have been the one harmed, or the harm may have happened to a loved one, or the person may have witnessed a harmful event that happened to loved ones or strangers. Post-traumatic stress disorder was first brought to public attention in relation to war veterans, but it can result from a variety of traumatic incidents, such as mugging, rape, torture, being kidnapped or held captive, child abuse, domestic violence, car accidents, train wrecks, plane crashes, bombings, or natural disasters such as floods or earthquakes (http://www.nimh.nih.gov/health/topics/post-traumatic-stress-disorder-ptsd/index.shtml#part5).

Diagnostic criteria for PTSD include a history of exposure to a traumatic event that meets specific stipulations and symptoms. Under the revised *Diagnostic and Statistical Manual* (DSM-V), there are four symptom clusters: intrusion, avoidance, negative alterations in cognitions and mood, and alterations in arousal and reactivity. Symptoms must exist for a month or more, cause significant functional impairment, and not stem from substance abuse or a co-occurring medical condition (APA, 2013).

Spirituality

Simply stated, spirituality refers to an awareness of one's state of being and one's spirit. It is associated with the transpersonal, looking beyond the level of the individual toward how each human is an integral part of a larger whole. Religion and spirituality are not the same, but they share a belief in something greater than the self, a higher power that connects us. This desire to attain oneness of spirit with the larger universe provides some clients with a sense of peace, well-being, harmony, and fulfillment. This connection to something greater than oneself is the opposite of feeling disconnected, alienated, lonely, and without purpose or meaning in life.

References

American Medical Association. (1984). *Diagnostic and Treatment Guidelines Concerning Child Abuse and Neglect.* Chicago: Council on Scientific Affairs.

American Psychiatric Association. (2013). *Diagnostic and Statistical Manual of Mental Disorders* (5th ed.). Washington, DC: American Psychiatric Association.

Bent-Goodley, T. B., Chase, L., Cirro, E. A., & Rodgers, S. T. A. (2010). Our survival, our strengths: Understanding the experiences of African-American women in abusive relationships. In L. T. Lockart & F. S. Danis (Eds.), *Domestic Violence: Intersectionality and Culturally Competent Practice* (pp. 67–99). New York: Columbia University Press.

Bent-Goodley, T. B. (2009). A black experience-based approach to gender-based violence. *Social Work, 54*(3), 262–269.

Bent-Goodley, T. B. (2007). Teaching social work students to resolve ethical dilemmas in domestic violence. *Journal of Teaching in Social Work, 27*(1/2), 73–88.

Boes, M. E. (2007). Battered women in the emergency room: Emerging roles for the emergency room social worker and clinical nurse specialist. In A. R. Roberts (Ed.), *Battered Women and Their Families* (3rd ed, pp. 301–324). New York: Springer.

Black, M. C. (2011). Intimate partner violence and adverse health consequences: Implications for clinicians. *American Journal of Lifestyle Medicine, 5*(5), 428–439.

Black, M. C., Basile, K. C., Breiding, M. J., Smith, Sharon G., Walters, M. L., et al. (2011). *National Intimate Partner and Sexual Violence Survey (NISVS): 2010 Summary Report.* Atlanta: National Center for Injury Prevention and Control, Centers for Disease Control and Prevention.

Brice-Baker, J. R. (1994). Domestic violence in African-American and African-Caribbean families. *Journal of Social Distress and the homeless, 3*(1), 23–38.

Cho, H. & Kim, W. J. (2012). Racial differences in satisfaction with mental health services among victims of intimate partner violence. *Community Mental Health Journal, 46,* 84–90.

Council on Social Work Education (CSWE). (2008). *Educational Policy and Accreditation Standards.* Alexandria, VA: Council on Social Work Education.

Davies, L., Ford-Gilboe, M., & Hammerton, J. (2008). Gender inequality and patterns of abuse post leaving. *Journal of Family Violence, 24,* 27–39.

Decker, M. R., Frattaroli, S., McCaw, B., Coker, A. L., Miller, E., Sharps, P., et al. (2012). Transforming the healthcare response to intimate partner violence and taking best practices to scale. *Journal of Women's Health, 21*(12), 1222–1229.

Eisbart, L. (2011). Mental health services for women and children residing in domestic violence shelters: A multi-cultural perspective. *Dissertation Abstracts International, 71*(8-B), 5119.

Fowler, D. N., Faulkner, M., Learman, J., & Runnels, R. (2011). The influence of spirituality on service utilization and satisfaction for women residing in a domestic violence shelter. *Violence Against Women, 17*(10), 1244–1259.

Fowler, D. N., & Rountree, M. A. (2009). Exploring the meaning and role of spirituality for women survivors of intimate partner abuse: A qualitative analysis. *The Journal of Pastoral Care & Counseling, 63*(3,4), 3-1-13.

Froeschle, J. (2009). Empowering abused women through equine assisted career therapy. *Journal of Creativity in Mental Health, 4*, 181–190.

Fugate, M., Landis, L., Riordan, R., Naureckas, S., & Engel, B. (2005). Barriers to domestic violence help seeking. *Violence Against Women, 11*, 290–310.

Goodwin, S., Chandler, D., & Meisel, J. (2003). Violence against women: The role of welfare reform. *National Institute of Justice*. Retrieved December 16, 2013 from https://ncjrs.gov/pdffiles1/nij/grants/205792.pdf.

Gillum, T. L. (2009). *The Intersection of Spirituality, Religion and Intimate Partner Violence in the African American Community*. Minneapolis: University of Minnesota, Institute on Domestic Violence in the African American Community.

Gillum, T. L. (2008). Community response and needs of African American female survivors of domestic violence. *Journal of Interpersonal Violence, 23*(1), 39–57.

Golden, S. D., Perreira, K. M., & Durrance, C. P. (2013). Troubled times, troubled relationships: How economic resources, resources, gender beliefs, and neighborhood disadvantage influence intimate partner violence. *Journal of Interpersonal Violence, 28*(10), 2134–2155.

Grossman, S. F. & Lundy, M. (2011). Characteristics of women who do and do not receive onsite shelter services from domestic violence programs. *Violence Against Women, 17*(8), 1024–1045.

Haj-Yahia, M. M. & Cohen, H. C. (2008). On the lived experience of battered women residing in Shelters. *Journal of Family Violence, 24*, 95–109.

Hampton, R., Carillo, R., & Kim, J. (2005). Dometic violence in African American communities. In N. Sokoloff (Ed.) with C. Pratt, *Domestic Violence at the Margins: Reading on Race, Gender, and Culture* (pp. 127–143). New Brunswick, NJ: Rutgers University Press.

Hegarty, K. L. & Taft, A. J. (2001). Overcoming the barriers to disclosure and inquiry of partner abuse for women attending general practice. *Australian and New Zealand Journal of Public Health, 25*, 433.

Hubbert, P. D. (2011). The transforming of the spirit: Spirituality in the treatment of the African American male perpetrator in intimate partner violence. *Journal of Religion and Spirituality in Social Work: Social Thought, 30*(2), 125–143.

Hughes, M. J. & Rasmussen, L. A. (2010). The utility of motivational interviewing in domestic violence shelters: A qualitative exploration. *Journal of Aggression, Maltreatment & Trauma, 19*(3), 300–322.

Institute of Medicine. (2011). *Clinical Prevention Services for Women: Closing the Gap*. Washington, DC: The National Academies Press.

Johnson, D. M. & Ziotnick, C. (2009). HOPE for battered women with PTSD in domestic violence shelters. *Professional Psychology: Research and Practice, 40*(3), 234–241.

Joint Commission on Accreditation of Health Care Organizations. (1992). *Accreditation manual: 1. Standards*. Oakbrook Terrace, IL: Joint Commission on Accreditation of Health Care Organizations.

Kelly, J. B. & Johnson, M. P. (2008). Differentiation among types of intimate partner violence: Research update and implications for interventions. *Family Court Review, 46* (3), 476–499.

Kim, M., Masaki, B., & Mehrotra, G. (2010). A lily out of the mud in Asian Pacific Islander communities. In L. T. Lockart & F. S. Danis (Eds.), *Domestic Violence: Intersectionality and Culturally Competent Practice* (pp. 100–128). New York: Columbia University Press.

LaTaillade, J. J., Epstein, N. B., & Werlinich, C. A. (2006). Conjoint treatment of intimate partner violence: A cognitive behavioral approach. *Journal of Cognitive Psychotherapy, 20*(4), 201–214.

Leong, F. T. L. & Lau, A. S. L. (2001). Barriers to providing effective mental health services to Asian Americans. *Mental Health Services Research, 3*(4), 201–214.

Lockart, L. T. & Danis F. S. (Eds.) (2010). *Domestic Violence: Intersectionality and Culturally Competent Practice*. New York: Columbia University Press.

McCaw, B. (2011). *Using a System's Model Approach to Improving Violence Against Women and Children: Workshop Summary*. Washington, DC: Institute of Medicine.

Macauley, B. L. & Gutierrez, K. M. (2004). The effectiveness of hippotherapy for children with language-learning disabilities. *Communication Disorders Quarterly, 25,* 205–217.

McDonald, P. W. & Dickerson, S. (2013). Engendering independence while living with purpose: Women's lives after leaving abusive intimate partners. *Journal of Nursing Scholarship, 45*(4), 388–396.

McNulty, M. C., Crowe, T. K., Kroening, C. VanLeit, B., & Good, R. (2009). Time use of women and with children living in an emergency shelter for survivors of domestic violence. *Occupation, Participation and Health, 29*(4), 183–190.

Morrison, K. E., Luchok, K. J., Richter, D. L., & Parra-Medina, D. (2006). Factors influencing help-seeking from informal networks among African-American victims of intimate partner violence. *Journal of Intimate Partner Violence, 21,* 1493-1511.

National Coalition Against Domestic Violence. (2008). *National of Domestic Violence Programs.* Retreived 12/15/13 from http://www.ncadv.org/resources/Publications.php.

Nelson, H., Bougatsos, C., & Blazina, I. (2012). Screening women for intimate partner violence: a systematic review to update the U.S. Preventive Services Task Force recommendation. *Annals of Internal Medicine, 156*(11), 796–808.

Nicolaidis, C., Curry, M. A., Ulrich, Y., Sharps, P., McFarlane, J., Campbell, D., et al. (2003). Could we have known? A qualitative analysis of data from women who survived an attempted homicide by an intimate partner. *Journal of General Internal Medicine, 18,* 788–794.

Postmus, J. L., Plummer, S. B., McMahon, S., Murshid, N. S., & Kim, M. S. (2012). Understanding economic abuse in the lives of survivors. *Journal of Interpersonal Violence, 3,* 411–430.

Potter, H. (2007). The complexities of the religious response to domestic violence: Implications for faith-based initiatives. *Violence Against Women, 13*(3), 281–291.

Power, C., Bahnisch, L., & McCarthy, D. (2011). Social work in the emergency department—Implemenation of a domestic and family violence screening program. *Australian Social Work, 64,* 537–554.

Randall, T. (1990). Domestic violence intervention calls for more than treating injuries. *Journal of the American Medical Association, 264,* 939–940.

Schacht, R. L., Dimidjian, S., George, W., & Berns, S. B. (2009). Domestic violence assessment proceedures among couple therapists. *Journal of Marital and Family Therapy, 35*(1), 47–59.

Sue, S., Fujino, D. C., Hu, L. T., Takeuchi, D. T., & Zane, N. W. (1991). Community mental health services for ethnic minority groups: A test of the cultural responsiveness hypothesis. *Journal of Consulting and Clinical Psychology, 59*(4), 533–540.

Taylor, J. Y. (2004). Moving from surviving to thriving: African American women recovering from intimate partner violence. *Research and Nursing Practice: An International Journal, 18*(1), 35–50.

Tjaden, P. & Thoennes, N. (2000*). Extent, Nature, and Consequences of Intimate Partner Violence: Research Report.* Washington, DC: National Institute of Justice and the Centers for Disease Control and Prevention.

Vatner, S. K. B. & Bjorkly, S. (2008). An interactional perspective on the relationship of immigration to intimate partner violence in a representative sample of help-seeking women. *Journal of Interpersonal Violence, 26*(10), 1815–1825.

Walsh, J. (2014), *Theories for Direct Social Work Practice.* Belmont, CA: Cengage Learning.

West, C. M. (2004). Black women and intimate partner violence: New directions for research. *Journal of Interpersonal Violence, 19*(2), 1487–1493.

West, C. M. (2005). Domestic violence in ethnically and racially diverse families: The political gag order has been lifted. In N. Sokoloff (Ed.) with C. Pratt, *Domestic Violence at the Margins: Reading on Race, Gender, and Culture* (pp. 157–173). New Brunswick, NJ: Rutgers University Press.

Conclusion

After finishing this book, I hope that you, my readers, will take away several key points to enhance your ongoing professional development: the utility of video-recorded interviews in learning and demonstrating social work practice skills; the importance of being able to identify and communicate to others the theories used in one's practice; the role of process recordings in supervision and the need to reflect on worker-client communication; and an appreciation of critical thinking and social constructivism in understanding how theory and experience influence how we interpret clients' stories. It is my feeling that these areas compliment and interact with each other quite nicely, so that as a whole, they create a meaningful way to teach and learn practice. We weave the fabric of our professional selves based on continual interaction with ourselves, our clients, and the world around us; to do so gracefully, we must have a deep understanding of what guides our practice—and also be able to verbalize those guidelines. I hope the ideas I bring together in this book help explain the intricacies of our work and how practice is a combination of both art and science.

Video-Recorded Interviews

Over the last few years I have experimented with using video-recorded interviews in class as a method of teaching practice. My approach is two tiered. First, I have students observe social workers interacting with clients and modeling interviewing skills by watching and discussing videos (that I have produced) in class. Next, I ask students to create their own video-recorded interviews and then bring them to share with the class. This gives them practice putting the skills they've learned into action and receiving feedback from their peers and faculty mentors. I also conference with each student once or twice during the semester, and this allows me to review the videos again to identify students' strengths and weaknesses and areas for continued growth. Each year I refine my teaching methods, incorporating what I have learned from the previous year. The feedback I hear overwhelmingly from students is that they understand how to integrate theory and practice better by using the video-recorded interviews.

I hope that after using this book, other faculty and students will confirm the benefits of this approach. I feel certain that there is no better way to make practice come alive in the classroom and for students to try out new skills. Students not only learn from watching the interviews that accompany the text, but also from doing their own videos, watching each other's, and using the classroom as an opportunity to give each other constructive feedback. Advances in technology have made producing these videos easy and fun. By reinforcing that students will make mistakes, as is true with the videos and "real" practice, students become less conscious of their own interviews. They understand there are no perfect interviews, and even experienced social workers can make mistakes. Students, who are at the very beginning of their professional careers, are permitted the freedom to experiment with practice skills, make mistakes, learn from them, and become more confident.

Identifying Theories Used in Practice

Another lesson I want students and faculty to glean from this book is the importance of identifying theories used in practice and articulating them to others when questioned. Although most social workers do not practice from a single theoretical perspective, it is imperative that we demonstrate our professional competence by communicating how we use theory in practice. For example, I prefer to say that I combine different theories in my work with clients, integrating cognitive, behavioral, psychodynamic, and narrative approaches, depending on the needs of individual clients and evidenced-based research. This answer explains more about how I practice than simply saying that I am eclectic. I also believe this shows a deeper understanding of theory, the foundation of practice, than a list of interviewing techniques such as solution-focused or motivational interviewing. These techniques, although useful intervention strategies, are not theories.

Throughout my years in the field, I have observed that there is often a difference between what practitioners say they do and what they, in fact, actually do. Although they may believe that they follow a particular theoretical model, on closer inspection and discussion of a case, it may become evident that they have adopted other ways of practicing. By a closer inspection and reading of process recordings, practitioners can reflect on their work and interactions with clients in the moment and gain insight into their approaches. This emphasizes the critical role of process recordings in identifying theories used in practice.

Process Recordings and Self-Reflection

In the book's introduction, I discussed what I think makes process recordings so important in supervision and lamented the tendency to move away from their use in social work education. I hope I have convinced readers of the need to return to this method of supervising and evaluating student work, both in the classroom and the field, a method that has formed the foundation of social work education in the past. Although process recordings are lengthy, there can be no shortcuts in helping students reflect on their work with clients. They are the best way for a supervisor to understand what has transpired between a client and student intern, and because they comprise a written record of the interview, process recordings can also be discussed in a meaningful way with helpful feedback.

When a student presents me with a summary of her work with a client, along with an interpretation of the problem and what needs to be done, I have no way of truly knowing what has gone on between the client and worker without a transcript or process recording. How can I provide the student with meaningful feedback about the interview when I can't look at the actual communication that occurred? What is the basis of my critique of how a student responds to the client in the moment or poses a question to explore a client's problem? Rather than working blindly, I find that when I can observe a student in a video-recorded interview and read the transcript or process recording, I have so much rich, descriptive material to work with on both a verbal and nonverbal level that it facilitates discussion of the case and leads to students really "getting it." We are no longer talking on an abstract level "about the case," far removed from what was said. Instead, we are "in" the case, and can have a concrete discussion about how a particular student listened, responded, asked questions, and read body language and nonverbal cues. As a group, we can also reflect on what went well, what didn't go well, what could be improved or done differently, and pinpoint any issues of transference or countertransference that might have surfaced.

Self-reflection is an integral part of social work practice and is another benefit of process recordings. By analyzing transcripts, students have the opportunity to study their interactions with clients, understand different feelings that surfaced during the interview, and question how they made assumptions or conclusions based on what was said. Although we are told to be value-free, we inevitably bring our values, past experiences, and theoretical biases with us when we work with clients, and there may be times when they interfere with a session. Together, ongoing supervision and the skills of self-reflection play a critical role in continued professional development.

Interview transcripts also spur discussions about how a student makes meaning from what a client says and interprets a client story in a particular way. What makes a student pay attention to one part of what a client says and ignore another? What causes a student to pick up on one aspect of what a client has shared and ask a question related to it and not explore another, equally important area? These questions ask us to inspect the issue of social constructivism.

Social Constructivism

I wrote this book using a constructivist lens that acknowledges the many influences that affect us growing up and form our individual experiences of the world: parents, siblings, and extended families, race, culture, work, communities, socioeconomics, friends, teachers, supervisors, theories learned, and many other aspects of diversity. All of these factors shape who we are and explain how we understand the world around us. As social workers, we bring a particular bias to clients' sessions based on these experiences, and on our education, that shapes how we make meaning of the stories that clients tell us. Self-reflection and critical thinking, as mentioned previously, are crucial practice skills that keep us aware of this bias and limit its impact on our work.

An underlying assumption of this book is my belief that there are many readings or interpretations of a text and that social workers must be open to multiple possibilities. I hope you come away with a greater appreciation of the importance of understanding your own biases in order to listen more fully to what your clients are telling you. Part of learning is staying open to other perspectives, being curious about other approaches, and inviting still alternative interpretations of case material. I have attempted to do this here. I believe this strategy makes practice more interesting and keeps us on our toes. We need to stay cautious about being so embedded in a particular theory or assumption that it dictates what we see, tells us what to look for to confirm our beliefs. At times, it's beneficial to suspend our theories and assumptions in order to see, listen, and understand based on what is in front of us, instead of on the ingrained prejudices of our theories and experiences. Theories can help us if we are not too attached to them; they can also hinder us if we are short-sighted and can't see beyond them.

Although I presented my analysis of the cases in this book, I encourage others to come to their own conclusions and to try out different interventions. In the process recordings, I included the social worker's reflections and observations and showed how the worker's own experiences affected the interview. This act of self-awareness allows the social worker to see how she was influenced by her own experiences and might have made false assumptions about the client based on past biases. Perhaps she wondered what made her pay particular attention to one thing her client said and not another, or even to avoid some topics. "How did this impact the direction of the interview?" she can ask herself. In other instances, the social worker may have questioned how she approached a significant intersection in the interview when she had to make a flash decision, in the moment, based on what the client had just said. This kind of self-reflection is vital, as it helps us as practitioners understand that there is often more than one path, and that how we proceed shapes the texture of our professional work.

I was able to cover quite a lot about theory and practice in this book, but still feel I have only touched the tip of the iceberg. I look forward to hearing how other instructors take the case material and go in other directions. I realize there are many other topics to discuss with each case; I, too, have identified additional worthy practice areas, some of which I inserted into the student questions at the end of each chapter. Through my research, I amassed great piles of articles and books related to the cases and found I had more than I could possibly get through or include in one book. I thought I could have written a book on each case, going into more depth, or I could have done fewer cases. In the end, I felt there was an advantage to having five cases that opened up diverse aspects of practice. Faculty and students can choose the cases and areas they want to discuss in more depth with supplementary readings and activities. Individual faculty members can tailor the materials to their own style of teaching and what they prefer to emphasize. No matter how much material I included, I realized I could never please every teaching need, and felt resolved in trying to do a "good enough" job.

The rest is up to you. I don't have statistics to prove this method of using video-recorded interview works better than other methods, but my intuition, my observations over the years, my experience using them in class, and a great deal of student feedback confirm my conviction that it's an incredibly compelling way to teach students about theory and practice in social work. As a next step, I would like to encourage research to study the differences in student outcomes using or not using videos in the classroom. This would help determine the significance of this method as an effective strategy to improve student competencies.

Interviewing Skills: Definitions

1. Acknowledging strengths: Acknowledging strengths can help clients improve their self-esteem and give them more confidence to take action on their own behalf. It empowers them by providing them with hope and a sense that they have the capacity and resources within themselves to improve their lives and overcome obstacles. When clients feel overwhelmed by difficulties, they may not recognize their positive traits, so the worker pointing them out can bolster the client's self-confidence.

2. Adapting intervention to family needs: The social worker recognizes that each family is unique and therefore tries to develop an intervention plan that takes the family's needs into account. This includes understanding the family structure, culture, norms, and communication style.

3. Advocacy: This is a macro practice skill that involves social action with or on behalf of clients. It includes obtaining services or resources for clients that they otherwise could not access. Advocacy also works to influence and change social policy that negatively impacts client systems.

4. Asking clients' permission to talk to parents: The social worker needs to keep clients' confidentiality in mind at all times. Before meeting or talking with the family of clients, the social worker must discuss this with them and make sure it is okay to do so.

5. Assessment is the process of understanding the client and his problem based on the information gathered. It is done in a holistic way that highlights the importance of context in the construction of meaning, and it is a collaborative activity that is done in tandem with the client. Some of the areas that are explored include the client's developmental history, present family as well as family of origin, school, work, medical and psychiatric history, culture, ethnicity, religion, friendship and support network, strengths, community, and significant events and people that have influenced the individual over time. Data collection refers to this process of collecting information that is used in assessment. The social worker learns more about the client with each meeting, which makes assessment a continuous process. To make meaning out of the information, social workers look to theories as well as other sources of knowledge that include: generalist social work practice, the ecological and the bio/psycho/social/spiritual model, human behavior and

developmental life span theories, family life cycle and family systems theories, knowledge of cultures, psychological theories, personality theories, and sociological theories on role and socialization.

6. Being authentic and genuine: This refers to the worker being sincere and honestly expressing what she is feeling, in a natural, personal way. These qualities help build positive relationships with clients.

7. Challenging moments: There may be times during an interview that are uncomfortable for both the social worker and the client. At these times, the social worker needs to contain both her feelings and the client's feelings. The social worker sits with these feelings and tries to understand them with the client. This can be hard to do, and many beginning social workers want to apologize or avoid pursuing uncomfortable subjects.

8. Clarification of problem: When sitting with a client, the social worker gathers details that further explain the nature of the problem. This is an ongoing process in which the worker collects new information and keeps an open mind to alternative interpretations and perceptions.

9. Clarification of role of social work: The social worker helps the client understand what services the agency offers and what will be her role as a social worker. There are times when the client needs reminding that the work is collaborative; it is the social worker's job to facilitate and not direct the process.

10. Cognitive restructuring is used to describe interventions aimed at helping clients change their belief systems.

11. Collaboration: Collaboration is when the social worker and client work together to define the problem, set goals, and plan possible intervention strategies.

12. Confidentiality: Confidentiality refers to the safeguarding of the information that is shared between the social worker and the client that helps to build trust. In the beginning, it is important to explain confidentiality and its limits to the client. The worker makes the client aware that what is said during a session will remain private and only shared if someone is put in danger. Reassuring clients about confidentiality allows them to express themselves more freely, knowing it is done in a safe environment where their privacy is protected. The worker may say to the client, "What is said here will stay here, unless you or someone else is in danger." If a client is involved in a legal case, the worker will want to explore additional limits of confidentiality.

13. Confrontation: Confrontation is used by the social worker when there are inconsistencies between what the client has said and what is known to be true. The social worker believes it's best if the client comes to terms with this, and faces the discrepancy in light of the facts. Workers can use confrontation to question a client's behavior that is harmful to the client. Also, a worker may confront a client's false assumptions or biases.

14. Containment: There are two types of containment situations, one in which the social worker contains herself from speaking or acting, and another when the worker contains the client from spinning out of control. In the first case, as a client begins to tell his story, the worker may have an urge to "help" before he completes the whole story. If the worker can contain herself and not speak too soon, the client can finish the story and express feelings without interruption. In the second case, when a client begins to get out

of control or expresses too much emotion, the worker will intervene to calm the client down.

15. Continued exploration of the problem: When continuing to explore the problem, the social worker listens for underlying feelings about the situation, who else is involved, and what resources are available to help resolve it.

16. Data collection: In the data collection stage, the social worker explores the problem in more depth. This involves getting information from multiple sources about the client's life and situation, and about the social systems that may impact the problem. Sources might include client records, bio/psycho/social history, self-assessment tools, and other professionals who have worked with the client. Also, through interviewing the client, the worker elicits information about the client, her perception of the problem, her social network, and her strengths. The social worker may construct a genogram or eco-map with the client in order to better understand the family history and social network.

17. Diversity: Diversity is most commonly used to refer to differences between cultural groups, but it also can describe differences in terms of ethnicity, race, class, religion, sexuality, age, health, disability, and gender.

18. Elaboration: Elaboration involves asking clients to describe what they are talking about in more detail. The social worker may ask the client, "I'm not sure I understand what you mean. Can you say more about that?" The social worker may also ask the client for examples of what the client is referencing: "Can you give me an example of when you felt that way?" Also, a social worker can encourage clients to continue telling their story through nonverbal communication that shows interest, such as leaning forward or a simple nod of the head.

19. Empowering clients: This is providing clients with information and skills to take action on their own behalf, advocate for their rights, and gain access to needed resources.

20. Empowerment: Providing clients with information and skills to take action on their own behalf, advocate for their rights, and gain access to needed resources. It involves helping clients have confidence in their ability to control their lives.

21. Encouraging work between sessions: The group leader may give group members assignments or tasks that involve practicing the skills discussed in the group session. Assignments could involve writing down observations, new ways of communicating, or new ways of sharing their feelings.

22. Endings: This is when the social worker prepares the client for the end of the session.

23. Engagement, beginnings: At the beginning of the first meeting with the client, the social worker welcomes the client, tries to make the client feel comfortable, and tunes in to her own and the client's initial feelings about the first meeting.

24. Engagement is the initial step in the problem-solving method and involves building a relationship and an alliance with the client and defining the problem.

25. Exploration of the problem: This is a way of gaining more information about a client's situation. When continuing to explore the problem, the social worker listens for underlying feelings about the situation, who else is involved, and what resources are available to help resolve it.

26. Exploring cultural differences: It is important for the leader to be aware of the role culture plays in members' behavior and assumptions. It is also important to explore cultural differences among group members. This helps to underscore the value and acceptance of diversity (Dorr & McDowell, 2004).

27. Exploring impact of past experiences on present behavior: Exploring the impact of past experiences on present behavior involves identifying any recurring patterns or themes in the client's life or family history that help to understand the present situation.

28. Exploring underlying feelings: The social worker asks the client her feelings on the subject under discussion.

29. Focusing on the process: At some points in the interview, the social worker needs to move the discussion from what is being said (content) to the underlying feelings in the social worker–client relationship (process).

30. Giving client feedback: This is when the social worker finds an opportunity to provide the client with information about his behavior and its effect on him or on other people. It can prove difficult, because the client may not want to hear or accept what the social worker is saying.

31. Goal setting: Goal setting is a collaborative process whereby the social worker and client come to a mutual understanding of what they want to accomplish (Dorr & McDowell, 2004).

32. Helping client to see another perspective: When clients can only see the problem from their own point of view, the social worker's task is to expand their understanding or perception of the problem. This may include discussing how other people think about or see the issue at hand.

33. History taking: History taking is a process of eliciting information about the client's problem, that is, when the problem began, how it has evolved and changed over time, its past and present context, and the client's previous attempts to solve the problem. History taking also involves learning more about the client's individual development, past and present family, and other interpersonal relationships.

34. Holding to focus: This is when the social worker helps the client stay on the topic under discussion. There may be times when, if a client is uncomfortable with the conversation, he may try to change the subject. This could also happen if a client goes off on a tangent or gets distracted. In these cases, the worker tries to redirect the client back to the topic.

35. Humor: Using humor helps the client express and release inhibited or stressful thoughts and feelings.

36. Identifying resistance: The social worker may notice that the client is withdrawn, quiet, negative or otherwise uninvolved in the process. It is important at these times to stop and discuss how the client is feeling about the helping process.

37. Identifying strengths: During assessment, social workers listen for client strengths they can use to help solve certain problems. As clients talk about their situation and their stories unfold, workers identify strengths that are embedded in the narrative. By focusing on positive attributes and characteristics, workers shift the focus away from deficits to inquiring about and affirming strengths.

38. Identifying underlying problem: Often clients may act out their feelings in self-destructive ways. The social worker's role is to help clients understand the relationship between the problem behaviors and their feelings.

39. Information-giving: Information-giving means informing the client about the social agency, the problem, and the resources for change. The social worker is knowledgeable about human development and human behavior and can help clients by sharing information that relates to a problem they are experiencing. For instance, a mother may complain that her four-year-old daughter is misbehaving and not understand how the birth of a new sibling has affected the older daughter.

40. Interpreting defenses: Defenses are ways that clients protect themselves from painful situations and feelings. It is a social worker's role to help clients understand this process and identify the situation and underlying feelings that they are protecting themselves from.

41. Introductions: At the beginning of the first meeting with the client, the social worker welcomes the client, tries to make the client comfortable, and tunes in to her own and the client's initial feelings about the first meeting.

42. Next steps: This is a phrase used when the client and the worker decide what they will work on next, and what actions they can take.

43. Nonverbal attending and listening skills: The social worker shows that she is listening through her body language, such as eye contact, facial expressions, nodding, and leaning forward. These nonverbal skills help the client elaborate and feel comfortable sharing personal information.

44. Normalizing feelings: Clients often believe that their feelings are unacceptable or abnormal. The social worker helps the client see that her feelings are a natural reaction to the given situation.

45. Offering support: When a client shares a story that is painful, it helps when the social worker offers encouragement. By acknowledging the difficulty of the situation, you provide support for the client and allow him to continue the story.

46. Opening up affect: Opening up affect is when the social worker encourages the client to open up more and elaborate on what he is feeling.

47. Paraphrasing: The social worker repeats back the major points of what the client has just said using her own words. This shows that the worker is listening and understands what the client has been saying.

48. Prioritizing problem: After the social worker and client have explored the problem(s) the client wants help with, they might need to prioritize what to work on first.

49. Problem definition: This is a collaborative process between the social worker and the client; they come to an agreement about what the problem is and what they will work on together (Dorr & McDowell, 2004).

50. Putting client's feelings into words: There may be times when a client has difficulty identifying the feeling he wants to express in the narrative. The social worker can help in these situations by responding to the client and using feeling words to summarize what the client has said.

51. Questioning: This is a way of gaining more information about a client's situation. There are many different kinds of questions, such as open- and closed-ended questions and reflexive questions. Questioning is often used in assessment as part of data collection.

52. Reaching for feedback: The group leader asks members of the group to share their perspectives based on their own experiences or thoughts about what they would do in a similar situation. It is important for the group leader to establish group norms about giving feedback that involve speaking from the "I," and being respectful and nonjudgmental.

53. Reaching for feelings: This is when the social worker tries to understand what the client is feeling when a particular subject or issue comes up. The social worker may use this skill when she senses that the client is avoiding, or is not in touch with, the feelings related to the current discussion. This may bring out strong reactions in the client, and it is important that the social worker is sensitive to what this means to the client.

54. Reassuring client: At times, the social worker needs to allay a client's anxiety by supporting her efforts to change or accept new resources.

55. Referral: This is when a client needs additional resources outside of the agency in which she's receiving services. With the client's permission, the worker makes the referral in order to help the client access other avenues for help.

56. Reflecting back feelings: This is when the social worker gives a short response back to the client that mirrors the feeling the worker heard the client express. It is used to let the client know the worker is listening.

57. Reframing: Reframing helps clients see themselves, their problems, and other people from a different perspective, generally in a more positive way.

58. Seeking clarification: At different times during a session, the social worker may ask the client to talk about her perception of a situation in order to make sure she understands the client's point of view. This is also useful when the worker wants to check what she heard the client say, so as not to make the wrong assumption.

59. Seeking client feedback: When seeking client feedback, the social worker asks for the client's perception of a particular situation, the client–worker relationship, or the helping process.

60. Self-reflection: The skill of self-reflection is an important part of professional practice. Social workers are expected to engage in personal reflection and self-correction to assure continual professional development (EP 2.1.1). Practitioners need to understand themselves on a deep level that includes deciphering their values, reactions to others, the influence of family-of-origin patterns, and basic assumptions about culture and difference. It requires setting aside time to ponder the meaning of clinical work—how our personal experiences and biases may trigger reactions to clients that are unwarranted. We learn a lot about ourselves from doing practice; sometimes we need outside help to sort out what issues that arise during our work.

61. Sensitivity to diversity: Social workers must show openness and sensitivity to every client's culture and ethnicity. There are many other ways clients are diverse: class, age, color, race, religion, gender, sexual orientation, immigration status, disability, mental or physical health, and appearance. Although social workers engage clients around diversity and appreciate difference in people's lives, society may marginalize and discriminate others based on difference. It is important to acknowledge the impact of this oppression on people's lives.

62. Showing empathy: The social worker maintains a nonjudgmental stance or remains neutral. The worker need not totally understand the client's situation, but she must show that she is trying to grasp what the client is feeling or experiencing. The social worker might say, "Tell me more about what your experience was" or "I want to understand more about what this means from your perspective."

63. Summarizing: Part way through the session, and again at the end of the interview with the client, the social worker summarizes what has been said up to that point. This helps reinforce for the client what has been discussed and ensures that the worker and client both understand the focus of the session.

64. Supporting ability to change communication patterns: The group leader recognizes a member's effort to change destructive patterns in relationships and to practice new ways of relating.

65. Sustainment: This takes place within the client–worker relationship and includes activities by the social worker to show interest, understanding, acceptance, and confidence in the client.

66. Taking a family system perspective: Although a social worker may be working with an individual client, the social worker also thinks about the client's family system and how it may contribute to an understanding of the problem. This involves seeing the individual as part of a larger system and how each system influences the other.

67. Understanding larger context: The social worker needs to explore the client's family, social system, and larger environment to better understand the problem and its context.

Full Transcripts
Transcription of Interview with Allen
Practice with Serious and Life-Threatening Illness
Allen: "I'm not a heart on my sleeve kind of guy."
Setting: Inpatient Hospital

Carol: I know I was in to see you earlier today and, um, I was about to leave and the nurses called and said that they were concerned about you that you had had a panic attack this afternoon after the doctor had been in to see you. So they asked if I would stop by and see you, and I wanted to just say hello and see how you're doing.

Allen: Thanks for coming by; yeah I guess, you know, I got a little wound up this morning. But they were really, uh, the hospital people were great. They took care of me right away.

Carol: Can you tell me what happened?

Allen: You know I don't know, I mean my body kind of went haywire on me, I guess I was thinking too much, about all the things that were, that are on my mind right now. You know it was getting hard to breathe and my heart was pounding and stuff, it was weird. I never really had anything like that before

Carol: You never had that before, so it must have felt like you were having a heart attack all over again.

Allen: Yeah, well, or getting there. It didn't make sense to be doing that the day before surgery.

Carol: No, it must have been pretty scary.

Allen: Yeah, it was. Yeah but as I say the hospital people jumped right in. They helped me breathe and helped me just get back in the moment. Because I guess, you know, I was thinking about the surgery, I'm thinking about the day after, all this stuff.

Carol: Too much.

Allen: Yeah, I got kind of overwhelmed. I mean I've had stress before, at work, or butterflies or something like that, but this was just different.

Carol: This was a lot more. More extreme, much more scary.

Allen: Yeah, they gave me some medication and that helped but you know they also helped me breathe and move and things like that.

Carol: Good, excellent. You said your mind was kind of racing and thinking about a lot of things. What were you thinking about?

Allen: Well, the surgery, the surgery is a big event, certainly to me. They try to downplay it and make you feel good about how everything's going to go, but you don't know and I don't know. I never had much more than a couple hospitalizations and nothing on this scale. Yeah, so I was thinking about that, and I met with the doctor today and a lot of stuff becomes, it becomes very much more real when he says what he has to say.

Carol: What did he have to say? What did he tell you?

Allen: Well you know, they're required to go through scenarios of what could happen, what I'll feel like, and also discuss different outcomes, and do the paperwork. Whether it's a health care proxy, advance directives. My wife is a nurse so we kind of, she knows about that stuff. I don't really.

Carol: So you've talked to her a little bit about it?

Allen: Yeah, we discuss it. She's very much involved in what I'm going through, so that helps.

Carol: That does help. It seems that the doctor coming in and talking to you about what to expect, and directives, triggered something in terms of your beginning to think more realistically about what was going to happen tomorrow, and that it really was a big deal.

Allen: Yeah, the health care proxy, the point of that is that if you don't come out of this or if you come out of this incapacitated, who's going to make decisions for you. I didn't really think about that before.

Carol: Pretty scary.

Allen: Yeah you always kind of think in terms of the next day; what I'm going to do tomorrow. But here, you've been talking around it for a week whatever or a month and then suddenly he says, "Who is going to make these decisions for you?" we have to put this in writing. I hadn't really thought about that.

Carol: Yeah, and of course a lot of the doctors, this is kind of something they do everyday and they don't think of it as a big deal. But for you sitting their and listening, it must have felt very different.

Allen: Yeah, I don't think they, I don't think it's the same reality to them at all. I'm sure they're trained to be sensitive about it, or maybe to be not so sensitive so that they don't spook the patient. It definitely got to me.

Carol: What is it like to be in your shoes right now?

Allen: Well, right, the doctor's point of view is the doctor's point of view and the nurse is seeing things differently and, you know, I'm the guy who's going to get cracked open tomorrow like a clam and they're going to do their thing. But that's just their environment, it's not mine, this is the place they're comfortable, but I'm thinking about my family, what my family's thinking about, thinking about how soon I can get back to work, you know, all those things.

Carol: Worrying about lots of things. Can you tell me a little bit about your family and how much you've been talking about this surgery with them?

Allen: Well I don't know, I guess we don't talk a lot about stuff we kind of talk around it, you know how it is. But, you know, my wife's a medical professional so we're pretty honest about that, but we still talk about it almost in technical terms.

Carol: So you haven't been able to share some of your fears about the surgery with her?

Allen: No and I kind of don't think I should, I don't want her to worry, you know, because she is a nurse she knows all the things, better than I do what could go wrong or how wrong it could go. But I'm supposed to be the strong guy.

Carol: Oh, so you're not supposed to have feelings?

Allen: Well I can have feelings but I want to be strong for them and confident. It's just another day to the doctors, it's another day at the hospital, and I'll get through it.

Carol: And maybe the panic attack was a way of your body telling you that you can't always be the strong man, that there are times when you have to acknowledge what you are feeling, and that that could be helpful to be able to work through some of this.

Allen: I guess that's somewhat the way I am anyway. I'm not a heart on my sleeve kind of guy or anything. You know I'm going to hold those, suppress those feelings. I try not to get too happy or too sad.

Carol: So that must have been very surprising to you when all of a sudden you were feeling so much and feeling out of control.

Allen: Yeah it was like my body kind of was revolting and it wasn't in my control and I guess that sort of causes it to feed on itself. It just went fast and got out of control quick.

Carol: I remember when we talked earlier this week you had mentioned that you father had died of a heart attack. I'm wondering a little bit more about that, if you could, tell me he was, how old when he died?

Allen: He was 56.

Carol: 56, and how old are you?

Allen: 58. Strangely enough it was his 56th birthday. He had a heart attack when he was, in his forties, he had a heart attack, but you know it had been 10 years or something. This was 30 years ago, medicine didn't really know how to cope back then, they didn't have the tools they have today, but we still we kind of thought when he came home from the hospital and he kind of resumed his activities so we put it in the back of our minds. He had a heart attack and died the same day.

Carol: It must have been terrible.

Allen: Yeah and you know obviously that's on my mind I don't want to leave my family behind so I've been trying to do what I'm supposed to do healthwise, eating, and trying to exercise.

Carol: And even given all that you still have a heart problem.

Allen: Yeah so maybe what they say about the genetics of it is true.

Carol: Genetic things, yeah.

Allen: It's just a good thing I guess that I've been paying attention, and that I live at this time they can do something about it.

Carol: So you said you've been thinking a lot about your dad while you've been here, and we talked a little bit I know the other day. I wondered if any of your thoughts around him and his death of a heart attack came into play at all this afternoon when you were feeling very anxious.

Allen: Yeah, yeah I guess it did, and that's what odd about this thing, you sit with the doctor and they lay it out for you and they make you sign papers that kind of take care of things if you don't make it through the operation. I mean you have some time to think about it, maybe that's not good. My father didn't have any time to think about it. I'm sure, he's a smart man, and he made arrangements for the family and all that, probably after his first heart attack. He had 10 years to think about it, do the right thing.

Carol: Were you aware that he had a heart problem those 10 years?

Allen: No, like I say it kind of it seemed like it went away. When it first happened I was like 10 or something so, I didn't really, it really wasn't anything real it was just dad's not feeling well he's in the hospital, and mom's acting weird.

Carol: So you don't remember any fear that he was going to die or something terrible was going to happen?

Allen: No. I mean it was weird that nobody was really talking to us but we were 10; I was the second oldest so if anybody was talking to anybody it was probably my older brother or something. My little sister and brother, what are you going to talk to them about, they're kids, I was a kid, so you know, that's not real to you at the time. But you know.

Carol: And then 10 years later he just dies suddenly without any warning.

Allen: Yeah and I thought, and I think he thought, he was probably doing what he was supposed to do, changed his diet. I think he was a smoker because I've seen pictures of him after college and stuff, he was a smoker, and I think he gave that up at that time. So he did all the things that I think he was supposed to do to the extent he could. And I'm doing the same thing and look where I am. It's a little frustrating. It was tough to lose him and I don't. ...

Carol: Can you tell me about that?

Allen: I don't want my family to lose me.

Carol: Of course not. It's a very sad thought. It was very sad for you.

Allen: So, I'm just trying to be positive and not be....

Carol: Can you just stay with your feelings for a minute? It seems like you're feeling a lot right now.

Allen: Yeah it's very real, you know.

Carol: It is very real.

Allen: I think probably I'll get through the operation OK, but they have to introduce a little doubt you know, and that kind of gets to you, you know.

Carol: And it's natural for you to be thinking of your father now, having lost him when you were a young man and you're facing surgery for a heart condition. It's natural that you would think about him.

Allen: Yeah, I kind of want to do better than he did. I got a lot of stuff left to do; I got to see my kids grow up. He didn't, he didn't have that chance, and I didn't have that chance. That's what I'm trying. I guess that's what got to me this morning, you know, thinking about all that, and at the same time trying to suppress it, which probably wasn't the right thing to do.

Carol: It seems like that maybe you can't always suppress you feelings, that there are times when maybe it helps to express them.

Allen: Yeah it does.

Carol: How are you feeling right now?

Allen: I don't know, sad, kind of sad, and kind of scared.

Carol: Is it OK to be sad and scared?

Allen: Yeah, I guess it's perfectly normal. I just have been trying to do my best to avoid it.

Carol: To avoid the feelings?

Allen: Yeah, I don't know how much good it does to let them out.

Carol: Were going to get a chance to see because you're feeling them right now.

Allen: But it makes everybody nervous.

Carol: Who's it making nervous now?

Allen: Well, just me mostly. I appreciate you being here, it's nice to have an opportunity to talk; because I can't really do this with my wife or my kids. It doesn't help them to see it. I'm supposed to be....

Carol: You're the strong one again. I know you keep saying you're the strong one, but you don't always have to be strong.

Allen: No I know.

Carol: Especially the day before your surgery, this is quite normal to have these feelings.

Allen: Well, like I say, I appreciate that I can share it with you.

Carol: And the thing about trying to hold them back and suppress them, they don't go away, they just keep building and building and then what happens is it kind of erupts in a panic attack. Panic attacks are often about suppressed feelings. So being able to acknowledge and understand your feelings and see them as normal really helps you to let them out and helps you to work through them and feel differently. Sometimes you have to feel sad and scared before you can feel better.

Allen: Yeah, well, I want to be mentally and physically the best for tomorrow that I can.

Carol: That's really important and we all want that for you too. Because going into the surgery with a positive attitude and really believing that it's going to be successful will make a difference. You play a role in the surgery as much as the surgeon, that you're there and part of the surgery

Allen: I do think that, I believe, I got to believe it's going to go alright.

Carol: And although this wasn't available for your father and he wasn't able to have this kind of intervention to live and see his children grow up, it's going to be different for you, you're going to be able to do that.

Allen: Yeah, yeah I am.

Carol: I know you are too.

Allen: Things are going pretty well so far in my life so I think this will go well too.

Carol: I think so too. Now you have got a few hours tonight, because the surgery is tomorrow. How are you going to get through tonight?

Allen: Well I guess my wife's coming back in, in a little while and bringing the kids, were going to sort of have dinner together and we'll watch some TV or something.

Carol: Very nice. Get your mind off of it?

Allen: Yeah, that'll be nice to just, it's kind of like when you're in the hospital you can't get away from it, you know it's just on your mind, its all around you. So it will be good; they'll come in and a couple of my family members who live in the area are coming in.

Carol: Good. Sounds like you have a lot of support. That's helpful.

Allen: Yeah it's good.

Carol: And we have some meditation tapes that are available if you're interested at all, and I could bring a couple down if you're alone and feeling a little anxious. You could listen to them and it would be a way to try to help you stay a little calmer and to breathe slower and be in the present moment so you're not thinking about tomorrow. Trying to stay focused just in the present will probably help you to not feel so anxious.

Allen: OK, I'll try that.

Carol: And just acknowledging what you are feeling and not being afraid to do that, that's normal.

Allen: It's been a big help that we've talked.

Carol: Do you think you would be able to share any of your feelings with your wife? What would that be like for you to do that?

Allen: Yeah certainly with my wife I can, it scares the kids, they don't like to see me cry or anything. Even if I cry in a movie or something, they think it's weird.

Carol: But it might help them to express what they're feeling too. It's not such a bad thing. Since we've been talking I feel you're a lot calmer now since you have expressed a little bit of your sadness.

Allen: I feel a lot better than this morning.

Carol: You feel very differently to me now. Which is again, a way of helping you to understand that it's not such a bad thing to express your feelings. It can help you.

Allen: Yeah I know. I know that. It's just hard to do.

Carol: I know. Well I felt this was very helpful, I'm glad I had a chance to talk to you again.

Allen: Well thanks very much. Are you going to be around at all later today?

Carol: Well actually I'm probably leaving in about an hour, but you know I'd be happy to be available for your family coming in tonight if that would be helpful. I'm on call. The nurses know how to reach me and I'm not far away so I'd be happy to come in to talk to them. And I'll be here tomorrow and I'll check in with your family and they'll be in a room near by. We'll be keeping them apprised of how you're doing and I'm sure it's all going to go very well.

Allen: Great.

Carol: Good, well I will see you tomorrow.

Allen: Alright, thank you very much.

Carol: OK, good luck.

Transcription of Interview with Betty

Practice with At-Risk Populations: The Elderly and Public Assistance

Betty: "If I don't get money here, I'll be out on the street."

Setting: Public Assistance Office

Ann: Hi Betty, I'm Ann. I'm one of the directors here. You're having a problem I guess. What's the matter?

Betty: Oh yeah, I've been...well it's my third day coming here. I mean I came in two days ago and I wanted some help, because I can't...I'm gonna get evicted probably and I can't pay the rent and I asked a worker for some help...and so she said I had to get a letter from the woman who hired me because I you know I do part-time work as a babysitter and I have to get a letter from that woman and I have to get a letter from my landlord...and so I went home and I got the letter, I didn't want to, but I did...and I came back yesterday and I gave the letter to a worker and the worker was very snippy she was really nasty, she didn't treat me right so I said I wanna see another worker so I'm here today and I wanna I've been waiting for two hours and I wanna you know...are you the boss?

Ann: Yes I am...I'm the boss. Now, when you came three days ago did you actually do the application form already?

Betty: No I just told her that I wanted some money and I needed money.

Ann: So no application was ever taken from you?

Betty: Well she talked to me for a little bit then she told me, yeah, she put something in her computer, I don't know what she was sitting at her computer.

Ann: So you don't know if you have an application filed at this time?

Betty: No I don't.

Ann: Are you currently getting food stamps?

Betty: No, no, no.

Ann: Or any benefits?

Betty: No, no, no.

Ann: So how have you been getting along every day?

Betty: Well I've been having a hard time. I've been...you know I work part-time like I said, you know, so I get some money from babysitting but my rent, my rent is....

Ann: Are you paying full rent or do you have a subsidized rent?

Betty: No, no, no. I'm supposed to pay full rent and I was able to do it when I worked full time, but now she cut my hours because, you know, the kid she does, you know, the kid's bigger now the kid doesn't need me so much and so she cut my hours. So I don't have that much money and the landlord said he would evict me if I didn't pay the rent.

Ann: OK, OK, and how many months in arrears are you in the rent? What do you owe the landlord now?

Betty: I owe him for two months.

Ann: Two months.

Betty: He's not very nice. He's nasty too he says he's gonna kick me out if I don't pay the rent and I'm gonna be on the street.

Ann: Oh OK. Well let's not worry about that right now today, because today we have to take care of getting you applied, you have to apply today if that hasn't already happened. Now do you have any dependents living with you?

Betty: No, no, no, no. I don't.

Ann: So it's just you?

Betty: I don't have any family. If I don't get money here I'll be out on the street.

Ann: Oh OK, and you've never applied for social security because you were working.

Betty: Well I couldn't get social security because I was doing babysitting and babysitters can't get social security.

Ann: OK, and you don't have any disability that you know of?

Betty: No, no, no. I don't think so.

Ann: Up until babysitting you've been working all along?

Betty: I've been working all my life. I'm not like one of these welfare cheats who sit on their butts all day. I've been working you know those other people in the office you know they're here for welfare they're sitting on their butts all day and I'm not getting anything.

Ann: Well, I know and I see your frustration but you know everyone's here because maybe the other people out there sitting or they may have been working at some point and came into hard times like yourself because that's what happens. I think when you come into the office a lot of people have the feeling that you know they're not getting treated right because they bring a lot of shame with it because they have to come here, but that's what the system is for. So, I don't know why your worker didn't describe or explain to you the application process and I'm very frustrated like you right now because we don't even know if you've applied but what we will do is once we find out about your application process we'll go back to the day you first came in to apply and that will be your start date we'll get any money owed to you back those days, alright.

Betty: Well, what kind of money will you give me?

Ann: OK, so depending on what you're eligible for you have to be, you know, hit the requirements for the federal guidelines for social security so you have to be over that age, and if you have any other disability, other than that if you have no dependents, there is no money available for you unfortunately.

Betty: Well, the government gives all this money to the liberals I don't know why I can't get some. I mean they get it all and they don't do anything for their own people.

Ann: I know I know.

Betty: I mean I'm a citizen and those people are just coming in illegally and getting all this money and why can't the government help its own people.

Ann: I know you're frustrated about that but there are certain programs where certain people qualify for certain things and the government doesn't let anybody go hungry.

Betty: What is the policemen looking at me. Is he gonna arrest me? I'm not a criminal.

Ann: No, I know Betty you're not.

Betty: So, why then, why do I need a prisoner why do I need a policeman?

Ann: OK I just want you to relax just a minute so I can explain to you why the officer is nearby. The officer is nearby because first of all your voice is raised and you're escalated and they don't know if you're gonna strike at me or anything.

Betty: Oh so you think I'm gonna throw like my cane?

Ann: Well, some people do get mad enough and do throw their canes at me.

Betty: Well I can see why, I can see why.

Ann: Well it is and there a very… it's a very frustrating situation, this process is terrible to navigate, especially to navigate alone, you go from one person to the next, you don't understand why your worker's changed, there's no explanation… it's a bureaucratic nightmare but people do need assistance and we're going to get you what you need today… so that today you go forward knowing where you are in the process and what benefits are available to you… the officer is gonna stand by unfortunately because of situations and the time that we're in with the government and people with difficult times… they are armed they're armed officers and they are scheduled to be here.

Betty: Well they can shoot me.

Ann: Well I don't think they're gonna shoot you Betty now c'mon unless you act up. Lets see what's gonna happen, but no our officers don't pull their guns or anything else, but they are here in case any situation gets out of control, and we're also what you call the city police as well.

Betty: Well they treat the poor like criminals don't they?

Ann: Well I think sometimes people feel like that when they come here they do, but sometimes the workers feel unsafe with some of the clients that come in that are facing extraordinary time or are off medicine and they can sometimes act out and be very aggressive and because of the numbers that come through here we have to keep officers in the building, so they're not gonna go away and they're not here to you know cause you any problems but let's see what we can do for you today to get you moved on because I mean I feel your frustration but you don't know who your worker was three days ago, can you recall who your worker was?

Betty: I don't know what her name was.

Ann: You don't.

Betty: She was so snippy I don't even wanna know.

Ann: OK, well have you brought the paperwork today that you need.… Have you brought the landlord's letter?

Betty: Yeah I brought it.

Ann: So if I bring you out now and we start you out with a new worker do you think that that would be OK?

Betty: Well if she treats me right, OK yeah.

Ann: Alright so I'm gonna go out now and your wait will not be any longer.

Betty: Well what kind, what kind of help can I get?

Ann: OK so what you'd be eligible for is the maximum that we could give you if you fit into where I think you do in this program would be three hundred and three dollars a month.

Betty: Three hundred and three dollars…I can't even pay my rent with that.

Ann: I know, I know.

Betty: My rent is seven hundred. What am I supposed to do? I'm gonna be on the street.

Ann: Have you applied or gone to…at this point you need to go to all your other resources…you have to go in the directions of trying to find subsidized housing, elderly housing?

Betty: OK, well how do I do that?

Ann: OK, so we have a bunch of resources out in the lobby for housing. Your worker can also direct you over to the local nearest place that can help you with the systems. There are also other Boston agencies. How did you get here, did you get here by subway or did you drive?

Betty: Oh no I don't have a car.

Ann: You don't have a car?

Betty: I walk.

Ann: OK, you walked, so then you're within walking distance from where you live, so then are you familiar with the bus line since you do, you know, walk places?

Betty: Yeah.

Ann: OK, so if we gave you the proper bus lines of where you needed to go and told you what directions you need can you get there, or do you think I could offer you an advocacy group that could assist with someone like yourself?

Betty: Yeah I could use…I don't understand all this stuff. I could use someone who knows.

Ann: OK, so have you worked with an advocate before?

Betty: What's an advocate?

Ann: An advocate is a person that is knowledgeable in each of the areas you need, housing, monetary, food, and also I mean I that you don't…well they are also there to help people that are noncitizens but I know that you've said you've been a citizen of the US all along…and they know what programs are available to you, they know how to navigate the system, which can be difficult. You're still gonna have to wait Betty. I'm sorry the zip codes that our office covers that are in our office is uh huge. They have poverty, high poverty areas so when you come into our office there's only x amount of workers and they have x amount of a case load so when you come in the wait can sometimes be up to three hours.

Betty: Oh my God.

Ann: And I know it's very challenging and it's very difficult for you but if you don't put the time in at the application process then you're never gonna get your assistance. So what you need to do is grow as much patience as you can handle, sit tight, and have a worker give you all the information and follow through with what you need to bring. What you need to bring is critical and if you don't bring it in hand mail it, do you have access to mail or a post office nearby so you don't have to sit for three hours.

Betty: Yeah, yeah.

Ann: OK, so what we're gonna do today.

Betty: But they're gonna lose it though, because I know they always lose things.

Ann: I know I know but we have to get something resolved for you today. You're gonna have to be turned on to an advocate, you're gonna have to follow through with an appointment with the advocate, you're gonna have to take some time to explain to them what's happening to you…that there's no more babysitting, that you're behind on your rent, no more hours at all…are you able to work at all.

Betty: I can still work.

Ann: Have you got any skills. What are your skills?

Betty: Babysitting, I've been taking care of children all my life. I'm good at that, yeah.

Ann: OK OK. Have you ever registered with any of the child care agencies of the state?

Betty: No.

Ann: OK, so that's another avenue you wanna go up you wanna investigate OK, because we run some we give vouchers out to day care…and it could be that you could assist in some of the day cares that are offered state wide because they need the help, because while you're on assistance they require certain clients to want to have work, you know there'll be a work requirement to get your money.

Betty: Really.

Ann: Oh yeah.

Betty: You mean that lousy three hundred and three dollars.

Ann: Well the three hundred and two dollars, the three hundred and three dollars Betty is used for someone who is elderly or disabled, so they're usually exempt from work and they're also required to apply for social security and any of the benefits that ever would have been you know awarded to them.

Betty: Well, my boss never put in any money on social security and I never did either.

Ann: Oh OK, so you haven't been paying taxes?

Betty: So I'm not gonna get social security?

Ann: Oh OK, so you're not eligible for social security, so but what's gonna happen is you still have to go and apply, they're still gonna, the screen we're linked to a computer system state wide into that computer system…so what's gonna have to happen is you're gonna have to go to the social security office, you're gonna have to file an application and it's gonna come back denied but that next application process is what will guarantee you to be able to get you into our program.

Betty: That's pretty stupid isn't it?

Ann: It is isn't it?

Betty: That's really stupid.

Ann: It's a bureaucratic…that's correct…the bureaucratic system seems to have a lot of those roads that lead nowhere and we share the same computer so you would think that we would know already that you're not getting a benefit…but unfortunately for us the state managed federal programs so what happens is each state has a management system to help manage their programs…so say if you were living in New Jersey on a yacht you may not get three oh three it may be a different amount in that state it could be lower it could be higher…so the program that since you have no dependents the program that you're eligible for or that you would be eligible for would be a program in Massachusetts where Massachusetts gives out three oh three is the maximum benefit, OK.

Betty: Can I get food stamps?

Ann: You'd be eligible for food stamps yes.

Betty: OK.

Ann: And also what they'll do is they'll screen you for an expedited...do you have any food at the home now.

Betty: Not much.

Ann: OK, so you have been OK...so with expedited we will get all you need.

Betty: What's expedited?

Ann: Expedited means a very quick, you'll have benefits this month. You'll get a flat rate which may not be your rate of preference it'll just be a flat rate

Betty: So you say this month, but how soon this month?

Ann: Very soon this month depending on where you social security number ends. You could have it actually when you're expedited you could have it as soon as tomorrow after 11 o'clock in the morning, OK.

Betty: OK OK OK.

Ann: Now that money will have to last you until you're approved or denied on your applications...so you wanna stretch that out so you only get the food stamp money once a month on a card OK...when you get a cash program the money is divided monthly, you get two checks so you don't spend it all at once...you're gonna get some money and two weeks later you're gonna get the rest of the money, half and half...but your food stamp money you have to manage it yourself and you have to be a good manager and you can only buy food products with the money.

Betty: I see some people buy liquor with food stamps, why can they buy liquor?

Ann: They can buy liquor and those places that are selling liquor to them uuhh are being investigated...so it may look like that to you and I know that people have these prejudice against all different people using their cards...as a matter a fact a very funny story is I went into my bank the other day to my bank machine and there was a man in there with three or four of those cards that didn't belong to him with codes written down taking money off of it, because you know what Betty people sell them for drugs.

Betty: That policeman should go get it.

Ann: I know, he should've but he can't...there is a squad, we have a fraud department and many many calls they are just as well over worked but the fraud department we have a 1-800 number for fraud...and anyone that knows that that's happening and the vendor if they're caught selling liquor on their EBT card and a lot of times what people mistake as being sold on the food card is it's the same card show for whether food or cash, so do you have a bank card?

Betty: No no.

Ann: OK, if you ever had a bank card when you go into a store to use your debit card they'll say on the store do you wanna do debit or credit, when you take your EBT card and you go to use it at a food store or a liquor store they're asking if your EBT if it's for food or cash...he could've been taking money out for cash and spending it on his own liquor even though it looks like it's being if someone were to video him in the corner it looks like he's used it as a food card...the cards are used for both but when you pick food only the food store deducts the money off the food side, you're able to go into a cash machine and get cash if you're getting the three oh three and food stamps...two hundred dollars would be allotted for your food and when you go to a grocery store you pick food when you use the card and it deducts whatever you bought your produce and your meats and whatever and then if you were using your card for cash then you can just use it to buy whatever but they're not supposed to obviously we don't promote that you use the cash the card at all for liquor, cigarettes, or anything of that nature, or gambling but you know people in desperate times will do desperate things, drug addicts will sell the rest of their money and go without food in order to get drugs, it's a terrible situation.

Betty: It's a terrible, terrible world.

Ann: It is but you have to worry about Betty right now. You have no roof over your head right now you're in fear of losing your unit, right.

Betty: Yes, yes.

Ann: And we need to get you heat assistance because it's getting cold you're gonna need heat OK.

Betty: Yeah.

Ann: Who pays for your utilities right now? Are you paying them or are they in with the landlord?

Betty: They're in with the landlord.

Ann: OK, so you need to make sure that the next place we get you if you go into subsidized, certain subsidies pay for your utilities certain don't...so this is why you need an advocate to help navigate for you, you have to know all the questions to ask...how long have you lived where you're living?

Betty: Oh I've lived there for years.

Ann: And so why do you think the landlord would not give you a little bit of grace period to pay him.

Betty: Well, he's gotten nasty...I guess you know he lost his job so I guess he's in trouble too.

Ann: OK.

Betty: So you know he's not, he used to be nice but he's not as nice anymore.

Ann: OK, so are there any other units in the building...does he take any subsidized units do you know, are any of your neighbors on subsidy?

Betty: No, I don't know...I don't talk to ...

Ann: Oh, you don't talk to them?

Betty: No I don't even talk to my neighbors I don't know.

Ann: Alright, well we have to get you together today so that when you leave here you feel like you've...your application has been taken, know whether or not you're getting food stamps, OK.

Betty: Yeah, OK.

Ann: So your frustration level goes down...now I'm telling you Betty you're gonna come back here another time and you're gonna be as equally frustrated OK...you have to try to keep your comments about your black people and all that...everybody here needs assistance OK, the workers are tired they have no right to treat you in a way that's disrespectful...you don't know what your benefits are but you also can't come in with any attitudes of prejudices towards the workers OK.

Betty: Yeah OK.

Ann: They have a lot of people in need right now so we have to all take care of each other and it's tough at times out there, alright.

Betty: Well you know you're pretty nice for a boss...I don't expect a boss would be nice.

Ann: Well you know there's a lot of us. We all work really hard in here and we all have the same goal we're all here to help people like yourself not here to be mean, and I'm not gonna lie some of my workers have an attitude they're tired and they're cranky, they treat people sometimes they desensitize and it happens to all of us some days I'm not on my greatest game either, but the common goal is that everybody get the benefits they need as quickly and as accurately as possible.

Betty: Yeah.

Ann: And alright, I want you leaving here understanding what you're getting. I don't want you coming in next week and if I'm not here saying I was back four days now and still left not knowing if I've applied, not knowing if I have food stamps, OK?

Betty: OK.

Ann: So, I want you to step it up a little, I want you to ask the questions and demand it of your worker and I'm gonna give you assign you a worker now so that you feel comfortable when you've left here that you know what you've applied for and you know what you have to bring back, OK, alright.

Betty: OK, I and I won't have to wait that long.

Ann: You may still have to wait Betty now I've told you that earlier and I know you're tired and you've been here but they may still be a wait...if it gets to be over an hour and you're uncomfortable I want you to go back up to the desk and tell them you've been waiting over an hour and see if your worker can come down and speak with you and let you know how long the wait is, alright?

Betty: OK, OK.

Ann: Do you think we can agree to that?

Betty: OK, OK.

Ann: Alright great, thank you.

Transcription of Interview with Emily

Practice with Children: Issues of Childhood Leukemia and Divorce

Emily: "Will they be scared of me, thinking they might catch it?"

Setting: Outpatient Hospital Clinic

Gloria: Hi Emily. How are you doing?

Emily: Good. How are you?

Gloria: Good. Do you know who I am?

Emily: No.

Gloria: OK. I met with your mom a couple of minutes ago. I'm Gloria. I'm one of the social workers here in the hospital. I work with kids that are usually first diagnosed. And I come into the room or wherever the kids are and I introduce myself and we talk a little bit about some things that might be going on for you, for your family, any questions that you may have. I understand that you just heard yesterday that you have leukemia, is that true?

Emily: Yeah.

Gloria: So I wanted to come in and check in how you're doing and any questions that you may have that I might be able to answer for you. How are you doing?

Emily: I'm doing OK. I'm just a little nervous.

Gloria: What's making you nervous?

Emily: I don't know a lot of things like how my friends are going to react, and if I can visit my dad or not because he lives in New York. I think he's coming in a couple weeks but I'm not sure.

Gloria: Does your dad know?

Emily: Yeah he knows. My mom talked to him.

Gloria: Have you spoken with your dad?

Emily: No. Not yet.

Gloria: What about your friends? Have you told them yet?

Emily: No. They think that I'm sick but they don't know what.

Gloria: How do you feel about your friends knowing?

Emily: I don't know I think it will be better because I know they'll also help me so that's good.

Gloria: That's great. Anything else that you are concerned about or worried about?

Emily: I'm concerned because I haven't really heard of this much. And so I don't know how they'll treat it or what I'm going to go through.

Gloria: What do you think this is about? What do you think leukemia is in your mind?

Emily: At first I didn't know what it was. I knew it was a kind of cancer but I didn't know exactly what it was. They explained it to me that it was cancer of the blood. I don't know. Does it mean like there's something in my blood or something like that? I don't really know much about it besides that.

Gloria: OK, would it be helpful to have someone explain it a little better and answer some of your questions?

Emily: Yeah.

Gloria: Well I can explain it a little bit what it is and some of the things the doctors are probably going to try to do, but I think it's better to have your doctors come in and give you a better explanation of what they think would be helpful to treat your leukemia. Leukemia is basically a disease in your blood where the cells in your blood are just not working OK. They're basically working too fast and we need to quiet them down so that they can reproduce at a normal rate. And the doctors need to give you medicine to make sure that happens. Have they told you for how long they need to give you medicine?

Emily: They said not too long, but pretty long, just that I should wait through, that it will go by fast.

Gloria: Have they talked to you about the medicine and the side effects and things?

Emily: Well, they talk about one side effect where I would lose my hair. I don't know about that, I'm kind of nervous about that.

Gloria: Yeah, tell me more about that.

Emily: I do some modeling on the weekends so I'll be nervous I will not be as pretty. Will my hair not grow back far enough and will it look bad?

Gloria: Sure that's hard, hard to imagine isn't it? What have you thought about, that you might want to do about this?

Emily: Well, I probably won't want to go back to school for a little while even though I'll miss it but, yeah.

Gloria: Yeah, your mom tells me that you're an excellent student and you're very active in school so I would think that not going back to school would not feel so great for you, would it?

Emily: I just hope it doesn't effect, because since I'm going to a new school, it's middle school, sixth grade, its kind of hard to make new friends. I don't know if this will affect it too much.

Gloria: Yeah, yeah what about your old friends from school, will they be coming to this school too?

Emily: Yeah, yeah that's good, none of them went to a separate school, so I know they'll stick by me.

Gloria: Do you have a best friend?

Emily: Actually, my closest friends are all my best friends, I don't have one.

Gloria: Yeah? Can you name a few?

Emily: Jenny, and Susan. Those are the two that I most hang out with. One of my friends really likes gymnastics so she can't really come over as much but she's still one of my best friends.

Gloria: Oh that's wonderful I'm glad that you have that. What else do you like to do during the weekends or when you're at school other than hanging out with your friends?

Emily: I like the sports that I play like soccer, and how I play the cello, that's fun to do.

Gloria: That's awesome, that's great. So do you think that going through the leukemia will affect you in those areas?

Emily: I hope not. I don't think it will much but, I hope it really doesn't because I like all those activities.

Gloria: How do you think that would feel if that affected you in that area?

Emily: I would feel really bad, I would, I'm not sure how I would go through that.

Gloria: Yeah, what do you think would help you get through that? What would be important?

Emily: If I could find something else that I would be better at.

Gloria: What else would interest you?

Patient: Well if I couldn't do soccer maybe I could do something like, I don't know, something less active like, I don't know.

Gloria: OK that's fine. Tell me about your family a little bit.

Emily: My parents left each other about five months ago.

Gloria: Really?

Emily: And so that was hard at first. I have an older brother, he's going into college and so I'll miss him but he hasn't gone to college yet so he'll still be able to come by.

Gloria: That's great, so your parents, are they divorced right now?

Emily: Not yet, but they're probably going to get a divorce.

Gloria: And this happened five months ago, that's very recent. How was that for you?

Emily: I felt bad because I liked my parents together, I like being able to see them in the morning.

Gloria: I'm sure, and now your dad moved away, that's hard isn't it. Do you wish your dad was here?

Emily: Mmhmm.

Gloria: I'm sure you do, this is hard isn't it, to have to deal with so many different things at the same time? So here you are, sick with leukemia and now you can't see your dad, many worries. So this is very difficult and I understand your dad is away and you're dealing with this leukemia now. What do you think would be most important for you right now?

Emily: Well I wish my friends would know, like, I really want them to know sooner so they can come and visit me so I can have something to do and get my mind off of it.

Gloria: Yeah what about in terms of your dad, what would you like him to do? And your mom?

Emily: I wish my parents would get together, I mean that would lift a huge load.

Gloria: I'm sure. Are you feeling this need to keep them together somehow?

Emily: Kind of, I've been trying to make it so they fight less because well my parents don't really want to see each other that much but when they do they usually fight.

Gloria: How do you try to stop them from fighting?

Emily: Well I try and distract them from what they're doing, but sometimes they keep me out of it, um but yeah I try to distract them by doing other things, asking them questions off topic.

Gloria: So when they're together it sounds like they're not in a good space, that they fight and they argue? And here you are in the hospital going through this. It sounds like somehow your parents are going to have to be together here in the hospital for you. How do you think that's going to go?

Emily: I hope they don't fight.

Gloria: What would that be like for you, here you are feeling sick and your parents arguing?

Emily: It'd make me very upset

Gloria: I'm sure it will. What do you think your parents need to know or need to understand so it becomes less overwhelming for you to go through this?

Emily: That if they would stop fighting it would help like a lot, it wouldn't make me feel as bad so.

Gloria: Right, right, in terms of you getting sick, do you have any thoughts about why this happened to you? Or why now?

Emily: I don't really know, like, how I got it or anything. I felt fine before the soccer game where I cut myself.

Gloria: Right right, do you think that this is something that might bring your parents together to look for you in a way of helping you get through this somehow?

Emily: I hope, that would be really nice.

Gloria: Is that your hope? Yeah yeah, what do you think they need to hear from you to understand that this is your hope?

Emily: That if they stop fighting it would make them feel better and then it would help a lot more it would help me because I know they both care about me. I guess if I told them that they would understand more.

Gloria: Have you ever tried telling them that? That you need them to stop fighting? What do you think would happen if you ever told them?

Emily: I think they would understand. I've never really felt the courage to say it.

Gloria: What makes you feel afraid of telling them?

Emily: I don't know, just because they seem so like wanting to argue I thought maybe they would just say they needed to.

Gloria: So what are they like when they're not together, when you're spending time just with your mom or when you're spending time just with your dad?

Emily: They're a lot different, they're very nice, they try to help me whenever I have a problem or like stuff like that, they help me practice cello and soccer.

Gloria: So it sounds like when they're not together you're able to have a good relationship with each of them, that's wonderful that's great. Do you think that will be the same experience here in the hospital?

Emily: Yeah.

Gloria: That when both parents are not together you're going to be able to do well?

Emily: Yeah.

Gloria: Tell me a little bit about the past, have you ever been healthy or have you been in the hospital before?

Emily: Um I've been in the hospital once before when I broke my arm, other than that no.

Gloria: OK tell me what that was like for you.

Emily: It wasn't nearly as bad because my parents didn't fight as much, they were doing very well together; it was like when I was in kindergarten. It was a lot better, it was easier. I didn't have as many friends then though, but because they were together it kind of made up for that almost.

Gloria: It sounds like having your parents together made up for not having as many friends. It sounds like both having friends and having your parents together are very, two very important things for you.

Emily: Yeah.

Gloria: Would you say that you have a lot more friends now than you had before?

Emily: Yes.

Gloria: OK what made that difference for you?

Emily: I don't know I guess I was just less shy as I got older, and more outgoing and so I made a lot more friends.

Gloria: That's wonderful, that's great.

Emily: Especially going into a new school, so many more kids it's a lot easier.

Gloria: Of course, what about your teachers?

Emily: They're nice, they're very helpful, it's kind of cool having several teachers because they help me in several different ways.

Gloria: That's great, how do you feel about going back to school when you finally feel well enough to go back?

Emily: I really don't know how people are going to react. Will they be scared of me? Thinking they might catch it after I'm done, something like that?

Gloria: Of course of course how differently do you think you're going to look? When you go back to school?

Emily: I don't know.

Gloria: Well you mentioned losing your hair.

Emily: Yeah.

Gloria: How do you imagine yourself looking without your hair?

Emily: Kind of scary.

Gloria: Scary, does that make you feel afraid?

Emily: Yeah.

Gloria: Yeah what do you think that would be like, telling your friends, or going back to school?

Emily: Well I don't how they would act, I'm scared about how they'll act or if they'll accept me anymore.

Gloria: What about your teachers, do you think they'll accept you or not?

Emily: I think because they're more adult they might but I'm not sure, I'm not sure.

Gloria: How do you feel about the workload in school?

Emily: Its OK, it's gotten a little bit more but not too much.

Gloria: Do you think you'll feel well enough when you go back to be able to do the work?

Emily: Yeah, yeah I think I will.

Gloria: That's great, good.

Emily: I want to continue getting good grades and just continue my life like I never had it.

Gloria: That's excellent, that sounds very optimistic of you. What do you think is going to help you get through this experience?

Emily: If my parents stop fighting and if my friends stick with me.

Gloria: How will you know that your friends will stick by you?

Emily: I don't know.

Gloria: Yeah, so they don't know yet, your friends.

Emily: No they don't know yet.

Gloria: Have you thought about how you might want to tell them?

Emily: Yeah, I don't know if I'll just find the right words now, like if I'll have to think about it now, or if I'll just do it right if I just tell them, I'm not sure how I'm going to.

Gloria: Who do you feel really the need to tell right now? Do you feel like you want to tell all of your friends? Some of your friends?

Emily: All of my friends.

Gloria: All of your friends. How do you usually communicate with them?

Emily: Well usually I see them at school but since I'm not going to school I'll probably call them or e-mail them on the Internet.

Gloria: How do you feel about us working on a way of telling your friends, if that would make you feel better?

Emily: Yeah that would help.

Gloria: You think that would help? Because you know that's something that I do, sometimes I work with the kids on ways that they can tell their friends at school or preparing them for going back to school because it can be a very scary process or it can make you nervous going back and not knowing how people are going to react and just feeling a little nervous. And that's something that I do with a lot of kids here in the hospital when they're ready to go back to school or before then, you know telling your teachers, telling friends family, and things like that. It sounds like you're a little bit concerned about. Would that work for you if we worked on that?

Emily: Yeah.

Gloria: That's great, what else do you think would help you right now, something you feel you need help with right now.

Emily: Um I need help with knowing how they're going to treat it and I need help with knowing, like I wish some fortune teller or someone, would tell me how everyone will react when they find out.

Gloria: Right, right, well you know that we can't tell how everybody will react to that.

Emily: Yeah.

Gloria: And sometimes people react in a certain way because they don't have the right information, about leukemia, or about what exactly is going on. And sometimes, in my experience working with kids, they feel like they have to tell the whole world. I don't have hair because I'm going through leukemia or because this is happening. And one of the things I tell kids is that you can decide who you want to tell, how much you want to tell, because this is your personal experience and you choose how much of that you want to share. It's really something we can definitely work one, and also I think it would be helpful to speak with the medical team so that they can come back in the room and really explain in a way that would be helpful to you what exactly the diagnosis is, how they plan on treating it, what the side effects will be, so that you feel better and clearer about what to look forward to?

Emily: Yes, definitely.

Gloria: I think that sounds like it might help, what do you think?

Emily: Mmhmm.

Gloria: Good good and lastly it sounds like working with your parents might be a good way of helping you relieve some of the anxiety around being here and helping you feel comfortable as you go through this because obviously having your parents both understand this and be on your side is going to help you get through this. I can certainly work with your parents on that, work with you, work with your family on it. How does that sound?

Emily: That sounds good.

Gloria: Yeah, great, how about if I come back maybe tomorrow and we can do, I don't know, some arts and crafts or something to pass the time and we can talk a little bit more about how you're doing and how things are going?

Emily: That would be really good.

Gloria: That works? Awesome. Good to talk to you.

Transcription of Interview with Lisa

Practice with Families: Parenting a Child with Leukemia

Lisa: "I'm going to crack, but not today."

Setting: Outpatient Hospital Clinic

Gloria: Hi Lisa, how are you doing?

Lisa: Um, I would say I've had better days.

Gloria: I'm sure you have. I'm Gloria. I'm one of the psycho-social clinicians here in the hospital, and, um, I wanted to come in and introduce some of the services that we offer for our newly diagnosed families.

Lisa: I guess that's what we are, isn't it?

Gloria: Yeah, I understand that you were diagnosed yesterday. Is that fair?

Lisa: I guess so yeah.

Gloria: Would you like to tell me how you arrived here? Sort of how did this all happen?

Mother: I would have to say it's, a lot of it is just a blur. I mean everything was normal. We were at my daughter's soccer game, and um, she fell down and she hurt herself and she got a small cut. And then, you know, we bandaged it up and then went home, and then the next night she was not feeling well. She was feeling kind of sick and coughing and kind of weak. And I thought well, you know, maybe she was just coming down with something. And then the next morning she wasn't any better and I thought, you know, better safe than sorry, I'll take her to the pediatrician, and so I did. The pediatrician decided to take some tests, some blood tests. And when the blood work came back, she didn't even talk to us. She just had somebody at the desk tell us to go, that we needed to go over to Children's Hospital, and so we did. And then I didn't know what to tell my daughter. We were just there waiting, waiting, and waiting. You know all these residents and interns, and god knows who they are, kept flowing in and out and asking the exact same questions as the person before, and nobody had any answers. They just had questions, questions, and questions. Then, finally, they all came, descended on us, and they said to us that she had leukemia. I still don't even, like, I can't even grasp that, like what? So, now the plan appears to be that she's going to have to stay and have some treatment, and I don't really understand what that is either. So, that's my day.

Gloria: Not a very good day.

Lisa: No.

Gloria: So, just to see if I understand this, you are at your pediatrician's office, she just rushes you to the emergency room, and, suddenly, you're told that your daughter has leukemia, and shock, something that you didn't expect.

Lisa: No, I still don't get it.

Gloria: The day before you had a normal day and lives, and, today, you're here in the hospital and don't really know sort of the plan ahead. I'm sorry that you're in this situation. That's unfortunately not a situation that parents want to be in. How is your daughter doing?

Lisa: She goes back and forth. Sometimes she seems to be fine, maybe not thinking about it, maybe it's not on her mind. Then, other times, she is really just so upset, but she doesn't know how to articulate what she's experiencing because she's only 11 years old. How can she reflect on what the long-term implications are when she's not even thinking abstractly yet? She's just sort of just goes about her day and does the best she can, so I guess that's how we'll do this as well.

Gloria: So what have you been told, in terms of treatment and how long she will be in the hospital?

Lisa: I have to say that's where I am kind of angry, because I am very unhappy with the process of learning about not only what is wrong but what will be done about it. It's unclear, there are conflicting messages, you know, one person says one thing, mainly nobody knows. All these people just keep coming in and asking questions and examining her and really being very intrusive, I think, about her physically. At one point, I did hear, although I don't know because other things contradict, but, what I did hear was that there would be this surgical procedure, which just sounds horrific, where they'll insert this port into her body. And it would be a direct access into one of the major arterys in order to allow for continuous administration of this chemical, toxin, which is intended to harm the cancer and will, of course, also harm her. You just think there has got to be a better way than putting something into a child and then poisoning it.

Gloria: Have they spoken to the different ways of accessing her, that it doesn't necessarily have to just be a port? It could be a central line or a PICC line.

Lisa: No.

Gloria: OK, because that's another thing that we can discuss with the medical team, because if it makes you feel a little bit uncomfortable about her having that foreign object implanted in her. There are other ways. Usually, the medical team tends to feel better about the port, but there are other ways if that would make you feel better, sort of getting more information about the other procedures.

Lisa: I think it would be helpful to just sort of be able to understand the pros and cons of various procedures. I mean, there's a piece of me that is there and then there's another part that's like, I don't want to think about this.

Gloria: How, when, why, how is this all happening? Of course, of course. Where are you now in terms of sort of the logistics of all of this? You were just at your pediatrician's office, emergency room, hospital. I'm assuming you have a life outside of here.

Lisa: Safe to say, I'm really struggling with how to organize everything. My son is with some friends right now and they're in the dark. I haven't shared and it's because I don't know what to say. I don't even, I don't know how to tell myself that this has happened, so how I can explain it to someone else is just beyond me. So there's that, and then there's my husband, and then that's another, uh, what a mess.

Gloria: Right.

Lisa: He has his own ideas about how this needs to be handled, and, you know, I didn't grasp what it is that we're doing, never mind second-guessing what is being done. In other words, he has ideas that physicians are, you know, jumping to conclusions, and that it's, um, something I failed to do is to get additional opinions before rushing in and getting the treatment here. And yet I don't know how on earth I was supposed to get an additional opinion when I went from the pediatrician's office to the emergency room, but that's just how he is. And now the decisions that we make, if there is ever a problem with Emily, it would be on my head, because I'm the one who had to bring her and I'm the one who had to sign the consent and I'm the one who had to make the decisions. And I think it's a lot easier to stand by and second-guess somebody's decisions in an emergency than it is to actually have to make the decisions. And to be with Emily and later with her brother. So, I mean, I don't mean to bad-mouth him. He means to be a good father, and he is a great father. A husband...very, very challenging. And so here I am trying to deal, it's a lose–lose no matter how I handle this. It will never be good enough.

Gloria: You know, I don't know if this helps in any way, but this is something that a lot of our parents struggle with.

Lisa: They do?

Gloria: Yes it's very common for this to happen where couples tend to have different opinions where we see families really struggle with making medical decisions. This is very difficult to do. Here you are in this position, attempting to make the best decision you can possibly make with the information that you know at the time. And the medical team usually tells you time is of the essence, and you're feeling overwhelmed just by having received the news, feeling emotionally really shocked and all of these different things that go through your mind and having on top of that to really make decisions that will affect your daughter and there's only so much that can be asked of you and you're doing the best you can.

Lisa: That's the truth.

Gloria: Has he been in, your husband?

Lisa: No.

Gloria: Where is he?

Lisa: He moved to New York, he had a job change, and there's a lot of conflict around that between the two of us. And so when he decided to take the position that he was offered in New York City we both agreed that it would probably be best that he go. So, he sees the kids every other week, and, since this happened he's been on the phone with me, and it's been very, very, very, very tense. He just, you know, rather than deal with the problem, rather than help me, he needs to blame someone. He's very angry. I would imagine I'll be angry eventually, but, at the moment, I'm just not there yet. He's angry at the physicians, he's angry at me, mainly angry at me, and then I have to deal with his anger at the physicians, and I just, that's something I don't need on top of all the rest of this.

Gloria: Of course not, you're needing support right now, to get through this. What about you, in terms of your feelings about all of this and having your daughter affected by all of this?

Lisa: When very bad things happen I tend to not be aware of what I'm feeling, I just know, I go numb, and I contend with it later, especially when my children are around I just focus on them and what they need and that helps me actually to deal with myself because I'm not dealing with myself just yet. And so I would imagine sometime in the future I'm going to crack, but not today.

Gloria: Right. It's that inner strength that you need to be strong to get through with this. Have you told anyone else what is happening? Do you have any support systems around?

Lisa: Well, yeah, I've told a couple of my friends. It's funny though, you know, when I share with them their reactions are so extreme that I almost wish I hadn't said anything because they kind of overreact and I don't, and then I feel like I need to take care of them and help them come to some understanding and in some ways that can be a little bit helpful but mainly I just feel like I don't have, and then I feel like maybe they're pulling away from me because they don't know how to help me and so they figure the best thing to do is just give me some space and in some ways that's true but in other ways it would be really nice if they could help.

Gloria: Sure, sure, and I can't begin to tell you how many of our parents struggle with those same concerns.

Lisa: Really?

Gloria: It's very natural for all of these things you talk about to be happening right now.

Lisa: It doesn't feel natural.

Gloria: It's part of the process I guess, and as horrible as that feels and seems, it's some of the natural things that our families do struggle with. And that's why we want to be able to provide some type of support to help families to cope with all of this, because we understand that this is a very difficult time.

Lisa: I feel like in some ways, you know, it's very nice that you coming in and chatting with me, and I appreciate your time. But, at the same time, what is the point of…I feel like in some ways the hospital is kind of giving me you so I can gripe about how I'm feeling, but what I'm feeling is that I don't have good information, and I don't have a coordinated treatment team, and I don't have an idea of what is going to happen, and I don't have clear good information to make good decisions. And you're a social worker and that's lovely and you can help me with my feelings, but the thing that helps me with my feelings most is good information. So this is kind of, not to be rude to you, but a waste of my time in some respects, because I need to figure out the best way to help my daughter.

Gloria: That is excellent that you tell me. Because that's part of what we do today, to sort of understand what it is that would be beneficial to you. And what you're telling me is that gathering more information and helping understanding how to help your daughter would be beneficial to you. And that's something I can work with you around. I work closely, very closely with the medical team, and any concerns that families bring up, that families feel the medical team needs to help them understand, or that we need to collaborate better with the medical team, I tend to facilitate those discussions with the medical team. Sometimes families request, I don't know, weekly meetings with the medical team on the floor, and I would facilitate that where I would be present, the family would be there, the medical team would be there.

Lisa: You know can I ask you? The medical team, speaking of that, you know in some ways I'm not interested in working with a team, I'm interested in working with the person who ultimately will help me make the decisions. And I feel like all these people floating in and out and asking questions and intruding and examining my daughter for their own interest, for their own curiosity, for their own training purposes. What is that all about? I want to work with a person or some people who actually have something to offer, rather than people who need her as an opportunity to expand their training.

Gloria: Right, right. When I speak of the medical team, it's usually the resident, the attending on the floor, and the fellow, and that would include me as a social worker. We also have resource specialists who are people who can help families with financial needs, transportation needs, any of those things that are beneficial at some point.

Lisa: When you say financial needs, what do you mean?

Gloria: I mean some families sometimes need financial assistance, and we have different agencies throughout the nation that can help families that are going through different cancer diagnoses with financial assistance while they're in the hospital.

Lisa: Oh, so I wouldn't be applying for public assistance or something.

Gloria: Not necessarily, but, if any point that becomes something that you feel is needed for your family, we have resource specialists that can help you with that process.

Lisa: Oh my god. So, in other words, in addition to my daughter being ill, there's a good chance that we will come into financial ruin.

Gloria: Um, that's not necessarily what I mean by that. What I mean by that is that if at any point you feel that it would be helpful for you family to apply for those benefits, we have people on the team that could help you with that process. It's just a way of you feeling like, if there is something that I need, at least there will be someone out there that I can go to that could help me with this process, so that on top of feeling overwhelmed about everything that's going on right now I don't have to go outside of the hospital or different places looking for someone who can help me with these resource needs that I may have at some point.

Lisa: What about my daughter's academics. She's a very committed student, I mean we're talking, I mean its unclear to me tragically, I have no idea what exactly this entails in terms of time, but it seems at least a few weeks, which is really a big chunk of time when there are only 180 days in a school year.

Gloria: Right, right, what are your concerns in terms of school for her?

Lisa: That she's not going. That she'll, you know, fall very behind.

Gloria: Right, right. Well I can tell you that here in the hospital we also have assistance for that. Some of the kids, while they're receiving their inpatient treatment, we can facilitate tutoring services where we work closely with the school that they're attending, so that the school can send the materials and work with the tutor. That is at no cost for you, it's facilitated by the town where she is going to school, and that tutor will come in to the hospital and work with her, of course depending on how well she feels. And you and the tutor can coordinate what that looks like. And one thing that happens sometimes is that when kids leave the hospital and they're receiving outpatient treatment, some days they don't feel well enough to go to school and some decide to go back to school half days and some go back full time. Some families keep the tutor so the child can receive tutoring those days that they're not going to school so that they don't feel like they're completely behind either. So that's something that helps too.

Lisa: Well, that's a lot.

Gloria: Yes, and I'm sorry if I'm bombarding you with too much information.

Lisa: No that's alright, I guess I wanted information. Not sure what I'm supposed to do with it yet.

Gloria: What would you say are your major concerns right now?

Lisa: Well um, how to be most helpful to Emily and to my son. I can only imagine what this is like for him. You know he's planning to go to college soon and, you know, it's a tough time and he's applying and we we're in the process of writing his essays and I can't imagine what this is like for him to, you know, in some ways losing me, I'm a big resource for him in this process. It's always a challenge to balance your time, my time, between the two children, and so, in this case, he's sort of left out.

Gloria: Left out right, and, you know, that's unfortunately something that we see a lot, with siblings, where they experience that loss of their families, and feel left out. And so for that reason we tend to try to facilitate services for siblings as well so the parents don't feel like they're not providing any type of care for their other children.

Lisa: What does that mean, services?

Gloria: That means that we do have other clinicians on the team that could work closely with your child that could identify what his needs are right now. If he needs help in writing college essays or if he needs help applying to different colleges or different things that you may not be able to assist him right now we have clinicians on the team that could help him with that. We really here in the hospital try to do whatever we can to try to alleviate some of the stress that the families go through.

Lisa: That's amazing, thank you.

Gloria: Sure, sure. In terms of Emily, what do you anticipate will be difficult for her as she goes through this process?

Lisa: You know I don't know what the process really involves, but you know it's physically painful obviously that's not going to be a picnic for her. She's very resilient. You know if things are kept relatively normal for her, you know if people don't treat her like she's a fragile ornament or something, you know and maintain a sense of humor and normality, I think she will probably do OK. I think you know not feeling well and losing her hair, oh my god, those will be big, big, big challenges.

Gloria: Right, right, how important is her hair would you say?

Lisa: Her hair, and I mean she's not especially vain or anything, but you know, a little girl, her hair …

Gloria: She's 11 …

Lisa: It's a big deal, and she's got a nice head of hair! It is important to her. She has a lot of interests that have to do with being physical. And that's one of my worries in addition to school. She plays the cello, and she plays soccer, and she does modeling on the weekend. She's a very active little person.

Gloria: Very active.

Lisa: Being sick and being physically changed, and, god knows, she'll probably lose weight. I just can't even imagine what that's going to be like for her, or me.

Gloria: What do you anticipate will be most difficult for you as you witness that change?

Lisa: Not being able to help her.

Gloria: Not being able to help her. (Pause) I can understand that. That's very difficult.

Lisa: Most things you can make go away, but this doesn't sound like something I can have any control over at all.

Gloria: Yeah, absolutely. What do you think you can have control over?

Lisa: Well, I can try to import some of the nicer aspects of her life to the hospital setting, you know like make sure that she maintains connection with her father, try to reduce her understanding of the conflict that we're experiencing. I know that's been a challenge for her over the years to know that her father and I don't get along as well as we'd like too. I think bringing her friends, although I don't know how her friends' families will feel about that, but to the extent that I can get them to remain actively involved with her, and remain her friends. I think that's going to be enormously important to her to not just be abandoned. To lose so much, it seems like this whole thing is about one loss after another loss; her physicality, her athleticism, her school, her friends, loss of her hair. Yeah that will be challenging.

Gloria: Absolutely, and it seems like you're very in tune, exactly right on target with the things that she may experience at this time.

Lisa: I think I'd prefer not to be in tuned. It just seems like a very big challenge.

Gloria: Yes, yes, what do you anticipate would be helpful for her, that we could provide for her here in the hospital?

Lisa: Well I think if she has long stretches of time where she is just left to sit by herself and watch TV or something that would be awful, and so, you know, if there are groups of other girls who are going through similar things it would be really important for her, you know can she get involved with other girls, other boys, other children. Can she be kept busy, you know, she's an active person, to just sit and stare at the wall for hours on end would be just terrible for her.

Gloria: Right, right, well let me tell you a little bit about what we can offer for her here in the hospital. First of all, I think that given the many losses you've mentioned that she's gone through, I think it would definitely be beneficial for her to be in some type of psychotherapy and I don't know what your feelings are around that.

Lisa: I'm not sure, I don't know. I've always been suspicious of people trying to get into my daughter's head. I don't really go for that.

Gloria: OK, OK, and we also have groups like you mentioned where she can be with other girls who are going through leukemia, similar experiences, similar age range, where she can express herself and it doesn't necessarily have to be psychotherapy. It could be someone who could come in and just sit with her and do different craft projects and talk about how she is feeling without it necessarily being framed as psychotherapy.

Lisa: She would love that.

Gloria: If that would be something you would prefer. I think finding some way of helping her talk about how she is feeling, talk about the difficulties of going through this, might be beneficial. Also, her father, how often he will come in? Where are we in terms of that arrangement? Will he be part of this process?

Lisa: I'm not sure. He's a very good father and I think he will do his best. I think in this kind of situation, this is not his strength, this is not his strength. He will, I don't know, time will tell I suppose.

Gloria: I feel like I've given you some information, I don't know how you're feeling about what we've talked about so far.

Lisa: I'm feeling good. No I'm not, that's a lie. I'm feeling a little more reassured that there are a lot of resources, although vague about what exactly the form they'll take and at the same time I feel like I've taken in as much as I can take in at the moment. I don't know if you have some written materials, or if I can have the opportunity to catch up with you again when I have some more clarity on what my questions might be, and a chance to digest.

Gloria: Absolutely, absolutely. That's definitely possible. It's often the experience some of our parents that they feel like the first few days they are just bombarded with so much information that there is only so much that they can take at once. I can certainly come by at another time and we can go over some written materials, I can maybe stop by and leave them for you to take a look at them when you have some time and we can certainly talk about the resources available, things like that that might be helpful for you. Do you have any questions for me so far?

Lisa: Well I think we've gone over most of them at this point.

Gloria: Great, great it was a pleasure meeting you. And I look forward to working with you closely.

Lisa: Thank you.

Transcription of Interview with Nicole

Practice with Domestic Violence

Nicole: "I'm scared for my life and want to be around for my kids."

Setting: Domestic Violence Shelter

Carol: Hi Nicole. My name is Carol Dorr and I'm the intake coordinator here at Safe Haven. I wanted to welcome you here and see how you're doing. I understand you've been here two hours now. I wanted to touch base with you to see how you're doing.

Nicole: Right now, I'm doing alright. I'm a little worried right now and I don't really know what I'm doing here.

Carol: Tell me a little bit about how you came here today. What was happening before you came?

Nicole: It's a long story, but, right before I came here, I had an argument with my fiancé. He said something that really scared me. He's never said it before, but I thought it was time to come here and get help.

Carol: Can you tell me more about what he was saying to you?

Nicole: Today he told me he was mad. I was studying at the library, because I'm in school, with a study partner who was a male. I told him he was only a study partner. I have no other dealings with him. We need study partners, and he became very upset when I told him I was with my study partner. He told me he would kill me if I ever went back to school to study with my study partner. He doesn't even want me in school anyways.

Carol: How come?

Nicole: I don't know why. He said there's no reason for me to be in school and that he'll take care of me. He said there's no reason to go back to school because I have two kids.

Carol: How old are your children?

Nicole: My older son is not his, but he's 4, and my daughter's 3, and she is his. He wants me to stay home, but I'm tired of staying home. I'm young. I'm only 25. I don't want to stay in the house all the time. When we first got together it wasn't like that, and now he gets angry when I want to do better things for myself.

Carol: Has he threatened you before?

Nicole: He's never told me he would kill me, but in the past he's hit me. He's pulled my hair. I don't know what I did to deserve this.

Carol: You haven't done anything to deserve this. This is frequently what a lot of women who have been abused feel. That they must have done something to cause the abuse, but that's not true. It's not your fault. Can you tell me a little bit about how long it's been going on or what it got started?

Nicole: At first he wanted to go through my phone and say I was with other guys, but I was with him every day. The one minute I go to the corner store he tells me I was talking to guys at the corner store. It's not my fault guys are in front of the store. One day he thought I was out with some guys when I was out with my friends and he slapped me. I was crying and I told him I was going to leave him. He told me I would never leave him and he slapped me in my face. That was the first time. I can't take it anymore. I can't continue to go through that.

Carol: Of course not. I'm glad you decided to call us. It sounds like you've been suffering in this relationship for quite a while now.

Nicole: Yeah. I'm just really scared to leave him right now, because my family knows we're engaged and I don't know how we're going to break this off. Everyone loves him. He puts on a show like he's so nice for everyone else. That's who he was when I first met him, but I don't know what's going on.

Carol: This is frequently a pattern with abusers. They can be very charming on the outside and very abusing at home. Your describing of him being controlling and possessive is also common to abusers. He seems to be really fitting into this pattern.

Nicole: He always degrades me. He tells me that I'm fat and I don't do anything. That's why I went back to school, but that's not even good enough for him. I just want to do good for me and my kids. I want to see us have a good life. I really want to stay with him, because

I want the proper environment for my children. I don't want men in and out of their lives but I can't do it anymore.

Carol: It seems that you have many strengths. I'm impressed you're going back to school, in spite of the pressures from him, and continuing to want to do what's good for you and your family and your children. And that's very important. What often happens is the abusers try to put down their partners so the partners feel weak and helpless and dependent. You have a real strength because you're trying to get out of that relationship and better yourself to support your family. That's really wonderful.

Nicole: I love my kids.

Carol: I can see that you must be a very good mother.

Nicole: Yes.

Carol: How are the children doing? Have they been hit by him or abused by him or observed your being hit?

Nicole: I don't think they've ever observed me being hit, but I can't say they've never heard him screaming at me. They live with us. I hope not. My older son, sometimes I feel he's even meaner to him, his name is Terrell. Sometimes I feel he treats Terrell so mean.

Carol: That's another good reason for your leaving. For yourself and your children, because you don't want them to have to be victims of his anger and his abuse. I think that's good that you came here. In terms of the history of the abuse, can you tell me a moment that was the worst that you had?

Nicole: I was in the shower one day and he came in the house. I was in the best mood ever, and I get out of the shower and said, "Hi honey, how are you today?" He said, "Where have you been today?" I said "Sweetheart, I called and you didn't answer the phone. I was in the shower." He said, "I just called and you didn't answer," and I said, "I was in the shower." He started to hit me and my head hit the tub. It was crazy and I was really scared, but the kids weren't home.

Carol: You must have been very scared.

Nicole: I was really, really scared.

Carol: Have you ever needed to go to the hospital?

Nicole: No, I never went to the hospital. I made up excuses for my bruises and handled it myself by putting ice on the bruises and sun glasses.

Carol: It must be horrible.

Nicole: It is really bad.

Carol: How are you feeling right now as you're talking about it?

Nicole: I want out. I feel like it has to end at some point, if for anyone I guess for my kids. I'm scared for my life and want to be around for my kids.

Carol: You mentioned he's charming to your family, and your family likes him. Is that right?

Nicole: Yes. They love him.

Carol: They don't know about any of the abuse?

Nicole: No.

Carol: Have you shared this with anyone?

Nicole: The only person I shared it with was my best friend. Her name is Chevon, and she's actually the one who told me about this place. She can't stand him and she knows he's been hitting me for a very long time. She wants me to leave him alone. She says I can do better. I tell her the things he says and she says they are not true.

Carol: It's important to be in a better environment where you feel cared about. That's partly why you are here and I hope you feel safe here.

Nicole: I hope so too.

Carol: Safe Haven is a place for women who have experienced abuse, like yourself. There are presently eight other families here with children as well. There are a few rules that are important for you to understand while you are here. It's very important that no one knows where you are right now and that no one knows the address. That is for your safety and the safety of the other women here. You'll have a social worker assigned tomorrow and she'll go over more of this with you. I'd like to show you around in a few minutes to let you see some of the other offices and resources here. We do have a department that helps with legal issues. We have another one with finding homes. There are many different resources here. We do have an evening meeting every night for the mothers to get together to discuss their experiences and provide support for each other. There are a lot of services to help you get a new start and rebuild your life and get out of the abuse.

Nicole: Will I still be able to go to school?

Carol: Absolutely. As a matter of fact, we may be able to find some scholarship money for you and financial help.

Nicole: That would really help because he was paying for a lot of the things I have. That was another concern I had.

Carol: Anything else? Any other questions you have before we stop and I show you around the home?

Nicole: No, I think I'm all set. I don't have any questions.

Carol: Well, I'm really glad you came here, and I really feel we can work well together and get you a new life.

Nicole: Thank you.

Terms Used in Theory

1. **Attachment**: This refers to the quality and style of relatedness between people and is part of psychodynamic theory. It's a developmental concept that looks at how people form relationships in the present based on how they related to caregivers during infancy and childhood.

2. **Brainstorming**: Brainstorming is another technique used in cognitive therapy for improved problem solving. Clients are prompted to create as many solutions to a problem as possible. Once the client has created an exhaustive list of ideas, he evaluates each one with the social worker to determine which seems the best choice at the time.

3. **Cognitive-behavioral theory**: The basis of cognitive-behavioral theory is that people's behavior is affected by the ways in which they think. A part of this thinking is self-talk and the need to be aware of the repetitive things we say about ourselves and our lives, such as, "I'm not good enough," or "I don't deserve this." The self-talk has become like a tape in our head that plays constantly and often without our realizing it. This approach explores the thinking, feeling, and behavior triad. Its purpose is to help people understand the connection between what they feel and think and how they behave, and to modify their behavior by better understanding these interactions. For example, if a couple comes in describing a fight they had the night before, the purpose would be to understand what they were thinking and feeling before they started to argue. The social worker plays an active role in the interview, asking detailed questions about the sequence of events and the client's feelings, thoughts, and behaviors. The client is helped to understand some of their self-defeating behaviors and irrational thoughts. Reframing is one technique used to help a client view a situation in a different way. For example, a woman feeling badly about herself after a divorce is helped to understand that rather than seeing herself as a failure, her husband was not able to appreciate her unique and wonderful qualities. Another technique is creating positive statements, called affirmations, to replace the negative self-talk. Often when clients are feeling anxious about an approaching event, it can be helpful to rehearse or role-play the situation with the social worker in advance. This

may include a client going to a job interview, or asserting herself with a boss or friend, or perhaps even practicing small talk at a party.

4. **Cognitive therapy**: Cognitive therapy helps clients interpret events and construct reality in new ways, and engage in more effective problem-solving and decision-making behavior.

5. **Defense mechanism**: In psychodynamic theory, defense mechanisms are unconscious and automatic processes that serve to protect people from unwanted or threatening thoughts or feelings.

6. **Denial**: This defense mechanism is a refusal to recognize the existence of an anxiety-producing thought, emotion, or conflict.

7. **Developmental theory**: Social workers use developmental theory to understand clients. Development occurs throughout the life cycle from birth to death and explains changes taking place in the individual on different levels—biological, psychological, social, and spiritual. Both individuals and families go through a series of stages as part of development.

8. **Differentiation**: Differentiation is a key term in family emotional systems theory. It refers to the family's ability to accept change and difference on the part of its members, allowing autonomy. Differentiated people can separate themselves from emotional entanglements. They are flexible, adaptable, thoughtful, independent, and more self-sufficient.

9. **Displacement**: This is another defense mechanism that happens when a person redirects feelings from their original source to an object that is felt to be safe or acceptable. It can happen when families feel overwhelmed and helpless in coping with a life-threatening illness and become angry with the doctors. Because it is difficult to get angry at the illness, the situation, or the person who is sick, a family member may displace this anger onto medical staff.

10. **Ecological theory**: The ecological model is holistic and defines problems contextually. It views problems as being the result of problematic transactions between an individual and her social and/or physical environment. The individual affects the environment and is affected by the environment. The social environment includes family, neighborhood, groups, organizations, and larger social systems. The physical environment includes problems such as poverty, lack of adequate space, poor living conditions, and lack of opportunity to experience nature. In this model, the person can influence the environment in many ways, such as temperament, self-esteem, genetic predispositions, and mental or physical illness. Problems are not seen as residing within the person or the environment. Instead, the problem may be described as a poor fit between the two. In looking at the transactions between the person and her environment, the social worker may construct an eco-map with the client. The eco-map is an assessment tool through which the social worker and the client can identify problem areas as well as sources of support and stress in the environment.

11. **Family development**: This is also referred to as family life cycle. Similar to child and adult development, families also have predictable stages they go through, although they are not identical for every family and are influenced by racial and ethnic diversity. Understanding the family life cycle helps social workers identify problems that may surface in a family

that relate to these stages. Each stage involves a transition and is associated with tasks that must be accomplished before going to the next stage. Some families negotiate the stages more easily than others and some families may struggle with one stage more than others, for example, families with adolescents. These stages are complicated by divorce, separation, and family illness. Carter and McGoldrick (1999) describe the stages as: leaving home; single young adults; the joining of families through marriage: the young couple; families with young children; families with adolescents; launching children and moving on; families in later life.

12. **Family systems theory**: Families are considered systems because they are made up of many parts that are interrelated and function as a whole. Psychosocial assessment from a systems perspective looks at understanding problems in their context and includes information about a client's family. Family emotional theory (or multigenerational theory) and structural family theory are two examples of family systems theory.

13. **Intellectualization**: This is a defense mechanism that occurs when a person avoids talking or thinking about feelings, and instead uses more abstract and higher forms of speech, devoid of emotions.

14. **Intersubjectivity**: Intersubjectivity is a term used in psychodynamic theory to refer to worker sensitivity and awareness of the client's experience. A worker who has achieved this level of relatedness with a client will have an easier time reading the client, in essence is aligned and attuned with what the client feels. As a worker notices changes in a client's mood and general well-being, the worker can use this information as a way to measure client progress.

15. **Mindfulness**: This is a type of meditation used in mind–body approaches to healing and behavioral medicine. Two key words that help describe qualities of mindfulness practice are "awareness" and "attention." By focusing on the breath, the practitioner pays attention to what is happening in the present and maintains an awareness of this experience from moment to moment.

16. **Motivational interviewing**: This style of interviewing has qualities of psychodynamic, cognitive, and behavioral theories. It is often used with clients who are ambivalent about changing their patterns of behavior. It takes a collaborative approach, emphasizes the importance of empathy and reflective listening, and uses questions in a creative way to assist a client in changing unhealthy behaviors.

17. **Narrative theory**: Constructivism and meaning-making play an important role in narrative theory by bringing special attention to the nature of reality and what is true. Narrative therapy looks at the importance of understanding how clients construct meaning and talk about their lives and how practitioners use theories to interpret their stories.

18. **Positive psychology**: A branch of cognitive theory, positive psychology looks at the importance of positive emotions and happiness as a means to alleviate suffering.

19. **Projection**: This defense mechanism unconsciously protects an individual from unacceptable thoughts or feelings by making him believe that it's another person having those thoughts.

20. **Psychodynamic theories**: Psychodynamic theories attempt to understand what motivates behavior, why people behave the way they do. The Psychoanalytic Method

originated with Sigmund Freud and continues today as a theory of human development that is concerned with personality, abnormal psychology, and treatment. Ego psychology and object relations are two examples of psychodynamic theories. Ego psychology pays more attention to ego functioning and ego defenses, whereas as object relations theory emphasizes the quality of interpersonal relationships.

21. **Rehearsal**: This is a strategy in cognitive therapy to help clients prepare for a challenging or difficult situation. The social worker instructs the client on what to say and do, and the worker may also role-play the situation in advance to build the client's confidence.

22. **Systems theory**: Systems theory represents an overarching theory that provides social workers with a conceptual framework or lens in which to view the world. A system is made up of many parts that are interrelated and function as a whole. Social workers engage systems of various sizes from the individual to families to groups to organizations and communities.

23. **Taking a family system's perspective**: Although a social worker may be working with an individual client, the social worker also thinks about the client's family system and how it may contribute to an understanding of the problem at hand. This involves seeing the individual as part of a larger system and examining how the different parts influences each other.

24. **Triangles**: In structural family therapy, triangulation refers to the process in a family when a two-person system brings in a third person to relieve tension in the relationship. This can happen in many different ways. A triangle can occur when parents bring a child into their problems, projecting their issues onto the child, who becomes the symptom bearer. Sometimes children may act out to bring attention to them to take the couple away from their own problems. Other times, a child who is uncomfortable with the parents' fighting may interrupt the fighting to distract the couple. These are all examples of how a family manages conflict.

25. **Trust**: Trust is a psychodynamic concept that looks at the types of relationships people form with others. When a client is overly suspicious about people's motives, these feelings might relate back to insecure attachments with parents in childhood that make the client mistrustful in the present. A lack of trust could also be related to early disappointments with caregivers, which made the client feel he couldn't depend on others or that others were out to hurt him. Parent–child relationships based on warmth, mutuality, consistency, and support help children form strong identities and develop a sense of trust in relationships. On the other hand, children from homes that lack these qualities and instead harbor instability, anger, frustration, abandonment, and loss, will form insecure attachments and be distrustful of others.

26. Ventilation is one of the ego-sustaining interventions that encourages the client to express feelings about a problem for relief.

Index